"*The Inner Journey* 1.   .. a profound and brilliant masterwork. A. H. Almaas presents a clear and comprehensive overview of the Diamond Approach that reveals the breathtaking sweep of this work. The book guides readers through the powerful dynamics and subtle dimensions of the soul, then takes us through the various obstacles and stages to its transformation. Revelatory for those already familiar with his approach, yet accessible to new readers, this book is sure to become a classic of spiritual and psychological literature. Indispensable."

—DON RICHARD RISO and RUSS HUDSON,
authors of *The Wisdom of the Enneagram*

"A brilliant synthesis of the best in traditional spirituality with the best in modern psychology. Almaas is among that select company who can combine spiritual depth with a profound and insightful intellect."

—RICHARD SMOLEY, author of *Inner Christianity: A Guide to the Esoteric Tradition*

Books by A. H. Almaas

Essence with *The Elixir of Enlightenment: The Diamond Approach to Inner Realization*

Facets of Unity: The Enneagram of Holy Ideas

The Inner Journey Home: Soul's Realization of the Unity of Reality

Luminous Night's Journey: An Autobiographical Fragment

Diamond Mind Series

Volume 1. *The Void: Inner Spaciousness and Ego Structure*

Volume 2. *The Pearl Beyond Price: Integration of Personality into Being: An Object Relations Approach*

Volume 3. *The Point of Existence: Transformations of Narcissism in Self-Realization*

Diamond Heart Series

Book One. *Elements of the Real in Man*

Book Two. *The Freedom to Be*

Book Three. *Being and the Meaning of Life*

Book Four. *Indestructible Innocence*

Diamond Body Series

Volume 1. *Spacecruiser Inquiry: True Guidance for the Inner Journey*

For more information on A. H. Almaas and all of his publications, please go to: www.ahalmaas.com

The Inner Journey Home

Soul's Realization of the Unity of Reality

A. H. Almaas

Shambhala · *Boston & London* · 2004

Shambhala Publications, Inc.
Horticultural Hall
300 Massachusetts Avenue
Boston, Massachusetts 02115
www.shambhala.com

©2004 by A-Hameed Ali

All rights reserved. No part of this book may
be reproduced in any form or by any means, electronic
or mechanical, including photocopying, recording, or by
any information storage and retrieval system, without
permission in writing from the publisher.

9 8 7 6 5 4 3 2
Printed in the United States of America

◎ This edition is printed on acid-free paper that meets the
American National Standards Institute z39.48 Standard.
Distributed in the United States by Random House, Inc.,
and in Canada by Random House of Canada Ltd

Almaas, A. H.
The inner journey home: soul's realization of the unity of
reality / A. H. Almaas.—1st ed.
  p. cm.
Includes bibliographical references (p.   ) and index.
ISBN 1-59030-109-9
1. Spiritual life. 2. Self-realization. I. Title.
BP624 .A46   2004
204′.4—dc22
2003017239

Dedicated, with love, to humanity, in its inexorable, though excruciatingly slow, development toward maturity and completeness.

Contents

Editor's Preface ix
Acknowledgments xiii
Introduction xv

PART ONE: SOUL

1. Soul or Self 3
2. Organ of Experience 15
3. Organism of Consciousness 26

PART TWO: PROPERTIES AND FUNCTIONS OF THE SOUL

4. Noesis 45
5. Potential 63
6. Morphing Dynamism 76
7. Impressionability of Soul 94
8. Living Presence 108

PART THREE: ESSENCE AND SOUL DEVELOPMENT

9. Soul and Essence 131
10. Animal Soul 141
11. Normal Development of the Soul 151
12. Ego Development of the Soul 164
13. Liberating the Soul 185
14. Primitive Structures of the Soul 200

Part Four: The Inner Journey of the Soul

15. The Inner Journey 221
16. True Nature 247

Part Five: Dimensions of True Nature

17. Divine Love and Light 271
18. Being and Knowledge 292
19. Awareness and the Nonconceptual 324
20. Logos and Creative Dynamism 348
21. The Absolute and Emptiness 376

Part Six: Actualization of Reality

22. The Journey of Descent 413
23. Reality 441
24. Separation of Soul, God, and World 459

Epilogue 481
Appendix A. Western Concepts of Soul 483
Appendix B. Eastern Concepts of Soul 495
Appendix C. Soul in Sufism 517
Appendix D. Essence in Childhood Experience 529
Appendix E. Soul as Autopoietic System 555
Appendix F. Consciousness Research 561
Appendix G. Logoi of Teachings 567
Notes 583
References 697
Index 705

Editor's Preface

> Every name from which a truth proceeds is a name from before the Tower of Babel. But it has to circulate in the tower.
> —Alain Badiou, *Saint Paul: The Foundation of Universalism*

IN THE COURSE of a person's transformation of identity, the meanings, resonances, and connotations of words in his or her thinking inevitably shift. This is so even in our ordinary experience: A romantic encounter may find us saying, "I thought I knew what love was!" Insight in meditation might leave us exclaiming, "I thought I knew what emptiness was!"

The meanings of words as they appear in a living discourse—whether it is scientific, artistic, or philosophical—also change over time. Changes of usage occur within shifts of context: as understanding progresses, the new conceptual and historical matrix in which discourse occurs alters the sense of the words and concepts that operate in that matrix.

In time, A. H. Almaas's thinking as presented in *Inner Journey Home* may contribute to a transformation of the meaning of the word *soul*. His original thinking on the nature of the self has already appeared in *The Pearl Beyond Price* and *The Point of Existence*. The present thinking on the soul deals with the fundamental underpinning of these works. A powerful understanding of the nature of the human being that facilitates psychological and spiritual liberation, Almaas's approach to the soul also honors the human being as a mode of reality that cannot be reduced to an object. The perception and understanding of the soul as a multidimensional living field addresses many questions in consciousness studies and brings to bear an understanding of self-organizing systems.

As well, Almaas's understanding is resonant with the deepest levels of various traditional spiritual teachings, even though it does not depend on those teachings. For example, the nonexistence of the separate self, which appears in Buddhist as well as other teachings, is elucidated here through discovering the qualities of the soul. The impressionability of the open field of the soul allows it to be "conditioned" in the negative sense, but enables it also to be consciously articulated in its life in the world, without losing contact with its deepest primordial nature and without identifying with separating boundaries. The perception of the nonseparateness of the soul from the world or from Being itself comes to pass not as a result of an effort to arrive at that perception, nor from a corrective orientation (although these factors might be present), but primarily from direct and open investigation of one's experience, and thus of the soul herself. The soul discovers her very nature to be free of separating boundaries.

Almaas's use of "she" as the pronoun for soul is a good example of how the process of understanding affects the way words are used. The changes in discourse can in a sense go backward as well as forward, as the logic of the traditional uses of words is revealed through insight. Although this usage may appear awkward, sexist, limiting, or simply strange, it makes more and more sense as our appreciation of the nature of the soul develops. The use of a personal pronoun is necessitated by our knowledge of the soul as the conscious substance of the person. You are not an it! We see also that the various qualities of the soul are archetypally associated with the feminine.

The method of inner work developed by Almaas is not connected with a religious or mystical tradition, although it draws on the wisdom of several traditions as well as on psychology and various scientific orientations. Because the main method of this work is open and open-ended inquiry, the orientation of the work itself has a scientific sense to it: the extensive practice of suspension of identification with the content of thoughts, for example, is done not primarily with a certain end state in mind, but more in an experimental mode, as part of an inquiry into one's experience. Here it resembles Husserl's phenomenology, which attempted a scientific (in the sense of suspending one's assumptions and beliefs as much as possible) inquiry into consciousness. The practices and inquiry are done always with reference to understanding and its effect on the soul, and always with reference to one's actual lived experience in the moment. The application of psychological understanding helps to make conscious and thus render transparent various mental structures, removing the veils of identification with those structures, not by an effort to move one's awareness somewhere else, but simply by understanding the patterns and the status of those patterns relative to other modes of experience. As openness of mind develops, the process of understanding and disidentification with the soul's ego structures becomes increasingly fluid, even as the uncovering of increasingly primitive or archaic structures presents a challenge to the soul's ability to persevere in her open inquiry. This perseverance is supported by an increasingly clear love of the truth of reality itself; one's intimate experience of what in Sufism is called "nearness to God" brings growing courage and devotion to the soul's process.

The freedom of Almaas's body of work from the structures of a traditional teaching allows an extraordinary openness to his and his students' inquiry, which in turn allows an ongoing movement from identification to spaciousness, from recognition of structures to understanding those structures, to freedom from those structures. Because there is no specific state or level of awareness postulated as the goal of the practice, the ability to hold on to a specified identity of self moving toward a specified goal is increasingly challenged. In the penetrating inquiry on identity that we have used as an example, we not only come to the state or dimension of nonconceptual awareness (free of identification), but also become aware of the precise movements of the consciousness toward identifications that occlude this awareness. The method allows us to inquire into the content of identifications and into the psychological significance of the patterns of identification (and thus the emotional charges around these patterns). With some clarification of these patterns in the soul, we are free to inquire further into the phenomenon of the arising of identification itself, seeing through the soul's propensity to identify.

Almaas's approach shares with the scientific orientation an emphasis on precision, clarity, objectivity, and a sense of the infinite potential of our knowledge. Because this knowledge arises in the context of an orientation toward total openness grounded in present experience, and arises ultimately from a ground that is completely free of concepts and beliefs, the precision and specificity of the understanding can be very powerful: remaining in touch with the open ground, the concepts produced or revealed through the inquiry can never become solidified or reified. Therefore the concepts do not form stable structures that can be "nailed down," so to speak. Our continuing investigation into our experience of any quality of the soul leads us to a deeper, broader, and more dynamic understanding of that quality and its relation to the whole. Thus Almaas's understanding of the objectivity of various qualities of the soul can, like all conceptual structures, be taken as solid and reified, but in the course of our investigations we see that the appearance, wisdom, and function of the specific manifestations of various qualities depends on the state of the soul's realization and on what is needed in the soul's process at that moment. We see that the qualities of the soul naturally reflect its multidimensional nature, and thus appear and function differently in different contexts. Reading this book with the idea of being able to completely specify and "nail down" its concepts will definitely result in some frustration on the part of the reader. This is so especially for the second and third parts of the book, whose descriptions of the dimensions of reality encountered on this path, and other aspects of the path of the Diamond Approach, only hint at the vast and intricate play of appearance and understanding the soul enjoys as she becomes increasingly simple and free in her nature. We return to the beginning, then, and see how the soul's realization and understanding change not only the meanings and connotations of our words and concepts but also the understanding of what words and concepts are. This frees us from being limited by them, even as it frees us to use them with precision.

Then it is possible for the appearance of reality as logos to become the matrix of our knowing, and the never-ending revelation of the articulated world to become our perception. The vastness, intimacy, and depth of the soul's nature is the heart of this appearance and of this revelation.

Alia Johnson

Acknowledgments

THIS BOOK HAS BEEN LONG IN THE MAKING. When I first finished writing it, toward the end of 1998, I thought it would be published within three years, but that was not meant to be. The manuscript turned out to be long and unwieldy, and many of the ideas in it rather controversial. In the opinions of some individuals who read the manuscript, these ideas would perhaps be unpalatable to many readers.

As a result of this feedback, the book received a lot of help from many individuals, who gave generous and useful feedback and suggestions on both subject matter and structure, language and presentation. I would like to thank Larry Spiro, Debbie Ussery (Letofsky), Harry Hunt, Laura Lau, Leigh MaCune, and Nancy Baker for this invaluable support and assistance. I also want to thank Janel Ensler for her supportive administrative overseeing of the general endeavor, and Robin Everest for her timely work toward the end of the editing process. Our main editor at Shambhala, Kendra Crossen Burroughs, managed with exemplary excellence various complex challenges in the process of editing and putting the book into production. The freelance editor, Jacob Morris, provided excellent copyediting.

My chief editor, Alia Johnson, took it as a major project in the midst of her full teaching schedule, and worked with it with her usual dedication and love, for she felt personally connected to the material. The book contains many deep and subtle topics, with intertwining themes, and she still sculpted it into its final readable form, the accessible book you find in your hands. My gratitude to her and her dedication has no bounds, and I am sure the reader will reap the benefits of her valuable service.

Lastly, I am grateful for the support and care of Shambhala Publications and its skillful and kind staff in welcoming such a major project and doing the work necessary to produce and publish it. I appreciate both the generosity and the attitude of service that has characterized our relationship.

Introduction

IN THE CONTEMPORARY WEST we find ourselves in a world in which the soul or self, the world or cosmos, and Being or God, are understood to be separate aspects of reality. They are so understood in two senses: first, in the scientific, religious, and philosophical discourses of the day, and second, in the actual experience of the modern person. Regarding the latter, the actual experience, some part of the alienation of the self from Being, and the sense of being a separate entity in a world of entities, is a result of ordinary egoic development. It has been argued in many places, however, that the alienation from the sense of Being or the divine is particularly prevalent and thoroughgoing in the modern Western world, and that it is due to the rational, scientific, and materialistic worldview that dominates in the modern West, in conjunction with the end of a more or less universally assumed context of belief in God. In this book we try to show that it is more accurately due to a worldview that not only separates the areas of self/soul, world/cosmos, and Being/God, but almost universally does not question or investigate such separation in the spirit of truth that has been such an important part of our cultural history.

The orientation of this book moves toward a living understanding of the fundamental unity of reality. We believe that it is possible to communicate a vision of reality that heals the current prevalent dissociation of self, world, and Being. We also understand that the alienation of the self from Being is a source of much suffering and hardship in the world, and hope to contribute to alleviating that suffering through this new understanding of the nature of the human being and the path to reclaiming our connection to Being. Our approach is not a theoretical one based on an externally defined discovery of unity, as for instance the whole-systems approach that is so significant and valuable in some current scientific discussion. Although these discussions are important and resonant with our understanding (see appendix E), our discoveries come from a systematic investigation of the nature of reality starting with the direct knowing of the nature of self or soul. This revelation inevitably leads, as is known in all authentic spiritual and philosophical traditions, to an understanding of the nature of the cosmos and the nature of Being or the divine.

The present book has two main elements: first, mainly in the first half of the book, is a detailed discussion of the nature of the self or soul, which understanding has developed in the course of several decades of systematic research and investigation of personal experience, the practice of traditional spiritual methods, and research and application of modern psychological understanding. Our investigation has culminated in a largely original description of the soul, involving a detailed description of the actual phenomenological nature of the soul as well as a description of how the soul's development creates the structures that come to be known as the self. In the endnotes and appendixes, we connect this understanding with detailed comparisons and references to modern and traditional notions of self and soul.

The second element of this book, largely in the second half of the book, is a simple overview of the path of the soul's journey to the realization and embodiment of Being, as developed in the Diamond Approach, and again referenced to the best of our knowledge to various traditional and psychological sources. Here we explore the essence of the soul, her true nature, its aspects, dimensions, and integration into the soul. In the second half of the book, the exploration of the essence of the soul develops into an explication of the inner journey as it reaches and integrates the ultimate true nature, the final ground of all existence. We discuss this journey in terms of five coemergent boundless dimensions of Being, clarifying our understanding of both normal and enlightened awareness, and how they relate to each other. We refer to the inner journey discussed to this point as the journey of ascent, in which the soul ascends the various subtle dimensions of Reality.

To complete the story of the soul's path we discuss the journey of descent, in which the soul integrates the ground of true nature, with its five dimensions, into everyday life, which brings the soul to a realization of nonduality. This takes us to a discussion of mature and complete human realization, in which the human being becomes not only a microcosm and mirror of Reality, but its agent, organ, and servant. We end with an exploration of how the three facets of reality—the triad of soul or self, God or Being, and cosmos or world—are related to each other in enlightened awareness, and unfold our vision of Reality as it is revealed in the inner journey of this particular path of wisdom.

This book presents the larger view of the Diamond Approach, its metaphysical underpinnings, its overall structure, and its metapsychology. This will clarify its logos, which structures its methodology and which in turn is grounded in the articulated understanding of the five boundless dimensions of true nature. The reader will notice that certain segments of the view are discussed in detail while others are described only briefly. This is because we have discussed many subjects in detail in previous publications, so we only refer to them in this book, giving the appropriate references. Thus this book can be used as the central organizing presentation of the Diamond Approach. The elucidation of the path of the Diamond Approach appears in many previous books, to which we refer readers for more detailed discussion of various aspects of the understanding of the Diamond Approach.

Since this book is a presentation of the structure of the path of the Diamond Approach, the main body of the book does not refer to other teachings, and does not quote other authors. This is true of all chapters. Quotations and cross-references are left to the endnotes and appendices. Hence, the reader can approach this book in two different ways. The reader can read only the body of the book, learning about the Diamond Approach in and of itself. Or the reader can read the body of the book and the endnotes and appendices as they are referred to in the main body, learning about the Diamond Approach within the context of other teachings and sources. The choice will obviously depend on the reader; if he or she wishes to understand the Diamond Approach purely and independently from other sources, and see it as it is without regard to its relationship to other teachings and writings, then reading only the main body of the book is the preferred option. But some readers prefer scholarly references, and connections with other teachings and sources; for such a reader, reading the endnotes and appendices in the order given in the text will be the preferred option. Our suggestion is that the reader read the book twice, once with and once without the endnotes and appendices.

The extensive endnotes fulfill several functions, including:

1. To elaborate in more detail some points and questions that are not in the main theme of this book, but are related to it.
2. To substantiate some of the ideas and findings through quotations from other more established teachings, or from scientific and psychological sources.
3. To show how and where the Diamond Approach uses, integrates, modifies, and develops findings from other sources, both spiritual and psychological.
4. To relate some of the concepts, ideas, and observations of the Diamond Approach to other teachings and fields of research. This may help the reader to understand them more accurately or completely by situating them in different and perhaps more familiar contexts.
5. To demonstrate that the Diamond Approach is similar to many well-known wisdom traditions in its general outlines, but also to illustrate differences.
6. To situate the Diamond Approach and its vision and view within the larger context of the wisdom tradition, as a particular path for human integration.
7. To demonstrate that even though the Diamond Approach expresses a particular approach to inner transformation and liberation, similarly to all other wisdom teachings, it is particularly an expression of the specifically Western tradition of seeking inner truth.

The book contains several appendices. Some develop ideas in the book and endnotes in more detail and with greater technical precision. Some address questions and themes that are tangential to the main body of the book but nevertheless amplify and develop its meaning. Some apply the Diamond Approach to other fields or areas, and some attempt to relate our understanding to other fields or cast them in the language of other fields or teachings.

Like other publications of the author, this book is not a rigorous philosophic treatise or an attempt to prove any theory or idea scientifically or logically. Even though the book utilizes philosophic discussions, logical reasoning, and scientific findings and procedures, it presents a teaching that developed experientially, as the expression of an inner transformation of consciousness that the author has undergone, as have some of his associates and many students who have participated in the teaching.

As a human individual I am the author of this book, but not the source of the teaching presented in it. The real source of the teaching is the true nature of Reality, the essence of our soul and what ultimately we are, the elixir that alone can transform our consciousness and life. By writing and publishing this book, and the others before it, I am fulfilling a facet of my personal function as a discriminating and expressive organ, and an appreciative servant, of this wonderful and magnificent truth of Reality.

PART ONE

Soul

1 Soul or Self

ANCIENT WESTERN THINKERS UNDERSTOOD human subjectivity or consciousness to include a spiritual dimension. Socrates originated the understanding of soul as comprising all of the individual consciousness; Plato and others further developed it. Although in ancient Greece there were variations in the notion of the soul among the various schools of philosophy, in general the human being was conceived of as a soul inhabiting a body. In Hellenic civilization, the concept of soul specifically referred to the totality of the nonphysical dimension of the individual. The soul—called "psyche"—comprised all of one's subjectivity, including what we now call mind, heart, spirit, consciousness, will and so on.

In contemporary thought, in contrast, the most common uses of the word *soul* involve either religious concepts of a particular aspect of a human being with spiritual characteristics, or nonreligious concepts, such as those appearing in transpersonal psychology, indicating various different aspects of the human being involving depth, presence, and some spiritual element.

In the Diamond Approach we have come to use the word *soul* as the best description of what a human being actually is, in a sense that is connected with these older concepts of soul, as well as with notions of soul held by various spiritual traditions.[1] However, our understanding of the human being as soul takes into consideration such contemporary knowledge as modern psychology, philosophy, and systems theory, in addition to our understanding of various religious and spiritual teachings, Eastern and Western. As we will explore in detail in the following chapters, our study of the soul has illuminated in great detail the nature, functioning, and development of the soul both in terms of the normal development of the self and in terms of the soul's spiritual nature and development. As we understand it, the soul is not separate from what is normally understood as the self, and in fact includes the normal self and its conventional or superficial levels of experience as well as its pure and perfect spiritual ground. Having taken an inquiry-based phenomenological approach to the study of the soul, we have discovered the nature of the human being to be a dynamic, living organism of consciousness, an ever-changing, open, multidimensional field whose experience can come to know and actualize all dimensions of Being.

Can the Self Lose Its Soul?

In modern Western culture, the soul is generally seen as something otherworldly, invisible, and distant from normal experience. In fact, the common notion is that soul is something someone can lose or exist without, as in the expression "he lost his soul," "he sold his soul to the devil," and "this woman's got no soul." The common usage of the word *self* refers to the individual or the person, specifically as distinct from others. Merriam-Webster's dictionary defines *self* as "the essential person as distinct from others." We can say, then, that the prevalent meaning of these terms is that a person is a self that can have or not have a soul. If we are religiously oriented we may think we are a soul that has a self, but this is not the prevalent modern view.

As noted above, many ancient thinkers did not make this distinction. For them a person *is* a soul; this notion of soul originated with Socrates and subsequently became the primary Western conception. (See appendix A for a detailed discussion of Western concepts of soul.) The ancient Greeks generally used the term *soul* the way we now use the term *self*, to refer to an individual person, with two differences: the first is that the Greeks conceptualized the soul as distinct from the body, while we generally think of the self as including the body. Some think of the self as the body, but rarely is the self referred to as distinct from the body. The second difference is that the Socratic notion of soul included the spiritual potential, which the modern concept of self does not, necessarily. In some sense, the modern concept of self did not exist in ancient times. There was no such thing as a self that could lose its soul.

The contemporary concept of self is actually vague and unclear; it does not refer to exactly the same thing for all individuals or writers. This indefiniteness and unclarity is reflected in the use of the concept in Western psychology. The field of depth psychology, especially psychoanalytically based psychology, is only recently becoming focused on studying the human being as self, and there is not yet a uniform meaning or agreed-upon definition of the concept. Some authors use the term *self* to refer to the total individual, including mind and body; others use the term to refer to the functional self, yet others to the feeling or subjective sense of self. Some refer to a mental construct, and others call the "self" specifically the self-image or self-concept.[2]

The original Socratic concept of soul became what we now call self, denuded of the substance and richness of its original meaning. The ancient concept of soul included both of the modern concepts of self and soul, but excluded the body. For these ancients, especially those following Socrates, the individual self was inseparable from its essential and spiritual elements.[3]

If we consider common expressions like "he lost his soul" and "she sold her soul" metaphorically rather than literally, we recognize in them a wisdom about the true condition of self and soul. Even though we are considering the soul as what the human being actually is, and therefore as not subject to being lost, we see that there can be meaning in the notion of losing the soul. For the self to lose its soul, or not to have soul, can mean to become superficial, to lose or be without the depth and substance that is possible for an individual, the source of moral and spiritual strength and character. We can see this in the term *soulful*, which we normally use to describe someone with a depth of feeling or a sense of inner richness. In other words, to lose one's soul means to lose contact with the inner depth and richness of being human. This understanding refers back to the classical and Socratic Western understanding of soul, in which the surface self and the inner spiritual richness are seen to be two levels of the same reality, which is our human subjectivity. Generally speaking, the common expressions we mention above are meant and taken relatively. There are degrees of loss of soul, degrees of alienation from the spiritual depths of the human soul. We typically use the above expressions only to refer to severe alienation or rejection of inner depth or spiritual integrity.

In contemporary life, rather than conceiving of human beings as fundamentally souls, we conceive of them as what we now call self, and this conventional sense of self is one that is normally not so much in contact with its soul; it is a self alienated from the soul's inner richness and spiritual depth. The ancient Greek philosophers would have considered such a self to be an alienated or spiritually depraved and unregenerate soul. In our times, the expression we normally use to refer to ourselves, *self*, refers in actuality to self without reference to soul, without an assumption of spiritual nature.

We do not imply here that contemporary humankind is more alienated from its spiritual depths than people in ancient times. We are discussing only how the classical Western concept of soul has metamorphosed into the modern concept of self. In this book we present an understanding that unifies the ancient, more multidimensional concept of soul with the understanding of modern civilization. This unifying vision can support our notion of ourselves as souls and thus present new possibilities for realizing the depth of human potential.

The ancient philosophers whose works are available to us saw the realization of the truth of one's nature as the normal potential for a human being. Our cultural ancestors referred to themselves as souls, meaning that their view of the human being included a spiritual dimension. Regardless of the degree of embodiment of such inner depth, many individuals lived within the atmosphere of this rich and multidimensional view of humanity.

In that atmosphere, the spiritual—at least the possibility of inner purity and perfection—was always close, not absent or distant as it is in the overall orientation of our secular era.

The Death of Soul in Psychology

In current Western culture, the self is the subject of the field of psychology. The dearth of notions of soul in Western contemporary thought is nowhere more apparent than here. While some approaches to psychology include a spiritual or some inner dimension—for example, Carl Jung's analytic psychology, Roberto Assagioli's psychosynthesis,[4] and the larger category of transpersonal psychology—it remains true that the majority of approaches to psychology conceive of the individual as a self without a spiritual dimension. These include behaviorism, experimental psychology, child research, neuropsychology, cognitive psychology, and psychoanalysis and its various schools, such as ego psychology, object relations theory, self psychology, and developmental psychology.

It would be surprising if this were otherwise, since psychology developed within the context of Western thought, in which the split of soul/self from the world and from the divine was assumed. Hence it is bound to be a study of soul/self that does not include considerations of the spiritual dimension of this facet.[5]

Thus psychology, at least in its main thrust, is bound to have no consideration of soul. It emerged within a current of thought that is philosophically grounded in the separation of the self from the divine, and merely took further the separation of the self from its spiritual essence, within a mentality already grounded in this separation.

These considerations indicate a direction for the field of psychology to consider, if it is to regain its understanding of the whole human being including the spiritual dimension. This orientation has the potential to unify the two extreme ends of the schools of psychology, those of cognitive and experimental psychology on the one hand and transpersonal psychology on the other. More precisely, psychology can regain its relevance to the understanding of soul by connecting to the study of God or Being on one hand, and cosmos or world on the other, that is, to spirituality and to science.

We cannot attempt to reclaim soul for our modern understanding by returning to the ancient ways of studying soul. To abandon the wealth of knowledge developed by the various schools of psychology in the last century or so would deprive us of the powerful tools for self-knowledge developed by modern psychology. The vision needed for a new psychology must hold the ancient way of understanding soul while at the same time embracing and employing modern understanding and methods of research. Our vision must not separate psychology from spirituality or from science. As we will see, the view that recognizes the true connection of the soul to the universe can and must embrace scientific knowledge.

The study of God/Being—that is, of religion, spirituality, and philosophy—has itself become alienated; it has become peripheral, disconnected from the needs and aspirations of the masses of humanity, and even from the majority of those carrying the main currents of Western thought. As part of the development that Nietzsche called the death of God, Western thought has become increasingly secular, and our understanding of the world and ourselves has turned steadily toward science and psychology. The development of modern science has captured human aspirations for at least the past century, although for a few decades psychology has increasingly been attracting our aspirations for meaning and salvation.

Isolation of God and Being

For most people, religion and spirituality are isolated compartments in their lives, if they are relevant at all. It is true that there is a growing interest in spirituality in the Western world, as evidenced by the proliferation of Eastern schools and gurus here and even of shamanic and ancient mystery schools. However, many individuals engaged in such paths experience their inner work as separate and isolated from the rest of their lives. A central concern of students in many spiritual groups and schools is how to integrate their inner paths with their everyday lives, their work and relationships, and the fact of living in our modern secular society. Contemporary society seems to lack a context, or a fundamental fabric of holding understanding, in which a spiritual life could be an integral and natural dimension of daily life.

The isolation of religious and spiritual matters is more apparent in the disciplines of thought than in general society; the concern with spirit is absent from most science and psychology. On the other hand, religious teachings depend upon received doctrine, not upon the findings and the methods of science and psychology. Hence, most teachers of spiritual practice disavow logical and experimental scrutiny. Religions generally resist the intrusion of both scientific findings and psychological insights. Many spiritual teachings and mystical traditions tend to emphasize the realization of truth independent of the logical and reasoning mind. This orientation has developed to the extent that many people believe that logical thinking and reasoning are the enemies of mystical experience and knowledge. The popular (though incomplete) understanding of Zen, for instance, is that one needs to discard the reasoning mind in order to become enlightened.

Our Western spiritual understanding has grown distant from its roots; Plato's and Pythagoras's spiritual training required the utmost rigor of logic and precision of discrimination. Pythagoras taught spirituality through instruction in mathematics, and Plato instituted mathematics as part of the curriculum of his academy. Logical debates were part of Plato's spiritual training, a practice inspired by Socrates.[6] The originators of our Western thought conceived of mystical experience and logical discrimination as two sides of the same capacity for knowing. The contemporary assumptions are radically otherwise; the major thrust of thought now is that mystical experience and logical thought are not only divergent but also incompatible.[7]

Contemporary thought concerning spirit tends to reflect the modern dichotomy between self and soul. Religion is the realm of priests and ministers, functioning as specialists to advise and aid individuals in a particular area of their lives. Most spiritual teachers seem to participate in this dichotomy, seeing themselves as caretakers of the soul or spirit, and leaving concerns of the self to psychologists. (This view is changing somewhat, but the dichotomy is still the rule.) It is interesting in this light to remember that the major religious traditions have developed in such a way that their primary concern is either preparation for the afterlife, in theistic religions, or enlightenment that brings freedom from existence, in Eastern religions. Concern for such matters as the redemption of the present world, as fulfillment and completeness of life, can arguably be seen not to be the primary perspective of the major spiritual traditions.

Soul without Self

We see, then, that just as psychology has adopted a self with no soul, spirituality has adopted a soul with no self. From the perspective of many spiritual approaches, the spiritual aspect of the human being is seen as quite separate from or even incompatible with the self, which is defined as that which leads the primarily bodily life, concerned with enhancing the self and material well-being. Thus most realms of religion and spirituality have developed an imbalance, in which there is a dichotomy between the spiritual and the material, and the material is rejected in favor of the spiritual. This tends to alienate the "man of the world," the worldly people who constitute the majority of humankind and who live from the perspective that ordinary, everyday life is important and potentially fulfilling. (We have discussed this matter extensively in the book *The Pearl Beyond Price*, which explores how an integration between the worldly and spiritual can be effected without compromising either.)

The perspective of soul with no self, the sense that the spiritual is distinct and divorced from the psychological, also characterizes some areas of Eastern thought. In Eastern or Western spiritual work, this imbalance manifests as working on spiritual development without taking care of one's psychological conflicts and aberrations. So one may develop with deep spiritual experience and insight, but retain some neurotic and emotionally conflicted manifestations.

In the past, religious and spiritual traditions dealt with these manifestations through moral and ethical purification. Because of the increasing secularization of society, these practices are generally not applied strictly and completely. However, psychological understanding shows us that even moral and ethical purification might not be effective in dealing with deep-seated neurosis, or with what is called structural weakness in the ego. Our present understanding of how unconscious beliefs and motivations manifest in distorted attitudes and behavior can help us see how one can be scrupulously devout and moral but at the same time be addictive, abusive, or otherwise psychologically unhealthy. Events across the range of modern spiritual institutions demonstrate this amply; we have seen how spiritually elevated or brilliant teachers and personalities can behave in psychologically aberrant ways; this has included Tibetan lamas, Zen masters, Indian gurus, Sufi teachers, Catholic cardinals, Hasidic rabbis, fundamentalist evangelists, and so on. There is no reason for us to assume that this is a contemporary phenomenon rather than a long-standing one that is coming to light.

It is obvious that such aberrant behavior indicates a psychological disturbance that is bound to influence and distort our spiritual attainment. This points to the need to include our sophisticated psychological understanding in our spiritual training. Using this understanding to serve our spiritual development might help us to appreciate that the specialization that created the field of psychology can be fruitful in surprising ways.

The problem with modern psychology is not a matter of wrong development of thought, but the way this thought is used in the larger context of the understanding of human life. It seems that the time has come for a new integration of the understanding of psychology with spiritual understanding. This will take us to a higher point of our spiraling evolution, an integration in which the currents of thought that have separated are reunited at a new level. The work discussed in this book contributes to this integration, utilizing the methods and knowledge of modern psychology as part of a view of the human being that sees no dichotomy between self and soul. We can now approach psychology from within the original Socratic notion of soul, a soul that includes the spiritual essence and depth in human potential.

A New Metapsychology

We are developing here a new metapsychology, one that views our overall psychological experience from a ground that does not dichotomize it from the spiritual dimension. Our metapsychology is based on a knowledge of the soul, not only a knowledge of the self, with its ego and its subsystems, or its overt behavior.

This higher ground of understanding that unifies the psychological and the spiritual is a facet of a larger integration, one that also integrates it to the scientific method and its view of the world, a world that is in turn connected to our spiritual understanding. This unification addresses the common modern perspective in which the soul or self is seen as separate from the world or the cosmos, and separate also from God or Being. More precisely, our new metapsychology is embedded within, and is an expression of, a metaphysics that brings to a new level of unity thought and research in relation to the three facets of reality, soul/self, world/cosmos, and God/Being. In this metaphysics, spirituality and science are seen as two facets of the same thing, which involves recognizing a ground where the spiritual and the physical, in addition to the psychological, are seen to be meaningfully related.

More than any other factor in our modern life, the dissociation of soul/self from the divine realm or Being and from the world terribly impoverishes us. The transformation of our identity from soul to self has indirectly impoverished our world; robbing us of our spiritual potential, this development left us increasingly identified with and thus dominated by the physical dimension of the self. And the more we experience ourselves as mainly physical, the more we see our world as fundamentally physical. This view of the world is in most of modern society the prevalent one: the world is simply matter.[8] Rather than inhabiting a comprehensible but ultimately mysterious living world, we inhabit a material universe, explainable only by physical science. The world or cosmos, separate from soul and from God/Being, is only matter. It is a dead world, an inert universe waiting to be explored by our scientific reason.[9]

For many people in the modern world, and for virtually all thought that is considered scientific, the dominant orientation is materialistic. When the soul is considered to be and experienced as a self, an objectifiable entity whose most fundamental identity is the physical body, we are bound to be materialistic, caring for material well-being, wealth and possessions, security and comfort more than inner depth and fullness.

Materialism is naturally the central philosophic position of our science, for our science is first and foremost a study of matter. Even the study of life involves the consideration of exclusively material components and physical processes. This orientation is actually a logical necessity for the separation of cosmos/world from the rest of Reality. It is clear that if we sincerely desire an amelioration of the rampant materialism of our times, we need not only to become more spiritual—namely, to regain our soul—but also to realize the unity of our Reality. And since the closest and most accessible facet for us is that of soul/self, we need to begin there.

Thus, to explore our unified vision of Reality, we begin by addressing the question of soul, a soul that we will come to understand includes what is conventionally called self, but also the spiritual depths and possibilities of humanity. We will refer to the human being as soul, meaning the self as we all know it, but this self is understood to be inseparable from what we in contemporary times call soul and spirit. We will use the two terms, *self* and *soul*, interchangeably, but use *soul* when we want to emphasize the spiritual nature or inner depths—or connection to such—and *self* when we want to emphasize the everyday identity and self of contemporary people, or the linguistic sense of differentiating a person from other individuals. We will often be somewhat ambiguous about which aspect of the soul/self we are emphasizing, because the surface and the depth of the soul are not a definite polarity, but form a continuum in which experience is in a constant state of flux. Holding this very ambiguity in our language can help us to overcome habits of thought that arose in all of us from our absorption of the conventional dualism of soul/self. At all times, our concept of soul/self includes all possible inner experience of the human individual. It is our interiority, the organ of perception, experience, and action.[10]

How do we study the soul? Scientists study their objects of research through controlled experiments. This method has created unprecedented advances in human knowledge and material well-being. Yet this approach relies exclusively on the use of the logical mind, applied to data collected with the senses, and with tools that function as extensions of the senses. The rational mind that is used to conduct science is typically split off completely from knowledge that involves direct knowing. It is the rational mind that chooses the object of study; it is this mind that decides what experiment or procedure to do; it is this mind that conducts the experiments, and it is this mind that draws conclusions and constructs theories.

One of the main functions of the use of scientific instruments, technical procedures, and logical analysis is to ensure that the information received through the senses is accurate and objective, or that we interpret them correctly. Thus the instruments and technical procedures utilized by physical science perform two primary functions: extending the range of the senses and correcting their faulty input. Even with very sophisticated technical and analytical support, however, the central mechanism of collecting data for scientific understanding remains the physical senses. Our scientific method cannot dispense with the function of the physical senses, just as it cannot dispense with the logical discursive mind.

However, the experience of the senses is not what the explorers of

Reality in the wisdom traditions call direct experience. In fact, the wisdom traditions of humankind, Eastern and Western, ancient and modern, speak of sense experience as exactly what is immediately present in the way of direct experience. When they speak of direct experience in intuitive knowing or spiritual contemplation, they mean that the mind itself, the medium of knowing, is in direct contact with the object of knowledge.

Of course, this kind of knowing is not recognized by our science; its view and method are precisely based on isolating the observer from what is observed. The philosophical position of science—its exclusive reliance on the discursive mind and the physical senses for knowing—cannot be the ultimate arbiter of truth if science is to be integrated with an understanding of the self and of God or Being. According to the senses, there are no such things as soul and God; they cannot be verified scientifically. Is there a more fundamental dimension of knowing, a real dimension that can support both science and spirituality? We will argue in this book that there is, and will begin our exploration with an unquestionable fact about the human soul, the fact that we have a capacity for knowing, any knowing. More precisely, we need to begin with ourselves, our body and mind and all their capacities of awareness and knowing. At least at the beginning, we have only ourselves as the agents of knowing, the organs of perception, and the locus of the revelation of truth.[11] By investigating ourselves, questioning how we are aware and conscious, exploring how we perceive and know, wondering how we can discern truth from falsehood, we can begin to study the organ of awareness employed by all ways of knowing, the spiritual/mystical mode and the logical/scientific.[12]

2   Organ of Experience

THE WORK OF INNER REALIZATION requires not only an external supportive context and environment but also the development of an inner vessel, the internal context for the journey.[1] Some Eastern traditions conceptualize this as the inner mandala that constitutes the totality of the personal field of experience; the corresponding notion in the Western tradition is usually seen as the soul. In fact, in our approach,[2] recognizing and understanding the soul as the inner vessel of the work of transformation is the best way to begin the inner investigation. The initial awareness of soul gives us the appropriate orientation, because it begins to show us what we will be exploring. In particular it helps us to recognize what is the "I" that we want to know and understand. When we are aware of the soul, we are aware of what we are actually investigating, the actual medium of experience, rather than merely the contents of experience. As we understand the soul, we appreciate what it is that needs to wake up, to recognize and realize its nature, to develop and become refined. We can know directly what it is that goes through the transformation.

In the Diamond Approach, students are taught various practices that develop the capacity to recognize and orient to (and later from) the direct experience of presence, of the field of awareness. In addition, ongoing open inquiry into one's experience, both of the content of mind/emotion/body and of the field of presence experienced by the student, and the effects of the latter on the former and vice versa, constitute a learning and orientation that support the ongoing revelation of various levels of the truth of the soul's reality and of Reality beyond the individual soul. The transformations in the sense of self that result from these practices turn out to be systematically consistent with various developments in traditional spiritual teachings.

In the Diamond Approach, we use the term *soul* to refer to the whole self, including all its elements and dimensions. Thus, when we work on ourselves we are working on our souls. Our true or spiritual nature does not need work; it is primordially pure and complete. However, we need to work on ourselves in order to become sufficiently open and clear to even glimpse this nature. What is it that becomes open and clear? Many will say it is the mind, but then what do we mean by mind? Is it our thoughts and thinking mechanisms, or does it include our feelings and emotions, our capacity to will and choose, our faculties and potentials? If by mind we mean all of our experiences and perceptions and the various capacities, faculties, and potentials, then we are back to our notion of soul. Our use of *soul* refers to the totality of our subjective experience, including whatever mechanisms and capacities, conscious or unconscious, are involved in that. We prefer not to call it "mind" because Western thought does not conceptualize mind in this way, but considers it only one of our faculties. Also, the notion of mind does not have a clear meaning or reference. So in our usage, soul contains mind, as mind is understood in Western usage. We will discuss the relation between mind and soul more extensively in chapter 4 and in the second half of this book.

Whenever we do any work on ourselves, or engage in any way in the inner journey, we are invariably working with our soul. There is nothing else to work on. When we can recognize the soul explicitly, our work becomes more exact and to the point. Understanding the soul clarifies what needs to be done and how it can be done. If you are an artist, a sculptor, for instance, and you want to sculpt, you need to know what the material is that you are working with. When you know what the material is and what its properties are, you know what you need in order to proceed with your sculpting. If you do not know anything about the material you are working with you will be at a great disadvantage. Without knowledge of your material, even if you are able to do some sculpting your work will not be easy, effective, or elegant.

In the same way, to know what it is that needs the work, to know the properties and characteristics of what goes through the inner transformation, will increase the accuracy of orientation of the work; we will see more clearly which way to go, where we are going, and what tools we need. It amplifies efficiency and cuts away all kinds of extraneous things; we will tend to not waste our time dallying around with questions and concerns that are not fundamental. It will clarify the priorities of the work, and of our life in general.

In some teachings, when the teacher is speaking from a certain perception of reality, inner or spiritual work is spoken of as a matter of not doing. This orientation might be seen as surrender, faith, or receptivity. However, these attitudes reflect some of the properties of the soul, and so even from the point of view that the inner work is not a doing, knowing the properties of the soul is still of immense benefit.

When we work on ourselves without knowledge of what the soul is, it is easy to miss the comprehensive, multidimensional, complex, and alive nature of what we are working with. Without knowledge of the soul itself, we would be considering in our inner work parts and fragments of the soul, but would lack the perspective of the wholeness and totality of the individual. This lack particularly reduces the capacity for working in an integrated and integrative way.

Knowing the Soul

To know and appreciate the soul is the point of entry into the Diamond Approach, but it is also useful in undergoing any path of inner transformation. In this book we will see how what arises in the path of realization is intricately connected with the qualities of the soul.

With this knowledge, we have a clear orientation for inner work, in particular an integration of the many developments and experiences, short- and long-term, that are involved in the path of realization. Knowing the properties of the soul also informs the seeker how to skillfully approach what can and cannot be done in a given situation when confronting certain issues and situations. We are able to understand what methods will work best and how these methods work. We are able to appreciate the rationale behind various methods of inner work; for example, understanding the ground of soul as awareness whose essence can be known to be emptiness helps us to understand how to work with methods which involve space and emptiness. On another level, understanding ego development helps us to understand the particular issues that arise as ego structures are challenged by meditation and other spiritual practices.

In addition, even a partial experience and understanding of the soul brings us to an appreciation of the rich, beautiful potential of the soul's development, realization, and liberation. This direct knowledge of what is possible for our soul is tremendously inspiring and orienting.

Recognizing and understanding the soul is itself a large part of the inner development. We spoke in the last chapter of the separation of the soul from the world and from God or Being. Actually, as we will see, only the soul can know and understand Reality in these three facets, so awakening the soul is of the utmost necessity for actualizing our vision. The soul is the window into Reality. The soul is actually much more intimately linked to Reality than we normally perceive, as we will see further on.

Even though we are always the soul, for the soul is what we are, the direct knowledge of the soul is not so accessible. It is like the water we swim in, while we are thirsty and looking for it. We not only swim in this water; our bodies are largely made of it. In terms of knowing the soul, we have been so identified with being the normal self, the self that has lost awareness of its spiritual ground, that we cannot even envision what it will be like to recognize ourselves as soul. The degeneration from soul to self, which in actual lived experience is no different in our era than in others, involves such fundamental and far-reaching alienation that to reverse it requires an extensive path of transformation. The direct experience of the soul involves penetrating or bypassing many layers of beliefs and concepts about ourselves and about reality; for most of us the full perception of soul occurs only occasionally, so rarely that most of us do not even comprehend at such times that it is our soul we are experiencing. Therefore, even in a path of inner transformation it is not possible at the beginning to directly recognize the soul.[3] Understanding develops gradually and in stages as one progresses in one's work.

Furthermore, even when the direct experience of the soul begins to arise and unfold, it is still not easy to understand what we are experiencing. This has to do with a particular characteristic of soul, a characteristic that differentiates her experientially from essence or spirit, even though the latter is her inner truth and deeper potential. The experience of the soul is vague, ambiguous, indefinite, imprecise, and impressionistic. More accurately, when we understand the soul precisely we recognize that she is not something definite but something amorphous. This is one reason such experience and understanding is often most effectively expressed in the languages of poetry, music, and art, which are suited for the communication of multivalenced meaning and nonlinear understanding. Thus we see many of the teachings of the Western traditions—Christian, Jewish, or Sufi—expressed in poetry or stories. This indirectness of expression retains the possibility of communicating things whose nature is not precisely or completely definable.

The ambiguity and amorphousness of the experience of soul are connected with the fact that it is in the very nature of the soul that everything in it is interconnected with everything else. The soul's nature is holographic; that is, each of her manifestations implicitly expresses all other possible manifestations.[4] Everything about her is flowing into everything else, with multileveled reverberations, so we cannot make a specific boundary in order to study this or that part specifically. In other words, it is not possible to isolate one component of the soul and study it separately from her other components. The soul is inherently and basically a nonlinear phenomenon. Therefore, to understand one quality or faculty of the soul it is necessary to have some feel for the totality of the soul. As we will see, every time we discuss one aspect of the soul we find ourselves unable to restrict our discussion from flowing into other questions and concerns about her. Whenever we genuinely begin to penetrate to the direct experience of the soul we are bound to move toward holographic wholeness.

Another reason for this ambiguity is that the very fabric of the soul, at the ontological level of presence, is flexible, impressionable, and dynamic. The soul is dynamic: she is in constant movement, is changeable, active and interactive, responsive and adaptive. We can have a very definite experience and feeling in which we know this is the soul but we cannot create a definite boundary and separate this experience from others. When we experience essence, on the other hand, we can precisely study and differentiate love from awareness, truth from will, peace from joy, and so on. But when it comes to the soul it is different; to study the aliveness of the soul we cannot help but study her dynamism; to study her dynamism we have to explore her impressionability; to investigate her impressionability we begin easily to see it intimately connected to her capacity of imagination; our exploration goes on in this flowing stream.

Locus of Experience

What is the soul in the most general sense? First, soul is the locus of our own individual awareness. It is our own self-awareness as a localized phenomenon. This has two meanings, external and internal. To understand the first we need to recognize that pure awareness is nonlocal, nondimensional, beyond time and space, and soul is the expression and manifestation of this awareness in our time-space universe. The soul is awareness, but not simply awareness. It is awareness localized in an environment; it is our individual awareness. It is the locus of our experience of ourselves, the place where we experience ourselves, the location in Reality where we experience the self.

This point is difficult to comprehend, because we ordinarily think of the site of our awareness as dictated by the location of the body, which is ordinarily the case. However, this perspective implies that the body is more fundamental than the soul, and here we are interested in exploring whether this is the case. This perspective is directly challenged by out-of-body experiences, frequently reported by individuals under anesthesia or in near-death experiences.[5] Reports of such experiences indicate that one can be aware of the body from a different physical location; for example, these reports frequently mention looking down at the body from above. The reports of out-of-body experiences indicate that we can be aware of our environment from the perspective of a different location than the body.

A similar perspective arises when we experience pure awareness, or any of the boundless dimensions of Being. In these experiences we are aware that our presence is everywhere; it is omnipresent. Even though we are aware of our presence everywhere, and not only inside the body, our perception is located in time and space. This is interesting because in such experiences we can be acutely aware that we are not the body, that the body is part of the manifestation of the omnipresence, like any other physical objects, but our experience continues to be localized. It is clear that this question is relevant when we contemplate out-of-body experience, whether in life or after death. This understanding shows that awareness is localized, which is necessary for perception, and under these conditions it is not the body that is responsible for the localization.

Under normal circumstances the body and soul are coextensive and hence function together to locate awareness. The more important meaning of locus—related to the first—is the second one, which is that the soul is the site where all of our experiences, of everything and on all levels, happen. So my experience happens within my soul; it does not happen in someone else's soul. Although this observation is the basis of the notion of an individual soul, its relevance is that the soul is our personal inner field of experience, the matrix where all inner events and processes happen. In other words, the recognition of soul as individual locus not only leads to differentiating one soul from another,[6] but also to the important insight that soul functions as the container of all experiences. The soul is literally the vessel that contains and holds all of our inner events.

Our normal experience does not generally include the perception of the soul as a vessel. Most of us tend to think of ourselves as a self that has experiences, thoughts, feelings, sensations, actions, perceptions, and so on, but we are not necessarily aware of a unified field or vessel that holds all these. The content of our experience seems to us to consist of events—thoughts, feelings, perceptions, and sensations—that come and go, like clouds passing through some obscure medium. We are not aware of this medium, and most of the time do not think that there is such a thing. In this way most of us most of the time are products of our times; we rarely even contemplate this question, because we believe we already know what is happening: we believe that inner events and external perceptions appear in our nervous system, which transmits signals to the brain, which then decodes and recognizes the content. Our basically materialist scientific view impels us to think of our experiences in terms of the mechanisms of the body, and so we conceive of our experience happening similarly to how things happen in a computer. In a computer the various events occur in and between wires and chips, and within their connections, but there is no unified container or fabric for all of the events.

If we are pressed to consider the question of where our experiences happen, we sometimes think of them happening in our mind, sometimes in our body, or both. We are not clear that we are each a field of sensitivity, a matrix of awareness, and that differentiating this inner matrix into body and mind is experientially arbitrary. Both physical sensations and mental images arise within the same matrix of awareness, the soul.[7]

When we are finally able to experience the soul directly, we can recognize that she constitutes a medium in which all of our inner events occur, a unified container and vessel that is the very fabric of our subjectivity. We can actually experience her as a sensitive field, a field of consciousness or awareness, where all experiences arise and pass away. We can imagine the soul as completely coextensive with the body, forming its experienced interiority. Whatever we perceive as happening within us, whether a thought, an image, an emotion, or a sensation, occurs within the body, but more intimately within the soul, because the soul functions as the sensitivity or awareness of the body.[8] This kind of perception leads us to the understanding of the soul as the inner vessel, necessary for the inner process of transformation. It is then clear why the development of this perception will help hold and support our inner journey.

To understand the soul as locus of experience is important for the direct experience and development of the soul. Without this understanding we simply remain in the normal experience of the ego. In this egoic experience there is the experiencer and there is what we experience; the locus is not perceived. Thus, to perceive the locus of experience is to begin to recognize the soul.

Agent of Experience

When we recognize the inner vessel, and see that it is the locus of all experience, knowledge of the soul begins to unfold. Since the soul is the field where all experience happens, it becomes possible to see that there is no experiencer experiencing the inner events, apart from the soul. This field is a field of sensitivity; it is the consciousness that is conscious of such experience; so the soul is the experiencer. It is a field of sensitivity—we will shortly discuss this sensitivity in its relation to consciousness, awareness, and knowing—capable of what we call experience. It can experience anything arising within itself, within its field. Soul, we see here, is basically an organ of experience. We normally think of ourselves as the experiencer of our experiences, but we do not know what this experiencer is. When we recognize the soul, it becomes clear that this experiencer is the same thing as the field where all experience happens. The experiencer is the locus; there is no duality between subject and locus of experience.

We also normally think of ourselves as the perceiver of outer objects and events. Once we recognize the soul as the inner field that contains inner experience and events, it becomes easy to see that the soul is also the perceiver of all events, outer as well as inner. Outer manifestations can be seen to be outside the soul but our perception of them occurs within us, within our sensitive interiority, our soul.[9] The soul is the recipient of perception; these perceptions might arise through the windows of the senses, but it is the soul that is the subject that actually perceives and recognizes such perceptions. The soul in this functions similarly to the eyes that receive the light, also similarly to the brain that deciphers the light signals, but most primarily it is the consciousness that finally sees and recognizes, the consciousness that becomes impacted by what it sees, and responds accordingly.

In recognizing the soul we recognize the real self that we intuitively know is at the center of all experience, and the agent of all functioning. Our intuition transforms into a direct perception of what we have sensed to be not only the site of all inner experiences and perceptions, but also the agent of all experience, perception, and action. The soul is the experiencer, the perceiver, the observer, the doer, the thinker, the chooser, the responder, the enjoyer, the sufferer, and the inner site of all of these.[10]

We arrive here at the classical notion that each of us is subject, and that when we experience this subject individually it is the soul. The innerness of experience is the soul.

Since the soul is the site and agency of experience then everything that arises in the soul can be seen as part of the soul. Thoughts, images, emotions, feelings, sensations, perceptions, insights, knowledge, and states of consciousness are all the soul. They all arise in the soul as waves in a field, as particular manifestations within it. At this point in our discussion this might not be an easy jump, but it will become clearer as we study the basic properties of the soul. The point is that the content of experience does not only occur in the soul, but that it arises in her as her manifestations. Thoughts do not come from outside; neither do feelings or images. They come from the soul and go back to the soul, always within the soul. Even our perceptions of external objects and events are part of the soul, for our perception is an internal event even though the object of perception is external. So all these are the soul, or more specifically its manifestations. To sum up, the soul is the locus, the agent, and all the varied content of experience.

To understand that the soul is the agency, the site, and the varied content of experience will bring us a great deal of clarity about experience. Under normal circumstances, we are aware of simply having experience, but are vague and indefinite about the basics of such experience. What is experience? How does experience happen, where is it, and what exactly is it? To recognize the soul is to become clear about such fundamental questions.

This brings us to a further fundamental truth about the soul: Since the soul is the experiencer, the fabric and container of experience, and the content of experience, then the experiencer is not separate from this content. The subject of inner experience is the soul, but so is the content, the object of experience. In other words, as we recognize the soul we begin to see the nonduality of subject and object of experience, at least with respect to inner events. For instance, if we consider an emotion that arises in our consciousness, the agent or experiencer of this emotion is not a subject that experiences it as an object, an object separate and different from this subject. The subject is the field and the emotion is a manifestation of this field, in this field. The emotion is nothing but the field itself with a certain manifestation or frequency arising in some region of it. The field is a field of sensitivity, so it is sensitive to this change in frequency or vibration.

There is no distinct separate observer experiencing the emotion. The soul, a medium or field, is in its totality aware of the emotion. The soul is the agency, the medium of experience, and the experience itself. The three are not separate; they are the same thing. When we recognize the unity of the three we are truly recognizing the soul. This differentiates the experience of the soul from that of the ordinary self, whose experience is egoic. For egoic experience, the three are different and separate. The site of the emotion or other experience is not clear, or not perceived at all. The site is experienced generally and vaguely as inside. The object, the emotion in this case, is an event separate and distinct from the experiencer, who is a subject over and above this object.

The picture of the soul that we are presenting is actually nothing but a description of the phenomenology of our ordinary experience. When we experience an emotion—sadness, for example—we do not actually feel ourselves to be an objectified subject and the sadness as some object, in a different place from this subject. The awareness of the sadness happens right at the site of the sensation of sadness. If we are experiencing the sadness in the chest, then the sensitivity that is actually in touch with the sadness is also at the chest. In fact, it is coextensive with it. In what we are calling egoic experience, however, we tend to conceive of ourselves as an observer looking at the sadness, and typically this observer is somewhere in the head.[11] But this observer is not the sensitivity that is actually and directly feeling the sadness; this sensitivity is right at the site of this emotion.

Discerning this sensitivity, we discriminate the field that is the soul, and begin to appreciate the primordial characteristic of the soul, the phenomenological nonduality of its experience. When we recognize that the soul is the experiencer, what is experienced, and the field of experience, we understand why it is called in some traditions the "organ of experience."

In this chapter our discussion of the soul has been general, presenting only the broad outlines of our understanding. To further elucidate this picture of the soul, and to study its functions and development, we need to discuss basic characteristics and properties of the soul.

3   Organism of Consciousness

WE HAVE DESCRIBED THE SOUL as a sensitive medium, a field of sensitivity. What is this sensitivity? What is the soul actually a field of? Only the direct experience of this field will satisfactorily answer this question.

Until we directly recognize the soul as a medium of consciousness, we are aware of the sensitivity of the soul only as a function. Our scientific thinking as well as our normal experience understand this sensitive field only by observing the function of sensitivity. Even though studying the properties of the soul as functions does help us to approach an understanding of the ground of these functions, the field itself, it requires direct experience to study the field itself. Otherwise, we are simply aware that we possess sensitivity, a capacity for experience. We are aware that we are conscious, that we can be aware, that we can perceive and know.

Consciousness

In order to understand the soul's sensitivity, the central property we need to study is consciousness. However, in ordinary experience consciousness is always a consciousness of something. We are not ordinarily aware of consciousness itself, but always of its function. We may believe that soul is conscious, and hence it is a conscious field, but continue to think of consciousness as a function the soul possesses and can exercise. In most conventional and scientific perspectives, consciousness is regarded as a function, not as an actual self-existing phenomenon. It is like the seeing of our eyes, or the walking of our physical body. If we think that the relation of consciousness to the soul is like that of walking to the body, then there is something fundamental we are not aware of regarding the soul. The body is a differentiated and organized field of protoplasm. What, then, is the body of the soul?

The most typical contemporary view is to think of consciousness as a property of the body. This notion naturally leads to the scientific theory of consciousness as an epiphenomenon of the development of brain complexity.[1] This view is clearly a manifestation of the extreme of materialistic reductionism, which we have seen to be a result of the separation of soul, world, and Being. Our direct and sustained experience—and that of hundreds of thousands throughout the ages who have investigated soul and consciousness—reveals the soul as a conscious field, a sensitive medium, which as we discussed in the last chapter can be experienced as separate from or in a different location than the body, and at many levels of spiritual experience is known directly to be more fundamental than physical reality.[2]

The soul is sensitive because it is fundamentally an organism of consciousness, and consciousness is sensitive. Just as the body is an organism of living protoplasm, the soul is an organism of sensitive consciousness; just as the body is an organized field of protoplasm, the soul is an organized field of consciousness. Before we discuss the organization of this field, we must explore the notion of a field of consciousness.

In the scientific sense a field is a spatial region with a particular effect or force. A field, a kind of fabric in space, usually invisible to our senses, is responsive to particular stimuli. The electromagnetic field, for example, will respond to electric charges and magnets, and these in turn will respond to it. In other words, an electromagnetic field is a pervasive spatial sensitivity, and so is a gravitational field. What is most significant for our discussion is that a field is not a collection of particles or parts. It is homogeneous, in that the field is active at all points of its space. We can think of a field visually as a liquid or gas that occupies a particular spatial region. Yet this analogy is not complete because a liquid or gas is a collection of atoms or molecules, while a field is a completely unified medium, in which the particular region of space possesses specific properties that make it responsive to a certain set of stimuli or forces. This is how Einstein thought of gravitation in his general theory of relativity.

The soul is a field in this sense, a region of space with particular properties responsive to a specific set of stimuli. The field of the soul is not physical, electromagnetic, or gravitational; rather, it is related to awareness and consciousness.[3] When we recognize the soul we find it to be a locus of consciousness, where this locus is an extended field. The field normally extends through the body, and is often experienced as coextensive with it.[4] However, the field of the soul has no particular shape or size. It is completely formless and amorphous, and can take any shape or form. Depending on the particular state of the soul, this field of consciousness can easily be perceived as bigger, even much bigger, than the body, or it can be perceived to be condensed or contracted into a field smaller than the body. The felt sense of the field of the soul usually takes the shape of the body, largely because the soul identifies herself with the body. The soul actually forms herself according to the body image, as we will see in chapter 11. When we are aware of the soul and have some distance from our body image, we begin to see the amazing flexibility and malleability of the soul, and we begin to experience ourselves assuming all kinds of shapes and forms. Although this description might sound like something out of the *Terminator* movies, it is not such a strange idea; most people feel this sort of expansion and contraction and shifting of qualities all the time. When we are happy and secure we tend to feel large, expanded, and light, when frightened or depressed we tend to feel contracted, small, and heavy. When we regress, as can happen in times of emotional stress or in psychotherapeutic sessions, we can feel ourselves assuming different sizes and forms, depending on the age to which we regress. We can be aware that our physical body does not change its size and form—unless we are undergoing a psychotic episode and hallucinate actual body changes—but still feel ourselves to be as small as a two-year-old, or even like a tiny infant.

The Holographic Soul

As we have mentioned, a field is not composed of parts; so the soul has no parts. We can compartmentalize particular regions of our field of consciousness, but this is not the same as the soul having parts. We can compartmentalize even empty space itself, by enclosing a region with a box, but this does not mean that space has parts that can be separated from each other. Thus all the properties of the soul are pervasive throughout the field, and her functions can be active at any region of this field. In other words, the soul is holographic—each region, regardless how small, possesses all the properties and capacities characteristic of the soul as a whole.[5] It is not easy to recognize this, but when we do we are on our way to true inner liberation. The liberation of the self or soul involves recognizing the true nature of the self. This can take place not only through recognition of the most fundamental nature of the soul, such as realization of pure awareness, for instance, but can also be approached by paying attention to and recognizing much more direct and immediate experiential phenomena than are typical of egoic experience. Our rigid identities and concepts of self compartmentalize our experience of the soul in such a way that we cannot see how her properties and capacities are available to us regardless of the state of consciousness in which we find ourselves. For example, when we are identified with a self-concept of being stupid, our soul forms into a dull and contracted state. But if we recognize that no region of the soul is devoid of any of her properties, and one such basic property is intelligence, then our identification with such a self-concept loses its rigidity, and we find it easier to access our natural intelligence.

In a later chapter we will further explore this property of formlessness and its corollaries. Here, we will begin to explore the qualities of consciousness. When we refer to the soul as a field of consciousness we mean a medium composed of pure consciousness. The capacity to be conscious of something, in the sense of being able to have an awareness or perception of something, reflects the fact that the soul is first and foremost an organism of consciousness. We can be conscious because we are consciousness. That is, what is usually thought of as a process or product of the soul, the function of consciousness, is not only a function but also the very ground itself of the soul. We are always this consciousness, and are always feeling ourselves as consciousness, but do not recognize this because we are paying attention exclusively to the content of our consciousness; we are constantly listening to the stories we tell ourselves about who and what we are. These stories become the mental lenses through which we look at ourselves and everything else. (See *The Point of Existence*, chapter 6.)

In addition to the property of being a field, the other fundamental property of consciousness is that it can be conscious of itself. In other words, we do not need to be conscious of something to be conscious. We can be conscious of consciousness itself; that is, not the property of being conscious but of the field or medium that is consciousness. The experience of pure consciousness is the experience of consciousness without an object. It is simply consciousness directly sensing itself. It is consciousness aware of itself as a field, a field characterized basically by the fact that it is conscious of itself.

Imagine you are a fluid, like mercury. Imagine that each atom of this mercury is acutely sensing itself, conscious of itself. Each atom is a ball of excitation, and this excitation is identical with the awareness of this excitation. This excitation, which is awareness of the excitation, is pervasive in the whole fluid. Now imagine that each of these atoms is composed of smaller particles, each of which is an excitation that is identical with the awareness of this excitation. Imagine that there is no empty space between these particles; so it is a medium that completely occupies space. Imagine now that each of these smaller particles is composed again of smaller and more elementary particles, again completely occupying the space. Keep imagining these particles to be smaller and smaller, but imagine that the excitation does not change in intensity, but continues to be a soft and soothing sensation. The size of the particles keeps getting smaller until we arrive at the limit of size, zero, but now it is still an excitation that is identical with the awareness of the excitation. As we arrive at the absolute level we arrive at the true notion of field, a medium that is composed of no parts, no particles. Yet it is a field of excitation, a field of sensitivity, aware of itself as a field of excitation. It is a field of a smooth and soft medium, smooth and soft because the particles are of zero size, but a field conscious of itself throughout its region. It is not conscious of itself in the sense of one region being aware of another region. No, it is conscious of itself at each point of its region, at all points of this region, homogeneously and continuously.

This experience of pure consciousness is like a quality that is aware only of its quality, like the color blue that itself is a seeing capacity but sees only blue. To recognize the soul is to experience ourselves first and foremost as pure consciousness, as a self-aware medium.

The soul is not only this homogeneous medium constituting a field; it is an organism constituted of consciousness, like the body is constituted of protoplasm. Just as the body, even though it consists entirely of protoplasm, is differentiated and organized into various organs, systems, and functions, the soul is also differentiated and organized into various qualities, properties, and faculties. The body's organization is generally fixed for relatively long periods of time, but the soul is much more fluid and changeable. We will discuss this in detail in the next few chapters, but now we will continue our discussion of the soul as a field of consciousness. We brought in the question of structure and organization merely to point out that even though consciousness is the ground and substance of the soul, the organism that is constituted by this consciousness is what is structured; that is, the substance is consciousness, and the form the substance takes is the organization of systems, functions, properties, and qualities.

When we begin to experience consciousness directly, a whole new world opens up. Rather than the normal sense that we are seeing the world as an external object, we begin to perceive the universe from within. The inner journey becomes a journey of discovery that opens us to magnificent, exhilarating inner experiences and perceptions, but also brings our knowledge of the world and of existence into a sharp, clear focus. Inner explorers travel to a world much more exciting and thrilling, much more beautiful and meaningful, much more satisfying and fulfilling, much more amazing and magnificent than any outer explorer will ever behold.

Many religious perspectives tend to turn the inner journey into a heavy sanctity, a dull morality, a perverse holiness. Given this tendency, it is no wonder that so many people are no longer interested in religion. But when we explore the soul, rather than leaving it in a static relationship with an external divinity, we penetrate to the ground of the self, to the conscious field of the soul, and begin to know consciousness directly. Then the inner reality becomes a delight and a wonder, and we approach more and more closely a lived understanding of the relationship of our soul to what has been thought of as the divine; thus we approach an appreciation of the source of all discovery and creativity.

Presence

If the soul is a field of consciousness, a medium aware of itself, then how is perceiving this different from our normal experience of being conscious of our inner experience? In other words, how is pure consciousness different from the normal subjective consciousness, which also feels like a field of sensitivity?

The primary difference between ordinary inner experience and direct knowing of consciousness is that when we discern the inner field that is the soul, we experience it as a presence, independent from and more fundamental than all the content of consciousness and all characteristics of subjective experience. When we recognize pure consciousness, then, what we become aware of is the presence of consciousness, its existence, its ontological truth. We are contrasting the recognition of presence with awareness of the objects of consciousness as well as with awareness of consciousness as activity or process. Experience of pure consciousness is awareness of the thereness, the isness, of consciousness. Consciousness is fundamentally presence, presence conscious of its own presence.

The presence, the hereness, the beingness of consciousness, is not something extra to consciousness; neither is consciousness an extra property of this presence. This is one of the primary discoveries in the inner journey: presence is always consciousness, and pure consciousness is always presence. This is similar to how photons are always light, and light is always photons. It is not that photons have the extra property we call light, or light possesses an extra property we call photons. Light and photons are two names of the same thing, emphasizing two different ways of viewing the same reality.

When we apprehend consciousness in itself, independently of the function of consciousness of objects, we experience presence. The term *field of consciousness* is an attempt to describe the ontological presence of the soul, her being. Furthermore, as we recognize that consciousness is fundamentally presence, the knowledge of our depth begins to open up. This is because our inner depth is nothing but the experience of our consciousness, and presence is nothing but the nature of this consciousness. Recognizing presence teaches us a great deal about consciousness, soul, and essence of soul. In this recognition, we can know ourselves in our fundamental mode of existence. We begin to see, perhaps for the first time, that what we are is more fundamental than all the content of our experience. We are more fundamental than our sensations, feelings, emotions, thoughts, images, symbols, ideas, concepts, and so on. We awaken to our essential nature, which is more fundamental and more basic than our body, heart, and mind. We experience the fabric that is ontologically fundamental, necessary for the existence of all that we have taken to be ourselves. We begin to recognize our real self, our soul. More precisely, by recognizing presence we become aware of the fundamental ground of our soul; we discover the inner fabric that holds all of our experience; we are enlightened to what we are beyond time and space.

The pure, simple experience of presence is not a matter of insight, intuition, or understanding. It is not an emotion, a feeling, a thought, an image, a vision, an idea, or any content of normal experience. (See *Essence*, chapters 1 and 2; *Diamond Heart, Book 1*, chapter 2; *The Pearl Beyond Price*, chapter 4; *The Point of Existence*, chapters 2 and 3.)[6]

The presence of soul is not available to our awareness in normal experience; normal experience is that of the soul that has collapsed into a self, through the process of dissociating from the ground of its Being, which is presence.

To be aware of our soul as presence is to be presence. To be presence is to be aware of our beingness. To be aware of our beingness is to simply be. In this state our knowing of ourselves is direct, independent from thinking, imaging, remembering, reasoning, or any mental or perceptual activity. Our positivist science and psychology cannot conceive of this possibility, because they are based on the split that dissociated them from Being, as Heidegger brilliantly demonstrated. The pervasiveness of this split in our culture has conditioned us to believe that knowing can only happen through mental activity, and only through the duality of the subject and object of ordinary experience.

Presence is not a feeling, even though it can have an affective component. The affective component in presence is not the quality of presence itself, but the differentiation of some inherent spiritual qualities, like love or compassion.

We know presence by being presence, by simply being. In other words, we can experience Being explicitly as a category of its own, and not only as an implicit dimension characterizing existents. We can experience the dimension of presence explicitly, directly, and clearly. The development of the modern positivistic scientific paradigm owes a great deal to Descartes, who made a particular contribution to the separation of soul from God and universe, in a sense setting self above and against the universe, as a separate entity that can study it.[7] It is no wonder that modern mainstream thought cannot conceive of presence as a category on its own, and can conceive of Being only in the abstract, as an implicit characteristic of existents. Modern thought is dominated by the philosophical paradigm that conceives of the world as matter, and of the self as matter that possesses consciousness.[8] This perspective has supported our amazing scientific and technological advances, but it has also robbed our knowing of its most fundamental dimension. Many developments in more sophisticated current thought are confronting the limits of this view.

Being is more fundamental than the thinking mind and more fundamental than feelings and emotions. It is the ground of all manifestation. And we can focus our knowing on this dimension, rather than on manifestation, the content of normal experience and perception. When we do that we find we are presence. As presence, I am because I am. Before we go into the subtle question of identity, whether presence is an "I" (which is discussed in *The Point of Existence*), the point we are emphasizing here is that presence is known by presence. In this dimension, being and knowing are one, not yet differentiated. From the perspective of a culture whose perspective is dominated by the dissociation of self, world, and Being, this unity of knowing and being seems like a novel idea. The dissociation of Being from the self or soul has separated rational/representational knowing from spiritual/mystical knowing. The articulation of rational thought characterizes our logical and discursive knowing, which relies primarily on thinking; and spiritual knowing is now thought of as involving nonrational, direct experience. In our modern understanding, what we think of as knowing is only knowing that relies on the discursive rational mind;

we have largely forgotten that direct and mystical experience is also knowing, or gnosis. Gnosis is knowing by being, by identifying with what we know. This kind of knowing has for the most part in modern culture been relegated to religious and spiritual teachings. And since consciousness is the very faculty of knowing, the only way we can truly know it is through gnosis. We can only know consciousness purely by being it, by identifying consciousness with consciousness. This is the experience of presence, which we know by being the presence.

We discussed in chapter 1 the possibility of an integrated and integrative understanding of knowing, which unifies discursive rational knowing with direct knowing. We see the seed of such knowing here, in our present description of the recognition of pure consciousness, which is the discovery of presence. There is direct experience, but there is knowing. The directness of the experience comes from the fact that it is the experience of presence, and the knowing comes from the fact that it is the experience of consciousness. The inseparability of consciousness and presence gives us the seed that can grow into a way of knowing that integrates the discursive rational with the mystic and intuitive.[9] This understanding is part of a much larger perspective that becomes revealed only in very deep and subtle dimensions of Being, which we discuss in the second half of this book. When we know our consciousness in itself, we find presence. We are presence. Because consciousness is presence it is not only a function.[10] This is why we recognize pure consciousness as presence. This recognition is one of the great discoveries on the path of transformation. Consciousness is Being. Being is consciousness; it does not have consciousness. And the other side of this momentous discovery is that Being is conscious: that is, we can experience our beingness directly. To know presence is a matter of our consciousness seeing itself directly and immediately. We normally look at ourselves, including our consciousness, through the filter of our self-concept and worldview. This is not a novel insight. All the wisdom traditions of humankind have seen this. Modern depth psychology understands the structures and details of this as we see in the various developments of psychoanalysis: ego psychology, object relations theory, and self psychology. When we can experience ourselves without this filter we experience ourselves directly, immediately, and intimately. What we find is that only consciousness is left, and if we want to describe the mode of experience of this consciousness, the best term we have is *presence*.[11] To summarize, the field of the soul is subjectively and psychologically consciousness, but phenomenologically this consciousness is presence. Experiencing presence is like taking our normal consciousness (which feels so rarefied that it is practically imperceptible), increasing it greatly, and condensing it. If we keep condensing it, allowing our sensitive consciousness to intensify, it becomes more and more vivid and substantial, until it is more liquid. It is like taking clear transparent light and liquefying it. When the condensation reaches a particular threshold, the consciousness will attain a body, an immaterial substantiality. This condensed consciousness, this sensitive substantiality, is now vastly aware of itself; for it is intimately in contact with itself, instead of being so dispersed that only its function is visible to us. We are always the conscious field of the soul, but now we feel present as presence, because we are here and now, not dispersed through our mental content and spread over external distractions. There is now a fullness, almost a density, but a transparent and light density. This fullness forms a field that pervades and underlies all of our subjective experiences. This fullness is also an intensity of sensitivity, a heightening of consciousness. The sensitivity pervades the whole field, for it is not something additional to it. The fullness is nothing but the condensation of consciousness.

The conscious fullness is presence, and we know it because it is consciousness so self-collected it is conscious of its fullness, its presence. It senses itself at each point of its expanse, and it feels itself as presence, as the beingness of consciousness.

Organism of Consciousness

As noted above, the soul is not simply a field of homogeneous presence. Its ground and fabric is the presence of consciousness, but it includes many levels and facets of this consciousness. Presence knows itself directly, without reflecting on itself, and without a self-object dichotomy. It does not look at itself; it knows itself by being itself. It knows itself by being naturally self-collected in such a way that it is spontaneously self-abiding. By abiding in itself it knows itself as presence. The soul has the capacity to know herself in this way, by collecting herself and abiding in her own presence. But she also has the capacity for self-reflection, so she can know herself self-reflectively, a mode of knowing that can—and usually does, in egoic experience—develop into dualistic knowing, knowing through the self-object dichotomy.

The soul can differentiate into many dimensions, many facets, which can operate in an organized way to fulfill specific functions. The consciousness of the soul differentiates into what we know normally as mind, heart, and will, with their respective capacities and functions.

The soul is an organism of consciousness with differentiated properties, faculties, and functions. She can act on and interact with herself and with the environment. An analogy may illustrate this view more clearly. Our physical body is an organism. It is composed of many facets and dimensions. It possesses various organs and systems, each with its specialized functions. It has the dimension of anatomic organs, like the eyes, genitals, and hands. It has the dimension of physiological systems, like those of digestion and circulation. It has the dimension of complex organic compounds, like hormones, enzymes, neurotransmitters, essential proteins, amino acids, and so on. It has the dimension of simple molecules, like the minerals and their compounds. But it also has the dimensions of atoms, quarks, and so on.

However, we can see that at a particular level of organization the systems and organs of the body, with their essential fluids, are all differentiations of a basic medium, protoplasm. This original medium is the ground of the body that has differentiated in many ways, becoming finally a complex living organism. The body is an organized and self-organizing field of protoplasm. The body is an organism of protoplasm. It is basically protoplasm, but not simply protoplasm.

When we think of the soul as analogous to the body, consciousness corresponds to protoplasm. Thus the soul is an organism of consciousness, just as the body is an organism of protoplasm. The consciousness or presence of the soul differentiates itself into many dimensions of increasing complexity and organization. (See appendix B for a discussion of the Yogachara system of consciousness.) Each dimension possesses many facets, each with specialized functions. All the dimensions and facets are organized holistically and synergistically to function as one organism. This organism is all fundamentally consciousness, but in its differentiated manifestation as soul this consciousness can know itself not only in direct perception of its fundamental nature as consciousness, presence, and Being, but also it can know all of its differentiations and manifestations. The soul can know its various qualities and structures directly, as well as reflectively and conceptually. The higher organization of the soul gives her the ability to perceive and experience complex events, but also the ability to reflect on her experience and perception, to think, imagine, remember, feel, will, decide, choose, and so on.

Soul and Essence

This analogy can help us understand the relation between soul and essence. If the soul is basically pure consciousness, then how is it different from essence? In previous publications we have described essence as presence, and as pure consciousness. (See *Essence*, chapters 1 and 2; *The Pearl Beyond Price*, chapters 35 and 38.) We also discussed it as the ontological ground of the individual, as the essence of the self and its spiritual dimension. Since this sounds like our description of the presence of the soul, a reader of these books might rightly be confused.

Essence is the essence of the soul, her true nature, which we have seen to be her ontological dimension and ground. Essence is pure consciousness, which is experienced phenomenologically as presence. So when we experience the ground of the soul as pure presence of consciousness, we are experiencing our essential nature, essence. Essence and soul meet as pure consciousness. As we have seen, though, soul is not simply pure consciousness.

We have seen that consciousness is to the soul as protoplasm is to the body. Hence, essence is the substance of protoplasm, a medium of pure consciousness. However, as discussed in previous publications, essence manifests in various qualities we have termed *aspects*. These aspects are particular differentiations out of the basic presence, pure consciousness. They are differentiations only in quality, so they always remain as presence. Each aspect is a presence capable of being self-aware, and the only difference from the protoplasmic presence is that this awareness is also an awareness of the particular quality. These qualities are usually implicit in pure nondifferentiated presence, but manifest explicitly in the soul as aspects like love, compassion, joy, peace, truth, strength, impeccability, sincerity, and so on. They are the perfections of our true nature, whose presence is necessary for the soul to develop and function fully and completely. In terms of our body analogy, the aspects correspond to the essential fluids and organic compounds of the body. They are like the complex proteins, amino acids, fatty acids, hormones, enzymes, neurotransmitters, and the like, which are all necessary for the growth, health, and full functioning of the body. This is only an introductory discussion of essence and its various aspects, to utilize our analogy, but we will discuss this matter extensively in chapters 5, 8, 10, and 19. We will also see in the next few chapters that although both essence and soul are the presence of pure consciousness there are subtle differences in their experience, because soul is an organism while essence is not, but more like the fundamental elements.

However, the analogy with the body is limited. For the body, the differentiation of protoplasm and the resulting structures of organs and systems, with their functions, are relatively stable and fixed for the duration of one's life. Not so with the soul; her organization is extremely more plastic than the physical body. The differentiation and organization are in constant states of shifting, change, and transformation. It is inherent to the soul that no organized structure is fixed, or needs to be fixed. This is partly because the differentiation and organization of dimensions and functions do not develop as stable and localized fixed structures, like the anatomical organs or physiological systems of the body. All the dimensions, facets, and functions of the soul are coextensive with all of her presence, and thus any region of the field of presence possesses all these dimensions and faculties. To know the soul directly we begin to see that our mind is not only in the head. All of the medium of the soul, any part and all parts, has the capacity of mind. We normally experience mental activities happening in our heads, mostly because of a particular connection between cognition and the brain. This connection does not dictate that mental events happen in the head, but rather that some specialized mental functions require the operation of the brain. We can actually know and contemplate in any part of the body. We can experience emotional states also in any part of the body. It is also known—in meditative or contemplative experiences—that inner seeing and hearing is not necessarily located in particular parts of the body. In other words, the functions of the soul that directly concern the physical dimension of experience tend to be localized in different and specific parts of the body, but inner events are not necessarily limited to this organization. Dimensions, structures, and functions of the soul are not differentiated and organized once and for all, remaining as structures that can exercise functions when needed. The differentiation and organization happens as need arises for a particular function or capacity. When the need passes away the organization dissolves, or merges into another one that becomes needed for the next experience or task.

We experience this as a flexibility and changeability of our inner field of sensitivity. At times we are all heart, full and consumed with emotions and feelings, with very little presence of mind. At other times, we are mostly mind, lost in thoughts or imagination. At still other times, we are mostly will, deciding and choosing, with various degrees of presence of both mind and heart. Most of the time we are a combination of the three, with constantly shifting proportions and qualities of presence and functioning. At times of intensification and self-collecting of consciousness, we are mostly presence, serene and settled, not preoccupied with anything in particular. This plasticity and constant transformation is why some of the ancients thought of the soul as a chameleon. It is also one of the reasons why it is so difficult to have a full knowledge of her. The possible organizations are infinite.

There is nothing like the soul in physical reality; it is like a kind of magical medium or substance that can appear and manifest in the form and capacity needed. She is in a constant state of morphogenic transformation, morphing according to the situation, like the changelings of science fiction. We are not normally aware of this magical show, mostly because we are not in touch with the inner field of presence. We are only aware of the products of the soul's continuous morphing, as thoughts, images, emotions, and sensations.

Appreciating this morphogenic plasticity of our soul allows us to glimpse the promise of freedom inherent in our nature. Before we explore this promise of freedom, we will first explore how this magical transformation and display occurs. To do this we must understand how pure consciousness, which can only know itself, becomes able to manifest forms and cognize them. We will first explore how consciousness of presence differentiates into awareness of content and cognition of it, and then how this content arises. What is the inner content of experience and how does it arise?

PART TWO

Properties and Functions of the Soul

4 Noesis

WE HAVE PRESENTED OUR VIEW of the soul as an organism whose substance is consciousness, a field of conscious presence. At its most fundamental dimension, this consciousness is the simple capacity to be conscious. However, in our normal experience we are generally conscious of a plethora of changing contents of experience. Although this capacity to discriminate various contents of consciousness, including physical, emotional, mental, and spiritual phenomena, is an obvious element of our normal consciousness, we will see in this chapter that this capacity has surprising significance for the soul on the path of inner realization.

Many meditative and spiritual traditions emphasize the movement from experience dominated by conditioned conceptual thought to experience characterized more by pure awareness or content-independent awareness. In this chapter we will discuss a form of knowing that characterizes all our experience all the time but is often not emphasized in the work of realization. We will discuss the mode of the soul's experience called *noesis*. We discussed in *Diamond Heart, Book 4*, the notion of noetic forms, concepts appearing in awareness that are forms of the manifestation of Reality. *Noesis*, as we are using it here, is the soul's capacity to be aware of itself not only as pure awareness, and not only as the content of experience, but to be aware directly of forms arising in the field of consciousness. This capacity for discriminating awareness that is not governed by the alienation of the subject-object view, and that does not separate discriminated content from the field of presence/consciousness in which it is arising, turns out to be a powerful tool for the soul's realization of its own nature and the nature of Reality.

We normally think of knowledge as information stored in the

mind, or in a book or a computer or some other place. In ourselves, this stored information is clearly related to past experiences, impressions, and thoughts. In this chapter we will begin to use the word *knowledge* in a new and somewhat unorthodox way. What we here call knowledge is much more basic, more fundamental to the workings of the soul, than the phenomenon of stored information. Knowing is a fundamental characteristic of every moment of our experience. Our sensation is knowledge of sensation; our emotion is knowledge of emotion. Our seeing is knowledge, our hearing is knowledge, our thinking about the past, present, and future is knowledge. Our questioning is knowledge. Our sense that we don't know something is knowledge; we know that we sense that we don't know. Our wrong beliefs and even inaccurate perceptions are knowledge in this sense. We "know" plenty of things that aren't true. A realization of conscious light is knowledge. A pain in your stomach is knowledge of pain in the stomach. A feeling of fear is knowledge of that fear. Even knowledge that we think of as "unconscious"—that is, things we become aware of through a certain kind of shift in our attention—is revealed to be a kind of knowledge.

These examples point to the way we are speaking of *noesis*, the soul's capacity for discrimination of direct experience. With the exception of a certain level of awareness that we discuss below, to experience something is always in some sense to know something. We are speaking here of what is in common between knowing that your elbow itches and thinking about the theory of relativity, what is in common between knowing the taste of an apple and recognizing the vast and beautiful emptiness of the inner space of the soul. It is what is in common between knowing the taste of the apple and knowing that you like that taste. It is what is in common between knowing the vast beautiful emptiness and being aware of your sense of appreciation, meaningfulness, and having arrived at a home-like depth. It is what is in common between thinking that your friend has done something disrespectful to you, knowing that you feel hurt and angry, and knowing the feel of the physical tensions and impulses which are part of your reaction, and knowing the words you want to say to your friend.

In *Spacecruiser Inquiry*, chapters 4 and 5, we made a distinction between basic knowledge and ordinary knowledge. Our discussion here brings us closer to an appreciation of what we call basic knowledge. Basic knowledge is the knowledge aspect of our actual present experience, while ordinary knowledge is that knowledge that is more formed and qualified by abstractions and memory. Connecting our discussion here with the previous chapter, we can see that this knowing of experience must be happening as part of phenomena arising in the field of consciousness that is the soul. This presents a challenge to the perspective that typifies ordinary experience, the assumption of the subject-object dichotomy.

We generally think of perception, even perception of our inner states, as a subject being aware of an object. I am a subject, an "I" or an observer, experiencing something in my chest, abdomen, head, or some other internal place. Let's say I am feeling a sense of warm kindness in my chest. From the usual perspective, I assume that the observer is separate from the object of observation, the warm kindness. Often we experience the "I" or observer somewhere in the head or at the back, although we might not notice this sense of location. Thus our typical sense of such an experience is that we are a self that is experiencing warm kindness, without necessarily identifying the self clearly. The self or "I" is assumed to be separate and distinct from the feeling of warm kindness. The feeling might be definite and clear, but the self is vague and in the background.[1]

However, in the course of many meditative and some philosophical approaches to knowledge, we begin to move from this conventional view, to challenge this assumption of a separate observer. When we say, "I feel compassionate," or "I have a headache," or even "I see a dog," we know we can become clearer about what is this compassion, where in the head it hurts, or what sort of dog we are seeing. But the "I" who is feeling or hurting or seeing is, as we said, usually vague and in the background. We don't think to ask, what is this "I" who feels or hurts or sees? This is a central element in many paths: beginning to explore what is the location of experience, and to appreciate the field of awareness itself as the ground and medium of perception and experience. Direct recognition of the conscious presence, which is the soul, gives us a new ability to understand our capacity for inner perception. When we recognize that this field is a presence that is ontologically more fundamental than inner content, we understand that the content must be arising within this field.

Inner content does not enter consciousness from somewhere else. It arises in the field of consciousness itself, as the field modifying itself at the particular region the content arises. In other words, content arises within the field of consciousness as part of the field. Content is composed of particular forms the consciousness assumes at certain regions of its presence. Such a form could be a feeling, like warm kindness or anger. It can be a thought, a word, or a string of words. It can be an image, with or without colors. It can be inner movement, as in the kinesthetic sense. It can be inner sounds, tastes, or smells, as in imagination or memory. All these are inner forms that arise in our consciousness. We normally think of them as entering our consciousness, happening to us, or that we actively produce them. We do not see them as forms arising through our inner field of consciousness plastically changing itself to create them out of its very substance. We do not see this process of inner creation because we are not in touch with the field directly, so we end up perceiving only the forms it takes. By coming in touch with the inner field of presence, we have the wonderful opportunity of seeing how our consciousness functions to create its own inner forms.

Not only does our field of consciousness manifest forms by morphing itself; it also perceives these manifestations. These forms are perceived not through the operation of looking at them from a distance, but by immediate awareness. Our soul is aware of her inner content by being inside all of the manifesting forms. Her conscious field completely pervades all forms completely and thoroughly, since it constitutes the totality of each form. And, being pure consciousness, the soul knows these forms directly and in the present moment. This is what we call *noesis*.

The content of experience is composed purely of forms of consciousness, forms of the very fabric that is the soul. So in becoming aware of the content, the soul actually is simply continuing to be aware of her field, but now this awareness includes not only the presence of the field, but the structure—the patterns, designs, morphogenic variations—this field is assuming.

How does the phenomenon of our experiencing the feeling of warm kindness appear from this fundamental dimension? The feeling appears as the field itself changing at the location of the chest, the vibration of this region of the field changing in such a way that we experience a particular sensation of warmth we can recognize as kindness. There are two steps in this process. First is the perception of change; the second the recognition of what this change is. The first is perception, the second is discriminating knowing. We will explore the first form of perception, pure perception.

Noesis versus Pure Perception

The first level of pure perception, prior to these two steps, is the level of perception with no discernment, no discrimination at all, simply pure consciousness aware of awareness itself and nothing else. This ground of pure awareness is the fundamental ground spoken of in many spiritual traditions, and is the medium in which all levels of knowing appear.

The capacity to discern differences in the field of our awareness is a fundamental element of our consciousness. But here we need to make a difficult and subtle distinction: in describing this capacity, we want to discriminate it from the capacity to actually recognize the forms that arise. So in what we are calling pure perception, associated with what is traditionally called nonconceptual awareness, there is the perception of differences within a field without recognition of those differences. There is awareness that there are different forms, but in pure perception these forms are not discriminated in such a way that they can be recognized or named.

This is consciousness with no mind involved, awareness with no knowing of any kind. There is merely the awareness of shapes, colors, movements, qualities; there is no recognition, knowing, or understanding of what one is perceiving. There is differentiation but not discrimination.

We refer to this perception without recognition as nonconceptual awareness, for recognition and knowing require concepts. There is awareness of content but no recognition of it; recognition requires a further step in the functioning of consciousness. The traditional metaphor for this pure perceptivity is the mirror. The mirror analogy describes the soul's primordial and original condition, which is the pure nonconceptual awareness of experience. This is the fundamental ground of any experience, which is the pure nonconceptual bare awareness of experience before recognition, reaction, categorization, or any such phenomena occur. Becoming conscious of this nonconceptual awareness is an important aspect of inner work, and something we begin to understand from the first glimpses of recognizing the soul. Simply understanding that the soul is a medium that is aware of experience within its own field, we begin to understand the mirror-like quality of the soul.

A mirror reflects forms without adding anything to them. It merely registers the shapes, colors, and movements of the forms. Our consciousness functions like a mirror with respect to the forms that arise within it. This nonconceptual awareness is fundamental to the soul, a function that underlies and precedes all other functions of consciousness.[2]

Thus we recognize here the quality of mind that is emphasized in many traditional spiritual teachings: the ground of nonconceptual awareness, of pure perception. We do not normally notice this dimension of consciousness, because our knowingness arises too fast for us to catch it. In ordinary experience, our knowing mind, in addition to our labeling, categorizing, and remembering mind, functions almost simultaneously with pure perception of objects. Normally, we perceive and know in the same act, thus always believing that consciousness functions only as the normal perception that always has some recognition of form.[3] It is clear, however, that the pure capacity for perception, before recognition, is a necessary ground for all our experience, including experience of our inner content.[4]

This ground of nonconceptual awareness that has the capacity for perception is the deepest ground of the field of the soul. It is this ground in which arise the forms of consciousness that constitute the inner experience of the soul. We see from this perspective that the mirror metaphor is helpful but not completely accurate. It is accurate only in the sense that it can register what arises, without any reaction or response. However, our previous discussion shows the limitation of this metaphor: a mirror can only reflect what appears in front of it, while the consciousness of the soul creates (or becomes) the forms.

Our consciousness is like a magical mirror that creates the forms that appear on its surface. A better metaphor is a more modern one: on a television screen, images appear within the screen, and unfold as a series of forms, shapes, colors, and movements that constitute a story in the experience of the viewer. Yet even the television screen is not a perfect metaphor, for our consciousness does not only produce the forms; it also perceives them. If we think of the light in the television screen as consciousness, if we imagine that this light perceives the forms it is projecting, then we come closer to understanding pure nonconceptual awareness.

The Soul as Riemannian Manifold

Our inner consciousness is a whole universe, a magical universe.[5] Our inner sensitivity operates in relation to the three spatial dimensions, but it also manifests in many other dimensions that we can experience directly. Our soul's consciousness has perceptual capacities corresponding to our five physical senses. Our tactile sense appears as sensations and feelings; our visual sense appears as visions and images; our auditory sense appears as remembering sounds, hearing inner sounds, imagining or hallucinating sounds; our smell sense appears as remembering and imagining smells and aromas, but also as inner smells characterizing many inner states; our taste sense appears as remembering and imagining tastes, but also as inner tastes of our inner states, common in spiritual perception. Our kinesthetic sense is already felt as an inner experience, but can also reflect our memory and imagination, plus the inner movements of thought and feeling. The awareness of the movement of thoughts, and of changes of inner states, involves the capacity for awareness of the passage of time. Our consciousness is a universe of many dimensions.

Viewing our consciousness in terms of its dimensions, we see that it is not a three- or four-dimensional field, but a multidimensional manifold, a manifold in the sense that it is a dynamic structure of dynamic structures. This manifold is characterized by a nonlinear—Riemannian—geometry, in that all the dimensions open up to all the others in nonlinear ways.[6] Even in ordinary human experience, we can be aware of many different levels of experience in a given moment. For example, we might be aware of an activation in the muscles, a certain state of alertness accompanied by deep breathing; at the same time we feel an emotional sense of excitement and anticipation. We also might be thinking and planning some action while in this state. If we are aware of more subtle levels, we might be aware of a sense of strength, of the presence of strength as essence, and a kind of clarity and spaciousness and sense of universal will holding and moving our experience. We might at the same time be aware of the fundamental presence of Reality and the dynamism of our experience and of everything in Reality. Everything connects with everything else in the soul.

An inner form may have only one dimension, for example, a simple sensation, or any combination of dimensions. All our inner experiences are manifestations of forms within the manifold of our consciousness, where these forms are nothing but the very fabric of this consciousness morphing itself at particular regions. This view is not only a more faithful rendering of our inner experience, but clearly reveals the purpose of inner work. This purpose is realizing the awareness of the field of consciousness itself, which makes it possible for us to inhabit our inner field completely, in all of its richness and freedom.

Basic Knowledge

So far we have seen two elements of the soul's experience: the most fundamental dimension of the soul, nonconceptual awareness, functioning as the bare possibility of perception, and the understanding of this field of awareness as a multidimensional field of sensitivity which is a dynamic nonlinear manifold. With this foundation of understanding, we can now add the next element of the workings of the knowing soul, and see more how we are using the word *knowledge* to further our account of the soul's journey. The next element is the element of recognition and comprehension of forms. In normal experience, what we experience as recognizable forms is inseparable from what we know about them; but when we can be directly aware of the presence of consciousness and of things arising in that field of conscious presence, we see that recognition is an actual discriminable step in the process of knowing. This step is not simply the discursive mind turning its attention on what is perceived, and recognizing things. From what we discussed above we can see that the arising of forms and the knowing of them do not really involve a separate observer reflecting on experience.

What we are calling "basic knowledge" is the fundamental element of knowingness that is inherent in all our experience. Every experience we have of any sort is knowledge. When a form arises in the soul this form is inseparable from the cognition of this form. The whole experience is nothing but knowledge, composed of knowledge, and dependent upon knowledge. We can easily see this by simply contemplating our experience, any experience and at any time. Our hearing of a sound is the knowledge that we are hearing sound; our knowing that there is hearing and sound, our recognition of the quality of the sound—all these are knowledge.

When we experience a sensation, there is knowledge that there is a sensation. We are not merely aware of a differentiation in our awareness; we have discriminating knowledge, or recognition. We know it is sensation. We also know the specifics of the sensation. In fact, is there anything else in our experience of the sensation other than the knowledge that there is a sensation and the specifics of the sensation? Our experience of the sensation may elicit associations, memories, ideas, and beliefs we have about it. However, we can discriminate two kinds of knowledge in this situation: the present-centered, direct knowingness of the sensations, and the remembered knowledge about them. The former, the direct knowledge that is implicit in all experience and fundamental to the soul, is the basic ground of knowledge; the latter, which we call ordinary knowledge, is a subset of the former.

Knowledge is part of whatever happens in the field of our consciousness. If we feel pressure in the stomach, what is the pressure but the knowledge that there is pressure and the knowledge of the specifics of the pressure? Every impression involves knowing. Every experience is knowledge. Is there an experience of fear that is not the direct knowledge of the fear? Knowledge is the very fabric of experience.

Nonconceptual awareness is the ground in which forms arise, and the capacity for knowing makes it possible for us to discern the forms. The question of how much ordinary knowledge determines the moment-to-moment knowledge of the soul's experience of itself is not simple. As we have noted, we cannot always easily separate remembered knowledge as it arises in associations, projections, memories, and information, from the direct knowledge of content. There is no absolutely clear line between basic and ordinary knowledge. Many thinkers who appreciate the extent to which our experience is constructed by our accumulated knowledge believe that all experience is construction. Those who strongly hold this extreme view assume that the direct knowledge we are discussing is completely formed by ordinary knowledge, mostly at subliminal and unconscious levels. We do not hold this view; we observe that although our ordinary experience is largely constructed through ordinary mind—which accounts for the preponderance of techniques in wisdom teachings which challenge these constructions—it is not completely so. (See *The Point of Existence*, chapters 5 and 6.)

Sharing many other spiritual and philosophical perspectives, we are aware that there are patterns and forms in Reality—including, for example, forms in the physical world—that are not determined by personal conceptual constructs. Even certain feelings, states, and senses of meaning can hardly be said to be completely determined by conceptual constructs, even though in the course of coming closer to the ground of direct experience we become increasingly clear about how these are affected by ordinary knowledge, history, and so on. One category of inherent forms that are seen not to be constructed, for instance, is what we call noetic forms, including what Plato called Ideas. This question of to what extent the knowledge of the soul is determined by constructions will be discussed further in chapter 18.

Traditional spiritual and philosophical teachings describe the process of realization as waking up to Reality. One sees frequently the simile of seeing through the veils of our ordinary experience being like seeing a rope and thinking that it is a snake, then waking up to the fact that it is indeed a rope. Many practitioners with certain kinds of experience assume and believe, and many teachers write or speak as if, when we are in touch with the pure ground of consciousness there will be no snake but also no rope! There will be simply consciousness. Our observation here is that the form of the rope is definitely still there when we are not in the thrall of constructed concepts; we are able to see, and perhaps to recognize, the form, but our perception is not veiled by construction. Even if we have ordinary or constructed knowledge about the rope and what a rope is, the more we are close to basic knowledge, the more the perception is fresh, direct, immediate, and objective.[7]

The experience of the soul, then, is not only a field of awareness, not only a field of differentiated but not conceptualized forms; it is also a field of discriminated forms. This is so for both inner and outer events. If we look around and see people, that is knowledge arising in our field of awareness. There is knowledge that I see, there is knowledge that I see something, there is knowledge that what I see are people, and there is knowledge of a nose, of an eye, knowledge of red, knowledge of green, and so on. All this is knowledge. We ordinarily do not recognize the forms we are aware of as forms of knowledge, because we take the naïve positivist position that they are objects that we can know. We believe that we are simply perceiving and recognizing objects that are actually there physically, or are passing through our consciousness. From this perspective, for example, an emotion, like fear, is something which is arising and I recognize it, the end result being the cognition of fear. From the perspective we are presenting here, the fear is a form manifesting within the field of consciousness, made out of consciousness. It is an extension of the consciousness, a form that the consciousness presences itself as. This form is not only a form of consciousness, but because the consciousness is also characterized by knowingness it is a form of knowledge, a manifestation of knowledge.

The soul, then, is not simply an organism of consciousness, but is also an organism of knowledge. When we recognize knowledge as the fabric of all experience, we cannot hold on to our habitual dichotomy of experiencer and experienced, knower and known. The knower is knowledge, the known is knowledge. The knower is the field, and the known is a form that this field assumes without ceasing to be the field. When we experience fear, our consciousness is the very sensations of the fear. The fear is the conscious field forming into fear, and knowing itself as fear. We might be experiencing fear in the belly, as some kind of vibration, an uncomfortable shakiness and irritation. Our consciousness is manifesting itself as fear in a particular region, and as consciousness we are aware of the fear in that region. We cannot actually separate the fear from the knowingness of the fear; they are the same arising in the belly. We do not actually know the fear in our head, even though we say we know it in our mind. The phenomenon of experience presents itself as an emotional form in the belly, a form that is itself the knowingness of what this form is. Of course we might experience fear in the belly without recognizing it as fear; but when we do recognize it, the recognition occurs at the same location as the fear, in the belly. This recognition often manifests as the form becoming clearer and more delineated.

In the conventional perspective, when we are not yet in touch with the inner field of presence, we experience an observer that observes the fear. The knower is separate from the known, maybe the knower is in the head, and the known is fear in the belly. However, in reality there is no duality of knower and known. We think there is duality only because we are not aware of the fabric of the soul. When we are, then we can see that the sense of the knower in the head is a manifestation in the conscious field, but so is the fear in the belly. They are both manifestations of the very same field of consciousness. Seeing this, we can recognize that the real knower is not the one in the head, but the consciousness that discerns the one in the head. We recognize then that the separation of the knower and the known is due to a certain perspective, a belief. Nevertheless, even this perspective is a thought form that the consciousness itself manifests. Nothing occurs in our experience that is not the manifestation of our consciousness, and here we are noting that this manifestation always involves knowledge. So both knower and known, whether appearing unified or as the self-object duality, are knowledge. Even when we are not directly aware of the field of knowledge, it is easy to see that both knower and known are knowledge. Can we separate the knower in our experience from our knowing of it? Can we separate the known in our experience from our knowing of it? Of course not, for all is knowledge, basic knowledge. (See *Spacecruiser Inquiry*, chapter 5, for more discussion of basic knowledge in its relation to other dimensions of experience.)

There is nothing but knowledge in our experience. The moment there is no knowledge, there is utter unconsciousness without knowing that there is unconsciousness. Knowledge contains all experience, including illusion. All of Reality is a field of knowledge, a field that is constantly and continuously morphing itself into forms, shapes, and colors, but these forms only express the knowledge, without ever ceasing to be knowledge.[8]

From Basic Knowledge to Ordinary Knowledge

In the normal cognitive process, we abstract certain forms and patterns from the overall unified field of knowledge and retain them in memory. The accumulation of these abstractions is what we ordinarily call knowledge. Our cultural environment largely determines which forms and patterns we focus on, isolate, and abstract. Thus ordinary knowledge is largely culturally determined. But knowledge can free itself from these constraints and apprehend what is. This is spiritual awakening.

As we stated above, ordinary knowledge is a subset of basic knowledge. It originates in perception and experience, but then forms structures which strongly influence and further structure our moment-to-moment experience.[9] Even ignorance and falsehood are knowledge. When we know we are ignorant of something, this is knowledge. If we are ignorant of something but believe we are not ignorant, this mistaken knowledge, this belief, functions as knowledge in our experience, even though it is false. If we see a rope and believe it is a snake, we respond exactly as if we know it is a snake. Here we are making a distinction between truth and knowledge, again acknowledging that we are using the word *knowledge* in a particular and unusual way in order to convey the insight that knowledge is an inherent part of the soul's experience.

When we begin to experience and actually comprehend that knowledge is a characteristic of the field of consciousness that is the soul, this comprehension has many powerful effects on the soul's experience of herself and the world. For example, it has the effect of changing the sense of separating boundaries around the various forms of which we are aware. The boundaries of what is experienced as the self become less opaque, and as the awareness of a field of conscious presence begins to come to the fore, the forms we perceive in the world become much less solid and separate. We become aware of knowledge as something that characterizes all our experience, and appreciate increasingly that the field of our awareness is a medium that contains all content of experience, from the thoughts in our minds to our perception of birds in the sky. The partitioning boundaries that had defined the different forms in our experience begin to melt and we become increasingly aware of continuity in all phenomena.

Encountering our experience as knowledge is one way we come to be in touch with the soul. When we are not in touch with this level of consciousness, we have the experience that some things in our experience are information, some things are issues, some things are feelings, some things are objects, and so on; this is the ordinary egoic dimension of experience. We can see how this perspective is related to what we have discussed as the dissociation of the triad of self, world, and Being. The normal experience of these various elements as separate from each other begins to be corrected as we become aware of the ground that connects them. The connecting ground is presence, consciousness, and basic knowledge.[10]

Rational Thought

When knowingness is present, then all of the dimensions of experience divulge meaning and significance. Basic knowledge is a dimension of consciousness that intersects all other dimensions, and provides our experience with its human character. It is the significance of this dimension in the human soul that led the Western philosophical traditions to refer to her as the rational soul. However, "rational" did not mean what it means in our modern times; it meant what we have been describing as basic knowledge, what the Greeks termed *noesis*. This is the capacity of our human soul to discriminate and recognize the forms and patterns in our experience.

The dimension of basic knowledge is a ground for the development of the capacity for thought. As we focus on, delineate, and isolate a particular form in our consciousness we recognize it as a piece of knowledge. Our memory retains this impression as an image, a pattern involving several dimensions in addition to the visual. It includes the cognitive discrimination and whatever inner sense—for example, the kinesthetic sense, the emotions, and the sense of an essential state or space—the original experience had. Concepts form regarding, and words become associated with, some of the simple forms that we retain. Because they arise within the conscious field, these retained forms and their associated concepts and labels are manifestations of basic knowledge. However, the concepts now refer to partial, limited impressions of past experience. These images, symbols, words, and concepts become the basic content of ordinary knowledge. They form the basic blocks for the soul's capacity to think. Thinking is basically the relating of previously perceived elements of basic knowledge with each other. The original demarcations or boundaries that define concepts, words, and images originate in basic knowledge. Thinking can then become a dimension on its own, by the process of relating these mental elements with each other, in conjunction with further perceptions in present direct experience, or basic knowledge. This new dimension develops to many degrees of abstraction; we abstract from the original abstractions, and create new concepts and symbols that relate to the relationships of the original abstractions, and to groups of them. This process develops many degrees of differentiation and integration, in an evolving spiral of self-organization. The original plasticity of the soul manifests now on this dimension in a much freer way than we know in direct experience. The use of thought in imagination makes it possible, for instance, to theoretically solve practical problems, like building a bridge, for example. It makes possible all kinds of creative work, such as music and literature, and makes it possible for us to consider the past and the future. Emphasis on rational thought has led to many advances in our practical life, but when it occurs without direct experience of the field of consciousness, it contributes to the loss of the fabric unifying the basic triad.

Although discursive knowledge is a subset of basic knowledge, it does not include some very important dimensions of consciousness. The more abstract it becomes, the less of the inner sensory dimensions it includes, until it is constituted only by the mental knowing dimension, a cognition that relies only on representational concepts and words. The most important dimension it loses touch with is that of pure consciousness; it loses most of the sensitive presence of consciousness. It becomes a disembodied knowing, where only the outlines of the forms of experience remain, and their interrelationships. This is what thoughts are. These thoughts arise within basic knowledge, embodying basic knowledge, but generally lose touch with the ground of this basic knowledge, and become disembodied knowledge.[11]

The functioning of this thinking capacity evolves various rules and principles that we call logic and reason. Although knowledge is not static, but is always in a state of change and transformation, these transformations are not chaotic or haphazard; they follow fundamental patterns that reflect the self-organizing intelligence of the soul. In fact, as we will see in later chapters, they reflect basic patterns of Reality, including Being and universe and their relationship to the soul. The recognition and abstraction of such fundamental invariant patterns develop into our rules and principles of logic and reason. We leave a more complete treatment of this interesting subject to chapter 20, but it is important to realize that logic and reason are not contrary to direct experience; they arise from and reflect its inherent patterns.[12] The difficulty tends to arise when they become estranged from their source and ground, and are applied in an abstracted and rigid way. When the patterns of our thought are not informed by basic knowledge, they can stray from Reality.

The question of the status of mystical knowing is clarified when we appreciate basic knowledge. Becoming aware of what is called mystical knowledge is the opposite operation from the development of discursive knowledge. Basic knowledge is being and discrimination at the same time. Discursive knowledge develops by emphasizing the discrimination aspect of basic knowledge, while mystical knowledge emphasizes the direct feel and touch of basic knowledge. It focuses on its Being side. In reality, basic knowledge is *gnosis*—the common word for direct knowledge of Reality—especially when it is not patterned by ordinary knowledge. Gnosis can possess degrees of discrimination, depending on how much we focus on the discriminating outlines in the field of knowledge. The less we focus on these demarcations and the more we are immersed in the direct feel of the field, the more that gnosis will be mysterious, intuitive, even vague and indiscernible. Gnosis can be divested of its discriminating characteristics such that only a bare minimum remains; this involves deep, direct experience, usually without the capacity to say much about it. This movement toward knowledge without discrimination goes as far as total mystery, where we are touched deeply, totally immersed in the depth of awareness with no content, or even with no sense of awareness.

We see here how basic knowledge is the source of mystical experience, intuitive perceptions, mysterious revelations, and how by emphasizing the basic textures and forms of the field of knowledge, at the expense of its discriminating demarcations, we can become convinced that mystical or spiritual experience is inherently beyond recognition, beyond mind, and beyond discrimination. The fact is that the more we are disinterested in discrimination in our direct experience, the more our spiritual experience will appear in the form of inexpressible revelations, perceptions beyond description, and experiences that transcend mind and reason. This approach to mystical knowledge is inevitable to the extent that we remain under the sway of our normal discursive mind and its abstract knowledge; then our only access to gnosis is by setting this mind aside, and with it cognitive discrimination.

Recognizing how thought, reason, and logic on the one hand, and mystical revelations and spiritual transcendence on the other, are both related to basic knowledge can help us move toward a new integration of knowledge. We have the possibility of recognizing the ground that unifies mystical perception with rational thought, a unification that is not simply an addition or sequential application, but a coemergent operation. Some Greek philosophy and Christian philosophy in the West, and various Eastern philosophers, have appreciated this unified nature of the various dimensions of consciousness composing our soul. Yet it is clear that modern thought has developed in the context of emphasizing abstract thought as increasingly removed from direct experience, allowing new heights in the abstracted operation of reason. The integration of this thought with a return to attention on basic knowledge, on the understanding of actual present experience of self and world, will take this understanding of unity to a higher level of integration on the evolutionary spiral.

This integration of the cognitive faculty allows us to approach our experience and perception with rationality and reason functioning as part of basic knowledge to inquire into the various forms that knowledge manifests. Since reason reflects objective patterns of the field of knowledge, this kind of inquiry can penetrate these forms and disclose how they conform to these general principles of basic knowledge. And since reason here is not dissociated from its ground, the presence of consciousness, it becomes a tremendous aid in investigating experience and perception and leading us toward new and more harmonious knowledge. Applying rational thought to direct experience can become a more balanced and complete method of scientific investigation.

Our particular method of inquiry, the Diamond Approach, is one such development. This method of inquiry unifies reason with its ground of basic knowledge to explore the inner experience of the soul, both psychological and spiritual. And since this method originates in a dimension of knowing in which reason and pure consciousness are not dissociated, the approach does not dissociate rationality and spirituality. For a detailed discussion of this method of inquiry, see *Spacecruiser Inquiry*, where we develop the understanding of this method in extensive and explicit detail. This is one particular development, but the logos of this integration of knowing can be developed for application in any field of knowledge.[13]

5 Potential

BASIC KNOWLEDGE IS DIRECT EXPERIENCE, but much of this direct experience is patterned by our ordinary knowledge, by the contents of the mind, which are in turn the product of our personal history, which unfolded in a particular cultural milieu. (See *Spacecruiser Inquiry*, chapter 5.) Nevertheless, basic knowledge is deeper than ordinary knowledge; it possesses its own objective patterns and principles. The objective patterns and principles of the physical world, for example, are described by the natural sciences. In the spiritual world, objective patterns and principles that manifest in mind and soul are seen and understood by the wisdom traditions. Science inquires into the surface manifestations of basic knowledge—its horizontal dimension, so to speak—and spirituality inquires into its depths—its vertical dimension. Each arrives at detailed, extensive, and useful knowledge. Both attempt to discover basic knowledge that is uninfluenced by opinions or projections, or determined by prior constructions. By exploring the wholeness of basic knowledge—both the vertical and horizontal dimensions—we may be able to arrive at a more fundamental dimension of knowledge that embraces both. The important point here, however, is that when we explore the forms of basic knowledge it reveals to us its truths, its invariant patterns and universal principles.

A thought experiment might illuminate the meaning of basic knowledge, and what we mean when we say that this knowledge may unfold in a way that reveals its true phenomenology. Let us imagine that we are in a completely dark room, a room full of all kinds of objects. There is a light source in this room, with a dimmer switch that can be turned up or down. We are also wearing clear eyeglasses with shutters of different colors. The colored glass of each shutter has some transparent designs painted on it. We begin to slightly turn the light on, by sliding the dimmer slowly, to the dimmest illumination. We begin to see the vaguest outlines of some of the objects in the room. This is the beginning of basic knowledge. We see what is actually there but we see only dim outlines with and within shadows. We may mistake what we see, for we still cannot differentiate the shadows from the real objects. We have also the complicating factor of wearing the multi-shuttered glasses. Our knowledge here, then, is incomplete because of the dim light and distorted by the colors and designs of the shuttered glasses. But all of what we see is knowledge, nothing but knowledge. We turn the dimmer up slowly and steadily, and every once in a while remove one of the shutters on our glasses. Basic knowledge increases steadily, becoming more full, and more accurate. Each time we remove one of the shutters we are surprised by what we see, amazed how wrong our assumptions were, or how accurate were our intuitions. These are the insights and satoris, the quantum leaps in knowledge. As we keep turning the dimmer up and removing shutters and seeing more, the more clearly and objectively we see, and the more we know. Our knowledge is steadily becoming both complete and objective, both full and truthful. When the light is completely turned on, and we have removed our glasses, we see everything just as it is.

Seeing everything as it is is nothing but full knowledge, complete perception of the forms that knowledge happens to be manifesting. This includes perceiving the container of the forms, the room with its walls, floors, and the space within it. But it is always knowledge. Knowledge can be full or diluted, complete or incomplete, distorted or objective. The situation of having only a little light with shuttered glasses is the situation of conventional experience, what we have been referring to as egoic experience. The shuttered glasses are our self-concept, the shutters are the various ego structures that constitute the sense of self, and the design on each shutter is the integration of the history that went into the development of the structure. This mind experiment does not illuminate the whole situation, but may help us see how we are always in knowledge. How much of it we see, whether it is distorted or not, is always knowledge.[1]

Potential Knowledge

In this mind experiment the totally dark room is knowledge that is nonmanifesting, potential knowledge. Entering this room when the light is turned off, we may sense that there are many things in here. With a developed sixth sense, so to speak, we will have a sense of a considerable potential knowledge, without knowing the details of this knowledge. We intuit great amounts of unarticulated knowledge, because all experience is knowledge. The room that is our soul is full of knowledge, but we know it only globally, without differentiation. We can feel the objects in the room and know there is a great deal of knowledge here, but cannot discern the forms of this knowledge.

This mind experiment can give us a sense of what we mean by potential knowledge. So far we have used the term *knowledge* mainly to mean the discriminating knowing of the forms of our experience. However, since everything is knowledge, the very substance of the forms is also knowledge. Knowledge is not only awareness of the details, but it is literally everywhere. There is knowledge even in regions where we do not discern forms. In other words, in the knowledge dimension of consciousness the soul is knowledge. The whole fabric, the conscious presence itself—not the patterns and forms—is pure knowledge. For how can there be forms of knowledge manifesting out of, without dissociating from, a medium, if this medium itself is not knowledge?

Knowledge is not only recognition of forms; it is more basically a particular mode of consciousness, in the sense that love is a mode of consciousness. This mode of consciousness is what makes it possible for our soul to know, and to manifest forms of knowledge.

In other words, the forms are literally forms of knowledge, constituted by knowledge. The forms are sculpted knowledge. It is as if knowledge is the potential of the dark room that can manifest, lighting up in a display of forms of knowledge. It is difficult to envision this kind of knowledge, mostly because what we have for a long time taken to be knowledge is only a subset of a much larger field of knowledge, a subset that has become increasingly alienated from its ground of pure knowledge. When we are able to experience our soul directly, and recognize the knowledge dimension of consciousness, that of basic knowledge, we may have the opportunity to discern the nature of its mode of consciousness, the essence of knowledge. This is a particular experience of the soul, where we experience the soul as pure knowledge. This is not a matter of experiencing and cognizing a form arising in the field of the soul; it is experiencing the field itself as knowledge. It is presence, and the presence is knowledge. The soul experiences herself as a presence aware of its presence, with an awareness inseparable from and coemergent with presence. Simultaneously with this awareness of presence there is, inseparable from and coemergent with this awareness, the recognition of this presence as knowledge. It is like a medium, such as a perfumed oil, made out of knowledge. It is as if the atoms of the oil are knowledge. It is both the capacity of cognition, the faculty of knowing, and the presence of knowledge itself. This is similar to our understanding of consciousness, in which we see that the presence of pure consciousness is both a medium of sensitivity and, because of that, the capacity to be conscious of something.

What we are pointing out here is that one of the specific ways of experiencing the soul is as an infinite, ever-flowing fountain of knowledge. We can experience the soul as an overflowing fountain, sometimes out of the heart, and the content of this fountain is knowledge. Sometimes we experience this knowledge as an ocean, or many oceans, as happens in the visions of the heart's imaginal capacity. The knowledge, because it is the very substance of the soul, feels real, organic, alive, and nonlinear. In this experience of our soul we have the perception that there is available for human beings, as part of the potential of being human, an infinity of knowledge. We not only come upon knowledge, we not only discover knowledge, but we can do these things because we are knowledge: real, alive, and relevant. When the heart of the soul finally opens there becomes accessible to us an infinity of knowledge. We then only need to turn our attention to a particular inner subject, and the knowledge begins pouring out, endlessly. This substance of knowledge, this essence and presence of knowledge, begins to manifest the forms of knowledge relevant for our study.

Soul appears here as potential knowledge, the essence of knowledge that is the potential for all knowledge. The subjective experience is that of the presence of the soul as an infinity of knowledge. This sense of knowledge is not mental, not cerebral. It is not an idea that I am pure knowledge, not an insight that I am knowledge, not an image of knowledge. The very conscious substance of the soul is knowledge. We feel it as real knowledge, intuitive knowledge, direct knowledge, useful knowledge, relevant knowledge, with the characteristic organic and nonlinear qualities of the soul.

When we feel the soul as an infinity of knowledge it is not a matter of experiencing an infinite content of knowledge, an infinite number of forms and manifestations of knowledge. That would be basic knowledge. Pure knowledge is like the experience of holding a book and feeling, "This is knowledge," without opening the book and seeing what the specifics of the knowledge are. We just know, "This is knowledge." This is a very specific feeling, a specific taste that tastes like knowledge.

It is easy to become flabbergasted with this sense of knowledge, and with the sense of infinity of knowledge, of the infinite potential of knowledge. We might have assumed that we had a great deal of knowledge, but with this experience of consciousness we recognize how meager is our knowledge, and how it will always stay meager, puny, in contrast to the immense infinity of potential knowledge. There is then in the experience a sense of immensity, power, and amazing energy that can manifest as knowledge, all kinds of forms of knowledge, in many fields and in numerous dimensions. When we open up to pure knowledge, access to real knowledge becomes easier. We are then in touch with the knowledge potential in consciousness, the inexhaustible source of all possible knowledge. When we need to learn something specific about the soul, about mind, about essence, about Reality, we can simply turn our attention there and we will discover that we are guided. Knowledge flows out, unfolds; our eyes will begin to see the right objects, our ears will hear the relevant words, we will somehow pick up the right books, we will find ourselves in the right circumstances. Everything around us will begin to point to the relevant forms of knowledge we are seeking. Pure knowledge will differentiate; the flow from within will manifest, as insights, realizations, understanding. And the more we explore, the more there is of it, an infinite ocean of knowledge.

The direct experience of pure knowledge, however, is the experience of the potential of infinite knowledge, of a form of conscious presence that intuitively feels and tastes like the sense and knowing that there is an infinity of new possible things to know, an infinity of new experiences, an infinity of realization, an infinity of insights, an infinity of qualities. It is like looking through a telescope into the night sky. At the beginning we see few stars; when we increase the magnification we begin to see that these stars extend infinitely, more and more of them, as far as any magnification can allow. We become humbled by our potential; we see how we have always been scratching the surface of Reality. It is again as if this medium of knowledge is composed of an infinity of atoms, each one an insight, an experience, a realization, a particular knowledge about a certain manifestation. It has a sense of power, a sense of exploding, a sense of potency, a sense of a fountain that is exploding with brilliant light.

Practically speaking, this means there is the possibility of knowing endlessly new things about the soul, for the potential of the knowledge of the soul is infinite.

Soul as Potential

By discussing the experience of soul as pure knowledge, or potential knowledge, we enter more specifically into the identifying experiences of the soul. When we experience ourselves in these ways, we know we are experiencing our soul directly, instead of the indirect and alienated way of egoic experience. In other words, these ways of experiencing soul indicate that we are experiencing the soul herself, the organism of consciousness, instead of one of the inner objects of the soul. We experience then the conscious field of presence itself, rather than the forms that arise within it. These forms of experience indicate to us that we are recognizing our soul, a recognition necessary for the development of the inner vessel, and most helpful for our inner journey. By understanding them we understand more clearly and fully the locus, agency, and field of the soul.

These forms of experience reveal to us the basic properties of soul, properties always implicit in the soul, but here experienced explicitly, identified and understood. If the soul is like a mirror and all experiences are like the images in the mirror, then these properties are those of the mirror, and not of the images that appear in it. We will find them in all of our inner experiences, because the images of the mirror always contain the properties of the mirror. These properties are the universal characteristics of the soul, underlying all of our experience, and the sources of all our inner faculties and functions. They characterize soul herself, and hence differentiate her from essence. They also reveal the relation of soul to essence, and to ego.

We have first explored the most fundamental of these properties, functioning as the ground of all inner experience. We discussed the field of pure consciousness and presence, and then differentiated it into nonconceptual mirror-like awareness and basic knowledge. The last one we discussed, pure knowledge, even though it is fundamental in that it forms the ground of basic knowledge, is yet specific, although it is not easily recognized as present in all inner experiences, as in the case of basic knowledge. It arises as a particular experience of the soul, rare and unexpected. Also, it points to other experiences of the soul, specific and particular like it. Pure knowledge is, nevertheless, a fundamental property of the soul. Some properties of the soul, such as consciousness and basic knowledge, can easily be seen to be always present in experience; but others, such as presence and pure knowledge, are not so easily recognized, and tend to arise as particular experiences, at least at the beginning stages of the inner journey. We will continue exploring some of these fundamental properties, and begin where we left off.

Pure knowledge is potential knowledge; experiencing it we understand how soul is the potential for all knowledge. This points to a property even more inclusive for the soul, potential itself. We can see the soul's potential as knowledge, but not necessarily. It is always knowledge, but we can view it differently, from different angles, emphasizing different qualities. Therefore, another way of experiencing the soul is not as potential knowledge, but as simply potential. Again, this is an unusual and unexpected kind of experience. We do not ordinarily think that we can experience potential directly; we do not envision that potential is a category of direct experience, that it is a quality that can be experienced similarly to love or clarity. We normally think of potential as a concept that we know indirectly, implicitly, by recognizing there is more to us, that we have more possibilities than we have actualized and realized. We think of potential as a concept referring to the totality of our particular potentials. We may even intuitively sense the possibilities lying dormant in us, waiting to be awakened and actualized. However, when we finally experience potentiality directly and fully, we understand our soul, and our potential, in a completely new way, an unexpected and wonderful way. We learn something fundamental about soul, something we cannot see by knowing of our potential inferentially or intuitively.

The experience here is of the conscious presence characterized by potentiality. The presence is the presence of potential. Just as potential knowledge is the presence of pure knowledge, potential is the presence of pure potential, as a category on its own, as a fundamental quality that we experience here explicitly and directly. We experience ourselves as pure potentiality. We do not experience ourselves as having potential; we experience ourselves as potential. We are the potential for all experience, all perception, all knowledge, all qualities, all capacities, all functions, all processes, and all developments.

In this experience we do not surmise that we are potential; we know we are potential by being potential. Our presence is the presence of potentiality. Here, presence and potential are the same thing. This shows that when we recognize that a particular individual has a great deal of potential, we are actually recognizing that person's soul, seeing its potentiality.

As in the experience of pure knowledge, we are not necessarily experiencing the specifics of potential. We cannot in this experience point to one thing or another, and say this is one of my potentials. We might be experiencing a particular element of our potential—we always are—but this is not what we mean here. The experience is more that the substance of the presence is made out of potential. We feel ourselves as a teeming fullness, recognizing that all this presence has implicit in it something that can grow and develop. We experience our consciousness as if composed of millions of living atoms, all in one space, with intuitive knowledge that each one of these atoms can become a million atoms, and each of these another million and so on, infinitely. Each one of these is an experience, an insight, a discovery, a function, a state, a form, and so on.

We also have the sense that the awareness or aliveness of each of these atoms can develop and multiply in various and infinite ways. There is an exploding sense, an unfolding sense, for each little part of it, each infinitesimal region in the field. Yet the field is not composed of discrete atoms. It is a continuous unified medium. It is a very dynamic, seething, pulsing medium, with an endless possibility of unfoldment, expansion, and experience.

It is like experiencing ourselves as the seed, rather than the tree. We experience the teeming aliveness inside the seed and recognize that this has the potential to become a tree. We do not experience the tree; we do not yet know what it is like to be a tree, or any particular kind of plant. We simply experience ourselves as the potential for something. We are full, full of potential, but more accurately we are the fullness of potential itself. In other words, we experience ourselves as the essence of potential, as pure potential.

Experiencing our soul as potential, we recognize that we are, more than anything else, the potential for experience, and for whatever is possible in experience. Soul is at the root pure potential, potential for consciousness, knowledge, experience, life, growth, learning, expansion, and so on. We do not merely have the potential for all of these, we are rather potential itself, pure potential. This points to a profound possibility of freedom; for we are not the particulars of our potential—the experiences, forms, qualities, and capacities—we are potential itself, free from the particulars, for our nature precedes them and underlies them. We begin to recognize that the soul constitutes an unlimited possibility of development in all dimensions. The soul is actually a potentiality, free in all ways and containing all possibilities.[2]

We do not here experience ourselves as a particular manifest form, but as the unlimited possibility for all forms, teeming with inner reality that can manifest in endless ways. We feel rich with aliveness, with energy, with possibilities. It is almost like feeling oneself to be a fertilized egg with the strong sense that a lot can come out of this, a lot of life. We do not see the forms that manifest, we simply feel the raw potential itself. In fact, all the other properties, qualities, experiences, forms, capacities, and functions that we discuss in this book are nothing but the unfolding of this potential.

Everything we experience is the forms this potential manifests, unfolding one after the other. All of our life is nothing but the unfoldment of this potential. Our potential is not only the gifts and special qualities and capacities that we have. This is the normal meaning of potential, but this is only part of our potential. Our potential is everything we have ever experienced, everything we will ever experience, everything we can ever experience. From the perspective of this pure potential we recognize that human potential is infinite, and miraculously free.

We also can see that it is the potential of all human beings. Human beings are not different at this basic level of potentiality. We all have the same potential, which is the potential of humanity. Practically speaking, however, we are different in terms of how accessible it is to us. This depends on our environment, our circumstances, our history, our times and culture, our physical constitution, and many other factors. Our environment, including our bodies, may constrain us, not only by putting up barriers and difficulties in the way of our potential, but also in not eliciting our potential by providing the opportunities and the supports we need. Our potential arises mostly as a response to needs, and its unfoldment requires not only activation but also holding and support.[3] We will discuss in more detail the necessary conditions for the arising and development of the particulars of our potential in chapters 11 and 12. (See chapters 4 and 6 in *Facets of Unity*, and chapters 18 and 27 in *The Point of Existence*.)

Therefore, even though we all have the same potential we are different in terms of our capacities and opportunities to actualize it. Generally speaking, it is difficult to accurately assess a person's potential.

Life is full of surprises in terms of who ends up actualizing which potential, and how much potential. Sometimes we think a particular individual has a great deal of potential, we see much promise, but then not much comes out of it. With others, we cannot glimpse much there, but then we are surprised how they have surpassed others who seemed to have had much more promise. Other times we can tell someone has tremendous potential, and it does pan out. But the substance of the soul is universal to all human beings, and it is pure and infinite potential.

All the seeds have the same potential, but they are not going to grow to be the same identical trees. Some of the seeds might be damaged, so even though they have the same inherent potential they are unable to unfold it. And how they will grow, and how well, depends a great deal on the environment and the weather.[4] In the experience we are discussing, the particular elements of potential are not manifest, not developed yet, but we are directly aware of the immensity of the treasures within, the infinite energy, power, knowledge, insight, development, and so on. There is a sense of infinity, limitlessness.

It is not possible to conceive of the totality of what is possible for the human soul. It is infinite. That is why our knowledge and understanding about the soul is bound to be partial and incomplete. As a result, each spiritual tradition has some knowledge and wisdom about the soul. None is complete.[5] They are not identical in their understanding, and they will disagree about many things regarding soul. They generally do not disagree as much about Being, or ultimate Reality. But when it comes to the soul, our experiencing consciousness, there are important differences, and significant contradictions. Different traditions explore different properties, capacities, and dimensions of the soul. The emphases vary greatly, but this does not mean that some are right and some wrong.

Essential Potential

The soul's potential includes all of our human capacities, functions, possibilities, and experiences. It includes all the dimensions of experience and consciousness. The potential has no limitations; it includes all that we think of as positive and all that we think of as negative. It is the potential for ego and its development, but also the potential for essence and its realization. It is the potential for ignorance and violence, but also the potential for maturation and enlightenment. In this book we will study many of the important elements of this potential. Many of these elements are well known, like the potential for thinking, learning, emotional life, and so on, so we will not explore them in any detail. Many are explored by other researchers, as the potential for ego development, cognitive development, cultural and artistic development, and so on, so we will have little to say about them. We will focus on the basic properties of the soul, her essential potential, and her potential for knowing and connecting with Reality.

The central and most important potential of the soul is her essence, for essence in its various aspects and dimensions forms the ground and provides the Platonic forms for all of our higher states of consciousness, and the higher faculties of experience and action. We need to understand this particular potential to understand the nature and fullness of the soul, and to understand Reality and the relationships between its triad of facets.

We discussed in chapter 2 that soul and essence meet at the level of pure consciousness. They are both pure consciousness, that is, they are identical at this level. This is the reason we use the term *essence* to refer to the true nature of the soul. They both come from the same ground, where essence constitutes this primordial ground and nature of the soul. Essence, hence, can be considered the deepest potential of the soul, her spiritual potential, the richness of her depth. Essence, therefore, does not have potential the way the soul does. Potential is a quality and characteristic of the soul, and hence soul is always growing and developing. We cannot say the same about essence, which is primordially pure and complete; our realization and understanding of it grows and develops, but this does not mean essence does.

Essence is always pure, eternally immaculate, everlastingly perfect. This is the reason why many wisdom traditions speak of realization as recognizing the inherent perfection of Reality.[6] Our true nature is primordially pure, complete; it does not need to develop or be clarified. This can lead, and has led, to much confusion about the inner journey, whether it is the discovery of a primordial perfection or the process of perfection. This also resulted in the conceptual dichotomy of gradual and sudden paths of enlightenment.

Understanding soul and essence, and the relation between them, clarifies such confusion. Soul grows and develops. She does this by actualizing her potential. The central potential she needs to actualize is her essence. Realizing her essential nature she is enlightened. Her essence is her deepest and most central potential, but it is a particular potential, one of the elements that constitute her potential. Essence does not have potential, for it is the ground of all potential, the ultimate nature. Realizing essence we recognize we are primordially and fundamentally immaculate and complete. The soul develops, and her spiritual development is the actualization and realization of essence.

But in the state of self-realization, development does not make sense, for we are then essence, which is perfection and completeness itself.

By realizing and actualizing essence the soul is enlightened, but this does not mean she has no more potential to actualize. Her potential is infinite, in terms of forms of experience, capacities, functions, knowledge, contribution, action, and so on. The realization of essence, however, throws the soul wide open for the development of her potential. There are then no inner inhibitions to the arising and development of her potentialities, but this development depends on actual and particular needs felt by oneself and others. It depends on opportunities and situations in life.

The soul can develop before enlightenment, by actualizing many of her potentials, as we see in the actualization of creative and intellectual potentials. Spiritual realization is not the only development, and does not imply or guarantee other kinds of development. Realized individuals, as a result, can be developed in various ways and on many levels in relation to the various human potentials. However, the soul's freedom and the fulfillment of her deepest longings depend on the realization of her essential potential. Only with the actualization of essence can the soul be free, completely authentic and totally serene. Essence is her true nature, without which she is estranged, lost, inauthentic, empty, and twisted. Regardless how much of her potential she actualizes, regardless how much a genius she becomes, artistically or scientifically, if she does not realize her essential nature her experience continues to be characterized by emptiness and strife, on the same level as most human beings. This is why the wisdom traditions think of their work as the most significant for humanity, as transcending any artistic, scientific, cultural, or intellectual kind of education and development. The essence of the soul stands apart from the rest of all of her potential, for it is the only possibility she has for finding true liberation and fulfillment. This is independent of history, culture, civilization, progress, and so on. Humanity can advance technologically, intellectually, artistically, and in many other ways. Such advancement can contribute a great deal to improve the lot of humanity in general, but the need for and value of the spiritual journey will perennially remain.

6 Morphing Dynamism

HOW DOES THE POTENTIALITY INHERENT to the soul become actuality? How does potential for experience become experience? How does potential for forms of knowledge become actual knowledge, manifest and perceptible forms? What is responsible for the inner infinite riches of the soul becoming manifest? The soul must possess a property or properties that allow her to translate her hidden treasures from the obscurity of potential to the light of actuality.

We generally believe that we know how experiences arise; we assume that they are responses of our nervous system to stimuli. When our stomach is empty for a period of time, a signal goes to our lower brain, which interprets it with the result of the feeling of hunger arising. When we lose someone important to us, our brain registers the loss in the limbic system that then activates certain hormonal and neuronal processes in our viscera, and a feeling of sadness arises. We read an article about a subject that interests us; our neocortex registers the ideas and images, and responds with a new flurry of brain activity that results in new images and strings of thoughts. It is all orderly, mechanical, and cybernetic. While this is a valid view of experience, corroborated by physical observation and experiment, it is one side of a complementary phenomenon. It does not explain the whole phenomenon and does not account for many of our subtle perceptions. Analogous to the understanding of light being both wave and particle, this aspect of the understanding of experience is the particle side of the understanding. Furthermore, since we have been focusing on the wave side of experience, we want to understand how our experience comes about from the perspective of the soul being a field of sensitivity. In other words, how does the process of the arising of our experience look to us when we do not hold the Newtonian view? We will discuss later how external stimuli contribute to the arising of experience, but here we want to explore how they are translated into the inner images and sensations that compose our direct experience. In this chapter we will focus on the inner mechanism that leads to the arising of inner forms and events, whether or not they are in relation to external stimuli.

Changeability

Our inner field is pure consciousness that is also pure potential for experience. How does this potential become actuality? How does the seed become a tree? To explore this we first need to remember that our soul is not a particular state or condition; it is the medium and locus where all states and conditions arise. The fact that all inner states and events are forms within and part of the soul means that the soul is in constant change. This is clear when we contemplate our experience. We notice that experience is in constant and continuous change and transformation. One thought follows another, one feeling leaves only to vacate the space for another. Inner sensations and movements are never still. Our inner space is like a multiple intersection at the center of a major city, where all streets and lanes are busy most of the time, with an incessant flow of traffic of various kinds and sizes of vehicles. Our inner space is not only busy with content, it is in incessant movement, transformation, development, evolution or devolution, expansion or contraction, and so on.

These are the external forms of our soul's field of consciousness; she is rarely at rest, rarely settled. And when she is settled, this is only a momentary state like all other states. This is why some see the soul as a chameleon, transforming from one condition to another. This points to an important property of the soul, related to its potential: its changeability.[1]

This changeability is more fundamental than most of us are ordinarily aware. Our very identity is always in a state of flux. We do not even have to look at our lives over the long term to see this; we do not need to remember how we were babies, then children, then teenagers, then young men and women, and so on. We need only contemplate our experience in a given hour. Our self-images are always changing;

we go from one image to another. Even though we have an overall sense of self, this sense is composed of constituent sub–self-images, as object relations theory has shown. These component self-images arise and dominate our identity, depending on situations and events. At one moment your sense of yourself might be an adult, then a few minutes later you might feel like a little child, unreasonable and demanding. One moment we are loving humans and a few minutes later we might be hateful monsters. These incessant shifts in self-image account for much of the changes in our states, our mental and emotional conditions.

Even though our inner experience changes a great deal more than we think, we are normally so caught up with our self-concepts that we do not notice the dynamic nature of our ongoing experience. We know that we have many thoughts and feelings, and they are in constant change, but we do not see the significance of this observation because we are so identified with the self-concept based on our body image, which is relatively stable compared to other facets of experience. This identification allows us to believe that we are stable, that we are the same person, while the phenomenology of our inner experience does not actually support this belief. Both outer perception and inner experience are always changing, and if for a moment we allow this observation to affect our self-concept, we might become attuned to the dynamism of our soul.

Flow

If we reflect on our experience, at any time, we can see that it is actually not just changing from one thing to another, but it is in constant flow. In other words, when we attune ourselves to the changing panorama of our experience we begin to be aware not only of the fact that inner events are transitory, always changing from one thing to another, but also of a sense that this change is actually a flow of inner events. We recognize it is a stream of impressions, feelings, thoughts, images, sensations, states, and the like. This statement would appear to be a truism, since it is obvious on reflection that our experience is a flow of events, outer and inner. However, an intellectual recognition of the fact that experience is a constant flow and change is not the same as knowing our experience directly as that flow and change. In the direct experience of the soul, we know directly and intimately the sense of a direct attunement to the flow. We are not only cognitively noting flow, we are the flow. The flow becomes experientially more significant than the particular experiences or inner events. We actually experience ourselves as a flowing river of impressions. The river becomes the foreground of experience, and the events recede to the background.

We are normally not attuned to the sense of stream because we are absorbed in the particular form that is momentarily manifesting. Our consciousness is generally so focused on the particulars of present experience that we are not aware of the flow of the forms. So we see two factors that predispose us toward an atomistic way of viewing our experience: first, our identification with the relatively unchanging self-concept, and second, absorption in the content of experience. We are aware of the atoms of our experience, the particular atom that happens to be the specific experience, but not aware of the stream of atoms constantly passing through. If we disengage slightly from the specifics of the experience we can see that there is a stream of experiences, a flow of impressions.

As we disengage somewhat from the self-concept and the content of experience, awareness of the flow brings us closer to recognizing the soul herself. To be attuned to the flow of inner events indicates that we are more aware of the consciousness which is manifesting the various states and experiences, relative to the content of the states and experiences themselves. We normally focus on the forms, one form after another, and are unaware of the substratum, the medium that is flowing and transforming. If we disengage from the focus on the specific forms and experiences, and simply observe them coming and going, we might become aware of the phenomenon of streaming, the sense of flow. This phenomenon of streaming and sense of flow is not merely the experience of various states happening one after the other. Sometimes, for example in sitting meditation, we might observe experiences flow one after the other, and we call that streaming. This is the external experience of streaming, not the streaming itself. We are still perceiving the flow through some conceptual filters. The experience of inner space with emotional states or thoughts arising in it is not the flow.

As we become more steadily attuned to the flow of experience, the particular forms and specifics of experience begin to appear as manifestations of a flowing medium. The flow takes center stage in our awareness, and this can precipitate the recognition of the medium underlying the various forms of experience. We no longer experience a succession of experiences, but a flowing medium whose flow is the manifestations of the experiences. It is not then a succession of events, but rather a current that carries events. The flow is of the substance of the soul, the medium of consciousness that underlies the specific experiences. The river of consciousness carries various forms, or more accurately, manifests these forms.

We begin to be aware of the nature of this medium, the basic properties of this field. We experience it as fluid, flowing, streaming, changing, and transforming. The presence is not rigid; it is not a fixed mirror that reflects passing forms. It is not like a static screen that displays the projected images of a movie projector. It is more like the light that streams out of the projector, a fluid presence. And as we saw in chapters 3 and 4, it is a self-aware presence, aware of its presence and of the forms that manifest within it. The soul is a fluid, alive substance—not a material substance, but a substantial presence. The change and succession of experiences are felt now as flow, the flow of this presence, as a river that bubbles and spatters, producing various forms we call experiences.

Here then we are exploring one of the basic properties of the soul: it is not only a medium, a presence, but a flowing medium, a fluid presence. It feels like a flow of life and vigor, of energy and power. The flow is an intrinsic property of the presence, and that presence is felt as one's own personal consciousness. It is this flow that is responsible for the changeability of the soul, which underlies the fact of our experience as a succession of events.

The experience of soul as flow possesses many degrees of subtlety, each reflecting a particular depth of this experience. At the beginning, we experience flow topographically, similar to the flow of a stream of water. We experience the medium of the soul as a fluid that flows through our body. We experience it as streaming from one part of the body to another, as in the flow of energy up the spine. We might be aware that the flow is faster in some areas than others, more sluggish in some regions, more blocked in others, completely stuck or absent, or free and smooth. This can alert us to various tensions and rigidities in our bodies, reflecting fixations and identifications in the mind. This can be very helpful for our inner work, as we recognize the areas where our soul cannot flow as places that need to open up. As we work on them, and they relax and open, our soul may begin to flow to these areas, bringing them to life, and including them in her range of experience. Our soul then inhabits more of our body, and we feel more present, more embodied, and our experience is more available, and more open and flexible. Our experience in general becomes more fluid, more flowing, and we feel this as greater freedom and release.[2]

At a deeper level of experience the sense of flow does not have the sensation of fluid going from one part of the body to another. There is a feeling of flow, there is something streaming, but there is no displacement in space. We can experience this globally, diffusely, and feel a sense of freedom, energy, and dynamic vigor. When we are directly experiencing the flow of the soul in our activity, we feel we are flowing, not hampered, not stuck. Our energy is unified, our mind focused, and our body moves in an integrated, fluid, and smooth fashion. We are completely involved in whatever we are doing, whether it is physical activity, artistic creativity, dancing, social activity, lovemaking, hiking, swimming, painting, writing poetry, playing music, or even the free flow of insights and knowledge. The central feeling is the sense of freedom and release, the experience of spontaneity and pleasurable absence of control. It is usually an exhilarating and thrilling ride.[3] Our minds and bodies are unified in this experience, synchronized and harmonized, so we tend to function and perform smoothly and easily. And our performance might actually be superior to other times. Athletes, artists, writers and, others familiar with this condition tend actively to seek it. Even though this is an experience of the flow of the soul, we do not necessarily recognize the soul through this experience. This experience of flow normally appears to us as one kind of experience, and not as the flow of experiences. It is actually a flow of experiences, for our experience is constantly changing its form and inner pattern. Yet most people view the whole occurrence as one experience because of how different it feels from other times, and because the flow is completely continuous, totally connected and integrated.

Our experience of flow can go deeper, which can help us understand the previous levels of flow within a more comprehensive and fundamental view. We can feel the flow as combining the previous two kinds of experience, but integrated into one gestalt. We can experience flow as the stream of experiences, without these experiences being disconnected. At the same time the flow is not a displacement of medium from one location to another. The whole field feels flowing, but not spatially, not horizontally. We feel the flow of experiences as a fountain or a bubbling spring, instead of a river or a stream. This is a more subtle perception than the stream image, and is more accurate regarding the source of the impression of flow. There is neither destination nor source, but merely the flow outward of the arising of experience as a continuous flowing fountain of conscious presence. The fountain effect is a sensation, a feeling, an impression of flowing. The streaming fountain is a bubbling stream of experiences, where the bubbles and eddies are the forms experience is taking.

It is like creation out of nothing, like a water fountain that does not have a source. The water emerges from nowhere; an experience was not there, and now it is there, while the flow is always present. This is a wonderful way of experiencing our soul: ever fresh, ever new, a source that is also the destination. This type of experience of flow occurs when our inner journey is well underway. It indicates that we are free from the constraints and limitations that keep our experience bound to certain forms, to limited dimensions of possibility. Our potential is literally flowing out, and our consciousness is a fountain of impressions, perceptions, insights, and realizations. We not only have occasional deep experiences of our spiritual depth and nature, but our experience of our soul is a continuous outflow of many new and fresh realizations and perceptions. Our soul is manifesting her inner treasures continually, in an ever-fresh stream of new discoveries; our life is not merely punctuated by deep perceptions and significant experiences and insights, but is more the flow of these significant and deep perceptions and insights. This flow is the inner core of our life, the very substance of our immediate experience.

The experience of flow as a continual fountain of manifestation whose very body is the presence of soul brings an awareness of freedom and spontaneity. The soul experiences release, ease, and freedom from inner constraints. Along with the sense of lightness and freedom, of spaciousness or emptiness, the soul manifests now as a continual stream of discoveries, new perceptions, dimensions, and capacities. So opening the flow of the soul brings freedom, liberation, and effortlessness, as well as richness, fullness, and texture.

Unfolding

Experiencing the soul as a bubbling stream brings us closer to understanding how our experience occurs, how potential becomes actuality. When our potential is streaming out freely it discloses, as part of this flow, how it manifests into actual experience. The sense of a bubbling or shooting fountain indicates a movement out, a displacement from the inside out, or from the depth to the surface. It is felt as a displacement of a fluid, vertical instead of horizontal. This is the experienced sense of flow, conveying the impression of a hidden potential that is making itself apparent, as if it is coming out of hiding and exposing itself to the light of experience. This impression is accurate, but still not completely objective. This experience of flow is the beginning of the disclosing of the actual mechanism of manifestation. We can glimpse this mechanism by contemplating the experience of the outflowing fountain of perception.

When we inquire into this outflow we may see that there is no displacement of fluid or substance from depth to surface. (This perception might also occur spontaneously.) There is actually no displacement of anything; the sense of flow appears because we are not yet completely abiding in the conscious presence itself. The center of our experience remains mostly at its surface, which is constantly changing and transforming, which gives us the impression of flow. When we are fully the presence itself we recognize that the forms appear not because they emerge from deep underneath and bubble up to the surface. Rather, the field of presence itself opens up and reveals another layer to itself. The process of uncurling, unfurling, and opening up is often experienced as a sense or image of an overflowing fountain. This is similar to a rose opening up as each petal uncurls and spreads out, all at the same location.

84   Properties and Functions

The flow is not a displacement of something to somewhere else; it is not an outflowing of something from something else, but an unfolding consciousness that is manifesting its potential by steadily opening up. We can experience our soul as a rose unfolding and opening up, revealing the implicit forms in her potential. Our soul is an unfolding living rose with an infinite number of petals, each petal an experience, a perception. The vision of the rose may arise during and represent a stage of the inner journey, but it is not an exact rendition of the process of manifestation. The importance of this vision or inner experience is the recognition that we are unfolding and growing. Our potential is freely manifesting, and we are actualizing our possibilities, with a sense of organic growth, living expansion, dynamic deepening, and continuous unveiling.[4] Our life becomes then a process of unfolding and opening; one experience leads to a deeper experience, one realization leads to a more comprehensive realization, one perception leads to more vast perception, one insight leads to a more encompassing and accurate insight. Facets of our potential reveal themselves in new forms of perception, in new dimensions of experience, in ever-increasing depth and width of realization, in the emergence and development of new faculties and functions of perception and action, and so on. In other words, our inner journey is not only free and rich; it is continually increasing in freedom and richness. The unfoldment of the soul brings not only change but also growth and expansion. It is not only the flow of experience, but also the deepening and widening of this flow, transcending one dimension of experience and knowledge after another.

The process of the soul's unfoldment is yet more mysterious: in this process of manifestation the consciousness of the soul is actually opening at each point of its expanse, where each point then reveals a new manifestation. In the experience of the unfolding flower the perception of displacement remains, but it is a displacement occurring in the same location. This apparent movement is not from one place to another, not from depth to surface, but from center to periphery, in some sense. There is movement without spatial displacement, similar to the generation of concentric waves when we throw a pebble into a still lake. Concentric waves form and expand out from a center. One wave follows the other, the previous ones dying away as new ones are generated. Looking at the situation from the outside, it appears to us that water is being displaced from the center outward. If we submerge ourselves in the water and do some experiments, we realize that there has been no horizontal displacement of water. The waves are actually water being displaced vertically, up and down, but the displacement happens in a wave, where one horizontal location is displaced vertically then a succeeding one, and so on. The outer appearance is that water is displaced horizontally.

No body of water actually migrates from the center to the outside. It appears so, but the body of water remains in its place, and because of a force spreading outward we see a wave. Analogously, in the unfoldment of the soul the apparent movement of a medium is actually not happening. In the actual unfoldment of the soul, there is not even the equivalent of the vertical oscillation of mass as happens in concentric waves in water. Rather, the medium of the soul, at each point of its spatial expanse, opens up and unveils a new form. The global effect of all of these unveilings give the impression of one unified experience, the impression that one form that is now present has taken the place of the previous one. And since the soul's medium is not actually composed of parts, regardless of how small, the change is continuous and universal.

The closest phenomenon to this perception is the changing picture on a movie screen. The light itself changes in terms of its streaming oscillations, and as a result the projected picture changes. When we see a dog running across the screen, we know that there is actually nothing running across the screen. The image of the dog does not move around because the light moves around; rather the light simply transforms at each point of the expanse of the screen, and the unfoldment of this change gives us the impression of a dog moving across the screen. In other words, the unfoldment of the soul is a matter of the medium of the soul unfolding globally, at each point and region of its expanse. We could say that the very atoms of the field illuminate differently from moment to moment (even though the soul is not discriminable into separate atoms). More precisely, each location of the field of the soul changes its wave characteristics, modifies its vibrational qualities, to transform one experiential form to another. These field-pervasive changes are reflected in the transformation of color, texture, viscosity, density, shape, luminosity, and so on. The subjective sense is that of an unfolding field, of a nonspatial movement. We feel this process as an opening up, an unwrapping, a displaying, a disclosing, a divulging, an unveiling, a revealing, a movement from nonmanifestation to manifestation, from potentiality to actuality.

The sensation of flow actually originates from the fact that our consciousness is continually unfolding, constantly creating its various forms. It is a ceaseless stream of unfolding.

We can perceive unfolding on an even more subtle level. We may experience the opening up of all the points of the field as a process of appearing and disappearing. One form mysteriously disappears as another form appears and takes its place. There is no origin of what appears and no destination for what disappears. It is like appearing from thin air and disappearing back into it. There is a stream of these acts of appearing and disappearing, giving us the impression of flow and unfoldment. This perception involves experiencing the consciousness of the soul from the dimension of emptiness, where the forms appear from and disappear into emptiness. And since emptiness is not an object, it is neither a source nor a destination. The forms merely move from nonmanifestation to manifestation. (See chapter 20 for a fuller discussion of this experience of manifestation of perception.)[5]

We are not ordinarily aware of this process of continual appearing, because we conceive of the flow of forms and events as occurring in time. We view it as a succession in linear time; this emotion followed by this feeling, then followed by this thought, then by this state, and so on. If we do not look at the experience of flow within the concept of time, as a succession of forms in linear time, we may realize it is basically a manifestation from nothing to something; it just keeps appearing. We can see manifestation then as self-arising, arising without a source.

When we are in the midst of the experience of flow, being the flow, the appearing presence with its various forms, time changes meaning. We are not then connected with linear time, clock time. Time becomes the flow itself.[6] We normally feel the passage of time by being aware of the flow of impressions. When we are the flow, the flowing appearance, then this flow is the context within which experience happens. Both time and space lose their structuring power, and the recognition of them is not separate from other events within the flowing appearance. The expanse of presence gives rise to the concept of space, and its flow gives us the concept of time. But experientially we feel the flow itself as real time, for we are actually in touch with the ground of our normal concept of time.

In other words, real time is the life of the soul, the unfoldment of the soul. Each period of it is a period of growth and development, not just a temporal space in which events take place. In fact, it is possible to see in this experience that a person's true maturity, the real measure of the soul's actualization of her potential, depends on the length of the period this person lives the unfolding flow of the soul. This is because this life is a life of steady unfoldment, a ceaseless manifestation of potential.

Real time does not necessarily feel like expanded time, or slow time, or anything like that. The flow can be slow or fast, but it's more like full time, rich time. We are really living, and not a second is wasted, but is completely and fully metabolized. Every minute is fulfilled, so time is completely there; all time is there in the experience of the soul. The flow of the presence of consciousness itself feels like time. The sensation of a rate of flow changes, in the sense that experience is going faster or slower. But the flow is always happening, and it does not really make sense to give it velocity. It is more like fullness of time, intensity of time.[7]

Morphogenic Transformation

Our discussion so far presents the notion that manifestation is simply appearing, or the continuity of appearing. Potential becomes actuality through a kind of magical show, a simple display of forms, in a continuous flowing fashion. Although this is an accurate way of describing how manifestation happens, this description can easily be taken dualistically. This is because it is difficult to envision manifestation without a source. The terminology of appearance and display is frequently used in nondual teachings, yet it sounds dualistic. It can be easily interpreted to mean that something that was hidden somewhere is now exposed. It was hiding and now it displays itself. Alternatively, this phenomenon is often described as a light source radiating new and different information in colors, forms, and so on, but in this description there is always the implication that the light or information is traversing spatial distances.

In the course of the soul's realization and understanding of change and manifestation, there appears another form of the experience of unfoldment that gives a more faithful picture of how potential becomes actuality. This experience is free of images involving spatial displacement. Self-arising becomes non-arising, for arising may easily invoke an image of spatial displacement. This is again another subtlety in the experience of flow, of awareness of the changing forms that express the flow of the soul.

We have seen that all these changes are the outward manifestations of the changeability of the soul. These forms are manifestations of the same field, a single medium. These changing forms reflect the continuous change in the field as a whole. Our field of consciousness is itself constantly changing, and this change is what we perceive as the string of inner events, as the current of consciousness, the flow of presence. In other words, the changeability of the soul is more fundamental than the passage of forms. It is a transformation, a transubstantiation. The very medium that is the soul is transforming its qualities and characteristics. The soul is not changeable; it is a changeling, like certain forms that appear in some science fiction movies and TV shows. It is in a continuous condition of morphing. When we see this continuous morphogenic transformation of the soul directly, in ourselves or in others, we see that it is so amazing and miraculous relative to our conventional notion of ourselves that it is far beyond what can be envisioned in fiction. The fictional portrayals of this phenomenon merely approach the truth of the continuous transformation that we can recognize as we learn to see the soul directly. The soul is continuously and spontaneously changing its phenomenology, its topography, its shape, its texture, its color, its feel, its luminosity, its depth, its clarity, its viscosity, its momentum, its force, its power, its level of consciousness, its perceptivity, and so on. The inner multidimensional Riemannian manifold is in a constant state of organic self-organization, not through one form passing and being replaced by another, but through morphing, by one form dissolving, melting boundaries, and this dissolution merging continuously into the emerging boundaries of a newly arising form. Dimensions interpenetrate each other, transform into each other, overlap with each other, coalesce and separate, all in a nonlinear, non-discontinuous manner.

This continuously changing formation is similar to the morphogenic transformation that the human embryo goes through. From a nondifferentiated initial condition, forms arise to change again into new forms. Organs emerge, develop, and become parts of whole systems, which systems formulate themselves, self-organize, and then interrelate in a holistic way. By birth the basic form of the human body is crystallized, except for a few things like the sexual changes that occur later. The body still goes through changes and transformations after birth, but they are no longer morphogenic on the level of body structures and systems. The body basically grows by getting bigger and the basic forms attaining their adult shape and size. Not so with the soul. Morphogenic transformation is a fundamental property of the soul. Its cessation would be psychic death.

So even though the soul transforms similarly to the way an embryo changes, unlike the physical body, it never assumes a final shape or form. The soul's capacity for morphogenic transformation is unlimited and unstoppable. In fact, what is called inner or spiritual transformation is nothing but the continuation of this basic property of the soul. Inner transformation frees the soul from the ego structures that constrain this property and orient the forms of experience toward a particular realm of experience. Ego structures cannot block this property, for our inner states are always in a constant state of change even in egoic experience. However, ego can constrain this morphing property to flow within a narrower range than that of which we are capable. Spiritual work eliminates these subjective inner boundaries, which liberates our soul to morph her field into whatever form our situation requires.

Our soul is then not constrained to form herself only into what we think of as a person with arms and legs. Our inner experience can be released from this body image, and we become free to experience ourselves as a flowing river of luminous consciousness, a bright star of presence, a rich planet of life, a rose of love, a lava flow of energy, a night sky of depth, a blue sky of inner rest, and so on. Our feelings are no longer constrained to the ordinary emotions of fear, greed, aggression, sadness, depression, and so on. We can now experience our inner feelings as a bright and happy sun of joy, a solid and stable silver moon of will, a warm honey of fullness, a fresh pool of innocence, and so on. Our mind will be freed from obsessive thoughts and limiting self-images, to manifest diamonds of clarity, jewels of lucidity, gems of insight, scintillating brilliance of knowledge, and so on.

Her substance or medium changes from instance to instance in terms of luminosity, texture, color, intensity, viscosity, transparency, shape, density, and so on. The soul changes structure and shape, from being a small and rounded baby to being a big strong adult, to a vast expanse of inner space, to an intense stream of thoughts, to a torrential rain of emotions, and so on. It changes its texture and feel, thick or delicate, smooth or rough, cottony or satiny, fluid like water or like mercury. It changes from opaque to transparent, or clear to dull. In fact, when we come to experience the soul's presence consistently, this is the way we perceive our inner experience. When we feel clear, it is not only that our mind functions more lucidly, but the very medium of our experience becomes clear and transparent. When we feel deep, we do not just experience a deep emotion, we experience ourselves as the deep night sky, vast and still.

The significant point for us here is the recognition that the soul manifests her inner potential through a process of morphogenic transformation. She does not throw things out of herself into some kind of space outside. She does not dismember herself and then mold each part into some form. Experiences do not fall into her, do not enter her from somewhere else. The elements of her potential arise by her morphing her substance, her conscious presence, into these forms.[8]

Under normal circumstances we are not in touch with the soul herself, with the conscious field of presence; rather we are in touch with the various states and forms that manifest in the soul. When we recognize the soul herself we recognize that her very substance is changing from one thing to another, which then we see as the changes of forms. This perspective allows for our normal experience, of changes of inner states and events, but gives these changes a quite different interpretation. They are products of a more thorough transformation, a morphogenic transformation. Our normal experience is, thus, the perception of the finished products of our soul's transubstantiation.

The perspective that is made possible by putting our attention on the nature and substance of the soul itself allows us to perceive the actual process by which forms come into being.

Lest we think morphogenic transformation is a process in time, we need to remember that it is actually a process of manifestation out of nonmanifestation. We experience it as a transforming field, but the transformation is basically a continual appearing, a magical display of potential into actuality.

Dynamism

We see that the soul is not a particular state, nor a static manifestation, nor a fixed form. The soul is inherently full of change, movement, flow, and transformation. Stillness and rest are only particular forms that the soul can assume, as are movement and activity. We have discussed this particular property of the soul as transitoriness, changeability, different forms of flow and unfoldment, appearing, manifestation, and morphogenic transformation. The question that remains is what makes these possible. All these point to an underlying property of the soul; all of them are manifestations of a particular characteristic that is fundamental to the soul. We refer to this property as dynamism, meaning that the soul is inherently dynamic, rather than static. This dynamism implies an energetic, vital, active, forceful dimension of the soul, a dimension that intersects all of her other dimensions. This dynamism is an active power, an inherent pressure toward manifestation, an implicit impulse toward unfoldment, a basic will toward revelation, and a fundamental love of display and self-expression.

Our perception of the soul's changeability and unfoldment helps us to recognize this dynamic dimension of the soul. All these manifestations of dynamism are nothing but the various ways it expresses itself. In other words, the pure conscious presence that constitutes the field of the soul is a dynamic presence, where dynamism is completely pervasive of, and absolutely inseparable from, this presence. The essential ground of the soul is not only her ontological dimension but also this pressure to manifest her potential.[9] The potential of the soul, in other words, is a dynamic potential, similar to the potential of the seed.

We can also experience this dynamism directly, as a pure quality, independent of its ways of expressing itself. This experience of the soul indicates that we are experiencing the soul herself, not only one of her forms. We can experience ourselves not only as a field of consciousness, but as an organism of consciousness, with an organismic sense of presence. We feel ourselves as a writhing, moving, pulsating, convulsing organism. The presence is full of pulsating energy, exploding power, dynamic momentum. The sense of writhing movement and convulsing activity is similar to how a healthy muscle feels when contracting and flexing. It is like the feeling of our body when it is full of life and vigor, and is moving in a robust, powerful way, as during intense exercise. The soul also feels both organismic and orgiastic the way genitals can feel during lovemaking, especially the pulsating movement and flow at the peak of orgasm. In the experience of dynamism there is fullness, robustness, power, energy, aliveness, movement, flow, but all as one integrated movement or action. There is a complete flexibility and flow to the movement, like a jellyfish moving in water.[10]

The sense of dynamism can be felt in many ways. We can feel it like a robust and vital movement of a healthy body, like the flow and rush of healthy and vigorous blood coursing through our veins, like a jellyfish forcefully wriggling and flopping its tentacles where this wriggling and flopping happens through the flow of the plasma in its organs. In the dynamism of the jellyfish there is movement, but the movement is not separate from the flow. The movement and the flow are the same thing, not separate. The dynamism of the soul, in other words, is a flow and a movement where these two are actually the same activity.

We can also experience our dynamism as the very substance of the soul being made out of a medium that is scintillating, exploding with life and consciousness. It feels like a pulsating, breathing medium, glowing with life and energy. It actually feels it is breathing, even though there is no oxygen exchange or anything like that. It is the sense of pulsation, of a teeming aliveness.

This dynamic fundamental dimension of the soul is the basic property, the inherent force that impels her toward manifestation. This dynamic pulsating quality to our consciousness appears to us as a flow, as the unfoldment of our potential. This dynamism is the intrinsic energy and power that makes it possible for our soul to manifest her hidden potential, to create her forms. It is a creative dynamism, literally generating her forms of experience by metamorphosing her very presence. It manifests the forms of all of our experiences through a morphogenic transformation of her very substance. In this morphogenic transubstantiation she expresses her excitatory pulsation, her motile dynamism. This dynamism generates forms through morphing.

7 Impressionability of Soul

Malleability

IT IS THE ESSENCE OF LIFE to change and unfold, evolving into new forms and functions. The life of the soul is inseparable from her dynamism and changeability. The pure knowledge of the soul manifests as the various forms of knowledge, giving pure life her inner content. This morphogenic property of the living soul indicates another basic property: malleability. The soul transforms by molding herself into the various forms of experience. She can move from experiencing herself as an adult man with arms and legs, to a chubby baby, to an empty sense of being a formless self, to a sense of being a bubbling fountain, to being a torrential rain of tears, to being an empty vast space, and so on. All these phenomena are the same soul changing her form to be one thing or another. Malleability is the property of the soul necessary for her to change from one form to another. This is what some ancient thinkers were referring to when they called the soul a chameleon. The soul actually is more plastic than a chameleon. Her plasticity and malleability are closer to the changelings in science fiction novels.[1] She can change not only her color, but the totality of her manifestation, across all the dimensions of the inner Riemannian manifold.

The property of malleability has a different significance than that of changeability. The soul cannot only change herself, she can be changed. She can be molded by her experiences, whether they have an external or internal origin. The forms she assumes are not always her choice; they can be imposed on her. At first, this may appear to be an innocent property, necessary for her in order to respond to situations and external stimuli. The forms she assumes are frequently dictated by external stimuli; her senses reflect the external environment by generating corresponding inner forms, and she also responds with corresponding inner feelings and thoughts to various environmental stimuli. This is obviously necessary for perception of and interaction with her world, a characteristic that begins to tell us the other side of how the soul's experience arises. The forms that the soul displays are, then, either a reflection of external forms, which is perception, whether faithful or distorted; or she can display her own forms, manifesting either for her own inner reasons or as responses to external perception, which is normally referred to as inner experience. The unfolding inner forms result from a complex interaction between the soul and her world.

The fact that the soul inhabits a world means that her inner forms are constantly shaped by external impacts. This shaping is necessary for learning and action. However, the soul's malleability also allows the impact of the world to mold her more than is necessary for learning and action. By malleability we mean not only pliability; we also mean that she can be shaped into a relatively permanent form, fixed beyond her normal needs for perception, learning, and action. She can be straitjacketed in a form. The soul is malleable and pliant like mercury; we can form mercury into any shape we like by putting it in a shaped container, but the moment we remove the container it is liberated of this particular form. However, the soul is also malleable the way Silly Putty is; we can mold it into a particular form that is relatively permanent. Both are true of the soul. However, these two examples are the extremes, representing polar opposites of development. She is more like water, which takes on a temporary form when we place it in a container, but which assumes a more permanent form when frozen.

It is easy to observe this malleability of the soul. For example, a strong and repeated experience in childhood can render one so stuck with the forms of that time that even though one becomes an adult, one may continue to feel and behave according to these forms, as if one is still a child having these experiences. A more extreme example is the intensity and frozenness of feelings and memories in posttraumatic stress disorder, resulting for instance from war trauma. The soldier will continue to feel and behave in ways that are not appropriate, because his inner experience of himself and world is frozen into a fixed structure that can last a lifetime.

The malleability of the soul allows her to be affected by her perception and inner experience, and this effect can be lasting. This phenomenon is everyone's common experience; it is a normal part of being human, and more basically part of being alive. Here, however, we are exploring exactly how this happens. We want to understand the basic properties of the soul responsible not only for her being affected, but also for her retaining such effects.

Impressionability

We refer to the soul's property of varying degrees of malleability as impressionability. The soul is impressionable first in the sense of being like a mirror that reflects external information, which is necessary for perception and experience. But the word *impressionability* indicates that the soul is not exactly like a mirror, for external impacts leave traces, impressions. We will discuss this impressionability in terms of how it changes throughout the development of the soul, and the implications and meanings of such changes, but for now we are interested in understanding it as a particular property.

The soul is impressionable the way earth is, for example. Walking on dirt, we leave impressions on the ground. Depending on our weight and the frequency of walking the same route, the impression can be more or less permanent, more or less indelible. If we regularly walk the same route, in time the ground will retain the impression of a trail. The more frequently we walk this route, the deeper is the impression and the more permanent. However, we can make just as deep and lasting an impression if we roll a heavy kind of machinery a few times, or even once, over the same area. Experientially, if as children we are regularly treated without much respect, we grow up feeling unworthy of respect and unable to have self-respect. Similarly, if our bodies or our minds were severely abused a few times, or horribly even once, the lasting impression might be just the same. The severity of the problem regarding respect depends on how frequently and how severely the soul encountered disrespect. This principle is true about both negative and positive impacts. If one experienced love frequently as a child, the lasting impression will be ease in the area of love. One then will relatively easily and frequently experience love, and be readily able to receive love.

The soul is not only malleable, giving her an infinite range and freedom of experience, but also impressionable, making her vulnerable to conditioning. Her experience can condition her, can create indelible grooves in her field that may last a lifetime.[2] This property of impressionability is clearly a mixed blessing. It gives us the possibility of infinite freedom and flexibility, of the openness necessary to unfold and actualize the infinite potential of our spirit. Also, the capacity to retain impressions gives us the potential for learning. The human potential for learning is unparalleled by any other life form. This potential is the basis for all learning. Actualizing this potential in the form of our great capacity for learning requires the capacity to retain impressions, and this capacity also allows our learning to become growth and development, whose source is both unfoldment of the great inner potential of the soul and interaction with the world.

At the same time, this capacity for retaining impressions—where memory is only one form of such retention—is also our vulnerability to influence and conditioning. The influence and conditioning involved in learning can become fixated in such a way as to limit or even preclude further learning, or the kind and range of this learning.

Understanding this property of impressionability clarifies both the capacity for learning and growing and the possibility of conditioning. In other words, the same property that gives us our distinguishing human characteristic, our developmental edge over all other known life forms, also lies at the root of our inner suffering. Furthermore, our infinite capacity for learning and growth determines the possibility for conditioning, and hence limitation of freedom and limitless openness to suffering. (For our distinction between learning and conditioning, see the discussion later in this chapter.) Our impressionability is both our boon and our misfortune. We are beings who can soar to unimaginable heights of freedom, creativity, and development, but can also plummet to the depths of suffering and degradation. We can be higher and finer than the highest angels, but can also be lower and more brutish than any animal or devil. Human history has amply demonstrated this. And it is clear that recognizing, understanding, and taking into consideration the basic properties that give us these possibilities can help us work with our human potential, which is both a promise and a dilemma.[3]

The property of impressionability is absent in essence, whose qualities are timeless and unchangeable. When we experience and understand essence, in any of its qualities and dimensions, one of the primary things we learn about it is its immutability, its spontaneously and primordially given properties, and hence its incorruptibility. It is not only pure; this purity is eternal and stainless, totally immune to the accidents of time. It simply does not make sense for essence to be corrupted or contaminated. In this regard essence is like space. Regardless what arises in space, space remains the same, totally pure and empty. This is why essence does not develop, while the soul does. Essence is timelessly perfect and free, while the soul has the potential for perfection and freedom. This potential is given to her by essence, which is her ontological ground and her timeless and absolutely precious potential. Through realizing and embodying her essential ground, the soul achieves her liberation and fulfillment.

Receptivity

The property of impressionability is what gives our human consciousness its quality of receptivity. The soul has to be receptive to stimuli, both outer and inner, in order for her to be impressed by them. As we discussed in chapter 3, the soul is also agency. She can be responsive and proactive. Here we see the opposite property, that of receptivity. Being necessary for perception and communication, receptivity is an obvious requirement for learning. However, the receptivity of the soul is not like that of a mirror. It is a dynamic receptivity, both because the soul can respond to stimuli and impressions, and also because the stimuli and impressions can leave traces, forming and structuring the soul.

Essence is not receptive. It just is. It is pure Being, and this presence can only have an active influence on whatever it touches. Soul can be both receptive and active, while essence can only be active. However, the action of essence is different from that of soul. It is not a sense of agency. It is active, but not proactive. It is the pure effect of its presence as it touches our consciousness. It is like a chemical substance that will readily interact with the medium it is in, if the medium possesses certain properties. It affects the soul merely by arising in it, but only if the soul is receptive to it. When the soul is receptive to essence the latter transforms and structures the experience of the soul. This is the basis for spiritual transformation.

The soul, then, is basically receptive, to both external and internal impacts. These impacts appear in the soul as forms of experience, and they also structure her by engendering further forms, some of which are lasting. Seeing an external object, for instance, will register in the soul as the image of this object, but this normally leads to the arising of further forms, in the form of associations to and feelings about this image. In other words, these impacts structure the experience of the soul, momentarily or in lasting ways. One of the phenomena that impacts the soul and structures her experience is essence, which is the most important element for her spiritual transformation. Essence is one of the soul's inner resources; others include the forms of her phylogenetic history, and her capacities, knowledge, memory, and so on.

The soul's receptivity, especially when seen in terms of essence's active relation to her, is the reason that traditionally the soul is given the feminine gender. Traditionally, soul is seen as feminine and essence masculine. When receptivity is thought of as a feminine property, this attribution makes sense. In fact, some religious teachings—Judaism, Christianity, and Islam, for example—take the view that the soul needs to become feminine in relation to essence, spirit, or God, in order to achieve her fulfillment and liberation. To attain completeness, she needs to be receptive to essence, rather than either being active toward it or receptive to the influences of the world. This perspective means that soul needs to be receptive to the influence of essence for the latter to structure her experience, which will allow the soul's experience to be formed by the dimension that is inherently perfect and free. We will discuss this in greater detail when we explore the development and maturation of soul in chapter 15.[4]

Learning and Conditioning

In the normal life of the soul she retains impacts of her experiences, as impressions that determine to a large degree her further experience and development. These impressions can be in line with her true nature, namely essence with its various qualities and the capacities it gives to the soul, thus allowing her further chances for development and growth. This is real learning, where the soul not only learns about the world, developing knowledge and skills that support her to grow and mature in it, but learns in a way that harmonizes with her true nature and potential for development. Such learning does not happen in a way that limits or blocks her openness, creativity, flow, flexibility, and freedom; that is, her potential continues to be available to her. This open and natural development allows the soul to learn about the world, and about life with other living beings, and to learn about herself in such a way that keeps her open to her greater potential.

The soul's retained impressions can also be disharmonious or even antithetical to her true nature, limiting or distorting her openness, creativity, flow, flexibility, and freedom. The retained impressions can become rigid and fixed structures, limiting her capacity for morphogenic transformation by constraining her malleability and her receptivity to the rest of her potential. Rigidity and fixation are elements of a larger category of disharmonious impressions: retained impressions that are disharmonious to her because they are false, inaccurate, and/or distorted reflections of her nature and properties. Distorted impressions create in the soul an opaqueness that obscures her inherent potential for luminosity, blocking the transparency of consciousness. In other words, any retained impressions that are not in harmony with her true nature and fundamental properties are bound to limit her access to her greater potential, to alienate her from the preciousness and freedom of her essential nature, and to inhibit her growth toward maturity and completeness.

Fixed, rigid, and inaccurate impressions constrain the soul's receptivity to her potential to be prejudiced exclusively toward the elements of this potential that are consonant with the rigidity, fixation, and falseness. The soul has the potential to be false, to manifest rigid and fixed forms, opaqueness, dullness, and darkness. When the retained impressions are such they will tend to channel her creativity and unfoldment of potential toward the elements of this potential that are compatible with these limited and distorted impressions. This is the problem with fixed and rigid impressions, and the forms that do not reflect faithfully her essential nature. This is a form of learning, but it is more exact to call it conditioning. Conditioning here means that she is structured in a way that is not wholesome; her experience is limited to forms that obstruct the free arising of her potential and its actualization.

The soul normally grows with a mixture of limited and wholesome impressions in various proportions, depending on the circumstances and environment in which she grows. The result is various degrees of actualization of potential, and various degrees of openness to such potential. Therefore, when a soul begins to feel the desire for expanded and truer experience, it becomes the task of the wisdom teachings to guide the soul to learn to shed her constraining retained impressions and influences, and to know her true nature and basic properties in a way that allows her to be open to the fullness of her potential. Real, effective teachings can help the soul to unfold in a manner that liberates her morphogenic dynamism to unveil and manifest the deeper and essential dimensions of this potential, which are necessary for enlightenment and maturity.

Since the maturation and potential liberation of the soul requires her open receptivity to the fullness of her potential, and particularly to her essential and ultimate nature, we recognize the need for her to regain her original inherent malleability and impressionability. But because of the limitations of the soul that has been conditioned and limited, this is an inherently difficult process fraught with conflicts, resistances, and fears.

Part of the difficulty is that there is a close relationship between conditioning and learning. Conditioning is the establishment of rigid and fixed structuralizing impressions in the soul, while learning means greater actualization of potential in response to experiences of internal and external environments. We will see in upcoming chapters that the two are not clearly demarcated, and that they can flow into each other. Developmental psychoanalytic psychology notes that ego defenses are frequently utilized to safeguard and further development, and that some of them lose their defensive functions at particular junctures in ego development and become elements of structures that support adaptation.[5]

We will see in chapters 11 and 14 that ego development, in particular, is largely the establishing in the soul of relatively stable structures, through the integration of myriad retained impressions. Furthermore, this ego development is a universal process that no soul escapes. It is part of the development of the soul on her way to the actualization of her potential. Even though we come to see how this development has moved away from our essential nature, it is a legitimate stage in the development of the soul toward completeness and enlightenment. Ego development is actually the process by which the soul metabolizes her experience of the world, and is necessary for her individuation and maturation as a human individual who expresses the true nature of the soul. (See *The Pearl Beyond Price*, chapters 11–15.) However, for most individuals in the vast majority of human societies, this process is arrested and does not move toward completion. It is arrested at the level of development of ego structure that culminates in our sense of being an individual with a psychological identity. This sense of being an autonomous individual with a capacity for psychological self-recognition is the outcome of the soul being impressed and structured with a self-image constructed through the integration of many retained impressions. (See *The Pearl Beyond Price*, chapter 2.)

Thus, ego development occurs mostly through the establishment of relatively fixed impressions. Furthermore, because ego development culminates in the establishment of an identity and sense of self that depend on the fixed impressions, it naturally leads to a limitation on our malleability and impressionability; dependence on the fixed impressions orients us toward identification with and attachment to them. We tend to perpetuate our self and its identity, limiting our openness, malleability, and impressionability. We generally experience as threatening and destabilizing the impacts of forms of experience outside the boundaries of our identity. In other words, we become both habituated and attached to the fixed impressions that compose our identity, at the expense of our basic capacities of openness, malleability, and impressionability.

As a consequence, we begin to regard complete openness and impressionability as undesirable, even threatening and dangerous. We unconsciously defend against it regardless of how much we understand its value and significance. This resistance is an attempt to protect our sense of identity. In resisting openness and impressionability, we unconsciously believe that we are fighting for our own personal survival and integrity. This becomes one of the primary difficulties in the process of inner work where we need to be open to new and novel elements of our potential. In fact, in order to be able to be receptive and impressionable to our essence, we need to be completely impressionable, for any limitation in impressionability will become a limitation in our receptivity to the true nature and ground of the soul. This is because our true nature is characterized by complete transparency, luminosity, and flow, and any opaqueness or rigidity is bound to limit our openness to it.[6]

This difficulty makes it problematic for the soul to learn to be truly impressionable and receptive, even though these are qualities necessary for her fulfillment and liberation. Learning to shed her rigid and fixed structures elicits a great deal of fear and vulnerability. She will become afraid of being controlled, determined, molded, made into something against her own will, lost, and so on. In other words, the normal soul, the soul structured through ego development, fears her impressionability and receptivity partly because she can be open to the wrong influences, which is frequently a justified fear. But the greater fear is the loss of her identity, which is the same as the loss of her relatively rigid ego structures.

The fear of being molded, determined, influenced, controlled, or losing oneself is more realistic in an intrusive environment, but most of us have a measure of intrusive elements in our environment. This is one reason it is important for inner work environments to be empathic, sensitive, adequately holding, and not too intrusive. Yet, this fear can be unmanageable for some individuals who had extremely intrusive environments in their early lives. The soul may have developed to particularly protect herself against intrusions and impingement by limiting her impressionability and receptivity. Such individuals have lost most of their basic trust that letting themselves be, surrendering to their experience without inner defensiveness or manipulation, will be positive for them, or even neutral. They will first need to deal with their distrust of simple inner relaxation and learn to trust the loving ground of their soul. (See chapter 11, and *Facets of Unity*, chapters 4 and 6.)

For the soul to let go of her rigidity means not only surrendering her defenses and protective strategies, but also the ego structures that give her the sense of self and identity. She feels that she will be naked, unprotected, and vulnerable. To be impressionable means to her to be vulnerable to all external and internal influences, without being able to pick and choose, or to control her life. She believes she will be prey to dangerous or unwholesome influences, influences that do not have her safety and well-being in mind. She is afraid not only of being harmed, but of being manipulated, even destroyed and annihilated. We all have such fears and such distrust. It manifests in many ways, some of which are:

- The need for control of one's life, experience, inner process, relationships, etc.
- Rigidity in structure and character. Rigidity can be a way of not allowing oneself to be influenced, not allowing what one considers external influences to affect one. Rigidity may be evident in inner psychological states, religious convictions, ideological positions, and political opinions, as well as in other attitudes, tastes, and preferences.
- Willfulness, an active way of being rigid and having control. Control can be both passive and aggressive.
- The general schizoid defenses of isolation and withdrawal. Schizoid defenses are utilized when we want to protect ourselves against vulnerability in general. If we are withdrawn, isolated, out of contact, or emotionally hidden, we believe we are not accessible to influences. Deep inside we may feel vulnerable, so delicate that anything can impress on our soul without our volition. Sometimes the delicacy can be extreme; some people are so vulnerable and so sensitive that you say one word and they lose their sense of themselves.
- Compulsive need for autonomy. The need for autonomy, to be who one is independent from others, can become so compulsive and obsessive that one always wants to be independent and autonomous, always different. This compulsive need for autonomy can militate against receptivity and impressionability, even though these properties are necessary for the soul to realize her essential nature that alone can give her true autonomy. In other words, by protecting oneself against influence, one becomes closed to the influence of one's own deepest potentials.

- Fear of intrusion and the need for empathy. When the soul is unusually sensitive to intrusion and requires a very exact empathy, she becomes unconsciously defensive against receptivity and impressionability.

Impressionability and Autonomy

A central component of the spiritual development of the soul relates to freeing her impressionability and receptivity so that she becomes resilient and malleable, as is her nature, but within a particular orientation. She becomes less impressionable to the external and more impressionable to the internal.[7] The receptivity never ceases; it is a property of the soul. In normal experience she is receptive to the world and its impacts in ways usually leading to the loss of her freedom, but she can attain inner autonomy by becoming more receptive to her inner nature, essence, or spirit. More accurately, external stimuli will continue to impact her, but will leave fewer or no lasting traces, and this way her forms of experience will be more structured by her own true potential. External impacts will have a determining effect in terms of what forms emerge, but not in lasting and fixed structures that impede her flow and unfoldment.

This brings us to the question of the impressionability of the soul in infancy, and how it is different from that in her maturity, when she is completed by the realization of her essential and true nature. The soul is completely impressionable at both infancy and full maturity, but in different ways. At infancy the impressionability can and normally does lead to inflexible and relatively permanent forms and structures in the field of the soul. The soul is not only impressionable but these impressions can remain as semi-permanent traces, as indelible impressions. The impressionability of maturity, when the soul is not only complete but has realized her true nature, is pure receptivity and malleability without the possibility of lasting traces. The soul is vulnerable in the sense of being open to all possible forms of her potential experience, but is actually invulnerable in terms of conditioning. Her impressions are momentary, transitory, and last only as needed for the moment. This condition of liberated impressionability is likened to the effect of drawing on water. The medium of water is quite flexible and impressionable, and readily takes whatever form we impress on it. But this form dissipates almost as immediately as it appears. Another image is that of making circles of smoke in air, as with a cigarette. The form of smoke circle exists only for a short period of time, and the medium of air gradually but quickly regains it original nature.

This realized impressionability is given to the soul by her essential nature, which is primordially immaculate and unchangeable. In the liberated state, the essential ground of the soul is now so fully and securely wedded to her that she possesses its incorruptible characteristics. She is still receptive, malleable, and impressionable, but this property is wedded to the immaculate and stainless character of her essence. This transforms the field of the soul into a medium similar to water or space, where it is in some way completely open, receptive, and vulnerable, but at the same time free and spontaneously self-liberating.

Why does the soul not possess this self-liberating quality in her infancy and childhood, when she is also quite impressionable and naturally coemergent with her essential ground? This is a complex question, and not easily answered. One way of addressing it is to relate it to the question of dependence and autonomy. In infancy and childhood the absence of maturity in the soul manifests not in distance from her essential ground, but in her total dependence on others; not only physically, but also emotionally and in all other ways. Because of this dependency she is at the mercy of her environment, her circumstances, and the ministrations of her caregivers. Her real need at the time for their physical support and nourishment, love and caring, mirroring and understanding, and so on, predisposes her toward losing touch with her essential ground. She is not enlightened, in the sense that her cognitive capacities are not developed enough for her to know and comprehend that she is her true nature, and she is not mature enough to consciously and cognitively realize her ontological autonomy. In other words, because of her phase-appropriate need and dependency she can lose connection with her essential ground. This loss tends to happen as part of a more comprehensive process, an important part of which is the retention of impressions. We will discuss this process in some detail in chapters 11 and 12. For a more detailed account see *The*

Point of Existence, chapters 6, 17, 18, and 19. In that book we explore in detail how the soul loses touch with her essential ground, and discuss how this process becomes primary in the development of narcissism. We enumerate the various factors leading to such alienation, a process that also includes the development of a stable self-concept through the integration of semi-permanent self-impressions. *The Point of Existence* is a study of self-realization, and the process by which the soul attains it by learning to recognize her essence as her identity.

The self-realization of our essential nature becomes the ground upon which true and unassailable autonomy develops. In *The Pearl Beyond Price* we discuss the true autonomy of the soul that she can attain only by realizing her essential ground. We explore autonomy as freedom of being oneself, independent of others and circumstances, by abiding in the presence of our true nature. This book also explores autonomy on the ego level, as a stage toward the true autonomy of Being. The ego development of the sense of being an autonomous individual is a stage that can lead to individuation on the Being level, which can happen through the soul metabolizing the content of ego structures that go into the construction of the sense of being an autonomous individual.

Self-realization of true nature and the ontological autonomy it gives the soul in her individuation both contribute to the development of self-liberating impressionability. Both of these attainments require the purification of the soul, a process by which the soul learns to be transparent to true nature, necessitating that she harmonize the various elements of her potential. The most significant and difficult part of this process is the integration and harmonizing of the spiritual and essential ground with the animal potential of the soul, with its instincts, drives, and desires.[8] This is necessarily a brief outline of the development of impressionability; the various materials that we have introduced into this discussion will become clearer and more precise as we continue our exploration in the present book.

8 Living Presence

THE SOUL IS NOT ONLY A CONSCIOUS PRESENCE; it is an unfolding dynamic organism of consciousness. She is pure potentiality, a potentiality that is inherently dynamic, whose dynamism unfolds the elements of her infinite potential through a process of morphing manifestation. The unfoldment of the soul produces not only constant change and transformation, but also movement toward a greater actualization of potential. The more potential manifests, the wider and the deeper is our experience, and the more expanded our sense of who we are and what we can do. A seed not only generates other seeds, or other kinds of seeds; it opens up and develops into a tree. The morphogenic transformation is not only a generation of forms, but also a generation of ever-expanding forms, forms of increasing complexity and organization. The mind expands not only in terms of the different functions it can exercise, but also in the development of these functions to greater and greater complexity and performance. Our emotional life develops and matures in intensity, depth, range, level, and kind. The way we experience ourselves evolves in an ever-increasing complexity and richness.

Growth

This unfoldment of forms progresses in an evolutionary manner, disclosing and actualizing our potential. It is not a chaotic or haphazard throwing out of elements of potential. This unfoldment usually involves patterns of self-organization. The soul continues to be an organism of consciousness, but her forms steadily move toward higher levels of organization. New elements of potential arise, new forms of experience and structure appear, and all of these continue to be organized into new structures. As the soul unfolds her potential she changes not by disposing of the old forms, but by integrating them into a more complex organization, in which more elements and levels are integrated into a functional whole. As forms emerge and develop they subsume the previous ones, creating a more complex organism.[1] This process happens in all the sectors and manifestations of the soul.

Mental development is a clear example of the appearance of increasingly complex forms.[2] At first we are capable of perception, then recognition, then we can use images and symbols, then concepts, then complex thought.

This again points to a basic property of the soul, a property implicit in its unfolding dynamism that we can understand and experience explicitly: the property of growth. The soul not only manifests her potential, but by manifesting it she grows and matures. As she unfolds she moves toward more inclusion of her potential, hence more completion of her experience. This movement is best described as natural growth, moving toward what we call maturation. We can be aware of growth externally, as a conceptual understanding of certain changes, but we can also experience growth directly, in our internal experience. We observe growth in the changing of the soul as she unfolds her potential in forms of ever-increasing levels of organization. This observable evolution of forms, of perception and experience, is amenable to empirical research, particularly in fields like systems theory. (See appendix E for a discussion of the soul in systems theory terms.) The growth of the soul can be explored scientifically in terms of the evolution of her forms, because we can observe it in our personal experience by reflecting on our individual history.

We see here that the potential of the soul is a potential for growth, for increasing development and maturation. It is not only a potential for greater numbers and types of forms of experience, but most significantly for a maturing organism. This is why we call the soul an organism of consciousness; it grows similarly to how a physical organism does; in fact, it is the essential archetype or prototype of a growing organism.

We can experience our soul as growing, as an organically growing consciousness. Growth is a particular experiential category, an experienceable concept. Our experience of the growth of our bodies gives us a vague notion of the actual sense of growth in the soul. We might be aware conceptually that our body is changing and getting bigger, but, especially in youth, we can almost feel it growing. We can directly feel the body transforming, alive, and pulsing. Not only do we surmise growth from observations across the axis of time, we can experience growth as a specific quality of our soul, of our consciousness. We feel a sense of being organic and alive, the way a growing tree is.

When we are in nature, for example in a redwood forest with living plants and tall trees, we can feel this sense of natural growth. When we are open and relaxed amongst these majestic and immense trees, we can sense their life, their organicity, their growing power and energy. If we try to identify ourselves with their life, with their mode of being, we might feel a sense of freshness, of moist aliveness, of dynamic vitality. They do not feel dead; they do not feel static, even though they are stationary. They do not move about, but we know they are alive. We know their aliveness because we can witness them growing and changing, but we can also feel their mode of aliveness. Their aliveness, or their mode of being, does not feel alive in the way an animal is alive. An animal is dynamic and organic in a different way than a tree, not only because it transports itself, but also because its feel, its consciousness, has a different sense of organicity.

When we can sympathetically feel the mode of being of a tree, like a redwood, we may sense that this mode is best characterized by the feeling of growth. We are not asserting that trees are conscious of their experience, but rather that when we are intimate with the organic living quality of a tree we feel a sense of growth. A tree is a growing organism; growth is a particular characteristic of the plant kingdom. When we touch a big healthy tree we can easily have a sense that there is growth, there is a growing organism.

The experience of the soul as a growing organism reminds us of the organic moist living quality of plants. There is the sense of a pulsating potential, of a dynamic energy, that we recognize as the feeling of growth. We feel the potential of the seed in its phase of opening up and manifesting. We feel fresh, moist, organic, and alive as if we are in the midst of a tropical jungle, with huge trees, rich with life and potential, teeming with vigor and energy.

We are differentiating the dynamic movement of growth from spatial movement. It is the experience of the unfolding characteristic of living organisms, in contrast to the sense of other self-organizing systems like clouds, storms, stars, or planets. These phenomena grow, develop, and structure themselves, but not in the same sense as organic life. The experience of growth is the experience of the forms inseparable from the process of the emergence of the forms, again inseparable from the sense of teeming potentiality. The experience of dynamism integrates potential, emergence, and form. There is the sense of a seed in the process of sprouting. The soul's sense of growth, then, is most analogous to plant life. (See appendix C regarding the Sufis' attribution of the quality of growth to the vegetal soul.)

The soul grows as she unfolds, actualizing her emerging potential. The soul does not stay the same. She is not primordially complete and mature, and hence she can have phases and stages of development. She can be primitive or advanced, simply organized or highly integrated, immature or adult and seasoned. She can be infantile, young, old, or ancient. She can be arrested in her development, underdeveloped, undeveloped, quite developed, or complete. All these are characteristics that apply to soul, but not to essence. For the presence of pure consciousness, these qualities do not make sense. Pure consciousness, pure presence, or pure awareness is the primordial ground, totally complete and spontaneously perfect. Essence is eternally itself; it does not grow, and growth makes no sense to it. This is a very important distinction between soul and essence, regardless of the fact that both are consciousness. Essence is pure consciousness, but soul is an organism of pure consciousness. Essence is always complete and perfect, but soul grows and develops; completeness and perfection is her deepest potential, but she needs to grow for this to be her permanent conscious condition.

Many wisdom traditions speak of pure consciousness as primordially perfect, eternally complete, not needing development, growth, or completion. These traditions tend to emphasize sudden enlightenment, or direct realization, where the methods of inner work involve simply recognizing true nature.[3] Because they do not discuss the kind of consciousness that can grow, like that of the soul, many practitioners of this kind of path end up believing that one does not need to develop one's consciousness in order to be realized. This view does not recognize that the fact that our ultimate nature is primordially complete does not mean that our soul can contain such completeness without first growing and developing. Our soul always has the possibility of experiencing the primordial ground and nature, and recognizing the nondual condition of Reality, but she cannot remain with this perception unless she is sufficiently mature and complete to live this realization. This is why enlightenment cannot simply be one definitive experience. Direct recognition of the ultimate truth does not by itself bring about enlightenment and liberation. In fact, the soul cannot actually absorb the significance and implications of such experience all at once. She needs a continual process of development, in which she grows and matures, and the fullness of this maturation will then coincide with the capacity to abide in the primordial perfection.[4] This process of unfoldment and learning is the process of growing and developing the inner vessel needed for our essential nature to manifest in a lived human life.

Life

However, growth is not merely development. Storms develop, stars develop, crystals develop, and so do all self-organizing systems. We do use terms like growing and maturing for the development of such systems, and systems theorists are using such terms more frequently. Nevertheless, the quality of growth we have been discussing does not appear in nature until organic life begins. The property of organic growth points to yet another basic property of the soul, that of life. In our discussion of the soul's properties, especially when we addressed unfoldment and growth, we had to resort frequently to the language of physical living things. We had to borrow terms—*organic*, *vital*, *robust*, *teeming*, *convulsing*, and the like—that are normally associated with living organisms. This is because the way the soul changes, transforms, unfolds, and grows is the way of life. The soul is actually the archetype of life, and hence we can understand life and living more completely by understanding the soul.

When we think of our lives, we think in terms of content. Our life is our situation, engagements, relationships, activities, projects, interests and pursuits, social and work structures, and so on. We think of how we spend our time, what things we do, what we value and pursue, our expressions and creativity, and the physical and human spheres within which all these take place. However, all of this content is actually the context, the matrix, where our life takes place. It is not actually our life. These are the external manifestations of our life, just as inner events are the external manifestations of the soul. Our life is what we experience of it. It is the totality of our experience. This means that my interests, for instance, are not my life; rather, my experience of my interests is my life. Suppose an important part of my life is tennis. Now, even though we use such expressions, my life is not tennis, but my direct experience of tennis. More precisely, tennis becomes my life only because of my experience of it. The parts of tennis that I do not experience, directly or indirectly, are not part of my life. Intellectually I can think of the totality of tennis as part of my life; this makes sense and is practically a useful way of thinking of it. But with respect to the actuality of my life, it is totally and absolutely constituted by my experiences. Everything else, as in the case of elements of tennis I never experience, is not my life, and when I die this becomes crystal clear. The other elements of tennis are potential for my life, and become my life only when I experience them. Of course they might indirectly influence my life by influencing what I directly experience. But even then it is the influence that enters my life, and not these unknown elements.

The fact of the potentiality of the various elements of the content of my life that I do not yet experience is what makes it useful to think of life in this customary way. However, this way of viewing life has its problems. It makes life seem to be out there, in the external objects and situations, while life is actually my personal intimate experience.

Strictly speaking, my life is my own experience of what we conventionally call life. The only thing that touches me is my experience. I can say that someone's actions and qualities touch me, but strictly speaking only my experience—direct or indirect—of this person's actions and qualities touch me. For something to enter my life, I have to be conscious of it. It is this awareness, this consciousness that is directly my life. I am looking at the vast blue ocean. I can say then that the ocean at this time is part of my life. Strictly speaking, though, it is only my perception of the ocean that constitutes this part of my life. The ocean enters my life through my perception and experience of it, and indirectly through the water I drink, the atmosphere I breathe, and so on. Like the person in the example above, the ocean is important for my life—besides being important for other's lives and in itself—for it is the source of my experience of it. My experience of the ocean does not stand alone; it definitely needs the ocean. Yet, the ocean in itself, as the physical phenomenon, is, strictly speaking, not part of my life.

Our life is not what we experience, but the experience of what we experience. It is the vision of the ocean, the sensation of coolness and wetness when I am swimming, the taste of bitter saltiness of the water. All of these are what actually constitutes my life. My life is my experiences of both outer and inner events. This is not a move toward solipsism, for it is clear that the ocean exists in its own right, independent of my individual mind, and enters the lives of many other people, as well as the lives of many other types of sentient beings. What we are trying to point out is that strictly speaking, as a little introspection or contemplation will show us, our life is the flow of our experiences. It is the flow of subjective forms, whether these forms reflect external events or inner ones. My image of the ocean is a picture in my consciousness; my sensation of the wetness of its water is an impression in my consciousness; the salty taste is also an experience in my consciousness. Our life is then, in this strict sense, completely subjective. It is the flow of perceptions and experiences, all occurring in my consciousness, in my soul.[5]

This line of thought demonstrates that in some fundamental and literal sense our life is our soul. Our life is constituted by the various forms that arise in our consciousness, which is our soul. Our life is actually the transformations and unfoldment of the soul. This is the essence of our life, the felt core of our experiences. To put it differently, our life is the life of the soul, where the life of the soul is her flow and unfoldment. This understanding brings our life closer to home. To recognize this truth helps us to feel our life directly, rather than knowing it as dispersed into various pieces of content. With this understanding and recognition, life becomes more direct, more experiential, more intimate. It is no longer the rarified life of the discursive mind that takes its life to be the external content it reifies and conceptualizes. The perspective of the life of the soul that we present here can allow us to know our lives as integrated into a unified current, an unfolding stream of continual actualization. Our life becomes full of meaning, for it embodies then the fullness of our soul.

As our inner journey progresses and our soul unfolds, this way of understanding life begins to prevail. We become so attuned to the actual field of the soul, so present as the conscious presence of the soul, that this field of presence becomes the center of life, the actual substance of life. It is then the current that fills and impregnates all the external situations that we conventionally call our life. We then are present in our contexts; we are the embodiment of life.

It is because we are the conscious current that streams in and through our external contexts that we tend to call such contexts our life. These contexts become more our life the more we fill them, the more that the current of life, which is the soul, impregnates them. In other words, as the knowledge and freedom of the soul grows, we have more life not because of how various or how rich is our external context, but because of how present we are in it. The external context does not give us life; we give life to it. We are the life that we live, and the deeper we realize this, the more we have life.

Physical Life

This perspective does not yet explain why we call our external context our life and why we refer to the flow of our soul as life. We could have just as well described it as the flow of basic knowledge. All of our impressions, of both inner and outer events, can easily be described as forms of basic knowledge, as manifestations of consciousness. We could have described this current as consciousness of a stream of events.[6] This description would be accurate but incomplete. Describing our ongoing experience only in terms of consciousness and knowledge seems thin; it leaves us cold, and seems to miss something fundamental. We obviously use the concept "life" for a good reason; it corresponds to something fundamental and significant in our direct experience. It refers to something not encompassed by the notions of consciousness and knowledge, even pure consciousness and basic knowledge. Where does this concept of "life" come from?

The conventional orientation may leap to our awareness first: life is a concept that is opposite to death; we call it our life because we are alive, not dead. Here we return to the modern view of Reality, a view that developed through the loss of the fabric that binds its basic triad together. We think of life physically: life is a property of our physical organism; and when our body dies, life ends. This perspective has a great deal of truth to it, in terms of normal perception and experience. Nevertheless, this perspective does not satisfy our current exploration, because we have seen that experience is not the experience of the body. Experience is always the experience of the inner field of sensitivity; it is always the arising of forms and events in our consciousness. If we now revert to believing that life is only life of the body, then we limit life to only a narrow segment of what we have discussed as life in the previous section. Life then becomes the life of the body, and consciousness an epiphenomenon of the brain. The stream of life becomes the excitations and responses of the body to its external contexts.

Let us explore the empirical belief, subscribed to by modern science and medicine, that the definition of life is that the body is not dead. The idea here is that for some yet inexplicable reason our physical organism can have life, and it can lose it. This life is not something on its own, not an entity, but a property that can qualify the body. Life is then similar to when the TV in our living room is doing its job, is functioning. When it stops functioning completely we say that it is dead. When our body functions in certain ways we say it is alive; when it stops we say it is dead. It stopped living.

In the life sciences it is thought that life arose in the universe when certain complex chemical compounds appeared and certain chemical reactions took place. Science still does not understand exactly what these conditions necessary for the emergence of life were, but the dominant perspective maintains that the whole thing was a purely physical occurrence, an electrochemical accident, to be precise. In other words, life is an epiphenomenon of matter; as matter reaches a certain complexity and interacts with itself under certain physical conditions, it begins to have a new property, life. It achieves a level of organization that gives it a self-organizing capacity, which then manifests as a particular unified functioning. When it malfunctions and loses integrity it dies, losing this capacity and beginning to disorganize and dissolve.

Most scientists believe that the initial conditions that led to the arising of life will be discovered at some point; this might very well happen. This scientific view clearly has a lot of truth to it, and may be completely accurate. It is accurate from the point of view of our empirical evidence, which is the sum total of our external observations of life.

The scientific paradigm regarding life holds that after life began, it then developed according to the theory of evolution. At some point this development became complex enough for life to have consciousness. Physical organisms began to have senses, capable of perception as we know it. This seems to have occurred at the transition from plant to animal life. Then, at a later point of evolution, after the nervous system and the brain evolved to a certain degree of complexity, consciousness became capable of inner life, of self-consciousness, not merely of perception. Biological evolution began with life, developed into life with perception, and progressed to life with consciousness conscious of itself—subjectivity or apperception. Our understanding of the soul, and the knowledge available through her unfoldment, does not contradict this view. This view of evolution is most likely accurate; at least it is adequate to explain our empirical evidence. However, this view does not adequately explain life, even the life of the body.

The knowledge of the soul brings another dimension to this perspective. It does not question the details of the progress of evolution; it does not even question that at certain stages of evolution matter needed certain conditions for life to arise, or that our brains needed to reach a particular level of complexity for inner life to be possible. It only questions the interpretation that life is an epiphenomenon of matter, just as it questions that inner experience—consciousness of consciousness—is an epiphenomenon of brain complexity. Direct experience and understanding of the soul shows us that life is not a product of matter, and consciousness is not an activity of the brain. The view of biological evolution theory that life arose as a new property of matter when it reached a certain level of organization is actually similar to what is known as the strong AI (artificial intelligence) position, that inner consciousness is an epiphenomenon of the brain. (See appendix F.)

One of the main competing theories to the strong AI position is that apperception is an emergent phenomenon. According to this emergence theory, consciousness is not an activity of the brain when the brain reaches a certain level of complexity and organization.[7] Consciousness needs a complexly organized brain before it can emerge, but it is an inherent potential to life, and not a product of brain complexity. It is a potential that waits for the development of the physical instrument necessary for its functioning. In other words, consciousness uses the brain to manifest its potentials of self-reflection and introspection.[8]

This theory, however, still relies on the standard theory of biological evolution, believing that consciousness (of consciousness) is inherent to life, while life begins at a certain point as a property that matter attains. Otherwise it would have to posit consciousness independent of biological evolution. So it posits that consciousness appears or develops when brain complexity reaches a certain level, as potential to a living organism. Therefore this theory can be seen ultimately to reduce consciousness to matter, because it reduces it to life, which is in turn reduced to matter.

To understand the relation of consciousness and life to matter we need to wait for our discussion of the relation of soul to world and Being. (See chapters 20 and 23.)[9] But for now we can begin to discuss this question by taking into consideration the new paradigms of systems theory. Some aspects of systems theory arose out of Ilya Prigogine's discovery that some chemical compounds can have self-organizing properties. His discovery won him the Nobel Prize and ushered in the new field of self-organizing systems, which had previously been thought to apply only to biological life. The main idea is that open systems in general, such as the human body, stars, planets, the biosphere, and storms, are composed of elements and structures that exchange information and matter with their environments. (See appendix E.) This is different from the situation of closed systems, for such systems always move toward dissolution, as stated in the second law of thermodynamics, that of entropy: left to themselves, the elements of a closed system move toward chaos. The new discovery was that some systems are self-organizing in the context of their exchange with the environment, and thus can keep the integrity of the system intact, at least for a period of time. These systems can also develop their organization, going from one level of organization to a higher or more complex one. In other words, they can regenerate themselves and develop to more complex self-organizing systems.

This understanding has developed to a whole field of scientific research that studies open self-organizing systems on many levels of existence. This theory is applied to the development of the whole universe since the big bang, to the development of galaxies, stars, planets, atmospheres, weather systems, chemical compounds and processes, life forms, cities, the human body, the mind, and so on.[10]

In other words, it was not an unusual accident that life emerged at some point in the evolution of the universe. Even granting that it is rare, biological life shares some basic characteristics with many other physical phenomena. The self-organizing properties of open systems, which science believed characterized only life, turn out to be common and in fact inherent to the whole of our universe. Our universe developed into its present state largely through this self-organizing property. From the perspective of systems theory, organic life emerged when self-organization reached a particular level in cosmic evolution.

Our question is, where does this self-organizing property of the universe come from? The soul is the self-organizing open system par excellence. Is it possible that when we understand the wave side of the universe, the complement to the particle side, we might find it to be responsible for the self-organizing properties of open systems in the universe?[11] This has already been posited by many thinkers.[12]

The understanding we come to is that neither life nor consciousness is an epiphenomenon of matter. Using the complementarity principle of quantum theory as a metaphor, we find that the wave complement to our physical universe is a field of consciousness that, similar to the soul, possesses self-organizing properties.[13] Consciousness, in its purity and ontological presence, is the basic ground, and self-organization is one of its properties or dimensions. Consciousness emerges later in evolution because it is more basic and fundamental, meaning less differentiated, and life emerges earlier because it is a property of this consciousness, an inherent part of its potential. It seems that if we take the evolution of the universe as the action of spirit or consciousness, as Hegel and others did, then we can recognize that the more primordial and less structured dimensions of spirit emerge later in cosmic evolution.

This means, first of all, that life is inherent in the universe; it is one of its potentials. It arises when the right circumstances evoke it, as part of the ongoing cosmic unfoldment. The second and more important point is that systems theory views the whole cosmic process of evolution upside down. It continues to participate in the modern scientific philosophic position that matter is primary, a position that results from and embodies the triadic dissociation we are trying to challenge and heal. This perspective sees life as a certain level of self-organization. Looking at the question from the perspective of the complementarity of matter and consciousness, it becomes possible to see self-organization as the particle view of life, where the wave view is that life is self-organization on the consciousness side. More accurately, the appearance of self-organizing systems in matter is the same thing as the appearance of a certain level of life, but viewed from the perspective of an atomistic universe. We observe then disparate elements that form a group or system with self-organizing characteristics, instead of beholding a medium that can self-organize itself. This is similar to experiencing the inner forms and events of the soul as having self-organization instead of seeing the actual field that is alive.

In our view, life is inherent to the universe, rather than merely being a potential that arises when self-organization reaches a high level of complexity. In our view the universe is alive, and has always been alive.[14] More precisely, when we investigate the universe from the perspective of its wave side, from its ground of consciousness, we find that life is a property inherent to the universe, characterizing some of its dimensions and forms. When we see the cosmos evolving through the development of self-organizing open physical systems, we are actually witnessing the life inherent to the universe, but from the particle side. The universe is not only alive; it is growing. This growth is what we see as cosmic evolution, which is explored by astronomy, astrophysics, physics, chemistry, biological evolution science, biological science, and now systems theory. However, these disciplines see the evolution of the universe in its particle aspect. As this life grows, an important stage of its maturation is the emergence of biological life. In other words, the emergence of biological life is the stage at which the universal life manifests explicitly and specifically. This lays the ground for the universe to experience its life consciously, which in turn prepares universal life to be conscious of itself, at the stage where introspecting consciousness finally emerges.

This understanding is self-consistent and accounts for the various stages of evolution. It explains the emergence of both life and consciousness in a unitary scheme, and does not leave as many loose ends as emergence theory does. The strength of this understanding does not actually lie in its self-consistency and power of explanation. It lies more fundamentally in the fact that this understanding is available for observation, through introspection and inner experience of the soul. We can experience that the universe is alive and growing, a repeatable experience given the correct control procedures.

Even though this understanding of the arising of life and consciousness in the cosmos might be correct from a certain viewpoint, our perspective here is that life is not a property of the body, but of the soul. Two specific observations are sufficient to suggest this possibility. If life is a characteristic of the body then it should be more apparently present the healthier the body, and should peak at the body's physical prime. We would observe more aliveness when our bodies are at their physical prime; namely, less at the beginning of life when the body is still developing, and even less at the end of life when the body is deteriorating. It is clear to observation that babies and young children are generally more robust and exude more pure life energy than most people at their physical prime. Life seems to be not complete at the beginning of our human life, but it is definitely present in a robust and full manner. Babies and young children are bundles of vitality and life—life within them seems to be uncontrollable and overflowing—while mature adults frequently are not. As has been explored by many existential philosophers and discussed by many psychologists, adults frequently experience their life force as being blocked, constricted, and twisted, not as vigorous as they know it can be. The life force does not seem to be experientially as available to adults in their prime as it is to young children. In fact many adults have to engage in sports or exercise regimes to feel the vitality and vigor of life. Adults engage in many more activities than young children, and they are more capable of self-organization, but this is different from the raw life force, the excitatory state that we feel more alive when experiencing.

At the other end of the spectrum we should expect older people to feel even less life force, less vigor and aliveness. This is generally true, but it is also true that we encounter some older individuals who seem to exude more life force, to embody more vitality and vigor than most adults in the prime of their life. We cannot explain this by postulating these older individuals are exceptions or that they must be lucky to be generally more physically healthy than the average adult. Frequently, such intensely alive older people are not physically sound; they might actually be sick and dying. But their life force shines bright with vitality and vigor. Even if they are unable to do much physically, their life force radiates through their emotional aliveness, their robust and active minds, and the quality of their energy and intelligence. The performer George Burns' vitality showed up not only in his continued ability to dance into his late nineties. His aliveness was also apparent in the clarity of his mind, the aliveness of his spirit, and the quickness of his humor. Another example was the teacher Krishnamurti. Anyone who had the good fortune to hear him talk toward the end of his life, when he was in his nineties and suffering from prostate cancer, could see the amazing and lively intelligence, the vital energy and clarity of mind, the dynamic robust presence. What is clear is that physical deterioration and infirmity eclipses the manifestations of life in most individuals, but not always. The fact that some individuals have more aliveness than others, even when they are older and their bodies more deteriorated, cannot be accounted for by the theory that life is a property of the physical organism. These are examples of the appearance of robust life when the physical organism is in decline.

These observations about old people and the obvious unusual aliveness of young children can more easily be accounted for when we recognize that life is a property of the soul. When we are in touch with ourselves, not conflicted with ourselves, not repressed or divided within, then we are more in touch with our soul, and hence with her inherent property of life. Young children are generally less conflicted and divided within themselves than adults; they generally have much less repression, and their ego structures are less rigidly in place, than those of adults. As we will see in chapters 12 and 14, where we discuss how repression and ego structures affect the life of the soul, we are generally less directly in touch with the conscious field of the soul in adulthood. We are less experientially open, more defensive, and more bound up with ego defense mechanisms in our adult years. Our losing touch with the sense of the soul explains why our sense of aliveness diminishes in some ways as we grow up; aliveness is a property of the field of sensitivity of the soul. And it seems that the few old individuals who retain an unusual aliveness must be more in touch with the fullness of their soul than most of us.[15] Their physical deterioration does not limit their contact with their soul, the wellspring of their life.

A second observation on this subject relates to the difference between a live person and a dead person. Many individuals report that when they are in the presence of someone who has just died—when they are with the corpse of the individual—they are surprised by their experience of the corpse. The body does not merely seem dead. There is a distinct sense that the body is missing something it had before. It is not that it is not moving, not that it is not breathing. It is clear that the corpse is missing something more fundamental. The body feels to them empty, only an empty shell. There is often a sense of something having departed that before had not been explicitly recognized. Death turns out to be not only the cessation of functioning, but also the absence of something that now seems very substantial.

This perception is heightened when there are other individuals present. The contrast between the presence of the dead person and that of the other living individuals becomes distinct and palpable. The living individuals clearly have something that is missing in the corpse. And it is not exactly what was expected. It is as if when the individual dies he or she is emptied in some fundamental and obvious way. A presence of some sort is gone. What is missing is not only energy, not only mind, not only movement. It is something that has all of these qualities, but much more. Here it becomes clear what life is. It is not merely the body functioning, breathing and metabolism and so on. Life is a manifestation of a presence, a fullness that is clearly missing from a corpse. Living people still retain this fullness, and one might be able to distinguish it clearly from the energetic condition of a living body. Exploring the contrast between a corpse and living people can be an occasion to recognize what people actually are, to discern that they are souls, and to see clearly the characteristics of these souls. They seem to exude something, to have some kind of fullness and luminosity that seems to radiate from their pores. The corpse is missing this quality, this presence.

The moment we recognize the living soul it becomes possible for us to see others as souls, and not just bodies. We may begin to see and appreciate the energy, the vitality, the color, the glow, and the intelligence of life in everyone. We can come to appreciate these qualities as manifestations of the presence of the soul, rather than viewing them as properties of the body. Recognizing in this way what a human being is naturally brings us to a deeper respect for people, and an appreciation of humanness.

When we are in the presence of the recently dead it is possible to see that when the body dies it loses not only aliveness but also something much bigger, something that has life. It loses the soul that gave it life, but that also gave the person many other characteristics, some in common with other persons, and some unique to this particular person. We might need to be attuned to recognize this loss, and we possibly need to be sensitive and receptive to see it clearly. However, this sense of the loss of the soul in a corpse is a common perception, and the sense that the corpse has been vacated is also common and unmistakably clear.

Death seems to come when the soul vacates the body. The loss of life is identical to the loss of the soul. It is clear then that life is a property that the soul gives to the body. As the soul leaves the body, she takes away life with her, for life is one of her basic properties. If we have subtle perception, we might be able to perceive that some kind of consciousness or presence has left the body. We might be able to sense or perceive this presence, depending on how sensitive we have been to our experience of soul. Individuals who have learned to experience their souls directly will generally be able to perceive the soul when she leaves the body. She is the same soul, whether occupying the body or not. This discussion might bring up questions about life after death, reincarnation, and so on, but these are not our concern here. Various wisdom traditions have detailed teachings about what happens after death. Here we are concerned with the recognition that life is a basic property of the soul, and that the presence of the soul in the body is what animates it and imbues it with life. It becomes very clear for us, in beholding a corpse and especially if we can perceive the departing soul, that death is the departing of the soul, and hence, life is not a property of the body. Life is not a property that a self-organizing system develops as it attains a certain degree of complexity and self-organization.

Life is immanent in the universe; it appears as its self-organizing property, and as it reaches a certain maturity of self-organization it manifests explicitly and fully as biological life.

Pure Life

We have discussed life by exploring things around it, by addressing evolution, self-organization, manifestations of aliveness, dying, and so on, in order to demonstrate that life is a property of soul. What is the direct experience of this property? If it is a property of the soul we can experience it as a type of consciousness, as a presence with particular characteristics. This is actually the case; for just as forms of experience turn out to be manifestations of basic knowledge, which is in turn an expression of pure knowledge, the content and characteristics of life are also forms and manifestations of the life of the soul, as a flowing current, which is in turn an expression of pure life. We can experience our soul as the presence of life, as a conscious field characterized by life. The manifestations of aliveness we have discussed are the experiential qualities of this mode of presence.

The soul is not only conscious, it is also alive; it is pulsing with life and vigor. When we experience the quality of aliveness we feel a pulsation, a teeming vitality, robustness, and vigor. The robust feeling of life characterizes the conscious presence of the soul, and appears now as a distinct quality or property. We discover that life, or aliveness, is a particular dimension of the soul, a basic property of its presence. It is actually a Platonic form, independent from bodies and from matter in general. It is always inherent and present in the soul, but we can experience it explicitly. In other words, just as we can experience our soul as pure knowledge, we can also experience it as pure life. We are then not only alive; we are life. We are fundamental life, present as life, life that can imbue the body with its vigor and dynamism and empower it to function.

Under normal circumstances it is difficult to experience life directly, because we are always experiencing it in association with the body, inseparable from the biological functioning of the physical organism. We might come close to the experience of this Platonic form when we are feeling especially alive, vigorous, robust, and dynamic. This can happen during intense exercise, sexual orgasm, or when we are confronted with a life-threatening situation or graced with wonderful news or a great occasion. We then can experience ourselves as more alive, excited about life, full of passion and vigor, strong and ready to take on the world. However, these experiences pale when contrasted with the direct and full experience of the soul in her property of life. In the direct experience of the quality of life, the aliveness and vigor are pure, distilled, and complete, without being related to a particular situation or even to the body.

Life feels like the dynamism of animals, just as growth feels like the dynamism of plants. (See appendix C for the Sufi connection of the property of life to the animal soul, and appendix A for Aristotle's view.) But the sense of aliveness feels much bigger than the body, not defined by it, and more fundamental than the physical mode of existence. Directly in touch with our aliveness, we feel like a river of life, a dynamic and pulsing consciousness. We experience ourselves as a fountain bubbling with aliveness, energy, fullness, excitation, passion, vigor. We sense ourselves as the presence of life, as life, as life outside of time. Our soul is life eternal, not in the sense of everlasting linear time, but outside of time, prior to time, independent of time.

With this aliveness there is vitality, there is energy, there is movement, there is warmth and heat, expansion and contraction. There is a sense of zest, of power, a sense of health, a well-being that pulses and undulates. There is a bubbling quality, as if our cells are exploding with it. We are the life force; we are the life.

What we see here is that life is a particular dimension of the conscious presence that is the soul, a basic and vital element of her potential. The soul qualities we have explored—changeability, flow, unfoldment, creativity, transformation, dynamism, and self-organization—all these are actually expressions of life. And when we directly experience life itself it is like experiencing all of these synthesized together as one feeling, one taste.

Recognizing the living quality of soul allows us to understand many significant aspects of the spiritual path. For instance, we see more precisely the similarities and differences between soul and essence. Essence is a conscious presence, like the soul. However, essence is only a conscious presence, while soul is not only a conscious presence but also a living presence. This is the main distinction between essence and soul. In some sense, we can say essence is more basic than soul, more fundamental, more primordial, because it is simpler; it is prior to life. It is beyond life and beyond death. From the perspective of essence, life and death are concepts. However, we can also say that soul is more than essence—she contains essence as her primordial ground, but she possesses other dimensions. Soul has infinite potential, which expresses itself as life. One of the main expressions of this life is biological life. The life of soul is also beyond death, because it is beyond biological life.[16]

In reality, soul and essence are two aspects of the same thing, just as the body and protoplasm are two aspects of the same thing. For us, for our experience, which is all we have, they are nondual, they are our nonduality. Because they are nondual it is not possible to differentiate them completely. More accurately, we can differentiate them but we cannot dissociate them, we cannot make them two separate and independent realities. How we see their relationship is bound to be somewhat arbitrary, depending on how we differentiate them in thought or experience. We can see essence as a potential of the soul, as its most primordial potential; but we can also see the soul as one of the aspects of essence, as the aspect of life. We can see essence as the ground of the soul, but we can also see the soul as the wholeness whose very fabric is essence. Both possibilities arise in direct experience and in advanced stages of the inner journey the difference between the two gradually dissolves. At this point we experience an essential soul, or a dynamic essence, indicating a complete and total coemergence of essence and soul, reflecting the primordial nonduality of Reality. (See chapter 23 for further discussion on this point.)

The distinction between essence and soul is not easy to make, because it is a subtle differentiation. The main difficulty arises from confusing consciousness with life. When one experiences essence as a conscious presence it is not usually easy to recognize that this is different from aliveness, for one has not differentiated life from consciousness. In our normal experience, consciousness and aliveness are inseparable. We rarely, if ever, experience one without the other. And when we experience pure consciousness we cannot differentiate it from life, because we tend to believe that to be conscious is to be alive. Even researchers interested in death experiences, or out-of-body experiences, tend not to explore the question of whether in these conditions the soul experiences herself as alive or only as conscious. These researchers generally believe that life ends with death, and that even though some kind of awareness survives the death, there is no curiosity about whether this awareness will be experiencing itself as only conscious, or conscious and alive the way it is in the body. The implicit assumption seems to be that the awareness will continue to be imbued with the sense of aliveness, as it is in physical life, even though the belief is that life ends with death. The main reason behind this situation is that even though everyone knows the soul, albeit not explicitly, the experience of essence is rare. When we experience essence we know what pure consciousness is, that it is beyond the sense of aliveness, more fundamental than life.

Understanding the property of life in the soul deepens and expands our appreciation of life for its own sake. We begin to recognize the intrinsic value of life, and especially the value of human life, for it is the life of the human soul, the soul with infinite potential. Appreciating and loving life is inseparable from loving and valuing the soul. We want our life to be full because it is the fullness of our soul that is our window onto the universe, our organ of experience. We not only want to be free and detached; we want to be free and detached and at the same time for our life to be full, rich, and fulfilled. And because we understand that consciousness is more fundamental than life, we realize that to be free we need to center ourselves in pure consciousness. We love pure consciousness because it is our very identity, truth, and substance, but we also love our living soul because she is what completes it. She is the daughter of primordial pure consciousness, but also its infinite potential.

PART THREE

Essence and Soul Development

9 Soul and Essence

IN CHAPTER 5 WE DISCUSSED the potential of the soul, seeing essence as the deepest and most precious element of this potential. But what do we mean by *essence*? It will be useful to clarify this concept, because spiritual and religious literature is not uniform in its usage of the terms *soul* and *essence*. Some teachings equate the two, some use only one of the terms, and some use both concepts but label them differently. Other teachings do not use either concept, or use more than these two.

We have described the medium or field of the soul as the presence of pure consciousness. In labeling the field "presence" we point to the significant fact that this field constitutes the ontological dimension of the soul. In other words, the existence of the soul turns out not to be only an abstract concept of being, but a direct experiential truth, a palpable presence. (See *Essence*, chapters 1 and 2.) This is the reason we frequently refer to this truth as Being, for it is the beingness of the soul. This truth is actually the basic spiritual insight of the inner journey and, in one form or another, common to all major schools of inner work.

This field of presence, which is a pure medium of consciousness, is the simplest and ultimate ground of the soul. This ground is not postulated but is discoverable in the process of any effective investigation; that is, if we investigate our experience of the soul and try to discover her final nature, her ultimate ground, if we become aware of what remains after all particular content and specific forms of experience are taken out or transcended, then we find this presence. This process is similar to the physicists' preoccupation with the most elementary particles of matter; they are trying to find the ultimate building blocks of our physical universe. The presence of pure consciousness turns out to be the ultimate building block of our psychic life, the ultimate ground of our soul. It is not particles or strings, but a field, a homogeneous medium, pure consciousness that turns out to be the actual ontological dimension of the soul.

In other words, if we investigate what the final essence of the soul is, the essence beyond particular manifestations, we find it to be this presence of pure consciousness. Therefore, we refer to this presence of pure consciousness as essence, meaning the essence of the soul. So essence is the ultimate ground of the soul, her final nature, her absolute purity. We also refer to it as the true nature of the soul, meaning that if we investigate our soul and are able to penetrate all of our beliefs and prejudices about her, and are able to behold her with total objectivity, without the slightest subjective posture or position, without any obscurations or veils, we find her as this essence, which is presence. Essence and true nature are the same thing, but viewed from different perspectives: when we view the ultimate and simplest ground of the soul from the perspective of its most basic constituency we refer to it as essence, just as the essence of water is H_2O molecules; and when we view it from the perspective of its final and most naked truth we refer to it as true nature.

There exist some minor disagreements among the various wisdom traditions about this essence or true nature. Some think of it as presence, some as awareness, some as light, some as love, and some as emptiness. But these views actually reflect fine distinctions and subtle discriminations in the experience and understanding of ultimate truth. We will explore these fine distinctions in some detail in chapters 17–21; meanwhile we can say that that essence is presence that possesses several basic dimensions, dimensions that give our experience of it various degrees of subtlety and discrimination. (See *The Point of Existence*, appendix B.)

In our discussion in chapters 4, 5, and 7 we focused primarily on three dimensions of this presence: pure nonconceptual or mirror-like awareness; basic knowledge inseparable from presence; and the creative dynamism of this presence. As we will see in chapters 17–21, we also understand this presence to possess the dimensions of pure love and pure emptiness. The subtle consideration of true nature as possessing several basic and fundamental dimensions is relevant mainly to the exploration of the nature of God/Being and cosmos/world. It is relevant to the exploration of the soul only at the deepest and most developed stages of her evolution.

Another distinction we make in our terminology is that between essence and Being. We refer to true nature as Being when we consider the ultimate ground of the universe or all manifestation, and as essence when we consider the ultimate ground of the individual soul.

However, our usage here is intentionally ambiguous, for the soul is not separate from all manifestation, as we will see in chapter 16, so we employ the terms mostly for emphasis. So finally, essence is the true nature of the soul, her ultimate constituency, which turns out to be the presence of pure consciousness.

Essential Aspects

Essence as fundamental ground of the soul is basically pure nondifferentiated presence, colorless and without qualities. Thus it is the manifestation of the true nature of everything in the soul. But essence rarely manifests in our individual experience in its pure and nondifferentiated mode; or more precisely, it is difficult for most individuals to recognize essence in its nondifferentiated state. However, essence manifests in other ways, by differentiating into presence with recognizable qualities.

We have discussed how essence is a presence of pure consciousness that also possesses the capacity to recognize itself as presence. This is the inherent coemergence and coextensiveness of the dimension of nonconceptual mirror-like awareness responsible for bare perception, and the dimension of basic knowledge responsible for cognition and recognition. So essence is presence that is inseparable from awareness of this presence, and is also inseparable from the knowingness of this presence. The presence, the awareness, and the knowingness are the same thing in the experience of pure nondifferentiated essence.

We have seen that this fundamental ground of the soul is aware of differentiation in a mirror-like fashion, but also that this differentiation appears within it as formations within a field. We have also seen that this ground possesses the capacity to cognize these formations, as noetic forms with recognizable characteristics. Some of these formations are simply presence itself with recognizable qualities. In other words, the noetic forms constitute all manifestations within the soul, but there is a special class of these forms, pure forms in the sense they are the differentiated manifestations of implicit qualities inherent in the nondifferentiated ground. These forms are not images, thoughts, emotions, sensations, movements, or any category familiar in our ordinary experience. They are purely spiritual forms, essential noetic forms.

Thus the essential ground, the coemergence of nonconceptual awareness and basic knowledge, possesses implicit qualities that we refer to as its perfections. In its nondifferentiated and fundamental mode it implicitly possesses peace, love, compassion, truth, authentic existence, pleasure, joy, strength, will, clarity, intelligence, impeccability, purity, contentment, fulfillment, satisfaction, spaciousness, and so on. They are not explicitly recognizable, but the presence feels complete and does not lack any of these qualities that the soul always needs.

These implicit perfections can and do manifest in a differentiated and explicit way in the inner experience of the soul. In other words, the soul can experience her essence in one of these differentiated qualities. Alternately stated, essence can manifest itself within as these perfect spiritual qualities, when the fundamental ground and nondifferentiated presence of the soul transforms a region of its field into this particular quality. The form that appears may have a shape but it might not; it may be bounded and limited or boundless and infinite. But it will have recognizable characteristics in all the dimensions of the Riemannian manifold of the soul. In other words, these noetic forms will be presence characterized not only by the three spatial dimensions, but also by color, texture, taste, smell, sound, viscosity, luminosity, density, and affect. They are noetic forms because each possesses a distinguishing cognitive component, which we call a universal concept. These forms are universal concepts, in that they are not personal or cultural ones constructed by individual minds. They are the spontaneous manifestations of true nature itself, and they can be recognized because true nature possesses inherent basic knowingness that it gives to the soul. (See *Diamond Heart, Book 4*, chapter 16.)

We refer to these qualities as essential aspects, or aspects of essence. Each is presence knowing itself as presence, but also and simultaneously recognizing this presence as the particular quality. Each essential aspect is actually the presence of essence, qualified with a particular noetic quality. It is the presence of essence, with the addition of one of its implicit perfections, now made explicit in experience. The noetic quality is not separate from the presence; it is completely indistinguishable from it. The knowingness of presence is now simply inseparable from the recognition of the quality. The knowing here is that of basic knowledge, so it is pervasive throughout the presence, not a recognition apart from it.

The differentiations are not man-made, not constructs of the individual mind, not even products of a cultural or collective mind. No person's mind is able to come up with such perfect differentiations. The direct perception of noetic forms shows us that the abstractions of ordinary mind are relatively gross and vague. The differentiations we perceive directly are the creation of the dynamism of our true nature, manifesting its perfections in explicit forms for the recognition and functioning of the soul. They are universal also in the sense that they manifest the same to all souls. The quality of inner peace is the same for all souls that experience it. Individual variations are minor, having to do with the shape and size of the field, its intensity, depth, brilliance, etc. The labeling of the forms can be different, depending on a person's background and circumstances; but what is labeled is the same noetic form. For instance, one may label the emerald presence as compassion, another might think of it as kindness, another as loving-kindness, another as a healing presence, and still another as sensitive empathic resonance. But all of these are actually universal characteristics of this essential noetic form.

Essential aspects are examples of Plato's ideas, but are not identical to the Platonic ideas. These latter are a larger category, the noetic prototypes of all manifest forms. The essential aspects form a special subset, the noetic prototypes or archetypes of essential or spiritual qualities. Furthermore, the essential aspects form a different category than the spiritual categories delineated by the various spiritual traditions, even though there is one degree or another of overlap with some of them. The recognition of these aspects as forming a particular set of spiritual qualities is, as far as we know, unique to the Diamond

Approach, and constitutes one of its strengths and major contributions to the research into matters of the spirit. At this point we can articulate more clearly the difference between soul and essence. Soul is the field whose true nature is essence. Soul can experience any of the essential aspects as an element of her essential potential. Essence and all of its aspects constitutes the deepest of the soul's potentials. But it does not make sense to think of an essential aspect as having a potential. It is itself, always and primordially. It can only know itself, which is nothing but the soul manifesting itself in the form of the particular aspect.[1]

This difference between soul and essence can help us to understand why we think of soul as always changing and developing, while essence is immutable. As we have noted, each of the aspects of essence is a Platonic form, eternally and primordially itself. Love is always and eternally love, so is peace, so is joy, so is intelligence, and so on. Each cannot be anything else, cannot evolve and cannot devolve. It cannot be contaminated and cannot be improved upon. Each aspect is aware of itself, and only of itself. It is the presence of a particular quality, and only this quality. It is a pure consciousness, a consciousness aware of its presence, but its knowledge is different from that of the soul. The soul can be aware of herself as pure consciousness, and then she is like essence, for she is then essence. The soul, however, can know herself as any of the aspects of essence, for all of these aspects are elements of her potential. On the other hand, an essential aspect is only itself, without the potential to be anything else. Its knowledge is similar to the soul only in the fact that it is capable of knowledge. It is capable of basic knowledge, but knowledge only of its own particular quality. This is clear when we experience essence in one of its aspects. Take for example the quality of personal love, whose affect is that of liking and appreciation, of recognizing what we love as wonderful and precious. This love is a manifestation of pure consciousness. It is a medium of consciousness conscious of itself. Its experience is the experience of a conscious presence, a presence that knows itself by being itself. Its knowingness is not discursive representational knowing; yet this presence is not only aware of itself as presence, but is also aware of itself as love. Love is a differentiation out of pure conscious presence, where presence now possesses a quality that distinguishes it from other essential differentiations.

It is analogous to the differentiation of colored light from white light; it remains light, but manifests as one quality from a spectrum that is implicit and nondifferentiated in white light.

Presence is now not only aware of its beingness and hereness, but also of the quality of love. Our consciousness is now manifesting itself, or a region of its expanse, with a quality that appears in all the dimensions of the soul's manifold. It appears in the inner touch sense as a soft and caressing texture, almost like baby skin or talcum powder. It appears in the inner visual sense as a beautiful and luminous pink, either as a shapeless medium or with a shape like a flowing pink stream, a pink cloud, or cotton candy, or a pink rose. It appears in the inner taste sense as a heavenly kind of sweetness, an uplifting taste that makes us realize why we associate love with sweetness. It appears in the inner olfactory sense as a the scent of rose or jasmine, delicate and so transporting. It appears in the inner auditory sense as the gentle delicate buzzing of bees, tinkling of bells, or a melodious enchanting sound.

All these phenomena might only be forms discerned by our nonconceptual awareness, in which case it is not knowing yet. Knowing involves the presence of the dimension of basic knowledge, coemergent with pure awareness of the form, which intersects all of the above subtle sensory dimensions, and synthesizes them as a unified gestalt with a particular affect. With the quality of personal love, this affect is that of liking, appreciation, and a happy enjoyment of whatever we perceive. This affect implies a recognition, a direct apprehension of a particular meaning. The multidimensional expanse of presence recognizes itself not only as presence but also as love. A kind of concept is present now, not mental, not discursive, and not a result of remembering stored information.[2] We know love by being love. Our soul knows it directly because it is a quality of her basic consciousness, not a thought in the mind. There is no dichotomy of subject and object here. I am not a self who is experiencing love. In the full experience of love I am love. The knower is the known, the presence of love. This presence is pure consciousness that is directly cognizant of the quality that pervasively characterizes it. I am love, and my knowledge of love is the presence of love. The presence is totally inseparable from the phenomenological characteristics of love, and the knowingness that it is love. This knowingness does not need to be associated with a word, but the word "love" may arise, in whatever language we speak. The knowingness is the presence of a wordless concept. It is somewhat problematic to use the term *concept* here, for we normally think of concepts as mental constructs. But here we do not refer to a mental construct; rather, we mean there is a recognition of a quality that is primordial and natural. This is basic knowledge, but basic knowledge of only one particular form, as an essential Platonic form.[3] This is a universal concept, or noetic form.

Essence is also incapable of self-reflective awareness or knowledge. It knows itself only in the mode of basic knowledge, specifically in the mode of identity. It can only know itself by being itself. However, this is also the freedom of essence. Because it is incapable of self-reflection it cannot be dual. It is always free from intermediacy, and hence from contamination by alienated constructs. It is the promise of freedom for the soul, because when the soul realizes essence as her ground she attains a center incapable of being contaminated. The conscious ground of the soul is then eternally immaculate and free.

The soul, on the other hand, is capable of basic knowledge in all possible permutations. She can experience any form within basic knowledge, including any and all of the aspects of essence. She is capable of reflection and self-reflection. Her knowledge is always changing and developing. She can change, and as we have seen it is inherent in her nature that she is in continual change.

Essence is the primary and most precious potential of the soul. The conscious realization of essence brings her true ultimate self-knowledge, authenticity, fulfillment, completeness, enlightenment, and liberation. But essence provides the soul with other advantages, some mundane and practical. Its dimension of pure awareness provides her with the capacity for awareness and perception, in whatever state she is in, spiritual or mundane, clear or dull. Its dimension of basic knowledge gives her the capacity for cognition, recognition, and knowing in all its dimensions. It is the prototype of knowing. The dimension of creative dynamism gives the soul the capacity for action, creativity, discovery, adventure, development, evolution, maturation, unfoldment, and so on.

And the aspects of essence provide the soul with the true inner richness of which she is capable. These aspects give the soul her experience of, and capacity for, all that is precious and desirable for human beings and their life: love, sweetness, warmth, friendliness, kindness, empathy, clarity, discernment, discrimination, intelligence, synthesis, will, steadfastness, commitment, contact, personalness, humanness, gentleness, subtlety, refinement, openness, curiosity, happiness, enjoyment, exquisiteness, balance, courage, justice, detachment, objectivity, precision, spaciousness, expansion, depth, capacity, initiative, passion, fulfillment, satisfaction, contentment, nourishment, generosity, even individuation, identity, and existence.

These essential qualities can be experienced directly, or through their effect on the soul. In other words, some of the descriptive terms refer to qualities of presence and others to the impact on the soul of this presence. The effect in the soul can be in her inner experience, her attitudes, or her actions and expressions. For example, the presence of the emerald aspect is the quality of loving-kindness or compassionate consciousness. It affects the soul by making her sensitive, empathic, and attuned. The presence of the ruby aspect is the presence of strength, and it impacts the soul by making her courageous, bold, energetic, and capable of initiative. The ruby or strength aspect also impacts the mind of the soul by sharpening her discriminating intelligence. The presence of the water aspect is the presence of the quality of humanness. It affects the soul by making her gentle, exquisitely ordinary, and vulnerable without fear. Satisfaction is the presence of a particular aspect, so is fulfillment, and so is contentment. Spaciousness is the experience of the presence of the space aspect, which affects the soul by making her open and receptive, not controlled by mental positions.[4]

In other words, essence, with all its aspects, provides the soul with the prototypes of her capacities and functions, as well as the qualities needed for her life with others. These qualities and faculties are needed for everyday life, but are also necessary for the inner journey home. In other words, our true nature provides us with all that we need in our inner and direct experience, both to live a functional and effective life, and to help ourselves and others reach spiritual maturation and completion. For a fuller and more detailed discussion of some of these qualities and their functions, see other books by the author.[5]

10 Animal Soul

IF THE SOUL IS ENDOWED with so much beauty and goodness, how does she come to suffer so much, to remain confused and conflicted most of the time, to become more wretched than any other living beings? How can she descend to the level of brutality, aggression, selfishness and self-seeking, grossness and crassness, and greed that we observe in the long history of humanity? It is rare that human beings exhibit luminosity, generosity, or inner beauty, even though most people love and appreciate such qualities when they see them, and recognize them as potential for all. The normal condition of human beings is a mix of the wonderful spiritual qualities we enumerated above, and all the wretched and miserable characteristics in which humanity seems to specialize.

This situation reflects the total potential of the soul. The soul's potential includes far more than the essential dimension. In addition to the capacities and faculties of action, imagination, expression, communication, conceptualizing, thinking, remembering, integrating, synthesizing, creativity, and so on, the soul possesses a whole other range of potential for experience. Qualitatively, her potential can be divided into two kinds: the essential-spiritual and the animal-primitive. We have been discussing the essential side of her potential, but the wretched qualities so well known to us are mostly due to the animal side, and the interaction between it and the essential. What do we mean by the animal side of the soul's potential?

It is inherent to the human soul that she can be like an angel, with all the purity of essence and its beautiful aspects, but she can also be like an animal, with all the primitiveness and irrational instinctuality characterizing the animal kingdom. We humans can be loving and selfless because this is part of our inherent potential, but we can also be driven by instinctual needs and drives to extremes of destructiveness, possessiveness, and self-centeredness; this is also inherent to our potential.

Because of the civilizing effect of life in human society, we rarely experience our animal potential purely and directly. We do, however, see its manifestations almost all the time. We can be both appalled and repulsed when we behold the extent of the potential of the animal soul. The human soul can be more animal than any other animal, more primitive than any primitive organism. This is because the human soul has this animal nature in its potential at the same time that it is malleable and impressionable to an extent that no animals are. The infinite range of openness and malleability gives us the capacity not only to experience the animal range of experience, but also to experience it with extreme intensity. We can reach heights of irrationality, primitiveness, destructiveness, grossness, and territoriality of which the animal kingdom is actually innocent.

We share with the animal kingdom a focus on the physical world; we are oriented toward and preoccupied with physical and other external phenomena. Partly as a result of this focus, we also share with animals the instinctual drives toward and passions for survival, food, sex, procreation, company, pleasure, power, dominance, possessiveness, territory, security, safety, comfort, entertainment, and so on. We are primarily driven by our survival, sexual, and social instincts. And these instincts operate in us the same way they operate in the animal kingdom, with drivenness, compulsion, and irrational passion for their gratification. When we experience the animal potential of the soul, what we call the animal soul, we are then full of desires, cravings, uncontrollable impulses, lust, and passion for what the world offers. We want with passion, crave with hunger, and desire with instinctual abandon. We desire instant gratification, but our appetite for such gratification has no bottom and no end. We want and want and want. We want to eat, copulate, possess, dominate, even nourish and nurse ad nauseam. Even when we believe we are being human because we want contact and sharing, our attitude about such fine qualities is animalistic, and worse. We are greedy for contact, and our need for sharing is bottomless. And whoever stands in our way had better beware.

The animal drives for shelter, survival, pleasure, and sex reveal their true primitive potential when we experience a barrier to their satisfaction. Our animal side can instantly become inhumanly brutal, grossly aggressive, crassly greedy, heartlessly selfish, and totally uncaring for others to the degree of complete disregard of what they feel. We can go about gratifying our desires with complete disregard of others, sometimes not even remembering that there are other living beings. When our survival or our objects of desire are threatened, we can lose all heart and rationality, and become so primitive, cruel, and insensitive that it would be difficult to find such behavior in the animal kingdom.

In other words, the animal soul does not reflect only the fact that we are partly animal because of our physical organism and its evolutionary history. The animal soul constitutes the potential of our soul that is the prototype of animality, in all of its primitiveness and irrationality. Because of this our appetites and desires can easily transform into greed and craving, and our aggression and power can instantly turn into rage, hatred, vengeance, and heartless destructiveness. Because of this it might be better to refer to this potential of our soul as the desire soul, rather than the animal soul, but most traditions have referred to it as the animal soul.[1]

Recognizing the nature of our animal potential seems to point to an interesting insight: our animality is not exclusively due to our physical organism.[2] The extremity to which the human soul can descend in its animal nature, an extremity unknown in the animal kingdom, points to the insight that animality, with all that goes with it, is an inherent potential in our soul, independent from our physical embodiment. The presence of the soul in the body, and more generally in the physical universe, simply evokes this potential forcefully and fully. The body on its own is a shell; without the soul it has no life and no desires. Just as the soul imbues it with life it also provides it with desires.

More specifically, physical embodiment activates in the soul the parts of her potential necessary for her to live in the physical world. These are the instinctual drives for survival, security, sex, and company. These are necessary for the soul to live in the world, for she needs her body to survive and flourish. However, things develop in such a way that these drives become greed, selfishness, and destructiveness. This development happens because these qualities are part of the potential of the soul. It is also partly due to other potentials of the soul, of which the most important is the essential. We will discuss this shortly, but here we want to emphasize that the desire nature is inherent to the soul herself, and not just due to the body. The source of desires is the soul, and the body is the stimulus that activates them.

The animal potential of the soul does not explain the extremes of wretchedness, narcissism, greed, possessiveness, hostility, cruelty, and heartlessness that characterize much of our human history and heritage. To understand this we need to turn to our spiritual potential and its relation to the animal one. More accurately, we need to consider the totality of the open-ended potential of the human soul. We have already mentioned the fact of the infinite potentiality and malleability of the soul that makes it possible for her to experience the animal potential in more extreme ways than animals normally do. The more important reason is that essence not only is the ground and true nature of human potential but is also the ground and nature of all manifestation, including the consciousness of animals. But human beings also have the potential to know this essential ground consciously, which potential is connected with the openness and impressionability of the soul. However, the openness and impressionability also mean that the soul becomes structured in such a way that contact with her essential nature can be lost: her experience is tied up with the content of the structure at the expense of awareness of the ground.

Animals do not have this extremely malleable and impressionable potential, so they cannot lose their nature in the way we can. Their impressionability is much more limited, so their consciousness cannot be easily structured in ways that are so alien to them. The human soul, however, can end up with only part of her potential in her conscious experience of herself, by developing a structure that excludes the rest. As we will see in chapter 12, ego development happens mostly by structuring the soul in such a way that leaves her animal potential partially accessible, and her essential potential missing. In fact, her animal soul is the dominant element that becomes structured into the ego-self, at the expense of the essential potential. The result is a humanized animal soul who is constantly suffering the deprivations of her essential nature. The conditioned human soul is, then, to put it bluntly, a twisted and distorted soul, and not just an animal soul. This distortion is what accounts for most human excesses, a distortion that twists power into hatred, strength into destructiveness, love into possessiveness, desire into greed, and so on.

This is why human beings can become embodiments of evil and destructiveness, even as they have the potential to be saintly, pure, and totally spiritual and selfless. To borrow the traditional terminology, the human soul has the potential of being either an angel or a devil. Most of us are somewhere between these extremes, with occasional excursions to one or the other. The struggle to balance the angelic side of our souls with the animal side lies at the heart of human nature. Much of our literature and art depicts this struggle as the quintessential human drama, the dilemma without which we are not human.

This struggle goes on because human society as a whole has not found an effective way to harmonize these two dimensions of the soul. Actually, the presence of both the angelic and animal potentials is what gives human beings the possibility of developing heart. What we mean here by heart is the possibility of the transparency of the soul to her essential potential.[3] We have heart when we have integrated our essential qualities to an extent where they affect our attitudes and actions. We are then able to be kind and loving, able to appreciate beauty and generosity, and are capable of creativity and selfless action. These reflections of our true nature are what we think of when we perceive someone as human.

The wisdom traditions have recognized that a human being is mature and complete—that is, fully human—when the soul has integrated her essential nature fully and harmonized it with her animal potential.[4] In other words, the struggle between the angelic and animal is characteristic of half-grown human beings, of incomplete human beings. This happens to be the station of the vast majority of humanity, but the complete human being, the being who is fully human, is one who has fully realized and integrated the two sides of the soul's potential. The fully human being retains animal instincts, for instance, but these instincts are integrated into a perspective of selflessness and compassion. Even though the wisdom traditions have understood this and developed ways and methods for accomplishing it, the paths are so steep and difficult that many involved in these traditions settle for an unbalanced development that usually involves suppressing and splitting off the animal side. The rest of humanity continues the struggle, balanced on the side of the animal, which is the path of least resistance.

Phylogenetic History

When we experience our animal potential fully, we do not necessarily experience ourselves as a person who is feeling intense lust and desire. When we experience the sense of the animal soul itself, it appears as a primitive mass. Experiencing the animal soul in itself, one feels oneself to be either a shapeless instinctual organism, with no human form or animal one, or sometimes as a primitive organism with a minimum of structure. The animal soul is a blob of a creature, full of lust and desire, hunger and aggression. The amorphousness of the animal soul has remained so because normal ego development tends not to deal adequately with this dimension of our soul. This is a reflection of the inability of our civilization to harmoniously integrate the animal soul.[5] It is usually repressed or split off from our conscious experience of ourselves, except for minor surges that we have learned to manage. Therefore, when we finally confront this powerful aspect of the soul we find a dimension of our self that is very energetic but has a minimum of structure. As we will see in chapters 12–14, our normal inner experience of ourselves in the shape of the body is actually the result of the development of ego structures that structure the soul through imprinting her with a self-image whose primary component is an image of our body. Hence, when we fully experience the animal dimension of our soul we are going beyond our normal structure, or more accurately, revealing a part of ourselves that has never been structured.

We can experience the animal soul in this most basic structureless form or with impressions of the forms of some primitive organisms and animals. For instance, when the animal soul is full of irrationally directed aggression, it is typical to experience it in the form of spiders, typically tarantulas, or snakes.

This brings up the question of the exact range of our animal potential. What does it mean that the soul can experience herself as a snake? This capacity of the soul is mysterious and magical, even incredible. It appears that our soul has the potential to morph herself into any of the forms in our phylogenetic history. Our observations, and those of our associates and students, seem to further indicate that the soul has the potential to experience herself in the form of all life-forms on Earth. Students report experiencing themselves as tigers, lions, hyenas, zebras, eagles, falcons, peacocks, sharks, whales, spiders, bees, lizards, and so on, all of course within modes of experience that involve certain specific qualities, but with the sense of these specific animal structures. The soul can also experience herself in more primitive forms, such as jellyfish, amoeba, even as a single cell. The range of the possibility of how the animal soul can be experienced seems to include all biological organisms.[6]

This phenomenon is mysterious because it is difficult to explain. We could explain it by saying that the soul has formed herself in all these images over the history of her life on Earth.[7] However, we are trying to understand our soul and the universe without resorting to reduction, and this explanation makes physical reality the ultimate blueprint of all experiences of the soul. We see the possibility that the soul inherently has the potential of all of these forms, regardless of her previous experiences, similar to how she has the potential for all of the forms and aspects of essence, regardless of her previous experience. We see the nonreductionistic possibility that the soul has these as her inherent potential partly because she is inseparable from the field of consciousness that is the ground of all of manifestation, and that this ground has the potential of all forms in manifestation. At this point this is only a suggestion, and we do not need to advance it as a theory.

During the spiritual journey one may experience some of these forms of the animal soul, depending on the degree of structure one is dealing with. When we are dealing and working with more structured parts of our soul we tend to experience animal forms high on the phylogenetic ladder. This happens, for instance, when we are investigating feelings and states of irrational and extreme aggression and destructiveness. By seeing through the distortions that have twisted our soul, the dissociation and splitting of our aggression, power, and strength, and coming to a place of acceptance, resolution, and understanding of these elements of our potential, the forms we experience may move from that of a heartless and primitive animal form that embodies hatred and vengeance, like a hissing black snake, into the more evolved, graceful, and beautiful form of a black panther, at peace with its vitality and power. We experience then our essential power and vitality, but in the animal form of a panther that is in harmony with its nature but also in a contented and peaceful state.

When we are dealing with the question of impressionability and its vulnerability, for instance, and are able to allow ourselves to surrender the structuring forms that have imprinted us, the soul will manifest with much more primitive forms, with very little structure. The soul may begin to experience herself with some structure that gives her some mobility and movement, like a jellyfish, wiggling and writhing, quite alive and vital, but without much range or structure. Or the soul may experience herself with even less structure and appear with the least structure for a living and mobile organism, as an amoeba that can have a modicum of locomotion, and the capacity to extend or retract pseudopodia. The soul may appear in these primitive forms of life sometimes when she is dealing with questions of inadequacy related to ego structure; this kind of inadequacy is due to lacking enough structure for adequate functioning or to beliefs that without these forms she will not be able to function.

Sometimes, however, the soul can lose all structure, and appear as an undifferentiated blob of protoplasm. It is as if the amoeba sheds its nucleus and membrane and becomes just a puddle of protoplasm. At such times, the individual feels no sense of psychological structure, no definition, no form or shape, no identity, and no firmness. When there is no understanding that this is simply the soul with no structure, this state can generate fear or panic, for it may indicate to the individual not only absence of identity, but also no functionality. When there is understanding, as in the orderly investigation of ego structure that leads to a relaxation of holding on to it, there might arise this condition of structurelessness, soul without fear but with relaxation and surrender.

The soul does not always experience these states this graphically in the form of animal or primitive organisms, but it is part of her potential to have these forms of experience, a fact utilized by some of the spiritual teachings in the formulation of their teachings and methods. The point we are making is that the soul has the potential to experience herself in various degrees of structure, from the most rigid and formed, to the most formless and shapeless. This is also important for the question of the evolution and development of the soul, in the sense that the soul evolves similarly to physical evolution, from the most primitive life form to the fully human level.[8] Furthermore, that evolution corresponds to higher and more complex organization of structure.

One significant observation here is the recognition that when the soul is completely structureless, before any development or maturity, the state feels fluid, and is similar to plasma or, more accurately, protoplasm. The actual texture and viscosity of the soul substance feels similar to egg white before it is cooked. We have seen that as the soul manifests more and more primitive forms of her potential she becomes more protoplasmic, like a jellyfish or an amoeba. When these structures finally dissolve what is left is a simple medium that feels like protoplasm.[9] This is the most primitive the soul can be and still feel like a living presence. To experience herself in the mineral or metallic state does not feel primitive and there is no structure. The sense of life is gone; only consciousness remains.

This is an interesting fact. It shows an isomorphism between the soul and the physical body. Just as the body is basically protoplasm, the soul is basically a protoplasmic presence. Presence here is still a field of consciousness, but lacks clarity and discrimination. It is like a somewhat dull consciousness, just as protoplasm is dull in luminosity in comparison to light.

It turns out protoplasm is the quality of the soul's presence that indicates the state of the soul before evolution. It is not exactly primitive; it is just the basic substance of the soul before she begins her journey of maturity. However, this does not mean that there is a time when the soul is in this condition and then must evolve to experience her more evolved forms of experience. The soul always has the infinite potential of all her evolutionary stages, but that her most dominant condition is one of the stages. Therefore, we cannot say that human beings in their infancy have only a protoplasmic soul. Far from it;

their presence is frequently delicate and luminous, but sometimes dull like protoplasm. This seems to depend on the particular infant.

The protoplasmic soul can be transparent to essence in its various aspects. This brings up another interesting observation, which is that when essence arises within this protoplasmic soul, the soul begins to evolve and develop inner cohesion and structure, and move toward integration and individuation. The presence of essence in the soul, with all of its aspects, seems to function similarly to the nucleus of a cell, with its DNA that patterns the differentiation and structuration of the cell. This observation is partly why we understand the evolution of the soul to include individuation, and why we think individuation is engendered in the soul by the impact of essence on her basic protoplasmic substance.

To end this discussion of the animal soul we need to note the important truth that the animal soul is not another soul, not a separate soul. It is one of the dimensions of the soul. We have, or more accurately are, one unified indivisible soul. We have many dimensions of potentialities. At any time, and at any of stage of development, we can experience any of these potentials, even though different forms of experience dominate at different stages.

11 Normal Development of the Soul

THE HUMAN SOUL IS BOTH ANIMAL AND ANGEL, without definite demarcations, at all stages of development in our life. This is obviously the case at the beginning of life, and since in infancy the soul has very little rigid structure, the human infant as a result can experience both essence in its aspects, and the animal desires and forms, without restraint or fixed identification. These forms flow in its experience depending on states of hunger and satiation, tension or relaxation, pleasure or pain, safety or danger. When its physical organism is in need, the animal component dominates and its behavior can become like an animal, lusty and aggressive, selfish and heartless. But its animal behavior tends to become extreme more when it is deprived or frustrated by the environment or the condition of the physical organism itself. The extreme or distorted animal reactions will tend to occur later on, not at infancy. It would be difficult to think of a few-days-old infant as exhibiting selfish or destructive behavior. But as the infant grows and becomes a young child, the kind of cruel behavior attributed sometimes to children begins to appear.

When the infant is not deprived, abused, or frustrated, its animality is normally mixed with its essential qualities, where a harmony can be observed, similar to what happens to animals in the wild. So when the infant or baby needs, for instance, the closeness of its mother's body and warmth, and it is not left unattended long enough to develop frustration, its wanting can manifest so full of love and tenderness that it melts the mother's heart. The same kind of harmonious mix appears in the state of the infant's soul when there is satisfaction, pleasure, comfortable rest, or loving holding.[1]

This seems to be the base state of the infant, the equilibrium set point to which its soul returns when tension and frustration are discharged and instinctual pressure is absent for an interval. However, the animal soul tends to dominate the infant's state. This is because of the infant's physical dependency and helplessness, as well as the almost universal absence of completely adequate caretakers. In other words, it seems that because of the universal presence of frustration the animal potential does not only dominate, but frequently manifests in its extreme forms. Another reason for this dominance is that it is phase appropriate. The soul at these initial stages of its development is completely mixed with the body, and experiences it without a body image yet. This close proximity of the soul field and the physical organism means that when physical impulses and needs arise there is no way yet for the soul to distinguish them from other levels of her feelings. At such times the soul cannot but act as if she is the body; whenever any strong physical impulse or need, or any strong impression in the soul's field, arises the soul is bound to completely identify with it. The soul would appear as all body then, all animal.[2]

However, this is not an accurate conclusion, for it is based on an adult mind observing the external manifestations of the infant. When the infant's needs are satisfied it will begin to act like an angel: peaceful, contented, and tender. Does that mean, then, it is an angel? In truth, the infant is both angel and animal, with the animal dominant in the first instance, and the angel in the second. During the animal identification the angel is frequently present in the sense the soul is still fully herself, and normally full of the qualities of essence, like strength, pleasure, will and so on, but completely coemergent with the animal form. The strong desire embodies the strength of essence, and the insistent need embodies the will of essence. These will vacate the field of the soul only if there is deprivation, frustration, or physical dysfunction, where such disruption will predispose the soul to react in a way that may disconnect her from the fullness of her essence.

The condition in which the soul begins her life is her natural condition, as we have described it in the previous chapters. Uncertain is how clearly and fully the soul experiences her basic dimensions and properties at this time. Because she is still not able to use concepts—as we know from cognitive developmental theory—her awareness is bound to be mirror-like.[3] Her knowing must be primarily that of basic knowledge, because she does not have the conceptual development for representational knowledge; even this is rudimentary at the beginning, requiring a capacity for primitive concepts that does not develop until around two years of age.[4] It is these two dimensions of the soul's basic nature that appear to us as her natural contact with essence in the early stages of her life.

Her malleability and impressionability are at their most extreme; hence she is quite receptive and undefended. Her dynamism is quite free and her forms are flexible, unfolding easily. She is at the same time quite vulnerable to conditioning because of an almost total dependence on her environment.

From this place the soul begins her life, and goes through various stages of development toward maturity. The major portion of this development happens in the first few years of life, resulting in the soul developing her physical, cognitive, emotional, and ego capacities. With a sense of inner identity and a coherent character structure, she becomes an individual human being who can think, reason, respond emotionally, and interact with the world and the people in it with increasing capacity and autonomy. The qualities, structures, and capacities of the soul develop together with various degrees of integration, but can be viewed as going through different lines of development, some going into adolescence and adulthood. There is the cognitive line of development, as well as the physical, the emotional, the relational, the logical, the moral, the ego developmental, and so on. Ego development can be divided into separate lines of narcissism, drive development, and object relations, comprising development of relation to self and others. These various lines have been studied extensively by many researchers in various field of study, with some thinkers developing systems that synthesize some of this wealth of research findings.[5]

Therefore, it will not be our task to discuss these lines of development in any detail. Our concern in this book is to study the soul and her relation to God/Being and cosmos/world, in such a way that reveals her nature and relation to these other two facets of the triad. Therefore we will use only the elements of this knowledge, drawn mostly from research in ego and cognitive development, that will help us open up the experience of the soul and its relation to the divine and the world.

The most relevant question for us concerns how this normal development of the soul is reflected in the experience of her essential nature, and how, as a result, this affects her view, cognition and everyday experience. More specifically, what concerns us is how this development translates into our experience and understanding of reality.

As the soul develops as an individual with character and identity, with the normal emotional and mental capacities, she slowly dissociates from her essential ground. A duality emerges between soul and essence that becomes bedrock reality, a duality that naturally and spontaneously separates the original unity of Reality. Soul, originally coemergent with her true nature, turns into a duality of self and spirit, and Reality becomes self, God/Being/spirit and world, three separate entities. The soul becomes a self, an ego-self, that may or may not believe it has spirit, soul or true nature. But this spirit is now something separate, mysterious, otherworldly, and something to which some of us want to attain. This spirit is now somehow mysteriously related to a spiritual world, where God or Being rules. The cosmos, on the other hand, becomes a physical world, mostly dead and inert with pockets of life and consciousness here and there.

The final outcome of this individual development is identical with the triadic separation that pervades Western thought. The possible implication is that Western thought has gone through a similar process of dissociation from an original unity. This means that the soul's development is parallel to the development of Western thought. It might be more accurate to view Western thought as having recapitulated the normal development of the soul, but we prefer the view that the two developments are both manifestations of the same dynamic in Reality. We explore this question further when we discuss the development of Western thought in chapter 24.

Our task now becomes clear; by learning how soul develops duality in a way that shows us how to reverse it we learn a possible path to the redemption of Western thought. The various wisdom traditions tended to see this development of duality as a going astray, as the fall of man.[6] However, we need not take such a view of normal human development. Since this development happens to all souls it makes more sense to view it as lawful and natural. And since Western thought has developed in a way that on the one hand alienates us from the ground of Reality, but on the other has resulted in various advances for humanity—scientific, technological, cultural, artistic, and so forth—the soul's normal development must also have its positive side, a result that would not happen otherwise.

This positive side is one thing we will need to explore, but the important point is that this development is part of the natural evolutionary pattern of the soul. That there is no other alternative for the soul will become clear when we recognize the implications of her childhood condition.[7] The soul cannot help but dissociate from her essential ground; the only variation is in the degree of this dissociation.

The dissociation occurs partly because the soul has not only essence, but also the animal soul, as an important potential; partly because of physical embodiment and living in a world that cannot perfectly satisfy her needs; partly because the initial condition and further development of her cognitive capacities strongly predispose her toward such dissociation; partly because of her extreme and conditionable impressionability and malleability; and partly because of the way ego development patterns the soul's overall normal development. There are other factors, some of which we will also explore.

In her primal condition, the soul is a wholesome harmonious unity, where there is no separation between soul and body and no dissociation of soul and essence.[8] Our view is not that the baby initially lives in heaven, but that it lives without the duality of self and spirit, soul, and essence. Most importantly, the primal condition is characterized by the nonduality of essence and soul. Individual babies are born with different dominant characteristics, but common to all is that there is no distinction between the soul and the essence at the beginning. This primal condition might, and possibly does, exist more purely and completely in prenatal life. It is most likely not completely harmonious in prenatal life, owing to disruptions that happen in the womb, but as we will see our exploration includes prenatal structuring of the soul.[9] It is also more complete in infancy than later and becomes gradually limited and disrupted in early childhood.

When the infant is in homeostasis, when it is not frustrated, mistreated, or sick, but is lovingly and appropriately taken care of, it seems to live not only in absence of duality of soul and essence, but with a great deal of obvious pleasure. This homeostatic baseline can get disrupted, but the soul's initial harmony is resilient and it reasserts itself spontaneously. However, the fact that disruption is a possibility, combined with the factors we discussed above, leads to a permanent state of disruption. The soul at some point loses her resiliency and the duality becomes impressed on her substance as a permanent structure. In other words, as a result of the soul's normal development her homeostatic baseline moves from wholesome harmonious unity to a largely conflictual and permanently dissatisfied state of duality. Stated alternately, when the adult soul relaxes and settles down at times of no instinctual or environmental pressures she does not go back to her original harmony, but can only settle into the dualistic ego state that has now become the bedrock of her identity and reality.

The original primary wholeness is not the same as the enlightened state, the completed state of the soul, even though it resembles it in some respects. The mature state of the soul, as we will see later, is also a nondual state, but one characterized by resilience against duality. The original nonduality is not strong enough to withstand the development of identification with ego structures. But it is more accurate to say that the original nonduality is lost as part of the natural evolution of the soul toward a higher level of integration of nonduality. The mature state of nonduality will have characteristics and capacities that either do not exist in infancy or exist in only rudimentary form. They are the result of a higher nonduality where the soul integrates the ego and cognitive capacities listed above with her essential ground. This is the story of the human soul, the mysterious drama that every human being undergoes.

The initial observation relevant here is that when a young child is terrified or very frustrated all essence is gone from its soul's experience. It can become not only a wild animal, but also a wretched devil. When it is again contented it becomes again one beautiful, nondual being. Its early life oscillates between these extremes and spans all the degrees in between. This observation indicates that the young soul is capable of losing contact with her essential ground.

Factors Responsible for the Loss of the Essential Ground

The soul's alienation from her true nature has been told throughout history through stories and myths, and explained with various religious and metaphysical systems. We will consider here only the factors that we know from direct experience and observation. We will discuss the factors that go into the development of this alienation only briefly since we have discussed these in our previous books in great detail. These myriad factors—some inherent, some common—converge to dissociate the soul from her essence, in various degrees of alienation. The most important are:

1. Inadequacy of early holding environment
2. Caretaker's narcissistic blindness
3. Extreme impressionability and malleability of the young soul
4. Nature of ego development in relation to the characteristics of the soul's essence
5. Cognitive immaturity of the young soul
6. Animal potential of the soul
7. Congenital and accidental physical limitations
8. Trauma and abuse

Inadequacy of Holding Environment

The soul is dependent and needy in childhood in many ways. In order to grow into her natural pattern she needs an adequately supportive and nourishing human environment. But this environment needs to also support her in being herself, in being true to her nature, if she is going to grow in a way that maximizes the actualization of her potential. In other words, she inherently needs an environment conducive both to her being herself and to growing in the way that is natural to her.

By adequate we mean that the environment needs to be, especially in the persons of the primary caregivers, not only welcoming and loving, but also caring, appropriate, empathic, responsive, and capable. When the environment—which includes the physical environment, the primary caregivers, and the social field surrounding them—is adequate enough, the child's soul feels held. Feeling held is a multifaceted state, but it includes feeling loved and cared for appropriately and adequately to the moment and to the stage of development of the soul. When the soul feels held this way she manifests and actualizes one of her basic potentials, a preconceptual state of trust. This state, which we refer to as basic trust, is inherent to the soul by the mere fact of her original innocence. She does not yet know of trouble, and hence she possesses a carefree and naturally relaxed attitude, an attitude that is not differentiated yet into a feeling. She is then in a state of nondifferentiated, nonconceptual trust, basic trust.

Upon closer scrutiny we recognize that when the soul experiences herself as adequately held, she feels herself embraced, bathed, literally held by a field of love, tenderness, and gentleness. What actually happens is that the soul experiences her environment as pervaded by a loving and gentle presence. For her, the caring holding is inseparable from this loving presence; in fact, she feels this loving presence to be inseparable from the environment itself. This is one of the dimensions of the ground true nature, invoked by the human holding and caring presence.[10] It is not that the infant's soul directly and fully perceives the ground of all manifestation as a presence of love, but rather that she feels held by a gentle love. She is probably unaware of much of her environment, except that portion directly in her perception.

In other words, when the environment is adequately holding it invokes the dimension of true nature that corresponds to this holding. Alternately stated, when the environment is adequately holding it is expressing this dimension of our true nature. The soul does not only feel the adequate and gentle holding physically and emotionally, but also in the field of consciousness that makes up her presence. Her presence, as a result, relaxes and lets go. She feels she is "in good hands." It seems that the effect on the soul, of the presence of this holding field of love, is specifically that of basic trust. She does not need to think about it, nor even recognize it; she only needs to sense it, as if the contact with it spontaneously and magically affects the soul and relaxes her in a way we would conceptually call trust.

In this condition she abides in her true nature, allowing her potential to unfold unhampered. When she trusts that everything will be all right, that her needs will be taken care of, implicitly and without discriminated cognition, she leaves herself alone, in the sense of not doing anything to change her state to gain holding. In this absence of inner attempts to do anything to herself, her abiding in presence is undisturbed. This abiding is necessary for the free manifestation of her inner potential, necessary for her learning and growth. By being, and not doing anything to her own state, she is not in her own way; she is not only receptive to what her potential unfolds, but she is also in a condition of maximum allowing for her dynamic creativity to function unhampered. Thus her dynamism manifests exactly what she needs at the moment for her further learning and growth. In other words, the adequacy of the environment supports her to be true to herself, and to grow and develop.

When her environment is not adequate in its holding of her—that is, it is unloving, rejecting, abandoning, inappropriate, unempathic, intrusive, unprotecting, harsh, abusive, non-nourishing, neglecting, or incompetent—her inner homeostasis is disrupted. She does not respond with basic trust, and does not implicitly feel things are all right or that her needs will be adequately met. Failures of the environment must be numerous and frequent, or intense for her to lose the capacity for basic trust. Because human environments are most often inadequate and sometimes grossly so, the soul slowly loses the innate trust she was born with, and learns not to implicitly trust reality. This developing basic distrust, this expectation that things will not be all right, that life will not turn out to the best, becomes slowly ingrained and impressed upon the receptive soul.

But even before basic trust is lost, when she experiences that things are not going all right, the soul organismically feels the inadequacy as an inner disruption. She feels not held, and the loving enfolding presence does not arise. The result is a bigger disruption than we would imagine. It means she cannot just simply be, she cannot continue to be presence. The disruption annihilates her sense of presence. She feels threatened, as if the bottom has fallen out. She instinctively contracts in response to the loss of her ground, and her dynamism manifests more difficult forms of experience. She may feel frustration, fear, terror, disintegration, anger, rage, sadness and, so on, depending on the extent of the inadequacy, the intensity of the resulting disruption, and the stage of her development.

When the environment is not taking care of her adequately, the soul tries to take things into her own hands, going into a sort of emergency overdrive. She manifests forms of behavior that aim to bring about the needed responses from the environment; when she grows up these become forms of behavior aimed at changing the environment directly or attempts to deal with her inner condition on her own.[11] Now the soul is no longer simply being, she is reacting. Her experience is no longer a continuity of being. When the soul loses her inner balance and tries to take things into her own hands, especially at times when such attempts are futile, she has to leave her place of abiding. Reacting is specifically not being, and so the continuity of being is lost.

When the soul moves or acts from a relaxed and trusting place, her presence flows into the appropriate forms and shapes effortlessly and easily. Her actions and movements are then a continuity of being, for she moves while abiding in her nature. There is smoothness, a sense of grace and harmony, and her presence exudes radiance and well-being. But when she reacts, she screams and screeches, flails about disharmoniously, and exudes anxiety, discomfort, and irritating energy. The former is a manifestation of the continuity of being, and the latter of the reactivity that disrupts this continuity.[12]

Reactivity has been understood by many of the wisdom traditions as antithetical to our true nature, and many inner techniques for transformation are one way or another to disengage from reactivity. We see here that the problem with reactivity is that it annihilates presence. It means the soul leaves her ground, and it further implies the absence of inner trust necessary for abiding in one's true nature. It reflects the position that if one continues to be present one will suffer more. Therefore, besides trying to control the environment, the soul learns to control her inner experience.

More precisely, the soul experiences the inadequacy of holding as an inner disruption, an undesirable and threatening difficulty. She reacts to this with an array of inner postures and strategies that end up dissociating her even more from her nature. The disruption and the reaction happen together, resulting in a dissociation from the ground of presence. Initially this happens every time the holding is not adequate enough, with the soul returning to her homeostatic state of simply being when the care becomes adequate again. However, repeated or continual inadequacy of holding, which is what most individuals endure, finally erodes the basic trust that makes it possible for the soul to resume simply being. The reactivity becomes habitual and structured into the soul, built into the very fabric of her developing character and identity.

The soul loses the ability to simply be; she even forgets what it feels like. Instead of experiencing a continuity of being, the soul experiences a continuity of reaction. This reactivity not only annihilates her being, but also obstructs her dynamism from manifesting the necessary forms for her harmonious and optimal development. The personal patterns this reactivity takes tend to become rigid forms that limit the soul's dynamic unfoldment, by channeling it through these forms. She loses her allowing openness, which is bound to constrict her creative dynamism.[13]

This dynamic is universal for the early life of the soul, but if it were the only one not all souls would dissociate from the essential ground. However, the process of dissociation is inevitable, as we shall see in our discussion of other factors contributing to the loss of contact with Being.

Caretakers' Narcissistic Blindness

As we have discussed, there are many kinds of holding. There is, however, a special class of these that have particular importance. These are the kinds of holding that invoke the specific potentials of the soul, mirror these potentials as they arise, and support them to be and to expand. As she interacts with her environment, the soul manifests particular parts of herself called for by her experience. Therefore, her environment needs to be not only receptive to her potential but also actively inviting of it. What the soul manifests of her potential will consequently depend in part on the range of experience of the caretakers, and their interest and skill in activating the soul's potential.

When a potential manifests, as a certain quality or capacity, the soul needs it to be seen, recognized, approved, and lovingly admired for her to see and value it. The soul is inadequately able to see and recognize herself at the early stages of her life, and is dependent on her caretakers to appreciate and value her. In other words, the soul needs this external mirroring in order for her to actualize the particular potential. Elements of potential do not arise in a vacuum so they need the calling forth by the environment, but they also need a positive mirroring in order to be integrated. (See *The Point of Existence*, chapters 27 and 28, for more detailed discussion of this need for mirroring.)

Furthermore, the soul also requires a great deal of firm but loving support for her to learn about her potential, how to recognize and use it, and how to exercise, develop, and expand it. She needs guidance, instruction, modeling, and setting of appropriate boundaries by confident and attentive caretakers. Without such support it is difficult for her to securely integrate her unfolding potential. (See *The Point of Existence*, chapter 25, for a more extensive discussion of support and the soul's need for it.) But when the environment, specifically the primary caretakers, who are usually the parents, provides her with adequate mirroring and support her arising potential, she can recognize it, value it, and integrate it into her sense of identity. She grows up with the implicit and confident sense that this is part of her. This secure establishment of her potential in her everyday experience is the actualization of it in her development. She develops by integrating her potential, as she learns, expands, and matures. This happens through the soul's identity being structured and patterned by her potential. In other words, the actualization of her potential is inextricably linked with the development in her identity of the ability to include the elements of this potential. Difficulties and issues in the development of identity are reflected in narcissistic disturbances and conflicts: intense and inappropriate need for mirroring, incessant and insatiable hunger for support, exaggerated or grandiose sense of self and its importance and capacities, and intense need for admiration and attention combined with lack of empathy for others and disregard for their concerns. This is because the difficulties in its development have left this identity weak, brittle, vulnerable, and easily disintegrated. So it constantly needs shoring up through an exaggerated, self-centered need for mirroring and support.

Identity is so important for the normal development of the soul that its disturbances can severely unbalance the total sense of self. In fact, the normal soul experiences a threat to the integrity of her identity as a threat to her survival. (See *The Point of Existence*, chapters 9–11, for more on the question of identity.)

At the same time, the sense of identity develops as cohesive and stable when it is mirrored and supported, but also and necessarily if the sense of identity includes the major dimensions of the soul. The less it includes of the major dimensions of the soul's potential, the weaker and less complete it is. This incompleteness is in itself a recipe for feebleness and vulnerability, for it means that elements of her own potential constitute a threat to the soul's narcissistic equilibrium, since this equilibrium is developed on the exclusion of these elements. That is why the parent needs not only to mirror but also to call forth the soul's potential.

When we recognize that most parents are ignorant of their essential potential we see that they will have a difficulty seeing it, and hence mirroring or supporting it, in their child. The result is that the most fundamental part of the soul, her essential ground and its aspects, will receive at best a minimum of mirroring and support. The soul develops without integrating this fundamental dimension into her identity, leading again to her dissociating her experience of her essential nature. Instead, the soul integrates only the elements of her potential that her human environment could reflect and support. Thus the parents' lack of self-realization is passed on to their offspring. (See *The Point of Existence*, chapter 18, for more detailed discussion of the various environmental factors involved in this dissociation.)[14]

The establishment of identity constitutes the development of a major and central ego structure in the soul, for in ego development the soul develops with an overall structure that constitutes a separate individual with a sense of identity, psychological characteristics, character, and preferences. The soul also develops the capacity to relate to others as separate individuals, with various degrees of autonomy and personal love. Cognitive development goes through the fantasy stage, to primitive conceptualization, to thinking and symbolic operations. The soul also achieves moral and aesthetic development. All these coincide, of course, with the normal growth and maturation of the body. We are listing these developments simply to note that they are developmental achievements.

12 Ego Development of the Soul

AS WE DISCUSS in *The Point of Existence*, there are other factors, besides the lack of mirroring and support that cause identity to develop without including essential presence. The sense of identity is connected to an ego structure, and hence its development is an important part of ego development. Ego development culminates in the soul developing a sense of being an individual person with a sense of identity. This means that the soul begins life without the most common things adults possess: individuality and a feeling that identifies this individuality to itself.[1]

Ego development progresses through integrating impressions accumulated from the soul's early experiences, primarily those with her primary caregivers. These impressions are basically memory traces of her interactions with her parents, first and primarily the mother. These memory traces are retained as images of the parent, of oneself, and the quality of interaction. The three constitute what is called an internalized object relation. The various object relations become integrated by the mind into larger and larger units until there finally results a superordinate self-image and object image. The overarching self-image, which contains all the memory traces of oneself (mostly vis-à-vis the mothering person), is a mental representation of the self that patterns the soul by impressing her with its content. In other words, the soul's field of consciousness becomes gradually structured in a semipermanent way by the development of this self-representation. The self-representation contains two primary ego structures: individual boundaries that separate the self from others, and identity by which the self knows itself. (See *The Point of Existence*, chapter 9, about the development of the self-representation, the two primary structures, and their relationship and differences.)[2]

The important point for our discussion here is that the self and identity develop through the integration of images and representations, dependent on memory traces of early impressions. This most characteristic feature of the ego development process has far-reaching implications, including:

1. Representations are the stuff of ordinary knowledge, which means the identity ends up being part of ordinary knowledge, not basic knowledge.[3] This means the soul will know herself through representational knowledge. Representational knowledge, especially through memories, is bound to be an indirect knowing. To indirectly know ourselves means, by definition, that we do not know ourselves as presence; to know ourselves as presence is nothing but to know ourselves directly and immediately. The hallmark of our essential presence is immediacy and directness. The development of the ego sense of identity means the loss of this immediacy, which is again a dissociation of the soul from her essential ground.

Furthermore, the overall self-representation, with all of its underlying ego structures, patterns the soul by impressing her field with the content of her history. The past ends up determining the forms the soul experiences in herself, conditioning her dynamic creativity to flow in largely predetermined grooves. This again means the soul's experience of herself is not immediately in the present, but mediated through past experience. This is both a mediation through the past, and a direct loss of the immediacy of the experience of the present moment. Essential presence is both an immediacy of consciousness and a completely present centered consciousness of oneself. This again dissociates the soul's experience from her essential ground of presence.

2. This dissociation is made even more complete by the phenomenology of essential presence. Because it is total immediacy and nowness, its principal feature, presence, cannot be captured in a representation, any kind of representation. A representation is particularly antithetical to that of the intimate and immediate presence of essence. Essence is presence in the moment; it is actually the ontological ground of the soul, her true beingness. A representation is a purely mental construction, regardless of how charged it is with affect, even when it is an attempt to represent essence. Hence any representation

can capture only some of essence's qualitative and quantitative characteristics, but not its nature, which is Being. We cannot put a conceptual boundary around presence and retain the resulting mental object in memory. Hence, presence cannot be included in the identity that develops through ego development, which is the normal identity of the soul.

Thus the nature of the ground of the soul and the nature of ego development combine, with great redundancy, to exclude essential presence from the identity of the ego-self. Thus the dissociation is not only contingent on environmental deficiencies, but it is unavoidable, since ego development is a natural stage for the evolution of the soul. (We discuss this point in exhaustive detail in *The Point of Existence*, chapter 12.)[4]

Ego development dissociates the soul from her essential ground in a still more complete way, not only constructing a sense of identity that excludes presence, but also patterning the soul such that her experience of herself is always through the self-representation. The self-representation does not simply remain in the mind as a mental content. Its various images and object relations with their associated feelings and attitudes become relatively fixed structures in the soul. To begin with, they are impressions in the soul because any experience is a form that impresses her field with various degrees of fixation. But when they are incorporated into the self-representation, the soul identifies with them and they become fairly permanent forms that structure the soul's experience.

The soul retains these identification systems to recognize herself. They also function to structure her capacities and faculties. The soul integrates her learning through ego development by synthesizing it with these identification systems, which structure the ongoing experience of the soul.[5] It is a truism in conventional wisdom, and a more developed understanding in Western psychology, that our experience of ourselves, our behavior, and our relationships are influenced by childhood experience. This is usually understood psychodynamically, especially in the notion that our painful or conflictual childhood experience survives in our unconscious and affects our conscious experience and behavior.

However, this is not the most basic way that our experience is structured by the past. The ego identification systems pattern the major elements of our experience; for example, as we have just discussed, our sense of being a separate person with an identity is due to ego development. But the effect of the development of the identification system is even more profound: our experience moves from being a field aware of the forms that arise within it to an experience of a subject that observes or experiences disconnected objects that seem to be floating nowhere, a nowhere that is sometimes referred to vaguely as mental space. We lose the unity of the experience of the soul, and our interiority becomes constituted only by the forms of experience that arise.

Since the self-representation is a content of ordinary knowledge, it is obvious that it is composed only of objects of ordinary knowledge, that is representations. Representation can capture the forms of our past experience, but it cannot capture the field of essential presence in which these forms arise. Therefore, when we experience ourselves and the totality of our perceptual field through the self-representation, we only see the forms included in it, abstracted from the underlying field that manifested them. Not only do we lose contact with our essential ground; but the living and field-like nature of the soul's experience is also changed, collapsed into the transitory and incidental, at the expense of the fundamental.

In other words, our basic knowledge becomes patterned by our ordinary and representational knowledge. Our experience is now conceptual, constituted by isolated objects of perception. We can see here that the positivistic and empirical view of things is due to ego development, and is the result of the patterning of the self-representation.

We can reach this understanding via a different route, by remembering that the self-representation includes two primary sectors: the self-identity and the self-boundary. The two together constitute the totality of our experience of ourselves as separate individuals. In other words, the self-representation patterns and structures our experience of being persons. This is the totality of our experience of ourselves.[6] Since these structures are products of past experience, all of our experience of ourselves, as long as this experience continues to be egoic, is influenced by our past, and hence it is neither immediate nor direct. It is all devoid of the essential ground of the soul.

Cognitive Immaturity of the Young Soul

There is a further redundancy in ego development that causes it to dissociate the soul from her essential ground. We know from research in childhood cognitive development that the capacity to conceptualize both self and objects emerges slowly and goes through several stages. One finding important for our present discussion is that newborns do not possess a capacity for self-reflection. The younger the child, the less self-reflection he has. The infant does not recognize where he comes from, is not aware where his actions and responses originate in his experiential field. The infant is the experiential field, and this field is aware of the content that arises within it. Since he has no precedents to compare with his experience, it does not occur to him to reflect back on himself and see the field. His mode of experience, referred to in spiritual literature as "witnessing," is not questioned until later.

The soul's earliest experience is, consequently, an identification with the field, or more correctly, an abiding in it, without discriminating recognition of this field. The soul begins her life abiding in essential presence, without her knowing this in a discriminated way, without an explicit recognition. The child is not unconscious regarding the essential presence. What is missing is not consciousness, but recognition.[7] This situation is similar to the that of the individual who is spontaneously happy without knowing it. It is common knowledge that when one knows one is happy, one loses the spontaneity and joy. This is because self-consciousness tends to obstruct the carefree attitude of the heart. This observation becomes precise knowledge in the understanding of the essential aspect of joy.

Since the soul is mostly not self-reflective early in her life, she does not recognize her true nature. She abides in it without recognizing it. Furthermore, even if for some reason she sees it she will not recognize it. She does not discriminate it in her experience as something independent from the various forms and shapes she experiences, because her discriminating capacity is not developed enough to do so.

By the time the soul is able to self-reflect in a sufficiently discriminating way, her ego development has already structured her experience to exclude the essential ground. It seems that the natural design of our soul is such that she cannot realize her true nature with a discriminating recognition, necessary for the enlightenment experience, until her cognitive capacities develop. In addition, the cognitive immaturity of the soul becomes a factor in the dissociation of the soul from her essence. To understand this we need to remember that for the soul to include something in her identity, she first needs to recognize it. This is the reason for her need for mirroring in childhood. The fact that she does not discern her essential ground of presence, does not recognize it, means she cannot include it in her identity. She cannot include it in her self-representation, nor can she retain it as a memory or an impression of herself.[8]

We see here that there are two things involved in this original absence of recognition—the lack or insufficiency of self-reflection and the limitation in the discriminating capacity.

Impressionability and Malleability of the Young Soul

It is evident that ego development is not possible without the impressionability of the soul. Ego development proceeds mostly through the building and establishment of structures. Ego structures are nothing but zones of the Riemannian manifold of the soul impressed by systems of representations in a semi-permanent fashion. This is made possible by the extreme plasticity of the soul, which allows the mental images and remembered forms to mold her field into their corresponding ego structure. In other words, an ego structure is a region of the soul molded by a constructed mental image.[9]

Ego structure depends on two levels of impressions in the soul. We have discussed primarily those semi-permanent impressions that are due to the self-representation and its subunits molding the field of the soul. This self-representation is built up using memory traces of earlier, more momentary impressions. However, some of these early impressions remain in a semi-permanent way, not through representational memory, but by the impressions being strong enough, or repeated frequently enough, that they directly condition the substance of the soul. These are the kind of impressions we discussed in chapter 7, the direct structuring of the soul field by her own intense or repeated experience.

These direct impressions also become integrated into the overall self-representation, and synthesized with the mental structures. The presence of direct impressions, due to the vulnerable malleability of the infant soul, shows that the soul can develop structure before her memory and that cognitive capacities develop to the extent of being able to hold and organize memories.[10] This means that there are two levels of structuring in ego development that become integrated together as one structure, the ego structure of the soul.

Because of this understanding we can assume that the forerunners of ego development extend back into prenatal life, to the beginning of life in the womb. We will discuss these prenatal structures in the next chapter; but we want to note here that these earlier structures actually function as the initial ground of the more familiar ego structures. Because of this, the exploration of one's ego structures will arrive at some point at preverbal and even prenatal structures of one's soul. This tends to happen in the inner journey because this journey takes us to dimensions of Being that are beyond conceptualization and memory.

Trauma and Abuse

Strong and/or repeated impressions tend to become fixed in the soul, becoming part of her overall ego structuring. These impressions can be positive or negative, pleasurable or painful. Some of the most well-known and problematic ones are those due to painful or intensely conflictual experiences in early life. These include abandonment and loss, hatred and judgment, severe intrusion and lack of empathy, and so on. A specific subset of these is abuse. When the child is subjected to abuse of any kind, the pain and conflict around events and situations are so powerful that the impressions are quite lasting. We can see this in the many individuals who were victims of emotional, physical, or sexual abuse, the effects of which can not only last a lifetime, but tend to structure their experience in painful and difficult ways.[11]

It is important to recognize how abuse imprints the soul, because many people tend to think that it is mostly a question of repression that needs to be undone and dealt with. This neglects the structuring effects of such powerful impressions, structuring that becomes part of the victim's identity and character. This means that to learn to fully be free from such history one needs to work on the structures that have developed through this abusive history and learn to disidentify from them, or bring them to a degree of flexibility and openness.

Traumatic events have similar effects, but are different in emotional content. Trauma is any experience that the soul is not able to tolerate with the resources available to her at the time of the event. A trauma can be physical, as in the case of physical accidents, bodily injuries, severe or chronically incapacitating sickness. It can also be emotional, related to the physical trauma, a response to a trauma in the immediate family, witnessing abuse or trauma happening to others, or being emotionally traumatized by other's cruelty and mistreatment, by an important loss like a death in the immediate family, etc. Trauma has such a powerful impact on the soul that its influence can last a lifetime and affects our life and experience profoundly even when we have no recollection of the trauma.[12]

Because the soul is incapable of tolerating the direct impact of traumatic event or situation, the organism becomes overwhelmed and goes into emergency mode. A dimension of the organism becomes frozen emotionally and energetically, a frozenness that ends up being repressed or split off from consciousness. This then influences conscious experience in ways that might not be obvious to the individual, as has been identified as posttraumatic stress disorder.

What is significant for our exploration here is that the soul cannot at the time tolerate the sensations, feelings, and visual images associated to the incident or situation. This intolerance makes the soul dissociate, a defense mechanism often seen in traumatized individuals. The soul deals with the intolerable situation by not experiencing it directly, either by totally blocking it out of consciousness or by retaining the memory while becoming numb to its emotional and feeling significance. But for the soul to do that she would need to limit and lower the intensity of her awareness. Since the essential presence is pure presence of awareness the dissociation will have to include dissociation from this inner ground of the soul for it to be effective. In other words, in order for the soul to dissociate from the traumatic event or situation it inadvertently dissociates from her essential presence.

Something similar happens in the case of severe abuse of any kind. In fact, any intolerable experience generally leads to dissociation of one kind or another, all of which result in dissociation of the soul from her essential ground. This dissociation then becomes structured into the identity and character of the developing soul.[13]

Congenital and Accidental Physical Limitations

For the soul to live in our world she needs an adequate body, for the body is her immediate environment, and she needs to feel held by it. When the body has limitations in its functioning, the soul is constrained in her ability to experience herself and in her range of functioning. In other words, the soul requires an adequate physical organism for her to fulfill the richness of her potential. The possible limitations of the body are myriad, and their influence in the soul happens in many ways. We discuss briefly only a few of these:

1. The most obvious is the effect of gross physical limitations, as in the case of physical disability or chronic injury. The soul will simply not be able to experience some of her potential. However, this is not the most serious physical situation for the soul, for her potential is unlimited and she can, as frequently happens, develop alternate areas of potential. In fact, some individuals seem to use their physical infirmity to an advantage, by compensating in ways that make their lives even richer than the average physically able individual. Yet many individuals are greatly affected by their physical handicaps, and experience severe limitations in their development, due to the physical limitation itself and the emotions and attitudes about it.

2. One factor that is becoming increasingly appreciated in modern psychology is that inner states depend on the chemistry of the body. Many hormones, enzymes, and neurotransmitters are found to be central in regulating emotions, moods, and inner mental states. When the body suffers from some kind of biochemical imbalance, one's inner state becomes disturbed. As a result, it has been found that many difficult inner conditions, such as some types of depression, anxiety and phobias, some forms of schizophrenia, etc., are due to such chemical imbalances, and that some pharmaceutical drugs can help alleviate these conditions by redressing the imbalance.

It seems that the soul is not able to experience and develop all of her potential when such limitations are present. For example, it is not easy for the soul to feel light and optimistic when it is suffering from a chemical depression, regardless how much inner work she does. The manifestation of some of the soul's potential inner states and capacities requires that the chemistry of the body be healthily functioning. This physical limitation can become a limitation in the experience of some essential aspects, even essence in general.

3. Recent findings further indicate that our physical organism is structured in such a way that at least some of its inner states depend on specific genes. There has been some indication, for instance, that happiness depends on the presence of a specific gene, as do maternal feelings. This means that some essential states are precluded from arising in the soul, because the physical environment can neither invoke nor support it. There is some indication that some of the limiting syndromes that individuals become trapped in might have their basis in one's genetic or hormonal make up, as in the case of some addictions.[14]

We understand the general situation to be that the physical organism is the immediate holding environment for the soul. The more complete and healthy is the body, the more of her potential is the soul able to actualize. The completeness and health is not a matter of appearance and general health, but more importantly of the inner functioning of the physical organism, and more specifically the functioning necessary for the experience and functioning of the soul, mentally, emotionally, and spiritually. For instance, the brain and nervous system need to be healthy for optimum experience of the soul. Some deficiencies in the functioning of the brain, for example, might not be apparent for everyday living, but might crucially affect the development of the soul. For instance, some deficiencies might limit the discriminating or the synthetic capacities necessary for many stages of the inner journey, or might make it difficult for the organism to discharge excess tension and go into inner relaxation.

Nevertheless, because of the immensity of the soul's potential, many physical limitations might not appreciably hamper her development, and may sometimes stimulate it. But it is clear that for the full development of potential a sound body is necessary.[15] Physical handicaps may contribute to the soul's dissociation from its essential ground, but they are more relevant to the overall development of the soul.

Animal Potential of the Soul

We discussed the animal potential of the soul in chapter 10. The animal forms that manifest in early childhood are included in the overall ego structuring of the soul because the animal instincts, drives, and impulses are important components of early experiences, as in the object relations that are internalized and integrated into the self-representation. In addition, these experiences tend to be very intense and dominant in early childhood, making them a major component of what is remembered and integrated.

The animal component of the soul structures her in even more global ways that tend to dissociate her from her essential presence: the early stages of development of the soul have to do mostly with physical indwelling. The infant soul's experience is dominated by her physical needs and impulses, because the body is in the time of its greatest vulnerability and need. The dominant need is the survival and growth of the body, and so physical and animal forms of experience dominate the experience of the young soul. Her most intense and regularly repeated experiences are those of hunger, eating, satiation, defecating and urinating, physical discomfort and its relief, physical holding and its associated nuances, and so on. Emotional and mental experience are present, but not dominant. Essential experience is also present, as in the arising of essential aspects, but even these spiritual qualities manifest in conjunction with, and in response to, these physical and animal processes and forms of experience. Both the baby's cognitive capacities and the actual need of this stage of development focus the attention on the gross physical processes and their associated states.

This means that the first, and hence the most impactful, impressions that structure the soul will be these animal and physical processes and forms of experience. Both the intensity and repetitiveness of these experiences make them the most dominant impressions in the soul. Since at this stage the soul is so completely impressionable, the soul develops mostly as an animal soul. The animal structures become the deepest and most dominant layer of her ego structure, underlying the more developed and mature layers of structure, the structures of emotional object relations. Thus the earliest object relations integrated into the ego structure are those dominated by the instinctual drives as they manifest in early childhood.[16]

This overwhelming focus on the physical and instinctual aspects of experience tends to dissociate the soul from her essence, especially as it becomes instituted in her structure. However, a specific feature of this deep structuring seems to be central in effecting such dissociation: the fact that the infant, toddler, and young child are completely dependent physically on their environment. This dependency becomes structured into the soul not in the normal sense of dependency that many individuals have, but in a more fundamental orientation toward experience and life. The infant's experience is that whatever the soul needs comes from her caregivers and the physical environment. In other words, what she needs can only come from outside her. This is typified by one of the most fundamental ego structures, the soul in the form of the empty stomach relating to an external breast. This deep impression in the soul permanently orients her toward the outside, always toward the most surface and physical reality, for the satisfaction of her needs.

As a result, whenever the soul experiences any need, any inner emptiness, the original template that the soul will morph her experience through will be that of an empty stomach wanting something from outside her. This outer-directed orientation characterizes the animal soul, and functions as the fundamental underlying attitude of the ego-self. The soul is then not only externally oriented, but she is always ready to move forcefully outward. This compulsive and rigidly structured outwardness, in both orientation and action, automatically dissociates the soul from her essence. Essence is the inner, the depth; fixated orientation away from it is bound to dissociate us from it. The compulsive outward movement literally means the soul leaves her essential ground for the object of her gratification. The end result is not only dissociation, but the fixated position that richness resides outside, when in reality, for the adult soul it is primarily inside. Because of this fixed animal structure, the soul will find it difficult to commit to her inner richness, even when she experiences and understands its unlimitedness, for this fixation is so deeply structured and crystallized that it takes a great deal of maturity and learning to break through it.

The overall process of the soul's alienation from the ground of her being combines all of the above factors, in a multileveled redundancy. As the soul reacts to the inadequate holding of her environment—which includes (a) inadequate mothering, (b) caretakers' narcissistic blindness, (c) the body's limitations, (d) and abuse and trauma—she dissociates from her essential ground. This reactive soul is patterned by the ego structuring process, through which—because of: (a) the mental nature of this structuring, (b) the soul's early cognitive immaturity, (c) the phenomenological-epistemological characteristics of true nature and ground of existence, (d) her early extreme impressionability and pliability, and (e) the outward orientation of her earliest and most powerful animal forms of experience—dissociation from her being is cemented in her identity and its overall experience. The soul becomes a normal self by dissociating from her essential presence.

The final outcome of this dissociation is not exactly a duality between soul and essence. Through this dissociation, soul loses her character as a soul. She is no longer a living organism of consciousness. She does not experience herself in her true condition. She is split up into two parts, two separate dimensions. One is the normal self, and the other is essence, or spirit. By losing contact with her essence the soul collapses into a self, a self that may experience spirit. The resulting duality is between essence and the ego-self.

The Gains of Normal Ego Development

The development of ego structure is necessary for further stages of the soul's development. It is important for the soul to develop certain dimensions of her potential, along with capacities needed for her full realization and maturity. We will discuss the most important of these achievements briefly, since most of them are fairly well explored by others. We will emphasize the ones that are not as well known, and also indicate how the various achievements are necessary for the further maturation of the soul.

Cognitive Development

The soul is born with only the rudiments of the various capacities of cognition, which then go through a process of development that has been mapped by many researchers. These include memory, imagination, discrimination, conceptualization, formal operations, organization, synthesis, comparative judgment, thinking, and so on. The movement of these developments, which seems to parallel the stages of ego development, is toward an abstraction of perception. At the beginning the child's experience is mostly nonconceptual; that is, there is perception of differentiation of forms without recognition or labeling of such forms. The child perceives differences and changing forms but there is no knowing, except in a very limited way. Then the child learns to discriminate—to differentiate one form from another, and to know what the form is. This is the development of basic knowledge.[17]

This development results in the capacity to recognize primitive concepts, or protoconcepts, to recognize a concept of an object, but not yet to know a formal concept where it refers to a whole category of similar objects of basic knowledge. This step leads to labeling, giving such a protoconcept a name: for example, "This is an arm, this is an eye, this is a dog."

The next step is to conceptualize, to understand the idea of an abstract concept, a notion of a category with specific characteristics. For instance, we know about chair in the abstract, as a concept that fits all possible chairs, rather than simply knowing about a particular chair. Such a concept is not actually a percept in basic knowledge. It is the transition to abstraction, which means to a mental creation. This is more of an abstraction than the creation of an image, for an image is always a replica of a percept, or a combination or development of a group of percepts. A concept, in other words, is much more independent from perception than an image.

The conceptualizing process is a process in basic knowledge, for all events are basic knowledge, but it creates something that is understood but does not appear in the way ordinary objects appear in perception. The word referring to a particular concept is in basic knowledge, but the concept itself is not. The concept is an understanding, a comprehension, an idea based on observing percepts in basic knowledge and categorizing them. This requires comparison and recognition.

The ability to conceptualize, combined with the labels we give to objects and concepts, makes it possible for us to think and to speak. Thinking is the relating of various concepts and images to each other to arrive at new concepts, which is new knowledge. This knowledge—composed of mental impressions or memories of primitive concepts, images, formal concepts, their relationships, and the resulting concepts of further discrimination and relating of various concepts—is what we have called ordinary knowledge in chapter 4. In other words, memory of elements in basic knowledge is the beginning of ordinary knowledge, but conceptualization and thinking expand this knowledge infinitely. This ordinary knowledge can now be used, in conjunction with observations of basic knowledge combined with fresh conceptualizations and thinking, to unfold basic knowledge, i.e., to have new observations. But it also expands ordinary knowledge.

We have seen that such "mentalization" of experience is necessary for ego development, but we see here that it leads to a new kind of knowledge, ordinary knowledge, and a new function, thinking. Thinking itself goes through stages, culminating in formal operations, which is working with formal concepts independently from perception. We have seen that this alienates us from basic knowledge, and its field of presence. Yet we see here that on its own it is a new faculty of the soul. We will see later that it leads to alienation only when used in a certain way, to know who we are fundamentally, but appreciating its nature and place in the overall economy of the soul we recognize it as a tool of tremendous potential benefit.

An aspect of this cognitive development is that the soul learns how to use reason and logic. This is the application, in the process of thinking, of abstract rules to our concepts. These rules help guarantee that our conclusions do not contradict basic knowledge, direct observation. We will see in chapter 20 that these rules of logic reflect invariant patterns in basic knowledge as it unfolds through the dynamism of Being.

This cognitive development is clearly important and useful for the experience, life, and development of the soul. We already know how it is useful in our ordinary life, and its usefulness is amply demonstrated in the development of science and technology. In fact, most of the achievements of modern Western civilization are direct consequences of this cognitive development.

However, this achievement is also necessary for the eventual spiritual maturation of the soul. The cognitive achievements contribute to our capacity for discrimination and reason, and our ability to relate and synthesize in general. We ordinarily apply this capacity for discrimination and synthesis only to our ordinary knowledge. However, there is no reason why we could or should not apply it to our basic knowledge itself. We only need to be in touch with the ground of this knowledge, essential presence, to do that. In fact, we believe this is the next stage of our cognitive development. Our cognitive achievements can be seen not only as the creation and expansion of ordinary knowledge, but basically as the development of our intellect to new heights of discrimination and synthesis that can now be integrated with basic knowledge on a higher level of understanding.

If we learn to connect with our essential presence and experience, and investigate it not through our ordinary knowledge, but with the enhanced capacities of discrimination and synthesis, we will have the opportunity to understand this presence more precisely and completely, which will then unfold it to reveal its further possibilities of depth and subtlety. This unfoldment is actually nothing but the essential or spiritual development of the soul, as we will discuss in the next few chapters.

This way our intellect will operate in conjunction with essence, allowing the soul to open up to the manifestation of essential intellect. The operation of essential intellect is nothing but the intellect taken to the essential level, where the soul can now inquire and understand with the help of essence and its various aspects. This is actually a manifestation of an essential form, a dimension of essence where all essential aspects function in the service of the intellect. We have referred to this essential manifestation as the essential *nous* in *Luminous Night's Journey*, and as the diamond guidance in *Spacecruiser Inquiry*, which is a book devoted completely to its exploration.[18]

The essential intellect or *nous* operates not only with the enhanced intellectual capacities of discrimination and synthesis, but even though it is essential presence it can operate in conjunction with the soul's normal intellect, with its logic, reason, and ordinary knowledge. Here, instead of ordinary knowledge obscuring our basic knowledge, the *nous* uses it to reveal and unfold the infinite potentials of basic knowledge. The essential *nous* can also operate in conjunction with reason and logic, applied to spiritual experience in all its dimensions and subtlety.

The essential *nous* is one of the natural secrets of the wisdom teachings; it was mentioned and discussed a great deal, but most contemporary investigators miss it for they do not understand it. They cannot understand it because they are subject to the dissociation of knowing and being.

We can mention one more thing about the functioning of the *nous*: it can combine with ordinary thinking to the extent that thinking becomes the flow of essence and its aspects, in a stream that scintillates with insight and understanding. Thinking becomes objective thinking, intentional, truly rational, steady, focused, and to the point. It is the operation of true nature in the process of discerning wisdom.

Individuation

Individuation is the primary achievement of ego development. We can say that the soul who is at the beginning an organism of consciousness becomes through ego development a person. The soul develops into an individual with unique characteristics and skills, a human being able to relate to others as autonomous human beings with their own characteristics and skills.[19] This unfolds many of the potentials of the soul, but also makes it possible for her to individuate further, on deeper levels.

We have discussed how this development leads to the dissociation of the soul from her essential ground, but we need to remember that this is a stage in development, getting the soul ready to progress to a further stage. The difficulty with ego development lies not in its basis on mental representations and fixed impressions, but in the identification with its achievement of individuality as if it were our final truth and identity. In other words, the problem is not with ego development, but in believing it is the terminus of the possible development of the soul, rather than seeing it as a stage that the soul needs to transcend. In fact it is our observation, and the observation of many researchers in the field, that the less successful is the ego development the more rigid is this identification. Healthier ego development results in a more flexible and permeable structure.

The next step is for the soul to continue this journey of individuation by including more dimensions of the soul's potential.[20] This happens by integrating her ego achievements into the essential ground of the soul. The sense of being an individual, which is based on identification systems of images and object relations, can now go through a transformation. The structures that constitute it can go through a process of clarification in which they are consciously understood. The soul can inquire into her ego structures, recognize them as structuring through mental impressions, and metabolize them into her essential presence.

The structures are based on memories and impressions that constitute the history of the life of the soul. By becoming aware of this history, recognizing its content as it actually was, and understanding instead of identifying with it, the soul can metabolize the important experiences in this personal history. The soul digests the truth and learning in this history rather than using it to define herself. This metabolism, which can happen only if the process of inquiry occurs in the presence of essence, integrates one's personal history and learning into the ground of the soul. The structures lose their structuring power and the learning and skills synthesized in them now become integrated into the soul directly, instead of indirectly through images and identifications. This process of essential metabolism develops the soul into an individual of essence. The sense of being an individual with unique qualities and skills does not disappear, but appears in the soul now as an essential presence that has a personal quality. (See *The Pearl Beyond Price*, chapters 11–15, for a detailed discussion of this process of metabolism.)

Through metabolizing her history, the soul individuates her essential presence. She now experiences herself as an ontological presence, but this presence is at the same time a well-rounded individual, a person of presence. The presence is characterized by the quality of personalness. The soul continues to experience herself as a person, but this person is presence, a true and essential structure. The soul is now structured by her own essence, rather than by images from the past. She is no longer dissociated from her essential ground; that ground transubstantiates itself into a personal essence. This personal essence allows the soul to act as an autonomous person with unique qualities and skills. The qualities are essential aspects, and the skills are the influence of these qualities on the faculties of the soul in a way that embodies her personal learning.

The personal essence is not a well-known manifestation of true nature, but it is a major potential of our soul.[21] It is the only essential aspect that makes ego development understandable as a stage of the soul's development. In fact, the individuation of the soul is the way true nature, in its transcendent ground, is able to experience its manifestations in the various ways available to life-forms. Here, true nature, transcendent to all manifestation, appears in the form of a human person who can walk, talk, and think, but is still the presence of this nature.

Normal ego development is a stage toward this essential individuation, necessary for the personal development of her potential just as the grain of sand is necessary for the development of the pearl. The individuation of the soul, which happens through metabolizing ego structures and everyday experience, is not only a matter of the arising in the soul of an essential aspect. This essential aspect becomes the structuring form, the essential prototype, for the soul to develop in such a way that she can be the personal embodiment of all dimensions of true nature, all the way to its absolute depth and subtlety. (See *The Pearl Beyond Price*, chapters 35–39, for a more complete discussion of how the soul individuates on the boundless and transcendent dimensions of true nature.)

Embodiment

Through her development of ego structure, and cognitive and other development, the soul learns about physical embodiment. One of the main tasks of normal development is facilitating the inhabitation of the body, which of course involves learning to live in a physical world. It is true that when the infant is born, it is a soul inhabiting a body. But the soul is not firmly indwelling in this body. She needs to cathect the body by learning about it from the inside out. She needs to learn how to function through it, and to learn about the unique properties of the physical world.

By becoming structured through ego development with the impression of the body and its various processes as a self-image that makes up the central element of the resulting structure, she begins her process of physical embodiment. The physical dimension has its unique properties, many of which are quite different from other dimensions of manifestation, and the soul seems to need to go through a particular process to be able to integrate this dimension into her experience.

However, this is only a stage of a more comprehensive development. The next step is that the soul needs to disidentify from the body, or more accurately from its image, and to recognize that the center of her identity is not the body but her true nature. This is actually part of the process of individuation above, for this individuation of being requires physical localization. The body image is metabolized in such a way that the body becomes one of the dimensions of the soul's existence. It becomes her existence on the physical dimension, where she recognizes this dimension as the most external of Reality. It is her physical individuation, coemergent with the individuation of all other dimensions of Being.

Thus we see that normal ego development serves the overall development of the soul partly through the achievement of indwelling in physicality.[22]

Self-Reflection

Self-reflection is important for self-perception and knowledge. In fact, many people believe that self-reflection is what differentiates human beings from other life-forms; they believe that it is unique to human consciousness. It is a potential of the human soul that arises as part of normal development. Without it a human being would be ignorant of his inner motivations, impulses, conflicts, and so on. It is necessary for self-examination, which includes the appraisal of one's beliefs, assumptions about reality, and so on. This is obviously important for the development of human understanding, and human knowledge in general.

This capacity is thus important for the soul's eventual self-recognition of her true nature. Through self-reflection we can find out that we do not know ourselves; without it we cannot explore what we know of ourselves, what we believe we are, which is a necessary requirement for undergoing the spiritual journey. The journey is to a large extent a form of introspection that is a development of the capacity for self-reflection.

Furthermore, this introspection goes through a development in which it ultimately becomes the soul's recognition of her true nature. At the deeper stages of her inner journey home, the introspective soul utilizes her essential *nous* in her inner investigation. This gives her introspective consciousness a discriminating capacity with objectivity, precision, sharpness, and brilliance that enables her to make very subtle discriminations in her awareness of herself. This reveals essential presence to her in various degrees of subtlety and objectivity until she finally discriminates both its ultimate truth and its completeness.

Self-reflection is necessary for the development of ego structures, and becomes a factor in the soul's self-conscious awkwardness and neurotic self-criticism. It also tends to dissociate the soul from her ground, for by reflecting back on herself, the soul takes the position of a subject that observes an object. Thus self-reflection develops into the dualistic mode of experiencing oneself. Yet it is necessary as a stage in the development and maturation of the soul toward self-realization. In the total self-realization of true nature, the soul is not self-reflective, for true nature does not look at itself. It recognizes itself by being itself. This capacity for discrimination is not present in early infancy. (See *The Point of Existence*, chapter 35, for a discussion of essential self-seeing and self-recognition.)

The soul does not lose her capacity for self-reflection when she realizes her true nature. She retains it as a capacity, rather than as the only way of knowing herself.

13 Liberating the Soul

THE SOUL'S INNER REALIZATION and essential development, which involves the transcendence of normal ego development, is a natural stage of maturation that integrates, and benefits from, the achievements of ego development. In this process the soul regains her original impressionability and receptivity, remaining receptive to her essential nature with all its aspects and dimensions. Impressions on the soul are increasingly dominated by essence and its truth, in contrast to external considerations, and thus she develops and matures under essential influence and guidance. She becomes impressionable to essence, receptive to its influence, loyal to essence, valuing essence. This transformation advances her from dominance of the animal soul to becoming a full human soul. Essence acts on her, impregnating and clarifying her consciousness. This marriage of soul with essence becomes deeper and more complete until it reaches the state of nonduality of soul and essence, which resembles the soul's original condition but now includes recognition, discriminating awareness, and understanding. The soul's marriage with her essence liberates her from vulnerability to fixated impressions, whether from external or internal sources.

This process has two threads: the soul's liberation from the rigidity and fixation of her structures in a way that retains the learning in them; and the soul's reconnection with her essential ground in a way that uses her cognitive achievements to recognize that ground as her true nature. The first is the process of liberation of the soul, and the second is that of her essential development.

These are actually two sides of, or two perspectives on, the same process: the first is of how the rigid structuring limits her development, the second how her essential alienation is a dissociation from her most significant potential necessary for further development. The two together become the process by which duality is overcome.

Liberation of the soul involves the full realization of her true nature, seen from the perspective of freeing her from the cramping and limiting influence of her previous stages of development, and the fixations she retained within them. It involves freeing her field from the constricting fixations and rigidities of her issues, conflicts, conditioning, and ego structures in order for this field to consciously realize its true nature with its primordial dimensions of nonconceptual awareness, basic knowledge inseparable from presence, and creative dynamism.[1]

Issues of the Soul

The process of liberation of the soul frees her from many issues and barriers. We can organize these into the following categories:

- The soul's physical preoccupation and external orientation. This is attachment to the external, which is what the world promises her, at the expense of her depth, her true nature.
- The passions and appetites, drives and instinctual compulsions. These are the forms external orientation takes.
- Attachment in general, with its grasping and tight holding.
- Psychodynamic issues and conflicts with their repression, ego defense mechanisms, and blockages. This includes the difficulties of early experience as they survive in one's personality and unconscious.
- Self-images and object relations. These constitute the content of the soul's identifications.
- Fixation and rigidity, which tend to characterize her views and attitudes, but most importantly her ego structures.
- Narcissism, which reflects the soul's alienation from her true nature.
- General ego structural issues, such as weakness and inadequacy. This includes schizoid defenses.
- Precocious development.

- Underdevelopment. Both this and precocious development may characterize some of the soul's ego structures.
- Structure in general, more specifically the need for one.
- Underlying all these categories are the fundamental issues of ignorance and duality. These are the central spiritual barriers usually identified by the various wisdom traditions. In *Facets of Unity*, we discriminate this fundamental barrier into nine fundamental delusions about Reality. (See part six of this book for further discussion.)

We will discuss the work on these barriers primarily in terms of work on the ego structures that are the carriers of these issues. We have explored the psychodynamic issues in our previous books *Essence*, *The Pearl Beyond Price*, and *The Point of Existence*. These issues are how structures first present themselves, allowing us to explore the content and history of these structures. Psychodynamic work focuses primarily on the defenses and repression related to these issues, an important level of work before structures reveal themselves as such. Furthermore, when inquiring into our normal experience, we find psychodynamic issues, structural issues, and epistemological considerations to be intertwined. In particular, it would be difficult to separate structural issues in particular from epistemological considerations that reflect the characteristics of true nature.

Working with Rigid Structures of the Soul

The soul's liberation frees her from the influences that limit the free outflow of her potential, and thus a central element of the path of liberation involves understanding the rigid structures that constitute a significant part of those influences. When the soul's creative dynamism is unconstrained by extraneous factors, free to unfold her potential, she develops and matures according to her natural pattern.[2] She develops by actualizing her arising potential within the crucible of its interaction with her everyday life; this way her development spontaneously integrates her experience and learning. This reflects her inherent property of freely unfolding in a creative morphogenic display, as discussed in chapter 6.

The relatively fixed structures with which she arrives to this point of her journey do not only obstruct the freedom of this flow, but tend to channel it in a manner that continues to manifest the forms of experience these structures allow. Her experience becomes repetitive, not only repeating the same experiences and patterns, but fixating her on the dimension of experience her structures define. She becomes unable to display her potential freely, repeating the old instead of unfolding the new and novel. She ends up moving in a gravity-bound orbit, witnessing the same kinds and patterns of experience. Different individuals vary in the rigidity of this repetition, but ego structures tend in general to confine the soul to a limited region of her Riemannian manifold.[3] Her dynamism constrained, the soul's experience becomes fundamentally static.

Liberation involves freeing this dynamism.[4] To free the soul's dynamism is to free her from being limited and constrained by rigidity and fixation, which means to find a way to deal with her structures so that there will be no such rigidity and fixation any longer.[5] This requires that we first recognize all the structures as structures and the realities perceived through them as not fundamental defining truths. For the soul to be able to recognize a structure for what it is, the structure must become conscious and fully manifest in our awareness.

This is not an easy undertaking, for structures can continue to effectively structure our experience only if they remain largely unconscious. In other words, in order for our ego structures to function as structures, we need to believe that they and their influences are fundamental truths about ourselves and reality. In fact, we arrive at the end of ego development with the crystallized belief that the views these structures define to the soul are fundamental and unchanging truths. Henceforth, the soul is resistant to investigating these structures, taking the view that their patterns are self-evident truths. Therefore, a more indirect approach is often preferable. A useful approach is to be empathic and attuned to the soul's ongoing normal experience and preoccupations, taking into consideration the natural need for mirroring, recognition, and understanding. At the same time our exploration employs and expresses the soul's longing to know herself as deeply and completely as possible. Taken together, these considerations, along with many more that we will discuss elsewhere, point to the value of approaching one's inner liberation by exploring one's everyday experience and its preoccupations.

We have observed that the soul is more willing to participate in the inner journey, and will in fact cooperate with enthusiasm, when this journey addresses her immediate experience and everyday concerns. Inquiry into this everyday content of the field of the soul will bring about understanding of this content. This understanding will at first involve the normal psychological insights and realizations, connecting with one's various experiences and at some point with psychodynamic material. The soul comes to understand the content of her experience in terms of its sources in childhood experience. This process uncovers a great deal of repressed content, much of which turns out to be difficult and painful.

Continuing the inquiry, with the help of essence and its aspects, the student will begin to question the more fundamental sources of this content.[6] This will at some point reveal the structures underlying the content; for example, one discovers that one's various psychodynamic issues are related to specific self-concepts. There is another reason the psychodynamic, emotional, and psychological work tend to reveal the underlying structures: Psychodynamic work relieves the issues of some of the pressure to remain unconscious, and releases much of the emotional charge associated to them through the history of their development. This makes it easier for the individual to become directly aware of the related structures. In addition, the soul has a new motivation for inquiry resulting from recognizing that the painful content does not simply go away; it has still deeper sources.

At some point, inquiry will reveal the particular structure or structures underlying the issues.[7] The soul will be able to see her conditioning. She can see that there is a rigid impression, a fixed structure that gives her identity, individuality, and functioning. It is then a short step to discerning the self-representation that patterns the particular structure; that is, she will become consciously aware of holding a particular self-image. By seeing the self-image while retaining the curious attitude of inquiry she may begin to see more precisely the history of this self-image, the specific object relations and their associated feelings that constituted its history. This will relieve her further from believing it is a fundamental truth of who she is. This can go as far as recognizing it as a mental image created, or remembered, by her mind. When she reaches this stage of understanding, the soul is open to who and what she is.

This openness of soul can only happen through the impact on the soul of a particular essential manifestation, inner spaciousness. Openness is the specific state that results in the soul when essential space arises in her. This openness is not a belief or an attitude based on beliefs. The soul arrives at it by letting go of a structure that defines her, without resorting to new definitions of who or what she is. If she does not manage to be this open, for instance if she is defensive, holding on to the self-image or immediately bringing up a different one, inner space may not arise, and she will not be able to liberate herself from the particular structure.

Assuming that the inquiry continues to the point of recognizing the mental and historical nature of the particular self-image, inner space arises and erases the self-image. The soul arrives here at a wonderful state of freedom, feeling unencumbered by the depressing and dulling weight of the previous rigidity and heaviness of the ego structure. She experiences herself unpatterned, as a clear and luminous spaciousness, immaculate and light, joyous and lighthearted. She is openness, lightness, a formlessness that is freedom. In the state of essential space, she has no structure, but is open to all the potential of her being.

As she continues in this essential state of spaciousness, with the curious and open-ended attitude of inquiry, essential presence will arise in one aspect or another to structure her experience, now from inside out. Essence will manifest in the soul in the aspect or aspects corresponding to the dissolved structure. In other words, the particular structure was either related to the loss of an essential aspect or was functioning in the place of one, and hence, when it is no longer in the way and the soul's dynamism is free again, it will manifest this particular aspect.[8]

A few observations about working with ego structures are in order at this point.

Ego Structure and Inner Space

There is a definite relationship between working through ego structures and the arising of inner spaciousness. This manifestation of true nature expresses its absolute dimension, with its emptiness. Inner spaciousness is not the same as ontological emptiness but is related to it in some mysterious way. The point is that because of this relationship, inner space stands for the total openness and lack of determination of true nature. True nature is ultimately formless, and hence any fixed or rigid structuring, as happens in ego development, is antithetical to it. In other words, ego structures, through their self-representations, specifically obstruct the ultimate indeterminacy of true nature, barring from the experience of the soul the aspect of inner space. More specifically, identifying with a self-image automatically blocks inner spaciousness. Therefore, when the soul finally understands a self-image and does not hold on to it, space arises.

With the arising of inner space, the soul regains, at least momentarily, her original openness to her potential. This allows her dynamism to morph out whatever elements of potential, essential aspect or dimension, are necessary for the experience and development of the soul. This is because the ego structure does not only obstruct the inner space. The fact of structure, or using a representation to define the nature of the soul, obstructs inner space, but each structure has its particular content and patterning that obstruct some essential aspect or another. Therefore, in the working through of ego structures space always arises, but the essential presence that manifests differs from one structure to another.

Nature of Liberation from Structure

It would seem in the process described above that a particular ego structure dissolves and is replaced by space and a quality of presence. This is true, but this does not mean that the particular structure has dissolved completely and will never arise again in the soul's experience. Ego structures do not simply finally dissolve, as the experience seems to indicate. They dissolve during the experience, but when the right situation evokes the related ego structure, that structure will probably arise. If the individual has worked through the structure the way we described it above, when it comes back it will be different. It will have lost some, or most, of its charge, and will have less power to structure the soul. The soul will recognize it more easily, and disidentify from it with greater ease. This will give the soul the opportunity to work through it further, to see something about it she missed the first time around, and to also understand it from a larger and more fundamental perspective, depending on the new stage of her overall development.

This process tends to repeat itself at the various stages of the soul's inner journey, especially when she is working through the major ego structures. The result is that the impression on the soul constituting any particular ego structure becomes steadily shallower and less powerful, more flexible and transparent, and less able to structure the soul in a fixed way. This is like sanding out a depression in a piece of wood. The more sanding, the less deep is the impression and the less important it is as a structure.

In other words, a structure does not dissolve in one experience, but needs many dissolutions at various depths, along with the clear arising and understanding of the relevant essential aspects. It is usually difficult to erase a structure completely, but consistent work will denude it of much of its charge and structuring power. It may continue to arise, but the soul will be able to readily recognize it as an image; hence it will have no power of structuring. It may continue as a recollection or an image that includes history, but a history that does not define one's nature. This happens to the overall self-representation and not only to constituent self-images. This major structure normally continues in awareness, but more as a carrier of history, a historical identity that does not structure one's true identity.

It must be clear from this discussion that one cannot change one's ego structure.[9] One cannot add new structures that are not part of early ego development, except maybe with dramatic, intense, and long periods of impression. And one cannot modify a particular substructure. In other words, one can neither create a new constituent self-image, nor change an already existing one. One can weaken or strengthen an existing structure; however, one cannot modify its form or pattern, because such form or pattern is the structure itself. For example, if one encounters an image of being unloving one cannot change it to an image of being loving. The arising of the essential aspect of love will not change this image. It will simply dissolve it for a period of time, and will make it less powerful and believable to the soul. When it arises again, it will be the same image of being unloving, but because it has lost most of its charge and power it will have less structuring influence on the soul, who will, as a result, be able to allow her dynamism to display the quality of love.

The image of being unloving will not change, for the form of being a person with no love defines the self-image in this case. If this form appears to change, it means that a new self-image has arisen, and not that the old image has transformed. In other words, the image of being unloving will continue to arise at certain times, even as the individual develops the capacity to experience and express love.

The transformation of an ego structure is not a changing of its topography, but primarily a thinning of its form and a diminishing of its power. How much the particular structure loses its conditioning and patterning power depends on how much one has worked with it, how deeply and accurately one has understood it, and how intensely have been the resulting essential experiences. The final outcome will be its metabolism, its absorption into the presence of Being, which happens after a long process of clarification, as we discuss in *The Pearl Beyond Price*, chapter 14.

It is important to recognize this to understand the true inner spiritual transformation. The transformation through which the inner journey takes the soul is not a change of her character, but a self-realization of true nature. This means one's field of consciousness ceases to be configured by ego structures, and becomes completely permeable to essential presence. One's identity ceases to be determined by one's history and becomes simple abiding in true nature. One's identity shifts dimensions, leaving that of historical content and abiding in timeless presence.

Enlightenment and Ego Structures

The previous paragraph might be interpreted to mean that one can be enlightened by simply experiencing one's true nature, that one does not need to work on ego structures, that ego structures might dissolve on their own through essential experience, or that ego structures do not need to dissolve as long as one is in this experience. Nothing is further from the truth.

In our discussion above about working with ego structures we saw that we arrive at our essential presence as we penetrate these structures. But it is also known that one can arrive at deep spiritual states by doing one technique or another, most of which do not seem to have anything to do with working with ego structures. First, these techniques do work with ego structures, but not in the same way or as directly as we are describing.[10] The important question for us here, however, is whether experience and recognition of true nature is sufficient for enlightenment and liberation, whether this means it automatically dissolves ego structures or does not need to.

First, experience and recognition of true nature, regardless on what dimension of subtlety and completeness, do not automatically dissolve all ego structures. It is our observation that ego structures, and for that matter psychodynamic issues, are not affected directly by enlightenment experiences. This is due to the fact that these structures and issues have mostly unconscious underpinnings. Unconscious elements of the psyche are not impacted by conscious experience directly, except maybe in exposing them to consciousness in some occasions. These structures are impacted only by awareness of them and complete understanding of their content. The enlightenment experience may give the individual a greater detachment and presence that makes it easier for him or her to confront these structures and issues without becoming overwhelmed by them, and hence have a better opportunity to work through them. The greater presence that may result might make it easier for the individual to abide more in true nature, and this way have a greater detachment from the influence of the structures. But the structures will not self-destruct simply because the soul has seen the light.

We understand that this view is counter to the claims of many individuals who profess enlightenment. The actions of many of these individuals should speak for themselves.

Furthermore, enlightenment and liberation, or the arriving home, is not only the realization of true nature. This realization is necessary for enlightenment; it is its experiential ground. Nevertheless, enlightenment also includes the absence of all structuring that may impede any of the basic dimensions of true nature, as those of basic knowledge and creative display of potential. Practically, this means the working through of all ego structures and issues. If there is a structure that one is not aware of, or has not worked through directly or indirectly, it is bound to obstruct or obscure true nature one way or another, at one time or another. Enlightenment has then two sides: the abiding in true nature and the liberation from all rigid and fixed structures. In fact, the more one is liberated from ego structures and their patterning influence the more one is able to abide in true nature.[11] In this chapter we are only discussing the liberation from structures.

We have described ego structures as developing in two ways, by direct impression of experience or indirectly through representations. We will now discuss various types or levels of structures. The inner journey generally moves in its inquiry from surface to deeper structures. The deeper are the structures the more basic or fundamental they are to the overall sense of self. Furthermore, the deeper are the structures the more primitive they tend to be, and the more they were created through direct impacts.

As the soul penetrates some of her structures, and these in turn lose their power to structure her, she automatically reverts to deeper structures for her sense of identity. Alternately stated, as some structures become transparent they reveal other structures foundational to them. For example, becoming conscious of the structure of being an unloving person will uncover the structure of being a person. This process moves normally with a parallel one, wherein essence manifests deeper and subtler forms and dimensions. The process of penetrating deeper and deeper structures, in conjunction with essence revealing deeper and deeper dimensions, does not stop until all structures are made transparent and flexible.

The deepening process reveals structures of decreasing definition. The deeper a structure the less formed or defined it will be, reflecting the well-known fact that ego development moves through increasing structuralization. The less defined and more amorphous is a structure the more primitive it will be, both in terms of phylogenetic history and its state. In other words, as the soul experiences her essence in deeper and subtler dimensions, increasingly primitive structures are encountered. One way of stating this is that the ego-structured soul goes through a deepening regression; reverting to earlier levels of development is the psychological meaning of regression. A possible inference from this might be that one needs to regress to retrieve one's essence, but this is actually not exactly the case.[12]

Regression and the Discovery of Essence

It is true that the ego-self regresses as it goes back in its developmental history toward more primitive established forms of structuring her experience and identity. In the inner journey, however, this is not a complete regression, because the work of inquiry happens in the presence of essence. In other words, one continues to be present in the moment even though part of one's consciousness goes back in time to earlier structures and their associated experiences. Even if the self regresses, essence is not retrieved as part of an earlier structure, or through a memory of earlier experiences. The structures themselves and their associated historical content are retrieved this way, but not essence.

For this reason a frequent sequence of events is that a particular essential aspect will arise in consciousness, before one deals with a specific structure related to it. This experience then precipitates a regressed state of the soul in one of her early structures.

We discussed in the last chapter that ego structures cannot capture essence in their representations. In fact, we have seen that this is one of the factors leading to the soul's dissociation from her essential ground. Therefore, we cannot retrieve essence by going to earlier structures, for the structures do not contain essence. Nevertheless, when essence reveals itself on deeper dimensions some of the barriers tend to be earlier and more primitive structures. In other words, we need to go back to these earlier structures because they happen to be the barriers to, and not the carriers of, these deeper dimensions of essence. This is partly because deeper dimensions of essence challenge ego structures in a more fundamental way. They challenge the ego-self's deeper foundations. The deeper and more fundamental foundations of the structured soul happen to be the earlier and more primitive structures. Another reason is that as more of the surface structures are penetrated, the soul will revert to earlier structures to shore up her overall structure.

However, this does not imply that the soul did not experience these aspects or dimensions of essence at those earlier times.[13] Even if she did, the work of realizing essence is not regression to earlier essential states, even though the process may include such regression. We can understand this by considering essence both in its essential aspects and its ground presence. Essential aspects are states of presence so they cannot be contained in a representation. What happens is that the ego structures and issues function as barriers to the dynamism of the soul; by morphogenically transforming her field, they prevent her from manifesting these aspects. They structure the soul in such a way that her creativity flows within the forms allowed by these structures. When these issues and structures are made transparent, which sometimes require ego regression, the barriers are not there anymore, and the inherent dynamism manifests these aspects.

Unlike essential aspects, the ground presence of essence is not a momentary manifestation. It is a timeless presence, beyond stages of development. It is always present, eternally our true nature. It is present in childhood and adulthood. The question is whether we directly perceive and recognize it. Ego structures obscure it and obstruct our consciousness from recognizing it. The earlier structures tend to do that more because they are the more fundamental scaffolding for ego. In other words, our disconnection from this ground happens earlier, generally speaking, than the disconnection from essential aspects. When these structures are penetrated, their obscuring and obstructing influence is reduced or ended and we simply become aware of our true nature. This is not a regression to our true nature, for it does not make sense to view timeless presence within the context of time. It is present even when the ego structures are obstructing us from perceiving it.

As we see, the question of regression is not a simple one, because essence is a different category of experience than the content of ego structures and their memories. Ego regresses, but this regression is not back to essence. We do not leave essence back in childhood, for it is outside of time.

Types of Ego Structures

We will discuss the structures in the order that they tend to manifest in the inner journey, from the surface toward deeper and more primitive ones: ego structures, primitive structures, preverbal structures, and prenatal structures.

These are the general structures that we encounter in the first stages of inner work. They constitute the final outcome of ego development, and dominate our normal everyday experience. They include the larger terrain of ego development, as in the structures of ego and superego. The superego has constituent substructures, as in the case of the ego ideal, the structures that regulate self-esteem, and so on. Ego has primarily two major structures that together give the soul her sense of self: self-entity (or separating boundaries) and self-identity. Together these give the soul the sense of being an autonomous individual. The superego is considered a more highly structured part of the ego. All these substructures are then constituted by subunits of self-images and their associated object relations.

The inner work normally begins with some of these component self-images and their object relations, moving gradually to larger and more general structures, but also sometimes to smaller subunits of structure. This work can take several years, and constitutes the initial stages of the liberation of the soul and the discovery of essence in some of its aspects. This stage culminates in the work on the major structures of the ego, those of self-identity and self-entity. These foundational structures in turn have their supports in the primitive and other types of structures.

What we call ego structures are the normal identifications of the self. Since they are the final and most highly structured outcomes of ego development, they are usually quite distant from the soul's ground of presence. As a result, when we explore these structures they always reveal themselves to be empty, devoid of inner reality. They are the most external structures, where the sense of inner medium of the soul is completely obscured from view, and her sense of agency is vague. We are a subject who observes and experiences objects, inner or outer. This is the conventional dimension of experience, the totally egoic realm of duality.

All these structures can be seen to compose a segment of the soul that we refer to as the central ego, meaning the central identification system that develops through normal ego development and that the individual soul identifies with consciously.[14] It is the final outcome of integrating the various object relations and their associated images into an overall self-image. It is the ordinary, normal, familiar sense of self and identity.

We are not here dealing with deep instinctual structures, but with the normal level of object relations: for example, "I am a bad boy who angers his father," or "I am a frustrated girl because my mother does not pay attention to me." This is why when we penetrate these ego structures they reveal themselves as empty shells, devoid of substance and reality.

14 Primitive Structures of the Soul

WE WILL CONTINUE OUR DISCUSSION of ego structures by looking at primitive structures of the soul. These are the structures we discover when the soul begins to be activated as a living presence. These structures are often the initial ways we recognize the soul in the inner journey to our essential home. The soul is structured, but only partially, by these primitive patterns. Because this incomplete structuring has not reached the level of ego structures, we can at these levels experience the soul as living presence. In other words, we here begin to experience the soul as a living presence, almost protoplasmic, that is somewhat structured but not completely dissociated from the essential ground. The primitive structures are partial and elemental, but also flexible and not as rigid as more developed ego structures. They arise in the early stages of ego development. When we are in touch with these structures we may experience much more aliveness and lability than in ego structures. The soul's experience is characterized by dynamism and flow, but not completely free and open.

Because of the primitive nature of these structures, we experience not only the protoplasmic living presence of the soul, but also her two primary potential forms of experience, the essential and the animal, more directly. More accurately, we may experience these structures as primitive and animalistic, but still full of essence in its various qualities, which is how the infant's soul experiences her animal forms.

In addition, these structures are primitive in their content, containing memories and imprints of early childhood experiences before ego structures were established. These structures are primitive partly because they were not integrated into higher level ego structuring; they tend to be split-off structures, separate from and alien to the central ego. Because of this these primitive structures may arise in experience independent of work on the structures of the central ego. This happens when a particular situation invokes a primitive structure, where the individual identifies with it at the expense of the central ego. It is as if one becomes another self, through one's identity shifting to a split off part of the soul.

Sometimes a primitive structure is only repressed, rather than split off, forming an unconscious structure of the central ego. This structure will then tend not to arise in experience until a person does work on the central ego, undoing the repression related to the more primitive structures.

Because these early primitive structures tend to be more flexible than the more mental ego structures, they will become readily unstructured when investigated. We then may experience them as an amorphous, blobby kind of presence, instead of the clear and crisp presence of essence. We group them into two levels, reflecting two degrees of primitive structuring.

The Soul Child

The less primitive group has more ego structure, and hence tends to be formed by the body image. These structures are formed by an image of being a young child, who is still somewhat in touch with its animal, instinctual, primitive impulsive emotionality, and with the remnants of some essential aspects. The primary structure is what we call the "soul child," which is the state of the soul before she was completely structured and became estranged from her primitive animal forms and her essential ground.

This is the structure popularly known as the "inner child"—the child of joy, the emotional child that is still in touch with its original qualities of aliveness, curiosity, mischievousness, openness, and so on. It is what is popularly called the emotional child, but slightly different. The emotional child is only the emotional part of the soul child. In reality, as children we were not only emotional; we were livings souls, full of life and vigor, adventurous and curious, joyous and playful, but also capable of exploding in rage and frustration, or going into fear and terror. Our emotions are still fully present, but so is our animal nature in its aggressiveness and excitement about life and its pleasures and objects.

At this level there is some ego structure, for there is a body image of a child patterning the soul, but the soul still retains her original aliveness and responsiveness. The soul child can experience essence but it is not its constant state. Essence appears in the soul child when it is experiencing satisfaction and contentment, or expressing one of its original positive qualities like those of boldness, brightness, or cuteness.[1] The dominant condition of the soul child is a soul presence patterned with the child's image, but presence mixed with emotions and impulses. It is fluid and emotionally labile in a passionate way. It is the core of the soul that becomes repressed or split off. It is not the dissociated essence, but a soul structure that still has some ability to experience it. In fact, it is the most developed structure of the soul in which we can still experience the soul as a medium. It is the most developed of the structures that still retains the basic properties of the soul. Nonduality between experiencer and experienced is still present to some degree.

This soul child becomes repressed and/or split off from the central ego early on, because it contains the main elements of the soul that were not adequately held by the environment. These elements include essential qualities, but the repression happens mainly because of the animal and emotional forms that the environment found unacceptable or inappropriate to the structures of civilized social life.[2] The soul child is the site of the classical passions of pride, covetousness, anger, envy, and so on, and hence clarifying these passions from the soul will bring an encounter with this structure.

One way of understanding the soul child is to contrast it with the central ego. The latter becomes the adult ego, but the soul child is the part of the soul that is split off and/or repressed, and hence does not have the chance to grow. It remains in its original condition of primitiveness and relative structurelessness. It has the aliveness and joie de vivre that characterizes children, while the central ego is the serious, civilized, and functional adult who mostly means business.

The soul child contains most of the more primitive structures of the soul, but it also contains the child structure in its various stages. So it includes the infant, the toddler, and the young child. The soul child is usually fixated at around age three or four, but can be as young as an infant or as old as seven years.

The Libidinal Soul

This is the animal soul at the beginning of ego structuring, where the soul's animal potential is all contained in one structure.[3] This is a much more primitive structure than the soul child, for it is not patterned by the human body image. This structure forms the more primitive ground of the soul child, and hence will generally arise as we make the soul child more transparent. It is a structure of a living entity, shapeless and formless, but has individual boundaries, for it appears as an entity. It feels like a primitive animalistic creature that is completely run by the instinctual drives and appetites. Its aliveness and dynamism are much more total than those of the soul child, appearing frequently as a writhing, wiggling, but powerful organism with no fixed shape or size.

Civilized society does not know how to deal with this aspect of the soul, so it relegates it to our subterranean depths, by repressing it in the unconscious or disowning it as a split-off part of us of which we are not normally aware. Because it is usually disowned by society and the individual, it becomes a pure animal soul, devoid of any human concerns or sentiments. In other words, splitting it off into a disowned and rejected part of the soul involves the creation of a soul structure that is separate from and not impacted by the other and more human elements of the soul's potential.[4] This dissociation from human concerns, which means absence of heart, appears in the experience of the libidinal soul in being irrational, guiltless, ruthless, completely selfish and self-centered.

In other words, the animal soul is originally run by drives and instinctual appetites, but it is not particularly destructive or grossly and intentionally selfish, but similar to animals in the wild. However, because it is disowned, it loses contact with the other elements of the soul, and becomes distorted and extreme in the intensity of its aggression, worse than actual animals.

Society has learned to civilize the soul not by transforming her animal dimension or harmonizing it with her overall psychic economy, but by disowning, controlling, repressing, and splitting it off; this recognition is among Freud's most enduring contributions to our knowledge. Our animal qualities are seen as bad, and the superego functions to control the impulses of the libidinal soul, so that they do not penetrate to consciousness or get acted out. This separates the animal dimension of the soul from true learning and civilization, and also from being impacted by spiritual aspects of the soul. Thus in the course of inner work, when we first get in touch with the libidinal soul we find it in this split off and hence distorted and exaggerated animalistic form. We feel then justified to continue our rejection and revulsion; but when we observe it with nonjudgmental awareness, it may transform to its original animal form, with its grace and power.

Society has tried puritanical control of the animal soul, but this has failed just as license fails. Only the balanced harmonious integration of the complete human adult can approach it correctly; only by integrating the soul's full potential, including the spiritual, can we truly civilize the animal soul.

The animal or libidinal soul is driven by two primary instincts or drives: the aggressive and the libidinal.[5] The aggressive drive includes the soul's power and energy directed toward survival and all of its correlates: dominance, rivalry, territoriality, etc. The libidinal drive includes sexual and erotic energy and impulses, animalistic wanting and desire, and the desires for togetherness, connection, and so on. These two drives appear in the animal soul within the context of two primitive object relations, again split off from each other. The first contains the aggressive drive and we refer to it as the "rejection object relation," and the second contains the libidinal drive and we refer to it as the "libidinal and/or frustrating object relation."

These two object relations make up a triad with a third, which we call "the central object relation." They are structured according to the earliest relation the soul had with her mother, or mothering person. The central object relation contains the mostly positive and good part of the relationship, while the other two contain the difficult or bad part. More specifically, the infant's soul splits her experience of her mother into three different parts. The object in these object relations is originally the breast, but becomes the whole mother at some point. It is as if the infant interacts with three breasts, or mothers, because of its primitive splitting. This splitting entails three senses of self that engage the three breasts within the three object relations. The primitive object relations tend to remain in their original form,

Primitive Structures of the Soul 205

split off from normal consciousness and without further structuring or development.

The rejecting object relation usually manifests as a small, weak, and frightened self, who is terrified of a big, powerful, hateful, and rejecting object. The self-image is not only small and helpless, but good and soft, while the rejecting object is big, powerful, and bad. When one experiences this object relation one tends to feel paranoid and frightened in relation to people who seem powerful or in a position to reject one. The splitting characteristic (seeing things as all-bad or all-good) manifests in the fact that the object is not only powerful and big, but bad and hateful, with no heart or compassion. In other words, the object is a purely bad one, indicating the operation of a splitting defense, for this pure badness is quite rare, if not impossible, in actual human beings. The understanding of this object relation begins when we realize that not only is the object bad but the self is all good, weak but all good. The self in this object relation is soft, good, and perhaps loving, but has no power.

This is not an easy structure to work through; its primitiveness is part of the difficulty, but the defensive nature of the splitting is the main reason for its persistence. When we understand this object relation and see its genesis in early experience with parents, especially with what is experienced as the bad mother, we recognize that the self feels weak and the object powerful because the self has projected its own power onto the object. The self takes the position that power is bad, especially when seeing hateful and destructive manifestations of it in its environment. She basically equates power and hatred, and projects both of these onto the object, usually onto a split-off object. In other words, the soul splits off her hatred and power and projects them onto the bad powerful object. She then feels herself to be without hatred, hence good and innocent, but because she equates hatred and badness with power she is also powerless. The object, on the other hand, becomes all-powerful, but hateful and bad. The result is a weak but good self terrified of a powerful and bad object.

We refer to this structure as the rejecting object relation because rejection is its primary affect. The self feels that it is rejected, or is going to be, with various degrees of aggression. Furthermore, when someone begins to experience this object relation, it is experienced as actual rejection or the fear of it. Only upon investigation does one recognize the primitive core of this structure. To understand this object relation involves recognizing the defense mechanism of splitting, and therefore coming into contact with one's split-off hatred and destructiveness. When one finally recognizes that it is one's projected hatred that one is afraid of, and deals with the fear and the splitting, one then begins to feel the hatred directly. The direct experience of the hatred can take the soul to a clear experience of itself as the animal soul: ruthless, irrational, heartless, hateful, destructive, and very powerful. The natural human tendency is of course to reject this structure; one wants to feel that it is alien to oneself, thus the impulse toward splitting. But with sufficient openness and objectivity one can experience it fully, as a powerful entity, an alien animal form full of brute instinct and ruthless determination to get what it wants regardless of consequences to others. The qualities of selfishness and destructiveness turn out to be incidental and unintentional; this animal entity is simply not going to tolerate anything that stands in its way. The ruthlessness of the animal soul is not personal and not intentional; it will simply wipe out whatever stands in its way without hesitation or qualms.

At the beginning we tend to reject these heartless and guiltless qualities of the animal soul. However, the heart is simply irrelevant for this animal form, which is purely instinct. The animal soul is not a cruel human who has lost her heart. As we come to understand this manifestation, we begin to see that its exaggerated destructiveness and hateful quality are actually reactions to frustration. Because the instinctual self is not allowed to be powerful and effective in getting its way, its power turns into destructive hatred and heartless reactivity. The particulars of this structure connect with one's early history in relation to power, control, destructiveness, as well as the need to protect the vulnerable and loving heart. When we are finally able to experience this animal form without either rejection or judgment or acting out, it transforms into its original animal form. This turns out to be an animal kind of power and energy, calm and confident, peaceful but ready to act with full power and energy. The opening of this experience removes the negativity associated with frustration. This is the time when one may experience oneself as a tiger or black leopard—strong, muscular, full of vigor and power, but calm and collected.

This is actually an animal form, inseparable in the soul from the essential aspect of power. It is the soul embodying her essential power to be herself truly and authentically. The animal form of black leopard possesses grace and beauty, where power and stillness are completely inseparable. Allowing herself to experience this structure without reaction or attachment, the soul releases the animal form and manifests herself simply as the presence of essence in the quality of power. The soul manifests stillness, immensity, and peacefulness, along with a sense of intense dynamic power.

The understanding that usually arises in working through the rejecting object relation and its related animal soul structure is that for one reason or another the soul had to disown this power early on, which turned it into destructive hatred, which was then projected onto the bad object. Thus the animal soul structure turns out to embody our essential power, which in early childhood was inseparable from animal desire.

The second primitive object relation in the animal soul is the libidinal or desire soul. It involves the same soul structure as in the rejecting object relation, which it manifests as a shapeless animal entity with tremendous aliveness and vigor. In this object relation, however, the soul is hungry and voracious, and lustily desires the objects of her satisfaction. This is the soul in the mode of going after the object, where the desire for the object and for the gratification of her desires are the same thing. She wants, and she wants fully, lustily, and passionately, with no holding back or sense of propriety. This primitive creature is bent on satisfying its instinctual desires for food, sex, territory, pleasure, and so on. It is single-minded in this desire, and all its power and passion are channeled powerfully to satisfy it. The libidinal soul is not only completely driven by powerful desires, but also indiscriminate in satisfying them. Any object will do, will copulate with whatever creature that comes its way. It will eat whatever seems full and meaty, with no considerations of manner or taste. This is the desire side of the animal soul, fully embodying and expressing her instinctual nature.

The libidinal object relation is the structure of this desire soul wanting a wonderful, yummy, and completely desirable object. The object appears here as beautiful and desirable in an animal instinctual way, full and luscious. Its prototype is the engorged, youthful, and turned-on breast, full of milk, thick juicy nectars, robust energy, and aliveness. It is a full and gleaming breast, desirable and inviting. It promises to give the soul the object she needs, the object that will satisfy her hunger and bring her erotic pleasure.[6] The libidinal soul loves this object passionately and wants to gobble it up with gusto and total satisfaction.

It is clear that the dominant genetic stage for this structure is the early oral stage, the characteristics of which pattern this early structure. What makes this structure become split off is not only its unabashedly animal and instinctual nature, but the frustration that results when the soul is unable to get the desired object. The affect coloring the libidinal object relation is the combination of total libidinal desire combined with the intolerable frustration of unrequited love and desire. The soul wants, but for various reasons cannot have, the object of her desire. It might be that the unconstrained animal nature of the desire makes the original object, the mother, unable or unwilling to receive such passionate desire; or that the good and desirable breast is not available when wanted; or that a sibling or husband has it, or whatever. The frustration in turn increases the desire, as happens with animal desires in general. The environment's disapproval of the animal nature of the wanting combined with the intolerable frustration lead to the soul splitting off this part of herself and the corresponding object relation.

When this object relation finally surfaces in inner work, there is normally a strong superego rejection and disapproval, often accompanied by intense feelings of disgust and revulsion at the extremity of animal instinctuality. The individual is afraid he will turn into an insatiable beast, voraciously eating everything and copulating with everything that moves. With consistent inquiry one may be able to experience the intense frustration and disappointment involved in this object relation, then become aware of the intense desire and wanting. This unveiling of the repressed material frees one's instinctual desire, and allows it to come into consciousness.

When this instinctual energy is opened, there arises the danger of becoming attached to its exhilarating, passionate aliveness, especially if the individual has lived a controlled and puritanical life. The insight that begins the process of working through this issue is the recognition of projection onto the libidinal object. One may recognize that the good mother or wonderful breast was beautiful and desirable, but the object he sees in his mind does not actually exist in the world. One may see at some point that the beautiful, luscious object, which is the true object of the soul's libidinal desire, contains all the wonderful, sweet, and fulfilling nectars of the essential heart qualities. The libidinal object turns out to be a strong, alive heart, full of a living presence that contains luscious juices that normally manifest in the heart when it is open to its essential qualities. One may actually see and taste the zesty pomegranate of passionate love, the rich golden honey and milk of satisfying nourishment, the apricot nectar of fulfillment, the luscious orange of essential pleasure, the beautiful fluffy pink of love, and so on.

The infant soul seems to project her heart qualities onto the good breast or the mother because she tends to feel these qualities when she actually gets the object. She believes that this yummy richness actually comes from the breast, like milk. This is partly because the soul is initially not completely differentiated from the libidinal object. There is also no differentiation at the beginning between the physical and the essential, and the animal orientation of the soul toward the external object becomes structured through this experience. But since there is rarely a complete and perfect satisfaction, the dissatisfaction becomes split off into this libidinal and frustrating object relation. When this object relation is finally understood in the inner journey, the soul regains her essential heart. She transforms from a hungry animal soul into a human soul with a rich and beautiful heart, a heart overflowing with richness, love, and fulfillment.

Both the rejecting and libidinal object relations arise at various levels of primitiveness and intensity. We have described them on the level where they are mainly contacted, that of the animal soul; but they may also manifest on the level of the soul child, in a less completely animalistic, instinctual way. On the level of the soul child, the alien hatred and power appear more as a child angry and hateful for being frustrated or neglected. It is the normal hatred that one experiences as a child, as part of various conflictual object relations. On the level of the soul child, the libidinal wanting appears mostly as the oedipal child passionately loving and wanting the parent of the opposite sex. There is desire and passion, but it is more discriminating than that of the animal soul; it is directed toward a human being, in fact toward a particular human being. We need to remember, however, that even though in our everyday life we generally encounter these object relations in the more structured and less primitive forms, their power and energy derive from the primitive animal level. Only by addressing this deeper and more fundamental dimension of these structures can we truly understand them and liberate our souls from their compulsive and limiting patterns.

The process of working through the primitive structures of the animal soul and the soul child requires that all three object relations be understood all the way to the clear, embodied experience and understanding of essential aspects related to them. We have not discussed the process of working through the central object relation, but this is the main structure that the inner work of the Diamond Approach addresses. To work through it means to render transparent its constituent self-images, which entails dealing with all the major ego structures. This involves working through the (normal) ego structure of being an autonomous individual with a unique identity. The autonomy structure is the subject matter of our book *The Pearl Beyond Price*, and the identity structure is the subject matter of *The Point of Existence*. Working through these ego structures leads to the self-realization of true nature and its individuation in personal life.[7] The two primitive object relations become clarified, and then are integrated into the clarified central object relation. More accurately, the soul develops into a mature and full soul, who experiences and recognizes essential presence as her nature and identity, but can also embody this realization in life, with her essential power and her rich, overflowing heart in harmony.

The primitive object relations have their forerunners in even more primitive structures, preverbal and prenatal.

Preconceptual Structures

The structures we have discussed so far are formed by impressing the soul with self-images in the process of ego development. The primitive forms, especially the libidinal soul, are less structured, but they do develop in the stages when memory and cognition are sufficient for the formation of mental representations. They include both direct impressions and mental images.

The preconceptual structures we will now discuss develop before there is cognitive development, so they are exclusively direct imprints of experience on the field of the soul. Strong impressions leave deep traces on the soul that structure it in a relatively permanent manner, forming the forerunners of actual ego structures. They develop before the soul has the capacity to identify with mental images and representations. They set the original template, the original general terrain of the soul's structure.

These structures are generally impressions of physical organs and processes that predominate at the beginning of life. Most of these seem to form the preconceptual foundation for the libidinal soul in particular. In fact, it is by inquiring deeply into the animal soul that we are able to discriminate these preconceptual structures, just as the primitive structures arise as we thoroughly explore ego structures. When the preconceptual structures arise they have a more physical component than the other structures; they tend to appear as various physical tensions and contractions. They do not feel like memories, so the visual component tends not to dominate. We simply sense that the substance of the soul is thick and inflexible, without mental content, with this thickness possessing shapes and forms. In the course of investigating these structures, memories might arise, but not necessarily. These memories tend to involve a telescoping of these early impressions with later but similar remembered impressions.

When we investigate the preconceptual structures they begin to reveal their meaning and origins, but this process generally feels vague and obscure. The fact that the soul was not so developed cognitively at the times these structures developed means they are impressions without a recognition or discerning of what the impressions mean or are. Therefore their experience is more like a regression than a remembering. The process of inquiry continues, but experience will feel amorphous, vague, and not so amenable to the normal discriminating faculty. In fact, it would be almost impossible to understand what these structures are and how they function if we were not able to be present in deep states of being, in particular at the level of nonconceptual mirror-like awareness, where there is differentiation of forms without discrimination or recognition. More precisely, we can effectively inquire into preconceptual levels of structure only when our field of consciousness can manifest in the nonconceptual dimension, because both lack concepts. But we also need to have integrated this dimension of true nature with that of basic knowledge; this integration makes it possible for our experience to be in the nonconceptual dimension, while at the same time the discriminating capacity can function, recognizing the forms and their meaning. Thus we can have cognitive insights even though we are investigating precognitive experiences.[8]

To investigate such a structure is to relive its original impressions, as a regression in the presence of essence in the nonconceptual and basic knowledge dimensions. One such structure may appear at the beginning as the experience of oneself as an empty bag with thick and muscular walls. The walls seem to have a living and dynamic quality, with undulations accompanied by sensations of hunger and satiation. It becomes clear that this is a stomach structure, with origins in the intense and recurrent sensations of hunger and satiation that are dominant in the first few months of life. This frequent and recurrent pattern leaves a deep and lasting impression in the soul, forming the core of the animal soul. This pattern is also the source of the outer-directedness of the adult soul. It is easy to understand how this structure develops when we appreciate the dominance of the feeding cycle early in the oral stage of development. The stomach contracts and releases many times a day, constituting the most intense and important process the infant's organism undergoes. This is bound to leave a deep imprint in the soul, an imprint that becomes one of the most lasting and influential ones throughout the whole of the life cycle.

The stomach wall structures the young soul, building a structure that feels like a bag with thick muscular walls whose affect is either hunger or satiation. Another form related to the stomach structure is that of the whole alimentary tract, beginning at the mouth and ending at the anus. This is a complex structure that feels like tubes and bulges connected together. Another structure is that of the mouth itself, where the soul feels like a big and hungry mouth and throat, which can only take in and swallow. We recognize we are dealing with this structure when we feel we want to relate to everything by swallowing it, whether it is food, knowledge, experience, people, and so on. We may find also anal structures, even urethral structures, but the oral ones tend to dominate because the oral stage precedes the anal. We might also find structures related to early illness, or early physical confinement, for example an impression of a cast on a limb, or impressions related to an incubator.

The process of working through these structures has the same stages as we have described. One becomes aware of a rigidity structuring experience, which upon investigation reveals an underlying emptiness; the understanding of this emptiness leads to the emergence of essence in one or more of its aspects or dimensions. Working through her early, preverbal, precognitive, or preconceptual structures tends to lead the soul's experience to very subtle and deep dimensions of true nature. It is these structures that, if not worked through, form a hindrance to the clear experience and integration of the basic, mainly noncognitive dimensions of true nature. However, because these structures tend to block the soul's openness to such deep levels of presence they also function as barriers to more discriminated aspects of presence, for essence is not organized like a layered cake but more as coextensive interpenetrating dimensions.

Prenatal Structures

Prenatal structures are a subcategory of preconceptual structures, but are earlier and more primitive, formed during uterine life. Since the soul is the animating consciousness, she is present commingled with the body throughout prenatal life. Various spiritual teachings put the conjunction of soul and body at various times in prenatal life, but the differences generally involve the first week or two, and mostly in regard to whether the soul is present all the time or intermittently at the beginning. Embryonic development is an intense growth process, during which organs form and function, the body systems develop, and the whole organism differentiates into an amazing complexity from very simple building blocks. This rich and eventful process impacts the impressionable soul, and some of these impacts survive as rudimentary structuring, depending on the intensity or duration of a particular process or physical structure. These impressions become the initial "grooves" in the soul, influencing and orienting future development.[9]

We recognize three sources of structure in prenatal life. First, since the sensitive field of consciousness is completely inseparable from the physical organism, intense physical processes with their anatomical development will impress the soul with more or less permanent structures. The impact of a new anatomical development, at the beginning as bulges and tubes but later on more complex and complete, leaves long-lasting impressions, impressions that become the initial blueprint for ego structures in general. Second, major prenatal events, especially difficult ones, will also leave long-lasting impressions on the soul. These include difficult initial implantation, the umbilical cord wrapping tightly around the developing embryo, and similar events.[10]

Third, the state of the holding environment, in this case the mother and her womb, may imprint the soul with either positive or negative impressions. This can be the general influence of the mother's health, her emotional state, and whether she takes medications, alcohol, cigarettes, or drugs. These will directly affect the state of the soul because the soul cannot differentiate herself from her environment. She will feel the mother's inner states, and will be affected by her physical condition, but will experience it happening in her own field; thus these impacts will form impressions that will later be integrated into her sense of identity.[11]

It is our observation that when inquiring into preconceptual structures, one eventually encounters structures that cannot be understood without considering the structuring impact of prenatal experience. These are even vaguer and more difficult to recognize than the other three types. For instance, in deep stages of the unfoldment of the soul you may experience yourself as wrapped with something thick and tight. You might physically feel as if you are in a straightjacket, tight and thick, but there are no accompanying memories, images, or specific feelings. You feel hemmed in, maybe vaguely depressed. Upon exploration you recognize that there is a thick and tight boundary around you that makes you feel contracted, but not as an emotional reaction. This may then reveal that there is some movement, some convulsing pulsation in the walls around you. You feel you want to get out, but it is not really up to you. This is an experience of a structure that developed in the womb toward the end of pregnancy, where the uterine wall, because of the size of the embryo at this stage, molded the soul's sensitivity strongly and continuously until it created a lasting impression. Unable to differentiate her own body from the wall of the womb, the soul incorporates its pattern into her own structure.

Being in touch with this structure can lead to birth experiences of various kinds, but the exploration of structures is a different category than a birth experience. The birth experience may give us the sense of freedom and release, and may have profound consequences for our development, but it might not make this structure transparent.[12] To work through a soul structure is first to recognize it as a structure that patterns our experience, and to see how this appears in various situations in our life. Then the particulars of this structure reveal an underlying emptiness, the understanding of which ushers us to some aspect of the experience of our true nature. This experience of true nature is the most important part of the process of working through a structure; without it the process will only have a limited therapeutic effect.

Another structure that arises for students is the placental object relation structure. One experiences oneself as an undefined entity of some sort, literally connected to a bigger something through something that delivers nutrition from the big object. This is not merely a self-structure; it is a whole object relation, but in a very primitive form, which one senses in a way that feels neither clearly physical or psychological. The affective mood of this placental object relation seems to be determined largely by the emotional and physical condition of the mother during pregnancy. This seems to function as the original prototype that develops in later ego development into the central object relation, for this object relation is crystallized around impressions of good enough mothering, where the soul was receiving something useful from the object.

Another structure is the amniotic sac; here the soul experiences herself as a thin and transparent sac full of partially clear fluid. The walls of the sac feel soft and flexible, however they function to give the soul a sense of boundary. This amniotic sac structure generally feels good, pleasant, and relaxed, but gives the soul the sense of being a separate entity, a separateness that becomes challenged by the boundless dimensions of true nature. This initial impression of being a bounded entity, the imprint of the early development of the zygote, becomes one of the forerunners of development, later filled out by ego structuring, into the separating boundaries of the ego that are normally modeled according to the skin contours of the body.

We have also observed a whole family of prenatal structures that are imprints from early embryonic development. These generally take the form of tubes and bulges of various kinds and combinations, reflecting the morphology of these early stages.[13] At the beginning the zygote differentiates and develops into three tubes, out of the three layers of the original disc. These tubes are dominant physical structures at a time when the soul is quite impressionable. The imprint of these prenatal tubes functions as a forerunner of ego separating boundaries. More accurately, the early tubular structure of the embryo imprints the soul with a form that becomes an initial body image according to which the sense of separating boundaries develops. This is, we believe, the reason that when we inquire into the ego separating boundaries we frequently find a structure in the shape of a tube along the body. The soul contracts and forms a tube, which sometimes feels like plastic, that gives her the sense of being an autonomous entity.

One of the primitive forerunners of the rejecting object relation is a soul structure that appears as feelings of not being welcomed or wanted. Upon investigation we can discern this structure in the form of something that wants to attach itself to something else but is not able to, as if it is repulsed. This is a prenatal structure that students frequently encounter, modeled on the process of the fertilized egg trying to implant but having difficulty in the process.[14] It is amazing how the sense of being rejected can start so early when there are no differentiated affects yet, just an impression of a physical process that develops, by integrating more highly structured experiences of being rejected into the rejecting object relation. This shows how far one needs to go to be liberated from these basic object relations that structure one's soul.

Prenatal structures can date to earlier times. Some individuals encounter structures that predate fertilization, as the sperm or ovum. The sperm structure normally manifests as an energetic condition when one feels that one needs to always be on the move, that one cannot rest, or some important opportunity will be lost. Investigating these feelings may take us to feeling small and running fast, running without looking back, but full of the total impulse to go fast and get someplace, without knowing where.

These examples of very early structures give us a sense of the depth to which the inner journey goes in the process of the liberation of the soul. This discussion also shows us the depth and extent of the structuring of the soul through which we become shackled before we are even conscious of our ourselves. We need to also point out that these structures are very subtle; we do not encounter them so clearly in our everyday experience. Though these primitive structures underlie our everyday experience, we cannot discern them until we have made transparent the more superficial structures built on top of them.

PART FOUR

The Inner Journey of the Soul

15 The Inner Journey

WE HAVE SEEN THAT ESSENCE is central to the process of the soul's inner journey of liberation and development. From the perspective of the relationship of the soul to essential presence, the inner journey can be divided into three subjourneys: the journey to presence; the journey with presence; and the journey in presence.

Three Journeys of Presence

The first journey is the entry into the path, undergoing initial preparation and setting the ground. This includes the work of developing one's orientation and inner capacities, and the initial work of learning to be present and to inquire into one's experience. This journey culminates in the discovery of the presence of Essence, and in learning to recognize it in its various qualities.

The transition from the first to the second journey is not marked by a particular experience, but by a process of discovery whose central element is the initial experience and recognition of presence. This has two phases. The first is the recognition of the medium of the soul, which is presence, generally experienced mixed with structures and impressions. This recognition is the discovery of a living presence that feels to us to be the core of the human being, what makes a human being both human and Being. On directly recognizing the medium of the soul, we feel we know what humanity is, for we are aware of its inner truth and potential. We may in fact feel in contact with all of humanity, for we feel the part of us that is the same in all humanity.

Through the recognition of the soul we develop the vessel of the inner journey, the consciousness that goes through the clarification and purification. (See chapter 2.) The second phase of transition from the first journey to the second journey is the activation of the subtle centers of the *lataif*, which is a system of centers through which the primary essential aspects operate.[1] We activate the *lataif* through concentration meditation and color visualization with music, in the context of a guided process of inquiry into the relevant elements of one's experience. These methods can open the soul to the arising of essence in its various aspects, and to her recognition of essence as immaculate and perfect presence. We have discussed in detail this process of the discovery and experience of essence as presence in our books *Essence* and *Diamond Heart, Book 1*. The recognition of essence as presence is the fundamental insight of the first journey, without which we cannot move to the second journey, the journey with presence. In this recognition we directly and immediately experience and know what our true nature is, beyond mind and history.

In the second journey, essence continues to unfold in its various aspects and dimensions. This is where most of the essential development of the soul occurs, as a process of her integrating the arising essence, which is the same as essence impacting her.

The process of essential development takes the soul from her initial condition at the completion of ego development, in which she is dissociated from her true nature and living mostly as the animal soul with a civilized veneer of ego structures, to the station of the human soul. In other words, the discovery and integration of essence transforms the soul from its condition of being primarily an animal soul to the state of being primarily a human soul, a soul with heart.[2] What transforms the animal soul to the human soul is her becoming receptive and transparent to essence. When essence manifests through the attitudes and actions of the soul we recognize that she now behaves in a more human way, with heart. This is primarily the task of the second journey of presence, the journey with presence. The soul journeys here in the company of presence, receptive to it and guided by it.

As the soul integrates her essence in its various qualities, she matures and develops her virtues, capacities, and faculties. The process of maturation includes two complementary sides. The first is that of individuation, centered around the aspect of the personal essence. This is the pearl beyond price, which the soul becomes in the midst of her life in the world. The pearl beyond price is the essential prototype of integration, and the soul experiences it as the presence of the soul as an essential person. This personal presence is characterized by maturity, individuation, and personal essential development.[3] It functions as the crystallizing point and the integration prototype around which the soul integrates all her personal experiences of her potential arising in interaction with the events of everyday life.

The pearl can also be seen as the essential structure that the soul develops as she metabolizes and transcends her ego structure. Ego structure gives the ego-self the sense of being an autonomous and unique individual. But this structure is constructed through fixed mental impressions in the soul; hence it both dissociates her from her essential ground and limits her development because of its rigidity and fixation. The essential pearl provides the soul with a sense of individuality and personhood that does not depend on fixed impressions, but on spontaneously arising forms of essential presence that structure her experience of herself and give her the capacity to function as a person. The soul matures and transforms into a person of essence. However, the qualities and actions of this person are quite fluid and flexible and are objective responses resonant to the needs and inputs of the environment. We have discussed this aspect and its integration in great detail in *The Pearl Beyond Price*, and in *Diamond Heart, Book 2*. The other side of the process of maturation of the soul under the impact of essence is that of the self-realization of true nature. During the second journey, the soul experiences essence mainly as an interior essence, as the preciousness that the soul inherently possesses, that inspires and guides the soul, and provides her with inner sustenance and support. At this point the soul still experiences essence dualistically. She recognizes essence as her nature, but does not feel herself identical to it. She is a soul who experiences her essence. A process then ensues, activated by the aspect of essential identity, the point of existence, that illuminates the barriers limiting the soul in her identification with her essence. This exposes the identity of ego as the primary barrier, because the soul still identifies herself historically and through ego structures. The process of going through these particular ego structures confronts the soul with the inherent narcissism of ego. The transcendence of this narcissism is self-realization. The soul realizes her essence not only as her nature but as her very identity. The soul begins to know herself as identical with essential presence. Here the duality of soul and essence begins to be bridged. The soul recognizes that she is the simplicity and exquisiteness of timeless presence. We have discussed in great detail the work on narcissism and the self-realization of essence in *The Point of Existence*, and the first half of *Diamond Heart, Book 3*.

The realization of the personal essence and that of essential identity are two different processes, each with its own stages and characteristics. The most important difference, however, is that the realization of the personal essence involves mostly a development while that of the essential identity mostly a discovery. The realization of the Pearl Beyond Price requires the soul to mature and individuate in her personal life, while the realization of essential identity is a matter of penetrating the false self and the discovery of the real self, essence as one's identity. Both the maturation of the soul into a pearl and the experience of self-realization of essence usher the soul into the third journey, the journey in presence. The soul is abiding in presence as presence. At this stage the journey is the development of nonduality. The soul's journey is inseparable from essential presence; this journey is the process of integrating everything into this nondual presence. This process again has two phases or two complementary sides. The first is the essential development of the soul, what we call the essentialization of the soul. It is the complete mixing with essence, where she is not only transparent to it, but this transparency becomes so complete that the two become one.[4] This is the nondual soul, where she and essence are one, a dynamic presence in which all contents of experience are forms of this presence displayed by its creative dynamism. The soul continues to be soul, but her medium is completely essentialized. She is completely the pure, immaculate, and transparent presence of essence, but now this presence has attained the dynamism and the morphing functionality of the soul. Alternately, she is the dynamic and living presence, morphing itself into the various forms and patterns of experience, but these forms are completely essential.

To illustrate, when the soul experiences herself as the love aspect of essence she experiences herself as the presence of love. She is love, and love is presence with sweet and appreciative characteristics. When the soul functions she has various degrees of transparency to this presence of love. Although she can be love before complete clarification, when she functions her actions will not be absolutely loving, for she retains limiting impressions that separate her functioning from the presence of love. However, when the soul is essentialized she is totally inseparable from the presence of love. She is completely transparent to the aspect of love, so transparent to it that she is completely indistinguishable from it, fully coemergent with it. The soul is a dynamic functioning medium, but now fully coemergent with the presence of love. Her action now is love acting. She is not only love, but she is loving in a complete and full way. She is a presence that expresses itself dynamically as loving action. The dynamism and the presence of love are inseparable, coemergent.

This essentialization can include all aspects. So the soul's action can be intelligent, compassionate, clear, steadfast, etc., in a total and full way. And this action can be physical, expressive, or mental. She is presence of essence, but also a dynamic living presence whose morphogenic transformations express the pure perfections of true nature. In this transformation the soul has progressed from the stage of the human soul, the attainment of the second journey, to the stage of the angelic soul, or the essential soul.[5] The second side of the development of nonduality in the journey in presence has to do with essential presence manifesting its ground of true nature. Essence here reveals itself not only as the ontological nature of the soul but as the ontological nature of all existence, all manifestation. True nature begins to reveal its omnipresence, disclosing that it is the ground and nature of everything. This appears as true nature revealing its boundless and formless dimensions that transcend the limited boundaries of the ego-self, even the individuality or personhood of the soul. The soul does not experience herself here as an individual soul, but as a boundless and nonlocal presence that transcends all spatial extensions, as eternal nowness that transcends all time, and as a mystery that transcends all determinations. She is all and everything, she is Reality.[6]

In the realization of the boundless dimensions of Being we learn about true nature in and of itself, free from the limitations of separateness, and beyond all forms and manifestations. Nonduality is now complete, for it has integrated the whole of existence, not merely soul with her essence. We will discuss this in more detail in later chapters. We discussed the boundless dimensions briefly in the last part of *The Point of Existence*, where the focus is on the self-realization of each of these dimensions, and the last part of *The Pearl Beyond Price*, where the focus is on the personalization or individuation of them. *Diamond Heart, Book 3*, deals with one of these dimensions in its second half, while the later books in this series all deal with this boundlessness and formlessness of true nature.

Issues of Essential Development

We see that essential development goes through stages, beginning with the recognition of the dynamic field and medium of the soul. Then essence arises in its various aspects, resolving the soul's issues and providing her with the real elements necessary for her life and development. Next the diamond vehicles arise, providing the soul with a personal, direct, and objective knowledge and wisdom about true nature and its relationship to the soul and her life. This wisdom transforms the soul further, and she becomes able to transcend her most fundamental structures and limitations, and to open up to the presentation of true nature in its primordial ground, with its formless and boundless dimensions.

In this process the soul, with the help of essence and its wisdom, confronts her various limitations, obscurations, and opaque structures. Essential diamond guidance sharpens her inquiry and gives it the capacity to penetrate and transcend these barriers. These limitations appear as issues of different types, reflecting the characteristics of the barriers and of true nature. The various types and levels of issues are interconnected; although many wisdom traditions focus on certain of these issues in isolation, it is actually artificial to dissociate them in one's personal work. We find that the various levels of personal issues follow a natural progression in the unfoldment of the soul in the inner journey, but only in terms of predominance; for they all continue to be interconnected throughout the whole journey. In the Diamond Approach, we organize them into the following categories, which we discuss briefly here in the order of predominance: psychodynamic issues, structural issues, existential issues, and epistemological/phenomenological issues.

Psychodynamic Issues

These are the barriers and limitations due to past experience and its repression. Conditioning is the result of impressions from the past, and tends to remain outside of consciousness, functioning automatically. Exploring psychodynamic issues reveals to the soul how many of its experiences, attitudes, and actions are influenced by unconscious conflicts, beliefs, and feelings. When one inquires into them, they reveal the related unconscious material. The soul then might recall various events in her early experience, including traumas and abuses, wounds and rejections, intolerable conflicts and deprivations.

Sigmund Freud discovered that the human individual manages to develop in spite of early intolerable difficulties by avoiding awareness of them through various methods of repression. This repressed material does not disappear but remains hidden in what he termed the unconscious, exerting a powerful force on conscious experience, actions, and dreams. One of the momentous discoveries of modern psychology, this made it possible to engage in therapeutic psychodynamic work, which is the retracing of conflictual and painful manifestations and symptoms to their unconscious roots, and then releasing the early conditioning. The ancient wisdom traditions did not have this understanding; hence their psychologies and methods could not and did not deal with this level of barriers to the soul's liberation and realization.

To explore an example of working on psychodynamic issues, we can look at one of the presenting issues of the strength aspect. The issue might present itself as a difficulty with anger and aggression, as a stance of passivity and weakness. Exploring this issue may reveal a fear of aggression, which then may remind the soul of the anger she encountered in her early environment, in the person of her father or mother. Making the fear conscious and remembering its source will help the soul to access her own anger, since she is in reality no longer a child who must be passive in the face of the anger of the more powerful adult. Exploring the energy of this emotion can reveal its connection to strength. Anger turns out to be a distortion of essential strength; that is, the quality of strength becomes caught up in the emotion of anger, which is itself caught up in the self-image of being a child in relation to the parents. In this example, the soul was afraid to own up to her strength because of fear of her parents' anger. So she abandoned and repressed her strength, and its resultant distortion, anger. Working through this issue opens the quality of strength in the soul.

Structural Issues

Simply dealing with psychodynamic issues is not sufficient for essential development, for the main barriers to essence are not psychodynamic. Developmental psychology discovered that the psyche develops through a structuration process, as discussed in chapter 12, where we saw that the sense of being an individual with identity and character is a developmental achievement. Furthermore, repression is the function of some of the structures built in early childhood; this is an important element of the connection between structure and psychodynamics.

Structural issues appear in two types. The first is the kind of issue familiar in psychological and psychotherapeutic work. These are the conflicts and inadequacies reflecting difficulties in the development of ego structures. They include difficulties of identity, ego boundaries, ego weakness, superego malformations, issues regarding relating and merging, isolation, and so on. Psychologists call these structural difficulties, which can be so severe as to manifest in psychoses of various kinds. In fact, every ego has some malformation or inadequacy of structure, since no one is blessed with perfect parents or a completely untroubled developmental history.

The second type of structural issue that appears in the process of realization and essential development includes issues not normally seen as problematic by psychologists. These issues center around the fixation on structure itself, concern with the presence of and the need for such ego structures. Such structures, even the deepest and most primitive universal structures, as we saw in chapters 13 and 14, are inherently limiting to the soul's potential and liberation.

We return to our example of working through the issues regarding the strength essence to illustrate the structural level of issues that expose the barriers to the soul's liberation. As the soul begins to be open to her aggression and anger, and allows herself to feel strong, she may encounter new difficulties. Now she finds new and deeper barriers to experiencing the essential quality of strength, even though she can be somewhat open to anger and aggression. Continuing her exploration, the soul becomes aware of a sense of weakness, which actually feels like an identification with weakness that the soul is not able to transcend. Further inquiry reveals an image of being a weak person that has become part of the soul's identity. This identification is not a matter of repression; rather, it is character and structure. Inquiring into this image, the soul may find that as a child she disowned her strength not only because of fear of others' anger, but because if she had felt strong she would have felt able to stand up to her mother, and even to be separate from her. This insight might reveal conflicts around separation from her mother, a separation that is appropriate at a certain stage of ego development. She may, for instance, discover that her mother could not tolerate the child separating from her, and wanted her to continue to be the mother's dependent little girl. Because of guilt and compassion for her mother, plus the fear of her wrath, the child resisted acting or even feeling separate. Therefore, in order to stay close to her mother the child abandoned and continues to ward off her separation drive, which necessitates disowning and repressing her strength.

Thus not only is the essential strength repressed, but as the child's self structures are being built, a part of this structure will include an identification of being without strength, of being a weak child. This first kind of structural issue relates to difficulties in the soul's process of structure building, part of which is the gradual separation necessary for establishing independent images of herself. However, in the inner journey, we do not stop here. As the soul begins to understand this issue and resolve it, her identification with weakness will become conscious and thus can be dissolved, especially as the strength essence arises, giving her the capacity to be separate and autonomous. Learning that real strength is presence the soul begins to recognize her essence and experience herself as its presence. However, this is a profound shift in her experience of herself, where now she knows herself as an ontological presence rather than as a mental structure built from historical impressions. Recognizing herself as this presence is a much more profound separation from her mother and other objects than her normal ego structure can handle, for this structure is always related to internalized images of others, primarily the mother.

To recognize oneself as presence involves a fundamental separation, a separation she has never consciously experienced before, in which she is separating from the whole dimension of images and ego structures. This is too radical a separation for any psychic structure, and she begins to feel she will fall apart and lose the integrity of her self and identity. In other words, presence exposes the mental and constructed nature of her usual sense of self, and reveals how it limits her capacity to be this presence. She needs to go beyond ego structure in order to be presence, but this movement discloses any weaknesses she has in this structure, and raises the possibility of its destructuring. This is the second category of structural issues that arise in the inner journey; these issues have been addressed in different ways by all the wisdom traditions. These issues reflect the soul's limitation of being structured through the mind, of having ego separateness and an independent self. They are connected to the basic delusion of ego, that it has a separate and autonomous self, existence, will, and so on.[7]

We see, however, that the two kinds of structural issues are connected, for the ease or difficulty in letting go of ego structures reflects the condition and the developmental history of these structures. Furthermore, they are both related to psychodynamic issues, for a large part of the history of this development is repressed, due to intolerable childhood experiences and conflicts. In dealing with these structural issues we begin to appreciate how they are connected to the other categories of issues.

Existential Issues

Existential issues are related to the normal limitations of being a human being living in a world with others. These issues include questions, conflicts, and suffering in relation to desire and desirelessness, gratification and frustration, intimacy and isolation, relatedness and aloneness, love and aggression, instinct and morality, limitation and finitude, transitoriness and mortality, choice and accident, meaning and emptiness, being and nothingness, fear and dread, and so on. These issues reflect the fact that the soul has both animal and essential potential, that she is unrealized without knowing it or knowing that there is any alternative. The soul lives an embodied life with its normal limitations and frustrations, which are compounded by her ignorance of her true nature.

These issues tend to arise naturally in life, especially during transitions and intense events, but they also are brought forth intensely due to the inner work. They arise especially as the soul learns to penetrate and transcend her ego structure. To follow our example, when the soul begins to see the limitation of structure and experiences herself as presence, the structure begins to reveal its nature as a mental construct characterized by past conditioning, ideas, memories, etc. The soul begins to experience an inner emptiness, a meaninglessness, a dread of falling apart, and terror of death and annihilation. These experiences of falling apart or being annihilated actually come to pass as the structures dissolve. The soul experiences disintegration and dissolution, disorientation, and a loss of identity; she feels lost and despondent. These existential crises are actually elements of some stages of working through ego structures that then lead to deeper realizations of true nature, moving to timelessness and formlessness.

These developments in turn bring about a profound sense of aloneness, for the presence of Being is not connected psychically to any internalized object relation; it is autonomous from the structured sense of self that consists of representations of the self in relation to others. At the beginning the soul inevitably experiences this transcendence as aloneness, which tends to bring a fear of loss of contact, relatedness, connection, and communication. However, deep and persistent inquiry reveals the intrinsic intimacy of essential presence, whose boundlessness and formlessness constitute a much more fundamental connectedness than that known by the ego-self. The soul contends with the notion of death and the fear of death, and learns, with persistent inquiry, that her true nature transcends both life and death, for it is the pure consciousness that forms the eternal ground of all phenomena. We see, then, that even though the inner journey confronts us, often painfully, with existential issues, the experience and understanding of essence provides resolution and a depth of wisdom not envisaged by existential philosophy or any form of psychotherapy.

Phenomenological and Epistemological Issues

The phenomenological and epistemological issues on the inner journey are connected to each other, and are also inseparable from the three above. The phenomenology of essential presence presents a challenge to the worldview of the conventional ego structures of the soul. Essence is known phenomenologically and not discursively: that is, it is apprehended directly through intimate contact and identity. For the soul to experience essence she must drop her normal experiential mode, which is dominated by ordinary knowledge, and let her consciousness immerse itself in basic knowledge. In other words, her epistemological stance needs to shift in order for her to experience her true nature, and especially in order to abide in it. She also needs to learn about experience without labeling, discrimination without abstraction, perception without conceptualization, even consciousness without content. Ultimately the soul must radically change her view of reality, which at times may entail abandoning the thinking process, letting go of her perspectives and her knowledge, and occasionally dropping the discriminating mind altogether. These developments bring up both existential fears and structural issues; they also involve dealing with intellectual attachment and pride, vanity and ignorance, confusion and dullness, and vulnerability and defenselessness. As well, the soul faces the inherent epistemological difficulty of making this kind of jump. This requires not only deep and subtle knowledge, discipline, devoted application, and concentration, but also a great deal of precision in perception and experience, courage in beholding the unknown, and an adventurous spirit. These issues are traditionally the most difficult barriers to realization and enlightenment, which are symbolized by mind-challenging paradoxical terms such as "the gateless gate."[8]

We find that the difficulty with these issues stems partly from their intertwining with structural and psychodynamic ones. As the soul continues to experience her essential presence and begins to recognize how profoundly this reality is beyond mind, she can again become terrified. To go beyond the mind is to go beyond the realm of ego structure, memory, and history: that is, beyond where her accustomed identity grew. The possible loss of identity and structure is greater than ever before, for now deep and primitive structures are exposed, substrata that she has taken all this time to be bedrock reality. The structural fears that arise can also be associated to earlier times of not knowing, vulnerability, and loss of control that accompanied trauma, sickness, loss, or abuse. The epistemological shift brings up psychodynamic material—emotions and conflicts—that make it difficult to stay focused on the purely epistemological task, or attend to the purely phenomenological characteristics of being, which are quite subtle.

To return to our example of the soul's process in the inner journey, we see that as the soul learns about the intrinsic aloneness of essential presence she begins to recognize that she leaves not only the world of object relations when she is presence; by realizing presence and understanding the separation of the red essence, she leaves the totality of her discriminating mind in this radical separation. This can bring up fear of losing her mind, of going crazy, of the unknown, and so on. She also begins to realize how her normal epistemological stance is a great barrier to the continuity and development of her essential realization. She feels the need to go not only beyond her memory but beyond all concepts, for she understands that such concepts are the elementary building blocks of the memories and images that compose her ego structures, structures that limit her realization. Of course, at this juncture true nature can provide the guidance and support to go beyond the conceptual mind; for it is the authentic reality that is transcendent to the mind and that functions as its eternal ground and source.

As the soul begins to realize her identity beyond mind, she may return to existential issues. Going beyond mind will initially appear to the soul as going beyond the world, which again raises fears and concerns regarding isolation, aloneness, possibility of loss of love and relationship, and so on. Most deeply it means separation; for at this point it becomes clear that the world stands for mother, who was the whole world at the beginning of the soul's life. In other words, an epistemological issue can bring up existential, structural, and psychodynamic ones, if these are not completely resolved. The wisdom and guidance of true nature can reveal the projections on and ignorance of the phenomenology of Being, an ignorance that the soul fills with her physical and atomistic view. True nature reveals that its Riemannian manifold embraces all of Reality, transforming the worldview of the soul, and penetrating her original and primordial ignorance. We have presented here the barest outlines of these categories of issues faced by the soul on her inner journey. We have discussed them in some detail in *The Void*, *The Pearl Beyond Price*, and *The Point of Existence*, and will discuss them further in the next few chapters.

Diamond Vehicles

The process of the soul's journey is assisted by the arising of certain structures of essential wisdom, which we call the "diamond vehicles." These vehicles show us that real wisdom can only come from true nature. They are often experienced as messengers from the source of the soul, teaching her about this source and guiding her return to it.[9] These messengers do not function like human messengers, but more like encrypted computer programs that, when their encryption is penetrated, unfold according to a specific content and logic, like a dynamic holographic multidimensional virtual reality. They arise within our field of experience to unveil in this field the deepest and most fundamental truths of its nature and ground.

The diamond vehicles function like spaceships, carrying our consciousness to exotic worlds. Each one takes us to a different universe, with different qualities constituting the building blocks of reality. They resemble spaceships in that they are vehicles that travel in inner space, taking our attention to the furthest reaches of Reality. They also resemble spaceships in how they are perceived: they appear as gem-like structures of various shapes and forms, with scintillating colored lights. Their impact on the consciousness of the soul includes deep hums and intense vibrations, filling her with awe, astonishment, transport, and delight.[10] The docking station for these spaceships is the medium of the soul itself; the substance of the soul is imbued with the particular sacred quality of each vehicle as it descends into consciousness.

The diamond vehicles are not entities separate from the multidimensional manifold of the soul, but manifestations of its infinite potential, appearing as this manifold morphs itself into these majestic structures, as it morphs its field into sacred space.

In the Diamond Approach, there is no attempt to visualize or create such forms in our consciousness. The teachers do not even describe the shapes precisely to their students. They are actual manifestations of true nature, which emerge when the soul is ready and her consciousness is oriented in a way that corresponds to a given vehicle's mode of consciousness and operation. The inner inquiry naturally opens the soul to such manifestations; the soul does not need to know about them; she does not need to even know that such things exist. In the experience of the author, these vehicles manifested totally without any expectations or prior knowledge. Their arrival was a total surprise, and their forms and functions are beyond any human imagination or intelligence.

Each faceted gem of the diamond vehicles is an essential aspect with the objective and precise knowledge of what it is from the perspective of essence itself. Each presents the precise knowledge and understanding of one of the perfections of true nature. Each is the universal knowledge of a ray of colored light differentiated out of the colorless clear light of true nature.

Each vehicle is a whole body of knowledge, a complete dimension of wisdom that relates to an important segment of the soul's experience and functionality, and particularly to what is needed for her inner journey home.[11] Each vehicle appears at some juncture of the inner journey, responding to the needs of the soul at this particular phase, and presents its overall view and knowledge, which is a new synthesis of the knowledge of the soul, essence, and their relationship. Then the specific and precise details of this objective knowledge are provided by each diamond of the vehicle. Thus this dimension of essential wisdom appears as the vehicle itself, a structure that combines all the essential diamonds of this dimension, and/or as the diamonds that appear singly, or as a few of them together, not in the vehicular structure. Each diamond presents an essential aspect on the level of its objective wisdom. This refines and completes the understanding of the particular aspect, which in turn deepens and completes the understanding of its relation to the soul, including further understanding and resolution of the soul's barriers against it.[12]

We will discuss each vehicle briefly, presenting the general outline of its dimension of wisdom. We cannot give a detailed discussion of each vehicle; such an endeavor would require a separate book as big as the present one for each of the vehicles. We briefly discussed the diamond vehicles in a previous work, *The Pearl Beyond Price*, Book Three, part 2. There, however, we discussed them only in the context of their relevance for the realization of the pearl beyond price. This realization is part of the development of the soul; it is specifically the process of her essential individuation. But the inner journey includes much more than this realization, even though this is a central and important one. It includes the self-realization of true nature in all its dimensions, the essentialization of the soul, and many other processes. We will briefly describe four of the various vehicles, referencing our other books in which various vehicles are discussed. The Diamond Approach includes ten primary vehicles.

Diamond Guidance

This vehicle is the essential *nous* that we discussed in chapter 4; it is the subject of our book *Spacecruiser Inquiry*. We also discuss this vehicle briefly in chapter 17 of *The Pearl Beyond Price*, where we refer to it as diamond consciousness. When the soul has an attitude of open and open-ended inquiry, desiring to know the truth out of love for the truth, this vehicle can appear with a form of wisdom that helps the soul to understand the barriers to her realization. Illumination and understanding appear as the vehicle supports the precise discrimination of basic knowledge in the soul's experience. Without excluding the usefulness of ordinary knowledge, this vehicle penetrates the opacity of the usual ordinary knowledge that tends to structure the soul's experience.

Markabah

Each diamond vehicle is associated with a presenting issue, whose resolution opens the soul in a particular way, correcting her orientation so that she can assume the necessary attitude and state for the descent of the particular vehicle. The issue for the Markabah[13] is the pleasure principle, and in general the external orientation that dominates the ego-self. Because the soul is structured in a way that dissociates her from her essential nature, in the normal course of ego development the soul becomes predominantly an animal soul with a civilized veneer. She inherits from the animal soul its external orientation, which is reinforced by the early dependency of the human infant, as we discussed in chapters 10 and 11. The soul is powerfully driven by the animal instincts, dominated by the need for gratification. Gratification is the pleasurable satisfaction of her desires, whether they are for safety and security, company and intimacy, sexual and physical pleasure, or for anything else she craves. Structured thus, the soul grows up adhering to two deep delusions: that the purpose of life is the gratification of her desires; and that the objects of gratification exist outside her in the physical world. She becomes enmeshed in a life of seeking instinctual gratification, ruled by the pleasure principle, which is seeking pleasure and avoiding pain.

The love of truth, which the soul has learned in the course of her inner journey and through which she has invited the assistance of the diamond guidance, comes up against this basic human orientation. The soul recognizes that to continue to love truth selflessly requires a huge shift in her view of life and her orientation in living it. She sees that truth must come before pleasure, and that she must look inward for what she needs. Most human beings are not willing to make this shift, and are not even convinced of its truth or necessity. The conventionally conditioned soul is not only wedded to the orientation of seeking pleasure externally, but this orientation is part of a larger one, which is her allegiance to the world and loyalty to its view. This orientation has its roots in the soul's very early experience of receiving pleasurable gratification from her mother. This early gratification creates an amazingly deep bond, such that the soul grows up deeply loyal to the mother who satisfied her needs and desires. Every soul with normal ego development grows up deeply, though often unconsciously, loyal to her mothering person, the first love object and object of gratification.[14]

Thus the soul has a much deeper loyalty to her initial object of gratification than most of us suspect. The power of this attachment does not become clear until it is brought up in deep levels of the soul's inner journey. In our work this issue arises in connection with the experience and integration of the diamond vehicle called the Markabah, the diamond vehicle having to do with pleasure. The soul's loyalty to the historical object of gratification and to the orientation associated with it is libidinal, emotional, and philosophical. The mother, or breast, was the first external object and hence the prototype of such objects. Each time the soul relates to an object of gratification, or a love object, the soul cannot help but relate to it in a way that is similar to how she related to her mother. She values it as a source of pleasurable satisfaction and fulfillment; at the same time, she has a deep and committed allegiance to it. But the fact that the first object of gratification is an object that the soul comes to recognize as separate from her and outside her, deeply conditions her to expect pleasure, satisfaction, and fulfillment only from external objects. This expectation becomes the libidinal foundation of the materialistic and worldly view of reality, the view that the animal soul adheres to totally. The first instinctual object and love object, the mother, becomes projected onto later objects, and onto the world, for mother was not only the first object but, at the beginning, the whole world for the infant. The externality of the first object makes the soul, at some point, project this onto all objects that she considers outside herself, onto the totality of manifestation.

The soul comes up against this deeply entrenched view of reality when she begins to learn to love truth for its own sake, especially when this truth turns out to be inside her, for it is the truth of her nature. She experiences a deep conflict between her love of truth and her love of pleasure and allegiance to its external sources. When the soul learns at some point to make this significant shift, and turns toward the truth, this turn becomes the state or station that invites the descent of the Markabah. This is the diamond body of pleasure, bliss, delight, and celebration, which arises as the soul's love of truth deepens and becomes a true turning away from the habitual egoic orientation and toward authentic loyalty and allegiance to the truth. The turn of the soul's heart is not a turn away from pleasure; it is simply the shift of allegiance from the pleasure of gratification and its sources, to the inner truth of the soul and Reality. The soul moves her allegiance toward truth, understanding its centrality and value irrespective of whether the truth is pleasurable or painful. This turn is the necessary condition for the descent of this diamond vehicle, which turns out to be what gives the soul the desire and the capacity to transcend her egoic pleasure orientation.

This becomes easier to understand if we remember the nondual unity of soul and essence; when the soul is turning toward truth and developing allegiance to it, she is already being impacted by the approach of this essential form, causing this particular issue to arise. As the soul works with this issue, which is being pushed to the surface in clear relief by the grace of Being in the form of the Markabah, and as she manages to make the turn because of her commitment to the truth which she has developed in her previous work, she finally becomes open to the direct and explicit manifestation of this form of grace.

In the process of the inner journey, everything is interconnected in a magical way. As the soul exerts her effort and sincerity and develops her love of truth, she awakens and invites more help from true nature, in the form of new manifestations of essence that then help her progress further.

The soul's turn toward truth must be heartfelt, genuine, and deep. When she finally reaches this station, she begins to hear the sweet and merry music of the chariot. By turning toward truth, even at the cost of pleasure, she discovers the true and timeless source of all pleasure and bliss. This vehicle manifests first as a merriment, a festive music, a colorful carousel of brilliant lights, as if the inner space of the soul has become a place where a carnival is taking place. There is an inner hearing of light and festive music, a sense of happy and lighthearted singing and dancing. First, as the vehicle is descending, it seems the carnival is at a distance; but it keeps getting closer until it is inside us, and we are participating in the festivities. Then we see colored lights, twirling and dancing like a carousel, with an inner state of happiness, merriment, and joy. As the Markabah descends, we feel a sense of celebration for our attainment, a celebration for having made the difficult turn. The presence of the Markabah appears first as a state of true and joyful celebration: celebration of our victory, celebration of the truth, and celebration of our true nature. It is as if the Markabah itself celebrates its own arrival. For this arrival is the victory of truth, the victory of nonduality; this turn inward to the inner truth of Being is inevitably the movement toward realizing the nonduality of true nature.

The Markabah is a dynamic structure of colored and faceted gems, light and lighthearted, a light and delicate presence. The turning of the Markabah inside the soul fills her field with a merriment that far surpasses even the liveliest festivals of the external world. Bringing undiluted and authentic joy, this vehicle is exquisite, beautiful, and delightful while at the same time being totally holy and sacred. This is the first stage of the integration of the Markabah; the second stage occurs when it sinks deep into the manifold of the soul and becomes deeply embodied such that its truth and depth of presence are revealed. We then begin to experience it with more density, substantiality, and fullness. We feel full and fulfilled, impregnated with a substantial but faceted and structured presence. The Markabah at this stage is impacting the depths of the soul, all the way to its level of animal soul.

Here the Markabah reveals itself not only as the body of celebration, but as the body of pleasure. It is a full and substantial presence, which is the presence of the very substance of pleasure. We begin to experience a pleasure we could never have imagined, wonderful, full, sweet, delightful, deep, intense, heavenly, and totally transporting and fulfilling. The soul begins to feel satiated with a deep and full ecstatic pleasure that transcends and surpasses any sexual or sensual ecstasy she has ever experienced before. And it is completely from the inside out. Furthermore, we begin to recognize that the pleasure of gratification is mostly a release of energetic tension, while that of essence is the direct substantial presence of unadulterated pleasure, which can be very intense and amazingly deep.

The Markabah is a structure of essence composed of all aspects in the diamond form except that in this dimension each aspect appears not only clear, faceted, and precise but also as the very presence of pure pleasure. Each diamond feels and tastes like a wonderful piece of candy, with an affect deeply and pleasurably satisfying, a state of consciousness that fills the soul with a pleasurable bliss that penetrates and suffuses all of her field, filling all the cells of the body with a glowing and fulfilling sensation. Each diamond feels like a heavenly and full-bodied presence that combines the pleasure of the best food, the greatest sensual and sexual contact, and the utmost of a loving fulfillment. Each diamond is a different kind or flavor of pleasure, so we feel compassion as pleasure, as well as love, strength, truth, clarity, will, and so on. The Markabah is revealed as the body of pleasure, a body composed of the purest and most authentic pleasure, in various qualities and flavors.

The Markabah thus discloses to the soul the truth about pleasure, happiness, and enjoyment. It is not only the presence of essence as pleasure but a faceted and precise presence, indicating wisdom inseparable from pleasure. The soul learns firsthand, through direct and immediate taste and touch, the eternal truths about happiness and bliss. She comes to understand that bliss is the inherent nature of essence, and happiness is what the soul feels when she is intimate with her true nature.[15] These truths are not new; they are in fact ancient, but have usually been cast in terms of moralistic teachings, involving reward or punishment, asceticism and renunciation. We find here the objective, exact truth of what pleasure is, how to attain it, and what obscures it.

The wisdom of the Markabah is a body of teaching centered around true nature as pleasure and delight; each diamond here is a viscous, faceted fullness that is presence but also pleasure. The teaching reveals that pleasure is our own nature, and that we attain pleasure and become eternally happy by turning toward the truth of this nature. Learning to be loyal to the truth, the soul is developing allegiance to her true nature, and thus the soul becomes spontaneously wedded to bliss and fulfillment. To find pleasure and happiness is to turn toward the truth of our nature, which is the ground of our interiority. In other words, pleasure is not to be sought, let alone sought outside us. We find it by simply being ourselves, by simply being.

The Citadel

The diamond vehicle we call the citadel functions as the true protector of the path, the truth, and its realization. The perspective of the citadel discloses that the true and lasting protection and defense for our essential realization is right living; living our lives and conducting ourselves according to the truth of our realization. As we increasingly see through our habitual identifications and recognize who and what we are essentially, we need to live according to such understanding if we want to support our realization and its development. Practice apart from everyday living is not sufficient.

To support the soul's inner journey, we need to live a life that holds our realization and our work adequately and objectively; we need to structure our life such that it recognizes, appreciates, and supports our ongoing realization. This life structure can involve participation in an inner work school, but such participation is not enough. We need to structure and develop the totality of our lives in a way that is sensitive to and supportive of our realization and our deepening development. Otherwise, our lives will support the ego-self, for the structures and habits and relationships of our lives have developed as extensions and expressions of the conventional self, the self we were before the deepening of our experience and understanding.

The soul discovers that to truly move toward the inner essential truth and to live the life of essence means abandoning her normal identity and its various external and internal supports. The soul's experience actually shifts to another experiential universe, where she will need to find different supports for her new identity and its life. Abandoning her old supports brings up deep fears and terrors, while discovering and implementing the new supports is usually counter to her habitual stances. Allowing the fear that arises from this and other issues connected with the citadel, particularly issues related to ego deficiency and the need to accommodate the desires and needs of other people, the soul can enter into a clear black space devoid of defensive functioning. The soul's allowing this space brings the possibility of the emergence of the true support for the path, the citadel.

As the citadel vehicle begins to manifest within the immediate field of the soul we become aware of its immensity, its forbidding power and deep immovability. Its upper part is diamond solid gold, and its base is diamond platinum. The sense is of solidity and immensity, power and invulnerability. It can fill the whole body, or become as immense as a mountain.

Gold is the substance of essential truth; diamond gold is the objective wisdom of essential truth. Platinum is the aspect of universal will, the will of true nature toward optimization and realization, so its diamond is objective wisdom of this support. Thus the central body of the citadel is objective universal support for objective truth, and its teaching is the recognition how to live one's life in a way that harmonizes with true nature's universal will, which is inseparable from objective truth. The citadel is an immense presence, dense and immovable.

Recognizing the citadel as the defender of essence challenges the defenses of the ego-self, which then brings up her fears and terrors, ultimately the fear of death. Specifically, all these defenses are seen to function as the avoidance of feeling defenseless. Inquiring into the defenses reveals the ego-self's underlying deficiency and inadequacy, for without the inner essential resources it has no real capacities. This universal ego deficiency turns out to be one of the main issues that the citadel addresses and resolves, with the wisdom that the soul is inherently deficient and truly incapable without her connection to her essential resources. Hence her only real recourse for supporting herself is living her life in a way that harmonizes with the truth her true nature has been revealing to her. Right living becomes the invitation for the citadel to take its place in the inner economy of the soul, as the essential defender of the truth and its realization. This again makes it possible for the soul to let go of her ego defenses and be open to the truth as the master of her existence and life. We discuss the citadel, especially in relation to the issue of ego deficiency, in some detail in *The Pearl Beyond Price*, chapters 29–31.

The Diamond Dome

The diamond dome is so called because it has the shape of a dome composed of variously colored diamonds. Its descent in the soul appears first in the form of a delicately faceted and transparently clear dome of clear light, of various beautiful colors, crowning the head. Its manifestation is frequently accompanied by a diamond *dorje* at the forehead.[16] The state has extreme clarity and lightness, with an amazing sharpness and precision in experience and perception. Its central teaching is objectivity in regard to knowledge of true nature in its various essential aspects. Each aspect manifests as a colored diamond, but each diamond is both the presence of the aspect and the wisdom of its epistemological mode, of how to know it. We refer to it then as the diamond body of knowledge, or of noesis, diamond gnosis.

It provides the soul with the wisdom of essential knowledge, disclosing how true nature is pure being inseparable from knowing. It is the objective teaching of how essence is true nature as basic knowledge free from ordinary knowledge. Hence, it clarifies the difference between basic knowledge and ordinary knowledge, and therefore between essential experience and egoic experience. We discuss this difference in detail in many of our previous publications; for example, in *The Pearl Beyond Price*, chapter 2, we address the difference between Being and ego.

The diamond dome is basically direct and objective knowledge about true nature; hence it is the wisdom of the path of essence. It demonstrates how each aspect of essence is a particular way of knowing true nature, and shows how the realization of each aspect can be a path on its own. In other words, it shows how the inner journey can be understood, in its totality, in relation to each of the aspects, and how a path can integrate various aspects in its conceptualization, or even the totality of all aspects. The presence of the whole of the diamond dome, as opposed to that of one of its diamonds, provides the complete perspective of not only all the aspects, but the objectively integrated teaching of all the aspects. Hence, it makes possible an objective balance in the inner journey, where the presence and wisdom of each aspect may arise at the appropriate stage or moment in the inner process. We discussed this perspective in *The Elixir of Enlightenment*.

The objective inner balance in the journey of the soul challenges her rigidity and fixation, exposing that at the apex of this tendency is her ego identity. It reveals how the unfoldment of the soul can move most optimally when it is balanced and not fixated, when there is a total flexibility in the inner forms that the soul can manifest and assume. This understanding challenges the ego identity, which normally requires rigid and fixed forms to recognize itself. The arising of the diamond dome exposes the ego identity as the primary issue for the state of essential balance, and hence as the central issue for the diamond dome. This diamond vehicle manifests here the wisdom of its various diamonds, revealing how each essential aspect can be a path toward ego death, the transcendence of the ego identity. (For detailed discussion of the ego identity see *The Point of Existence*, chapters 9 and 10.)

Ego death refers here specifically to the soul's experience of herself free from the identity structure that gives her the normal sense of self-recognition, particularly the egoic sense of having a center, or of the ego identity being the center of experience. Even without this center, she is still partly structured through ego development, but her center is now the peace and stillness of essential emptiness within which true nature presents its various qualities. We have discussed this process—as part of our discussion of the diamond dome—and its necessity for the development of the soul to embody the total pearl beyond price, the pearl that has personalized all essential aspects, representing the station of the complete person, in *The Pearl Beyond Price*, chapter 32.

The diamond dome embodies the wisdom of the necessity of ego death for the free unfoldment of the soul, and provides knowledge of how essence works toward this death. It reveals that essence is inseparable from knowledge, and ushers the student into the perception that being Being and knowing Being are the same. This perception is itself revealed through working through each of the essential aspects in such a way that the knowingness of each of the qualities is seen to be intrinsic to the experience of that quality. Working through the issues of the diamond dome reveals that, in contrast, the ego identity subsists through its inner activity, based on rejection, hope, and desire. The soul learns that being her essence is a matter of simply being, and that this essence is recognized by being it. No activity is needed for the soul to be herself. This insight brings about the end of the attitude of seeking that began the inner journey, revealing it as a continuation of the ego activity.

The teaching connected with the end of the search, as the soul learns to simply be, and the wisdom regarding being and activity, manifests as the diamond dome descends deeper into the soul. The wisdom of the diamond dome displaces the soul's ignorance about her instinctual channeling of such searching, and appears now as a turning diamond wheel of teaching. The turning wheel is the manifestation of the diamond dome that ends the inner ego search, and allows unfoldment as a continuity of being. The turning diamond wheel, by ending the search, shows how it ends the time of ego, revealing itself as the wheel of time. The diamond dome appearing as the wheel of time reveals that it is an objective teaching specifically appropriate for the age in which it manifests. For a further discussion of the wisdom of the diamond dome see *Diamond Heart, Book 2*, chapters 1–9.

16 True Nature

AS THE SOUL INTEGRATES the various essential aspects and the diamond vehicles, transforming into an increasingly essential soul, essence begins forcefully to reveal that it is the true nature not only of the soul but of all Reality, of all forms and phenomena, all manifestation. The soul has had glimpses of this truth throughout her inner journey, but now it becomes necessary to integrate this truth. She is at the stage where this integration is the next step in her development and completion. The penetration of the major ego structures, those of self-identity and self-entity or boundaries, made possible through the wisdom of the diamond vehicles, readies her for this transition. Essence expands beyond her individual location and reveals itself as the essence of everything.

What does it mean that essence is the essence of everything?

To be the essence of something means it is its ultimate substance, its final nature, its most absolute level of existence. To use a physical metaphor, we can see that the essence of the body is protoplasm, but this is not its ultimate substance. To find the most fundamental level of existence of the body we have to go to the most elementary particles composing it, where these building blocks are the final and ultimate ones. *Essence* also means the simplest level of existence of something.

Essence is the essence of the soul in this sense, and it reveals itself at this point to be the essence of everything. But "true nature" has another significant meaning: the true nature of something, as we are using the term, is the most absolute and objective truth about what it is. When we have penetrated all that obscures our direct knowledge of anything, including the essence of the soul, when we have seen through all our inaccurate ideas, beliefs, positions, projections, and

248   The Inner Journey of the Soul

distortions, everything that obscures our awareness and knowing of it, we find anything we contemplate to be characterized by this true nature.

We have seen that essence is the true nature of the soul in both of these senses: it is her ultimate existential mode and ground, and it is the most objective truth of what she is. In the same way, essence reveals itself at this juncture of the inner journey as the essence and true nature of everything. Essential presence is the ontological ground of all phenomena. It is their ultimate substance. It is the true nature of plants, animals, rocks, atoms, elementary particles, energy, light, oceans, planets, galaxies, whatever universes exist, and so on, and the true nature of all thoughts, feelings, sensations, images, and all processes involving any of these objects. Nothing is outside the compass of true nature.

We saw in our discussion of the soul that her essence is not composed of distinct isolated parts, not composed of atoms. Essence is a homogeneous and indivisible medium, a true unified field. Seeing this indivisibility, it is actually a short logical step to recognize that it must be everywhere, as the essence of everything. More fundamentally, however, we increasingly appreciate the characteristics of true nature; it is timeless and infinite, beyond time and space, transcendent to all manifestation, and so on. Here we can explore these characteristics more specifically, to develop our understanding of the transcendence of phenomena, especially of time and space, from the perspective of true nature itself.

Absolute Transcendence

One way of picturing this situation is to consider the situation of dreaming. Suppose Jack is having a dream in which he is a scientific explorer, involved in various kinds of explorations. He dives deep in the oceans, goes deep into the earth, climbs mountains, penetrates atoms and elementary particles, dissects animals of various kinds, analyzes people's minds, studies groups and societies, travels around the earth, and even uses advanced space travel to explore distant galaxies and star systems. In his dream, he lives in a wide universe and encounters all possible phenomena. However, even though he encounters so many things in a practically infinite universe, this whole universe with all of what is in it is actually all in Jack's dream. The universe and its inhabitants are all the creative production of Jack's consciousness. In the dream are space and time, physical objects and psychological phenomena, even spiritual perceptions, but all these are in and part of Jack's mind.

Jack's mind, or consciousness, is the ultimate ground of this universe, its most absolute existence, its final constituency, its true nature. The objects of this universe are not exactly Jack's mind, but they are inseparable from it, are absolutely dependent on it, and are actually manifestations of its possibilities. They are forms manifested by Jack's mind, but his mind is much more than any of these, and can end this whole universe and create a new one. More precisely, Jack's mind transcends this universe and all of its inhabitants.

It is in this sense that true nature transcends all phenomena.

Since Jack's mind holds the totality of his dream universe, we may say that his mind is infinite and boundless. It is beyond the time and space of the dream universe, because these are dream creations of this mind. He can dream of going back billions of years in time, or advance as much in the future, for his mind transcends this dream time. His dream might seem to last for years, when it is actually seconds of waking time. In other words, Jack's mind transcends the time and space of his dream universe.

Similarly, true nature transcends our actual time and space.

Can we say Jack's mind is composed of parts, of atoms, or is it an indivisible field, a continuous medium? It is an indivisible field that holds all of its dream universe as it transcends this universe along with its time and space. But what does it mean that it holds all of this universe, and transcends its time and space? This takes us to the most interesting question, which is most illustrative of true nature: What is the size of Jack's mind? Is it small or large, finite or infinite, boundless in space or endless in time? When we think of this dream universe, we tend to think that it is infinite and boundless in space, and endless in time. However, we have seen that the sense in which Jack's mind transcends the time and space of its created universe is that it comes before them; the time and space of this universe, as well as its other content, are its creation. This transcendent ground, Jack's mind, cannot be measured from the point of view of its content. It is immeasurable not because it is of infinite extent, but because spatial distance does not apply to it. There are no distances in it because space is its creation. We cannot apply the concept of space to Jack's mind itself. In fact, because it transcends space it has no spatial distances, a truth easily proven by the fact that Jack can dream himself traveling instantly to any point of his dream universe. Jack's mind actually has no distance from any of its creations, and at the same time has no spatial extension. From the perspective of the objects in his dream universe there are distances between them. However, if a person in his dream, Jackie, is able to recognize her true nature in the dream as Jack's mind, and abide in this mind, she will experience no distance between herself and any of the objects in the dream universe. She will perceive objects in space, but from her place of abiding as Jack's mind she will experience or recognize no distance, no separation whatever between any object and another in this universe. It will be a completely paradoxical experience; perceiving objects in space but having no concept of distance because she recognizes herself as Jack's mind that has no spatial extension.

To say that true nature transcends space means that it cannot be thought of in spatial terms. True nature has no spatial characteristics: extension, distance, shape, or size.

With respect to time, Jack's mind encompasses all possible time in his dream universe. But does his mind possess time extension? Does it have duration? Normally we think of Jack's mind in the "real" world as occurring in time and space, without having spatial or temporal extension itself. The question of temporal extension is more difficult to imagine, and it is not as straightforwardly clear as in the case of spatial extension. We ordinarily think of Jack's mind as atemporal, but existing in our time. It has no duration, but duration passes on it. Yet it includes all time in its dream universe.

Jack's mind transcends all time in the dream universe; it is beyond time. In terms of the dream time, it is timeless; yet it holds all time. It is in all the times of the dream time. For Jackie, her experience of self-realization of her true nature is paradoxical also in terms of time. She sees time passing by but she feels no time because her nature, what she is, is beyond time. She is outside of time, immeasurable by time, but nevertheless she contains all time. Hence, she is all time but not in time. She has no temporal distance from any time; that is, no time separates her from any period of time in the dream. This is because Jack's mind is timeless but contains all time in his dream universe.

True nature, similarly, transcends time because it is outside of our time. It contains all time, yet it possesses no temporal extension, no duration. We cannot look at it within the concept of time for time is its creation, its product. It is ontologically prior to time just as it is ontologically prior to space. This is what we mean when we say true nature is timeless. However, actually experiencing this timelessness—knowing one's own mind and nature from this perspective—is a far cry from recognizing it conceptually. It is paradoxical, as we described Jackie's experience in the dream, and it is just as miraculous and mind-blowing.

We now have some idea of what is meant by transcendence. It is the experiential recognition of one's identity as beyond time and space, as timeless and spaceless.[1] The soul experiences the luminous intensity of true nature, a formless sense of consciousness aware of itself without a self-awareness consisting of shape, size, location, or duration. Since there is no concept of space there is no sense of being small or large, finite or infinite, bounded or boundless; and since there is no concept of time there is no sense of time or timelessness, of being old or young, or of time passing or standing still. There is only an ineffable freedom.

The Unmanifest and Manifestation

However, this state is not the normal experience of self-realization; besides there being no ordinary mind, there is no orientation or functioning in this state. The normal experience is that of formlessness inseparable from forms, similar to Jackie's experience in Jack's dream. The pure experience of true nature, in its absolute timelessness and spacelessness, is the experience of the unmanifest. In other words, true nature in its true and transcendent truth is unmanifest. The universe, with its space-time, and its underlying spiritual dimensions, is the manifest.[2]

From the perspective of Jackie in the dream, Jack's mind is not manifest; she sees only its creation, or its appearance as forms in time and space. And when she is self-realized she experiences herself as this mind, but nondual with its manifestation. She is timeless and spaceless, but contains all time and space. In fact, she is timeless and spaceless at the same time that she is all time and all space. By being the timeless and spaceless truth, she is, at any instant of time, all time and all space, all of existence.[3] Such is the experience of true nonduality in self-realization.

Full nonduality is not a matter of the nonduality of soul and essence, but of the total nonduality of true nature and manifestation. The nonduality of soul and essence is only an instance of the true condition of things, an individual and hence limited nonduality. But as we have seen, the realization of this level of nonduality functions as the entrance to the full nondual condition, reflecting the soul's function as a bridge between the two worlds, that of duality and of nonduality.

We now have two questions to consider. First, what is the nature of true nature? What are its characteristics? Second, how do we experience true nature in self-realization, in the midst of manifestation?

The Timeless Characteristics of True Nature

It is questionable to think of true nature as having characteristics, for it is completely indeterminable. It possesses no explicit qualities, no recognizable differentiations. We know that we are experiencing true nature in its full self-realization in that we feel a state and its impact, but we cannot describe it in positive terms. The tendency is to describe it negatively, in terms of what it is not. More precisely, to attribute to it a particular quality gives it a determination from which it is actually free. Any quality or attribute can only be a form it momentarily displays. It cannot be delimited, though people have attempted to describe it throughout the ages. Therefore, the classically given characteristics are such things as its lack of determination, limitation, quality, color, size, shape, form, duration, etc. This approach to describing true nature does avoid various pitfalls, but it is not completely faithful to the experience. Since it is possible to experience true nature, it is possible to say definite things about it. Our understanding of true nature leads us to see that we can say much about it, but what we say can only be a pointing, a path toward greater penetration and precision of experience. In others words, our description is functional and not delimiting, pointing to nuances that direct our mind to become even subtler in its experience. A discussion of the characteristics of true nature is, then, only an attempt to communicate a direct experience, and not one of packaging it in a conceptual wrapping. Any such description will inevitably be tentative and open, and will be transcended by a more subtle description that itself is not final. There can be no final and complete description of true nature, only attempts to point it out to the reader or listener. And in fact this is all that is necessary, for what is important is its direct experience and realization.

We have discussed how true nature is timeless and spaceless, but this does not say much about the actual experience of timelessness and spacelessness. Such an experience is so miraculous and magnificent that describing it in metaphysical language ends up sounding empty and drab, heavy and dull. We say that true nature is without qualities, but we also say it is infinite. Here, infinity is not the endlessness of time or space, but rather of lack of limitation. It points to the pure potentiality of true nature, from which arises the universe of myriad things. This infinity can be experienced, but it is very difficult to describe such experience except by giving its impact on body and mind. We can say it is stupendous, it is mind-blowing, it is amazing, it is bedazzling, and all this is true. But such descriptions simply express how we are impacted by the revelation of the infinity of true nature; they do not describe true nature itself.

Because of this difficulty, many wisdom teachings take the view that the transcendent true nature is unknowable.[4] In our view this is both true and false. We can definitely know and experience true nature, fully and completely. We can experience ourselves as timeless and spaceless infinity, and respond with wonder. We are then the ground of everything, the source of all manifestation, the essence of reality. We are total freedom and bliss, with no conceptual limitations. We are what makes anything exist, the source of all that appears, and the very substance and nature of everything. At the same time we are totally autonomous, absolutely independent of any form or quality.

Yet this is not the experience of true nature in its absolute transcendence. It is the experience of true nature nondual with its manifestations. Here we are experiencing ourselves as true nature; we are recognizing true nature in its fullness and completeness. Yet we are experiencing it with the forms and colors that it manifests. We can discriminate true nature from its manifestations, yet in reality we do not know whether true nature will be like this when there is no manifestation. So, in actuality, we cannot know true nature in its absolute transcendence. This is so because there is no such thing as experience of true nature without some manifest form.[5] The form might be empty space, but this is still not true nature. In fact, as we will see shortly, when there is no form manifesting there is no awareness at all, for awareness requires some differentiation, and hence the presence of forms.

The situation is even more subtle, leaving ample room for humanity's mystics, theologians, and philosophers to rack their discriminating brains, split hairs, and develop many and various systems of metaphysics. The experience of true nature in self-realization has two sides: true nature and manifestation, the ground and the forms that arise out of (or within or as inseparable from) the ground, respectively. Either side can dominate experience. In egoic experience manifestation dominates, completely displacing the awareness of true nature. In self-realization we are aware of true nature as the essence and ground of all the forms. But true nature can dominate the experience in increasing degrees, where the awareness of true nature can outshine the forms of manifestation so completely that it is virtually standing alone.[6] We can experience ourselves as true nature and perceive manifestation, with its time-space context, as receding away, or thinning away, until we are aware only of true nature. Our recognition of true nature feels utterly complete, and so powerful that it dispels any traces of the discursive and conceptualizing mind. Here we can be said to know true nature fully and completely. This knowledge is tantamount to full enlightenment.

Nevertheless, there is a limit to this complete experience of true nature. Regardless of how dominant is the presence of true nature, there is always a manifest form in awareness, even if it is the slightest differentiation, the barest glimmer of light in darkness, the subtlest sense of a differentiated quality. We might have our eyes closed, so that we do not see external forms. There might be no sounds, and our mind might be completely still. Yet, there is bound to be a sliver of light, a nuance of a sensation, the barest outline of a form or hint of a quality. The fact is that when there is absolutely no differentiation, no difference in perception, there will be no distinctions to be aware of, and no movement to indicate change. The complete absence of distinctions and movement amounts to no perception, for perception requires some differentiation. If there is absolutely one thing with absolutely no differentiations within it, then there is no perception and no sensation. Perception and sensation depend on awareness of distinctions.

This experience of no perception, internal or external, is reported by advanced practitioners of most wisdom traditions.[7] This indicates that we cannot know true nature in its absoluteness, because as we move away from manifestation and toward the transcendent truth we lose consciousness of anything. Such a conclusion is supported by the fact that the movement deeper into pure true nature, as awareness relieves itself of the perception of manifestation, is an experience of being increasingly enveloped by darkness, a divine darkness that feels like grace. The sense of the experience is that the light of true nature darkens the consciousness of the soul, liberating her from the perception of phenomena, as it draws her nearer. The soul feels increasingly close to the source as she feels more enveloped by darkness. At the point of complete nearness, that of unity, the darkness is complete, and there is no perception or awareness of anything, including darkness.[8]

Knowable/Unknowable Transcendence

Clearly, the nature of this process and its accompanying experience can lead us to the conclusion that the absolutely transcendent truth is unknowable. When absolute transcendence is taken to mean true nature totally apart from any manifest form, this is true. However, we see this as one possible understanding of this process. While it is true that our experience is such that we feel we know less and less as we are enveloped in the divine darkness, we are actually becoming increasingly intimate with the divine light, the absolute transcendent truth. We perceive and discriminate less, but this decrease of discrimination is not an increasing ignorance. It is the increase of a different kind of knowledge, a knowledge that is in its nature beyond discrimination, beyond the recognition of qualities and attributes. It is the simplicity of the source, which is so single that its knowing is an unknowing. As we become more enveloped in the divine darkness we are actually enveloped in divine light, for the divine light is dark. It is black light, the source of all light, not colorless but pre-color. We might think that clear light is the ultimate light, as is asserted by some Buddhist schools. However, clarity is an attribute, albeit a fundamental one. It is the absence of color, but not the ontological antecedent of color. Black light is the luminous divine darkness, the source of all light, and the origin of awareness.[9]

As we approach the transcendent light, we see less because we are accustomed to seeing white, colored, or clear light. When we do not see these, we believe we do not see and do not know; in fact, we are seeing black light and knowing the transcendent light. As we are enveloped increasingly in this beautiful and intimate darkness we see less and less of the manifestation, and more of this light, which is pure night. Hence, the increasing darkness can actually be recognized as an increase in the direct and intimate knowing of the transcendent true nature. It is because of this that there is an intensification and deepening of the sense of intimacy, love, contentment, peace, that mystics are known to experience in the divine darkness. When we completely know it, when we are totally one with it, when we are the transcendent light, we see nothing and experience nothing. It is a condition of absolute cessation of the light of knowledge and consciousness, for true nature is beyond such light. True nature is the source of light. What some call a complete lack of knowledge is, in some sense, a complete knowledge of transcendence.

What do we expect transcendence to be? It is absolute nonmanifestation, and true nature requires the mirror of forms in order for it to reflect and know itself the way we understand knowing.[10] Transcendence knowing itself is simply absolutely being itself, where the beingness of itself is completely absolute, and hence there is no hint of self-reflection, not even self-awareness. Self-awareness is already the beginning of manifestation.

We might view this pure experience of transcendence as indicating that the source of awareness is inherently not aware of itself, that it is aware of itself only when it manifests the world with its light of consciousness.[11] Another view is that true nature is inherently a mystery, a pure black light where there is nothing but light, this light preceding not only what we usually know as light, but also Being itself. Since its nature is mystery and indetermination, increased intimacy with this dark light will not produce more knowledge; it will instead produce more mystery. To experience mystery is to know the mystery as mystery. It is absolutely empty of any determination, devoid of any quality or form, and so to know it is to have no experience. This total absence of experience is not darkness, but rather total and absolute knowledge. It is the absence of all obscuration, but also the absence of all manifestation. Since there is no obscuration, no obstacles, not even the distraction of the forms of manifestation, why would we think of it as ignorance or darkness? Why think of it as not knowing or unknowing? Since the transcendent true nature is inherently mysterious and indeterminable, this is the absolute limit of mystery and indetermination. It is absolute knowing. It is the mode of knowledge of transcendent true nature, Being without mirrors, not even the mirror of awareness.

We can easily arrive at the same view by considering absolute absence of differentiation, or quality. It makes more sense that this condition is total knowing, because the approach to it is increasing, and increasingly direct, knowing of the divine light.[12]

Nonconceptuality of True Nature

Regardless which view we take of the experience of cessation, and of the knowability of true nature in its absolute transcendence, we need to remember that true nature is essentially indeterminable. Nevertheless, the more completely and absolutely we know true nature, the more we are enlightened and liberated. We need to know it because it is our nature and the nature of everything, and it is a deep need and desire of the soul to intimately understand and live this nature. Most of the soul's experience and realization is bound to be in the domain of immanent true nature, realized as the essence and true nature of everything. The self-realization that we can live is not that of cessation, but of the nonduality of true nature and manifestation. True nature is indeterminable even in such immanence.

True nature transcends the various categories of experience because it is beyond all form. In itself it transcends all conceptual dichotomies. It is neither small nor large, neither finite nor infinite. But these are not the important dichotomies that the soul comes up against as she dissolves into true nature. She rather encounters at this juncture dichotomies significant for her existence, life, and functioning. The most fundamental dichotomy that is challenged by the experience of true nature is the dichotomy of being and nonbeing. The soul has known essence as presence, true being. But as essence reveals itself as the true nature of everything it reveals its nature more completely. Essence is revealed here as both fullness and emptiness, both presence and absence. Each has been a true and authentic realization of true nature, but even this fundamental distinction turns out to be a form that differentiates out of the original mystery, a mystery beyond all differentiation.

True nature is absolute being, but also absolute nonbeing. It is both presence and absence of presence. It is both but not exactly, because these are conceptual elaborations of which true nature is innocent. We say it is both being and nonbeing, or neither, only because these are fundamental concerns for the soul. Being is the last thing the soul needs to surrender as she opens up to her true nature. As she does this she learns about nonbeing. She experiences the emptiness and ontological absence of her existence, and everything else in manifestation. So she may believe that true nature is total emptiness, absolute nothingness, complete absence of existence.

The experience of true nature as nonbeing or emptiness does not mean that there is no reality, no soul or manifestation. This is a nihilistic perspective that experience and understanding do not support. The wisdom of emptiness or nonbeing is an attempt to understand the final ontological mode of things. We normally believe that things exist when we perceive them. This belief is accompanied by a subtle underlying feeling or sense of what existence is. Things feel real in a substantial way. We consciously or unconsciously feel that the existence of things is a substantial solid quality. Existence becomes the existence of substance and solidity, which becomes opaqueness if we continue in this direction. In other words, we not only perceive that things appear to our perception, and not only believe that this appearance is objective and independent of our imagination and mental construction, but feel at the same time a sense of substance to this appearance, a sense of solidity. Existence for us then is not only the true appearance of things in perception but the imbuing of what appears with a quality we call Being.

In the true experience of emptiness, the subjective feeling and belief in the substantiality and solidity of things is exposed for what it is, a subjective feeling based on a belief. Emptiness reveals to us that things do not possess such substantiality or solidity. Their mode of being is not what we have called existence. More accurately, their ultimate nature is not existence, but nonexistence. They appear, but are characterized by nonbeing. Experientially, phenomena appear and we perceive them along with their usual qualities, but we do not feel that they exist. They are felt to be empty of the solidity and reality that we believed they possessed. In other words, the true nature of things is that they manifest, or appear, but that is all. In appearing they do not give us the feeling and belief that they are real or that they exist in the way we have assumed. We are accustomed to believing that things exist in the way we normally experience matter, solid and opaque. In reality, things are insubstantial, transparent, and light, similar to thoughts or mental images. But they are also luminous, so they are more like light. However, even light as we ordinarily know it does not express the absolute lightness and emptiness of things. Things are actually diaphanous forms, holograms floating in nothing, glimmerings of this nothing.

The nothing is not exactly something substantial, something that exists. The nothing is simply the perception of the nonbeingness of things.[13] In other words, emptiness is the term used here and in many mystical writings to refer to the fact that things do not exist the way we ordinarily think, but that they are luminous forms whose mode of being is nonbeing. When we investigate their existence we end up in complete nonbeing, total absence. We do not find phenomena to possess ultimate existence. Thus we see that the ground of all manifestation is nonbeing.

This is not the conventional sense of nonexistence, which is closer to nihilism. Clearly, this understanding is subtle and difficult. Yet we do understand it when we experience the true nature of things.

When we recognize that emptiness characterizes all objects, that it is inseparable from them in the way a shadow is inseparable from the object that casts it, or similar to how wetness is inseparable from water, it is easy to see that it is the ultimate nature of things. This view is supported by the fact that all forms are transitory while emptiness is not. Emptiness is not something in itself, so we cannot say that it is everlasting or eternal; but since it is absolutely inseparable from all forms, and all forms are transitory, emptiness is the only factor that is permanent, or unchanging. Actually, what is permanent is the flow of forms and their inseparability from emptiness. However, this is not the only possible view of true nature.

With more discrimination in this experience of the emptiness of everything, we may observe that there is another characteristic that always accompanies the emptiness. In the experience of true nature in its nonduality with manifestation, we observe that forms are not only transparent and empty of substantial existence, but that they are also luminous. Emptiness never appears simply as the emptiness of forms; such experience is always accompanied by luminosity, although the luminosity may not be consciously or directly perceived except upon investigation. Upon further inquiry we can recognize that all forms appear as forms of transparent radiant light. Thus we see that it is not only emptiness that is apparently unchanging; so is luminosity. In some sense, emptiness reveals the transparency of things, disclosing that they are forms that clear light, or transparent luminosity, assumes. We find, then, that luminosity, clarity, or clear light is a permanent ground of all phenomena. At the same time we cannot separate the experience of this clarity from that of the emptiness of all things. Emptiness characterizes the ground of clear light, so we cannot say that clear light exists in the conventional sense. This observation may lead us to take the view that true nature is clear light inseparable from emptiness, or empty clear light.

The perception of luminosity in nondual realization may allow us to recognize clear light as a form in itself. It is the everlasting ground of all phenomena, but it can also be experienced as a state in itself, as clear essence in the soul. When we experience it thus we experience it as presence. Clear light, or transparent luminosity, turns out to be the ground presence of essential manifestations. It is pure being, authentic nondifferentiated presence. When we experience it in its inseparability from emptiness we recognize true nature as the coemergence of being and nonbeing. But this state is totally nonconceptual, and this conceptual description does not communicate the experience completely. Here we experience everything as radiance, as the presence yet absence of existence. It is a completely paradoxical perception if we look at it conceptually. Experientially it is simplicity itself—clarity, lightness, and freedom. We cannot say we exist, and we cannot say we do not exist. In fact, it does not occur to us to say one or the other, because in this experience the concept of existence, or being, is gone without even a memory of it. True nature, here, is nonconceptual, has gone beyond all conceptual dichotomies, including those of being and nonbeing.

We recognize this nonconceptual presence-absence as the ground, essence, and true nature of everything. It is the eternal ground, transcending all forms and phenomena as it manifests them.[14] It is the reality of all phenomena, their essence and true condition. The realization of this ground is the recognition of true nature in its fullness in the condition of manifestation. It can be considered the experience of absolute manifest Reality, in contrast to true nature in absolute transcendence.

Boundless Dimensions of True Nature

Emptiness and clarity characterize true nature in manifestation, but we need to remember that true nature is beyond time and space, beyond manifestation. So how does this transcendence become reflected in manifestation? Contemplating this question will bring to mind other characteristics of the experience of self-realization of true nature.

The luminosity of the coemergent true nature is not simply the perception of radiance. The luminosity is the factor of awareness in true nature. It is intrinsic to the manifest true nature, for without awareness there is no perception of manifestation. True nature is then awareness, which means that awareness is fundamentally clear transparent presence coemergent with emptiness. Through this luminosity, true nature is inherently capable of being aware of the distinction of forms arising within it as expressions of its own field. Hence, true nature is inseparable from bare awareness. Yet it is not simply awareness, for it is the potentiality for all things.

We can be contented with our present understanding of true nature as fundamental awareness where clear presence is coemergent with emptiness, or of true nature as a self-aware coemergence of being and nonbeing. Many wisdom traditions do just that, for this is one valid way of viewing the situation. Yet, we can also easily see that true nature possesses other inherent properties. Recognizing that true nature is always inseparable from the forms it displays points to another perpetual characteristic, that of dynamic creativity. Since there are always forms manifesting, manifestation or display of forms is an ongoing characteristic of Reality, and also since all forms are a display of true nature itself, it is easy to see that in the nondual view true nature is inherently dynamic, endlessly displaying forms. In other words, true nature is not only coemergent awareness but also dynamism itself. True nature is, then, awareness inseparable from dynamism, just as it is inseparable from potential.[15]

The continuous display that true nature enacts always appears in the context of time and space. True nature is timeless and spaceless, but manifests everything in time and space. It forms the ground and essence of all manifestation, but as we saw in our example of Jack's dream, this ground is one and indivisible. The ground true nature is one unified field that underlies and constitutes all existence. In itself true nature has no dimensions, no spatial or temporal extensions. Yet because all forms manifest within true nature, we will experience it as a boundless, infinite field of coemergent presence. We perceive the presence of true nature as an infinite field of awareness or consciousness, unbounded and unlimited.

True nature in manifestation appears, then, to be omnipresent. It is everywhere, as the indivisible field of presence forming the ground and substance of everything. In self-realization, the soul will experience that she is everywhere, she is everything, she is infinite, she is boundless. In other words, dimensionless true nature will appear in manifestation to possess infinite and endless extension in space. Its original spacelessness appears in manifestation as infinite space. True nature has no distance but it is all the distances in manifestation.

Since true nature is also beyond time, it will appear in manifestation to fill the totality of time. All time appears in true nature, inseparable from it; hence, true nature is all time. However, true nature is timeless, and this timelessness will appear as no time. The experience of true nature as no time, in manifestation, is that of nowness, the present of presence. True nature is always in the present, even when it is in the past or future. In other words, true nature extends through all time, yet it extends as the present of all time. In reality, we can only experience the present of time. Past and future cannot be experienced as such. To go to the past is to go to the present of the past, and going to the future is going to the present of the future.

True nature appears at all times as the now. The now is nothing but true nature experienced in manifestation. This now extends through all time. It is an eternal now. More specifically, we experience true nature in manifestation as the eternal now, the now that extends through all time. For true nature, all time occurs now because now is the recognition of its timelessness within manifestation. The now holds all time, just as it holds all space, for it is nothing but the timeless and spaceless true nature. The now is nothing but the omnipresence, present through all time. Presence of true nature is indivisible, spatially and temporally. In other words, now is Being, and Being is now.

From this we see that our ordinary concept and experience of present time is a reflection of the eternal now. The present moment is the time we experience our presence. Our presence is ultimately the presence of true nature, but we do not see it because we are enraptured by the forms of manifestation, the forms that presence takes. Put differently, we can say that the present moment is the intersection of time with the eternal now. Time touches the now at the present moment, giving us our concept and experience of present time. But this touching expresses the fact that the now touches all time, for it is all time. But it touches all time only at the present of any time.[16]

Even though the now holds all time, it has no duration, no time length. Hence, any instant is the present, which is the now, which is all other instants. From this discussion of the reflection of timelessness and spacelessness in the space-time manifest reality, we see that all instants are contained in one instant and all points in one point. This is the most subtle way we can describe the reflection of transcendent true nature in manifestation. If we pursue this line of inquiry, we can only get into deeper paradoxes, but we see at least that true nature is the experience of boundlessness and nowness in the condition of self-realization.

From the above considerations we see that even though true nature is fundamentally free from spatial and temporal extensions, it appears in manifestation as the experience of infinity and eternity, boundlessness and nowness. However, the mystical experience of boundlessness and infinity, and that of eternity and nowness, is not the most direct experience of true nature; rather, it is the experience of true nature from the perspective of the time-space grid of manifestation. This is why true nature is usually described as infinite expanse, omnipresence, omnipotence, omniscience, endlessness, infinity, eternity, and so on.

In the view of the Diamond Approach, true nature reveals these characteristics, and many others, by revealing itself as consisting of many dimensions, each illuminating some of these qualities. In other words, rather than viewing reality as true nature appearing in manifestation with such characteristics, we view true nature as manifesting itself with many dimensions. More accurately, we view reality to be a Riemannian manifold with many dimensions of Being: the physical dimension of time and space, the dimension of subtle energy, and the subtle dimensions of presence. The latter are those structuring the presence of true nature. This view takes us back to our understanding of the soul as we presented it in chapter 3. We will expand on this view and how it relates to the soul in chapter 20.

We are presenting this view here only to appreciate that we can come to know true nature by studying its dimensions of manifestation. These dimensions express the fundamental characteristics of true nature, such as omnipresence, awareness, dynamism, gnosis, and so on. Thus to understand the timeless and spaceless characteristics of true nature as they are reflected in manifestation we need to focus on what we, in the Diamond Approach, refer to as the boundless dimensions of Being, the subtle dimensions of true nature that reveal its boundlessness.

Various teachings formulate this understanding in their discussions of several dimensions of reality or realization, of increasing depth and subtlety. Traditions differ in the number and characteristics of the subtle dimensions they discriminate, thus creating different metaphysical systems. The Diamond Approach recognizes five basic subtle boundless dimensions as being of primary importance. These begin to manifest after the soul integrates the diamond vehicles and their wisdom. True nature simply expands beyond the limited perspective of individual experience and reveals itself as the essence and ground of all manifestation, not just of the soul. True nature reveals its manifest structure through the revelation of these dimensions. The dimensions are all simultaneously the dimensions of true nature; all are always present in manifest presence, just as length, width, and depth are always present as the dimensions of physical space. To understand manifest true nature completely, we need to understand all these dimensions and how they coemerge to structure our experience of its field.

Even though true nature is composed of five coemergent boundless dimensions, these dimensions generally manifest in the inner journey one by one, in a specific order. The order seems to be of increasing fundamentality and subtlety, moving from the dimension closest to ordinary experience to the one nearest to transcendent truth. These dimensions arise in an order that reveals the characteristics of manifest true nature in increasing depth, subtlety, and precision. The latter levels are simpler than the ones preceding them, possessing less structure and hence less accessibility to our ordinary consciousness. Yet they are all true and authentic dimensions of true nature, spanning the totality of its Riemannian manifold.

When a boundless dimension manifests, it relocates the consciousness of the soul to a whole different realm of reality, where she experiences herself and the world in a completely new way. All the elements of her world continue to appear, especially the objective ones not constructed by her mind, but they begin to appear on a different dimension. So the body, physical reality, emotions, thoughts, images, actions, essential aspects, and diamond vehicles all continue to appear, but in a different light. They appear explicitly as manifestations of true nature, with the quality and characteristics of the particular boundless dimension. The elements are all grounded in and inseparable from a boundless and infinite field of presence.

Therefore, the experience of each of the boundless dimensions includes the perception that all of reality is one. All manifestation is one Reality, unified by the boundless dimension that forms the ground and substance for all forms. Hence, self-realization on the boundless dimensions is the experience of unity, oneness, and nonduality. It is the knowledge of the indivisibility of true nature, reflecting its nondimensionality, but appearing in the multidimensional manifestation as oneness and unity. The experience and understanding of this indivisibility becomes subtler as deeper boundless dimensions arise, moving toward the truth of nondimensionality.

Each boundless dimension brings about a whole universe of experience, perception, insight, and wisdom. The wisdom becomes available through the precise and objective presence of the diamond vehicles. As the soul encounters the boundless dimensions on her inner journey, all the diamond vehicles arise again on a new level, on the level of presence characteristic of the particular boundless dimension. They function together, teaching the soul and transmitting the wisdom of this dimension of true nature, experientially and with precise discrimination. Their combined wisdom functions to help the soul self-realize the particular boundless dimension, and to integrate it into her ongoing everyday life.

Journeys within the Journey

We can view the inner journey home as comprising two parts, the journey of ascent and the journey of descent. The journey of ascent includes the journey to presence and the journey with presence, as described in chapter 15. These two journeys include the discovery of the soul, that of essence in its aspects, and finally of the diamond vehicles. The last part of the journey of ascent is the revelation of the five boundless dimensions. The integration of each of the five dimensions is like a journey on its own, similar to the two first journeys. It includes understanding the body, emotions, and thoughts on this dimension. It also includes the integration of the soul, essential aspects, and diamond vehicles.

The essential development of the soul proceeds all over again, now within a new ground and attaining a new identity, the boundless true nature itself.

The journey in presence includes this part of the journey of ascent, i.e., the integration of the five boundless dimensions, but also the journey of descent. The journey of descent includes the integration of the five boundless dimensions into a unified whole, recognizing and understanding them as dimensions of the same true nature, coemergent in such a way that they simultaneously structure the full experience of nondual self-realization. In the journey of ascent the soul climbs up the ladder of Reality until she reaches the most subtle dimension of true nature, the absolute. Then she descends by going back and integrating the various dimensions she has passed through in the journey of ascent into this most subtle dimension.

The journey of descent includes other processes and realizations. The most important is the manifestation and recognition of the diamond vehicles specific to this journey of descent. The last vehicle, the diamond vehicle of freedom, reveals the knowledge and wisdom of true nature from the unified perspective of the five dimensions, through the revelation of transcendent true nature and its relation to manifestation through the five dimensions.

Each of the next five chapters offers a short summary of the characteristics and wisdom specific to one of the five dimensions. To give the detailed knowledge and understanding of the boundless dimensions would require five volumes, each the size of the present one, one for each of the dimensions. We will present the five dimensions in the order they normally arise in the Diamond Approach, in order of increasing subtlety and simplicity. Each succeeding dimension is more fundamental than the one preceding it, but as we will see they are all necessary for the full experience of self-realization.

PART FIVE

Dimensions of True Nature

17 Divine Love and Light

THE PRIMARY OBSTACLE to the arising and integration of the boundlessness of true nature is the ego principle, the idea that the self is a separate and autonomous entity or person. The soul's development leaves her deeply convinced that she is separate from other souls, and from Reality as a whole. She believes that she is an island that comes into contact with other separate islands.[1] This sense of separateness is due to the ego structure of self-entity that provides the soul with the experience of herself as a bounded entity. (For a precise discussion of this, see *The Point of Existence*, chapter 9.) One of the primary achievements of ego development is the structuring of the soul according to the surface contours of the body. The soul perceives herself as a discrete entity because of the discreteness of her experience of her body and other objects. This discreteness has been shown by developmental psychology to be absent in the infant's mind.

The Boundedness of the Ego-Self

The soul's increasing realization of her essential nature spontaneously puts pressure on this structure of separating boundaries, illuminating it and causing the soul to feel an exaggeration of the sense of separateness. One of the ways this inner pressure manifests is that the soul begins to feel constricted, even though she is deeply in touch with her essential nature. She feels limited in a way that causes existential suffering. She longs to be completely essential; she yearns to melt into the sweet juices of essence; but whatever she does, whatever practice she engages in, whatever attitude she takes, nothing works. She feels trapped inside her own skin while she strongly intuits, and frequently knows from direct experience, that her real condition is complete release and total marriage to her beloved, the truth of essence. She is filled with tears and deep sadness for not being in the carefree condition that she knows is her potential, and pained with the anguish of separateness from what she deeply loves.

At this point the soul may reach depths of despair about ever being released from the trap of isolation; whatever inner efforts she makes only dig her deeper into this dilemma. Eventually she begins to see the futility of doing anything to free herself, even the spiritual practices of meditation, prayer, concentration, contemplation, inquiry, attention, and so on. Whatever she does is her own individual action, exercising her own will and intention, and it is becoming clear that this is an expression of the dilemma itself. It is all based on her own individual desire. To desire is to be the individual she is, to long and yearn for her freedom is to be the same limited person, and it is this individual that does the spiritual practices and works on herself. This separate person is, in fact, the same individual who wants to surrender, and because she wants to surrender she cannot; for by wanting it she is being the individual who turns out to be inseparable from the separating boundaries of ego.

A major insight of developmental psychology is that the sense of being an autonomous individual is based on the ego structure of boundaries; at this point the soul may begin to recognize this fact in painful and intimate personal experience. This is the contribution of the diamond dome; it is part of the wisdom of this vehicle that all such inner activity is the expression of ego activity, as the cycle of rejection-hope-desire, and that such activity is inseparable from the sense of being an individual entity. This is the issue of the inner search, as we discussed in chapter 15 in the description of the diamond dome. (A more detailed discussion of the ego activity can be found in *The Point of Existence*, chapter 8.) The wisdom of the diamond dome brings recognition that the inner hopelessness occurring at this point is objective, that the dilemma is due to this inner activity. The helplessness is due to the fact that such inner activity only entrenches the soul into being the separate individual. More important, the helplessness is objective because no action on the part of the soul can release her from this trap. What is needed is not activity, not a doing of any kind, but a giving up of the struggle. The soul needs to recognize that she actually can do nothing here; she needs to forget about trying to release herself. She needs to forget even about wanting or desiring the release.

The resolution does not usually arise through an inner decision based on understanding. It cannot be a surrender based on a strategy. It is more that the understanding truly renders the soul helpless, and by finally accepting her helplessness she simply lets go and forgets her inner struggle. She accepts that she will accept whatever happens, for it is the will of the inner truth, not hers. It is at this point that the soul beings to realize, usually to her surprise, that she is feeling at ease. She may feel a delicate and light presence entering her head from the top, seeping into her body and consciousness. She tastes a delicate sweetness, sees a beautiful golden white light, and feels caressed and bathed by a soft and loving medium. The delicate and sweet light releases her inner tensions, softens her heart, and soothes her anguish. She cannot help but melt into the gentle hands of this loving and caring presence. There is then no contraction at all, no concern whatever; the body is soft and relaxed, the heart open and happy, and the mind rested.

The Boundless Ocean of Light and Love

The important part of this new experience is that the soul begins to see that the delicate presence of this loving light is not only inside her. It is all around, everywhere, bathing and blessing all manifestation. All forms look as if they are melted and surrendered, softened and released. Everything looks luminous, beautiful, and in complete harmony. She recognizes that essence has now manifested in a boundless form, as the presence of oceanic love that is at the same time light and consciousness. It is conscious love, loving light, the coemergence of presence, light, and love in a soft and delicate ocean that suffuses everything and cleanses it from all her projections. All objects appear immersed in its grace, and all essential aspects manifest as sweet substances condensing from it.

She may experience herself as the conscious sweet light, and in this state she is a witness of all phenomena without being any of them. She witnesses her body sitting, walking, and talking, but she is pure consciousness that is not the body. There are many variations on this state. One is to experience herself as an infinite and boundless sweet light that forms the ground of all manifestation. All forms arise from it and dissolve back into it. She is not the body and not an individual entity, but the boundless presence of consciousness. Another variation is to experience herself as everything, all manifestation, for this is the state of nonduality of manifestation and true nature. She is true nature, but since true nature is the substance of all phenomena, she is everything. This everything is a state of oneness, in which all forms make up one field, since they are constituted by the same indivisible ground.

The common factor in all these forms of realization is that the soul recognizes true nature to be boundless, infinite. She experiences herself in a radically different way; no longer does she know herself as an entity amongst other entities; rather, she is the infinite ocean, beyond all individuals and objects. As such she is not an individual soul; this will generally bring up deep issues and fears, challenging some of the deepest of her ego structures. One initial fear, based on lack of true knowledge, may surface even before she experiences the boundlessness of her nature. This issue appears as the fear and concern of losing whatever is associated with being a separate individual entity. She fears losing her separateness, which reveals the deeper fear of losing her individuality, her autonomy, her personal quality. But one of the most alarming expectations here is the fear of losing her individual experience. She believes that if she is not a separate entity, an individual, she won't be around to experience anything, especially the wonderful beauty and majesty of her true nature, and Reality. She fears that if she is not an individual entity she won't have experience.

Exploration reveals that the concept of experience has been unconsciously fused with that of being an individual entity, that the soul believes she has to be an individual self for her to have experience at all. The realization of boundlessness reveals the delusional character of this conviction, as it sweetly melts away the ego boundaries that give her the sense of entitiness. A subset of this is the concern about not having her own experience, because she believes experience can only be her own. This fear is not exactly the loss of "I," but of "my." This possessive tendency turns out to be a distorted expression of the need to have personal uniqueness and autonomy. This reflects a lack of objective understanding of the personal essence, the true individuation of the soul. This understanding is provided by the stupa diamond vehicle, which challenges the soul's deep belief that in order for her to feel her personal autonomy and uniqueness she needs the separating boundaries of ego. Furthermore, the stupa unveils the timeless wisdom that personal autonomy and uniqueness are characteristics of the personal essence, which does not require boundaries or in fact any ego structure. The soul can be personal, unique, and individuated when necessary, as one of the possibilities of true nature. In other words, because the boundless love is a dimension of her true nature, it is not antithetical to her personal attributes; in fact such attributes are part of its potential.

The Body of Light

As the soul comes to this understanding, her boundaries may begin to merge with the divine effulgence. She becomes part of the ocean, a big drop of the ocean. The drop is a dense liquid honey, or amber nectar, as if the ocean of light liquefies at the location of her body as a big wonderful drop of grace. She sees and feels herself surrounded by grace. Her essence feels like an inseparable part of the ocean, but denser than the rest. As this development began she was afraid of losing her experience; she sees now that the outcome is a more clear and free essential realization.

She now sees the way out of the dilemma of boundaries: actual merging with the divine and losing the sense of individual experience. Essence becomes clearer, more lucid, and very graceful. The soul becomes a drop of grace, of full and substantial presence, but utterly free and fulfilled.

A great deal of understanding may unveil at this juncture, especially if the diamond guidance has already been integrated and now functions on the dimension of divine love. Its graceful presence attains a soft and divine quality; its faceted diamonds become more fluid and softly glowing. The boundless love is not like someone loving something. It is more of a full and rich presence, softly and delicately textured, with a heavenly affect, sweet but wonderful, uplifting but totally pure and selfless. It bathes all forms, infusing everything with the most sublime love, and blessing appearance with the garb of divinity.

Boundless light is not only love, but a dimension of love beyond the human, beyond the individual. It is not for anyone, and not by anyone. It is for everyone; true nature is manifesting everyone, and everything, as pure love. And one of these forms of love is the soul herself. The soul recognizes here that she is a manifestation of the love of true nature. She is love and light, a consciousness with total goodness. When she recognizes her light nature, she lights up and glows like a self-luminous bulb, but when she does not, when she is deluded by the ego structures, her light dims and only the external outlines of her form remain in awareness. These become boundaries and she feels herself as a bounded and separate entity. The dimming of the light of the soul causes the soul to experience herself as a separate entity. Only a minimum of this light remains, as her ordinary consciousness, trapped within the skin of her body. Everything now looks opaque and discrete, and appearance becomes a physical world littered with separate objects, dead objects that have lost their luminosity.

When her rigid structures are made transparent through the unfolding of her process, the soul feels this as an increase in consciousness and presence. At a heightened level of intensity this presence reveals itself as luminous light that now overflows her personal boundaries; the overflow that melts these boundaries is actually the overflow of divine love and grace. Thus it reveals itself as the boundless ocean of Being and love, consciousness and light, the substance and true nature of everything. She experiences herself as a form held by this loving light, inseparable from it. She is an offspring of the divine light, one of its loving and exquisite manifestations. But her light can grow so intense that even her sense of being a form of light becomes outshone, and she recognizes herself as the light itself, in its boundlessness and infinity. She is then the true nature of everything; she is the ground. More exactly, she is everything, as one divine being, where substance and form are wedded into an inseparable Reality. She is ultimately true nature itself, in its divine boundlessness and omnipresent grace. All things are equal, equalized by the unity of appearance.

One insight possible at this stage is the experiential recognition that the structure of being a bounded entity is based on identification with the body. The soul begins to see the crystallized nature of this deep conviction that she is the body. However, in the course of penetrating the sense of boundedness through the grace of Being, she is in for a pleasant surprise. As she witnesses the revelation that all forms are forms of love and light, she recognizes that one of these forms is her own body. Her body turns out not to be what she thought it was, not what she was identified with. In effect, she has been identified not with her real body, but with an idea, an image of her body, a reified concept of the real thing. Now her body reveals its own true nature, as a body of light. It glows with the inner luminescence of light, a light that possesses the fluidity and softness of love.

Boundless Goodness

At this juncture, the soul is discovering an important feature of the timeless truth of true nature. She realizes that true nature is goodness itself, and the source of all goodness. It is unblemished goodness, incorruptible goodness, indestructible goodness. Goodness is a fundamental characteristic of true nature, a timeless potential that it might reveal at any time or any place. This divine goodness is not limited; it is not parceled out to individuals. It is totally boundless, unlimited and endless, for it reflects the transcendence of true nature that appears in time and space as boundless and infinite. It is boundless goodness.[2] The dimension of divine love reveals that true nature is absolute goodness; it is inseparably both light and love. Its presence and impact on the soul is fundamentally that of blessing and grace, in all ways and in all dimensions.

Such goodness is often not obvious or recognizable, but our lack of perception does not diminish or sully this goodness. The soul often does not perceive this goodness because of her obscurations; but although the goodness can be obscured, it is never destroyed.

The fact that true nature is fundamentally characterized by goodness means that the manifest world possesses an inherent goodness. There is goodness in the world—not in the discrete and reified forms of the world, which are obscured expressions, but in the depth of the world, in its ultimate nature. The soul can see this only when she is denuded of her obscurations, and surrenders completely to this perception. Denuding herself from the false garments of ignorance and identification, surrendering the illusion of a separate self and her own will, the soul will find this goodness. If she lets herself truly fall, all the way, not into the hands of one person or another, one form or another, but absolutely and fully, she will be received with grace and love. Unfailingly.

The dimension of divine love is the experience of true nature in its fullness, in its richness, in its abundance. The ocean of love is a rich and richly textured medium, like a boundless ocean of ambrosia, fluid and outflowing. Its outflow is manifestation, an unfolding juicy womb constantly birthing the universe. It is a total generosity, a giving out of substance, existence, life, forms, qualities, capacities, all as manifestations of love. The universe is so rich, so abundant with goodness and wonderful qualities and forms, that when the soul beholds it she cannot help but be completely fulfilled and satisfied, overflowing with deep and sweet gratitude. She now recognizes how impoverished her normal world has been, how empty and barren, and how unreal. She recognizes that this inherent abundance and richness has always been lying in her depths and at the base of all manifestation, but she did not see it because she was looking through filters that specifically filtered out the ground true nature. Belief in her separateness and pride in her independence have functioned as the primary obscurations that disconnected her from this heavenly world. Heaven, it turns out, is always here, but only the purified and sincere soul can enter it. And the price is her head, her independent selfhood.

Origins of Heart

Divine love is the dimension of true nature responsible for the arising of qualities, feelings, and affects in experience. It is not only light, which is consciousness, but also love. Love is the primordial feeling, the source of all affects. Light differentiates into colors; love differentiates into various affects. Divine love is golden white, white for light and golden for love. It is typically experienced as an ocean of golden white, a homogeneous medium, but it can differentiate within this field into the various forms of manifestation, with their myriad shapes and colors. An important and special differentiation is that of the essential aspects, where the very substance of the medium assumes, either throughout the entirety of its manifold or in some local regions, different colors and textures. The differentiation of the field into colors reflects the prismatic differentiation of light, but it is also concurrent with and inseparable from the differentiation of the sweet feeling of love into the various affects that characterize the essential aspects. Each of these essential aspects manifesting on the dimension of divine love has the sweetness of love as ground, but with an added subtle differentiation. The emerald green divine love has the warmth and tenderness of compassion; the ruby red love embodies the spirited vitality of strength; the silver white love exudes the confidence and steadfastness of will; the luminous black love is deep with the stillness of peace; the luscious apricot love is redolent with the deep feeling of fulfillment; and so on. These are the original differentiations, which we see here as the differentiations of love. Love is the basic and fundamental feeling of the real world, and it differentiates into the richness of the essential universe. It unfolds into a universe of affects, adding the richness of feeling to experience. We now have warmth, intimacy, depth, lightness, joy, happiness, celebration, benevolence, kindness, power, immensity, awe, wonder, freedom, release, expansion, clarity, excitement, aliveness, sharing, melting, exquisiteness, and many other free and authentic feelings of the heart.

When the light is dimmed, the original affects are also muted, but the latter can also become blocked and distorted. The muting, distortion, and blockage of the original affects mushrooms into the many feelings and emotions that characterize human experience. We now have frustration, barrenness, anger, rage, hatred, sadness, pain, fear, deprivation, loss, jealousy, envy, pride, and the many other well-known difficult emotions of the human heart. We see that love actually forms the ground of the human heart, even though sometimes we cannot find it in ourselves. Love is the ontological ground of the heart and the original source of all feelings. Without divine love there would be no affect, no capacity for feeling, and no such thing as essential heart.[3]

On this dimension of Being we experience all manifestation as heart. The whole universe appears as the heart of Being, the love of

God. All manifestation is love; its differentiation is the richness of the heart of Being. Hence, it is not only glowing and graceful, but also absolutely harmonious and peaceful. Everything appears to consciousness as plenitude and harmony, the way a full, fulfilled, and peaceful heart will feel. The harmony gives appearance an aura and feeling of beauty. Reality appears magnificent, radiant, and resplendent, full of color, abundant with light, rich with feelings. The affects are deep and full, the colors luminous and rich, the aromas heavenly and delightful, and the smooth and soft textures can only melt the body and quiet the mind. This full, rich, melting experience is just what the heart of the soul has always wanted existence to be and life to embody.

The soul, particularly the animal aspect of the soul, is generally ignorant of the possibility of this realization. As we have discussed, because the ego-structured soul is dominated by the animal potential, which has an external orientation, it sees abundance and richness only outside itself, and only in certain locations. Divine love reveals that richness and abundance, all that the soul desires, is not only inside, but everywhere. It is a nonlocal phenomenon that reflects the nondimensionality of transcendence in manifestation. All Reality is full and overflowing with richness and wonderful fulfilling qualities. The soul does not need to seek emotional gratification anywhere in particular. Fulfillment is available everywhere, for the very substance of everything is fulfillment. Therefore, to truly and fully integrate this dimension will liberate the soul from the inner compulsion to seek; there will be no more inner emptiness, no more inner psychic hunger. The soul will be full and overflowing, and the abundance of her true nature will manifest in her as overflowing generosity. She cannot help but give, not because she wants to, but because she is authentically so rich she cannot help but overflow. Her generosity is fundamentally boundless, bounded only by her material circumstances. And she gives joyfully, with total gratitude and celebration.

Ease and Surrender

Because this dimension of true nature is of the most pure and gentle love, it impacts the soul in ways she has always longed for but could not fully attain. Its softness is soothing, lulling the mind into rest, the body into natural relaxation, and the heart into serene openness. When touched by this amazingly soft and flowing medium one cannot help but let go and relax. Tensions naturally release, anxieties subside, concerns diminish, and activity becomes easygoing and carefree. One spontaneously feels at ease, as if touched by a heavenly soothing hand, letting go like a baby responding to its loving mother's intimate holding and comforting.

A distinguishing characteristic of this dimension is a sense of being at ease and carefree. The body melts, as if it has been on a prolonged vacation in a tropical paradise, with one's every need completely taken care of. There is not a worry in the world; instead there is complete security and safety, fullness and abundance. The soul lets go of all of her protective and defensive devices and strategies, for in this realm there is no danger possible, and the heart is so secure and serene that even the concept of trouble does not exist. It is actually quite similar to how the human infant feels when it is completely taken care of, completely loved and cherished, with abundance of loving care all around, unquestionably available. The infant is then totally relaxed, the mind peaceful and empty, with no care, no tension, and no frustration. The infant feels, implicitly and without cognitive discrimination, that it is totally and unconditionally held. It is held physically, emotionally, energetically, and in all other ways. Similarly, the soul in this dimension feels the same, as if the universe is its loving and totally caring mother. The real world here, manifestation suffused by divine love, actually feels like the loving and caring hands of one's mother. One feels in good hands, with all states of fulfillment.

The ease characterizing the experience of the soul in this dimension is because it is the kind of love that the soul specifically recognizes as unconditional care and loving holding. It is not a conceptual recognition. It is almost like an instinctual recognition, but it is on the soul level and not just the body. The soul infused by this divine love feels secure, safe and at ease because she feels held and protected in preconceptual ways that her mind can never completely articulate. She cannot help but feel trusting. But this is not a discriminated kind of trust. It is more of preconceptual basic trust, where the soul naturally and spontaneously relaxes, lets go, and surrenders. Surrender is nothing but a melting away of all her rigidities and fixations, concerns and cares.[4]

When she feels held by this ocean of love, as one of its inseparable expressions, she knows herself as one of its loved offspring. On the other hand, when she experiences the ground of love as her identity, it is a different kind of experience. She is then the divine presence itself, the infinite and boundless heart of God.

All these characteristics and features of this dimension of true nature deeply challenge beliefs and positions strongly held by the soul, instituted in her structure and identity. An important example is the implicit position that the ego-self takes of believing the world to be basically unsafe, and at best neutral. This attitude of basic distrust impels the soul to continually resort to strategies and devices to protect and defend herself. We are specifically referring to the defensive attitude of autonomy, where the soul feels that she needs to take things in her own hands, that she will not be automatically taken care of, that if she is not alert, even paranoid, things will not go as they should; her life will fall apart. We have discussed the development of this deep lack of trust in chapter 10. (More extensive discussion can be found in *Facets of Unity*, chapters 4-6.)

Thus the presence of this dimension of true nature in the experience of the soul is specifically associated to the nonconceptual attitude of basic trust. Such basic trust is necessary not only for the ease and security of the soul, but also for her connection to her true nature and for her unfoldment and development. We discussed in chapter 11 how the loss of basic trust leads to the soul's reactive dissociation from the nondual simplicity of just being. At the present stage of the soul's journey, at least in the Diamond Approach, the discovery and integration of divine love gives her a great support and momentum for the further stages of this difficult journey. The more deeply she integrates divine love, and the more completely she learns its wisdom, the more trusting she will be that her unfoldment will proceed guided and held, that her needs on the journey will be met and her difficulties resolved. She develops both trust in and a carefree attitude toward the path, allowing her to let go of the effortful seeking activity, and inspiring her that she need only love truth and reality, and then simply relax and be. She learns that her unfoldment is supported by the real universe itself, that it is not in her own hands, and that it is infinitely better that it is in the hands of loving divinity. Such basic trust and confidence on the path spurs the journey forward, accelerating the unfoldment of the soul and the revelation of her true nature and its wisdom.

Since divine love inspires trust and surrender, it functions as the melting elixir in the various difficult stages of the soul's development. The ego-structured soul is too scared and distrustful to let go of her major defining structures, which makes surrendering difficult. The distrust causes her to identify with these structures even more rigidly, for they are the building blocks of her autonomous existence and functioning. However, when divine love appears in her experience it makes the letting go of this identification and the surrender of these structures much more possible, certainly easier. The presence of divine love, with both its love and light that transcends words and promises, holds the soul and assuages her fear and terror. The most fundamental structures are those of separating boundaries and self-identity, and their underlying ego activity. The loving light of the divine dimension appears when these structures are released. It appears with the integration of the diamond dome, which brings understanding of inner seeking and its ego activity, as well as cessation of this activity at the center of the ego. It arises again with the integration of the stupa, for this is the stage of understanding and transcending ego boundaries and their sense of separateness. The loving light appears as well at the dimension of the diamond will, at which stage the dissociating representations of the ego-self and its identity are transcended. Such deepening levels of surrender finally invoke the full presence of divine love, as a boundless dimension of Being. (For discussion of some of the issues and questions relevant to these levels of surrender, see *Diamond Heart, Book 2*, chapters 1–10.)

The Prince of Darkness

The absence of adequate holding in early childhood marks the specific stage at which the soul becomes estranged from divine love. Not only does the soul develop basic distrust, but she begins to lose the precognitive experience of holding and the oceanic sense of presence as her environment. She reacts and takes things psychologically into her own hands. This reaction is generally suffused with bitterness, disappointment, frustration, and hatred. She develops the position that there is no inherent benevolence in the world, within various degrees of distrust. The arising of divine love, at this stage of the inner journey, and its appearance as an eternally omnipresent feature of existence, generally activates the early deprivations and frustrations around the need for adequate holding. We discuss this in other places, but here we want to focus on one particular feature of such regression or activation. The loving and divine features universally activate in the soul an intense distrust, rejection, even hatred. Most people seem to associate the boundless loving light with divinity, and hence with God's presence and benevolence. Its presence at such stage activates the experience of early absence of adequate holding, and the various conflictual feelings about it; the soul remembers and experiences the effects of early deprivations and frustrations, and also intense hatred. It is generally quite a surprise to the soul to discover upon intimate inquiry that this hatred turns out to be directed specifically toward the love and goodness of the new state. The individual feels full of black crystallized hatred, and wants to intensely direct it toward the universal love. He hates the universal love itself, its goodness and benevolence. He wants to destroy it, annihilate it, obliterate it. He cannot stand hearing about it, seeing, or feeling it. Instead of feeling happy and grateful, he feels venomous enmity and opposition toward it. He sees it as the enemy, and is gripped with a hateful desire to take vengeance.

Inquiry into this surprising reaction to the arising of boundless divine love reveals that the soul is identified with a specific demonic form. The soul actually begins to feel as if she has hooves, horns, a tail, and burning red eyes. The soul assumes the form of the devil, just as it is popularly known.[5] One may at this point experience oneself as a huge and powerful presence, in the shape of a black devil intent on opposing and destroying everything good and beautiful in existence. It is not easy to acknowledge and experience oneself as an all bad destructive force, which accounts for the issues of splitting that are associated with hatred and how it is the distortion of the power of Being. The important point for us here is that the emergence of true nature in the boundless love dimension activates this powerful hatred toward the very goodness of the divine. It becomes personified in the figure of the devil, but the process of its working through takes us to its genesis in early frustration that appears in the soul in the form of a furry jackal.

This hatred of goodness typically manifests as hatred of God or Being. The vengeful, destructive hatred reveals deep bitterness and intense disappointment in God or Being or whatever the soul believes to be the universal force. The soul felt betrayed and abandoned in early childhood when she did not receive the loving holding she needed. She expected that there was a benevolent force in the universe, whether her family believed in God or not; but she did not experience it coming to her aid when she needed it. The human environment failed, and no universal force or presence appeared and soothed her. She felt totally on her own, a deeply felt condition that became integrated into her ego structure and now underlies her life and action. She remembers how much she has struggled and suffered, has felt lost and despondent, without the appearance of a true helping or guiding hand. It does not matter whether one believed in God or one was an atheist; these intense feelings arise now as there appears to the soul a universal presence that inhabits and suffuses the whole universe.

All the deprivation, loneliness, loss, pain, and frustration from early childhood become channeled now into a form that expresses them in the face of the arising divine love. The old pain and abandonment, with its rage and hatred, appears as this reaction: "Where have you been all this time? If you are so loving and benevolent, why did you not come to my rescue? Why did you let me, my ignorant and inadequate parents, and everyone else I know, suffer miserably without help or even comfort? You have abandoned us all! You are no good. Go away, I hate you! I do not want to see you or hear of you."[6]

Inquiry into these intense feelings reveals their origins in the oral stage; this clarifies the oral nature of the soul's need in this ego structure. One may then move to dealing with the absence of adequate holding in early childhood, the fear and terror of disintegration and annihilation, and how distrust developed. The process leads to deep hurt and abandonment and the understanding of the origins of the Beast, or hatred of the good, in the early oral frustrations and deprivations. One of the steps in this process of working through is the recognition of how this issue depends partly on the reification of universal or divine Being. Being is personified; the soul's relationship to it assumes the form of an object relation between a separate individual soul and a separate powerful entity one may call God. The resolution is the integration of the black aspect of power in a diamond dimension, and the wisdom of how true nature does not operate like an individual entity. This deepens one's understanding and appreciation of the boundlessness, omnipresence, and omnipotence of true nature, and its divine and loving features. One sees that true nature is an ocean of love, that is always present regardless of the experience of the soul, and that there are universal principles through which it operates, different from the functioning of separate entities.

The Beast turns out to be a particular crystallization of the ego principle, the conviction about and identification with separateness. Separateness is what truly opposes divine love, and the devil's hatred is the final natural outcome of such separateness.[7] (See *Facets of Unity* for further discussion of this process.)

The soul suffused by divine love, forming an inseparable expression of its bountiful resplendence, is the divine offspring, the prince of light. The soul disconnected and alienated from Being, especially from its loving light, becomes the prince of darkness. It is important to see that even the Beast is the result of the reaction of the soul to her experience. It is not an ultimate form, nor an eternal one. Hence there is no eternal damnation, and no absolute evil.

Resolving the issue of the Beast has a salutary effect on the soul's relation to her true nature. It opens up a deeper level of appreciation, love, and valuing of essence, and allows the soul to see it as sheer beauty, as what makes everything beautiful. Essence's value becomes more objective, in the understanding that essence is valuable not because of what it does and gives to the individual soul, but because of its mere existence. True nature, the essence of the soul, is valuable, is worthy of appreciation and love, not because it gives her something, not because it adds to her, not because it liberates her, but because it is beautiful. Its value is in its beauty and perfection. Its truth is its value, and this truth is the essence of all beauty. The beauty of a form turns out to be its transparency to true nature. The more a manifest form expresses and embodies true nature with its timeless features, the more the eyes of the soul behold it as beautiful. Beauty is a reflection of truth, and truth is ultimately true nature.[8] And the dimension of true nature that reveals this essential beauty is that of divine love.

Jabba the Hutt

This realization, and many others on this dimension, erode the soul's attachment to worldly things. For the soul can clearly see that all richness belongs to the divine presence, and all abundance is of the very nature of truth. Attachment is based on the separateness of self, which is one side of a larger illusion, the belief that the world is composed of discrete objects. Not seeing the indivisible boundless ground of everything, the soul sees manifestation as composed of discrete objects. One can then possess or lose one object or another. And since this dismemberment reflects the absence of the unity of Being, with its richness and abundance, it is bound to be colored by a sense of impoverishment. Impoverishment becomes desire and greed, and possessiveness develops into grasping and attachment. Therefore, instead of the soul experiencing herself living in abundance and seeing richness everywhere, she inwardly feels, consciously or unconsciously, that she is deprived and empty. She ends up being ruled by desire, greed, possessiveness, and attachment. Instead of the beautiful and rich display of love, the world of dismembered objects becomes the promise of possessions, power, and objects of gratification. The boundless Good is dismembered into material goods, to be attained, possessed, and hoarded. The natural richness and its associated spontaneous generosity becomes an economy of scarcity, where each is for his own, each is looking out for himself, and each fights and competes with others for as big a piece of the pie as one can get through cunning or brute force.

This worldview is the direct result of not seeing the unity of Being, and not recognizing the inherent richness of its nature. It is actually founded on the perception of reified reality, what we have become accustomed to calling the world, or physical reality. The physical world as we ordinarily see it is basically empty, and populated only by material objects. It is a material reduction of manifestation, with forms that are visible, but without their ground and true nature.

This world produces the worldview of ego, the ground for greed and aggression, possessiveness of material objects, and adulation of power.

The emergence of divine love challenges this view and highlights the ego structures that embody it. A major form that becomes highlighted at this point is that of a greedy, power-hungry, fat self, a separate self fattened by objects of the world, and interested only in what the reified world promises. Such a self has no spiritual aspirations, and no appreciation for subtlety and refinement, except perhaps for objects that signify material wealth. It is a level of the animal soul, but more exactly a higher structure of this animality. It is an animal in a human form, or almost human. But it is one that loves excess, that simply wants more and more of all material things, for its own material wealth, pleasure, and power. It is selfish, self-centered, self-seeking, gross, and primitive in its interests and aspirations.

All ego-selves include this structure; human beings differ only in the degree to which it dominates their overall sense of self. It is the ego structure expressing exclusive cathexis of the physical world, where the soul is caught by the illusion of the world, believing the reified world can satisfy her needs.

We can say that in some sense it is the ego's counterpart of the divine being, the boundless richness and abundance of the dimension of divine love. It is an attempt to be rich and self-sufficient, to have abundance and plenitude but from within the materialistic worldview of the ego. An apt image for it is that of Jabba the Hutt, from the *Star Wars* film series created by George Lucas. Jabba is a ponderous, very fat semi-humanoid creature, having the body of a slithery worm-like animal with semi-human face and upper body. He is grossly fat, insatiable in his greed, and dangerous in his treachery. He likes to collect slave girls, dancing girls, and different kinds of aliens and animals to serve him, protect him, and satisfy his sensual desires.

In the actual experience of this structure one feels like a shell made of fluffy fat, but empty and greedy. One is only interested in things of the world, and things of the spirit hold no interest. But the emptiness points to the inauthenticity and unreality of such form, revealing it as a psychic structure. Recognizing this, one may then see that the world one relates to from this perspective is itself empty and devoid of any real significance or substance. It lacks all the characteristics of divine love. It lacks richness, abundance, beauty, fullness, love, benevolence, softness, vividness, and color. This turns out to be the condition of the material world, for it is a world alienated from its true nature, and hence empty of all of its beautiful features. We discuss the way of working through this issue in *The Pearl Beyond Price*, chapter 36, in which we refer to divine love as cosmic consciousness. The inquiry into and resolution of this ego structure becomes the main issue for the self-realization of the dimension of divine love. The final resolution is the self-realization of divine love: that is, the soul transcends her individual manifestation and recognizes herself as the unity of Being, as the boundless ocean of love and light. We have discussed the issue of Jabba the Hutt only in order to highlight the fact that since divine love is the dimension of the richness and abundance of true nature it will spontaneously challenge sectors of ego structure that specifically contradict such properties.

Self-Realization and Personalization

In this chapter we have discussed mainly the issues relating to the discovery and characteristics of the dimension of divine love. Besides what we have discussed, the soul goes through two long and difficult processes in her relation to it. The soul goes through these processes each time she comes upon a new dimension of true nature: as a new dimension arises, first the soul works through the identifications, structures, and positions that function as obstacles to this dimension. Part of this work is the understanding and penetration of all obscurations that are associated to the characteristics of the particular dimension of Being.

Then two intertwined processes ensue that determine the development of the soul in terms of integrating the new dimension and absorbing its wisdom. The first process is realization, as we have begun to discuss in the issue of Jabba the Hutt, with regard to the dimension of divine love. This process involves dealing with the narcissism related to the dimension, that is the particular related expression of the inherent narcissism of ego. We discuss in *The Point of Existence* this narcissism that reflects the soul's alienation from its true nature, and we detail the process of working through the associated ego structures, which culminates in the self-realization of whatever dimension of Being the soul happens to be integrating. We do not discuss this process in relation to divine love in the above book, but we do in *The Pearl Beyond Price*. It culminates in the soul recognizing herself as the divine love. She does not experience herself as a form inseparable from the boundless love, but as its very omnipresence. Divine love becomes her very identity. This realization ushers her into the experience of herself as the unity of existence, with all of its richness and abundance. She does not experience this as herself in terms of being an individual soul. Rather it is the transcendence of her individuality and entitihood. She leaves her identity with the individual soul and becomes the boundless presence. More accurately, the individual form goes through a process of death, and the rebirth is the arising of divine love as the oneness of all existence. A similar process happens on all the boundless dimensions of Being.

The second process that the soul goes through in relation to all the boundless dimensions is their personalization. The central element of this process is the transformation of the soul from a separate entity into personal essence on the particular boundless dimension. The soul learns that she is a personal manifestation of the particular dimension of true nature, as a form that expresses it while being inseparable from it. To use a familiar metaphor, in the self-realization of the boundless dimension the soul realizes that her identity is the boundless ocean. She is the ocean of Being. In the personalization process she learns she is a particular and unique wave in this ocean. She regains her form as an individual soul, but not her separateness. She is an extension of the ocean, part and parcel of it, expressing it personally, giving it the possibility to walk, talk, and function as a person.

We discuss the personalization of divine love in *The Pearl Beyond Price*, chapter 36; this process involves some early object relations with one's parenting objects, especially the loving relation with them and their inadequacies. The rediscovery or recognition of the loving bond leads to a loving connection between the soul and her true nature. Such connection is not an object relation, because there is no object in the Piagetian or psychoanalytic sense. It is more of an experiential recognition of the true and objective relation between the individual soul and true nature.[9]

True nature is the ground that manifests all forms, expressing its infinite potential and richness. Such forms include physical forms, such as bodies, inanimate objects, and phenomena like waves and storms. There are also the essential forms, such as aspects and diamond vehicles, among others.[10] Then there are individual souls. Individual souls, especially human souls, embody the full potentiality of true nature. Physical forms do not; they embody only one possible form that true nature can take. Essential aspects express true nature itself in its various perfections. But the soul is like a microcosm of manifest true nature.

The soul is a particular local form that has the potential to glow much more intensely than physical forms, and more completely than any essential form. It is a manifestation of true nature, embodying its potential and dynamism, but doing so in time and space, in the world of manifestation. It is a particular wave of the ocean of Being, but a special wave. Its specialness is in its potentiality, reflecting the infinite potential of transcendent true nature itself.

Each boundless dimension reveals more of the nature of the soul and her objective relation to true nature on the one hand, and the world of manifestation on the other. We will discuss the contribution of each dimension in the following chapters, but reserve for the last chapters in the book a full discussion of the nature of the relation between true nature and the soul. Divine love reveals that the soul is an inseparable offspring of true nature, a child of the divine. The soul is a body of light, a drop of grace that embodies the total potential of the transcendent, but in a particular and individual manner. She is a potential necessary for the emergence of further possibilities within true nature. This dimension also reveals that the soul is the expression of the love and grace of true nature, and the carrier of this love in the world of manifestation. The soul is the manifestation that can consciously experience true nature in all of its fullness and splendor, contemplate its knowledge and mysteries, reflect on its miraculousness and majesty, and celebrate its beauty and magic.

The soul is the organ of experience and expression of true nature and, hence, the organ of consciousness of Reality.

18 Being and Knowledge

AS THE BOUNDLESS DIMENSIONS EMERGE, they take the soul nearer to the transcendent state of true nature, with each succeeding dimension a little nearer to the primordial simplicity, each one a little simpler, with fewer qualities and features. Divine love is manifest true nature with the quality of love, true nature as heart. Love is a differentiated, recognizable quality, a discriminated quality of Being. The next dimension to emerge is simpler; it arises through the transcendence of the quality of love. We have already seen that love is the source of affective qualities. This gives us a hint of what the next dimension will be like. We refer to it as pure being, or pure presence. Divine love, like all qualities of essence, is being or presence; and all these qualities are definitely pure and undefiled. Here, however, purity is not simply the absence of defilement; it is the absence of differentiated qualities. Pure presence is presence with no qualities, with no discernible color, affect, or taste. It is simply being, with nothing added. It is the simplicity of presence, before presence manifests its qualities and aspects. In a sense, it is like divine love with the love removed, and only the sense of presence or light remaining. But when there are no qualities, the light is not white light. It becomes clear, transparent, colorless light, like clear water or empty space.

Pure Presence

In the realization of pure presence, the soul understands presence in its most pure and simple state. She finds it to be so simple that she cannot say anything else other than that it is presence, or beingness. Presence here is without qualities, devoid of recognizable characteristics such as love, compassion, truth, joy, and so on. It is presence, and that is all, no more and no less. Since her true nature here is simply presence, it is devoid of opaqueness. From this perspective it becomes clear that the manifestation of a quality or color adds something to true nature; it adds a slight opaqueness. Even when there is color the medium of presence can be transparent, but with color it is not as transparent as when it is colorless. When there is color, or quality, one sees the color, or feels the quality, in addition to simply being aware of presence. Hence one's awareness is slightly divided between the sense of presence and the color or quality. It is not exactly a division, for in essential realization the presence and the quality are inseparable, but the mind can still discern two things, on two ontological levels. They are coemergent and coextensive, but the presence and its quality or color can be discriminated.

In pure being, there is no possibility for this discernment, for it is no longer a matter of coemergence. It is singleness, simple unity. This simplicity means total transparency, complete colorlessness. The medium is completely see-through; there is nothing to obstruct the awareness. There is not even any quality for the awareness to reflect on and recognize. It is presence, however, with the sense of the fullness of beingness. Presence is substantial here, and full. We feel and recognize the fullness of the presence that we are, and everything is. Yet it is a purity, an amazing transparency, a medium that is clear through and through. Such colorless transparency can be thought to possess the quality of clarity, but then clarity is nothing but the absence of qualities. In fact, pure presence is a searing clarity, yet this clarity is nothing in particular. It is the qualitiless characteristic of simple presence, its transparency, its lack of opaqueness.

Oddly enough, the sense that this pure presence is without qualities does not make it indescribable; we can point to its transparency, simplicity, clarity, lightness, blissfulness, and emptiness. Yet it is free from all the qualities of the essential aspects. More exactly, it is qualitilessness because it transcends the essential aspects and qualities. It is presence empty of any of the differentiated qualities of essence that characterize its aspects. It is essence before aspects, presence before qualities. Instead of richness, there is simplicity; instead of abundance, there is light emptiness; instead of vivid colors, there is transparent colorlessness. In place of the deep fulfillment of divine love there is the unencumbered lightness of being, and in place of the nectary juiciness of pleasure there is the lighthearted blissfulness of simplicity.

The transition from divine love, with its rich and fulfilling qualities, to pure presence, with its transparent simplicity, generally activates many issues and resistances in the soul. Although the realization of pure presence is undiluted bliss and freedom, it is a momentous loss for the soul that has become accustomed to the richness of divine love. The soul is not familiar with such simplicity and emptiness, and may resist it regardless of how wonderful and free it actually is. She has been attached to richness, color, quality, abundance, texture, flavor, and so on; these attachments now become obvious. Since the beginning of her essential development, and even before that, she has loved such rich textures and colors, the fluffiness and softness that goes with them. She loved and enjoyed all the sweet intimacies and juicy pleasures of life, and her essential development has magnified those pleasures a great deal. To the soul who has been enjoying this blessing, the transition to pure presence seems to mean losing love and all its wonderful qualities: sweetness, intimacy, richness, fullness, warmth, depth, texture, variety, color, and so on. Hence the soul resists the state of simple presence, resulting in contraction and disconnection from Being.

The transition also seems to mean the loss of heart, the loss of the soul's capacity to love and to feel loved, the capacity to feel and respond. This can make her feel that she is losing her humanity, that she will end up being an unemotional thing that she associates with deadness, the lack of fun, and the absence of the warmth of human relationship. These expectations may bring fear and trepidation as well as guilt and self-recrimination. The soul feels that she is now heartless, uncaring and unloving, lacking human warmth and compassion. Her essential development has brought her to the realization of the full and beautiful qualities of essence, culminating in the boundless richness of divine love. Pure being is a higher dimension, but she may sense only that it is the loss of essence and divine love. She views transcendence as loss, and responds with many reactions and conflicts.

At a deeper level of significance, moving to the simplicity of pure being means to her that she is leaving the world, for the world is a universe of colors and qualities, differentiations and discriminated forms. She feels she is leaving the manifest world, which means both a loss and an abandonment. So she may feel grief and wounding, and/or guilt and self-recrimination. Psychodynamically, leaving the world is equivalent to leaving her mother, for mother is the original object, the original world. Many childhood issues tend to arise in this context, especially issues of separation, rapprochement, inadequacy, and loss of merging.

All these reactions, beliefs, and issues are due to the soul's ignorance of the truth of true nature. The reactions come from what the soul associates with the experiential simplicity of pure presence. Pure presence is a dimension of true nature, and so is divine love. There can be no contradiction between them; in fact, they are simultaneously present, along with the other dimensions, structuring manifest true nature. Thus at some point in the integration of pure presence the soul begins to experience it as inseparable from and coemergent with divine love. Pure presence is revealed as simply the ground for divine love, the inner essence of its richness. More important, if the soul truly loves truth for its own sake, and has actually integrated divine love and thus come to a place of basic trust, she will not panic at the possibility of the above losses. Instead she will with trust and ease inquire into the new dimension, to discover its truth and wisdom. When she surrenders to this manifestation of Being she will realize that pure being does not lack anything. Her fears of loss are simply associations, and are not truly warranted by the experience of pure presence. Remaining with this presence, she recognizes its complete purity.

Nondifferentiated Presence

Pure presence is a state of completeness. It is a simple and pure condition that has no excitement, no drama, and makes no big deal about anything. It is the simplicity of fully being oneself. It is being, without any movement out of the completeness and serenity of being. There is no gap in one's identity, in one's sense of oneself; in this condition there is no deficiency, no need, no want, no desire, and no fear. This completeness is not arrived at by completing a process or a project; true nature is eternally complete. It is so complete that there is no excitement about the completeness. It is so complete that there is absolutely no seeking, no looking somewhere else, not even an interest in being aware of the completeness. It is so complete that there is no inner gap that would motivate the soul to even look inward to see the completeness. There is no waiting for anything, no anticipation. When the soul is established in the state of completeness, divine love arises spontaneously, as the only action completeness can take. Pure being is so perfectly complete that it does not arise out of itself to do anything. Its implicit contentment manifests as an outflow of divine love with all of its qualities.

The completeness is not a matter of having anything or everything. It is more fundamental; it is the completeness before manifestation. It is the source of all qualities, for these qualities simply emerge out of it, as it morphs itself into these qualities.

Awareness of being the source and being perfectly complete discloses then the timeless truth of our essential nature in its original transcendent condition. It has all the essential qualities in it, but here they are implicit. This complete, pure presence does not lack any quality because it naturally possesses all qualities. The dimension of divine love basically reveals the qualities, makes them explicit. But before they are explicit they are present in their fullness and completeness in pure being, for pure being is complete being.

Pure being is complete being because it is transcendent being, the source of all. It is the original and primordial presence of true nature, before it manifests through the display of its qualities, qualities that it possesses totally but implicitly in its completeness. As transcendent being, it is not differentiated into qualities. Pure being is nondifferentiated presence, presence before differentiation. Pure presence is simply true nature before it differentiates into its discriminated aspects of presence. The central insight here is that pure presence is nondifferentiated presence. The implication is that it is like white light, and the aspects are like its prismatic colors. However, pure presence is not white, but colorless. It is clear light. It is clear light because it is not a reflected light and not a refracted light. It is a self-existing light, which appears directly in awareness as clear light, and is experienced as pure transparent presence.

The dimension of pure presence is more fundamental than any of the essential aspects, and more fundamental than divine love, because it is prior to the arising of the differentiated qualities of presence. Differentiated means not complete; a particular essential aspect has only one element of the completeness of pure presence. We see here that simplicity is actually more complete than richness, even though we might see richness as more abundant. We also recognize here that the deeper we go into our realization of true nature, the nearer we are to its transcendence, the simpler it will appear in experience.

One significant insight we may have here is that pure being is the ground for all essential aspects, for all qualities of Being. The qualities are simply the differentiation of the implicit perfections of true nature into explicit qualities of presence. True nature prismatically differentiates its presence into these qualities. In other words, these aspects are true nature itself, but true nature that has manifested itself in an explicit perfection that it timelessly possesses in potential, implicitly. It is the pure presence of true nature, with an added quality, a color and flavor. The added quality, which has timelessly been implicitly present, pervades the transparent purity of Being.

Through her opening up to the dimension of pure presence, the soul realizes the deeper ground of her essence, nondifferentiated presence. By being undifferentiated it is not only simpler but more fundamental, more basic, forming the ground and background of all manifestation. It is the ground not only of essential qualities and forms, but of all forms, all manifest differentiation. In other words, manifestation turns out to be nothing but a differentiation of pure presence. Pure presence, a homogeneous manifold field, structures this manifold by differentiating it into the various forms of manifestation. Manifestation is not something that comes out of true nature; rather it is true nature that spontaneously structures itself into the myriad forms constituting manifestation. Thus it is said that manifestation is coemergent with true nature, a state referred to traditionally as nondual reality. It is nondual not because it is two making up a unity; rather it is primordially one, one field with inherent patterns that we recognize as the forms of manifestation. It is the nondifferentiated ground where all differentiations appear, the space empty of differentiation necessary for differentiated forms to be seen. So if we penetrate any form, regardless of its size, we will encounter the infinite expanse of true nature.

We see here two kinds of differentiation, making up two levels of manifestation. The first is the differentiation of true nature into its own qualities, aspects, and forms of essence. True nature is perfect in all ways, but it has special perfections that are eternally present in it in an implicit way, the way white light inherently contains the colors of the rainbow. These are the perfections of love, truth, compassion, contentment, peace and so on, the diamond vehicles and other essential forms and dimensions. Being timeless qualities, they are independent of human mind, history, and culture. True nature presents these depending on historical situations, but the qualities themselves are timeless and primordial. True nature manifests them by differentiating its own field into the forms, colors, and flavors implicitly inherent in its pure presence. Such level of differentiation is purely spiritual, forming the objective and true universal realm, and hence hidden to the physical senses.

The second kind of differentiation of pure presence is differentiation into the myriad recognizable forms—the physical, emotional, and mental forms. This is the totality of physical manifestation, in all of its levels of structure and process, plus the ordinarily experienced inner forms. So it includes the physical universe with its galaxies, stars, planets, atmospheres, elements, atoms, elementary particles, forces, the bodies of all living creatures, plus the normal experience of these creatures, their sensations, feelings, thoughts, images, and so on. Strictly speaking, the ordinary inner mental forms can be classified as a third level of manifestation, but since they are not timeless and do not reflect the perfections of true nature we include them with the physical forms in one level of manifestation. These two levels of manifestation are coemergent with pure being, which forms the ground level of manifestation, as a pure transparent infinite expanse.[1]

Pure presence does not disappear totally when it differentiates itself into manifest forms, whether spiritual or physical. It remains as their eternal ground, their inner essence, giving them the sense of presence; it is their true being, their true ontological ground. A good analogy here is embryonic differentiation: as the original protoplasmic substance differentiates into the various kinds of cells, organs, and systems, this substance does not change from what it is, into these forms. It differentiates into the myriad forms, but remains as their ground, their final biological substance and nature. The developed embryo is a body with organs and systems, but it is all protoplasmic substance.

Pure being remains as the inner constitutive substance of all forms, spiritual and physical. We tend not to be aware of it when we experience these forms, because we are focused exclusively on the features of these forms, to the exclusion of their being, their ontological dimension. When our consciousness is somewhat liberated from this exclusive focus we can discern their ontological nature, their presence. Normally it is easier to become aware of the presence of the spiritual qualities before that of pure presence, because we can recognize the qualities more readily than presence. But since the spiritual qualities are qualities of presence, we can easily discern their presence. This presence is actually pure presence, but we are not discriminating it from the quality it is assuming. In other words, a differentiated aspect is pure presence clothing itself with the garb of a particular quality.[2] In essential experience we experience both the garb and the garbed, the quality and the presence. The presence is pure presence, but we do not see its purity because it is veiled by the quality. The pure presence is always present, cannot not be present, for it is the ground true nature without which there would be no manifestation and no experience.[3]

Unity and Oneness of Being

In actual experience, this means that in the realization of pure presence we are aware of an infinite expanse, totally transparent and absolutely clear. We can be aware of manifest forms, but they are external to the presence, as if they are ripples and waves in an infinite ocean of clear light. Pure presence is their inner essence, true nature, and constitutive substratum. And since it is actually the timeless and spaceless, true nature appears in manifest experience as boundless and infinite, pervading everything.

It is possible to discern two types of experience related to pure presence. One is the experience of it as the inner expanse, which is also the nature of everything. This is the experience of unity, in which there is only pure presence. It is easy to understand such experience of unity when we remember that presence is the ontological dimension of any and all forms. If we take any form, the human body for instance, then presence is its being, its very existence. When we look at the limbs and organs, it is also their existence. It is the existence of the liver, and not only the body as a whole. It is the existence of each of the cells of the liver. It is the existence of each of the molecules of each of the cells. It is the existence of the atoms of each of the molecules. It is the existence of the elementary particles of each of the atoms. We can divide these elementary particles to smaller and smaller elements, and it will be the existence of any of these elements, regardless of how minute. We can divide until we reach the limit, zero, and it will be existence of the limit. In other words, as we analyze down to smaller, more elementary, simpler forms, pure presence will always appear as the nature and beingness of the form. At the limiting calculus of such an analysis we see that there will remain only existence, only being. There will remain only pure presence.

We normally experience this in the form of "pure presence is everything, and everything is pure presence." We see here that pure being is ultimate being, it is true being. By Being we do not mean any particular being, but the being of all beings. Being is true existence, but it is not any existent. Being is the true existence of any and all existents. Existence is not something that characterizes existents, nor something that qualifies the forms of manifestation. Such view of existence is part of the egoic worldview, where existence is an abstract property that the mind gives to the forms of manifestation. The ego-self can only conceive of existence or being as an extension of an object, a property it has, while in the enlightened view existence is absolutely more fundamental than any and all existents and forms. In reality, the forms are qualifications of true existence. We see here that true existence is a metaphysical truth, for it is the ontological ground of all existents. Forms are then differentiations of this fundamental existence. The ego sense of existence is only a reflection of this existence, an abstract idea of it, while it is the ground of all experience, and the actual immediate sense of sentience.[4]

Since there is no differentiation in its presence its experience is totally immediate. There is no differentiated form experiencing it in the experience of self-realization. Its purity is its simplicity, which is also its complete immediacy.

Experiencing oneself as the immediacy of pure presence, or as the expanse that is the inner nature of everything, we experience the state we call "unity." It is the experience of true nature as if from the inside, from its own side, and not from the side of manifest forms. We see that it is an indivisible expanse, a single medium with no inner distinctions, similar to the empty sky.

The other kind of experience, that of oneness, is experiencing pure presence from the vantage point of the manifest forms. We experience ourselves as the oneness of all these forms, that all the forms constitute one Reality, whose nature is pure presence. We are aware of pure presence as the constituting ground of everything, but we are not in the midst of the expanse of true nature, but in the midst of the surface of manifestation. In unity, the forms are still visible, but barely, appearing as distant surface phenomena. True nature almost completely outshines the manifest forms. In oneness, true nature and the manifest forms are both strongly present, as two sides of the same Reality. Both unity and oneness are nondual conditions.[5]

In oneness we understand that the forms are basically the outer structuring of true nature. Pure presence sculpts its own medium into the myriad forms. We see here a different sense of the term *differentiation* than the one we have used. We have used the term *differentiation* to mean something similar to the prismatic separation of the colors of the rainbow, out of white light. But now we mean that there is an expanse, a field that becomes structured by the appearance within it of outlines and patterns. These patterns are due to the appearance of nonpartitioning boundaries that outline the forms. The nonseparating boundaries distinguish the forms from each other without dissociating them from their ground of pure presence. In other words, in the state of oneness of Being, Reality appears as the expanse of true nature structured into a multidimensional Riemannian manifold. The structuring happens through the appearance in the clear expanse of the shapes and colors of the forms, outlines that span the various dimensions of the manifold. The expanse, which is a homogeneous medium, becomes differentiated into the myriad forms: the sky and the stars, the birds and the trees, the mountains and the rivers, the thoughts and the feelings, and so on. Oneness is basically a differentiated unity, a unity in multiplicity. (For further discussion of these considerations regarding this dimension, and other questions, see the second half of *Diamond Heart, Book 3* and the first half of *Diamond Heart, Book 4*.)

Now and Eternity

In the soul's realization of this dimension she dies to being an individual soul and recognizes herself as the infinite and boundless expanse of pure presence, whether in unity or oneness. But this presence, because it is the ground of all differentiations and forms, is also the ground of all change and movement. Movement is basically the flow of differentiations, the succession of different forms that the moving body takes or perceives. Movement is actually a type of change, which is also the flow of differentiations, the succession of different outlines that the particular changing form assumes. All differentiations occur in the expanse of pure presence, as its differentiating self-structuring. Hence, all change occurs in pure presence. This is the case for all kinds of change: action, movement, expression, transformation, evolution, development, growth, maturation, decay, living, and dying. In other words, not only objects but processes occur as the self-structuring of true nature.

One important process is the passage of time. We perceive time only by perceiving change. In fact, time is a measurement of change. When there is no change whatsoever, and no movement, then time is at a standstill. In fact, it is easy to see that time is the flow of successive differentiations in manifestation. Therefore, since all differentiations are within the boundless expanse of true nature, time occurs in pure presence. All time—past, present, and future—happens within the expanse of pure presence. And since we experience presence only in the present, presence is the present of all time, including past and future. As we discussed in chapter 16, true nature is timeless, beyond the concept of time. We see in its dimension of pure presence that it contains all time.

We experience the presence of true nature here inseparable from the present. The present is a differentiation of time, which is a differentiation of pure presence. Thus we experience pure presence as the presence of the present. The presence of the present is now, the nowness of the present. In the self-realization of pure presence, when we are aware of the passage of time, we experience presence as the now. Now includes all differentiations, and hence all the changes in differentiation. Now, therefore, includes all time. It is the now of all time, which we experience as pure presence at any time. The now is not only this instant, it is all instants. More accurately, an instant is a snapshot of differentiation, the next instant is the next snapshot of differentiation, and so on. All these snapshots are differentiations, a flow of differentiations where the awareness of flow depends also on differentiations.

All time flows in the now. All time passes now. Now is always, for it is pre-time. It is pre-time because time is differentiation; and now is pure presence, which is pre-differentiation. Being pure presence, one is present at all times, just as one is present at all places. Time and space are coordinates differentiated within the now. Time-space is the self-structuring of now, which is Being.

We discussed this point in chapter 16 from the perspective of transcendence. The understanding of differentiation of pure presence is an alternative perspective that clarifies different questions. This perspective reveals the objective relation of time to true nature. The experience of the now is not an experience of time. It is not the experience of the present. It is more exactly the experience of pure presence, which can happen only in the present. But since all distinctions and the changes of forms are here differentiations in pure presence, the present is an expression of pure presence. Pure presence is the ground of differentiation, so the now is more fundamental than time. It is actually quite interesting and magical to experience how now extends through all times, how it contains all time. We actually feel our presence as the ground of all, and intuitively containing all time. We feel that our presence contains all the universe at all instants of its time. But no time passes in pure presence. Pure presence as now contains time, the passage of time and all times.[6]

When we experience ourselves as a form in the now, as when the soul experiences herself as the offspring of Being, we experience ourselves not as now, but as eternity. As an inseparable form of pure presence we are aware of the changes all around us, but because we are constituted by pure presence, time passes us, but does not touch us. We are eternity itself. Experientially, eternity is the state we experience when we are aware of the passage of time, but feel untouched by it. Timelessness, on the other hand, is the transcendence of time. There is no awareness of time at all, for there is no differentiation, and hence no change.

Therefore, time is in the midst of now, but eternity is in the midst of time. But time passes neither on now nor on eternity. Time passes in the now, and by eternity, for eternity is the offspring of the now.

Being and Nothing

Since pure presence is nondifferentiated presence, complete with the totality of implicit perfections of true nature, all essential potentials are present in it undifferentiated from each other. Before the advent of the boundless dimensions the soul experiences these essential potentials in two primary categories. One is the presence of fullness, the other the presence of emptiness. The soul experiences essential aspects in forms like nectars and diamonds, for example, but they normally appear in empty spaciousness. The empty spaciousness is one way that essence manifests, as inner space, of various colors and grades, forming the clearing where the various forms and substances of essence emerge. (See *The Void*, part four, for a detailed discussion of this point.) We can think of space as a particular essential aspect because it is possible to differentiate it clearly. However, it is not only differentiated from each other aspect, it is also clearly differentiated from all other aspects, making it fundamental in a way that no other aspect is. It functions as the essential clearing or medium where all aspects arise. It functions as a spacious emptiness where the fullness of Being emerges. Its special status becomes objectively clear in the boundless dimensions, especially in that of pure presence.

Pure presence contains inner space, but the space is undifferentiated from the rest of its perfections. Pure presence thus discloses the inherent synthesis of the fullness of Being and its emptiness. Before experiencing this dimension, the soul has experienced presence as a fullness, a substantiality, almost material, although not physically material. Such fullness or substantiality still appears as the characteristic of pure presence, for it is what gives this dimension its sense of being presence. However, this substantial and full presence is undifferentiated from the emptiness of space. Because of this the experience of full presence on this dimension is indistinguishable from inner spaciousness. Pure presence is at the same time an emptiness, a spaciousness, a nothingness. We feel ourselves, and the whole manifestation, as a fullness of presence at the same time that we feel we are nothing. We simultaneously feel full and empty, substantial and like nothing at all. We are the hereness and fullness of reality at the same time that we are its immateriality, its insubstantiality, its utter lightness.

Fullness of Being and nothingness of space are two inseparable sides of the same presence, of the same perception and sensation. Each side may dominate experience, depending on the particulars of experience. Sometimes we feel ourselves as the boundless truth in its full beingness; at those times, we feel the whole world as the fullness of Being, real and substantial. We are the solid ground of everything, the true existence of all forms and appearances. At other times, we feel light and empty, like a boundless nothingness. Everything is nothing, where the nothing is what truly is. Nothing has any substance or sense of existence; all forms appear as empty appearances, like a mirage reflected in the clarity of nothingness. We feel like nothing, totally light and empty. But it is a wonderful emptiness, for it is a lightness and delight, a freedom and release. There is no heaviness or depression of any kind, not even the weighty fullness of presence. We are lighter than light, emptier than space, a nothing that is the ground of all things. Sensing ourselves, there is nothing to find, just a lightness and an infinite openness. At the same time by remaining with this nothingness we realize it is also fullness, beingness, and presence.

The dimension of pure presence is the beginning of the paradoxes of Being, where logical dichotomies no longer hold. Being and nothing are not two things here, for they have not yet been differentiated for the conceptual mind to make them into a dichotomy. Inner essential space appears here as an indistinguishable side of presence, as the nothingness of Being. Its direct feel is somewhat different from the way we have experienced it before, on the preceding dimensions. Space has felt to us similar to physical space, even though pervaded by the clear awareness and psychological spaciousness. It has felt somewhat linear, Euclidean. Now we feel it free from linear Euclidean dimensionality. It feels as if it has no straight lines, no sense of distance, almost no sense of extension at all. We feel like nothing, a nothing that extends forever, without this nothing having any sense of dimension. It is a nothing that underlies and constitutes everything, and hence there are no limitations or boundaries anywhere. Yet, we do not sense any inner structuring that will give us the sense of length, width, and depth. It has no coordinates, at least no Euclidean coordinates. It is like a space that has been destructured, that has lost its spatial structuring. We have no sense of orientation and no sense of its absence, no sense of direction and no sense of its absence. It is like an exploding nothing where we have a sense of exploding only because we still perceive forms arising.

In some sense, nothingness is the unstructured and unimpeded nature of pure presence. We experience this nothingness psychologically as total openness. We feel we are completely open, with no limitations, boundaries, restrictions, differentiations, or any recognizable features. We are the total openness of true nature, open for any arising and perception. The openness is both phenomenological and psychological. We feel our presence phenomenologically as sheer openness, nothingness so total that it does not impede anything. Hence, we experience ourselves as lightness, buoyancy, transparency, unlimitedness. This lightness often brings an affect of ever-fresh blissfulness and delight, freedom and release. At the same time we are psychologically open, not resisting anything, not preferring one thing over another; we have no positions or identifications.

Ontological nothingness is phenomenologically openness, whose psychological effect is total openness to everything. The soul integrates here the openness of Being necessary for the free emergence of all potential, which is her psychological freedom. Her openness now is the openness of true nature, primordial and without limitations, making it easier for her to know her true unlimited nature.

At this point it is easy for the soul to recognize that the fullness-nothingness, with its openness and transparency, is familiar to her. A little inquiry may reveal to her that it is nothing but her ordinary awareness, the awareness that she has always had, without which there is no perception or experience. She has always known it, for her conscious experience is inseparable from it. Yet she has not recognized it before, partly because she has always exclusively looked at the content of her experience, the objects of her awareness. She has never simply looked at her awareness itself; she has always deeply thought of it as a function, and not an ontological reality on its own. Now she recognizes that this awareness has always been the ground of her perception and experience. She recognizes her awareness for what it is, a presence that is also nothing. She recognizes its fundamental status and its timeless characteristics, and how it is her own true presence and ultimate nature.

This recognition is an explosive insight, a momentous awakening. Pure presence is now revealed, felt, and known as the very presence of awakened awareness, the very reality of awakeness. Soul awakens to her true nature, and experiences her presence as the presence of awakened awareness. She is now awake, bright, clear, lucent, and transparent. She is also full of bliss and delight, beyond mind and reflection. She is drunk with awakeness, delighted with lucidity, and free beyond bounds. The primary awakening is the recognition of her ordinary awareness, which has always been familiar to her, as her true nature. Such recognition intensifies ordinary awareness to a phenomenological and psychological experience of awakeness. Ordinary awareness becomes awakened awareness, which now reveals itself to be the true nature of all phenomenal appearance. She recognizes that her ordinary awareness is actually both presence and openness, fullness and nothingness, inseparable and undifferentiated. She also wakes up to the fact that she has never lost her true nature, that her nature has always been with her, in all her conscious experiences, and that she can never lose it. True nature is so near to her that it does not make sense to lose it, an insight that intensifies her joy and delight, and shows her that she has always been free, always herself. She can lose touch with many of the differentiated qualities of her true nature; but its undifferentiated ground is always what she is.

Origin of Knowing

Recalling our discussion in chapter 3, it would seem that pure presence is nonconceptual awareness, the ground of experience and perception. This conclusion is true but partial. Pure presence is undifferentiated, so it has no discriminated conceptual categories. However, one discrimination remains: nondifferentiated presence is conceptualized as presence. Thus this dimension of true nature retains one concept, the concept of being. The fact that we experience it as presence means we recognize it as beingness. It has no other recognition, but still the recognition of being is a recognition. Being free from all determinations, and hence from all existents and beings, it is true nature with the self-recognition of its own presence. True nature knows one thing here, only one thing. It knows it is. And it knows it is by being. More precisely, nondifferentiated Being is true nature with one concept, the concept of being. This lack of differentiation in pure presence divulges that Being is the original concept, the root of mind and knowing.

The first thing that true nature knows is its being, its presence. This knowing is knowing of its being, a knowing not differentiated from its being. Being, in this dimension, is knowing of being. In other words, in this dimension, manifest true nature is being, which is knowing of being. More accurately, in this dimension of true nature, knowing is being and being is knowing. Being and knowing are both present in pure presence, but undifferentiated. We can say that being is the original knowing, before which there is no knowing.

What do we mean here by knowing? Knowing is recognition, apprehension, which implies some kind of concept. On this dimension, the concept is the simplest possible, the bare possibility of concept. The simplest concept is that of being, which experientially appears as presence.[7] The simplest concept is not a mental concept, not an ordinary representational concept. The concept is presence itself, for concept has not differentiated from consciousness. It is a kind of protoconcept, but even simper and more fundamental.[8] When there is concept and concept is not differentiated from pure consciousness or awareness, we experience such concept as being, which is consciousness coemergent with the concept. The simplest possible concept, in other words, is the experience of nondifferentiated presence. It is not a thought, not a representational concept, but a direct discriminating awareness of presence, inseparable from the presence. This is pure basic knowledge, basic knowledge before any differentiation. We actually see here the origin of basic knowledge, and its objective nature. Basic knowledge is a capacity that exists in its simplest and hence most direct and immediate form in the realization of pure presence. Pure presence is actually basic knowledge before any content, for any content will be a differentiated content.

Since there is no differentiation in pure presence, its knowing is the first knowing, the origin of cognition. We see that the origin of cognition is the experience of being, or more precisely, the dimension of pure presence. Knowing begins with being, which is the knowing of being. It becomes clear to us in the realization of the dimension of pure presence that the origin of the cognitive capacity of mind is the knowing of Being. This means that knowing begins as immediacy of experience, a directness of consciousness with a discrimination of the condition of consciousness. Knowing begins as completely inseparable from what is known. Even more, knowing begins with the nondifferentiation of known, knower, and knowledge. Furthermore, knowing begins with the knowing of Being, where Being is known, knower, and knowledge. The timeless truth here is that fundamentally the knower is Being, the known is Being, and the knowledge is Being. We see of course that as cognitive differentiation develops and expands, knowing tends to develop in the direction of discrimination so completely that what is discriminated is experienced as not only discriminated but separate; ultimately this separateness develops to such an extent that knower, known, and knowledge become three distinct things.

Thus we see that at the beginning of mind there is being, which we experience as undifferentiated presence. We can say that true nature reveals itself at some point in its ontological manifestation as the beingness of all things by clothing itself with the concept of Being. It manifests its nature beyond mind as being-knowing by manifesting the first concept, a concept that pervades the entirety of its manifold. It is then pure being, which is pure knowing, which is pure knowing of being, which is pure being of knowing. Such is the fundamental gnosis, which is the origin of all knowing. To put it succinctly, with being, mind begins.

Universal Concepts

Why are we emphasizing that Being is the origin of mind, when we are speaking of the experience of pure presence? This is actually simple to understand. We have seen that pure presence is not only undifferentiated but that it implicitly includes all perfections of true nature. We have also seen that pure presence differentiates into a particular category, that of the essential aspects, as the explicit manifestation of the perfections of Being. But we have just discussed how in this dimension of true nature being and knowing are inseparable, undifferentiated from each other. Thus when pure Being differentiates into the perfections of Being, its inseparable basic knowledge also differentiates into the basic knowingness of these perfections. Pure presence is presence because it inseparably includes the knowingness of Being, which knowingness now differentiates into the inherent knowingness of the aspects of Being. The differentiation of presence is spontaneously and instantaneously the differentiation of knowing. Therefore essential aspects arise in the dimension of pure presence not only as differentiated presences, but also as discriminated, knowable qualities.

Pure presence is the ground of all the aspects, aspects that now arise as the inseparability of presence and differentiated knowing of the qualities. This basic knowledge differentiates at this point through the manifestation of the inherent perfections of true nature as differentiated concepts. However, these differentiated concepts are inseparable from Being, just as the knowingness of Being is inseparable from Being. They are merely the differentiation of the ground into patterns of color, affect, texture, flavor, and so on. Now, however, we see something new about this differentiation. The color, affect, texture, flavor and so on, are all synthesized into a coherent whole, which is the differentiated concept. The differentiated concept is the totality of the gestalt of the differentiated quality, which the soul realizes is a basic knowingness of the quality. In other words, the differentiation emerges spontaneously synthesized into a coherent gestalt through a cognitive dimension.

Pure being is true nature inseparable from its basic knowingness, which is itself a cognitive dimension. More precisely, pure nondifferentiated presence is true nature in its transcendence appearing clothed and embodied with its own inherent knowingness. This inherent knowingness is initially simply the knowingness of its presence, but here it differentiates into the explicit knowingness of the inherent perfections of this presence.

Each aspect arises in this dimension as presence, but presence inseparable from a differentiated knowing. Each differentiated knowing is a differentiated concept, as if the original concept has differentiated into many subconcepts. In this dimension of pure basic knowledge, knowing and concept are the same; cognition is simply the presence of a basic concept clothing presence. This concept is nothing but the expression of a cognitive dimension that structures the manifold of true nature, in parallel to the other dimensions, those of color, texture, affect, and so on. It is the differentiation of the cognitive dimension, while the simple knowingness of Being is the nondifferentiated cognitive dimension.

Essential differentiations are discriminations; that is, they are differentiations that can be discriminated, cognized, recognized, known. Each essential discrimination is what we have termed an aspect of essence, where it is presence inseparable from the knowingness of the particular quality of perfection. When essential aspects arise in this dimension, they arise in a very clear and precise way, in sharply faceted diamonds of the aspects. In fact, one of the ways of connecting to this boundless dimension of pure presence is through the aspects, where a more complete and more precise understanding of the aspect takes the soul into the realization of this boundlessness. For instance, the soul might encounter a particular terror when dealing with this dimension and might recognize after some inquiry that her terror has to do with projecting her own hatred outside her. When she recognizes the projection, she owns up to her hatred. Upon further inquiry she is likely to find that this hatred is a distortion of her power, which then arises as the essential aspect of power. Here it arises as a large, faceted black diamond, with the full quality of presence characteristic of this dimension. She feels a full sense of presence, powerful and immense, yet clear and precise, with an exact understanding of power. She feels she is powerful enough to be herself, that nothing can scare her away from being herself. As she relaxes into this presence, and the presence reveals its wisdom to her as a quality of pure being, she begins to be aware of a nothingness that is undifferentiated from beingness, a perception characteristic of this dimension. The diamond presence expands to reveal the full nothingness and openness of this presence.

As the diamond expands and reveals its inherent nothingness, it becomes clear that it is a form that nothingness takes, that the quality, with its specific countenance, is a transparent garb that Being takes, but that it is inherently completely nothing. The recognition of nothingness of this presence highlights the quality in a new way. The quality appears now as an ephemeral, transparent, and insubstantial form, a cognitive form. The sense of it is similar to our experience of our normal thoughts and images when we become aware of them, that is, ephemeral and intellectual. We recognize here that the black diamond is similar to what we know as a concept, a cognitive form. It is the concept of power. This is the precise and objective recognition and understanding of the essential aspect of power on the dimension of pure presence. We see here the basic concept itself, which turns out to be the black diamond. The sharpness of the diamond indicates the precision of understanding the aspect on its own level.

The moment we recognize that the aspect is a concept, the transparent black diamond form becomes increasingly nothing, until it fades away. As it fades away we find ourselves to be the boundless presence of undifferentiated being. And we understand that we are not only powerful enough to be ourselves, but that we are boundless power itself; for we are boundless and infinite Being. We can be ourselves; we are not afraid of being ourselves, because we are the infinite Supreme Being itself.

This process is repeated for each of the essential aspects, where each aspect appears as a huge, sharp diamond of a particular color and quality. As we directly and experientially recognize that each aspect is a concept, it dissolves and reveals the nondifferentiated ground of pure presence. Each essential aspect reveals itself to be a conceptual differentiation of pure presence, conceptual not in the representational sense but as a discrimination in basic knowledge. Each aspect is a differentiated and discriminated form in basic knowledge. Each of the aspects reveals itself as a universal discrimination, a natural cognitive differentiation of true nature itself. In this dimension it becomes crystal clear what essential aspects are and what their relation to true nature is. It is also very clear that an aspect is a universal manifestation, in the sense that it is not the conceptualization of one person's mind. It is the conceptualization of the mind of true nature itself, for it is the discriminated differentiation of the basic cognitive dimension of true nature. We recognize that each essential aspect is a universal concept, a concept that embodies in an explicit way a particular perfection of true nature.[9]

We refer to these diamonds as "concept diamonds," for they are actually the original concepts, the original conceptual differentiation of pure presence. We need to stress again that by concept we do not mean ordinary mental and representational concepts, which are elements of ordinary knowledge. We are discussing concepts that precede the personal discursive mind, elements of pure basic knowledge that are free from the reflection of ordinary knowledge. We also refer to them as "no-diamonds," meaning nothing-diamonds, referring to the fact that they are discriminated differentiations of nothing and also to the fact that because they are differentiations they do not exist independently. They are empty of an independent essence, for their true essence is the boundless pure presence that is the indivisible ground and nature of everything.[10]

Noetic Forms

The various concept diamonds are the diamonds of the vehicle of the diamond guidance in the dimension of pure presence. This vehicle may appear now as the revealer of the truth of this dimension, and of Reality from the perspective of this dimension. It reveals that the dimension of pure presence is that of universal or divine mind, the mind of Being, just as the dimension of divine love is the heart of Being. It reveals what mind is, what cognition is, what thinking is, what reason is, and so on. And it reveals them on their many levels and complexities, as well as the relation between these levels.

First, we will return to the question of differentiation. We saw above that essential aspects form a special type of differentiation. The level of boundless presence presents another type of differentiation, a more general one, which comprises the totality of manifestation. In other words, boundless pure presence differentiates itself into the various forms that populate manifestation, on all levels of manifestation. Essential aspects are a special category that embodies the perfections of Being. However, just as in the differentiation of essential aspects the original simple knowingness differentiates into the various recognizable qualities, the same happens in the differentiation of the myriad forms of manifestation. The basic cognitive dimension of pure presence differentiates into the various forms of phenomenal appearance. What is new in this differentiation is that because we now know that pure presence possesses a cognitive dimension, the forms that manifest are not only differentiated outlines in the manifold of presence. This Riemannian manifold reveals now that it has a cognitive dimension, which points to the important realization that these forms are also cognitive forms.

On the dimension of pure presence, all forms can be discriminated, recognized, cognized, known. In other words, all forms are cognitive forms. However, they are knowable not discursively but directly, as manifestations of basic knowledge. We can know anything and everything here, given opportunity and true capacity, but we can know them directly, immediately, intimately. Because of this we call them noetic forms, referring to the *nous* of direct knowing.

On the dimension of pure presence, manifestation consists of noetic forms, forms capable of precise and sharp discriminating knowing. We can know any form, whether it is a star, a planet, a rock, an animal, an organ of the body, a molecule, an atom, a feeling, a state, a thought, directly and sharply for what it is. If it manifests we can know it. We can know it exactly and objectively, with specific details and minute discriminations. We can know it because it is fundamentally a noetic form, because it is fundamentally knowable. It is fundamentally knowable because knowing is a fundamental dimension of the ground true nature and any form is a manifestation that participates in this dimension.

We find in this dimension the source of all knowing, and all knowability. Pure presence is the cognitive, more precisely the noetic, dimension of true nature, which makes knowing possible. For all knowing is ultimately the knowing of Being, the knowing of isness. We recognize the source of knowability in the fact that all forms, objects, and processes, are noetic. We do not mean here a vague "mystical" kind of knowing, intuitive and impressionistic, but rather a discriminating exact recognition of the form, its qualities, properties and functions, its components and systems, and so on. We see here the possibility for the precise knowledge of objective science.[11]

Universal Mind

The mind that knows is pure presence itself, which knows its own differentiations. It is the knowing of Being, the knowing of true existence, differentiated into the knowing of beings and existents. It knows through the soul, for it needs to be localized for there to be discriminated knowledge of forms. It provides the soul with her knowing faculty, with her mind and intellect, just as the dimension of divine love provides her with her heart and feelings. This means that it is not an individual soul that knows, although that is how things appear. When we know the boundless dimension of pure presence, which is the dimension of pure basic knowledge, we recognize that it is basic knowledge that knows. Basic knowledge is a dimension of true nature, and not limited to the individual soul. It operates through the soul; for the soul is its organ of perception, similar to how the eye is the organ of seeing for the body but it is not exactly the eye that sees.

The boundless dimension of being-knowledge is inherently knowing; its very substance is knowledge, for it is the original knowledge of simple being. We have seen that knower, known, and knowledge are the same in this dimension. True nature here is the knower, the known, but also knowledge. It is pure knowledge without differentiation; it is the very substance of knowing, which is knowledge.[12] The whole expanse of this dimension is spanned by knowledge, constituted by knowledge, knowledge undifferentiated from the experience of presence. The expanse is the space of pure basic knowledge, untouched by ordinary knowledge. The expanse functions as the background against and within which noetic forms manifest themselves.

All manifestation is simply the expanse of basic knowledge that differentiates itself into the myriad noetic forms. All forms of the phenomenal world appear as noetic forms, forms that knowledge takes. This means that all manifestation appears in this dimension as knowledge, basic knowledge but knowledge nevertheless. We discussed in chapter 4 how the field of the soul is pure knowledge, that all its experience is nothing but a constant flow of forms of knowledge, that all thoughts, feelings, sensations, images, perceptions, actions, and so on, are nothing but manifestations of knowledge within a field whose very medium is knowledge. In the realization of the dimension of pure presence, we experience the whole world, not only our subjective experience, as knowledge. We live in knowledge, surrounded by knowledge on all sides. There is nothing but knowledge; knowledge inside, knowledge outside, even inside and outside are nothing but knowledge. There are no such things as rocks and mountains, sky and oceans, animals and people. They are all forms of knowledge, noetic forms inseparable from the boundless field of knowledge. We are knowledge, so are all beings, all souls, and all manifestations of Being.

When we realize this truth of Reality, all the world begins to shimmer and glow with the light of knowledge. Everything appears not only as an indivisible unity but also luminous and resplendent with the transparent light of knowledge. We see the usual phenomenal forms, but they appear as forms of light, lucent and iridescent and full of color and meaning. The world is meaningful, but not reducible to any specific meaning. It is simply all meaning, all knowledge, true and direct knowledge. There is brilliance, radiance, clarity, lightness, fullness, and presence. The universe is a multidimensional manifold where all dimensions intersect the dimension of knowledge at all their points. Hence, knowledge pervades the whole manifold, making it into a magical self-luminous holographic world of exquisite meaningful deep knowledge. The colors, textures, and flavors of physical objects express the essential qualities themselves, this way the phenomenal world expresses the perfections of Being. The darkness of the night expresses the depth, stillness, and mystery of the black peace essence; the redness of blood and fire reflects the vitality and vigorous energy of the red strength essence; the yellow of the sun and of flowers embodies the lightness and delight of the yellow joy essence, and so on. In such experience the two levels of differentiated forms appear as a unified gestalt, unified by the boundless presence of basic knowledge.

The whole universe, appearance or manifestation, appears as mind, but divine mind, universal mind.[13] Nothing falls beyond the purview of this universal mind, for it is all manifestation. We are all in God's mind, as God's thoughts; so are all objects both inner and outer. We may recognize here how our individual minds are reflections of universal mind, microcosms of the macrocosmic mind.

Ordinary Mind

The soul possesses memory, which makes it possible for her to retain impressions of basic knowledge. Her first memories are bound to be of elements of pure basic knowledge, direct and simple experiences and perceptions. However, she cannot retain the fullness of the impression, but most importantly, she cannot retain the knowingness of being. Pure basic knowledge is both protoconcept and sense of presence, but memory cannot retain the sense of presence, as we discussed in chapter 11. So it retains only the concept, the defining outlines of the element of knowledge in question—the shape, color, texture, affect, and cognitive garb. Basic knowledge further manifests in the soul the capacity to label such concepts. The label is usually a word, which is another form of basic knowledge that refers to the remembered one. Memory and labeling become the initial steps of the process of representation. Conceptualizing develops into full-blown formal concepts that refer to categories and categories of categories. Memory can then connect one concept to another, remembering relationships and correspondences, beginning the process of thinking.

The discussion in this section adds to a similar discussion about rational thought in chapter 4; we address thinking more completely in chapter 20, where we discuss the dimension related to change and flow.

Linking categorical concepts, thinking then develops more abstract concepts, such as evolution, thermodynamics, communism, and so on. They are abstract because they are further removed from basic knowledge. This activity of abstraction has no limit, and can develop to amazing degrees of abstraction and complexity. We end up with an increasing accumulation of concepts, of various degrees of abstraction, and an amazing network of connections and interrelations. This accumulation is normally called knowledge, but we refer to it in our work as "ordinary knowledge," differentiating it from basic knowledge. It is important to not forget that basic knowledge is the origin of ordinary knowledge. The latter is in fact a subset of basic knowledge, for it consists of mental forms, which are nothing but a certain type of noetic form. But ordinary knowledge is a special subset that becomes influential in the development of basic knowledge. The mind begins to not only directly know but to relate what it knows to its memories and ordinary knowledge. Basic knowledge gradually loses its purity, becoming increasingly contaminated with ordinary knowledge. The individual mind does not only relate and associate memories and concepts to immediate perceptions and experiences, but in time begins to experience and perceive through its ordinary knowledge. For example, the soul's perception of a sunset is not simple and direct; it includes, in ways that the soul becomes increasingly unconscious about, associations of past experiences of sunsets, the memories and impressions surrounding such experiences, information about the sun and its setting, and so on. So the soul ends up viewing the sunset through a segment of its ordinary knowledge.

The loss of immediacy is even more radical. We discussed in chapter 12 how the soul develops through the establishment of ego structures, which become her defining identity and character. We have seen that such development dissociates the soul from her true nature by interposing the totality of her ordinary knowledge, which includes all her history of experience, between her and her experience. Experience becomes a combination of basic knowledge and ordinary knowledge, mixed to various degrees. Ordinary knowledge, in particular, develops the patterns of basic knowledge by seeing new connections that allow the emergence of new forms of basic knowledge. Obvious examples are inventions, the development of new procedures and processes, and the development of new kinds and areas of knowledge, culminating in our scientific knowledge.

Ordinary knowledge also influences basic knowledge in ways not as wholesome as these. By interposing itself between the soul and her basic knowing, it increasingly dissociates the soul from the immediacy of her presence. Ordinary knowledge can dominate consciousness so much that the soul forgets the importance of basic knowledge, and hence the central significance of the sense of presence. We need to remember that it is characteristic of ordinary knowledge that it cannot carry the sense of presence. This sense is a concept, but it is the simplest concept, the first concept, which forms the basis of all knowing, and memory cannot hold such simplicity. This concept has no differentiated outlines for memory and ordinary knowledge to carry.

Reification

Another significant reason for the unavoidable alienation from the presence of Being, related to another characteristic of ordinary knowledge, is that in pure basic knowledge all noetic forms are manifestations of the same ground, differentiations of the same field. They do not appear as separate objects; each forms an inseparable segment of the universal pattern. Their unity is in their omnipresent ground true nature. However, when memory retains an impression of such a noetic form it is generally difficult for it to remember its oneness with other forms. Furthermore, since memory cannot carry the sense of presence, because this sense is nothing but the immediacy of experience, it actually cannot carry the oneness of the form with the rest of manifestation, except perhaps as a vague intuitive continuation of the sense of oneness. It may remember for a short time the intuitive experience of oneness, but the normal uses memory wants to make of what she carries generally do not include the sense of oneness. And when the recollected concepts multiply and become complex, this memory becomes impossible.

The obvious result is that the individual mind ends up with a collection of disconnected concepts, memories of discrete elements and objects. Noetic forms that were initially inseparable components of an infinite pattern, constituting the oneness of Being, end up in the mind as separate objects, composing a dismembered world. The discreteness actually exists only in the individual mind, never in the field of Reality itself. Furthermore, the mind uses these discrete units to view this field, a lens that when finally established gives the mind the impression that basic knowledge is composed of discrete entities. This process is supported and enhanced to completeness, normally in early childhood, when ego development structures the soul using these disconnected and discrete memory elements as building blocks for its structures. The veil through which the soul learns to view her experience does not only function as an intermediary that dissociates her from her sense of presence, but also as an epistemological scalpel that dissects each noetic form from the oneness of Being. Her experience becomes then of discrete objects, which she grows up believing to populate manifestation.[14]

The process of turning the basic knowledge of an inseparable noetic form into a discrete object in the mind is referred to as reification.[15] Ordinary knowledge cannot help but reify its experience, and this process of reification seems to be a natural stage in the soul's cognitive development, necessary for the development of ordinary knowledge and discursive thinking.

The normal mind reifies concepts, which originally are noetic forms inseparable from the oneness of existence. Therefore, ordinary knowledge is composed of a collection of reified concepts. It is important to realize that what is reified is a concept, a concept that is abstracted from the oneness of pure basic knowledge. Furthermore, reified concepts exist only in the individual mind, never in Reality. The most important consequence for the soul is that she ends up living in a reified world, a world populated by reified concepts. She no longer sees reality, but believes in and sees a world composed of objects. She believes she sees reality as it is, when in fact she is perceiving her own reified concepts. In a very real sense, she lives in her own small mind, or more accurately, within a world structured by the reifications that she projects on it. She is deluded by the belief in discrete objects, a delusion that becomes the basis of her sense of separateness and her deep conviction in it.[16] This delusion develops into the crystallized conviction that each object exists ultimately and independently, that reality is actually composed of ultimately and independently existing discrete objects, one of which is the soul herself.[17]

Inquiry as a Path of De-reification

We now come full circle to the barrier of separateness, the ego principle. We see that the ground of this barrier is reification, for the separate individual self is a reification of the soul.[18] The ego principle is basically the principle of reification. From our discussion in this chapter we see that the general barrier to the experience and realization of the boundless dimension of pure presence is reification. Adhering to the view of the reified world we cannot see the real world of oneness and unity, and cannot experience the pure presence of our true nature. It also becomes obvious that a potentially powerful path toward the realization of true nature is one that can penetrate the reifications of the mind and reverse the process of reification. Many wisdom teachings, including our approach, are based on this insight.

In our approach we begin with what the soul normally experiences. These are mostly reifications and the products of reification. The soul, however, is not aware of this at the beginning of her inner journey, and will generally not take it to heart if told directly. The process of the path is an inquiry that attempts to penetrate the boundaries of reified concepts.[19] The inquiry is an exploration to understand the truth of experience, which initially amounts to the truth of reified experience: that is, the understanding of how it is a reified concept, how this reification affects experience and obscures the basic truth. Inquiry leads to the discovery of truth, which unfolds as an ever-deepening understanding of the forms of our experience. This understanding is fundamentally a matter of seeing through the products of reification, allowing them to shed their reifying boundaries, and hence regaining the directness of basic knowledge.

An important element of this inquiry is understanding how one's history, ego structure, beliefs, and worldview determine and pattern one's experience. In other words, it is an exploration of how the soul's ordinary knowledge influences and contaminates basic knowledge. As inquiry penetrates this influence it makes the boundaries of the soul's reified concepts more transparent, allowing her experience to become more immediate. For as reified concepts become transparent, their original corresponding noetic forms lose the opaqueness that makes them appear as discrete objects. As they become transparent, the light of Being begins to shine through them, revealing the true condition of appearance. Such development of immediacy is the purification of basic knowledge, which appears as the discovery of truth. Truth simply means what the forms of basic knowledge actually are, free from the influence of ordinary knowledge. Because the liberation of basic knowledge from the limiting influence of ordinary knowledge is a gradual process, the revelation of truth is also gradual. Truth shines forth with increasing intensity and brilliance, as the light of basic knowledge, until it reveals itself as the presence of essence. Essence unfolds its aspects and dimensions, supporting and guiding the inquiry and understanding, and showing the soul what it means to experience pure basic knowledge; for essential presence, in any of its qualities, is basic knowledge undefiled by ordinary knowledge. The diamond vehicles further penetrate the reifications that obstruct the timeless wisdom of true nature, finally penetrating the reified concepts of entity and identity.

Essential presence unfolds its subtle boundless dimensions until it finally appears as the boundless pure presence. Here the aspects appear as the concept diamonds. The concept diamonds, it turns out, specifically challenge and penetrate the reification of essential aspects. For a long time in her journey, the soul cannot help but engage in the process of reifying her experience, including her essential experience. In fact, essence first arises as if within the soul or outside her, as limited forms of presence, because it is arising in a mostly reified field. Hence, it is very difficult for the soul not to reify the essential qualities, and put them in conceptual packages. If this continues without challenge it will ultimately close the door to essential unfoldment. But the true attitude of inquiry, of loving truth for its own sake, keeps this door open, allowing essence to finally reveal its aspects in the form of concept diamonds. These, one by one, reveal the largely unconscious reification of the aspects, precipitating the soul into the realization of herself as the pure omnipresence of true nature, as we have discussed above in the example of the black peace diamond.

The dimension of pure presence clearly reveals the process of reification, and challenges the major reified concepts of egoic experience. Here the soul learns the objective wisdom about unity and oneness, knowledge and Being, and the nature of the barriers to realization. It becomes clear that the barrier here is not exactly concepts themselves, not the process of conceptualization, not even the conceptualizing mind. It is the reification of concepts that makes them opaque, and causes them to appear in experience as discrete objects. We need to remember that basic knowledge is the source of concepts; in fact, it is full of concepts, but concepts that carry the immediate knowledge of Being. There is no knowing that is not conceptual, including gnosis, basic knowledge itself. The barrier to realization is the reification of concepts, not their arising. The process of conceptualization is involved in reification, but as we will discuss in the next chapter, it is important to distinguish between conceptualization and reification.[20]

We have not discussed in any detail the various major issues that need to be resolved for the realization of the dimension of pure presence. Lack of space makes this impossible, but we can mention that among these issues are those related to self-realization and reification, and how the ego sense of identity is grounded in reified concepts. We discuss this in some detail in *The Point of Existence*, chapter 39. We also discuss the process of personalization of pure presence in *The Pearl Beyond Price*, chapter 37.

19 Awareness and the Nonconceptual

KNOWING DEPENDS ON PERCEPTION; without perception there can be no knowing. Perception is, hence, more fundamental than knowing. Perception involves the capacity for simple awareness, the sensitivity that makes it possible for us to see, hear, smell, taste, and feel.

We saw in the last chapter that the dimension of pure presence turns out to be nothing but our simple everyday awareness, even though we ordinarily do not recognize it as such. This does not mean that it is pure awareness. It is more accurate to say that it is our ordinary awareness, recognizing that this awareness includes the cognitive dimension, which is inseparable from our ordinary awareness except when discriminated through meditation practice. We ordinarily perceive and know, or perceive and do not know what we perceive, together. We normally cannot separate awareness and knowing.

Yet the awareness responsible for perception is more fundamental than knowing and cognition. This becomes clear when we experience another boundless dimension of true nature, pure awareness. Pure awareness is again a field: boundless, infinite, and continuous. It is similar to that of pure presence, but without the cognitive element. Since the source of cognition is the knowing of being, pure awareness is not a sense of being. We do not experience it as presence, for the experience of presence involves the concept of being or existence. Since pure awareness is a continuous medium or field, we can say it is presence, but it does not feel like presence because it involves no recognition of being or nonbeing. There is only the pure awareness of manifestation, without knowing of what one is aware.

Pure awareness is like a mirror that reflects what is in its field but does not recognize or know what it reflects. Pure awareness is the capacity to perceive prior to knowing or recognition. It is implicit in normal perception, in which we perceive and know at the same time. We do not normally recognize this dimension because we always experience it along with the cognition.

In various wisdom traditions pure awareness is referred to as nonconceptual awareness or nonconceptual presence. To call it nonconceptual presence is problematic, for even though it manifests as a field and ground, it is beyond any conceptual category, and presence implies the concept of existence. Pure awareness is free from all concepts, basic concepts and representational ones. There is no knowing in it, neither basic knowing nor ordinary knowing.

Pure awareness is perception without cognition, seeing without recognition, hearing without comprehension. When this level of awareness is dominant in our experience, we can be looking at someone and see a shape and color, lights and shadows, but not register that we are seeing a person, or indeed have any notion about whether there is such a thing as a person. We do not recognize the shape, or even know that there is such a thing as a shape. We see the colors but do not register that there is such a thing as color; we see the lights and shadows, but have no sense or meaning for what we see. We may hear someone talking but have no comprehension of the words; we do not actually know that there is such a thing as words. We hear sounds, without recognizing that there is such a thing as sound. The mind responsible for knowing and discrimination, and hence recognition and memory, is not operative here. We are simply aware, without the sense that there is someone who is aware, without even the idea that there is such a thing as awareness. There is simply pure perceptivity, mirror-like and absolutely innocent.[1]

Such a state is not chaotic, not dull, not confused, but the absolute opposite. Recognizing the presence of her true nature as simply a field of awareness, the soul recognizes pure awakeness. She feels awake, bright, and clear, as if she has been perceiving from within clouds, and now she has raised her head above the cloud layer. There is stupendous clarity and inconceivable transparency. She has awakened to her true nature prior to all knowing. Because the presence she experiences now does not include cognition, she can experience her true nature free from all knowledge, all memory, and all association. She experiences a boundless and infinite field pervading all appearance, totally transparent and completely clear. It is simply the presence of awareness, not as a function, but as a field, a manifold, whose very substance is nothing but pure sensitivity, pure perceptivity, pure awareness. There is a vast expanse, transparent and lucent, limpid and bright, which forms the ground of all manifestation.

Since all the boundless dimensions of true nature are coemergent, they function as ground for manifestation, or appearance. Here we are isolating one of these ground dimensions, pure awareness. This dimension functions as a ground similarly to divine love and pure presence, but because it is only awareness, it also functions as ground for these two dimensions. Both of these boundless dimensions imply awareness, and at this dimension we make this awareness explicit. As ground, it pervades all forms, constitutes all forms, and transcends all forms. We discussed the notion of ground in the last three chapters, so we will discriminate here only how this ground is different from the experience of previously discussed dimensions, and focus on what it adds to our understanding of true Reality.

Pure awareness is similar to pure presence in that it is a nondifferentiated field, but also in being clear and transparent. Its clarity and transparency are more striking, more crisp, and more intense than that of pure presence. This difference brings us the sense of awakening, as if one has awakened from a long sleep, or has emerged from a previously unperceived cloudiness. Also, the absence of knowingness makes us feel bright and awake without any content to this awakening. We feel an intensity, a brightness, a crispness that simply obliterates all thinking and rumination. We become like a transparent light bulb, and the whole universe becomes boundless clear light.

Since in pure awareness there is no knowing and no recognition, there is no memory and no association; there is nothing old in the experience. Everything seems as if perceived for the first time, absolutely new and fresh. We do not feel this as newness, because that would be a contrast to something old, but more as a sense of intense freshness, as if our consciousness is pervaded with the crisp, delicious coolness of a mountaintop breeze in winter.[2] We feel cleansed, unburdened, and the cool freshness is an unspeakable ecstasy. A delicious tingle fills the totality of our consciousness. We are awareness, pure and simple, with no memory, no history, no identity, and no heaviness.

Nonconceptual Awareness

Pure awareness is presence in the sense that it is a field or medium that pervades everything, and underlies all manifestation. Yet, in the experience itself we do not have a sense of recognition that we are that. Even though the awareness is the presence of a field, the direct sense is of no presence, no existence, and no substance. The immediate experience is totally paradoxical: we are aware of awareness as a pervasive field, and at the same time this field does not feel like the presence of anything. We are here and now fully, yet experience a total absence, a lightness that is the very absence of any existence. We cannot say awareness exists, yet we cannot say it does not exist. It is both and neither, and not even that.

Since pure awareness is beyond knowing, the experience is totally nonconceptual. There is awareness of awareness, which is the presence of awareness, but this presence is not felt as presence. Nonconceptual awareness is beyond the concept of being, so we cannot experience or describe it as being or presence. We might then think that it must be nonbeing, but nonbeing is also a concept, the opposite of being. Being and nonbeing constitute a pair of mutually defining concepts; like all conceptual pairs, neither exists without the other. Experientially, being is presence and nonbeing is absence; the latter is often referred to as emptiness. Because pure awareness is free from the cognitive element, it transcends all concepts, but it is specifically the transcendence of the concept of being. By transcending being it also transcends nonbeing, emptiness. Experientially we feel it as simultaneous presence and absence, being and nonbeing. But this is only when we begin to view it conceptually. When the experience is full and complete we cannot say it is both presence and absence, nor neither. In fact, it does not occur to us to say anything about it, for to speak is to conceptualize, while here we are absolutely in the moment, beyond all mind and speaking.

One way to arrive at the experience of nonconceptual awareness is through negation. We first negate presence or being, and we experience absence, or metaphysical emptiness. This negation comes not from a denial or rejection or attempt to go beyond, but simply through one's awareness expanding or deepening past being and presence. Then we negate absence, arriving at nonconceptual presence, which is pure awareness. This occurs experientially in the path of the Diamond Approach, where the student moves from pure presence to pure absence, recognizing the ontological emptiness of presence and all phenomena predicated on presence. The revelation of truth continues to pure awareness, beyond presence and absence. Traditionally, the most common route in this process is the transcendence of the discriminating mind, by going beyond any discriminating cognition and simply pointing to what is.[3]

Thusness

In recognizing that pure awareness is nonconceptual, we discover new and surprising truths about Reality. We see that our being is fundamentally beyond mind, beyond discriminating knowing. We see that, since nonconceptual awareness is the ground of all manifestation, Reality is independent of our minds, and manifestation is not the creation of our thoughts. Without manifestation there would be no awareness, and since awareness is ultimately nonconceptual, the forms in manifestation are not conceptual either. This is a radical discovery. It illuminates the Reality beyond our individual minds, revealing that the differentiation in manifestation is beyond mind. We do not need discriminating knowing to perceive differentiation. Differentiation is inherent in manifest reality, and it ontologically precedes the dimension of basic knowledge, the *nous* dimension. The basic knowledge of pure presence simply adds discrimination to the already present differentiation of forms in manifest reality.[4]

In other words, pure awareness, a nonconceptual presence and truth, is the ground of all manifestation, more fundamental than any knowing. But this nonconceptual field that gives the soul both her fundamental ground and her capacity for perception, differentiates into the various forms of manifestation, the shapes and colors, the tastes and flavors, the changes and movements. These forms appear differentiated in pure awareness, but such differentiation does not imply recognition, rather it means simple differences, a perception of patterns of color and shape that we do not recognize as having any meaning and do not even isolate as forms. We simply see an indivisible transparent medium with patterns of color and shape, but we do not even recognize these as colors and shapes. We perceive these patterns without abstracting out forms from these patterns, without even isolating any details in the patterns. We see the patterns of appearance in their totality, but without mentally registering that we are doing so. Cognitively contemplating our perception we can then say we saw patterns, shapes, and colors. (See *Luminous Night's Journey*, chapter 6, for a detailed description of this perception.)

This understanding usually appears in the experience of the total inseparability of ground and manifestation. It is the experience that there is one indivisible Reality, not two as ground and manifestation.[5] The manifestation is not something apart from the ground, but it is the ground itself. One perceives everything forming an indivisible, boundless, and transparent block of ice, with forms simply as carvings in this block. There is a sense of eternity, for time is also conceptual, but mostly it is the sense of seeing what is, Reality as it is, before memory, association, and commentary. It is the virgin Reality that has never entered time. Discriminating mind cannot enter there, nor thought, nor memory.

In this experience, there is only true nature, for all forms are nothing but true nature, as its own differentiation. Conceptually, we can discern true nature as the pure undifferentiated awareness that is the ground of everything, and everything as manifestation, but in immediate experience there is no such discrimination of the two. Reality is what is, in its thusness.[6]

We describe this situation by saying that nonconceptual Reality is inherently differentiated as the world we normally see, but in the immediate experience of pure awareness we do not recognize the elements of our world, even though we clearly perceive them. In other words, differentiation is a step prior to discrimination. To put it more analytically, true nature manifests as a nonconceptual ground that differentiates into all the forms of appearance, and its dimension of pure presence develops these differentiated forms into discriminated ones.

Differentiation creates differences, but discrimination makes these differences knowable. The new point for our discussion is that the nonconceptual ground functions as ground by differentiating into the various forms. If that were not the case we would then have a ground that is separate from the world of differentiation, which is a contradictory position from the point of view of the perception of the nonconceptual ground.

The Crystal Dimension

We call this dimension of nonconceptual Reality the crystal dimension. The forms of the world appear in this dimension of true nature as shapes and colors nonconceptual presence takes. There is no knowing, but these forms are the same ones that become knowable at the dimension of pure presence. At the dimension of pure presence we saw them as noetic forms. But since these are the same forms that appear at the nonconceptual dimension, we refer to them in this dimension as prenoetic forms. They are prenoetic just as pure awareness, nonconceptual presence, is prenoetic presence. It ontologically precedes the knowing dimension, but is a ground for it. In other words, all forms appear as fundamentally prenoetic because they can and do become noetic when true nature manifests its noetic dimension. In normal experience, the nonconceptual and noetic dimensions are present simultaneously, for we both perceive and know in the same instant of experience. (See *Diamond Heart, Book 4*, chapter 16, for a more detailed discussion of noetic and prenoetic forms.)

Experience at the nonconceptual dimension of Reality includes all the forms we normally perceive, outer and inner. These include the physical forms, the oceans and mountains, stars and galaxies, trees and animals, molecules and atoms, and so on. They include all our subjective experience: the thoughts, images, feelings, and sensations. But they also include all the spiritual forms, including essential aspects and diamond vehicles. Essential aspects arise at this dimension differentiated, in the sense that they have different colors and textures. Yet, we do not recognize what they are, or what they mean. We cannot, in fact, differentiate them from the physical and emotional forms. We cannot tell that they are pure spiritual qualities and the others are physical or emotional, for all forms of manifestation are nothing but a differentiation of the same reality, nonconceptual presence. In other words, we can experience essential aspects at this level of experience but we will not be able to recognize what they are. We can tell that the pink quality is different from the green one, but we cannot tell that the pink is love and the green is compassion. The recognition of the qualities requires the noetic capacity of the dimension of pure presence.

Just as the essential aspects arise in the dimension of pure presence as faceted gems, in the nonconceptual dimension essence manifests in a similar way. The absence of knowingness makes consciousness more objective and less emotionally reactive, and the qualities tend to appear as crystals rather than gems. The diamond vehicles become crystal vehicles, which are simply the diamond vehicles on the nonconceptual dimension of Being. The crystals and crystal vehicles become the emissaries of the wisdom of nonconceptuality, of reality beyond mind. The diamond guidance, for example, appears in the crystal nonconceptual form and guides the soul's consciousness to the integration of nonconceptual presence. This is a subtle manifestation, not easy to understand. What does it mean that we learn the wisdom of nonconceptual truth? What is wisdom on the nonconceptual level?

The crystal aspects and vehicles function partly by challenging various barriers and obstacles to pure awareness, which are mostly conceptual positions taken to be ultimate truths. These positions appear on the conceptual level, but the guidance demonstrates how they become obstacles to the realization of the nonconceptual. As these barriers are understood, the crystals arise as the aspects and vehicles needed for the resolution, but appear as manifestations of nonconceptual presence. In other words, basic knowledge unfolds in such a way that takes consciousness beyond it.

One example of such a barrier is the conceptual position that there is a difference between spirit and matter. There is no such distinction on the nonconceptual dimension, but it is such a deeply held dichotomy that most people believe it is an ultimate truth. When one is experiencing or approaching the experience of nonconceptual awareness, this conceptual position may arise as a contraction of awareness, or some emotional issue. Often it appears as the fear of loss of the world, as we begin to see that there is no physical world the way we normally know it. It may arise as a rapprochement issue, the fear of loss of mother if we leave or go beyond her, which is equated with losing the world. These are ultimately conceptual issues that reflect the lack of understanding of the nonconceptual ground of Reality. The crystal guidance appears to illuminate these issues, and as they become transparent various specific crystals may emerge. The merging essence crystal arises because merging essence stands in the unconscious for the mother one is afraid of losing; the truth gold crystal emerges as well, pointing to the fact that there is nonconceptual truth we are not seeing. Their emergence will coincide with the arising of the recognition of our position as a conceptual one. We see it for what it is, a conceptual position and not an ultimate reality. When we see this, the conceptual position dissolves as the crystals dominate consciousness. We do not feel them as merging love and truth, but as nonconceptual presence that then reveals itself to be the nature of everything.

The perception transforms to a new clarity and transparency, eternity and spacelessness. We see the physical world as this nonconceptual presence, and nonconceptual presence as the physical world. Ultimate truth and manifest reality are completely one, totally coemergent. We cannot separate the spiritual presence from the physical forms; they are actually one when our mind is not in the way. It is true that nonconceptual presence is vast and boundless, but it is at the same time the rocks and the thoughts, the sky and the birds. All forms are nothing but formations that nonconceptual presence assumes, without them becoming anything else but this presence. The flower is ultimate Reality, so is my ear, so is your nose.[7]

The crystal aspects and vehicles manifest to challenge and highlight the conceptual barriers that oppose their corresponding nonconceptual truth, and as they dominate consciousness they move it to the nonconceptual dimension. It is important to see that nonconceptual truth is not mental ideas or images, but the solid bedrock of reality. It is more real and fundamental than what we ordinarily consider to be physical reality. Furthermore, because it is actual presence it can appear within conceptual experience, but such experience cannot approach it in its customary way. In other words, when nonconceptual presence arises it does not mean there will not be conceptual elements in the experience. They can and frequently do coexist, as presence on different dimensions. We may experience nonconceptual presence and still have conceptual thoughts in our mind, or speak using words. If this were not the case it would not be possible to learn and develop wisdom while one's awareness abides in this dimension.[8]

It is easy to understand this when we remember that all the boundless dimensions of true nature are coemergent. The noetic dimension is coemergent with the nonconceptual dimension. Experience can be dominated by one or the other, or both. In nonconceptual experience, nonconceptual presence dominates, displacing knowing, but rarely completely. At moments one may be totally on the nonconceptual dimension, where there is no recognition at all, but normally even in very deep experiences of realization there is some knowing. It is like the experience is of an infinite ocean of nonconceptual presence, but there is a slight wave somewhere that still retains some noetic capacity. This makes it possible to understand the ocean in a way that allows us to express it in actions and words. Our clear understanding of the situation may dissolve the wave, so that for a time there is no cognition at all. But cognition will always return, even though it may not dominate. Our ground may continue to be nonconceptual, with enough conceptual consciousness remaining for understanding and communication.

In this nonconceptual dimension, or crystal dimension, all forms are perceived as nonconceptual manifestations of true nature. This includes both physical and essential forms. The whole of Reality appears now as transparent, fresh, clear, empty, but full of colors and shapes. Such perception can appear with such exquisiteness and precision that all forms become faceted. All around us we see glittering jeweled forms, the environment as a multicolored jeweled palace, brilliant with light but claiming no existence. (See *Diamond Heart Book 4*, chapters 7–17, for further discussion of the nonconceptual dimension and its mode of wisdom.)

Transcending Conceptual Dichotomies

Much of the work of realization of the nonconceptual dimension is a matter of recognizing the basic mental dichotomies, and recognizing them for what they are. They form the solid bases of our mental universe, and hence function as the final underpinnings of the structure of self and world, a structure that we generally accept as reality. Our ordinary mind adheres to these dichotomies as if they are solid and ultimate reality, unquestionable and eternal.[9] This view of reality inherently supports the structure of the ego-self, for this structure is built using images and representations that are ultimately conceptual, but also depend on the basic dichotomies for their reality. As long as we adhere to them as truth they structure our experience in such a way that reality appears to conform to them. It is difficult to challenge the fundamental dichotomies, for we cannot see them as conceptual fabrication until we stand on the nonconceptual ground. Only true nonconceptuality, which is the ground of pure awareness, can expose them for what they are, through contrast. Some approaches to realization try to penetrate the conceptual dichotomies through thought and reason, but how can a dimension of being comprehend a deeper and more fundamental dimension than itself? Access to the deeper dimensions is what frees the soul from its inherent limitations of thought.[10]

We have discussed the dichotomy of matter and spirit, and indicated others. The most basic fundamental dichotomy is that between being and nonbeing, or presence and emptiness. It is true that presence and emptiness are not simply cognitive experiences in the normal sense of the word. But because we know that we are experiencing presence, which is being, and emptiness, which is nonbeing, it becomes clear in pure awareness that such experiences retain some conceptual colorings. These colorings are subtle, for the concept of being is so pervasive in experience. The fact that they appear as opposites reveals them to be conceptual, even though it is the conceptuality of basic knowledge. The sense in which pure awareness neither exists nor does not exist is not related to whether it ultimately appears in experience, but to how it feels in experience. It does not feel like existence and it does not feel like nonexistence. It is both presence and absence, but actually neither, for it is innocent of conceptual coloring.

We have also discussed the dichotomy of reality and appearance, essence and manifestation. This dichotomy is not normally relevant for ego experience, which holds the view that manifestation is all of reality. But as one progresses in the inner journey and discovers the underlying spiritual presence, perception begins to reveal that what we have taken to be reality is only manifestation, and that there is an invisible ground for this manifestation. This view continues, and is useful, until we finally grasp the nonconceptual. Then we recognize the conceptual nature of such perception, and that Reality is one, totally and completely. There is only true nature, which is Reality in its totality. Reality is thus.

The dichotomy of the spiritual and the material actually forms the core of the dichotomy of reality and appearance. Related to these is the dichotomy of the sacred and the profane. On the nonconceptual dimension there is only the sacred, and the sacred is not named sacred. It is not named. Yet even though there is only the sacred, this sacred is also the negative, the hostility, the physical, and the mundane. The nonconceptual is such a fundamental ground that no known or knowable category of experience or thought can escape it. It is absolutely sacred, for its purity is never touched by mind or body. It is eternally present, continuously pervading all and everything.

It is particularly difficult to penetrate the dichotomy of being and doing. Many students are able to experience the nonconceptual ground, and to integrate its timeless truths. But most of them find it quite difficult to function from this place. They can be this presence, but when they take action—physical, emotional or mental—they separate from it, and return to a conceptual level. Such disruption of realization can be quite painful and disconcerting; it makes many doubt their realization, and causes some even to believe that their realization is fake. Inquiring into this issue reveals the conceptual dichotomy of being and doing. Quite simply, it is difficult for the mind not to discriminate being from doing, stillness from movement, action from repose. It can understand and accept pure awareness as presence, and recognize itself as this presence. But to act, to express, to communicate, brings up a dynamic dimension that the mind cannot help but think is distinct from simply being. The inquiry into this dilemma leads the soul to the understanding of how manifestation occurs, and how this is related to movement and action. This is the subject of the next chapter, so we will not discuss it here. But this does not resolve the dichotomy, for being continues to be contrasted to doing, stillness to movement.

Integrating the wisdom of nonconceptual Reality leads one to include it more and more in one's everyday functioning. This development is supported by a pearly form of the crystal dimension, leading the student increasingly to recognize the conceptual nature of the dichotomy between being and doing, and to see how in the nonconceptual there is simply no such thing as being and no such thing as doing, no such thing as stillness and no such thing as movement. All these are abstractions from the nonconceptual patterns of perception. When the discriminating mind is not in the foreground, the student may suddenly attain his satori, and his nonconceptual eye is completely opened. He may notice at some point that he is walking, but he finds no difference between that or standing. It feels the same to him; he could be scratching his back, but he feels no meaningful distinction between his hand, his back, the movement of his hand, the itching sensation, and the transparent clear presence. In fact, the question of whether there is a distinction or not does not occur to him until he contemplates his perception. One perceives that the boundless presence is what does everything; more exactly, the boundless presence is everything, including the movements and actions. More precisely, there is no such thing as movement and action; there is only Reality, fresh and virginal, beyond any description. To integrate this realization, and especially to establish it as a permanent station, is very difficult and rare, as many of the great masters of antiquity have observed.[11] (We discuss the process of integration of functioning into the realization of nonconceptual presence in *The Pearl Beyond Price*, chapter 38, in a way that illustrates different aspects of this work.)

The most frequently noted dichotomy on the way toward nonconceptual freedom is that of good and evil, or more exactly, good and bad. Without concepts there is no sense that one thing is good and another is bad. First, there is no separation between forms, because separation happens only through the reification of concepts, and there are no concepts here to reify. Because of this there cannot be a comparison between them, all forms are equal in being pure awareness. Second, since there is perception of difference between forms but no recognition of what the difference is, it is not possible to value one form and not another. All appear equal. The moment we recognize something as good in contrast to something else as bad, we are definitely existing in the conceptual realm. Recognizing that the distinction between good and bad is ultimately conceptual, pure awareness emerges and equalizes all forms and experiences as manifestations of true nature.

Experientially, the notions of good and bad are connected mostly to pleasure and pain, happiness and suffering, gain and loss, expansion and contraction, and so on. In the unutterable bliss of nonconceptuality, these dichotomies disappear. An important part of this process for the soul is the development of nonattachment. The understanding that arises with the help of the crystal vehicles is that attachment depends on the dichotomy of good and bad. These vehicles teach the soul that nonattachment is nothing but the effect of the nonconceptual presence on the consciousness of the soul. They teach her this wisdom by challenging this dichotomy, which she has adhered to as long as she can remember, and showing her how it is not a fundamental truth, not a timeless truth of Reality. The soul has the opportunity at this point to perceive the development of attachment. It starts with the differentiation of nonconceptual presence. As long as these stay simply as differentiations no attachment is possible, but the differentiations become discriminations, knowable concepts. As long as they remain simply knowable concepts, noetic forms, attachment is still not present. But the concepts become labeled and eventually reified. They become discrete forms, which obscures the unifying ground. The labeling and reification make it possible for the first time to compare the forms, resulting in judgment. This judgment is the beginning of the dichotomy of good and bad. This judgment leads to preference, generally of the good over the bad. Preference based on the entrenched belief in the ultimate truth of this dichotomy becomes a rigid and fixed preference. Such fixed preference easily becomes attachment, which is holding on to what one so prefers, or rejecting what one does not.

Understanding attachment, and the freedom from attachment that arises through the impact of nonconceptual presence, liberates the heart from its habit of orienting according to fixed preferences. The heart becomes transparent to the operation of essential intelligence, functioning from a ground of nonattachment. Its love and joy are now free, totally unattached. It can love fully without having to possess what it loves, liberating its joy and delight, which become the celebration of Reality, immaculate presence, and pristine awareness. The soul learns from direct experience that nonattachment is nothing but the nonconceptual presence in the heart, as the heart of enlightenment, the crystal heart. Such heart responds openly, spontaneously, without premeditation or prejudice. It responds without hesitation to the objective needs of the situation, with a nonconceptual intelligence that needs no inner recognition.

As the discriminating mind dissolves under the impact of nonconceptual presence the dichotomies merge into each other, and all polarities reveal their underlying unity as the uniformly blissful field of awareness.

Beyond Oneness

We saw in the previous chapter that pure presence is the dimension of unity of existence, which appears in various degrees of unification. We discussed unity free from multiplicity, and oneness that is unity in multiplicity. Unity and oneness are the most well-known mystical experiences, but as we move into the nonconceptual realm we begin to see the concepts that are still attached to true nature in these perceptions. To perceive that all forms make up a unity, that they are not separate and discrete objects, but a unified field, indicates the presence in our consciousness of the dichotomy of the one and the many, and that of oneness and separateness. In other words, to experience oneness is to still experience true nature through a concept, the concept of one, as contrasted to many. One and many is a basic conceptual dichotomy; it is difficult for the mind to conceive perception without it.

There is oneness in the nonconceptual dimension, in the sense that we do not perceive the forms of manifestation as separate and discrete. Yet, we do not experience oneness, we do not feel that everything is one. It is not that we feel everything is not one, but rather that we do not experience one and do not experience not one. There is no one and no many in nonconceptual awareness. There is just the suchness of things, or more accurately, it is thus. Reality as such is neither a oneness nor a multiplicity, but an indivisible truth that we experience without thinking it is an indivisible truth. The experience of unity and oneness is simply the contrast to that of separateness and multiplicity. In reality, there is no such thing as unity or oneness, for Reality is beyond any such categories. It is what it is, before any knowing and commentary.

A related dichotomy is that of duality and nonduality. Some refer to Reality as nonduality, to emphasize that there is no separateness between observer and observed, manifestation and source, and so on. Yet, in reality there is no such thing as nonduality. Nonduality is the creation of the discriminating mind, just as duality is. At best, it is a concept that attempts to describe the nonconceptual, but it fails just as all other terms do.

One dichotomy whose dissolution many find difficult to assimilate is that of meaning and meaninglessness. People feel that they need meaning in their lives, that without meaning reality has no value and no significance. In fact, some individuals kill themselves when they fail to find a sense of meaning in their lives. Yet, meaning, any meaning, is not ultimate. The inner journey leaves all meaning behind when it moves to the nonconceptual, and at this stage the soul needs to acclimate to life without meaning.

At the stage of recognizing true nature, the soul realizes that it is the ultimate meaning of existence and of life. She understands that when she is not in touch with her true nature her mind thinks of it as absence of meaning, which she then tries to find, pursuing a particular style of life, philosophy, activity, or interest. As she realizes her essence she finds that the need for conceptual meaning disappears. She finds that meaning is being, the fact of her existence. But at the stage when the soul moves to the nonconceptual, even being is gone, for being and nonbeing are both conceptual. She may first see this as meaninglessness, as the sense that life has no meaning. Meaninglessness becomes the true condition of things, for any meaning is simply a story the discriminating mind concocts. But precise inquiry into this meaninglessness reveals it to be simply the transcendence of the concept of meaning. Meaning requires recognition, cognition, and now we are simply beyond that. Reality is simply thus, pure awareness without commentary. In other words, to see Reality as ultimately meaninglessness, even when this is idealized as total freedom, is to still view it within the concept of meaning. Reality is neither meaningfulness nor meaninglessness, neither the presence of these nor their absence. It is simply independent of anything that the discriminating mind can grasp. So when we use the term *meaningless* to refer to nonconceptual Reality we need to realize we are referring to the transcendence of meaning, not the opposite of meaningfulness.

Enlightened Indifference

The dichotomy of purpose and purposelessness is related to that of meaning and meaninglessness. Before we realize nonconceptual truth we find it important to have purpose in our life, and purpose gives meaning to our existence. Yet, to have purpose indicates the adherence to meaning, and to the belief that our life can have a good or bad direction. It involves the conviction that we can see a movement from a cause to a result, from one type of action to another, and that this movement is ultimately real. Because of this, we can judge the direction of our life, and gauge our success in accomplishing our purpose. This in turn becomes attachment and suffering. In appreciating the nonconceptual dimension of true nature, we understand that such discrimination is not ultimate, that when we realize true nature we are free, and this freedom transcends any purpose. We actually discover that we need purpose because we have not recognized the true purposeless ground of existence. That purpose is the creation of our discriminating mind, and that our freedom and fulfillment require no purpose. Everything is perfect the way it is; every instant is perfect just as it is.

In the realization of the nonconceptual dimension, we do not experience purpose in life, nor do we experience the need for it. In fact, we do not even experience purposelessness, for Reality is beyond both. We do not strive toward anything, and do not aspire toward any result. We have no motivation, but act intelligently and compassionately. We act this way not because we want to, not because we have compassion or love as our motivation, but because we are true nature, and true nature is the source of such qualities. It acts the way it acts, always in a nonconceptual perfection, but when we cognitively contemplate this action we think of it as loving and compassionate. In other words, one who is realized in the nonconceptual does not experience himself to possess a motivation for action, and does not feel a purpose for his life, but looked at from the outside people will think that such an individual is motivated by love and compassion, and seems to have a clear direction and purpose to his life and action.[12] (See *Luminous Night's Journey*, chapter 4, for a discussion of the issues relevant in the attainment of motivelessness.)

What is traditionally referred to as purposelessness and motivelessness, and sometimes as indifference, but more accurately understood as the transcendence of purpose and motive, is not something to try to emulate. One cannot say that there is no such thing as purpose and motivation, and that it is therefore fine to live a haphazard and meaningless life. That attitude would abrogate one's human nature, for as long as one still lives in the cognitive sphere one's life requires purpose and meaning. Purpose, motive, and meaning are necessary for human beings, because they are emissaries of the timeless truths of nonconceptual Reality, before they are recognized for what they are. Only when we have integrated the nonconceptual can we say we do not need meaning, purpose, or motive. Otherwise, we will be stuck in the meaninglessness and purposelessness that are the opposite of meaning and purpose. Here there is no transcendence, only disconnection.

Universal Heretic

To be established in the nonconceptual is to attain an inconceivable freedom. The soul realizes her nature in such a way that she does not need to know what it is. She does not need to know she is enlightened. She is beyond the concept of enlightenment and liberation. She is innocent, not knowing she is enlightened, and not caring to know. She has attained liberated indifference, for the fullness of realization takes her to such completion that there is no distinction between falsehood and truth, soul and essence, enlightenment or delusion.[13] There is no reflection on one's realization, no excitement about it, no narcissistic congratulations, and no need to talk about it. One is, Reality is thus, and one goes about one's business.

The aspirant's mind is open and free, totally unencumbered by any position, philosophy, or system. He has no perspective that he takes to be ultimate and final. Yet, he is free to use any system. Since he is established in the nonconceptual he sees all perspectives for what they are, conceptual perspectives, and hence not ultimate truth. But because he can use his discriminating mind, he can see when a given perspective is useful or necessary for some functioning or teaching, and is free to use it. Nevertheless, he uses it without having to believe it is ultimate and can drop it whenever it becomes unnecessary. He needs no perspective for his own experience, for he lives where no perspective can enter. Although he understands the need for the correct perspective for those who have not attained the nonconceptual, he recognizes that what is necessary for the soul's freedom is not a particular perspective, but liberation from all conceptual limitations.

He is free from all positions, and the need for positions. He may have a system or a detailed teaching, but he recognizes that truth is beyond any such system, and cannot be captured by the conceptualization of any teaching. He uses one system or another, a particular conceptualization or another, because he knows how to use it well, and not because he believes it is the most correct, or that it is ultimate or final in any way. He understands that the point of any teaching is liberation and realization, and not any system or teaching. In fact, he recognizes that all teachings, even the most sublime paths, are simply stories; their sacredness is in their effectiveness and not in the tenets and knowledge of the teaching. Because he is free from the discriminating mind, he is free from any and all teachings. He has gone beyond, beyond even the most sublime teachings.

Under normal circumstances, an individual in serious spiritual work follows a particular teaching, a certain path that involves a perspective, a detailed knowledge of Reality and the path to it, along with various attitudes and methods. He needs to faithfully follow the teaching, for a real teaching is the objective manifestation of true and essential knowledge, the *nous* of true nature. Yet, to be fully liberated he must go beyond any knowing, and his realization must be independent of his discriminating mind. This will be possible only if he does not adhere to his path as the final description of reality—not because the description is necessarily wrong or inaccurate, but because true nature is ultimately beyond any description, any system or teaching. This possibility of detachment from the path he has faithfully followed is granted when true nature manifests its nonconceptual presence. It appears as nonattachment in his heart, and as total openness in his mind. He is open to see that the teaching he has been following has been, at least partially, conceptual. He can now see all teachings, and all systems and wisdom traditions, simply as useful stories that explain Reality and the path of liberation, but that liberation itself is beyond any and all stories, any and all teachings, any and all knowing.

This is not usually easy for good students who have not only followed their chosen path faithfully and diligently, but have deeply appreciated and loved it, and seen its amazing beauty and preciousness. At this juncture in the inner journey, many conflicts may arise, great doubts about one's path, and even about one's personal realization. If the student has been following a path that emphasizes a certain dimension of Reality, or postulates God as the reigning divinity, this juncture can bring about a great crisis of faith, involving guilt and intense self-recrimination, because the inner unfoldment is now revealing to him that God, or whatever divinity he has believed in, is actually a concept. That Reality, or God, cannot be seen as "God" or anything. It cannot be named, and it cannot be made into a special category. There are no special ultimate categories, because there are no ultimate categories.

No sacred cows survive the realization of the nonconceptual, and one's realization becomes independent from any belief or teaching. He recognizes that who and what he is is ultimately beyond any category, including all the spiritual categories. He realizes that Reality is not a description, and that any description, any teaching or belief system, regardless how useful and accurate, falls short of Reality as it is. He recognizes the uniqueness of his realization without having to compare it with others, and appreciates the differences between the various teachings without having to rate them. His realization has gone beyond conceptual categories and, hence, beyond comparisons and ratings. He believes in nothing, and adheres to no teaching or religion as final and ultimate. He has become a universal heretic, embracing all, yet free of all.[14]

In the Diamond Approach, this realization is related to the crystal vehicle of the citadel. It is the timeless wisdom leading to nonconceptual certainty. One attains here a certainty beyond doubt, because it is independent of belief, of knowledge, and of any intellectual or experiential category. One is oneself, and sees Reality as it is, with a nonconceptual conviction. The person's realization has gone beyond knowing and, hence, beyond any doubt or questioning. It is not that he feels certain because he is convinced, for he is beyond convincing. He is not convinced of anything, not even of the truth of his own personal and ascertained experiences and perceptions. He is certain because there is nothing to be certain about, and nothing to doubt. In fact, there is no such thing as doubt, for the mind that doubts is the discriminating mind. This realization becomes what we call certainty only when he contemplates it conceptually. He understands that certainty is unquestionable only when it is nonconceptual, when it is not certainty about anything, but simply the solidity and rootedness of one's realization of nonconceptual truth.

With such nonconceptual certainty he does not need to gauge or rate his realization according to any teaching or wisdom tradition. His realization is totally autonomous, and he accepts it with its uniqueness, just as he accepts the uniqueness of other teachings and realizations. He is free, and this freedom is unutterable delight and uncontainable joy.

Master of Knowledge

We saw in the last chapter that the dimension of pure presence exposes reification, for it reveals the original concepts that have been reified. However, this dimension inherently presents its differentiations as discriminations, as noetic forms. In other words, the possibility of reification will always be present because of the very nature of the dimension of pure presence. The mere fact that pure presence includes forms that can be known, makes its realization insufficient for total freedom. Our mind will naturally reify noetic forms, and such reifications will ultimately alienate us from our essential presence and dismember its boundlessness.

Pure presence can take us beyond ordinary knowledge and penetrate its reifications, but the tendency for reification will remain. As long as the mind is present, and can recognize forms, it will reify them. It will even reify omnipresence, even though it is not a form with shape and size. To go beyond the tendency for reification we need to go beyond the mind that reifies, and beyond the concepts that can be reified. In other words, freedom from reification can be total only when we do not see any concepts, only when we do not recognize any forms. And this can happen only on the nonconceptual dimension of true nature.

In the process of inquiry into our sense of self, we first see how our soul is patterned by past impressions. Such impressions perpetuate the past, with its conflicts and ignorance, as patterns of identity and character. Then we recognize that the past continues in representations, which first appear as images and object relations taken from past experiences. Going to the dimension of pure presence, we recognize that these images and representations are composed of reifications, of both basic and ordinary forms of knowledge. Pure presence penetrates these representations by showing that they are reifications, revealing the omnipresence that underlies and constitutes all forms. Yet the tendency toward reification does not disappear, though it may diminish a great deal.

The separate self will continue to arise, less rigid and opaque. When true nature presents its nonconceptual dimension, we begin to detect a deeper source of this sense of self. We see that the soul cannot be completely free from the shell of reifications because as long as there are concepts available to it the mind will reify them to create such a shell. Nonconceptual presence exposes the ego identity, the shell of the separate self, as composed not only of reifications but of concepts. We realize that every time we recognize ourselves, even when the recognition is basic and immediate knowing, the mind takes the concepts of this recognition and builds reifications that then coalesce into the shell of ego.

Understanding this level of the creation of the shell of self we realize pure awareness, and our being and identity become established as nonconceptual presence, beyond mind and concepts. We are, without knowing what we are. In fact, we do not even know we are. We simply experience freedom, without recognizing it as freedom. We are simply free, aware of our nature without cognizing it as "our" or "nature." (We discuss this process in greater detail, exploring some of the psychodynamic and structural issues involved in this process of self-realization, in *The Point of Existence*, chapter 40.)

We see that inquiry can penetrate deeper than the cognitive realm. It can do this when the inner guidance appears on the nonconceptual dimension, as the crystal vehicle of guidance. Crystal guidance not only reveals the presence of reifications, but goes further, pointing to concepts themselves and how they become barriers to pure awareness. By challenging the various concepts and conceptual positions it moves consciousness beyond them, to nonconceptual presence.

Crystal guidance functions in another, unexpected way. Beyond the exposing of concepts and dichotomies, its crystalline structure illuminates barriers that developed before the arising of conceptual knowledge. These are the structures of the soul that were established very early in life, before the cognitive capacity developed enough for the establishment of representational structures. We discussed these primitive, prenatal, and preverbal structures in chapter 14. These structures are simply impressions in the soul; they are not cognitive. Because it is the expression of nonconceptual awareness, crystal guidance penetrates these preconceptual structures and challenges their opaqueness. These structures manifest in consciousness and reveal how they are barriers to realization and liberation. Crystal guidance, along with the various aspects manifesting as crystals, brings about the precise and objective understanding of this dimension of obscurations. Such understanding can be simply the recognition of the nonconceptual as the ground, but can also manifest as insight and basic knowledge.

We have described how this occurs: pure presence with its noetic capacity can manifest coemergent with that of nonconceptual awareness. In other words, the inner guidance of Being can arise as the coemergence of pure awareness and basic knowing. Pure awareness penetrates the preconceptual obscurations, and basic knowing discriminates the specifics as insight. The nonconceptual dimension of the inner guidance challenges and highlights the nonconceptual differentiations in these obscurations, allowing the noetic dimension to discriminate these differentiations. The insight is basic knowledge, but it is a discrimination that nonconceptual differentiation brings into awareness. As the noetic guidance illuminates the obscurations they melt away, and allow the soul to experience herself on the nonconceptual dimension.

In reality, essential guidance can operate with all the dimensions of true nature, for it is the expression of true nature. It can operate with one dimension, or with two or more of the dimensions, in coemergence. Depending on the need of the inquiry, one dimension may dominate, and in the gradual inner unfoldment one dimension after another dominates in its functioning. Thus we see how the dimensions of pure presence and pure awareness function conjointly in the inner guidance.

When the soul fully understands and integrates the dimension of pure presence, she becomes open to all knowledge, to all the timeless wisdom of Reality. When she attains the dimension of pure awareness, she goes beyond knowledge, and attains nonconceptual freedom. She is now free from the constraints of knowledge. However, if she has been able to realize both dimensions and integrate them in her realization, she will be free to use knowledge without constraints, and without danger of reification. She will be able to recognize concepts and their reifications, to see the usefulness of conceptual knowledge as well as the dangers of the discriminating mind. She is open to knowledge, but is established beyond it, and hence she is not afraid of it and not constrained by it.[15] She has attained the station of master of knowledge.

20   Logos and Creative Dynamism

ORDINARILY WE PERCEIVE A WORLD OF OBJECTS, many of which move in space, such as a moving animal or a hurtling meteor. Many of the objects we perceive transform, for example a human body or a tree. Our inner experiences of sensations, feelings, thoughts, and images are constantly moving and changing. The usual view of these phenomena, as reflected in our scientific theories, is that our world is composed of objects that populate space; these objects are in constant change and/or transformation that occurs in time, as a linear progression from past to future. Yet our experience of true nature and its boundless dimensions demonstrates that there are no such things as discrete objects, that all objects are manifestations of the same field of presence, but that we see them as discrete objects only because we are not aware of the ground of presence that both underlies and constitutes them. Knowing the boundless dimensions of Being, we realize that the normal perception of movement and change of objects is an outcome of a particular point of view, the specific vantage point of egoic experience, and is not necessarily objective or ultimate. So how, from the perspective of true nature, which recognizes that ultimately there exist no discrete objects, do we perceive movement and change?

We have discussed three boundless dimensions of Being, all of which possess characteristics of movement and change. Divine love is not a static realm, for it is always flowing and transforming its myriad forms; pure presence is also not static, for its noetic forms are in constant metamorphosis. And it is the same with pure awareness: its perceptual prenoetic forms are in perpetual movement and change. Without the characteristic of change there would be no perception or knowing, and hence no experience of any kind. We have ignored this characteristic until now because we wanted to explore it in some detail, as the expression of another of Being's boundless dimensions. This dimension, like the others, is inseparable from all the other dimensions. Its specific characteristic of change and transformation is responsible for the dynamic changeable property of Being in general. In other words, Being is inherently dynamic, a dynamism that appears as a particular dimension whose specific property is that of dynamism, change, and transformation.

However, perception of change and transformation is different on the boundless dimensions than in normal egoic experience, revealing the relation of dynamism to Being or true nature. We understand this relation exactly, precisely, and completely when we experience this dimension of dynamism. Phenomena, both external and internal, appear similarly to the previous three boundless dimensions; but here the characteristics of dynamism and change dominate the experience, giving us the opportunity to experientially understand their relation to Being. The dimension of dynamic being is a boundless dimension, appearing as an indivisible and infinite field of consciousness and presence. All forms, external and internal, appear as forms that this conscious presence assumes. The fact that all forms are basically shapes and colors that Being assumes changes our perception of change and transformation, and our view of such processes.

We begin to gain an entirely new and different perspective on all processes that involve time; these processes include not only change and transformation, but also development, growth, maturation, evolution, decay, decline, movement, action, behavior, functioning, expression, speaking, thinking, and so on. We begin to understand time—its flow and the origin of this flow. The new perception and understanding are unexpected and exhilarating. This perception is reflected in the insights of many ancient philosophers and spiritual teachers.

Change and Movement

From the perspective of the dimension of dynamism, it turns out that there is no such thing as movement. Since there exist no separate objects there are no objects that move. There is only the appearance of movement. We have discussed this in terms of inner objects in chapter 6, when we were exploring the changes of inner experience. But in the boundless dimension of dynamic presence we experience Being not only as a boundless field of presence, and see all manifest forms—both inner and outer—as expressions of this presence, but, furthermore, this presence is dynamic and mutable, perpetually changing its appearance. The various manifest forms are nothing but the patterns and shapes that this infinite fabric of presence takes. There is no such thing as a separate object that moves in space from past to future. What has been seen as a moving object is seen here as a manifestation of a particular location in the field of presence, a shape that keeps appearing but in different locations, giving the impression of a moving object. We go back to our example of the cinema screen from chapter 6. We see a man moving across the screen, but in fact there is no movement. The totality of the picture changes from one frame to the next. Because this change of the frames happens gradually, and because the change occurs faster than our eyes can discern, we see a continuous picture of a man walking. Yet, we know it is a picture that is simply changing from one instant to the next.

In the movie the change actually occurs at all the points of the plane of the screen. Each point on the screen is going through a transformation, and the total effect is our perception of a man walking across the screen, but more exactly in some kind of a scene that is itself changing. The walking man is actually part of the whole picture, and the whole picture changes. In reality, there is no man, just a picture changing its details. This is quite similar to the perception of movement in the boundless dimension of dynamic presence. Because of its dynamism, the field of presence is constantly changing its appearance. This appearance includes all that we ordinarily see in perception, but now we feel and recognize that it is one indivisible appearance, one picture. We also recognize this oneness of appearance across all the modalities of perception, and not only visually.

In other words, we experience the oneness of Being similarly to the dimensions of divine love, pure presence, and nonconceptual awareness, but with the highlighted property of dynamic transformation of the appearance of this oneness. The changes in this fabric completely account for all the changes we ordinarily perceive as movement, transformation, and so on. However, in egoic experience we do not perceive the oneness of all phenomena, because we are not aware of the ground of presence that underlies and constitutes all their forms. Therefore, we perceive the changing forms without perceiving their underlying ground. The result is that we perceive separate and independent forms that move or change. We see a man walking in the street rather than perceiving a dynamic field that takes the form of a street with a man walking in it. We end up taking the view that there is such a thing as a man, and hence all kinds of discrete objects, and separate phenomena and processes. We miss not only the sense of oneness and unity of existence, but also the throbbing and vital dynamism.

The dimension of dynamic presence reveals that Being is not only the ground and ultimate constituent nature of everything, but that it is the only thing that changes. In other words, change is never local or individual; it is always universal. The totality of the universe, in all of its dimensions, changes as one indivisible Reality; the perception of these changes, when combined with ignorance of its true nature, gives us the impression that there exist objects that move and change.

Since each point of the field of presence perpetually changes, giving the appearance of movement, development, transformation, and so on, we can say that no man has ever walked on the face of the earth. In fact, no human being has ever taken one step. No being, human or animal, has ever moved a limb. No being has ever changed, grown, matured, developed, evolved, declined, or decayed. No one has ever been born, lived, or died. It is only the appearance of true nature that changes. We call the changes of some locations of this appearance movement, of other locations transformation, and of yet others development or evolution. Depending on the characteristics of the changes of a particular location of appearance, in its relation to its neighboring locations, we may term the change transformation, development, evolution, decay, decline, and so on.

More accurately, the ordinary concepts of change and movement are based on reified concepts of objects and phenomena, the products of a process of reification that dissociates us from the direct experience of our ground true nature. The reification is exposed when we recognize how change occurs from the vantage point of true nature, as on the dimension of dynamic presence. We begin to see the reality of change, which reveals that there is no such thing as movement.

Change entails a transformation of appearance over the entire field of presence, similar to cinema frames changing; however, it is a continuous change, not a series of discrete changes as in the case of an actual cinema film. By revealing the nature of change the dimension of dynamic presence also discloses the true meaning and sources of development, growth, evolution, and all processes and phenomena that have a continuity in time. Before we discuss these we need first to explore in some detail the experience of change in the dimension of dynamic being. We experience this universal transformation in various ways, according to the subtlety of our realization; these have been reflected by the various wisdom teachings of humankind.

Continual Creation

One of the most common ways of perceiving the phenomenon of universal transformation is the recognition that objects do not move from the past to the present. Such movement depends on reification and absence of the perception of the unity of Being. It also implies the belief that each object is old, that it has existed from some certain moment in time, and now time passes on it, this way changing or moving. We instead see the object coming into existence each moment. It comes into existence and passes away as a new object takes its place. The new object looks exactly identical to the one before it, or almost so. In other words, the object is always being replaced by a newer version of itself. The movement is not from the past to the present, but from nonexistence to existence, from nonmanifestation to manifestation. This way the object is always new, for time never passes on it. Since the new object is identical to the one before it, and the change happens too quickly for the eye to discern, we can easily believe it is the same object, and then conceive of the concept of time to account for its changes. Yet in reality, the object is coming into creation continually; it is being continually and newly created, instead of being created—coming into existence—at some point in the past and after that existing in time.

Continual creation is the process through which each object exists. Since objects are not separate from each other, and they all form one continuous spatial tapestry which is the appearance of Being, continual creation is the process by which this appearance changes.

All of existence is continually coming into being, where it is always a new existence. The universe is never old; it is always new, for it is renewed instant to instant. This includes absolutely everything. It includes both animate and inanimate objects, the earth and the sky, the planets, the sun and the stars, the galaxies and the space that contains them; it also includes all the thoughts, images, memories, feelings, sensations, and all phenomena at all levels of being. And all of this constitutes one manifold, continuous and continuously coming into being.[1]

We can experience this directly when we have realized the dimension of dynamic being. We do not simply perceive objects in space that move in time, but we experience ourselves as an infinite and boundless presence that continuously transforms itself into the various objects and forms of the universe. We experience ourselves as the ground and nature of all forms, but also as the substance that is in continual and eternal transformation, and through its transformation objects appear, continue to appear, and cease. All forms arise within this boundless manifold, as manifestations of its potentialities, but this manifold never becomes anything different from itself. There exist no objects, just the appearance of objects, which are nothing but in their totality the appearance that Being takes from instant to instant. All objects are Being itself manifesting as the universe. In other words, using monotheistic terminology, the universe is a theophany, and its changes are the life of God.[2]

Timeless Translation

Going back to a particular object, we see how change and movement occur. There are several possibilities for the eternal recurrence of the object. Let us view the body of a cat. This object is always coming into appearance, as a new body. The new body may come into being as exactly the same as the one before it. We say the cat has not changed or moved at all. Or it may come into being with a slight change, a change that keeps increasing each time a new body comes into being. We say the cat is moving in place. It is simply changing its posture and moving its limbs. Another possibility is that the new body will come into being in a slightly different location of space. Each time it comes into being it also appears with slightly different positions of its limbs. The cat keeps coming into being in different locations, with different postures, giving us the continuous impression of a cat walking. The situation is actually more total than this. It is not that the cat appears in different locations in a particular room. The whole room, with all the objects in it, is also continuously coming into being. The whole scene is continually coming into being, including the observer, and the inner experience of this observer. It is one total picture, nothing excluded, always and continuously coming into existence.

Movement turns out to be the impression of translation in space and time, when it is actually a timeless and spaceless translation. The cat did not move from one place to another. The totality of the appearance of Being transformed into a new appearance where the cat now appears in a different location. We see how this boundless view of change accounts for the normal perception of change and movement. We will come back to the question of growth, development, and evolution after we discuss further properties of dynamic presence.

Universal Transformation

We can know universal transformation in various ways. The way we have described it above is one of the subtlest, similar to our discussion of morphogenic transformation in chapter 7. Being is indivisible and is constantly changing its appearance. We can also experience the same process similarly to how we saw inner experience unfolding in chapter 7. Each of these ways discloses a significant aspect of the eternal dynamism of true nature.

In fact, the above discussion mixed two ways of perception. One is pure transformation. Nothing is created and nothing is annihilated; Being simply transforms its form. The other is that this transformation is not a change, but a new creation. Each instant a new universe is created, while the one before it is annihilated. We perceive the process of universal transformation as a continual process of creation, coupled with a continuous process of annihilation. We directly perceive creation happening, instant to instant. The experience may emphasize the creation process or its opposite, the annihilation process. In other words, we may be struck by the newness of the universe, how it is continually renewed and re-created. Life and experience is always new, full of possibilities, and open to unexpected surprises. Or we may be struck by the enormous power of Being that is always annihilating everything. We are aware of the new creation, but our focus is on the end of this creation, which is that it never stays, never remains, but is always moving toward cessation. We then recognize the folly of holding on to anything, for all forms are evanescent and transitory; this insight helps the soul to develop nonattachment.

We can also experience universal transformation as a process of manifestation. In this perception we are aware of the purity of true nature, a homogeneous unity beyond any form or color. We perceive the forms of the universe manifesting out of this timeless ground, as if they are first hidden and unmanifest but then come out into manifestation. We then view the appearance of Being as the manifest reality, with the pure ground of Being as the unmanifest. This perception is clearest when we perceive the transformation process from the perspective of the absolute dimension, the subject of the next chapter. There are many grades of subtlety to this perception, which we will discuss in the next chapter. We experience the absolute as the unmanifest, the source of all manifestation, and perceive everything manifesting out of it. In fact, we witness the whole dimension of dynamic presence as manifesting within the vast mystery of the absolute, which is concomitant to the continual manifesting of the totality of the universe. More accurately, we experience the dimension of dynamic presence as the manifesting manifestation. Its emergence is the emergence of all creation, with all of its dimensions and forms.

It is simplistic, even mistaken, to think of nonmanifestation as the forms existing somewhere and coming into manifestation through the manifesting power of the dimension of dynamic presence. This would simply be a process of vertical translation, modeling the process of universal manifestation on the physical view of reality. Being is much more mysterious and magical; it simply manifests what is potential to it, in effect, creating it out of nothing. Forms exist in potential, the way a tree exists in the seed. But there is not even a seed, just the mysterious emptiness of true nature. Before manifestation, there is only the unmanifest, the absolute mystery and depth of Being.

Furthermore, manifestation is always new. It is not like the universe is manifested and then continues in time. No, it is always manifesting, in different forms and shapes, giving us the impression of change and motion. Manifestation is a similar process to creation, but bypasses the dualistic reification possible in the view of creation. Such reification is possible, and quite common, in the view of creation because creation is easily viewed anthropomorphically. In addition, manifestation is a universal process. The totality of what *is* manifests at once and continues to manifest with local variations of forms.

Because of this subtle understanding of the process of manifestation it is sometimes preferable to refer to it as "appearing," where "appearing" is not only a terminological difference, but actually a different and unique way of experiencing universal transformation. Everything seems to appear, to continue to appear, and to keep changing its appearance. Here there is the sense that there is absolutely nothing, and out of this nothing everything simply appears. This implies several things. First, the process does not take time, for appearing is instantaneous. As the forms appear they immediately disappear, and a new phenomenon appears. Both appearing and disappearing take no time; it is all instantaneous. We see a process only in the fact that appearing continues to happen, in conjunction with disappearing.

Another interesting implication of this perception is that we experience Reality clearly as appearance. In other words, it is very clear in this perception that the forms are only the appearance of Reality, and not its substance. We experience the totality of the universe, including the rocks and mountains, as light and ephemeral, possessing neither substantiality nor solidity. Everything seems to be of the nature of light, or even of thought. In fact, everything is of the nature of image, insubstantial and totally empty. Everything spontaneously appears, without ever establishing itself as something solid. We feel light, transparent; everything is free of gravity. The nature of everything is unrestricted freedom.

Yet it is all one appearance, one image, one picture, that keeps appearing with modified patterns and colors. We come close here to our metaphor of the movie screen, where the scene simply appears, and continues to appear. In fact, the question of disappearing is irrelevant. We do not say the picture appears and disappears on the screen.

We simply witness a picture that appears, and continues to appear but with modified shapes and colors.

We may see this appearing as a process of arising. The form arises out of formlessness. In this way of perceiving there is more of a perception of process, of an object that gradually arises and takes form. Such perception is closer to our normal way of experiencing, where we experience emotions, for instance, as arising and taking form gradually, not forming totally instantaneously. It is a gradual process of formation, where the object gradually comes into perception, the way we perceive a person emerging from water after being submerged into it. We can perceive our thoughts in this way, especially our ideas.

Both arising and the continuity of appearing give the impression of flow. Reality is flowing out, from formlessness to form, from nonexistence to existence, from nothing to appearance. Flow becomes another way of experiencing universal transformation, where we experience the totality of all forms of existence as one tapestry that is flowing out; the outflow is continuous but changes its patterns and colors, giving us the impression of change and movement. In the experience of flow we feel more intimately the direct sense of the dynamic presence. We experience all of Reality as one presence, sculpted and formed into the various objects and phenomena of existence. The totality of this field of presence is moving, flowing out within a particular pattern. This patterned outflow appears as the changes and movements we ordinarily perceive. In other words, in the experience of outflow we directly feel the process of creation. Being does not create something out there, apart from itself. It simply flows out of its own inscrutable depths, into the forms, colors, and shapes of the world.

We feel a sense of flow, as if a mass is flowing out, forming itself into the shapes and forms of existence. We may experience our body as a flow, as a mass of presence flowing out, and as it flows out it assumes the particular topography of our familiar body, with its colors and shapes. We may even experience this flow emerging at different locations of space, this way experiencing our motion as a flow, a flow of presence into the forms our body assumes in its various postures that the particular movement requires. We may even experience the flow of our body and its movement as an inseparable part of flow everywhere, where the whole universe is flowing out, as if Being is a fountain of abundance producing the world in its outflow. There is a sense of richness, energy, and power.

The outflow is, however, not a spatial translation. It is rather an unfoldment, where each point of space is always opening up and flowing out, the totality of this unfolding constituting the dynamic universe. In other words, the boundless presence is an unfolding presence, through whose unfoldment the universe comes into being and changes. We recognize here how the potential of Being becomes an actuality. Being simply opens up and unfolds, revealing in the process the universe with all of its variety, changes, and movements. It does not only flow from nonmanifestation to manifestation; it flows within a pattern, a pattern that differentiates this flow into the continual creation of all forms and phenomena. The flow and unfoldment create both the objects and the changes and movements of these objects, whether these objects are external or internal.

Dynamic Presence

When we experience the process of universal transformation as a flowing and unfolding presence, we begin to recognize the dimension of dynamic presence itself. The various ways of experiencing universal transformation in the above discussion reflect how we experience the coemergence of dynamic presence with the other boundless dimensions, and the degrees of subtlety of experiencing these dimensions. But when we experience it specifically as the flowing and unfoldment of presence we come upon the particular dimension of dynamic presence, at least in the logos of the Diamond Approach. Our experience focuses here on the dimension of true nature responsible for change and movement, which provides us with a more complete and detailed understanding of the changeability of existence.

We experience ourselves here similarly to the soul, as a flowing and dynamic presence, teeming with energy and pulsing with power. Yet, we are not a limited soul, but a boundless presence that is dynamic and vital, full of life and creative power. We may actually recognize here that the qualities that our soul possesses, those of flow, unfoldment, dynamism, potentiality, creativity, and morphogenic transformation come to it from this boundless dimension of dynamic being.[3] In other words, when we experience our soul as a living dynamic presence we are actually experiencing the dimension of dynamic presence but in a limited and individual way, as related to our particular physical body. Dynamic presence does not dismember itself into individual and separate souls, but simply appears so due to our limited understanding of our true nature. Because of this, the realization of the dimension of dynamic presence challenges our conviction that our souls have to be separate for them to be individual, and brings about the precise understanding of the relation of individual soul to universal soul, or dynamic presence, this way liberating us from this deep and constricting conviction.[4]

Such understanding can be the entry point to the dimension of dynamic presence. Here we experience ourselves as boundless and infinite, pulsing and throbbing with energy and vigor. We experience true nature on this dimension as presence that is energetic, active, and dynamic. It is pulsing and throbbing, full of force and power.[5] The sense of dynamism is strong. We experience it in various ways, but mostly as a presence that is not static at all, but vigorous and alive. The vigor is exhilarating and energizing, giving a sense of power and creativity. We feel it as presence, as the immediate sense of substantial being, but this presence has an excitatory quality that brings a tremendous dynamism to our experience. We sense the immense underlying dynamism of the universe, as the force, will, and energy of Being responsible for all manifestation, change, and transformation.

The experience of dynamism is independent of its action of creation of manifestation. It is simply the quality of presence, the energetic feel of the field of consciousness. It is not that the presence is moving or flowing, even though this feeling happens in conjunction with manifestation. It is simply the sense of dynamic power, similar to the feeling of the immense power that we sense when sitting in a big airliner, when its engines are idling just prior to take off. All other dimensions of being have the sense of stillness and beingness, but this dimension feels energetic and dynamic in addition to having the sense of beingness. It is actually an amazing experience, completely paradoxical for the normal mind.

We feel this incredible throbbing dynamism usually in conjunction with the particular function of this dimension, which is creativity. We experience Being here as a presence whose action is the creation of everything, all objects and all experiences. Its dynamism perpetually expresses itself as the unfoldment of the manifest world, with all of its physical and spiritual dimensions. It is a dynamism that is eternally manifesting the potentialities of true nature as the richness of the experiential universe. It is always displaying these potentialities as the outflow of the richness of Being, as the unfoldment of true nature's presence. Such creativity does not separate the creator from the created, the displayer from the displayed, the manifester from the manifestation. It is one indivisible presence that is perpetually displaying its richness and color as the universal manifold of all possible existence and experience.[6]

The Only Doer

In this dimension, we not only experience presence, awareness, and knowingness, but also the particulars of perception and experience, and the patterned flow of these particulars. We experience, in other words, the generation of the very experiences we are having, and the generation of all objects of experience. We perceive how experience happens, which turns out to be the same as the generation of manifestation. More precisely, we do not perceive a difference between the perceiver, the perceived, and the act of perception. All of these are generated together, as the specifics of the unfolding unified field of presence. We recognize ourselves as the generating dynamic presence, but also as the generated forms and experiences.

In the same act true nature generates forms and perceives them. It is the creator, the created, and the process of creation. Creation is simply generation, a continuous unfolding of forms and experiences. One way this appears to us in the inner journey is the recognition that there is no such thing as individual action. When we realize that there is ultimately no separate and autonomous soul we see that there is no such thing as independent action, personal choice, or volition. We began to understand this in working with the previously discussed boundless dimensions, in the form of questions about action and functioning. In fact, one of the primary difficulties in integrating these boundless dimensions of Being is the question of functioning, of how expression, action, and behavior happen. We understand functioning completely when we realize the dimension of dynamic presence, for we see how all change and movement occur. Since change and movement are limited ways of perceiving universal transformation, we see that individual action is a way of viewing a particular transformation of a certain region in the field of presence. Since an individual is only a form taken by a particular region of the field, one's action is actually the action of the field. One's behavior is nothing but the manifestation of the dynamism of Being, just as one's choices are made by the same dynamic presence. Volition becomes a concept that we cannot apply in this experience, for there are no autonomous entities that can have volition. All is done by the dynamism of Being, all chosen by the dynamic presence, and there is only one will, the dynamic will of true nature.[7]

In other words, there is only one doer, one mover, and that is true nature. Furthermore, the universal doer has only one act: the act of continuous creation. This doer does not take individual or specific actions, for it is not an entity in the space-time of manifestation. It is the force that in one unified act manifests the totality of existence. What we call action, doing, behavior, and functioning are actually imaginary things. In reality, there are no such things. More precisely, we may experience the unity of Being moving our hand, or circling the earth around the sun. It is accurate to think it is the action of the one doer, and not any particular individual being. This subtle and rare perception is still not completely accurate, for we are not seeing the unity of all actions, all movement, all changes. When we see the unity of action, as in the dimension of dynamic presence, we recognize that it is not a doing, but simply the manifesting or creation of all Reality as one unified fabric. This unified fabric is always unfolding, and unfolding in a pattern. We discern some of the dynamic elements of this pattern and call them action, behavior, and so on. In reality, there is no such thing as one person moving her arm, nor even God moving the person's arm. The expression "movement of the arm" is simply a convention that abstracts out a particular subpattern from the universal dynamic pattern and reifies it as such movement. In other words, individual action is a reification of a subprocess of the overall unfolding of the universe, inseparable from this overall unfolding.

The Pattern

The manifest world unfolded by the creative dynamism of Being possesses certain characteristics that humanity has seen as harmonious and orderly. Modern science relies on this order for its research in discovering, understanding, and applying natural laws; spiritual traditions rely on an inner order that makes sense of inner development. In other words, it is important to realize that appearance is not chaotic or haphazard. It is the universe that we perceive and within which we live, the universe that our science has recognized to faithfully follow natural laws. Manifestation appears orderly and meaningful, changing and transforming in orderly and meaningful ways. It unfolds within an order that we recognize as both meaningful and harmonious. The dynamism is constantly unfolding the universe in a particular orderly pattern. The unfoldment is a patterned unfoldment, and its pattern is the universe we perceive. This implies that dynamic presence has its own ordering and organizing principle that manifests the world always in what we recognize as the natural order of things. We may think of the functioning of this dimension of true nature as it unfolds the universe in what we consider an orderly fashion, as a fashioning and ordering of the universe. In fact, some of the ancient traditions thought that the creative ground orders, runs, and steers the flow of the universe, besides bringing it into existence. This was exactly how the ancient Greeks understood things to be, and called the ordering principle "logos," or reason.[8]

This original Greek usage of this term *logos* is identical to our meaning when we use it to refer to this dimension of true nature. The term *logos*, however, means much more in Western history, which is a further reason we prefer to use it to refer to the dimension of dynamic presence. The logos is the boundless dimension of true nature that is both presence and creative dynamism. Logos refers to the fact that true nature is inherently dynamic and creative. Logos is the creative matrix of all manifestation. Logos is the manifesting dimension, but it is also all manifestation, for it manifests everything from its own substance, its own presence. True nature in its absoluteness is totally transcendent, as we will see in the next chapter; but it possesses a dimension of itself, one of its inherent potentialities, that makes it inherently dynamic and creative. One way of saying this is that true nature creates the universe through its logos,[9] while in reality the logos is only a facet of true nature, and not something separate from it. It is true that it is the dimension responsible for creation and manifestation, but this is due to our focus on this dimension, which in reality is always coemergent with all other dimensions of true nature.

In experiencing the dimension of the logos we experience a boundless presence, transparent and full of being. We see all of manifestation, both physical and spiritual, as manifest within it, constituted by it. We see all of manifestation as the details and specifics of the logos. These details and specifics form a universal and infinite pattern. It is one pattern, interconnected and indivisible. Discerning this pattern we recognize the universe of experience in its totality, for all objects of the universe are subpatterns within the overall pattern. At the same time, the pattern is in flow, in progress, its flow detailing the development and evolution of the universe. The flow is an unfolding of the presence that not only generates the forms of the world but their changes and movements. In other words, the pattern is dynamic and evolving. Putting it in the language of modern science, the pattern fills the four dimensions of space-time. More exactly, since there is no time in the usual sense here, the pattern is not only of the details defining the objects but also of the details determining their changes and movements. Furthermore, this pattern includes the invariant patterns that govern all natural and spiritual processes. For instance, it includes the pattern that objects fall toward the earth, detailing the laws of gravity. It also includes the pattern that when a person identifies with a particular self-concept, they become dissociated from the immediacy of their essential presence. To summarize, the logos is not only the dynamic force generating existence, but the pattern of this existence that reflects the pattern of this generation. The logos pattern, in other words, is the original order of all things.

The Logos

We have discussed how the characteristic of change is present in all the boundless dimensions, even though the logos is the specific dimension of creative dynamism. We can experience the logos from the perspective of any of the other dimensions; that is, we can experience the pattern with love, knowledge, or nonconceptual awareness dominant. We can see the pattern nonconceptually, without recognition of the meaning or significance of its specifics, or we can see it with knowledge and discernment of these details, or we can see it as the force of love that generates the universe and makes the world go around.[10]

When we experience the logos from the perspective of nonconceptual awareness we arrive at the various paradoxes for which Zen is famous, as discussed in the last chapter. When we experience the logos with knowledge, we recognize a whole dimension of wisdom that makes sense of some of the fundamental teachings of the Western traditions of wisdom. Most important, the pattern is one that can be discerned, can be known.[11] This is of extreme importance for the development of knowledge of both universe and Being/God. If the pattern is not knowable then neither is our universe, and there is no truth to find in experience and perception.

The experience of the logos is then not only the flow of all objects and phenomena, but the flow of knowledge. Just as we saw in chapter 18 that on the dimension of pure presence all manifest objects are noetic forms, we see here that they are dynamic and flowing noetic forms. The manifestation and evolution of the world is the flow of basic knowledge, knowing inseparable from dynamic unfoldment. And since this flow is orderly and patterned, the flow of knowledge is orderly and harmonious. In other words, the flow of basic knowledge follows the pattern of the logos. The Greeks equated logos with reason, because the logos has an order, or a rule, that steers its unfoldment. Reason is originally the order of the logos, the principle or principles that order its pattern. In other words, the flow of basic knowledge is reasonable, makes perfect sense. We may refer to this as basic reason, differentiating it from ordinary reason, in correspondence with ordinary and basic knowledge.[12]

We also discussed in chapter 16 how each object in manifestation is a noetic form, a universal concept, and how we can perceive the conceptual nature of these forms. On the dimension of pure presence we can experience each noetic form as having the nature of thought. That was the basis of calling the dimension of pure presence universal or divine mind; all objects are thoughts in God's mind. But the logos is a dynamic flowing presence full of knowledge, so these divine thoughts do not simply exist; they move and flow. In other words, we can experience the logos as thinking, as the reasonable flow of concepts and thoughts. Each concept is an object in our world, but they all flow in a rational (reflecting the order of the logos, reason) pattern.[13]

With this discussion we are approaching the experience of the process of manifestation as universal thinking. We experience the whole unfoldment and flow of phenomena and events as thinking, as rational thought. This may sound like a dry intellectual experience, but in fact it is a powerful and beautiful perception. The whole universe appears luminous and transparent, composed of luminous forms of variegated colors, qualities, and flavors. This whole amazing and enchantingly beautiful panorama is unfolding with intelligence that imbues the flow with a glittering brilliance. At the same time it flows in patterns that are clear, precise, and discernable. The clarity and precision give the experience an exquisite aesthetic sense that is inseparable from the amazing insights that constitute the basic knowing of the forms. The forms are like words, discernible concepts, and the process of flow feels like thinking. This thinking is rational thought, for it is the orderly flow of knowledge, a knowledge inseparable from the intimate directness and richness of presence. The experience is that God/Being is creating the world by thinking it. The thinking occurs in all the sense modalities, for each concept is a noetic form in the multidimensional manifold of the logos.[14]

A subtler form of this experience is one that combines the logos with pure nonconceptual awareness. We perceive the flow of prenoetic forms in the process of creation as a flow of colorful images. In other words, the forms do not have knowingness, only the differentiations that compose them. In effect, we recognize the process of manifestation as imagination. All the manifest universe, and all experience, appears as the content of imagination. It is not our personal imagination, but universal imagination. We can say that the logos imagines the world into existence.[15] The sense of imagination reflects the fact that in this experience we perceive the forms as images devoid of substance or solidity. The dominant impression, however, is the unity of manifestation, which appears as one image. Everything is purely image, purely an imagined form, but we are part of what is imagined by the logos.

The Speaker

In the Western tradition the most common understanding of the logos is that of the Word, made famous by the gospel according to Saint John.[16] It is easy to understand this when we see that it is closer to direct experience to describe the creative unfoldment of the logos not as the flow of knowledge but as expression. Being is inherently dynamic and it expresses this dynamism by creating the universe as a revelation of its potentialities. This is similar to personal self-expression, which reveals one's potentials; but in this case God creates the world as theophany.[17] By unfolding the manifest world, Being expresses its properties of creativity and dynamism, and its qualities of love, joy, and compassion.

Being expresses itself through noetic forms, each of which we can directly experience as a word-concept. A word-concept is not a generic or category concept, but one word that is not just a meaningless word, but embodies a concept of a particular object. On the dimensions of pure presence and the logos, these word-concepts are actually the objects themselves, as concepts in the divine mind, or words uttered by the logos. In other words, the logos creates the world through a kind of utterance. The utterance is not simply the enunciation of sounds as we know them, but the outflow of orderly expression that uses word-concepts for this expression. More precisely, the logos speaks the world into existence. The logos is a speaker, in fact, the original speaker. It creates through the word.[18] And since the logos is not only the creative agency but the manifestation itself, it is composed of words. It is composed of living words, each of which is a presence, a noetic form, an object.

More accurately, since the manifest world is also the logos, for it is the logos's unfolding particulars, and the world is composed of word-concepts, the logos is composed of word-concepts. It is both speaker and speech. It utters the words and is the totality of all the words. However, the manifest world is one indivisible field of dynamic presence, and not disconnected forms and objects. The presence of the logos is then a unified field of words, spoken all at once, for creation is of the world as a whole, instantaneously and continuously. The logos does not utter the word-concepts in succession, it utters them all at once, simultaneously, as if it is uttering one word. In other words, the logos is a word that contains all words. We can understand here why the logos can be referred to as the Word. It is the word of the divine being through which all comes into being. The logos is the Word of Being, the speech by which Being becomes a speaker, and by which the manifest world comes into being.

The logos is the speaker in another way. Just as it reveals the potentialities inherent in Being through the primal revelation that manifests Reality, it also manifests these to the soul as inner revelations. This has been the understanding of the various wisdom traditions.[19] In the Diamond Approach, inquiry invites the logos to unfold the soul's experience. The Diamond Guidance aligns the inquiry with the intelligence and dynamism of Being, opening the soul to the revelations of her true nature. The experience of the individual is usually a sense of unfoldment of the soul, where the mysteries of Being are revealed to her as she knows and understands herself. She discovers one quality of true nature after another, one dimension after another, one capacity after another, as the logos reveals them to her. In other words, the guided unfoldment of the soul is precisely the orderly pattern of the logos as it manifests in the individual soul. They are the same process, but seen from two vantage points, that of the individual soul and that of the universal logos. We can say that the logos speaks to the soul, informing her of the mysteries of Reality, but it is more accurate to say that the logos speaks the unfoldment of the soul.

We see a deep, fundamental connection between speaking and the operation of the logos, just as we have seen it between thinking and the creative dynamism of the logos. In reality, the creative outflow of the logos, thinking, and speaking are parallel expressions of the same phenomenon, which is basically the orderly flow of words as seen in three dimensions of experience: the actual experiential world, the thinking mind, and communicative speech.

Direct Transmission

Just as real, basic, or pure thinking is a way that the logos reveals truth to the soul, real speaking can do the same. This function is one of the major ways a teacher transmits the teaching to students. When the teacher has integrated the dimension of the logos in his realization he becomes able to function similarly to the logos. By speaking he reveals the truth of true nature and Reality. Such speaking is not simply the communication of ordinary knowledge; it is the communication of basic knowledge. By speaking, the teacher utters the words, which are word-concepts. By uttering such words, he does not only say the syllables. Each time he says the word-concept he sees the reality of this word, its color and shape; he feels the quality of essence to which the word corresponds; he tastes its flavor and feels its texture. His speaking is not only through the mouth but through the fullness of the manifold of the soul. By speaking about a truth of Being this truth arises in his soul, fills it, and overflows to his listeners. In other words, real speaking, or logos-speaking, is an invocation of the truth spoken within the soul of the speaker but also a communication of the same truth to the consciousness of the listener. The logos-speaker communicates the essential truth by embodying it in his presence and in his speech. Through his speaking a particular timeless truth, this truth fills his soul, pervades his gestures and postures, and fills his words with wisdom. The words do not carry only ordinary knowledge; they carry the substance and full presence of basic knowledge.

It is as if, by speaking, the logos-speaker pours the substance of truth, in the various qualities he is verbally communicating, into the consciousness of the listener. His words reflect the logos unfoldment he is presently experiencing within his soul, and these words directly, instantaneously, and spontaneously carry the meaning that is inseparable from the full, textured presence of this unfoldment. Recall from chapter 18 that knowing and being are inseparable in basic knowledge. In logos-speaking, the words and being are inseparable. By speaking the truth, the logos-speaker embodies the truth; and by embodying it he communicates it through all the modalities of expression: through his postures and gestures, through his attitudes and states, through his words and expression, but also and most importantly, through his embodied and unfolding presence.[20]

Such speaking is the direct transmission necessary for any teaching, and is the central method the teachers of the Diamond Approach use when teaching in group settings. By speaking about an essential aspect or dimension of true nature, the teacher invokes it in his consciousness and it becomes his presence. By communicating the inner orderly flow in the skillful and guided speech, he guides the souls of his listeners to align themselves with such unfoldment. It may seem as if he is pouring the substance and presence of truth into his listeners' souls, but in fact he is only inviting their souls to align themselves the way he is aligning himself. Through such alignment the listener's experience can begin to unfold, revealing the truth the speaker is communicating in the personal experience of the listener.

The complete process of direct transmission in logos-speaking is that the speaker communicates the truth from his own experience. This invokes it in the moment in his own presence. If he has also integrated the diamond guidance, his speaking will be guided and skillful, so that his communication is empathic and attuned to his listeners. His communication will also precisely guide his listeners through their own ignorance and positions, helping them to open up and be receptive to his transmission, which is more accurately an opening up to the unfoldment in their own soul. In other words, the direct transmission is an embodied speaking where both the logos and the diamond guidance are present and operating; the logos unfolds the experience and the guidance opens up the consciousness and aligns it with the unfolding truth. In reality, the diamond guidance is the discerning eye and intelligence of the logos.

Language and Manifestation

Speaking involves not only words, but a whole language, which means that logos is intimately related to language. Language includes grammar, syntax, and many other components. A language, as expressed in a sentence, possesses a structure, which structure imparts meaning. The structure of a meaningful sentence is an orderly pattern of words, an orderly flow of words, a patterned flow where the pattern and order is indispensable for meaning. In other words, for a language to have meaning it will need to have an orderly structure, which is reflected in its grammar and syntax.

We have seen that both thinking and speaking reflect the orderly flow of the logos, which is the flowing pattern of manifest reality. Thinking and speaking, in addition to writing and reading, are the carriers of language, the direct representatives of its structure. Hence, we see that a language must correspond in its structure with the pattern of the logos.[21] Since we have already seen that the words of a language must first arise from the word-concepts of noetic forms, we see now that the totality of a language, both its vocabulary and structure, must faithfully reflect the pattern of the logos if it is going to be useful and meaningful. This is not a new insight, for thinkers have known for a long time that a language is a reflection of the reality that consciousness experiences. But we have seen how thinking and speaking can and do dissociate from their origin and ground, the dynamic presence of the logos. This understanding can help us see that a language can develop originally from the intimate contact with Reality, through the direct experience of the logos, but that it can move away from its original ground, and become more abstract and distant from the immediate experience of presence. The more we develop intellectual concepts, and the more abstract our thinking and knowing becomes, the more dissociated the language will be from the reality of the logos.[22] But a language can never be completely estranged from the logos without losing its usefulness, for the logos is the pattern of Reality.

Harmony

We have been exploring the pattern of the logos, the order immanent in manifest reality, seeing how it is the ground and basis of rationality, reason, thinking, speaking, and language. But how does this order appear in experience, and what are the qualities of such experience? Such experience is the principal realization of the dimension of the logos, for it is the direct experience of the logos.

We feel a sense of presence and fullness, at the same time that we are aware of powerful dynamism and the sense of flow. The full presence is boundless, infinite, and at the same time luminous and alive. It is a conscious presence where awareness and the fullness of presence are inseparable, making up one unified field of consciousness. We experience all of the world of perception as the forms that this presence assumes at various regions of its expanse. All forms and objects are nothing but the field of presence itself, but with differentiating colors, shapes, and qualities. At the same time we perceive the sense of flow as the flowing out of all of these forms, not from one place to another, but from depth to surface, and more accurately, from nonmanifestation to manifestation. We directly feel the whole infinite field as a fluid fabric, flowing at all points of its expanse. We perceive the flowing as the changes and movements of the various forms in the field of perception. In other words, the flow is not only of the existentiating outflow of the medium of the logos, but also of the progress of all phenomena. We see the changes of the weather, the changes of the environment if we are in motion, the movement and changes of all objects around us as we move and they move, the changes of the body as it moves and gestures, the flow of our words if we are talking, the flow of our thoughts and feelings, the unfoldment of the inner states of presence, the unfoldment of the qualities of the boundless presence of the logos all around us, and so on. But we see it all as one flow, as one fabric that outflows, or continuously manifests.

We perceive the various objects and phenomena flowing together in a manner where there is no contradiction, no opposition, no collision, no competition, no jostling, no confusion, no interference, and no enmity. All the forms and phenomena of manifest reality—in all of its physical, mental, emotional, and spiritual dimensions—flow together with total and perfect harmony. At the same time, it is clear to us that the whole flow is not only harmonious but completely intelligent in an organic and synergistic fashion, where the harmony owes not only to the absence of discord, but also to the exquisite intelligence implicit in the details and specifics of the unfoldment. Everything interweaves with everything else in total intelligence and harmony, as if it is the work of a master designer. It is like the perfect symphony, the most complete cooperation, and the most total coexistence. The inner sense is of an intimacy and peace, a settled and contented heart, a relaxed and settled presence. The fullness possesses beauty and harmony, and a texture of blissful sweetness. The blissful sweetness may be that of a rich and richly textured love, that of the nectar of fulfillment, or that of the flowing delicate honey of surrendered contentment.

This is the effect of the dimension of love as it fills the field of the logos, giving us the impression that the universe is unfolding as the action of the love of Being. The logos is felt then as the heart of God, and we are all its inhabitants. At other times, the flow is more of universal revelation of knowledge. We feel and perceive knowledge arising everywhere: each form is a recognition, and each phenomenon an understanding. The flowing boundless presence is here transparent, but with an exquisite faceted sense to it, as if it is a flowing ocean of liquefied diamonds of various colors and hues. Such is the effect of the dimension of pure presence as it arises coemergent with the logos. At other times the flow is totally empty and light, even though formed and sculpted with the forms of manifestation. It is radiant and clear, with a sense of total freshness and newness, with an indescribable beauty and ecstasy that shatters the thinking mind and leaves it awed and dazzled. Such is the effect of nonconceptual awareness as it intermingles with the flow of the logos.

At other times we feel an immeasurable depth and a profound stillness, and experience ourselves as the true nature of everything, but a truth that is continually clothing itself with the creation. We experience ourselves as the source of all manifestation, and the manifest world as a flowing robe that we wear. The logos here is the apparel of the absolute that reveals the treasures hidden in its inscrutable depths. We are the truth, and all of reality is our ornament. The world is alive, breathing with the dynamism of the logos; and the world is real, expressing the truth of true nature. Such majesty and such beauty of appearance are the effects of the presence of the absolute dimension in conjunction with that of the logos.

Optimizing Force

The order and reason of the logos is not simply in the harmony of the flow, but in the intelligent development of this flow. We recognize that the dynamism of the logos possesses an optimizing intelligence, which makes it into a maximizing force. When we are able to stay in this flow for some time we begin to recognize its influence on our experience in general, and on phenomena at large. The logos does not simply flow from one object to another, from one phenomenon to the next, but in this flow there is development, growth, maturation, and evolution. Not only is there intelligence in this outflow that contributes to its harmony, but this flow is intelligent because it tends to fulfill the nature of each individual form. It fulfills the nature of each form by making it a better vehicle through which true nature can express itself. The flow is intelligent because it influences everything by moving it closer to intimacy with true nature. It moves everything closer and opens everything further to greater realization and embodiment of the qualities and dimensions of true nature.

We see this most clearly in its role in the development of the soul. We begin to understand why when the soul unfolds under the guidance of Being it does not stay in the same place or deteriorate. The unfoldment always reveals greater depth, clearer insight, more precise and universal truth, enhanced clarity, and more luminosity. In other words, the unfoldment of the soul always leads to greater and more complete experience of the qualities of true nature. We begin to see that this is due to the action of the optimizing dynamism of the logos, which manifests experience in such a way that it is always tending to reveal true nature in as clear, deep, and complete a way as possible.

More specifically, the action of the logos in the experience of the soul, especially when the soul is open and receptive to this action, is to optimize her experience. Because of this, the inner journey is simply the optimization of the soul's experience by maximizing her clarity, luminosity, awareness, love, truth, compassion, openness, joy, freedom, and so on. Furthermore, the guidance of Being simply orients the soul to be in harmony with the optimizing force of the logos, which appears in her experience as a deepening and expanding unfoldment.

The optimizing force of the logos functions throughout manifest reality, in both the animate and inanimate worlds. We do not always understand its direction, for its intelligence is cosmic and spans all time. But we can recognize signs of its functioning in the self-organizing properties of the universe, in various cosmological and terrestrial developments, in the arising and evolution of life, in the development of each living organism in its growth and maturation, even its decay and death. In other words, the logos is not only the principle of change and movement, but also of development and evolution, of growth and maturation, of both body and soul. This understanding may help us to recognize that the totality of the manifest universe is not only unfolding and changing but that it is also developing and evolving. And the direction of this evolution is the optimization of manifestation in order that all forms embody and express true nature in as complete and total a manner as possible, appropriate for the capacity of the particular form. We can easily understand this when we remember that the logos is the way true nature expresses and reveals its infinite potentialities.[23]

Since the logos is the harmonious flow of all phenomena, a flow that embodies an optimizing and loving intelligence, it is the source of wisdom regarding many of these phenomena that are of particular interest to human beings. Being the harmonious flow of interrelating phenomena, the logos contains the wisdom of their optimization. It can show us the truth and reality, and the possible optimizing direction, of such things as human relationships in their various forms, such as love relationships, marriages and divorces, friendships and work associations. It can reveal to us the wisdom regarding destiny, connection, union, even the various degrees of union with God. It can also reveal to us the wisdom of how to grow, develop, mature, evolve, and so on, and how to unfold knowledge and deepen heart. Because it is the harmonious order of all phenomena, it can guide us toward optimization of all concerns of human life, and of life in general. It can also provide us with a more complete understanding of the self, and support our realization that there is no self-existing and abiding entity called self, for everything is continually created new.

Real Time

Only a scant discussion is possible in the present volume of the various themes relevant for the dimension of the logos. Each theme is a study on its own. For further discussion of the dimension of the logos and some of these themes, see *Diamond Heart, Book 5*, and *The Pearl Beyond Price*, chapter 39.

We will end with a discussion of a theme central to the understanding of the logos. If the logos is the flow of all change and movement, where does this flow happen? In other words, does this flow happen in time, which is what will be ordinarily expected? But we need to remember that the logos manifests everything, so it manifests space and time, too. It manifests all of the perceptual universe at once, in one image, or one Word. This image includes space and time. No time passes on the logos: it is before time. Time is a phenomenon occurring within manifestation.

More precisely, time is the concept we develop to account for the fact that we observe changes and movements. If there were no such thing as change or movement we would not need the notion of time. In other words, we need time to explain processes, the fact that phenomena progress from one form to another. We invent the dimension of time to account for this prolongation of phenomena, for it is not in space. However, we have seen that change is not from the past to the present, but rather from nonmanifestation to manifestation. Each stage of the progress of phenomena simply means that new creations have emerged. We need time, and feel the passage of time, only when we are in the midst of the changing phenomena. But when we are outside of all phenomena, and are experiencing ourselves from the vantage point of the logos, we directly perceive how all phenomena arise, and that nothing moves from past to future. It simply flows out, always in a new edition. We recognize that no time ever passes on anything, for all forms and objects are eternally new.

An alternative view is that the logos is the source of the sense and concept of time. Because it is responsible for change and movement it is responsible for the passage of time. Its flow is actually what is happening that accounts for change and movement. We may experience this flow directly, and then we can recognize it as the flow of real time.[24] This is not clock time; it is the time that actually changes and moves everything. And because it flows, we can get a vague intimation of such flow in ordinary experience, which then we believe is the feeling of the passage of time. In reality, time does not pass; rather it is the logos that flows. Continuity of time is a vague intimation of continuously new creation.

21 The Absolute and Emptiness

IN ELUCIDATING THE PRINCIPLES OF KNOWING, Immanuel Kant thought of time and space as the most fundamental intuitive a priori categories, indispensable for all experience. Isaac Newton thought of time and space as absolute, underivable from anything simpler, and believed that they are God's direct creation. Albert Einstein, in his theory of relativity, challenged the absoluteness of Newtonian time and space, and demonstrated that they are relative, dependent on the frame of reference of the observer. However, Einstein's challenge concerned only the measurement of time and space, and did not address their existence and ultimate nature. Modern physics generally does not try to address the question of the reality and nature of time and space, remaining with Newton's original understanding corrected with Einstein's relativistic view. But time and space have always been among the deepest subjects of inquiry for both philosophy and spiritual understanding. We discussed in the previous chapter how time can be understood from the perspective of true nature, and saw how the concept of time originates from the flow and unfoldment of the logos underlying all change and movement. To appreciate how we can understand the ultimate reality and nature of space, and the origins of the concept of space, from the perspective of true nature, we turn now to the fifth boundless dimension of true nature, that of the absolute.

We have seen how the world of experience is continually generated by the logos, as an unfolding pattern of forms and phenomena. One way of experiencing this is to see that the manifest world is not a continuation from the past, but an arising in the moment. It simply manifests, as a new creation, a movement from nonmanifestation to manifestation. Such understanding can begin the inquiry into what nonmanifestation means. When we recognize the unfoldment of the logos as the appearing out of nonmanifestation, where does the appearing appear from, or in? What is the unmanifest, if there is such a thing? Can we step out of the manifest world and witness the process of manifestation?

The Unmanifest

The unfoldment of the logos is an outflow, a cosmic articulation, a speaking of the Word. All movement must occur against a background of stillness, and all speaking against a background of silence. Stillness and silence are the first properties of the unmanifest that the soul normally encounters in her inner journey. By simply witnessing the process of manifestation, and not going along with the normal enmeshment in the forms it assumes, the soul may find herself outside of her individual form, as the background against which all change and movement occur. She is then simply a silent witness, unmoving and immovable, a vast expanse underlying the process of continual creation.[1] In this process we discover a deeper dimension than the logos, deeper than all other boundless dimensions, a dimension of true nature that forms the ultimate ground of the other dimensions and the ultimate ground of all things. We discover where the unfoldment happens, which turns out not to be a place; we discover the source of all manifestation, which is also its ultimate and absolute nature.

We experience a stillness beyond all stillness, an absolute and total stillness, a condition prior to all manifestation, movement, and change.[2] We experience a stupendous silence, empty of all noise, whether outer chatter or inner rumination, whether outer manifestation or inner movement; for it is the condition before all expression, prior to thinking and speaking, prior to the Word. We become aware of being a field that cannot be called a space; for it includes all space and time as an unfoldment within it, but does not touch its pristine stillness and silence. We are the prior, prior to all. We are the immovable, the unchanging, the mysterious ground of all movement and change. Movement and change are the manifestation that arises within it without ever disturbing its stillness and peace, without ever touching its silence and emptiness. We are prior to all manifestation, the source from which creation emerges, and the mystery to which it returns. We are the beginning and the end of everything, the truth without which there will be no awareness, and no experience.

We experience ourselves as a vastness, an immensity, an expanse so deep it is absolutely dark. Though dark and still, inscrutable and silent, it is the source of all luminosity and light. And within this immeasurable immensity, we witness the process of creation. We see a dynamic presence, the divine logos, flowing out of the absolute, revealing its potentialities as the manifest reality, disclosing its mysteries as the multidimensional manifold of existence and experience. Yet, because of the infinity of the absolute we see this manifold as a surface phenomenon, as if the absolute is so pure and pristine that it glitters and shines, its brilliance forming a surface, colorful and luminous. This colorful and luminous surface of radiance is continually scintillating with colors and forms, shapes and patterns. We witness an unfolding surface of clear and variegated light, whose pattern is the totality of creation. The absolute is prior to light, but also its source and ultimate nature and mystery. The light is the unfolding logos, whose pattern is the totality of existence, a dynamic unified manifold. The scintillating light is one unified surface, with no parts and no partitions, a field of radiance full of intelligence and truth, reality and significance.

The background of this unfoldment, the absolute, is so totally dark it appears black, but luminous crystal clear black.[3] We experience it as beyond the world. The world looks like a transparent picture, as if it were a soap bubble with pictures on it. It looks like a reflection on the inside of a transparent bubble, within the infinite immensity of the crystalline absolute. This perception changes depending on how involved we are in the manifestation, or how concentrated we are on the absolute.

When we are witnessing within the manifestation but still being the absolute, we can perceive our body moving, doing what it does—eating, talking, and so on. However, all this is seen as completely spontaneous functioning, not belonging to a person or a self. There is no doer whatsoever. Everything is happening as functioning, each part is doing its functioning smoothly and spontaneously. The functioning is not related to a doer, a person, or a self. And it is not seen as separate from other functioning in the environment, for all functioning is a unified dynamic field. Furthermore, the functioning is the same as the phenomena, the perceived reality, the logos whose dynamic pattern is the universe. However, there is no I, no self, no center. The awareness and perception originate from the darkness of the absolute.

We feel unknown and unknowable, and in front of us phenomena appear with functioning. There is awareness of phenomena and functioning, but there is no involvement in it whatsoever. It does not feel like there is someone observing or aware of phenomena. It is as if Reality has two sides. The front is all of existence, the back is the darkness of the absolute. All of appearance, as the divine logos or being, is seen as external to the absolute. There is no one who feels he is doing. The doing is present, without being related to doer. The interesting thing is that there are functioning and perception without a sense of self. We realize that usually there is a continuous sense of self or "I." Now there is experience and perception of experience, but it is not related to an "I." The experience is far or distant from who I am, without who I am feeling like an "I."

Or we can experience ourselves in the midst of the manifest world, aware of the absolute as the background and underlying nature of all manifestation and perception. Here we experience everything around us as if it were one unified surface, luminous and transparent. We perceive everything—the floor, the walls, the furniture, and all people present—clearly as appearance, as the luminous beauty of the logos, radiant with golden truth, and rich with the nectar of love. Yet all this transparent surface is penetrated by the blackness of the mystery. This perception has a sense of beauty and magic, as if we experience the totality of the perceptual field as a luminous and transparent surface, with the absolute blackness peering through from all directions, giving the impression of being inside a transparent bubble in an infinite dark space. The luminous blackness peers through the walls, the floor, the bodies of people, through all objects and surfaces. Such experience depends on being completely in the present, where the mind is not thinking of other places and times, but is totally focused in the here and now. The mind is free of its normal knowledge, with all of its details about reality and the world. So there is only the perception of the here and now; everything that lies beyond is a mystery, unknown and magical. We realize that as far as perception goes there is only the here and now; everything else is memory and accumulated knowledge. And when memory is not filtering our experience, we directly perceive what is, the luminosity of the unfolding logos pattern, transparent to its underlying truth, the inscrutable brilliant darkness of the absolute.

It is clear in such experience that there is only the now, that the now is not caused by the past, but is continuously generated out of the absolute. There is the certainty that there is no continuity in time and no movement in space and time. There is only the continual manifestation of appearance, as a cosmic and universal act, all at once. There is absolutely no room in this perception for individual action. There is only cosmic continual appearing, beyond which is the mystery of the absolute. There is only the now, which is not continuous with the past, but with the absolute as source. It is interesting that not only sight is appearance, but also hearing, and the input of all the senses. Sound does not seem to come from various sources, for that implies a process in time. We perceive sound only in the now, as originating from the absolute. We see the absolute as the reality behind the appearance, penetrating the surface of appearance and suffusing it. A deep sense of peace pervades, within a blissful harmony.

As we abide in the inscrutable darkness of the absolute we recede, as if backward, from the world of manifestation. The soul feels: "I am perceiving the world and knowing I am not of it, not part of it, and not in it. When I reflect I do not find myself, either as a person or self. It seems I am some kind of emptiness that does not have any particular feeling, even of self. There is awareness of phenomena, but I am not part of what I perceive, and I am not anything in particular. I am pure subject, which is not an object. I am the source of awareness. I am not the witnessing, but I make witnessing possible."

There is everything, there is the perception of everything, but no self or person, and no reference to them. The mind cannot conceive of existence without reference to a center. There is no frame of reference here. There is lightness, openness, expansion, and joy.

As abiding in the absolute becomes deeper and more concentrated we experience ourselves even less in the midst of the manifestation. The soul experiences herself now more clearly as the absolute, a vast peace and an immense stillness. The logos with its universe appears clearly as a surface phenomenon for the absolute, as if it is its outside. The soul here recognizes her realization of the absolute as: "I am the absolute and the logos-universe is my robe. The manifest world is my shimmering apparel, adorning my majesty, and revealing my beauty. I perceive the oneness of existence as a thin surface of appearance, with all of its color and richness, and I am the luminous night peering though all." It is the perception of the perceived universe as appearance appearing continually and instantaneously in the absolute darkness. Appearance is perceived as grace, beauty, luminosity, and harmony. It is the oneness of the logos, full of golden love and presence.

As we go deeper into the mystery of the absolute we move away from the surface and experience ourselves as a vast immensity, a solid emptiness. We clearly perceive the universe as an unfolding surface of light. There is the sense of the manifest universe not only as appearance, but also as appearing from the absolute. So the perception is not only a matter of seeing the oneness of existence, but also that the oneness is a flow from the absolute. Appearing is the process of continual creation, out of the absolute. Appearing is time, is universal action. It is obvious and self-evident that there is no personal action, that there are no causes in time. The absolute is the only cause, the prime mover.

We can then sink deeper into the mysterious darkness of the absolute, leaving the surface manifestation. We experience ourselves receding deeper, and the universe of appearance looking smaller and smaller, until we see it as a small luminous sphere floating at the distance, in the vast silence of the absolute.[4] We recognize the vastness of the absolute, the immensity of its truth, and the smallness of the manifest universe, with all of its forms and phenomena. We recognize in this experience that if the universe is four-dimensional, it appears as a spherical surface in the vastness of the absolute, demonstrating that this vastness is at least five-dimensional. As will we see later, it is infinite-dimensional, which is the same as being nondimensional.

The absolute blackness may dominate even more, until we perceive the universe as a surface patch, a patch of luminous surface floating in the vastness. Everything else is absolute darkness. No thoughts, no movement, no self-reflection, only silence, stillness, and mystery.

The absolute is the unmanifest because it is prior to all manifestation, the source of the unfolding logos. It is not part of manifestation, but is the ultimate nature and mystery. We can experience it and realize it, but not when we are enmeshed and busy with the content of the manifest world. We can experience it when we recognize ourselves as the light that emanates from it, or as the witness that perceives this emanation. However, this view may not be satisfactory in terms of understanding the unmanifest; we may think that the unmanifest cannot be experienced, that only the manifest can. We will discuss this subtle question as we proceed in our exploration of the absolute.

Cessation

Beyond this experience, all light disappears, all awareness ceases. There is no perception of anything; there is simply no experience. When the soul is completely concentrated on the absolute there is nothing to perceive, for to perceive total darkness is not to perceive. Light is the awareness that arises out of this total darkness, revealing that the absolute is prior to light, awareness, and consciousness. This experience of cessation is the experience of complete ego death, for it is going beyond the world of manifestation, beyond even awareness of the world of manifestation. There is no awareness of self or soul, for there is no awareness at all, without this being unconsciousness or sleep.

When awareness looks out again, which we experience as the return of awareness, the manifest universe reappears. With the return of awareness the logos appears as the displaying of time and space, and all the phenomena of the universe. We are here the absolute, the luminous night, witnessing appearance arising within it, out of it, but we still experience ourselves as the immense stillness and stupendous silence underlying all existence and all appearance.[5] We feel fresh and clear, as if our consciousness has dipped into the cleansing energies of the source, and returned renewed and rejuvenated. This is similar to the rejuvenation we experience after deep sleep, except we are here clear and awake, bright and lucid.[6]

The experience of cessation can occur in different ways, usually before the discovery of the absolute, as the initial entry into it. It can be precipitated by the experience of mystical poverty, when we recognize how our attachments and compulsive desires disconnect us from our true nature. Letting go of these attachments, we realize we have to let go of everything. This includes not only the sensuous objects of the world and the satisfaction they promise us, but also inner riches: making a contribution, having a position, knowledge, a state, fruits of the work, a station, recognition, anything. As the soul lets go of all of her possessions, including her qualities and capacities, even her existence, she experiences the state of poverty. This state has a sense of having nothing, feeling nothing, being nothing, perceiving nothing. Accepting and welcoming the total emptiness of this state can lead to the state of cessation, where the last thing to go is perception.

Cessation can also happen as part of the love affair that the soul has with her true nature. As she opens up and becomes fully present, without defenses or pretensions, she may feel her intimate love for the absolute. Such love may appear as an ardent desire and longing, or a resistance and unwillingness to keep living in manifestation. She feels she would rather dissolve in the absolute and disappear than experience the various realms. Such longing may lead to a complete disappearance into the unmanifest absolute, as the soul feels enveloped by its delicious darkness, and caressed by its infinite mystery.

This intimate embrace can reveal to the soul that she is like a cloud of consciousness particles. As she dissolves she feels only a few particles, conscious of themselves and of black nothingness. As consciousness thins away it disappears in the nothingness. All perception and sensation are lost. There is then not even consciousness of nothing. It is as if unconsciousness. There is absence of consciousness. There is absence of existence, absence and no awareness of absence. It is as if the consciousness thins away like air and the awareness itself disappears. When there is no consciousness at all, there is no experience whatsoever, and no awareness of no experience.

Such dissolving is usually gradual, feeling like a delicious melting, a wonderful and lovely embrace. However, this experience is quite informative, for it reveals further mysteries of the absolute. As the consciousness of the soul thins away, she recognizes the effect of the surrounding blackness and nothingness on her presence. She feels herself as a thin and dispersed mass, so delicate and so fine, as if she is composed of the most minute atoms. Each atom is conscious of itself and of the surrounding emptiness. Each experiences itself as presence, and the surrounding emptiness as the absence of presence. In other words, the surrounding darkness is not only the absence of light and consciousness, but also the absence of presence and being. It is total nonexistence, absolute nonbeing. As this nonbeing comes into contact with the presence of consciousness it annihilates it, turning it into itself. The consciousness of the soul thins out much more, where the experience becomes of a few particles of conscious presence within an infinite expanse of nothingness. There is simply nothing around, not even the sensation of space. Just the distinct sense of oneself as a conscious presence, right at the precipice of annihilation. All around there is absolutely nothing, only annihilating absence. As the conscious presence apprehends this annihilating absence it comes into contact with it, and it instantly dissolves and disappears; only annihilation is left.

When the last atom annihilates there is total cessation, but in this last perception there is the clearest impression of the nature of the absolute: vastness so empty it is the absolute absence of all being, silence so still there is no manifestation. Nothing stirs and nothing reacts in this mysterious but luminous darkness. It is so empty of anything that it is absolutely transparent, a transparency that makes it the greatest clarity.

We see that the nature of the absolute is really the absence of being, the annihilation of presence. This discovery is actually not surprising, for all presence is nothing but the being of the manifest world. Presence emerges as the flow of the logos, as the outflow of being, whose field is patterned by the forms of the universe. And since being is a conscious presence that emerges from the absolute, the absolute must be prior to being and its contrasting background. Being, in other words, emerges out of nonbeing.[7] The source is a mysterious nonbeing, a nonbeing that is not simply an ordinary nothing, but a metaphysical nonbeing that holds the potential of all possibilities of existence and experience.[8] It is a breathtaking truth: the source and ultimate nature of all existence is nonexistence. Being, with all of its richness and variety, is born out of nonbeing. We begin here to understand the mysteries of Reality; we see that it does not correspond with the apparently obvious, normal perception of things. We begin to appreciate the stupendous mystery that is Reality, and the subtlety of truth, which can quicken the passionate love of the heart to inquire into the mysteries of Being.

Selflessness

In the process of dissolution of the conscious presence of the soul into the absolute, or in any experience of inquiring into the nature of the absolute, we discover that the last vestige of consciousness is a multimodal sensory one. As we see and feel the mysterious darkness of nonbeing we feel our presence as a kind of sensation. Our presence becomes simply the presence of simple sensation, sensing itself and the nonbeing of the absolute. As it apprehends the absolute it sees and senses it. The seeing becomes a seeing of darkness, which culminates in the total cessation of perception. The sensing becomes a sensing of absence of being, which culminates in the total cessation of sensation. As we learn to acclimate to the reality of the absolute, and experience it as our truth, we experience ourselves as its vast emptiness, as the infinity of the luminous night. We are then the absolute nonbeing witnessing the emergence of the forms of experience. When we look within we see nothing, just a darkness; and if the darkness dominates, there results either cessation or the extroversion of awareness to the witnessing of phenomena. Also, when we sense ourselves we find nothing, but this finding of nothing is the finding of no sensation. The absolute is so empty that it is empty of the sensation of anything, including the sensation of nothing. This is quite an unusual state, for we are accustomed to having sensations. But here we are completely ourselves, totally in touch with our depths, absolutely intimate with our subjective experience, but experience no sensation. We are aware only of the absence of sensation, which is possible only because there is some remnant of sensation in parts of the body that creates a contrast.

We learn then that the absolute is quite a mysterious presence. Presence of true nature is normally coincident with the consciousness of its texture, density, and viscosity, namely, with the touch of the presence. Presence, in other words, is mostly a sensation of being.[9] But when it comes to the absolute, it is precisely the absence of such sensation that characterizes its presence, and hence we cannot think of it as a presence similar to the presence of being. If we are going to refer to it as presence, we will have to say it is the presence of absence. But we will see as we continue in our exploration that this is not a completely accurate description. The absolute is more mysterious than even that.

In the inner journey of the soul, we learn that the presence of consciousness is the basis of all experience. It is the basis of the experience of both ego and essence. In other words, the experience of ego is not possible without the presence of sensation. Since ego development produces the ego-self, with a sense of self and identity, we realize that the sense of self depends on sensation. Without sensation there is no inner content for the soul to have a sense of self or identity. How can the soul recognize herself when she cannot sense her inside? Even the experience of true identity, the point of existence and light, is presence, and hence dependent upon sensation.

Therefore, the absolute is the absence of all the components that give us the sense of self. The silence and stillness of the absolute means that there is no inner content, no inner forms, not even sensation. There is absolutely nothing upon which to base a sense of self. There is no sense of boundary or image, no sense of center or existence, and hence nothing to give us the feeling of self. We experience ourselves as totally selfless, completely devoid of self. There is absolutely nothing, and such nothing is the source and nature of all our manifestations; it simply witnesses them. There is no sense of a self that experiences or is aware of manifestations or movements.

More precisely, to experience the absolute is to experience the absence of self, person, entity, soul, essence, substance, presence. We realize very distinctly that the sense of the entity of the self is actually a result of holding different things together with some sort of glue. The glue is the concept of entity, giving the illusion of entitihood. When this holding is relaxed, then nothing remains; there does not remain even a sense of being.[10] In other words, when we realize our deepest nature we realize it is pure and absolute selflessness. We have nothing inside, even though we are the source and ground of all existence. We are not a self, and do not have a self. We are the mystery of nonbeing, the absence of any basis for self or personality.

Because there is no inner content, not even sensation, there is nothing to reflect back on. The moment we reflect on ourselves, and look inward, there is nothing to perceive. Our awareness simply comes back to awareness of "external" phenomena. In other words, in the experience of ourselves as the absolute there is no self-reflection; in fact, the possibility of self-reflection disappears. Reality has a front and a back, phenomena are the front and the absolute is the back. However, since the absolute is actually nonbeing, Reality becomes simply the front. There is no back. There is no back to reflect on, no inside to look into. We are the freedom of the world, the liberation of all manifestation.

Alternatively, there is total absence of self-consciousness, on all levels and in all senses of the word. There is no awareness of self, and no knowing of this lack of awareness. This phenomenological absence of self-awareness becomes a psychological or emotional absence of self-consciousness. We cannot be self-conscious, because there is no self to be self-conscious and no self of which to be conscious. And without self-consciousness there are no personal issues or conflicts, no personal suffering.

The most interesting part of this lack of self-consciousness is the experience of spontaneity. Without self-consciousness there is no self-watching and no cautiousness about our expressions and actions. There is no premeditation and no rumination about what to do. Hence we are totally spontaneous, like young children. We are totally open and innocent, with no defensiveness and no strategizing. There is no holding back, no hiding, no protection, no pretension. There is complete openness, presence, and genuineness. There is no self-control whatsoever. So the spontaneity is total. The absence of control is absolute. We simply experience ourselves as freedom, lightness, delight, openness, and spontaneity. Without self-consciousness, action and expression are absolutely spontaneous, and hence totally free.[11]

Emptiness

In discovering this dimension of true nature we realize that this selflessness is the ultimate nature of everything. The absolute turns out to be the final ontological status of all things, the ultimate status of existence of all forms of manifestation. When we inquire into this final ontological nature we find nothing, no object of perception. We simply feel light and empty, free and unencumbered. And everything in manifest reality has the same quality of lightness and emptiness. All forms appear as diaphanous forms, empty of substance. It is as if all forms are holograms, forms of light, empty of any solidity or heaviness. Everything is transparent, with no opaqueness anywhere. The manifest forms—houses and furniture, mountains and rivers, trees and animals, men and women, thoughts and feelings—appear as particulars of a dynamic unfolding multidimensional field; but it is a field of total lightness, as if it is an emptiness that luminates and its lumination is the forms of appearance.

Such realization challenges our normal perception of the opaqueness and solidity of forms. When we perceive a rock we do not only see or touch a form. We see a totally opaque shape, and touch a solid and substantial object. By realizing the absolute nature of the rock—by perceiving the form of the rock while simultaneously recognizing its final ontological mode—the rock seems to lose both opaqueness and solidity. Loss of opaqueness does not mean we can see the physical objects behind it; it means we can see through its appearance to its deepest nature. We see through the color and shape, as if its appearance suddenly becomes thinner, so thin it is transparent. We can look inside, so to speak, but then we simply see nothingness, an infinity of space. This shows that the normal opaqueness is due to cognitive filters, whose absence makes all objects transparent to their inner nature, their final constituency. We do not necessarily see the atoms and the elementary particles, for these are merely the smaller constituents of physical appearance, which also become transparent to reveal ultimate nature.

The more important observation is that as the rock becomes transparent to its true nature our experience of it also changes in terms of substance. The rock not only looks transparent, it feels insubstantial. We lose our normal sense of it being a solid object, substantial and real. In other words, the sense of physical solidity, substantiality, and rock-like reality are also the result of cognitive filters. When we reify this particular form of appearance, separate it from the rest of manifestation, and think of it as an independently self-existing object, such cognitive conclusion imbues our perception of the rock with the feeling of substantial solidity. Without these cognitive positions, with total openness to the reality of the rock, our perception continues to be of the same rock, with the same shape and color, but we see it as transparent and we do not feel the customary feel or sense of solidity and substantiality. We perceive it to be of the nature of light, or of thought, light and insubstantial.

This perception does not mean that the rock is only a surface with a hollowed-out interior. We can test this conclusion easily, especially with our modern devices. Or we can break it into two parts. We then have two rocks, but then we see both parts as empty and insubstantial. Precisely put, when we perceive the insubstantiality of the rock we are seeing not through one layer of atoms to the next layer; rather, we are looking through any layer in the line of vision to its underlying ontological ground. We are looking vertically, not horizontally, so to speak. We are seeing through the ontological dimensions and not through layers of the same dimension, such as the physical one. But we are so conditioned to think of things only physically that when we see through the physical surface our mind tends to think of penetration from one physical layer to another. In other words, the rock is actually solid and substantial when we consider it physically. This is the particle view of the rock, using our metaphor of particle-wave duality. The wave view is that the rock is insubstantial, a phantasmagoric form. This view is the perception of the rock when we are able to also perceive its final ontological status, the absolute.

From the perspective of the absolute, all manifest forms possess this insubstantiality and lightness, and all in the same degree. It is not as if rocks are insubstantial but more substantial than water. When it comes to the absolute perception they are all equal in their insubstantiality; this insubstantiality is simply our perception of their ontological ground, which is the same absolute everywhere. They are all totally insubstantial, for their ultimate status is nonbeing. More accurately, all forms are a coemergence of two things: appearance and nonbeing. Their appearance is their being, but their ground is nonbeing. Their appearance-presence is always accompanied with their nonbeing. They cannot be without nonbeing, for the nonbeing of the absolute is the ground of their being. Such understanding is totally paradoxical for our thematizing ordinary mind; but it is actually how things are, and how we will perceive them when we are free from all cognitive filters.

The absolute demonstrates that there is no ultimate substance, for whatever substance we find will have to possess nonbeing as its final nature and constituency. The other concept we lose in our experience of manifest forms, besides that of substance, is that of realness. We normally have a subjective sense of reality in our perception of objects and people. We tend to believe that this feeling of reality is objective, and not simply our inner and subjective feeling. However, when we finally realize the insubstantial nature of things, we wake up to the fact that we do not possess this old feeling of realness in relation to these things. It is not that we realize these things are not real in the sense that they are not actually there or that we are mentally hallucinating them. No, it is clear to us that they actually and truly appear in perception, that they are not just the content of our personal minds. What we realize is that the customary sense of realness to which we are habituated is concomitant to the sense of substantiality and solidity we tend to perceive in these objects. When we recognize their ultimate insubstantiality they lose their sense of realness, for this sense is caused by the belief and perception of substance. Without ultimate substance they lose their sense of realness.

This realization helps us understand insubstantiality in subtler ways. We see that substantiality is actually not physical solidity, but the belief in the ultimate self-existence of the objects. In other words, we normally give substance to air, space, thoughts, images, light, and so on, objects that are not physically solid. Giving them substance means we give them a final ontological status of truly existing. This simply means that we do not apprehend that nonbeing is their final ontological mode. We do not perceive the absolute as their ultimate ground of existence. This subtle ignorance appears in our perception of physical objects as the sense of solidity, which psychologically makes us feel they are real and substantial. But the sense of realness appears in our perception of all objects, whether physical, psychological or spiritual; for we attribute to all these forms of manifestation an ultimate status of existence: that is, we do not recognize that their ultimate ontological status is nonbeing.

Normally we have a continuous subjective feeling of the realness of things, a feeling that gives our ego-self a sense of security, the sense that its supports ultimately exist. By perceiving the absolute nature of things this feelings ceases, for it turns out to be a psychological outcome of the belief in the ultimate self-existence of things. But this does not mean that objectively things are not real in the sense that they do not manifest independent of our thoughts. Things are noetic forms, even prenoetic, but they simply do not possess the kind of reality we have been accustomed to giving them. In fact, in such perception we see true Reality; we see how things actually are. We are truly in Reality, but it does not have the same psychological sense to which we are accustomed. Realness turns out to be a concept, and our perception has now gone beyond concepts, to the core of things. We experience freedom and liberation, and are finally released from the need to support our ego-self with the sense of solidity, substance, and reality. We do not need any supports, for reality has no supports; it is all a magical display of colors and shapes, of presence that is simultaneously insubstantial and rich. We are beyond the conceptual mind, and the dichotomy of being and nonbeing.

The traditional term for the ultimate absence of substance, solidity, realness, and existence is emptiness.[12] To be empty, a form is void of ontological substance, solidity, realness, and ultimate existence. Emptiness is a name for the absolute, which points to one way of experiencing it, or to its most significant truth.

To recognize the absolute as the ultimate ground of all objects and phenomena is to perceive their transparency, insubstantiality, and lack of ultimate being. Instead of opaqueness we experience a transparent expanse, spacious and open. Instead of substantiality we experience a lightness, a freedom, a total absence of heaviness. Joy is released, and contentment fills the heart.

Crystalline Absence

We call this dimension of true nature the absolute for very specific reasons. First, it has the sense and feel of absoluteness. When we are fully abiding in it we feel a certainty that this is the ultimate truth of everything, transcending all other certainties. We feel absolutely certain of this truth and that there can be nothing beyond it or transcendent to it. But it is also easy to see why it is the absolute dimension of true nature. If there were any other dimension it would have to arise in awareness; otherwise there would be no way of knowing of it. However, for a dimension or truth to arise in awareness puts it in the realm of the manifest, and the absolute transcends all the manifest.

Some teachings insist that the ultimate is a personal god that possesses a form.[13] It is, however, impossible to conceive of a form that transcends the absolute. Any form is bound to be within the logos, for the logos is an infinite field of oneness. To perceive or conceive of a form we have to see that it is an inseparable part of the oneness, for no form can be outside the oneness of being. To conceive a form outside of the oneness of being would mean that we conceive a boundary and end for this oneness, which contradicts the knowing of true oneness. In other words, any form must be an inseparable part of the oneness of being, and hence part of the unfolding pattern of the logos. It is bound to be arising within the absolute, with the absolute as its transcendent source.

Other teachings conceptualize the absolute not as the nonbeing underlying all being, but as the coemergence of being and nonbeing. In other words, such teachings use the term *absolute* to refer to the coemergence and inseparability of all dimensions of true nature, as a truth that is both presence and absence. However, such teachings always refer to the dimension of nonbeing as the essence of such truth, as the most fundamental and inner dimension of it. In fact, some of these traditions see nonbeing as the only permanent dimension of true nature, and all others as transitory.[14] We conceptualize true nature differently, as consisting of five dimensions, with the nonbeing dimension as the absolute. The fact that it is the unmanifest means that it is truly the only unchanging truth, for everything else is a manifestation out of it. We will also see that in some very deep sense there is only the absolute. The absolute is not only the ultimate nature of everything, but is itself everything. This is a very subtle insight, part of the understanding of the journey of descent. What is significant here is not what name we give to this mystery, but the fact that it is the most fundamental dimension of true nature we experience.

Nevertheless, we need to remember that all dimensions of true nature are ultimately inseparable. They are all coemergent even though they can emerge separately.

We have seen this in our discussion of emptiness, seeing that emptiness or nonbeing cannot exist on its own; it is always accompanying and characterizing manifest being. Yet, there is a deeper subtlety and mystery to the absolute, besides its ultimate coemergence with the other boundless dimensions. To explore this we need first to remember that in our discussion of pure awareness, in chapter 19, we saw it as nonconceptual presence that transcends the dichotomy of being and nonbeing. Does this mean it is deeper than the dimension of the absolute, and more fundamental than it? For we have been discussing the absolute as nonbeing. In actuality, the absolute is also nonconceptual, and beyond all conceptual dichotomies, including that of being and nonbeing. Does this mean we have two nonconceptual dimensions, and if so, what does that mean and how are they different?

This is part of the mystery of true nature, which appears as the ultimate mystery of the absolute. Experientially we recognize both pure awareness and the absolute as nonconceptual. Yet they are phenomenologically different. They differ as day differs from night. Pure nonconceptual awareness is clear, colorless, transparent light that feels like the coemergence of presence and absence. We see a vast expansive space, clear and colorless, bright and limpid. It is a space full of light, just like space in daylight. Yet, it is also a presence with the sense of solidity and fullness.

In experiencing the absolute, we perceive a transparent and clear space, but dark, so dark it is absolutely black. The blackness is not a color, but the absence of light. In other words, nonconceptual awareness possesses light while the absolute is ontologically prior to light. They are both transcendent to being and nonbeing, but they differ in their relation to light. We can say that the absolute is the mystery prior to light, but at the same time the source of light.[15] The first light that manifests in it is the nonconceptual light, pure awareness. In other words, both are empty of ultimate existence, but the absolute is much more empty. It is even empty of light, awareness, and hence can be experienced as cessation. Looking into pure awareness we see transparent and light-filled space, pervading all manifest forms, and constituting them. Looking into the absolute we first see darkness, but if we focus on it completely, our awareness spontaneously turns around and we find ourselves witnessing manifestation. We see the manifestation as possessing a ground of pure nonconceptual awareness, but this ground now appears as a manifestation within the absolute.

Another difference is that the nonconceptual presence of pure awareness retains the experience of inner sensation, while the absolute is precisely the absence of all sensation. We can say that nonbeing dominates in the absolute more completely than it does in pure nonconceptual awareness, to the extent of annihilating all sensation. Because of this characteristic the understanding of emptiness and insubstantiality is much clearer and more precise in this dimension. That is why it becomes the dimension of emptiness, while in fact it is nonconceptual and beyond being and nonbeing.

Because the absolute is not simply nonbeing, we experience it as a field, an expanse, and not simply nonbeing. To understand this we need to make a particular differentiation explicit. We have been using two terms interchangeably, namely absolute and absolute dimension. Strictly speaking, the absolute is the ultimate nature of Reality, and it is beyond dimensions; for dimensions are the experience of manifestation. Yet, we do experience the absolute as a dimension, boundless and infinite, an infinity that contains and holds all manifestation including the other boundless dimensions. We can say that the absolute is the unmanifest, the ultimate truth and mystery of Being, beyond all dimensions and qualities. But when it begins to manifest appearance, this manifestation appears as if in an expanse, an infinite and boundless expanse, that looks like black space. Manifestation appears always in the context of time and space. It always possesses an expanse in time and space. Therefore, when we witness appearance from the stance of the absolute we see an expanse appearing in a more vast, dark expanse, the absolute. We have the sense of the absolute as an expanse, as a vast infinite black space. The absolute appears in this perception as a boundless dimension that underlies all other dimensions. But in reality the absolute is beyond space and time, for it is beyond manifestation.

Strictly speaking, since all perception is in relation to manifestation, either within it or outside it but witnessing it, we experience the absolute as a boundless dimension. We discussed this mystery in chapter 16, when we used the metaphor of dreaming to illustrate how the truth beyond space and time manifests as and within space and time. From this we see that the absolute in its absoluteness, the unmanifest understood irrespective of manifestation, is beyond dimensions; yet it appears as a boundless dimension that constitutes the final ground and ontological nature of all manifestation and dimensions. In other words, the absolute dimension is constituted by the absolute, or its nature is the absolute.[16] This is similar to saying that the dimension of pure awareness is constituted by nonconceptual presence.

So the absolute dimension is the boundless, infinite expanse whose nature is the black mystery of the absolute. When we experience it we experience the absolute, because it is the absolute that is appearing as a dimension; whereas the absolute is not a dimension, but rather the ultimate mystery and source of all dimensions, the unmanifest true nature. Because of this differentiation it becomes ambiguous sometimes to say that the absolute is the unmanifest when we are experiencing the absolute dimension, because a boundless and infinite dimension is necessarily a manifestation.

What is the absolute nature, then, whether we are referring to the unmanifest absolute or the absolute dimension? We have discussed its qualities of stillness, silence, peace, nonbeing, and emptiness. But we can also experience it as an immensity, a solidity and presence. One way of understanding this is to use the notion of the three major centers of subtle physiology, the belly center or *hara*, the heart center, and the head center. When we experience the absolute through the belly center, we experience it as a solid and immense presence, more substantial than any physical substance.[17] We feel we are more fundamental, more basic, than anything else; all manifestation, including the physical world, appears as ephemeral and wispy. Yet, when we sense inside that we cannot find anything, there is no sensation of any quality. We are completely empty inside, so empty that our inside is total absence. The full impression is that we are so light and free because we are total absence; yet at the same time we are immense and solid for we are the most fundamental truth. We are both absence and presence, the emptiness of nonbeing and the fullness and solidity of being. Yet the fullness and solidity of being is not another quality added to the emptiness of nonbeing. The solidity feels more like full emptiness, solid absence. We are this solid nothingness, immense and immeasurable, and the universe is simply the glow of its intensity.

When we are precise and exact in our understanding of the absolute nature, the solidity can attain a faceted and crystalline quality. We experience ourselves then as a crystalline absence, a clear and absolutely transparent immensity. This experience is completely paradoxical. We feel totally solid and full, with crystalline sharpness and clarity, yet simultaneously we feel so light, so empty, so not there, that we are the absolute absence of anything. We are both simultaneously, a quality of experience completely incomprehensible to the conceptual mind. Yet it is the most beautiful, the most aesthetically satisfying, and the most dazzling of perceptions. We feel fully present, but our presence is so smooth and crystalline because it is solid absence, with no coarseness and no opaqueness.

When we experience the absolute through the heart modality, the absolute attains a sense of gentleness and simplicity. We feel the same fullness and emptiness, but now with a softness, a gentleness, and an amazing contentment. We feel light and simple, easy and at ease. The most characteristic element of the heart experience is an amazing sense of intimacy. Since the absolute is the being of nonbeing it is totally transparent and absolutely free of obscurations. The sense of absence means the absence of all qualities; hence it has nothing to hinder perception and contact. This means there is nothing, no intermediary, between our awareness and whatever we are experiencing. We are experiencing the absolute inside of everything. Such nearness to the secret chamber of any and all manifestation appears as the most total and the most exquisite intimacy. We are not intimate with anything in particular. We are simply experiencing the intimacy of nearness to the absolute nature of everything. We are near everything, because we are the absolute, the inner heart of everything. Our presence becomes the exquisite gentleness and intimacy of no barriers, no intermediaries, not even qualities to be in the way of the heart.

When we experience the absolute through the mind modality, it attains the greatest subtlety. It is total absence, with the slightest hint of presence. The presence is like a subtle glimmer to the absence, giving it a slight sense of presence that easily melts into nonbeing. The lightness is greatest here, so much freedom, so much space, so much openness. We are so free we are almost not here; it is like we have overcome gravity and feel no more heaviness of any kind. Even the slight, almost absent, sense of presence can attain a crystalline quality that gives it precision and brilliance. We feel so free and so awake, so clear and so bright; yet there is nothing there: total selflessness.[18]

Nondimensional Truth

When we precisely understand the nature of the absolute, the paradoxical coemergence of emptiness and presence, we understand how emptiness appears in manifestation. Emptiness is simply the insubstantiality, the nonbeing, of manifest forms. This nonbeing is what makes the absolute so light, so empty, so spacious and open. We begin to see that this absence appears at more superficial ontological dimensions as the experience of inner space, with its various degrees of subtlety. Since it is nothing at all, it appears as the total openness for anything to arise and as the allowing necessary for anything to be. Such openness and allowingness are the properties of empty space, which we experience inwardly as inner spaciousness and openness, and outwardly as the space where all manifestation occurs. In other words, space is the reflection of nonbeing in manifestation. Because we do not understand the paradoxical nature of true nature, as a coemergence of being and nonbeing, we conceptualize nonbeing as space and being as manifesting forms. Just as our ignorance of the timeless flow and unfoldment of the logos leads to our conceptualizing time to account for the changes brought about by this unfoldment, our ignorance of the spaceless nonbeingness of true nature leads to our conceptualizing space to account for the accommodating openness made possible by the emptiness of the absolute.

The absolute in its absoluteness, meaning the absolute understood independently from the constraints of manifestation, is beyond time and space. We experience its emptiness as space, but the absolute is not spatial. Space is characterized by dimensionality, which is basically extension. In other words, space creates the concept of distance, or in fact it is the concept of distance. In inner experience space appears as spaciousness, as infinite extension, as unlimited expanse. This sense of expanse provides for shape and size, which gives us the impression that true nature is an infinite expanse, a space that extends endlessly. In the experience of contact and communication we feel closer and more intimate with others, especially when there is psychological openness. But why does psychological openness mean more closeness and contact, more possibility of intimacy and coming together? We usually believe this happens because openness means there are no barriers. Yet why cannot we experience distance when there are no barriers, why does it automatically mean greater closeness and intimacy?

When we understand the nondimensionality of the absolute, we understand that the more open we are the more we are in touch with the nonbeingness of our true nature. The openness is the external manifestation of this nonbeingness. But nonbeingness is not an expanse; it is nothing at all, so how can it possess extension? It has no extension at all, it completely transcends the concept of distance. We experience this directly when we are more familiar with the emptiness and nonbeingness of the absolute. At the beginning it may feel like an openness, a spaciousness, or an expansive nothingness. When we know it more intimately we begin to see that it does not have the sense of extension, that it does not actually feel like space. The mind simply cannot comprehend this at the beginning, for it is nothing like anything it knows. We simply feel a simplicity and intimacy, a state that possesses no shape, no size, no extension. This is the essence of space, which is also the essence of the absolute. Therefore, when we feel more open with another we are more in touch with this extensionless condition of nonbeing. As a result, we experience less phenomenological distance from the other, which we feel psychologically as closeness and intimacy. And when we are fully in touch with the extensionless nonbeingness of the absolute, we experience no distance at all from the other. Because there is no extension, we experience no distance. The amazing result is the sense that we are totally one. We perceptually see the other at a distance, but feel no sense of distance; in fact the concept of distance is transcended. It is like our individual souls are spokes of the same wheel, but are aware of themselves only at the rim. At the rim it appears as if there are many souls, with distance between them. But when they become aware of their depth, at the center of the wheel, they feel no distance between them, for they are identically one.[19]

We experience ourselves as the other, totally. More precisely, we experience our inside as the inside of the other, the center of our heart as the center of the other's heart. We are the same identity, the same essence, which is the absolute. But this essence, because its nature is nonbeing, has no extension. In other words, we experience our true self the same as the true self of the other, and it feels more like an extensionless point.

Imagine the kind and intensity of love possible here. Love is the appreciative attraction between two forms of manifestation because of the pull of their true nature, which is one nature. The fact that it is one nature makes us feel this appreciative gravitational pull toward others. The pull is simply the indirect experience of the underlying unity, felt through the veil of varied manifestations. Now, since this nature has no extension, and no distance, imagine the amazing gravitational pull it exerts on two beings who are in touch with this nondimensional truth. They perceive spatial distance between them, but feel no distance at all. It is the most pure, the most intense, the most ecstatic, and the deepest possible love. It is the gravitational pull to be one point, a point of nonbeing. It is the appreciative and ecstatically transporting attraction that wants to dissolve all barriers to such singular unity. It is the attraction-desire to completely melt into each other, to melt together into complete nonbeing.

The Mystery

From our discussion of the nature of the absolute so far, the difficulty of determining what it is should be apparent. We can experience it as absolute nonbeing, the fact of lack of the permanent existence of manifestation; yet the next moment we experience it as fullness and solidity, as the most fundamental truth in Reality. We can say it is both being and nonbeing prior to their differentiation, but this is a conceptual elaboration on a truth that is beyond all concepts. We can say it is neither being nor nonbeing, but this is not experientially true, for we can experience it as one or the other, even as both. We cannot even call it truth, for truth is only a concept that refers to it without describing it. We experience it as total stillness and silence, but when we recognize that the logos is its manifestation, a manifestation that never becomes something other than the absolute, we begin to see how it is dynamic and alive. Yet it is alive while totally silent, dynamic while absolutely still. We can say it is unmanifest, but we cannot actually separate it from manifestation, for manifestation is nothing but the manifestation of its richness. We can say it is unknowable, but the fact is that we can experience it fully, and know it more than anything else in experience, but in a manner that we do not normally call knowing. This is because it is our most intimate nature and we know it as such when we discover it. We can say it is knowable; but every time we know something about it we discover something exactly the opposite about it. It does not stop bedazzling the soul and confounding her attempts at determining what exactly it is. Her mind is naturally interested in making such determination while the truth is simply beyond it.

After some time of attempting to understand it and to penetrate its secret we cannot help but be bewildered and bedazzled, and throw up our hands at the futility of our endeavor. We are awed and humbled, but this awe and humility turns out to be the true understanding of its nature. We may arrive at the realization that to truly understand its nature is to recognize it is indeterminate; we can even say it is actually the principle of indeterminacy.[20] In other words, the absolute is the indeterminate truth that underlies all determination; it is the source and potential of all determinations. All manifestation is simply determination, for each form is a determinate one, as is each quality and dimension.

It is interesting that the more we recognize the indeterminacy of the absolute, the deeper is its darkness, and the more luminous. We go further into its unfathomable depths as we accept its mysteriousness. Such darkness is pure bliss and realization, for even though it is the absence of all being and knowing, it is enlightenment. Its darkness is luminous and brilliant; it is the spiritual midnight sun. This darkness bathes us, caresses us, melts us, dissolves us, annihilates us, until we are all gone; there remains only the majesty of the luminous crystal night. We realize then that this darkness of being and knowledge is God's knowledge of Himself.[21] It is not normal knowledge, it is pure basic knowledge before any discrimination, before any conceptualization. It is nonconceptual knowledge, which is not what we ordinarily call knowledge.

Thus the indeterminacy of the absolute is the same as the divine darkness, the inscrutable nature of the divine, the ultimate essence of Being. It is not an ordinary darkness and lack of knowing and being; it is the majestic and luminous blackness of the divine essence, the absolute essence of Being, the most intimate truth of true nature.[22] It is the core of all existence, the depth of Being, the inner of all. Whenever we find an inner quality and dimension, the luminous night will be its innerness; whenever we find a deep truth the luminous night will be its ultimate depth. It is the inner of all, the essence of everything, the back of all fronts, and the ultimate ground and facticity of all manifest forms. It is indeterminacy, but it is also the ground of all determinations; it is nonbeing but it is also the ground of all being; it is darkness but it is also the ground of all light; it is unknowing but it is also the ground for all knowing. It is the primal darkness before there was light, and the eternal night that highlights the appearance of the day.

We can know it, but to know it is to know it as mystery, the ultimate mystery from which all being and knowledge arise. To feel the exquisite intimacy of its nonbeingness and to see the absolute blackness of its emptiness is to behold a majestic mystery, luminous and deep, awesome and enveloping, yet inviting in its annihilating touch and caressing in its melting embrace. We behold a mystery that we passionately wish to know, and we know that to know it is to cease being, yet we long to be embraced by its annihilation and love, to be taken in by its cessation. To know it is to cease, and to cease is to know it. To know it is to not know it, but to not know is to know it. To know it is to know it as mystery. It is the mystery that must remain a mystery, which cannot but be a mystery. Its being a mystery saves us from the obsessions of our mind, and from the false securities that our false self thrives on. We behold it as mystery, a mystery that by remaining a mystery liberates us from the traps of the manifest world. We learn to live in mystery, to be supported by ultimate insecurity, and to love the flavor of nonbeing.

The absolute is a luminous mystery, yet also the source of all knowledge and being. Everything we know is a knowledge of it; for whatever we know is a manifestation that expresses something about it. Even when we approach it as unmanifest and absolute mystery, nondetermination and nondelimitation, we gain tremendous luminous insights about it. When we see that it is nonbeing and being implicit and undifferentiated, it is an earthshaking insight; when we realize it is stillness and silence it is a balm for the heart; when we know it is nondimensional it uplifts the most ecstatic lovers; when we recognize it is mystery it dazzles our minds and hearts with joy and bliss. Although all these are correct in that they tell us something about the absolute, and lead us deeper into it, they are not completely correct, because the absolute is ultimately indeterminable. They are approximations on the right track, for they lead us deeper into its mystery. We learn a great lesson through this process, which is that the knowledge about what we have thought of as determinate and discriminated objects of knowledge is always approximate, and never absolute. We learn that no knowledge is absolutely exact and correct, for it is never the whole truth, and that there is no such thing as the whole truth. It is always relative, always approximate, yet it can be correct enough to keep us on the right track, and to take us further into the mysteries of truth. In other words, exact, precise, and objective knowledge about something is always relative to a task, an endeavor, a worldview, a perspective, a dimension. It can be useful and enhancing for our life and understanding, but its greatest function is to take us closer to the mystery. Everything reveals something about the mystery, but nothing reveals everything. By revealing something it takes us closer to it, and by its limitations it invites us to greater knowledge and understanding. We keep learning and moving deeper; the more we know the more we see that we do not know. For to move nearer to the mystery is to know it further; but to know it further is not to know it, but to see its mystery.

We learn that the whole universe, with all its manifest forms and dimensions, partakes of its mystery, for the universe is its appearance, its apparel, its offspring. Indeterminacy is the nature of existence because this existence reflects its source, the principle of indeterminacy. And when we know completely, when our knowledge is totally objective, we fully know it. Yet this knowing is the knowing of absolute mystery, and is our fulfillment and liberation.[23]

The absolute is knowable in the sense that anything else is knowable. We can experience it and know many things about it. We can have many insights and illuminations about its nature. Yet these insights and illuminations never fully capture it, never totally describe it, never truly delineate it. We can know much about it, but the more we know the more we realize how much we do not know, and how mysterious it is. In other words, our knowledge of it, regardless how deep and exhaustive, never exhausts its truth, never encapsulates it. It is knowable, for if it is unknowable then this is its determination, but it cannot be fully knowable, otherwise it will be determinable. It is the inexhaustible mystery. (See *Diamond Heart Book 5*, for more discussion of many of these points.)

Home

When we learn to accept the mystery that lies all around us, and to recognize that what we know, regardless how immense, is nothing but a blip in an ocean of darkness, we give up the search for security, we relax and let go. We learn to live in mystery, and recognize that the world we live in is full of mystery. We learn to love to know, for it is the knowing of this mystery; but at the same time we learn to love the mystery, for it is the rest of our hearts and the home of our souls. To know is to move nearer to our home, and to behold the mystery is to be at home.

Being at home is one of the most characteristic feelings the soul receives when beholding the luminous darkness of the mystery. The soul frequently has this feeling the instant she feels herself abiding in its luminous darkness. It is not a conclusion, not a reasoned understanding, not the result of understanding or consciously knowing something about the absolute. It is a spontaneous recognition that happens to most people when they find themselves in the absolute. We have the instant and joyous recognition that this is our true home. We finally feel completely at home; we understand why we love to feel at home, and why it is so difficult to feel at home. The soul realizes that she has been estranged from her source, exiled from her home. She realizes that she has been roaming the universe looking for her home, feeling uncomfortable and unsettled, lost and bereaved. She has been looking mostly in the wrong places, in manifest objects and places, when her home is within, totally within, within but beyond all of manifestation.

When we know only the manifest world we are estranged from our true home, living in exile, and always waiting, whether consciously or unconsciously, to return home at last, to finally rest and forget all of our woes and worries. Now the time comes, in the lap of the luminous darkness, in the depths of total mystery. We recognize this without anyone telling us, for in our hearts we have always known. Our minds have told us various stories about where home is, where rest is, where contentment is, but now we know with certainty that we are home at last, and wonder how we came to be lost. We feel like celebrating, full of joy and dancing with delight.

The Beloved

We find that home is the inner of the inner, in the most secret chamber of our heart. When we discover the absolute in our heart, which is a particular realization of the absolute, we find out that it is what our heart has always been looking for. (See *The Point of Existence*, chapter 41, for a discussion of the process of finding the absolute in the heart.) We learn that we have been erecting idols in our heart, when our heart is in reality the Kaaba, the throne of the divine essence, the absolute. We have been loving so many people, so many things, and filling our heart with them and then wondering how come we are not completely happy and totally fulfilled. But now we realize that we have needed to keep our heart vacant, emptying it from all other loves except the love of the truth. We did not recognize what should truly fill our heart, who our real beloved is, until now. When we see the luminous crystalline mystery in the depths of our heart our love runneth over; we are beyond ourselves with deep joy and passionate love. We finally recognize our true and one beloved, the one we have been looking and waiting for, and understand the reason for our previous lack of total contentment and complete fulfillment. All these loves were simply expressions of the true beloved, reminding us of Him, and because of that we loved them.

We see that all that we have loved, we loved because it revealed something about our true beloved to us. It was a reflection of the true beloved, a message from him, a beckoning toward him. But we did not see that at the time, instead filling our heart with these partial expressions. Now our true love has revealed Himself to us, and the heart instantly recognizes and rejoices. We realize we have always been in love, sometimes sweetly and tenderly and other times passionately and deeply. We have always been forlorn and sad, dejected and depressed. When we were in the company of an earthly love we could not feel the total intimacy that we knew our heart wanted. Our love has always been unrequited, because all the loves were substitute loves, at best partial manifestations of our true love. Now that we are united with our true beloved, our earthly love is balanced and seen in perspective. It deepens and expands, for we see how much beauty and majesty our earthly love reminds us of, and expresses to us. In other words, we realize that we love others and objects because we see something in them that expresses our true beloved. We have earthly love because all manifestation is the appearance and body of our true beloved.

Now our love affair is consummated and fulfilled. Our ecstatic and passionate love of the mystery draws us powerfully to its depths, and its annihilating love for us draws us deeper into its nonbeingness. We meet in the heart, the soul consumed with passion, and lovingly annihilated in the beloved's embrace. We become one, a crystalline luminous beauty, sable black and charming beyond description. Musk fills the air, and the scent of roses announces the total marriage.

Depth

We realize that our beloved is in the most absolute depth of our soul. We discover that our beloved is not only in the depth, but is the depth of our soul. We learn that the absolute is pure depth, depth with no end. The darker it gets the deeper we feel, and the more profound is the truth. The deeper and darker it becomes the more empty, the more free, and the more intimate. The absolute turns out to be the principle of depth, and all manifestation is surface.

We tend to think of depth in terms of feeling, thought, and knowledge. In the inner journey home we find out that these are actually part of the surface, for they are an expression of the horizontal world of everyday life. We discover that, in fact, true nature in all of its qualities and dimensions stands for depth in our experience and life.[24] We experience the unfoldment of our soul as taking our experience deeper because we are following the dimension of depth. When we arrive at the realization of the absolute we understand depth most clearly and distinctly, for it is the dimension where we know depth most specifically. The absolute, we can say, is pure depth. It is absolute depth because it is the source of all.

So our home turns out to be our depth, and our depth turns out to be our beloved. And it is absolute depth because it is nothing at all, complete absence, total nonbeing, which is the ground of all being. We discover that to be at home is to be home. To be in the depth is to be depth. To unite with our beloved is to be the beloved. To be at home as an autonomous self is a contradiction; for by becoming an autonomous self we got lost, and became estranged. To be at home is for the soul to recognize that the absolute, her home, her beloved, which is her depth, is also her nature and identity.

Ipseity

The absolute is such a mystery that even though it is total selflessness it is also the ultimate self.[25] What can that mean? We have seen that the absolute is the divine essence, the inner essence of Being. It is the final nature of everything, including ego and essence. It is the absolute nature of the soul, her deepest ground. To realize it is to recognize in direct experience that there is nothing that is not constituted by it. We feel we are constituted by it, that it forms our very substance and identity. We are it, and it is us. We feel and see it as a luminous crystal presence of black clarity. But at the same time we feel it is I, nothing but me, for there is nothing else that can be me. It is not like there is a cognitive sense or feeling of I, identity, or self. There is no conceptual quality of the beingness of the mystery. But there is a perception or apperception that it is none other than I. It is a perception of the luminous night being the beingness of me, without the feeling of me. The I is not the familiar I, whether ego or essence. It is like I know it is I because I am it. There is nothing else that is I. It is the sense of complete subjectivity. It is like recognizing the subject that is I, which turns out to be the absolute.

In other words, the absolute is both my nature and my identity. It is the nature of the soul and her very identity. It constitutes her manifestations but it is also her depth and deepest essence. Alternatively, we can say the absolute is our true self, our objectively actual self. But it is also the nature of the soul. That is why we like to refer to the absolute as ipseity, for the word *ipseity* means both nature and self. To recognize the absolute as ipseity is a profound experience, for it is the self-realization of this dimension of true nature. (See *The Point of Existence*, chapter 41, for a discussion of the process of this self-realization.)

The experience is of I as the ipseity, an infinite luminous night. And I, the mystery of ipseity, see the world of appearance as a luminous and smooth oneness. The oneness is of the logos, which looks smooth, luminous, and transparent. I am the ipseity, and the harmony of oneness is my robe. Joy and happiness fill the field of experience, joy at seeing the emergence and dominance of the ipseity, and happiness to know myself as the ipseity, the self that is the source and nature of everything.

This experience is the end of a very deep differentiation between the concepts of self and nature. True nature tends to be seen as the nature of the self and everything else, which means there is something that is not true nature, and this something has a true nature. Usually, this differentiation is completely gone only in the state of the absolute ipseity, where self and nature are the same, self-nature. We find our true self when we are completely selfless, and we discover our true identity when our normal identity ceases.

End of the Search

When the soul arrives at her absolute home, recognizes her true beloved, and realizes it as her ipseity, many insights, realizations, and feelings spontaneously arise. One's life begins to show its overall pattern, seen from the perspective of the inner journey home. This culminates in the personalization of the absolute ipseity, where we learn to be a human being, a person, and to still abide in the absolute. This is an unusual and rarely known realization, where the vastness of the mystery, without ceasing to be the mystery, finds itself walking with two legs, touching with human hands, speaking with a mouth, and so on. (For the details of this process of personalization, see *The Pearl Beyond Price*, chapter 38.)

At this point the soul is surprised by new feelings and realizations that occur spontaneously, as if brought home by the power of the self-realization. What spontaneously arises, without self-reflection or reasoning, is the feeling that the soul is at the end of a certain phase of life and work. She feels she has accomplished the task she had set for herself, or is in the last stages of finishing it. She recognizes her worldly accomplishments and her realization of her true nature. But the feeling is more general than the specific accomplishments. It is a sense of finishing something. There is a feeling of space or room left, open for new possibilities.

She begins to feel completely relaxed and settled. Upon inquiry she feels she has reached her destination, even though she did not know it was the absolute that she was looking for. There results a sense of having lots of time, energy, and space to spare. She may feel willing and happy to give her time and energy to others. She feels at home now; her search is ended. It is as if she has been on a journey, searching for her beloved and her true home, but she did not know it consciously, at least she did not think of it in these terms. She does not have to decide to stop the search; the seeking ceases on its own, for the drive for seeking is spent. She sees that she has been consciously or unconsciously seeking, regardless what she was doing or involved in, because she was actually away from home, estranged in the profoundest way. Now she is home, and the reason for her search is gone. It is truly gone, not because she understands there is no need to seek, but because she does not feel the seeking energy anymore. The seeking energy is simply the tension of separation and the love for the union.

Fulfillment saturates her experience, and she begins to experience a new order of contentment. Her contentment and happiness cease to be primarily caused by life happenings, for it is now the natural condition of the heart that has found its beloved. She feels mature, ripened, and free; she feels herself as the ipseity, with its immeasurable depth, luminous vastness, and blissful intimacy. (See *Luminous Night's Journey*, chapter 10, for more discussion of this process of ripening.)

Even this sense gradually and subtly passes away as the soul abides in the mystery of the absolute. As we become accustomed to this condition it becomes more ordinary and simple. The soul feels she is a complete but ordinary human being. She is aware of her nature as that of the inscrutable absolute, but feels completely ordinary and normal. There is no sense of the extraordinary, while in fact the self-realization of the absolute ipseity is quite an unusual realization. The sense of the big deal is due to the excitement of the discovery. After that, with the ripening, one feels simple and ordinary, and recognizes that the absolute is simplicity itself. It is so simple that it is absolutely nothing. It is so simple that it is impossible to know. The mind needs some complexity, some discrimination, to discern and know. When the experience is of absolute simplicity, there is nothing for the soul to know. This simplicity appears as simplicity of behavior, attitude, and speech. One is ordinary and appreciates the ordinary, for the most ordinary is the simplicity of the absolute. The simplicity may develop to the station of the invisible sage, the highest station, the sage who appears as a normal simple human being, but whose innerness is the luminous mystery of the absolute.[26]

PART SIX

Actualization of Reality

22   The Journey of Descent

THE SELF-REALIZATION OF THE ABSOLUTE is the end of the search, the satisfaction of the soul's longing. But it is not the completion of the inner journey. As the process continues, we continue to realize the absolute as our ipseity and the true nature of all manifestation. The soul becomes established in the absolute mystery, where its crystalline emptiness becomes the unchanging field of all her experience. For some, this station lasts for many years, and for others only a few days.[1] At some point, the soul realizes that she cannot simply remain at the transcendent summit of Reality; her unfoldment naturally takes her on another journey, the journey of descent.

Here the soul begins to have confusing experiences; she has known herself as the absolute ipseity, but begins to experience herself in more limited ways. Issues and limitations arise that do not make sense for her station of absolute realization, yet at the same time she recognizes that some profound learning is occurring. She has been content to remain at home in her nature, feeling the restfulness of no searching and the peace of no ambition. She is now finally melted in the arms of her Beloved, totally annihilated into its velvety emptiness. She has gone through the whole cycle of discovery and development, and now she is back at the origin of all manifestation, as the mysterious and luminous mystery at the root of all. She desires nothing, not even the exploration of the mysteries of Being. She is happy and satisfied with the spontaneous life of freedom, with no care and no burden.

Ascent and Descent

The soul feels any sense of movement away from total intimacy with the absolute mystery to be an intolerable loss. However, regardless of her resistance and protest, it finally dawns on her that she cannot stay where she is, and that it is not up to her personal choice. At some point she recognizes that her unfoldment is taking her to a place different than the transcendent absolute ipseity. She might feel the arising of a great sadness, tremendous grief. It may take her a long time before she realizes that there is no loss of the total intimacy with the absolute, that she does not have to actually leave her home to go on to these further stations. As she surrenders to the dynamism of Being, and ceases to hold on to her realization of the absolute ipseity, she recognizes and surrenders her attachment to the absolute realization. In this process she discovers that while it is true that she is on a journey of descent from the heights of transcendence, this journey is not a separation from the absolute. The descent is a descent into limitation, but it is the descent not of her individual sense of herself, but the descent of the ipseity itself. In other words, she descends into the limitations of the world not as a soul entity, but as the absolute mystery itself.[2]

Nevertheless, this process feels like separation and loss; it is more than the soul has wanted, and a journeying further when she wants to journey no more. However, she recognizes these manifestations of a sense of loss, separation, resistance, and grief, which became familiar phenomena in her journey of ascent to the absolute. Whenever the dynamism of Being unfolds her experience to another dimension of Being, the soul always feels that she is going to lose whatever she has realized. Every time her unfoldment takes her to a further dimension, she cannot but feel it as a separation from, a leaving of, and a loss of, the station at which she has stabilized. As the soul begins the journey of descent, the station she feels she has to leave is that of union with her ultimate Beloved and home, which she clearly knows as the deepest of all truths. She finally learns to surrender to the flow, mostly out of love for the absolute ipseity, for she recognizes that it is the source of all unfoldment.[3]

She recognizes that her inner journey to the absolute has been a journey of ascent, of moving from the lowest and grossest dimensions of experience to the summit of subtlety and truth. In this journey of ascent, the process has been primarily that of discrimination, separation, purification, and resolution. Her nature reveals itself as simpler, more subtle, and increasingly devoid of forms, qualities, determinations, and concepts. The journey moves toward absolute simplicity, through a process of continual shedding. All forms and dimensions are shed, to reveal the perfect simplicity and emptiness of the absolute. Absolute simplicity turns out to be absolute transcendence, the transcendence of all forms and dimensions of manifestation. Her journey has taken her deeper and deeper, steadily leaving behind more superficial dimensions, until she has arrived at the absolute depth of all experience, as the dimension of depth itself, which is simultaneously the transcendent summit of all dimensions and manifest forms.

The journey of descent moves back through the same dimensions of manifestation, from the vantage point of the absolute. In the process of descent, she learns that there is no leaving the absolute, but that the descent is simply the integration into the absolute of all dimensions of manifestation. The garments that the absolute has shed to reveal its absolute simplicity return now, but distinctly as garments, garments that do not hide or obscure the truth of the absolute. The descent is a conscious descent of the absolute into the various dimensions that it has manifested. It is a movement of recognizing the absolute as immanent in all forms and phenomena of reality. The absolute moves from being absolute transcendence, beyond and above all dimensions and forms, to being the inner nature and ground of all. Yet, the absolute does not leave its condition of transcendence; its transcendent mystery simply appears as inseparable and nondual with all forms and dimensions.

In the journey of ascent, the individual soul penetrates the various dimensions of creation and manifestation, which are the garments in which the absolute was hidden. The journey of descent, however, is the conscious donning of these garments by the absolute. The ascent is like a movement inward, while the descent is a movement outward; in the first the absolute regains its conscious awareness, and in the second it retains this awareness within manifestation. Hence, the descent is into manifestation, but not into exile and alienation. Therefore, just as the journey of ascent is that of shedding and separation leading to the simplicity of singlehood, the journey of descent is that of integration and union leading to the richness of wholeness.

The journey of descent is actually a further understanding and realization of the absolute. It is a matter of understanding the absolute as not only the transcendent truth but also as the immanent ground and essence of all Reality. This includes the view and understanding of all of the dimensions and forms of Reality from the vantage point of the absolute. Hence, this and the next chapter can be viewed as a continuation of the previous chapter's discussion of the absolute.

Just as the journey of ascent possesses two complementary facets, those of self-realization and individuation, the journey of descent has two facets as well: on the one hand, new dimensions arise, with their associated relative and essential forms, and the self-realization of these dimensions; on the other hand, the soul achieves the personalization of these dimensions and the maturation into greater individuation that integrates these new dimensions and their wisdom.

The dimensions that arise in the journey of descent are not exactly new dimensions, for they are all various degrees and forms of the integration into the absolute of the various dimensions of Being. They include the absolute as the central element of their truth, and hence can be called dimensions of integration into the absolute. They are new, however, in the sense that it is the first time the soul experiences and understands them. The present chapter will address this process.

In the journey of descent, the process of personalization and individuation progresses further, as we understand more fully the functional relationship between self-realization and individuation. This reveals the organic relationship between the triad of self/soul, God/Being, and world/cosmos, leading to the understanding of the wholeness of Reality. Such exploration will be the subject matter of the next chapter. Understanding the functional relationship between true nature and the individual soul clarifies the significance of the journey of descent for the soul, for it reveals her place and function in the cosmic context of Reality.

The Hidden Treasure

The dimensions of the journey of descent represent different degrees of the integration of the forms of manifestation into the unmanifest absolute. The unfoldment starts with the absolute dimension, where the absolute is transcendent to all manifestation, and moves to greater and greater integration of the manifest world, until it arrives at their total coemergence and nonduality. At the same time, each of these dimensions reveals a particular relationship of the absolute to manifest reality. By experiencing and understanding each of these objective relationships, we recognize something fundamental about the absolute truth, and its significance to the soul and the totality of Reality. This understanding in turn facilitates a more complete and thorough realization of the absolute as the ultimate nature of Reality.

In chapter 21, we differentiated between the absolute and the absolute dimension. In discussing the absolute dimension we did not differentiate between the various dimensions of descent, so our examples ranged over a few of them. We saw, however, that the absolute in its absolute transcendence is beyond any qualities and beyond differentiation. Yet it contains all possibilities of manifestation, including all essential qualities and forms. The absolute implicitly contains all the qualities and dimensions of true nature, unmanifest and undifferentiated. Recognizing this fact, we can begin to see the relationship of the absolute to all manifest forms. The soul may become aware of a mysterious intuitive grasp of the indeterminable truth of the absolute possessing simultaneously one of the essential qualities, like love or clarity. We experience our nature as completely the mysterious truth of the absolute, beyond being and nonbeing; yet we somehow know we are love. We can almost taste the sweetness of love and feel its soft texture, as if there is a hint of the love quality in the absolute; but there is actually no color of love and no explicit love quality. We are the absolute but we are also, implicitly, love. We can have the same experience and insight with compassion, clarity, truth, joy and so on. It is as if the qualities are present in the absolute, in their fullness, but not explicit and not manifest.

We learn from this that the absolute is the potential for all qualities of essence, that these qualities actually characterize the absolute but in a completely implicit, undifferentiated, and nonmanifest manner. It is like the essential aspects exist in some kind of a virtual fashion in the absolute. We also find that not only the essential qualities, but all possible forms, are virtual potentialities in the absolute. We learn, in effect, that all of manifest reality is potential in the absolute, in some kind of virtual existence. We recognize that the transcendent absolute, even though it is total absence, is pregnant with possibilities. The whole of possible manifestations is implicit in it, as a hidden treasure waiting to appear.[4] We refer to the absolute pregnant with its hidden treasure as the virtual dimension, which we recognize as the seed possibility for manifestation, and hence as the pre-beginning of the journey of descent.

We learn from this virtual dimension that all aspects and forms of essence are nothing but the absolute, inherent in the very fabric of the absolute. They are its inherent, implicit, nondifferentiated, and nonmanifest perfections. When they manifest they are basically the manifestation of the inherent perfections of the absolute, appearing differentiated and explicit. They are always the absolute appearing in its various perfections. The hidden treasure is simply revealed, as the inherent perfections of the mystery of Being.

The Absolute Dimension

The beginning of these manifestations is the beginning of the journey of descent, where the virtual dimension becomes the absolute dimension. In this dimension the absolute is totally transcendent, but now explicitly transcendent to its manifestation. We clearly see this in the way the essential aspects appear. They manifest as they normally do in any of the boundless dimensions of true nature, as faceted diamonds of presence, but a presence characterized by the ontological truth of the particular dimension. In this dimension they are characterized by the truth of the absolute, beyond being and nonbeing. They manifest as delicate, faceted, colored diamonds of presence; the presence, though solid and full, is totally empty. The absolute diamonds are like diamonds of nothing, diamonds of absence. They are solid with sharp facets, yet in our experience of them they feel as if nothing is there. They are so light and empty they have no substance at all, no weight. Yet they are solid and faceted diamond-shaped presence. The experience is completely paradoxical, exactly the same as the experience of the crystal absolute.

Each diamond is totally black, with no light or radiance within it, for it is made out of the medium of the absolute, which precedes light.

However, each is differentiated from the other by a hint of a radiance at the surface of the diamond. In fact, the faceted surface is nothing but a glimmering, a fine and subtle shimmering that appears with a shape and color. The shape is the faceted diamond shape, and the color is that of the essential aspect. The compassion absolute diamond, for example, is a black diamond of nothing whose surface is delineated by a gentle and faceted emerald glimmering. The glimmering is just a hint of light, a hint of color that differentiates the compassion aspect from the black vastness of the absolute. With the truth aspect, a gold shimmer differentiates a faceted diamond from the sea of darkness. The truth absolute diamond is all black, a solid nothing, but shimmers and shines at the surface with the metallic gold color of truth. Each essential aspect appears as a transparent colored sheen that differentiates out the particular quality. And each quality is absolute, complete and indestructible. The love is absolute love, the intelligence is absolute intelligence, the power is absolute power, and so on. This absoluteness and completeness is expressed both in the fact that the body of the diamond is the absolute itself, and in the exquisite precision and extreme sharpness of the diamond facets.

Hence each essential quality is a faceted diamond, a wisdom presence, a synthesis of the presence of quality and the timeless wisdom of this quality. Each is a differentiated perfection of the absolute: precise, clear, and objective. The sense of presence is exquisite and transporting, gentle, subtle, delicate, smooth, and absolutely light. We feel our presence as the utmost of refinement and subtlety, combined with a delicate and gentle precision. We feel our insides both smooth and totally open, both exquisitely fine and amazingly sharp. This delicious, blissful state is both awake and peaceful, clear and completely still. It is the absolute itself differentiating its own perfections through the minimum of emanation. This minimum of emanation imbues each diamond with a very subtle sense of its quality: the compassion diamond has a subtle and delicate warmth; the love diamond a fine and exquisite sweetness; the strength diamond a precise and still vitality; and so on. And all are but differentiations of the mysterious vastness of the absolute.

This is a boundless dimension of true nature, so not only aspects but diamond vehicles appear in it, but all as black faceted presences, differentiated and delineated with subtle colorful and faceted glimmering. Each diamond vehicle appears as usual in boundless dimensions, but its faceted medium is that of the absolute, with variegated subtle radiance. We also perceive all forms and manifestations, including the normal physical and mental forms, as simply forms of subtle radiance. There is only the mysterious darkness of the absolute, which glitters and shines in the most delicate radiance. This radiance takes the shapes and colors of the manifest world. All the universe, in all of its dimensions, is nothing but the shimmering of the blackness of the absolute. Nothing exists but the mysterious absolute, for all manifestation is nothing but its immaterial glimmering.

Here we see the immensity that is the absolute, and understand that the whole of creation is completely immaterial in relation to the absolute, comprising the faintest of its glimmers. Alternatively, it becomes clear in this dimension that the absolute is the very substance of everything, and what differentiates the forms is but a simple faint glimmer, a shimmer that can simply melt and die into the vast darkness of mystery. Yet it is a shimmer of the utmost exquisite beauty, revealing the jeweled and precious nature of the hidden treasure.

Emanation

In this dimension we behold all manifest reality as an emanation from the absolute. Everything is a radiance emanating from the still silence of the absolute. Everything emanates from the mystery, for everything is nothing but the variegated and beautiful radiance of the absolute. This is one of the objective relations of the absolute to its creation. Everything is an emanation from the absolute, hence the absolute completely transcends all manifestation. The absolute in this dimension is supremely transcendent to all its manifestations, including its qualities and vehicles.

We may think of this relationship as some form of duality, for there is the absolute and there is its radiance. However, it is not exactly duality, nor is it coemergence. The emanation is not separate from or other than the absolute; rather, it is the radiance of the absolute. If we only knew coemergence of manifestation with the absolute, it might be difficult for us to recognize the true relationship between the absolute and manifest reality, which is that the absolute is always transcendent to manifest forms, regardless of how nondual it is with them. The absolute dimension reveals this relation in a completely clear and unmistakable way: the absolute is always pure and transcendent regardless how immanent it is in manifestation. In other words, regardless of how nondual and inseparable is the absolute from manifest reality, it is always itself. It never leaves its mystery, never leaves its ontological status of transcending both being and nonbeing, never leaves its simplicity and emptiness.[5] More precisely, the absolute never changes regardless of the never-ending manifestation. Because of this we can express this dimension in the paradoxical statement that "the absolute never changes even though it is in constant transformation."

The wisdom diamonds of this dimension reveal another important relation of the absolute to manifest forms: there is only the absolute, for it constitutes the very substance of the forms of all manifestation. Forms are differentiated through the shimmering radiance of the medium of the absolute. Hence, because the absolute is total absence all forms are empty, with no substance whatsoever. In fact, the forms are not only empty, they are nothing but emptiness. Everything is immaterial radiance, whose ontological status is absolute absence.

Absolute Source

Another significant relationship that becomes clear in this dimension is that the absolute is the source of all aspects, qualities, and forms. It is the single source from which all emanates. We understand the absolute here not only as the ultimate source, but as the only source. It is simply The Source. All else is emanation. This perception is not only a metaphysical insight; it goes to the very heart of liberation. The soul has seen that the absolute is her ipseity, that she is actually the absolute; this self-realization allows us the view that we are the source of all qualities that we normally believe we need. We normally believe that we need love, compassion, intelligence, strength, and so on. In this dimension our view is corrected by seeing it is folly to seek them; for they all come from us, from our presence and identity.

As the absolute, we are not only the source of essential qualities, we are actually the source of the situations from which we want the qualities. We are the source of the relationships and activities and life situations that we perceive to possess such qualities. We are, in fact, the source of all creation, all manifest forms and phenomena. We are the source of all; we are the transcendent sun from which everything originates.[6]

Recognizing oneself as the source of all can be a very lonely realization. One is the transcendent source of everything, single and alone. However, this is only a reaction based on incomplete understanding of this dimension; for the absolute is not only singularity, but also the very essence of intimacy. It is the source that unifies all of manifestation, just as the center of a wheel unifies all of its spokes. In other words, the question of aloneness returns to her because of her recognition of the singularity of the absolute, that there is only I, as the single source.

Absolute Subject

To see oneself as the emanating source of all manifestation can lead us to recognize that we are also the subject of all perception. This insight is the specific experience of the self-realization of the absolute dimension. We are the emanating source, and from this place of source we witness all of manifestation arising as emanation. The glimmering is not only the emanation of manifest reality, but also and simultaneously the light of awareness of the absolute. In the very act of emanation the absolute perceives.

The self-realization of the absolute dimension is not simply the experience of emanation and the simultaneous witnessing of emanation, but also the recognition that one is the absolute that witnesses the manifestation. We are the subject, and all emanated manifest reality is the object of our perception. The sense of subject is the recognition that the absolute is none other than I. Here the absolute is Self, the inner nature and identity of all Reality. We recognize that we are the mystery at the heart of everything.

The realization that we are the absolute is different from before. We experience ourselves as the unfathomable empty solidity of the absolute. The absolute is subject in the most direct and immediate way. We experience ourselves not as "I am," but more like "I" or "II." But it is not a feeling of identity; it is merely being the mystery, complete abiding as the absolute, and recognizing oneself as such. We learn with certainty that we are always, have always been, and will always be the absolute. We cannot but be the absolute, for only the absolute is. When we are awake to our nature we recognize it as the stupendous silence at the heart of everything, the single source of all manifestation. When we are not awake to our nature we are simply forgetting our nature, and identifying with one of our manifest emanations. Yet, this is only a momentary distraction. We, the absolute, are the one that identifies or disidentifies from any manifestation.[7]

We also realize that "everything is mine, all appearance is a manifestation of me, an extension of my existence. I am the heart of everything, the inmost essence of all. All essential aspects and dimensions express my mystery. Each is a specific manifestation of an implicit perfection, manifesting through differentiation. Each is a pure messenger from me to the soul, reminding her that I am her home and nature and self. All aspects and dimensions point to me, their inmost essence." There is certainty in this, but this certainty is not mental conviction. It is the direct recognition of one's nature and self. The soul recognizes that every time she uses the pronoun "I" she is referring to the absolute as subject, for she realizes with certainty that "the word 'I' is myself. I am always referring to my truest self whenever I say 'I.' But 'I' here is not a concept. It is a nonconceptual recognition of my nature. I am not an entity, not a form, not a center, but the source of all. There is total unification. I am the singleness in the various experiences and manifestations. There is no ego, essence, soul, aspects, various ego sectors, and so on. It is always I manifesting in one form or another. It is not an integration, not a synthesis, not even a unification. It is merely recognizing the singlehood of the self."

Preparation for Descent

There are amazing and beautiful perceptions on this dimension, and great knowledge and timeless wisdom; for it is the wisdom of transcendence. But the soul feels mainly a sense of unfettered liberation and lighthearted spontaneity. The self-realization of this dimension can lead to the arising of other dimensions of descent; for this realization is the beginning of the journey of descent, the process of realizing manifestation and one's relation to manifestation. The descent is a movement toward greater and more complete immanence, experienced as coemergence and wholeness; in the process, several transitional dimensions arise. These dimensions reveal further objective relationships that the absolute inherently and eternally possesses in relation to manifestation. The dimensions that arise at this point also demonstrate the degrees of integration of manifest reality, and hence of descent into our familiar world.

A particular diamond vehicle appears and functions as a stepping-stone toward the journey of descent. We refer to this diamond vehicle as the *point diamond*, which is basically the appearance of presence in the form of a faceted diamond, except that its center is occupied by the point of essence, the essential identity. The faceted diamond can assume any of the qualities or colors of the essential aspects, but with the point of light and presence always at its center. The point diamond vehicle continues the process of self-realization of essential presence, which is begun by the integration of the essential identity of essence. The integration of essential identity gives the soul the capacity for the experience of self-realization, the ability to be and recognize herself as the presence of true nature itself. The point diamond is the clear and precise recognition and understanding of oneself as the essential presence. It is conscious and discriminated self-realization, being essential presence inseparable from knowing it as one's nature.

The wisdom of this diamond vehicle is the recognition and appreciation of one's uniqueness, and unique realization. But this manifests specifically as the recognition and appreciation of where one is. In other words, to authentically be oneself is to abide in what the logos's dynamism of Being happens to be manifesting as one's identity at the moment. This is because Being is always and constantly manifesting all of appearance, including the form and presence of the soul. Therefore, one's authentic and real truth at each moment is what the logos manifests it as. Therefore, to be true to the dynamic intelligence of the logos the soul only needs to recognize this manifestation and abide in it. The soul does not need to do anything to get anywhere; she does not need to direct her experience toward any particular end, whether it is the absolute or whatever. She cannot determine her own manifestation because it is the logos's dynamism that actually determines any experience and form.

Wisdom of Nonarrival

From this follows the wisdom of open and open-ended inquiry, of the freedom from searching for any particular state or realization. It is the wisdom of knowing that because the dynamic intelligence of true nature, expressed through its creative logos, is what is always manifesting all forms and experience, the best approach to Reality is to recognize what form or dimension is manifesting in the consciousness of the soul, and to abide there. Any attempt to determine one's experience, by the exercise of any practice, will be a manipulation and an interference in the flow of Reality, or at best a second-guessing of where the logos is taking our experience. Hence, the center of this wisdom is that of holding no end state to strive toward, but knowing that the ideal of liberation is the freedom of the unfoldment, of the surrender to the flow of the logos.

Since we are then not trying to direct our experience to go toward any particular state or condition, the dynamism of the logos is liberated to unfold according to its optimizing intelligence. The flow of our experience can be constrained by ego structures and identity, which is the normal constant constraint of the egoic life, or through conscious and intentional inner and spiritual practices that aim toward the generation and actualization of particular states. Both constrain our experience and are counter to the spontaneous outflow of the logos. This is true even if our spiritual practice is an attempt to realize the highest spiritual states, like that of the absolute or of nonconceptual awareness. What is left for us is the motiveless inquiry into the truth that the logos is manifesting, and the surrender to its flow. (See note 3 on page 684.) However, this practice of surrendering to and abiding in the true manifestation of the logos does not feel to the soul like an attempt to cooperate with the logos in order for the latter to take her to the condition of an ultimate state of enlightenment. This would simply be a manipulation, not a genuine surrender. It feels more like being real and authentic, or like a respect and appreciation for the truth that happens to be one's experience of oneself. It specifically feels like being oneself, for oneself is whatever the logos manifests it to be. We simply feel authentic, while the form of authenticity can be any form or dimension of the presence of true nature.

The wisdom of the point diamond is not only a matter of finding where one is and abiding in it, but of continuing to be where one is. In other words, it is the wisdom of abiding in the flow of one's experience. It is first the recognition of the thread of one's unfoldment, as the thread of where one is. This is the clear discriminated experience and understanding of the flow of one's experience. And it happens that when we do not manipulate our experience, consciously or unconsciously, it simply unfolds and reveals the mysteries of our Being. Since the optimizing intelligence is free to unfold the form of the experience of the soul, it reveals her nature in its various aspects and dimensions, all the way to the absolute, and further into the journey of descent. So the surrender to where we are quickly unfolds our experience into a continuity of being, which becomes a continuing self-revelation of true nature.

The important realization and wisdom in this diamond vehicle, which makes it quite helpful as a preparation for the journey of descent, is that we learn not to be attached to any particular state or condition, not even that of the absolute. We learn to flow with whatever the logos of our true nature manifests in our experience, and learn to respect and appreciate any arising state without a preference, comparative judgment, or view of an end state of realization. We become free from our conceptualizing mind and the ideals it uses to constrain and channel the flow of our experience. We become contented with whatever state into which the logos manifests our experience. Our experience becomes the clear, precise, and discriminated awareness of the flow of where we are, as the continuity of self-realization.

Without this wisdom it will be quite difficult to accept the revelations of the journey of descent, but this wisdom is also useful in all stages of the inner journey. In the Diamond Approach, it becomes one of the central pillars of its view and method. (See *Spacecruiser Inquiry*, chapters 10 and 11, for a more detailed discussion of the wisdom of the point diamond vehicle.)

The Core Dimension

The integration of the point diamond vehicle and its wisdom facilitates the shift from the journey of ascent to that of descent. There is now freedom from the fixation of self, for at this juncture identity is essential presence that can flow as any quality or dimension. Identity has been shifting for the soul, from ego identity based on historical impressions, to essential identity in any of the essential aspects, to boundless identity of true nature on the dimensions of divine love, pure presence, nonconceptual awareness, and finally the absolute. Through the self-realization of the absolute dimension identity becomes established as the absolute, for identity has no more place for it to unfold. Before this juncture the identity of the soul, her sense of self-recognition, has been in continual unfoldment, going deeper and subtler. Self-realization in the journey of ascent goes through stages as the dimension of what and who the soul is unfolds to deeper and subtler dimensions of Being. (See *The Point of Existence* for a detailed discussion of this shift of identity.)

In actuality the soul is always unfolding, for it is the nature of the soul to change and flow; however, the unfoldment of her identity is a subprocess that forms the deeper and most central part of the inner journey. It is the deepening of the center of the mandala while the unfoldment of the soul is the transformation of its general field. The center keeps deepening until it arrives at the dimension of depth itself, the absolute mystery. When this happens the identity remains the same. Who one is, what one is, is unchanging as the stillness of the absolute. We find ourselves, or the center of our experiential mandala, to always be the unchanging mysterious absolute, beyond being and nonbeing. The mandala is bound to be in continual change: the field of the soul will continue to transform and unfold. Yet, the center and ground of the soul, her conscious sense of her true nature, will always be the absolute. This is one of the implications of the dimensions of descent being all a matter of various degrees of integration of the manifest dimensions into the absolute. The inner nature of all these dimensions is always the absolute; thus, as the soul self-realizes these dimensions, the depth of her identity continues to be the absolute. This understanding becomes specifically clear at the next dimension of descent, that of the core dimension.

The absolute dimension can be considered the apex of the journey of ascent, but it is also the point from which descent commences.[8] The dimension that actually begins the descent is the core dimension, and hence we consider it a transitional dimension. More exactly, the core dimension is the first dimension of descent, and hence the first step toward the movement from transcendence to immanence. As usual, the clearest way of understanding the major characteristics of a boundless dimension of descent is to see it in terms of the relation of the absolute to the essential aspects, the manifestation of its perfections. In this dimension each essential aspect arises as a faceted diamond, whose core is the absolute. The core is a sphere of blackness and emptiness of the absolute, but the rest of the body of the diamond is constituted by the dynamic presence of the logos. This dynamic presence assumes the color and quality of the particular essential aspect. In other words, the core of the diamond is always black emptiness, but the external part changes color and quality depending on the arising aspect. The external layer is substantial and full, unlike the ethereal radiance of the absolute diamonds.

These diamonds are similar to those of the point diamonds, except that the center has changed from the radiant point of light to the dark emptiness of the absolute. This change reflects the fact that one's identity has shifted from essential identity to the absolute ipseity. With the essential identity, one's center and core can be essence in its various aspects, while the identity of the absolute ipseity is the only unchanging truth in Reality. In other words, one is now free from the unfoldment of identity, for such unfoldment has reached its ultimate repose. The point diamond liberates the unfoldment from the fixation of the self; realization of the core dimension integrates it with the absolute as the unchanging core. The central issue for the point diamond is the need to free one's unfoldment from influence. The central issue for the core dimension is identification, forgetting one's true self, one's inmost nature. In other words, it is identification with the soul, with the unfoldment. The resolution is seeing that it is the absolute that identifies, that forgets, and its deepest identification is with the unfolding soul. The core dimension reveals to us that we are the absolute, and that the soul is one of our expressions, an organ for our experience.

The experiential sense of a core diamond is of a substantial and living presence of essential qualities, but the depth and core of oneself always feels empty and dark, silent and still, mysterious and unfathomable. The primary wisdom inherent in these diamonds is that the absolute is the core nature of all essential aspects, and of all manifest forms. We see this in the experience of manifestation on this dimension, which is experiencing oneself as the vast emptiness of the absolute at the core of the oneness of existence. We experience all of manifest reality as a dynamic luminous oneness, whose depth and core is the mysterious black stillness of the absolute. We are one boundless body; the inside or the mass of it is crystal absolute, and the skin is the logos oneness. So we feel full and rich, and at the same time empty and light. There is a paradoxical juxtaposition of fullness and emptiness, color and darkness. The surface is fullness, color, and richness; the depth darkness, emptiness, and simplicity.

Just as the universe continues to unfold, so does one's individual soul; yet one's core and identity remains constant as the mysterious absolute. The absolute is clearly the inner nature, the depth and core of all manifestation. Being the inner nature and core of all manifest forms is the objective relation this dimension reveals the absolute to have with manifest reality.

The Ground Dimension

The next step in integration appears in what we term the ground dimension, where each aspect arises as a faceted diamond of a particular color and quality, which possesses two layers, inner and outer; the inner is the absolute and the outer is nonconceptual awareness. The inner layer is not a spherical darkness but a diamond-shaped black emptiness, of the same shape as the external layer. It is like two concentric diamonds, the inner is constituted from the medium of the absolute and the outer from the medium of nonconceptual presence.

The experience of an essential aspect on this dimension is that of being a nonconceptual presence—clear, precise, and objective. There is no conceptualization, no ideas of oneself, just simply being, where being is inseparable from awareness. Yet one experiences one's nonconceptual presence as grounded in something deeper, vaster, and more mysterious. We experience manifest reality again as a oneness of Being, but it is a nonconceptual oneness, where it is the absence of conceptual partitions, instead of the sense of oneness. At the same time, we are nonconceptually aware of a dark and mysterious ground that underlies this nonconceptual unity of appearance.

An alternative experience is that of awareness of one's presence as the vast crystalline mystery of the absolute, whose surface is a transparent and clear crystalline layer that contains all the forms of manifestation, in all of its dimensions. In this experience it is quite clear that nonconceptual presence or pure awareness is the ground of all manifestation, yet it is external to the absolute. More accurately, the absolute functions as the ground of all reality, including nonconceptual awareness. The absolute is the ground of all grounds, the ultimate ground. In other words, the emptiness of the absolute is the ground of all reality, so all manifest forms, whether relative or essential, are grounded in emptiness. This is quite a paradoxical truth, for it shows that nonbeing is the ground of all being. All forms, regardless of how real or substantial, are grounded in nothing. Such is the objective relation that the ground dimension reveals the absolute to have in relation to all manifestation.

The insight that emptiness is the ground of all forms is specifically significant for the inner journey, especially for the journey of descent. Through the absolute descending into the world we see that the world is grounded in emptiness, and hence is always insubstantial and lacks any ultimate existence. The soul learns that to live in the world from the perspective of the absolute is to never forget that the world is ultimately insubstantial, that it is groundless; for the absolute ground is simply absence. More precisely, its groundlessness is its truth and freedom and the liberation of the soul is in remembering that she can rely ultimately only on the absolute: it is the groundless ground. She can trust emptiness, for it is the ultimate unchanging ground that is certain to be found at the depth of everything. In other words, the ground of all manifest forms is that when we try to find their ultimate essence they disappear. The unfindability of their ultimate existence is their ground.

The ground dimension clearly and specifically reveals what ground of Reality means, and what the ultimate ground is. Ground of Reality means what underlies it, what forms its inner constitution, what we find as we penetrate its particular forms. It is what we find as we see beyond the forms, shapes, colors, and qualities. And what we find is the absolute whose essence is unfindability itself. A ground is also what supports the forms of manifestation, without which there will be no appearance of forms. Hence, the ultimate support for all manifest forms is not nonconceptual awareness, but the mysterious emptiness of the absolute. Emptiness, absolute absence, paradoxically supports all presence, all that appears to exist.

The absolute dimension shows us that the absolute is the source of all manifestation; the core dimension shows us that the absolute is also its core and inner nature; and the ground dimension reveals to us that the absolute supports all manifestation and grounds it in emptiness.

The Integrated Dimension

A further step toward integrating the dimensions is our direct perception of the simultaneous presence of all the boundless dimensions in all manifest forms, whether relative or essential. An essential aspect will arise as the integration of all dimensions of true nature in a faceted diamond presence. The integration is not complete yet, because the dimensions appear hierarchically stacked. Each aspect appears as a multilayered diamond, where the center layer is composed of the medium of the absolute, then the next layer of pure awareness, then pure presence, then divine love, and finally at the surface, the flowing essence of the logos. All the layers are of the color and quality of the particular essential aspect, except for the deepest layer, which is the sable black of the virtual dimension, beyond being and nonbeing. The surface layer is a flowing essential presence, essence not in the diamond form. So the presence is a faceted diamond while the surface is fluid and flowing. Flowing presence at the surface does not mean that the logos is the most superficial dimension. The logos cannot be included in the hierarchy of manifest dimensions because it is the principle of manifestation, which we can experience in any of these dimensions, and as the outflow from the absolute.

The integrated dimension points to the hierarchical nature of manifestation, revealed in the hierarchy of the boundless dimensions of true nature. As we will see when we discuss the coemergence of complete nonduality, coemergence does not reveal such hierarchy, but shows all dimensions as equal and equidistant from the absolute. Even though this is ultimately accurate, there is a fundamental and important understanding implicit in the view of hierarchy that is not so evident in coemergent nonduality.

We are referring to hierarchy in a sense that has nothing to do with dominance or control. It refers to the timeless truth that a deeper or higher dimension in the hierarchy is more fundamental than the one that comes after it. It forms its ground, core, and essence. In other words, as we investigate a particular dimension we can penetrate it to a dimension deeper than it, which both underlies and contains it. The deeper dimension is more fundamental and hence deeper or higher. It transcends the one below it. Furthermore, it means that experience or manifestation can continue without the lower one, for it can be on the deeper dimension on the hierarchy. For example, we can experience essential forms on the dimension of pure presence, where the presence and the knowing of presence are inseparable. Or we can go deeper to the nonconceptual dimension, where the essential forms are present, yet there is only awareness with no knowing of the presence. So pure awareness is deeper and more fundamental than direct or basic knowing. Our experience in most situations, however, needs and includes knowing.

The journey of ascent is characterized by the movement up the ladder of this ontological hierarchy. Each step is a penetration of a dimension, which is the same thing as the shedding of its characteristic mode of experience. The movement upward is also a movement toward greater simplicity, for what is shed is basically fundamental concepts and differentiations of Reality. And what we find through this shedding is that there is actually no leaving of the old dimension, but a movement to a greater ground that contains and supports the previous one. A metaphor that illustrates this is the dimensions that exist in our bodies. Molecules form a dimension larger and more fundamental than the dimension of organs. Yet, the dimension of atoms is larger and more fundamental than that of molecules, and the dimension of elementary particles is more fundamental than that. Each deeper or more fundamental dimension is simpler, but contains the one previous to it.

This dimension of the journey of descent reveals the fundamental truth that Reality is composed of many dimensions, all necessary for manifest forms and our experience of them. It also reveals their hierarchic functioning, which in turn points to the absolute as the apex or center of the hierarchy. It reveals the objective relation of the absolute to manifest reality as the center of a hierarchy of manifestation, and shows us that by descending into manifestation the absolute descends into an increasing number of dimensions. It also shows that this hierarchy of manifestation is not temporal or spatial, but ontological.[9] The integrated dimension reveals the manifest world as a Riemannian multidimensional manifold, and shows the hierarchical relationships of the functioning of its various dimensions.

The experience of manifestation on this dimension is that it is multilayered, where the absolute forms its center and core, its inmost essence. We see a oneness of appearance, flowing and rich with colorful forms and qualities, but possessing several grounds all necessary for such experience. We experience ourselves as this multilayered Reality, a macrocosm whose ultimate ground and essence is the absolute mystery. We are all and everything, all dimensions and all forms. Or we may experience ourselves as the absolute, a vast luminous mystery that clothes itself with layers of manifestation, each of them clothing itself with the next layer, until we arrive at the physical dimension. The universe appears to us as our apparel, composed of levels of luminosity. Another kind of experience on this dimension is to experience ourselves as one of the intermediate dimensions, such as the nonconceptual. Here, we experience ourselves as a nonconceptual awareness, and the world as our external mind. However, we find that there is a deeper ground that supports and contains us. We are not separate from the world, for it is our external appearance; and we are not separate from the absolute, for it is our deeper essence.

To understand the view of the hierarchy of the dimensions of Being, and its usefulness, is to understand the usefulness of the perspective of ascent, as the experience and exploration of each of these dimensions. To understand each dimension on its own, as we have done in the last five chapters, is to recognize and appreciate its specific and necessary contribution. Such understanding is necessary for understanding the principles governing the path of realization and liberation, which requires a full grasp of the functioning of Reality and of the soul. At the same time, the integrated dimension adds the insight that Reality is not one of these dimensions, but they are all necessary for both its existence and our experience of it. This insight points to the truth that realization is not a matter of realizing one of these dimensions of true nature, but of realizing all of them simultaneously, for that is the true structure of Reality.

The Quintessential Dimension

Transitional dimensions appear in various degrees of integration. We have discussed the major dimensions; the integration also appears in various combinations of these. The process is nonlinear, so the unfoldment moves back and forth for some time before integration is complete. One possibility of integration is the interpenetration of the absolute and another dimension, like that of nonconceptual presence or pure presence. Sometimes the three are combined such that they interpenetrate one another, almost completely mixed but still differentiated and recognizable. Various states arise, revealing the richness and wonder of Reality, where it is beauty pervaded by the mysterious blackness of the absolute. A significant state is that of the integration of the absolute with the blue aspect, which is the aspect of basic knowingness and consciousness. We then experience everything as a boundless blue-black absolute. We see a deep blue vastness that becomes darker at the depth, until it becomes the black absolute. At such place of interpenetration the blue and black completely mix and become one presence of deep blue-black mystery. This is a state of absorption and mental rest, consciousness without discrimination, where there is consciousness of the absolute without mental reflection or specific knowing. It is a condition in which mind and consciousness melt into the absolute.[10] This state points to the next integration.

The integration reaches its crucial stage at the quintessential dimension, where each essential aspect arises as a faceted diamond that has both the absolute and the quality pervading the totality of it. It is totally luminous black emptiness, at the same time that it is completely the essential presence with its color and flavor. For instance, the joy aspect arises as a faceted diamond that is luminous black and bright yellow at the same time. It is completely yellow, through and through, but the yellow is transparent and pervaded by the luminous blackness of the absolute. The yellow brightness is so transparent that it reveals its underlying absolute blackness. The yellow is not only at the surface of the diamond as in the case of absolute diamonds, but pervading all of it; yet it is so transparent that it reveals the black spaciousness that interpenetrates all of its field of presence. In other words, the yellow and black are coextensive, totally coemergent. The yellow is not only a color, but the quality of joy in its sweetness, lightness, spontaneity, and delightful presence; and the black is the absolute in its mysterious emptiness, smoothness, and stillness. The combined result is the experience of an exquisite sense of presence—both absolutely sharp and smooth, precise and delicate—richness, and total absence. And the quality of joy gives it a lighthearted and playful happiness, a playfulness that is at the same time an amazing stillness and depth. The interplay of qualities in terms of affect, sensation, texture, taste, and so on are simply beyond any imagination, ecstatic beyond any expectation.

The most characteristic quality of the quintessential diamond is the exquisite synthesis of presence and absence, fullness and emptiness. The two are absolutely coemergent, totally coextensive. We can differentiate them from each other, but we are aware of both as one. We feel so empty and light, as if our nature is simply total absence. Yet, in the same perception, there is a sense of full presence, sharp and precise. The result is an exquisiteness beyond mind and imagination, which is a sharpness and intensity of sensation that is inseparable from a heavenly smoothness due to the absence of any sensation. The effect on us is delight, bliss, ecstasy, transport, which is at the same time lightness, freedom, liberation, which is also precision, truth, reality, and significance.

The transparency of the quality is due to the presence of clarity; hence, there is the coemergence of awakened sharp clarity and empty stillness and peace. We feel still, deep, empty, and vast; and at the same time we are lucid, clear, and limpid, in a very sharp, precise, and awakened manner. We are awake to our emptiness, present to our absence. This is the general sense of the self-realization of this dimension. More precisely, the ontological nature of this dimension is the total coemergence and synthesis of pure presence and absolute emptiness. So it is clear and colorless presence, pure and independent of qualities, coextensive with the darkness of total absence. The quintessential aspects are simply the same nature manifesting with a particular quality and its color, in the form of a faceted diamond.

From this place we experience the world as luminous appearance, crystalline and rich with qualities, but whose nature is the coemergence of clear presence and black emptiness. It is a jeweled universe, glittering and radiant, but the jeweled forms are formations that the luminous emptiness assumes. More precisely, the universe is nothing but a self-luminous emptiness, where this self-luminosity assumes the forms of manifestation. It is as if the empty vastness, which is simply total absence, differentiates itself into the forms of the world by its own self-radiance.[11] The glowing radiance is not only at the surface, but pervades the vast emptiness. The radiance is awareness, but is felt also as pure presence.

Quintessence

We refer to the nature of this dimension as quintessential presence, or simply quintessence. Quintessence reveals the most true and objective relation the absolute has to the other dimensions of true nature. It is so integrated with them that there is no hint of separation or even differentiation. Complete coemergence means that the absolute so interpenetrates the field of the other dimensions that we cannot differentiate it from them. If we look at it in terms of its coemergence with the dimension of pure presence, for example, we see that quintessence is presence and absence undifferentiated from each other, clarity and emptiness undifferentiated from each other, being and nonbeing absolutely undifferentiated from each other. It is a clear medium, colorless and transparent, yet it is totally black and mysterious. Imagine a totally dark empty space without an iota of light; then shine throughout it a radiant transparent colorless light. However, even though this light illuminates its vastness it reveals its blackness rather than eliminating it. Furthermore, the clear light does not originate from some other place; it is simply the glow of the blackness, coemergent with the totality of its expanse. It is as if each point of this expanse is so empty that it is absolute clarity, a radiance. At the same time this radiance is not only light, but also presence and being. Its ontological nature is so absolutely absence that the absence glimmers with presence. In other words, when true nature reaches the extreme of nonbeing it cannot be differentiated from being.

The juxtaposition of clear light and the dark emptiness of the absolute frequently gives the quintessence an almost gray color, or more exactly, the color of the sky at dawn.[12] In this condition, the sense of spaciousness disappears, for the emptiness of the absolute appears as nondimensionality, beyond the concepts of space and distance.

We refer to the condition of this dimension as quintessence because it is the true essence of manifestation. Manifest forms require presence, for manifestation means being. More exactly, manifestation means the arising of the manifest dimensions, those of pure awareness and presence; for without light or presence there is no manifestation, only the absolute in its absoluteness. In other words, manifestation is the appearance of forms that the dimension of pure presence assumes, due to the flow of the logos. Yet manifestation is never separate from the absolute, for it is its radiance. Therefore, manifestation always has a ground composed of both pure presence and absolute, being and nonbeing.

And since in actuality there is always manifestation, there are always presence and emptiness. We can say that emptiness does not exist on its own; for it is always the emptiness of manifest forms, always associated with manifestation. There is no such thing as emptiness on its own, nonbeing on its own, without being. In other words, presence and emptiness together are in actuality the ultimate ground. And experiences of dissolution of presence in emptiness until there is total annihilation can only be an individual experience, for the world continues during one's annihilation. Therefore, we call the synthesis of presence and emptiness the quintessence, the deepest core and nature of everything. This does not contradict the truth that emptiness is the ultimate essence because it is the inner aspect of the quintessence. It only points to the fact that the underlying ground and nature of manifestation is always presence coemergent with emptiness.

438   Actualization of Reality

Like all the dimensions of descent, the quintessential dimension points to the fact that presence and emptiness always underlie manifestation. This particular dimension more significantly points to the fact that the quintessence of Reality is not simply presence and emptiness, but their coemergence. The ground dimension, for instance, has both emptiness and presence, but the two dimensions are not mixed all the way, not completely coemergent. They are distinctly differentiated from each other, a differentiation that is more clearly delineated in the integrated dimension of descent. In this latter dimension the lack of coemergence appears as a hierarchy of differentiated dimensions. The quintessential dimension reveals the more complete truth, that although the dimensions are functionally hierarchical they are not actually or ultimately differentiated. They are totally mixed, completely coextensive.

To understand this coemergence we use an analogy. Let's say that presence is the front of a coin and emptiness is its back. Now slice this coin into two coins. Again, the front is presence and the back is emptiness. Keep halving its thickness, each time resulting with presence at the front and emptiness at the back. Continue this process indefinitely until we arrive at thickness of zero. Now the front is presence and the back is emptiness; but now the front and the back are the same thing, for there is no more thickness. In other words, we arrive at the condition where presence and emptiness are undifferentiated. They are actually this way throughout the thickness of the original coin. This is their coemergence.

We need to remember that the absolute truth is nonspatial, and hence its inseparability from manifestation inevitably means coemergence. It is inseparable from any of its manifestations and therefore absolutely coemergent with all the manifest dimensions. It pervades everything so completely that there is no region, horizontal or vertical, where it does not reach. In fact, it is this understanding that led us to recognize, in chapter 21, that there is only the absolute. For if it pervades everything absolutely, then there is no region where it does not exist. If anything is not it, then it does not reach there, does not pervade it yet.

We see that the objective relation that the quintessential dimension reveals the absolute to have to manifestation is that it is coemergent with all forms and dimensions. In other words, it has no distance from any manifestation. It is actually not differentiated from anything. More precisely, the absolute has no relation to manifestation, for the possibility of relation does not arise unless there is differentiation. It is a matter of complete unity, absolute nonduality. We can also see that coemergence implies all the previous objective relations we have discussed in relation to the other dimensions of descent. Everything is its radiance, just as in the absolute dimension, except now we see that its radiance is not differentiated from its emptiness. It is the core of everything, just as in the core dimension, except now we see that the core and the surface are coemergent, and without any distance between them. It is the ground of all manifestation, just as in the ground dimension, except that now we see that the ground is undifferentiated from the manifest. It is the center and apex of the hierarchy of all dimensions of manifestation, just as in the integrated dimension, except that now we recognize that this hierarchy is not spatial; it does not even imply differentiation.

We reach the essence of integration in the journey of descent. Ultimate integration is perfect coemergence. But this means that there is no such thing as descent, for descent implies distance and differentiation. Alternately stated, the journey of descent culminates in the end of descent, but also the end of ascent. In the quintessential dimension the concepts of ascent and descent lose their meaning. They are useful for discriminating knowledge and understanding, for they are the differentiated discrimination of true nature. Yet, true nature is ultimately nondifferentiated, a primordial synthesis.

Immanence

The quintessential dimension stands at the opposite pole from the absolute dimension. The latter shows the absolute to be completely transcendent to manifestation, while the quintessence shows it to be fully immanent. It is so implicit in manifestation that it has no distance from it. Whenever we look at manifestation we see the absolute right there, underlying it, grounding it, coemergent with it, inseparable from it, even undifferentiated from it. All the dimensions of the journey of descent reveal the absolute to be immanent in manifestation, but the quintessential divulges perfect and complete immanence. The manifest world is the crystal radiance of the absolute that is perfectly coemergent with its emptiness, with no distance to separate them. Yet it leaves transcendence untouched; for even though the world is inseparable from the absolute, it cannot and does not contaminate its simplicity and emptiness. The absolute remains in its absolute purity, unmixed and undefiled, even though it is completely mixed with manifestation. This is similar to the situation of mixing dirt with water. The water appears dirty and murky, but it does not lose its nature at all; for it is always H_2O, regardless of the mixing.

The quintessence is the complete immanence of the absolute, yet it is transcendence. We can say that in the quintessence transcendence and immanence meet. Or alternately, the concepts of transcendence and immanence lose their differentiating boundaries at the culmination of the journey of descent.

The quintessential dimension also reveals how the generation of Reality occurs. It shows that it is not a matter of emanation, but of manifestation within the field of the absolute. The world appears within the absolute, inseparable from it, undifferentiated from it, without any ontological distance. So it is not emanated the way light emanates from the sun, but more like the picture appears on the TV screen. The emanating light never leaves its source, being coemergent with it.[13] Source and sourced are simply two facets of the same Reality. It is because of this complete inseparability of the manifest and the unmanifest that one of the main issues for this dimension is rapprochement, but now between appearance-world and true nature—absolute.

23 Reality

THE JOURNEY OF DESCENT reveals the relation between the absolute and the various dimensions of true nature. The quintessential dimension reveals it specifically as not actually a relation, but a complete integration, a perfect coemergence. All the dimensions of true nature—its absolute essence, nonconceptual awareness, pure presence, divine love, and creative logos—make up one truth, in a primordial synthesis. In the soul's personal experience she may perceive the absolute coemergent with awareness, presence, or love, but in actuality all the dimensions make up an indivisible unity. To experience a limited coemergence indicates a transitory dominance of some dimensions due to the conditions of the particular situation. But true nature inherently and primordially possesses all the five dimensions. This means that any essential aspect inherently exists in all the five dimensions simultaneously. An aspect is always a dynamic presence continually generated by the creativity of the logos. It possesses its own inseparable awareness of its presence and phenomenological characteristics, its cognitive flavor or universal concept, its affective coloration, and it is always fundamentally coemergent with its own ontological absence. In other words, the journey of descent shows us that an essential aspect is inherently nondual with all the dimensions of true nature, a differentiation of a particular perfection of this true nature.

Coemergent Nonduality

The perfect coemergence includes all manifestation, not only the boundless dimensions of true nature and its essential aspects. Any manifest form is nothing but a form taken by true nature with its five dimensions. Each manifest form is a differentiation of the coemergent true nature, patterned by the creative display of its logos. There is only true nature that continually changes its appearance as the changing forms of the world. A tree, for example, is nothing but true nature manifesting itself as a tree. The tree is simply the local changing manifestation of a particular region in the five-dimensional manifold of true nature. To see it from the perspective of coemergent true nature is to see a dynamic upwelling that continually manifests the particular tree as a form that possesses a five-dimensional ground. The tree appears to us transparent; we can see through its appearance to a multidimensional vastness. We see luminosity, presence, color, but also the deep darkness of the absolute.

We do not see the tree this way in the midst of our conventional world, where the rocks and grass appear as usual. It can occur as a passing experience, but the full perception is to see the tree as inseparable from a whole field, a field that contains all the trees, the rocks, the grass, the sky and clouds, everything in the line of perception. All these appear similarly to the tree, constituted by the same five dimensions, but all forming one three-dimensional tapestry. The whole tapestry is flowing and upwelling as a miraculous display of newly created forms.

The tapestry includes our bodies, our movements, and even our thoughts, images, and feelings. There is no inner or outer experience, for all is one manifestation, one unified appearance of true nature. We cannot truly call it an experience, for it is simply reality. Experience always involves a focus on a particular manifest form or phenomenon, while here there is simply the presence and awareness of the totality of all that exists, in a perfect nonduality. We perceive all forms, inner or outer, mental, physical, or essential, as nondual with true nature in all of its dimensions. We do not perceive these forms as external to true nature, or additional to it, but rather as its appearance. In other words, nonduality does not mean that there are two things that have a particular relationship to each other. True nature and manifest forms are simply two facets of the same reality. These two facets are in complete coemergence, where we can find each of the dimensions of true nature in any form, or any part of any form.

We call this condition *coemergent nonduality*, to differentiate it from the nonduality, where the different facets or dimensions are inseparable but not coextensive, as in the transitional dimensions of the journey of descent. In this view we cease to believe that there exists a manifest world and also a true nature, for the two are simply the two facets of the same truth, two facets that we continuously perceive to be coemergent. Reality is then nothing but true nature that is constantly displaying itself in various and changing forms.[1] Coemergent nondual presence does not exclude anything. It includes true nature in all of its dimensions and aspects, all of physical reality including our bodies, and our subjective experience with all of its content. We experience this totality as an indivisible truth, where all of its dimensions and forms coexist in total harmony, a harmony that appears in the orderly pattern of the logos.

Since we understand this condition to be the objective truth of things we term this wholeness *Reality*. It is what actually is in its true ontological nature. When we do not see it this way we are simply perceiving through some obscuration or veil, some belief or representation, or from a particular vantage point. In other words, we refer to it as Reality because it is the real; it is how things are when perceived with no subjective filters. We may perceive Reality as it is, completely objectively, or in one degree or another of approximation. Our experience and perception can vary with various factors, but Reality is always a coemergent nondual wholeness.

What does this understanding of nonduality mean about the world, God, and the soul?

The World

Is there still a world, then, as we normally know it? From the perspective of coemergent nonduality, there is a world, and it possesses many of the features of what we normally call the world, but differs from it in some fundamental ways. The world is nothing but the appearance of Reality, its face or external facet. In other words, there is a world of people, animals, trees, planets, stars and galaxies, atoms and elementary particles, and so on, just as we normally perceive them. What we normally term the world is basically the physical universe, life forms, human beings, their consciousness and their interactions. The view of Reality does not eliminate these forms of manifestation, but reveals them as the particulars of the manifest face of Reality. They appear as formations that true nature takes in the way it presents itself to perception. They are not separate and dissociated forms, but constitute a oneness of existence where the forms continue to be forms, differentiated from each other; they are nothing but particular patterns of the unified fabric of existence-appearance.

Furthermore, the forms that we recognize as constituting the world are not only inseparable from each other, but also inseparable from true nature in its various dimensions. In fact, they are coemergent with true nature, where true nature constitutes their ground, core, nature, and substance. What we normally call the world is nothing but Reality seen with obscurations veiling its underlying ground and substance. The conventional world is nothing but Reality shorn of its true nature. Only the differentiating outlines of the forms of Reality are then left for our conventional perception. Since we perceive these outlines without the ground that manifests them we believe they are separate and autonomously existing objects. The ground that is their source of manifestation is what unifies them, and so without it in our experience we simply perceive objects in physical space. This is the essence of reification, taking a manifest and inseparable form and holding it in the mind as a separate self-existing object. In other words, what we call the world is nothing but the reification of the forms of Reality, as we saw in chapter 18. It is the reified world, where the central effect of reification is the elimination of the ground of true nature from perception.

Coemergent nonduality simply reveals the world in its totality, both the forms and their underlying ground. What we perceive then is Reality. The forms of the familiar world continue to appear in perception, but now are seen as forms of a formless truth. And instead of seeing discrete objects in space we see jeweled luminous forms that are manifestations and extensions of a mysterious but self-luminous ground. Our mind is quiet and empty, and our body a diaphanous form that expresses and extends Reality into its environmental field.

Energy and Matter

We have discussed the ground of Reality as comprising five dimensions of true nature. We can conceptualize Reality slightly differently, by taking into consideration some important differentiations and distinctions in manifest reality. We have discussed the manifest forms as if they are all of the same kind, or on the same level; but there are physical forms, mental forms, emotional forms, essential forms, and so on. It might be helpful to differentiate two significant categories and explore how they are related to true nature. We then can speak of two additional dimensions to Reality, the physical dimension and the dimension of energy. Reality then comprises seven dimensions, the five boundless dimensions of true nature and the dimensions of energy and physicality.

We are not referring here to physical energy, which is part of the physical world. Rather, we mean the vital energy necessary for living forms, referred to in Sanskrit as *prana* or *shakti*. This differentiation is important because we can think of the human organism as the confluence of a physical body, an energy body (referred to sometimes as the astral body), and the soul, which includes her essence. The energy body is the dimension of vital energy necessary for life; we can access it through the activation of the *chakra* system. This system of energetic centers uses the vital energy—*prana* or *shakti*—for its functioning, an energy that the organism partly acquires through the breath. It is this energy that yogic systems utilizing *kundalini* for their practices try to cultivate and direct. *Kundalini* is the name given to a reservoir of dormant energy, visualized as a serpent coiled in the first *chakra* at the perineum. By awakening the *kundalini*, the *shakti* is activated, which then rises up the spine activating and energizing the *chakra* centers. The *chakra* centers become doorways to deeper spiritual experiences and dimensions.

In the Diamond Approach we activate this vital energy not through the familiar yogic practices of *kundalini* but through inquiry and understanding. Our perception is that *shakti* energy is a dimension that is patterned according to essential aspects, a dimension that has its particular psychodynamic and structural issues. In other words, it is a dimension of presence; but this presence is the presence of energy, like light but not exactly. It has no fullness or density, just vitality. And just like any other dimension of presence, it manifests in various colors, each color being that of an essential aspect. More exactly, essential aspects arise on various dimensions, and one of these is that of *shakti* energy.

Shakti energy is the raw energy of the emotional realm, for emotions are basically *shakti* with some conceptual coloration. By freeing oneself from identification with these emotions, their issues, and the concepts that underlie them, the energy is liberated and appears as the vital pure energy of *shakti*. This can activate the *kundalini*, which becomes pure vital energy that goes up through the spine activating the various *chakras*. Each *chakra* has, associated with its mode of functioning, psychological issues that must be worked through. The energy can become strong enough to penetrate to the head centers, appearing as the bejeweled, hooded cobra around the head.

When we experience this energy coemergent with essential presence, the presence attains new characteristics. Besides the increased vitality and vigor, the main difference is that the quiet blissfulness of essence becomes an intense ecstasy. The sense of pleasure intensifies, and can even be overpowering. It is similar to the pleasure of sexual orgasm, but felt as the affect of the essential presence.

In complete coemergence, Reality includes not only the boundless dimensions of true nature, but also the dimension of *shakti* energy and that of physicality. The physical dimension is more difficult to understand, because it is not a dimension in the sense we have been discussing. It is basically physical matter always in the form of one object or another in space. In fact, it is not possible to think of physical matter except in the form of an object. We do not find a continuous field of matter that takes the forms of the various objects.[2] When we observe physical objects from the perspective of true nature we do not experience them as physical the way we normally do. They lose their opaqueness and sense of solidity, and appear as diaphanous forms of presence. In other words, they simply appear as forms that the presence of true nature assumes. Yet they are not essential forms, and not like essential forms, even though all forms appear similar in the boundless dimensions of true nature. Thus it makes sense to think of these forms as constituting a dimension of their own. These forms have characteristics different from essential forms, or mental and emotional forms, even though from the perspective of true nature they are only forms that true nature takes. The main difference they have from essential forms is that two physical forms cannot exist in the same time and space. For instance, you cannot have two apples at the same exact location of time and space. In other words, physical forms displace each other. This is not true of energetic or essential forms, for they can coexist at the same time and space, as an overlap that is impossible for physical forms.

Another reason we consider physical manifestation to constitute a dimension on its own is that in conventional perception, where the perception of the ground of true nature is absent, physical forms have different characteristics from mental, emotional, and essential forms. Yet the underlying ground of the physical dimension, like that of the energetic one, is true nature with its five dimensions. Thus we might more accurately say that Reality is the coemergent nonduality of seven dimensions, the five of true nature and the energetic and physical ones. And we can more accurately state that what we ordinarily call the world is the physical dimension in combination with the energetic dimension. In other words, it is Reality shorn of its true nature.

The important insight for us here is that what we ordinarily call the world is not actually separate from true nature, and that only by perceiving an imaginary separateness do we experience the world as fundamentally physical. It is more accurate to think of a Reality whose surface is the world.

Being

We have used the concept of Being in two primary ways. The first is that of existence, of the ontological dimension of all forms. In this meaning Being is the same as presence, for it is the beingness of the forms. In other words, when we inquire into the ontological dimension of forms, the fact of their existence, we come upon the experience of presence. The existence of a form is its presence, which is a palpable category of experience and not an abstract idea. We have seen that the dimension that clarifies this fact most fully and precisely is the boundless dimension of pure presence. And because essential experience, all the way from the beginning of the journey of ascent through the realization of the dimension of pure presence, is always the experience of presence, we have tended to use the term *Being* interchangeably with *true nature.* However, we have seen that in the dimensions of pure awareness and that of the absolute, and in all the dimensions of descent, true nature is not simply presence or beingness, but rather the coemergence of being and nonbeing, presence and absence.

This brings us to the second sense in which we have been using the word *Being*. We have frequently used it to mean true nature, not just the beingness of forms. We used it to mean true nature in general, regardless of dimension or quality, regardless whether it is presence or emptiness. This is a larger category, but we have used the term this way because true nature is the ontological dimension of forms, regardless of whether this ontological dimension is existence or nonexistence. In other words, the ontological mode, or the mode of existence, can be presence or absence, or both or neither. The other reason we have used the term *Being* in this sense is simply following tradition. The tradition is not exactly that of equating Being with true nature in all of its dimensions, but more of equating it with Reality as a whole, whatever its nature or ontological mode. We have followed this classical usage of the term *Being* because in our view such usage is not different from our usage of it as referring to true nature. Our view, as we have been discussing in this chapter, is that Reality is actually true nature, for there is no reality separate or apart from true nature. Reality is nothing but true nature, in its various dimensions, coemergent with its own manifestation in the various forms. The forms are forms that true nature takes, so true nature is nothing but Reality seen in its subtlety. Alternately, Reality is nothing but true nature seen in its wholeness, totality, and completeness.

The second sense of *Being* refers then to true nature, but also to Reality. In other words, the traditional usage of the term *Being* is general and vague; we make it precise by seeing the inseparability of forms and their ontological dimension. Our discussion addresses the question of the relation between Being and the world. In such a question the second sense of the term *Being* is the relevant one. However, whether we take Being to mean true nature only or Reality as a whole, it is clear from our exploration so far that the world is not separate from Being. If we think of Being as true nature apart from the manifest forms, then these forms of the world are completely nondual and coemergent with Being. And if we think of Being as Reality, true nature nondual with its manifestation, then the world is simply the appearance of Being, again inseparable from Being. There is no world separate from Being.

God

How is the concept of God related to that of Being? The concept of God has not been static; it has developed throughout the history of the three monotheistic religions.[3] We will discuss it only in terms of direct experience, hence only from the mystical perspective. The concept of Being, and that of true nature, tends to be impersonal, where true nature is a ground of manifestation that spontaneously, though intelligently, displays all the manifest forms. This ground is beyond life and death, and has nothing anthropomorphic about it. Where is God, then?

First, we need to appreciate the truth of what we have been discussing as coemergent nonduality. This truth is a oneness that includes any possible form. Oneness of Being is boundless and infinite; thus, by definition, if we find any form separate from this oneness then it is not the oneness we are discussing. Therefore, because there cannot be any particular form outside the oneness of Being, there is no such thing as a God with a particular form. There cannot be a creator God that is a separate form from Being; and if there is such a form, then it is bound to be part of the oneness of Being, as a form generated by the creative dynamism of Being. And if we think of God as an infinite, formless, and boundless reality, as some religions believe, then He is one of the dimensions of true nature. Such formless reality is bound to be inseparable from the wholeness of Being, for this nondual wholeness is both a horizontal and vertical unity. To contemplate a formless reality separate from the wholeness of Being would indicate the possibility of separateness, which contradicts the fundamental truth of this wholeness. And we have seen in chapter 21, it does not make sense to think of a dimension deeper than the absolute, so this formless dimension will have to be the absolute or one of the other dimensions.[4]

The important thing about the concept of God, which is not accounted for by our discussion of true nature and Being, is that God is a reality that functions, wills, and responds, personally. Because God is personal and acts in a personal manner, we tend to think of this reality in anthropomorphic terms. We cannot ordinarily conceive of how a personal being who acts in personal ways exists without being a particular form, for personalness and personal action are attributes of individual, usually human, beings. But since it does not make sense for there to be a personal being with an individual form who can generate the universe of Being without its own form being generated by it, we can get into all kinds of convoluted ideas to account for the possibility of a personal God. Therefore, we need to resort to our direct experience to understand the notion of a personal God. This is what mystical teachings do.

In the particular path we are discussing, that of the Diamond Approach, there is a place for a personal God. The path includes attitudes, states, and conditions that are best conceptualized in terms of relationship to a personal God. But the important thing is that the perspective of the Diamond Approach makes it possible to have direct experiences that help us understand and appreciate what the concept of a personal God can mean. This is because this perspective includes, as an important part, a rare understanding of the personal. We discussed in chapter 15, and in more detail in *The Pearl Beyond Price*, our understanding of a particular essential aspect, the personal essence, which gives the soul the sense of being personal. The personal essence gives the soul the capacity for personal contact, personal interaction, and communication. We have discussed the sense of personalness in detail in chapter 5 of *The Pearl Beyond Price*; there we saw it not simply as emotional communication based on historical content, but as a particular essential quality, a platonic form that makes it possible for us to make contact with another soul directly and in an appropriate and attuned manner, a manner that considers and respects the uniqueness of each soul and her individual unfoldment.

We also discussed in the final part of *The Pearl Beyond Price* the process of personalization of the formless-boundless dimensions, which is the individuation of the soul on these dimensions. This is because the personal essence is also the aspect associated with the individuation of the soul, an individuation that develops as the soul's identity shifts to deeper dimensions. Personalization has another side, which complements the individuation of the soul on the boundless dimensions. This is the personalization of the boundless dimensions themselves. In other words, as the soul learns to be a pearl, personal essence, on a particular boundless dimension, it becomes possible for her to experience this dimension integrated with the aspect of the personal essence. More exactly, we can experience the dimension of pure presence, for example, not only as a boundless and infinite omnipresence, pure and undifferentiated, but as omnipresence inseparable from the personal quality. The personal quality of essence, the pearly quality, can pervade the pure omnipresence, in a complete coemergence. We then experience everything as a oneness of Being but with a personal quality. In other words, Being can be personal, but without having to be an individual form. This is the personalization of the pure presence boundless dimension.

Furthermore, we can have experiences of being this personal oneness of Being holding the individual soul, loving her and caring for her. However, the individual soul is not separate from the omnipresence here, but is part of it, a cell in the cosmic body. We can also experience this condition from the perspective of the individual soul. We then experience ourselves as a cell in the oneness of Being, its offspring, held by it but also loving and appreciating it, feeling grateful to it. This will feel like a personal love and a personal relationship between the individual soul and the personal Being.

The personalization of Being is a process that goes through all the boundless dimensions of the journeys of ascent and descent. It culminates in the personalization of the wholeness of Being, with all of the boundless dimensions in coemergent nonduality with each other and all manifest forms. We arrive then at a personal Reality, boundless and unified Being with a personal quality, a Reality with which we can have a personal relationship. Yet, it is not the normal idea of relationship, for there is no separation between the individual soul and the personal Being; and the personal Being is not an entity, not a particular form, but the wholeness of Reality.

One specific characteristic of the personal Being is that it includes in its coemergence the logos dimension. This dimension of creative dynamism gives our experience of personal Being the sense that it personally acts and responds. Being is what creates and sustains everything, through its logos dimension. It is what makes anything happen, what moves and transforms all manifest forms. It is the only doer. However, since it is now personalized we experience it as personal doing. In other words, personal Being acts in a personal manner, where this action is nothing but the creative display of the logos, now integrated with the personal quality of essence. In the self-realization of personal Being, we experience ourselves as the wholeness of Reality, so we do not only feel personal but realize we are a dynamic and active cosmic presence. We can actually experience ourselves, as this cosmic dynamic presence, moving the winds and the stars. We feel that all that happens in the universe happens through our personal will and intelligence. This is not the will and intelligence of the individual soul, but of the cosmic Being, the personal boundless and infinite Being.

Such cosmic personal functioning has a sense of being integrated and organized. In other words, it has a sense of self-organization that makes us feel that all the cosmic action is integrated into an interconnected coherent whole. This is due to the integration of the personal essence into the wholeness of Being. As we have discussed in chapter 4, and in *The Pearl Beyond Price*, the personal essence is the aspect associated with individuation, which means it is related to autopoiesis, self-organization, and coherent integration, which amounts to autonomy. The personal essence is the prototype of the maturation of the soul from being a formless and unstructured individual conscious presence to being an autonomous person with unique development, capacities for original functioning, and the ability for personal contact and communication. It is the prototype of the individuated soul, the true meaning of personhood. Thus the personal essence is the prototype of the self-organized, cohesive, and individuated functioning that we see in living organisms. It gives the mature soul the sense that she is the source of her actions, and that her actions are truly hers, original to her, even though the soul recognizes that she is an inseparable cell in the oneness of Being. This is the essential counterpart to the ego sense of being the agent and center of one's action.

These characteristics of the personal essence now appear in the new integration of boundless personal Being. Therefore, in the experience of this wholeness, we realize there is a sense of individuation, which is more like a feeling and recognition of organized and coherent functioning. We experience this oneness as a sense of individuated and personal wholeness, whose actions are coherent, self-organized, and organizing. This is almost like being a person, but a person with no particular form. We arrive here at a condition of Being where there is personalness, self-organization, individuation, cohesive functioning, and will, but with no hint of anthropomorphizing. This personal Being is not a form, it does not have arms and legs, or a white beard, and does not premeditate and discriminate in its actions. Personal Cosmic Being acts in total spontaneity, for its action is the dynamic creativity of the logos. It acts with total attunement and responsiveness for it possesses infinite intelligence, the boundless intelligence of true nature that appears in the orderly flow of the pearly logos. We find this condition of Being to be the closest, in our experience, to the concept of a personal God.[5]

God is not something different from Being, or true nature. It is one significant potential of the wholeness of Being, a particular way that this wholeness can manifest itself in our perception and understanding. Being can be impersonal, simply the true nature and ground of all; it can also be personal, as the creative Reality that is constantly generating manifestation and relating to it in a personal way.[6] Furthermore, God is not separate from creation. The world is the creation of the personal God, but it is also the face of God. The world, in all its dimensions and forms, is simply the appearance of the body of God, and also God's mind and heart. The world is a theophany.

The two facets, world/cosmos and God/Being, are intimately related. The world/cosmos is the appearance of God/Being, and God/Being is the nature and source of the world/cosmos. They are two facets of the same Reality. We can think of God/Being as true nature apart from the forms it manifests, which is one way some traditional teachings conceptualize the situation; but then the world/cosmos is the inseparable creation of God/Being, its external facet. In either case, there is no separation. In fact there is perfect coemergent nonduality.

From Macrocosm to Microcosm

The personal wholeness of Being is an integration of all the dimensions of Reality in an individuated or personal way. Therefore it is a cosmic pearl. Since it integrates all aspects and dimensions of true nature it is a diamond cosmic pearl. Since it also integrates these with all the manifest forms of reality, we refer to it as the *macrocosm pearl*. The macrocosm pearl is not simply the macrocosm, which is the wholeness of Being, Reality with all dimensions and forms coemergent in it. It is a personal macrocosm, a personal God. The macrocosm pearl possesses more structure than the macrocosm, or impersonal Being. This is parallel to how the soul is initially structureless, but develops into the pearl beyond price, which structures it into a real functioning person.

The form of personal essence is a luminous white pearl of presence. However, the macrocosm pearl is not exactly a pearl the way the personal essence is. It is not a form, not a rounded presence. It possesses the pearly luminosity and texture of the personal essence, as well as the faceted crystalline quality of diamonds, but it is an infinite, boundless field with no shape or form. It has the feeling of individuated totality, and the sense of coherent functioning, as if it is a functioning unit, but it is not a unit amongst other units.[7] It is simply a functional wholeness with a personal and self-organizing quality.

Understanding the macrocosm pearl takes us to the microcosm pearl, the individual personalization of coemergent nondual Being. This is the culmination of the personalization process that we discussed in detail in *The Pearl Beyond Price*, where the individual soul matures through the inner journey into an integrated and individuated essential person. The soul develops and individuates by realizing the personal essence, the pearl beyond price. This individuation develops by integrating into the pearl the various aspects and dimensions. By integrating the dimensions of descent it finally arrives at the full personal integration, the microcosm pearl. It is the individuation of the soul that personalizes all aspects and dimensions of Reality. We experience it in the form of a crystalline or diamond pearl, a faceted squishy roundedness, an exquisite synthesis of fullness of personal presence, clarity of awareness, sharp diamond facets, and the impossibly total absence of the absolute. We feel full and empty, personal and precise, integrated but totally spontaneous and free.

We experience ourselves as a differentiated form that the macrocosm manifests in a particular way. (See *The Pearl Beyond Price*, chapter 39, for more discussion of the microcosm pearl.) There are a few important insights here. The first is that the microcosm pearl is not a separate existence, not a self-existing unit; rather, it is an extension and prolongation of the macrocosm pearl. The soul experiences her complete individuation inseparable from Being, as a differentiated but not dissociated cell in the cosmic body. This insight addresses the question about the true relation between the facets of self/soul and God/Being. The soul is an inseparable individual expression of coemergent Being, and her individuation is the inseparable expression of divine Being.

The soul is not only an expression of coemergent Being, for everything is an expression; she is a special kind of expression. She has the potential to consciously experience herself as an expression of Being and to consciously experience and know Being in its totality; hence she is the only individual manifest form we know that has such potential. Also, she has the potential to become an individual replica of the personal Being, as an integrated totality, an individuated soul, a real person. Furthermore, this development is always unique. No two souls develop identically, though they begin with fundamentally the same potential. Because of this each soul possesses a unique function in the totality of Reality, with a specific contribution, and an original combination of qualities.[8] The microcosm pearl is actually inseparable from one's work, understanding, contribution, and life; for it is the unique integration of the soul's potential that makes all these possible and makes them what they are. One's learning and work is intimately connected to the pearl because these are some of the most important contexts where the soul develops into a diamond pearl. Therefore, part of the process of realization of the microcosm pearl is to recognize and appreciate one's realization, understanding, and contribution, which can pervade the microcosm pearl with the rich amber syrup of essential value. But it is also important to recognize one's development as a development out of the absolute, expressing and serving it. In other words, it is always the absolute, or coemergent Being, that is always developing the soul. More accurately, the development of the soul is simply the development of a particular special form that Being manifests. Such recognition increases the blackness of the absolute in the experience of the diamond pearl, deepening the amber of value until it is indistinguishable from the darkness of mystery. It is the ripe fruit of the evolution of the universe; our apprehension of it fills the pearl with the apricot nectar of fulfillment and the rich love of gratitude.

Freedom versus Service

The relationship of the soul to the macrocosm, and specifically to its absolute essence, becomes clearly delineated by the advent of a new diamond vehicle that manifests as part of the journey of descent, the freedom vehicle. It clarifies where lies the true freedom of the soul, and how this freedom is inseparable from the life of service. Among the many elements of the infinite wisdom inherent to this vehicle, one that is paramount to the soul in terms of her life and development, is the objective and precise wisdom regarding the soul's role in the cosmic manifestation. What is important about it for our life on earth is that it contains the objective wisdom of what an individual being is in relation to the cosmos, and what his or her function is in actuality. The freedom vehicle clearly indicates this wisdom, which reveals our presence as a direct manifestation and extension of the absolute into cosmic manifestation. It is the absolute, nonlocal, and nonextended; yet it is a form localized in the world of time and space. It is a bridge between timelessness/spacelessness and time/space. It is itself beyond time and space, but protrudes into them, bringing through its emanations the richness inherent in the absolute.

In realizing the freedom vehicle, we realize that each of us is an objective, precise instrument for the absolute. We exist as its eyes, its mouths, its ears, its arms, its legs, its genitals, its brains, its nervous systems, its mind, its intellect, its heart, and so forth. The complete and natural function of any of these organs, and hence of our bodies and souls, is to be an instrument of the absolute, allowing the absolute to behold and experience its own creation, its own display of its hidden treasures. To be fully ourselves is to faithfully serve the absolute, to purely and selflessly do its bidding. In serving it, in surrendering our wills completely to its dynamic will, we find our happiness and fulfillment. We cannot be happy by trying to fulfill our separate and self-centered wishes and desires, if they conflict with the natural outflow of the logos of true nature. Recognizing our selfishness and egotism, and understanding how these positions dissociate us from our true nature, allows us to align our wishes with the natural flow of Reality. First we need to align our identity with the absolute ipseity; but deeper still, we need to align our will with the will of the ipseity.

As the freedom vehicle we can recede and merge into our inner nature, which is the vastness of the absolute mystery. We are then the vast stillness and silence that underlies all that is, an absence without which no presence can be. But also, as the freedom vehicle we can manifest as individuals in the world, bringing forth and expressing the qualities of the absolute, and thus serving the absolute. In effect, we are either the absolute mystery or its absolute servant. There is nowhere else to be.

We begin to understand service precisely and objectively. To serve is not a matter of serving a person or creature. It is not a matter of serving a community, even humanity. All that is, all forms and sentient beings, exist for the absolute to behold its creative display. All beings are instruments toward this end. Because that is their true and objective function, their true happiness and complete fulfillment rests in totally fulfilling their function, in completely being themselves. For beings to completely be themselves is to serve their source, which is actually their innermost identity. To be happy is to do what they are designed to do, which is to be instruments for the absolute truth. There is no distinction between being authentically oneself and serving absolute truth. The two are absolutely identical.

We definitely need to serve other human beings and other sentient beings. But we need to remember what serving them means. To serve them is to guide them toward their greatest happiness and fulfillment, which means to guide them toward their true nature and their function in relation to this nature. This again is to serve the absolute truth. We serve it by assisting its various manifestations to attain the functions by which they can serve it, which is identical with assisting their self-realization. In other words, when we objectively understand and appreciate what service is, we realize that there is no true difference between serving human beings and serving God.

To truly serve humanity is to help humanity attain its full potential, in whatever small or significant ways we can. Humanity attains its full potential in fulfilling its pattern as the personal expression of true nature, as a species microcosm. The species microcosm is in the image of the divine macrocosm, but it is also its representative, its expression, its vice-regent, its instrument in the world. We discover that as human beings our function is to express the absolute, to be a mouthpiece for the absolute, a revelatory expression of it that reveals it. The greatest development of the soul is to serve the absolute by expressing it.[9]

To be an instrument of the absolute is to be its absolute servant, which is the same as being a complete, thoroughly ripened, and mature human adult. This is human happiness and fulfillment. This is the station of realization of the freedom vehicle, which is the reason we frequently refer to it as the body of service. We develop a new subtle body, which inherently recognizes its function as servicing the truth of Reality. It is a precise, clear, totally objective wisdom, completely free from subjective bias or reaction. This functioning may appear as a limitation when compared with the station of abiding in the absolute, and students tend to react to it in this manner, yet it is actually a deeper and higher realization. For in this station there is no preference at all; there is no need at all for any state or condition, not even for that of the absolute.

Our freedom is that we are the absolute in its mystery, but at the same time we are also the individual soul with all of her development, life, and maturation. We are essence with all of its dimensions and aspects, but we are also the adult human being, a matured and completed person.

24 Separation of Soul, God, and World

WE HAVE USED THE NOTION of the triad of soul/self, God/Being, and cosmos/world as part of the context of discussion in this book. We have followed this context as a particular thread that we picked up whenever our exploration of the inner journey gave us the necessary understanding to deeply or completely reflect on it. We can now collect our insights into a focused consideration of this basic triad.

We are not original in using the notion of the basic triad. Throughout the history of Western civilization many individuals who thought deeply, and desired to understand life and existence in its fundamentals, formulated their love of truth in questions regarding this triad of soul, God and cosmos. We can see this in ancient Western philosophy and metaphysics, continuing through the Middle Ages, and remaining an important element in philosophical investigation up to the present time, just as we can see it in the development of all the monotheistic religions, and their mystical currents. Formulating the triad in the terms of self, Being, and world brings it closer to the Eastern formulation of self, ultimate truth, and manifest world, promulgated by the teachings of Buddhist and Hindu philosophy and spirituality.[1]

In modern times, including our postmodern era, this triad appears in three specialized fields of interest or research, three distinct disciplines. Soul appears mostly in the field of humanities, especially in that of psychology, but as the study of and work with the psyche or self, and its inner mechanisms and manifestations. God is the focus of religion and spirituality, and when this is cast in the form of the study of 'Being' it becomes also a subject for philosophy. Cosmos or world is exclusively the concern of physical science in its various specializations. In other words, we find ourselves in the situation where this basic triad is not seen as a triad at all, but as three disconnected areas of interest with very little relationship or interaction.

Our interest is partly in whether the dissociation and specialization are fundamental or accidental; or, alternately, if they constitute a particular meaningful development.

It is a well-known historical fact that the dissociation of science from religion in the Western world has been a particular development and it cannot be denied that it is, in a great measure, an emancipation. It would be difficult to imagine the twentieth century's phenomenal advancement in both scientific knowledge and technology without this dissociation. This separation has also led to the development of what we now know as the modern field of psychology and its expression in various psychotherapeutic schools. A concurrent and related development has been the gradual secularization of society and the relegation of religion to a compartment of life, instead of being—but for few exceptions—the pervasive atmosphere that people live in, as it was for many ancient societies.[2]

One general result of this separation has been the material improvement of the life of most of humanity, a development that is usually lauded as the mark of our times. Clearly there are advantages to separating the fields of study into specialized units.

Yet, along with its benefits, this dissociation and its resulting specialization and advances have been widely criticized as having less wholesome consequences. Our exploration in this book not only casts doubt on whether this dissociation is still necessary—or if it has even been necessary until now—but also can help us to understand this process of dissociation.

The significance of the modern dissociation of the three major sectors of human life is more profound than most of us suspect. It is important not only for the overall development of thought, but specifically for the evolution of groundbreaking new paradigms that determine the development of cultures and societies, as well as advances in science and technology. This development has touched the foundations of our understanding of humanity, in terms of our beliefs about what is human, what human life is about and what it can be, and how we can attain happiness and fulfill our human potential.

Existential Emptiness of Modernity

The orientation of modern and postmodern times has been criticized by many thinkers and philosophers as having a general dehumanizing effect, due in part to our increased dependence on science and technology. Our material improvement, they argue, has happened at the expense of inner spiritual and moral richness, resulting in a pervasive psychic emptiness. The human effects of this development have been described by various significant Western thinkers, and also by broad movements in philosophy, psychology, and even physical science. We can see this, for example, in the work of Nietzsche, who described one consequence in his notion of the death of God. We can see it in the development of phenomenology and existentialism in philosophy, as exemplified in the work of Heidegger and his insight into how Western philosophy has forgotten Being. We see it also in the phenomenal increase of interest in Eastern spiritual teachings and shamanic approaches, in the revival of interest in the various Western mystical schools, and even in the latest rise of fundamentalism in all the major faiths. Even though what is called the New Age movement contains many superficial and distorted elements, it is an expression of the awareness of a certain lack and a sense of emptiness; it is a response to a felt need.

We can see the response to this need in the emergence and development of humanistic, existential, and transpersonal psychologies that recognize the underlying emptiness of the positivistically based mainstream of Western psychology. We see it in the rise and proliferation of many approaches and disciplines of the human potential movement, the growth movement, and the many consciousness groups and self-help approaches. These developments in psychology indicate an increasing awareness of the death of soul in our postmodern, primarily psychological, society.

What about psychology's ambiguous and hybrid status, in respect to those of science and religion? Has its dissociation from religion and spirituality helped it in its development, and what should its relation be to both religion and science if it is to achieve optimum development?

In many areas of modern life we see increasing disenchantment in science and technology when it comes to answering the deeper needs of human beings. For more than a century Western science and technology became the religion of secular culture, seeming to hold the promise of salvation for the human masses. This passion about science and technology has been evaporating in the last few decades; although science answers certain questions and meets many important needs, its inability to address others, just as important, has become painfully clear. This awareness has not diminished science or slowed down technology; but thinkers, philosophers, and historians now regard them in a more discriminating light, acknowledging them as materially useful and extremely beneficial, but seeing that other dimensions of human experience are open to other modes of investigation. The recent interest in alternative medicine and ancient Asian approaches to health can also be seen as expressing the awareness of a gap that is left by our scientific medicine.

Although Western thought has led to a great advancement of the human condition and a phenomenal increase in knowledge, the secularism that has attended these developments has led to a fundamental impoverishment of meaning. Many believe that our secular and materialistic culture is an unavoidable result of scientific and technological development.[3] We advance the thesis that the existential emptiness that seems to pervade Western thought and life is due to more fundamental reasons. Science and technology are not necessarily materialistic, and are not in and of themselves capable of alienating human beings from existential depths and meanings.

We find that approaching this phenomenon from the perspective of the fundamental triad of self/soul, God/Being, cosmos/world gives us a more complete and precise understanding of it and a much deeper appreciation of its genesis and development. We believe that the dissociation of the triad, fundamental to modern Western thought, is a much more primary cause for this existential emptiness and impoverishment of inner life. The dissociation that manifests in Western thought is part of what conditions the individual soul in such a way that she is dissociated from her being and from her world. This dissociation fractures our experience of ourselves and our world in a way that leads to alienation and existential impoverishment.

We see that the isolating separation of the basic triad has been a double-edged sword, leading to increased discrimination and specialization that has benefited humanity in a completely new way in its history, while at the same time stripping the three elements of their substance by denying their interrelatedness. Can we have our scientific and technological development and still retain the potential for existential depth and inner richness of life?

Our study in this book has clarified what each concept of the triad objectively stands for, which has helped us to recognize the true relationships between the three. We have seen that these concepts refer to objective, actual categories of universal human experience. We have also seen that the modern separation between them is not an inherent one, which means it is a particular development that the West has found. We have also shown how the elements of the triad admit of a natural connectivity, and that this natural unity can embrace the modern differentiation and its advantages. Unfolding the vision of the path of the Diamond Approach, we have been able to recognize a view of Reality that respects the advances resulting from the triadic dissociation, but appreciates them as developments from a differentiation out of a more basic unity. This view makes it possible for us to realize the fullness of each element of the triad; it reverses the alienating effects of dissociation, while at the same time being able to fully appreciate the advantages of specialization, recognizing them as the natural development of greater discrimination. In chapters 5 and 7, it was shown that precise discrimination need not lead to dissociation. We can apply this insight to the development of various fields of research. The specialized fields can be seen as the products of focal settings of the investigating consciousness and can be differentiated and discriminated infinitely without departing from an underlying unity that functions as the ground of all differentiations and discriminations. This is because discrimination is inherent to Being itself; and if we can maintain some contact with basic knowledge, we can make whatever discrimination we need without having to dissociate our personal experience from the dimension of presence.

This view does not imply a return to the original unity before differentiation, which could only disregard and nullify the advances of the human condition resulting from the developments of the last two centuries. Our view can help us to approach our situation with new synthetic understanding, because it recognizes a necessary inseparability of the basic triad and utilizes the particularly Western approach to truth of research and inquiry. The resulting understanding actually benefits by integrating into its view and methodology the major insights of the various branches of Western knowledge.

We see here an approach to redeeming the fullness of the elements of the triad. This is possible because the view that arises from this study can embrace the developments of Western specialization while understanding and embodying the underlying unity of the triad. It must be clear by now how this understanding can bring about a wholeness in our lives, where a fundamental fabric of felt and lived meaning, constituted by the five boundless dimensions of true nature, pervades everything in which we engage. Our study has shown the potential for us to be authentic and for our human potential to be fulfilled—physically, psychologically, and spiritually—while enjoying a meaningful connection to our world, a world that we can directly know as expressing a transcendental mystery, a mystery that we can participate in as the underlying foundation of our existence. This wholeness, rather than being antithetical to our Western civilization, can be a support for it to flourish in new ways, and a guide for it to address our human needs more fully and completely.

Our approach will be more effective if we can explore the history of development of the various branches of the triad in a way that illuminates their insights and accomplishments in relation to their underlying unity. This will be necessary for integrating our understanding of these accomplishments into the larger picture, for by understanding how a particular finding or development is situated within the unifying fabric underlying the triad, we can embrace it without compromising our wholeness. In fact, it will then only enrich our wholeness through the greater discrimination and development.

Historical Perspective

We have seen that the individuated soul is fundamentally inseparable from Being, while God/Being is inseparable from the world. The three are simply inseparable facets of the same Reality, which is a coemergent nonduality. As we saw in chapter 23, true nature is the truth of

Reality, the world of manifestation is its appearance, and the soul is its special offspring that functions as the mirror in which it experiences and knows itself. Separation between the three is nonexistent, and when we see such separation it is our perception that is faulty and our mind that is ignorant. The question now is how did Western thought arrive at the present dissociation of the basic triad if it is fundamentally a triadic unity, and can we find some meaning in such development? In its classical period, Western civilization flourished through the efforts of individuals who thought deeply, and desired to understand life and existence in its fundamentals, conceived their love of truth in questions regarding the triad of soul, God, and cosmos. There are strong indications, and many scholars have argued this point, that the ancients did not separate investigation of these areas into three distinct disciplines; rather, the wise men and women who concerned themselves with such fundamental questions saw them all as necessary, besides being inseparable, for deeper understanding and authentic human life. That is why the ancient philosophers and investigators were simultaneously psychologists, spiritual adepts, and scientists, among other things. It seems that it was an important part of the development of Western thought that the three facets became separated gradually into three distinct disciplines, what we now know as psychology, religion, and science.[4]

The differentiation and separation of the ancient tradition of wisdom along the lines of the basic triad and into three disciplines has had many positive consequences. But there has been a less obvious, though equally momentous, consequence: the gradual dimming, and for most individuals the loss, of the awareness of the fabric that held the three sides of the basic triad together. The wise ones of ancient times, like the spiritually realized individuals of all ages, sensed the ground of true nature that bound the three sides of the triad—soul/self, God/Being, cosmos/world—together. We are now generally not aware of it, neither are we aware of its absence; for we have grown up in societies that have for a long time implicitly taken the dissociation as real and final.

We are not glorifying ancient times, nor condemning our postindustrial era. We are aware that in ancient times only a few individuals contemplated the fundamental questions of existence, while the majority languished not only in material backwardness and depravity, but also in moral darkness and psychological ignorance. In contrast, our modern world has brought not only increased material comfort and great advances in medicine and health, but also greater opportunity for education and increased awareness of human values and rights. The isolating separation of the basic triad has obviously been a double-edged sword. It has led to increased discrimination and specialization, benefiting humanity in completely novel ways, while at the same time blinding us to the ground of true nature through a process of reification. We discussed in chapter 4 how normal and logical knowledge differentiated all the way to dissociation from its ground of pure presence, a dissociation that resulted in the forgetfulness of the Greek's notion of *nous*, direct and basic knowing, where knowing and presence are inseparable. This mechanism has been the primary way that Western thought dissociated the three facets of the triadic unity. For by dissociating knowledge from its ground of Being, both world and soul lose this ground of essential presence; and without this ground we can only see them dissociated from each other and from the concerns of religion and spirituality, while the latter then attempt to exclusively focus on the ground.[5]

One of the results of this dissociation is that many have turned to Eastern spiritual teachings to find answers and ways to reconnect to a deeper reality. However, we take the view that the recourse to Eastern thought and religion is not going to completely remedy our situation, regardless of how useful it is for some individuals; for the interest is strong only in a few cultural spheres in various locations. In fact, the major schools of Western thought and philosophy remain largely isolated from this Eastern influence. Furthermore, these approaches do not fully answer the Western thirst for complete knowledge, largely ignoring the accomplishments of Western civilization. These accomplishments, in addition to their material benefits, express very deep roots of the Western mind, a mind interested in life and the world in a way foreign to Eastern thought, a mind that developed from appreciating and embodying a particular approach to truth.[6] This is one reason many Eastern schools are trying to modify their teachings to make them more palatable and accessible to the Western mind, and why there has also been an increasing interest in ancient Western schools of spirituality. Moreover, it is Western culture that is actually spreading through the world, with its values, which are based on the triadic split.

Therefore, it would seem that a Western view that recognizes and appreciates the faceted unity of the triad is a necessity for our times. This view existed in Western thought in its classical period, in the origins of Western thought; and because this thought operated within a natural unity, a unity before separation, it might be useful for us to understand that thought, and see how such unity can arise again, but at a higher or new level that naturally embraces and utilizes the results of differentiation, discrimination, and separation. We see the possibility of such redemption in the appreciative understanding of the triad of self/soul, God/Being, world/cosmos as the trifaceted Reality, where all dimensions of Being are in coemergent nonduality. We see it specifically in the understanding of the five boundless dimensions of Reality, and how they are related to awareness, knowledge, change, and so on; for by understanding how knowing is intimately related to awareness and presence, it is possible for us to understand how the two can be differentiated without having to be dissociated. The differentiation can then lead to a greater discrimination in knowledge, as has happened in Western thought, while remaining near to its roots in the presence of Being. The differentiation can also lead to a deepening of mystical experience but without dissociating it from analytical insight that can both develop it and guard it against superstition and imagination. We can then have a differentiation that leads to greater discrimination without alienation, to a greater scientific and technological advancement without losing contact with the spiritual depths of Reality. Both science and spirituality can benefit from this. This view appreciates and learns from our Western roots in the *nous* and logos of ancient Greece with their implicit triadic unity, and their developments and augmentation in Judaism, Christianity, and Islam, without having to simply regress to the past. This way we can live a primordial unity and still embrace the useful contributions of Western civilization.

Parallels

We can see an intimate parallel in the development of Western thought to that of the individual soul. We find that the normal development of the soul, as reflected in the everyday experience of the average adult, recapitulates the development of Western thought. Our explorations throughout this book amply demonstrate this insight. We saw in chapters 1 and 12 that as the soul develops as an individual with character and identity, with the normal emotional and mental capacities, she slowly dissociates from her essential ground. A duality emerges between soul and essence that becomes bedrock reality, a duality that naturally and spontaneously separates the original unity of Reality.

Soul, originally coemergent with her true nature, turns into a duality of self and spirit; and Reality becomes self, God/Being/spirit, and world—three separate entities. The soul becomes a self, an ego-self, that may or may not believe it has spirit, soul, or true nature. But this spirit is now something separate, disembodied, otherworldly, and something to which some of us want to attain. This spirit is now somehow mysteriously related to a spiritual world, where God or Being rules. The cosmos, on the other hand, becomes a physical world, mostly dead and inert matter with pockets of life and consciousness here and there. In other words, the ego development of the soul includes a basic dissociation from the ground of Being. Such dissociation is at the root of the isolation of the triadic unity. We see, then, that ego development progresses similarly to the way Western thought has developed. Furthermore, we have seen that ego development can be understood to be necessary for the development of discriminating awareness. At infancy the soul is coemergent with her true nature, but her discriminating and cognitive capacities are not developed enough for her to recognize her true nature. Such innate ignorance seems to necessitate some kind of development where the cognitive capacities can mature to the extent of being able to recognize the ground of the soul in a conscious and discriminating cognition. This development turns out to include the normal ego development of the soul, in which not only does the soul differentiate and dissociate from its essential ground, but such differentiation and dissociation also seems to be an integral part of the process of developing the cognitive and discriminating capacities of the soul.

More specifically, as we have seen in this book, the dissociation of soul from essence occurs primarily by, and parallel to, the development of normal representational knowledge, which is conceptual discrimination divorced from the ground of Being. Ordinary knowledge develops by the soul abstracting out the outlines of concepts from basic knowledge, and holding their reifications in the mind. Such knowledge develops to greater discrimination as the mind creates more abstract concepts and concepts of these concepts, in an increasing complexity and abstraction. This is exactly how Western thought developed its capacity for greater and greater discrimination that finally led to our science and technology. Ego development occurs basically by taking these reified concepts as real constituents of Reality. The soul identifies with the reified concepts of her own experience of herself, which become her self-representations; by thus defining herself through representational knowledge she loses contact with her essential ground, which cannot be captured in representational concepts.

Western thought has developed similarly, by taking these reified concepts to be real constituents of Reality. In fact, this is the distinguishing hallmark of the positivist philosophy of Western science. By abstracting these concepts from the field of basic knowledge, and developing greater discrimination through greater levels of abstraction, Western thought developed science and technological advancement; but by taking such knowledge to be the only possible and valid one, it has dissociated itself from the presence that is the ground of basic knowledge. In other words, Western thought has dissociated science from religion through the same process by which ego dissociates self from essence. Ego development finally results in an ego-self separate from a disembodied spirit, while Western thought's development has ultimately resulted in a world separate from God. And just as ego development is the process by which the soul begins her individuation, leading to a practically and emotionally functioning individuality, a development necessary for living in the world, the development of Western thought has resulted in a science and technology that has been quite useful for living in the world. We see this further parallel particularly between practical ego functionality and technological scientific advancement. Many thinkers have observed this parallel between egoic functionality and technological efficiency, but they have stopped at that; yet it is clear to us that ego development is a stage in a larger process, and the parallelism needs to be extended to the further stages of development.

The Promise of the West

Before we discuss this further parallel we need to recognize that it is amply clear that ego development recapitulates the development of Western thought. It might be more accurate to view the development of Western thought as recapitulating the normal development of the soul, because this latter development is universal and basic to all humanity. Nevertheless, we prefer the view that the two developments are manifestations of the same dynamic in Reality, one individual and the other cultural. Both involve a process of differentiation that develops to the extreme of dissociation, and both show that such a process seems to be necessary for developing cognitive discrimination and efficient worldly functionality. The cultural development actually includes Eastern thought, and not only Western thought. To understand this we need to remember that ego development of the soul results in the duality of a functional ego-self and a disembodied spirit.

So what is the parallel in cultural development to the disembodied spirit? We have seen it as the dissociation of science and religion, but we can also see it in a larger global context. We can see it in the dissociation of Western and Eastern thought. More particularly, we can see it in the fact that the West has developed discriminating understanding to its extreme in science and technology, and the East has proportionally neglected that and developed the other side, the spiritual and mystical side. In fact, East is traditionally associated with spirit in many fairy tales and teaching stories, because it is connected with the Sun; however, such association also has mystical and spiritual roots. Eastern thought and philosophy have tended to emphasize the life of spirit, transcendence, nondifferentiation, nonconceptuality, freedom from the cycle of birth and death, and so on. It definitely has tended to move away from the greater discrimination of the cognitive mind, as clearly demonstrated by Zen and other Eastern developments. Although the differences between East and West are basically a matter of emphasis, there are enough differences in the currents of thought of East and West that we can say there has been a global expression of the pattern of differentiation and dissociation, where the West has tended to embody egoic functionality and worldly wisdom while the East has tended to embody spiritual depth and the wisdom of true nature.

To extend the parallel we return to our exploration in this book, where we saw how the soul develops beyond ego structure. The development of the soul progresses from the stage of ego development to that of essential development, which she achieves through an integration of her essential ground, but now with discriminating knowledge. The discriminating knowing itself develops through this integration toward basic knowledge, as finally embodied in the dimension of pure being, the *nous* of the ancient Greeks. The outcome is the essentially individuated soul, which can develop all the way to the microcosm diamond pearl. The microcosm diamond pearl is a soul that has individuated by the integration of her worldly experience and wisdom with the various aspects and dimensions of her true nature. It is also the individual self-realization of Being with precise awareness and discriminating basic knowledge. If Western thought has developed according to a universal pattern that expresses itself also in the development of the individual soul, then it could develop further toward a higher and more structured level of unity. In other words, we can view the dissociation of the triad in our modern and postmodern Western thought as a stage that can be followed by other stages, all natural to the development of thought. We can envision a further stage, parallel to the stage of essential development of the soul, and further still toward the stage of the microcosm diamond pearl. This will be a stage where Western thought redeems itself, just as the soul can, by finding the unity underlying its dissociation, by appreciating the value of differentiation and discrimination without having to continue the dissociation. This way it can redeem itself by integrating its discriminating knowing with its ground of Being, while still embracing and benefiting from the advancements that have resulted from its dissociation of this knowledge. Western thought then has the potential and possibility of moving to a further stage, where its science can be grounded in the presence of basic knowledge, of the *nous*, and where its spirituality can achieve the diamond crisp discrimination of this same basic knowledge. A true bridge will then appear between science and spirituality, to their mutual benefit and evolution.[7] Just as ego development is a stage of individuation that can lead to essential individuation, Western thought has arrived at ego individuation, expressed in worldly efficient functionality; this can yet progress to essential individuation, with this functionality grounded in the presence and truth of Being. Furthermore, we can view the development of Western civilization as a cultural movement toward individuation, which has arrived only at the ego stage. In other words, Western culture as a whole can be seen as developing toward being a pearl, a cultural pearl rather than an individual one. To be a pearl means to be integrated in a self-organizing and cohesive manner and to function in a harmonious unified balance, just as ego strength manifests and even more so the soul's pearly individuation. And because Western thought is not anymore confined to the geographic West but is spreading worldwide through the transport of Western technologies and values, this pearly development may turn out to be a global one. The fact that globalization is already progressing in many sectors of human interest can be seen as indicating a movement toward an individuated unity of humanity. Furthermore, globalization may include, as an important part of it, the meeting and unification of Western and Eastern thought, in a new and novel synthesis. In other words, the movement toward globalization is bound to include thought and culture, religion and values. Such movement can be at the level of ego development, or it can move to the essential stage. And since West and East have historically differentiated in a general manner into the egoic-logical and the spiritual-nonconceptual, respectively, it would seem that such pearly integration is a distinct possibility. That will mean humanity has the possibility of developing into a species pearl, an integrated and individuated human race. We actually see, by continuing the parallel, that humanity has the potential of developing into a diamond pearl, meaning a humanity that is not only integrated and unified as one harmonious people, but as a unity precisely and clearly aware of its true nature and its connection to the wholeness of Being.

It is interesting that one of the visions that many individuals have when they first discover their essential pearl is that of seeing it as the planet Earth. This vision partly indicates that the Earth is a unified integrated totality, a planetary pearl. For humanity to become a pearl will mean that humanity has the potential of being integrated with the Earth itself as one unified pearl. In fact, the environmental awareness that has been developing in many places, and the increasing wisdom regarding the ecosystem, may indicate a movement in that direction, or the possibility of such a movement. This view may sound far-fetched, and in many ways it is. However, the new paradigm of self-organizing systems directly supports it. This new branch of science, the study of self-organizing systems, understands both the Earth and the ecosystem as self-organizing, self-regenerating systems. The same understanding applies to societies and nations. The soul is also a self-organizing system. For the soul to develop into a pearl means that its self-organization has matured to the stage of being a person, which is a very high level of organization and structure.

We find another parallel here, between the development of the soul and Earth as a whole. Therefore, the potential development of humanity toward pearly organization can be seen as one level of the development of the Earth's self-organizing system. We need to remember in applying our parallels that the development of the soul rarely progresses beyond ego structure. It usually requires a conscious commitment, a great deal of intentional work, a tremendous wisdom, and the essential guidance of Being for the soul to progress to the essential stage. Therefore, even though Western thought possesses the potential to redeem itself in a genuine movement toward triadic unity, this is statistically improbable. There are, however, many indications of this movement, as we have discussed above, which may mean that it is a real possibility. But we view it as a long-term possibility, which may take thousands or hundreds of thousands of years, perhaps, or even more.[8]

In our view, the development of Western thought has not been haphazard, nor was it fundamentally a wrong turn. The various wisdom traditions tended to see the ego development of duality as a going astray, as the fall of man. However, since this development happens to all human beings, it makes more sense to view it as the lawful and natural development of the soul. And if it does in fact express the same evolutionary movement that Western thought has gone through, then the present stage of Western thought, that of triadic dissociation, is a lawful stage of development. If we recognize it as such, and appreciate it within the context of a larger process of evolution, we will have a better chance of moving toward its redemption.

Vision of Reality

In discussing our approach we have communicated a vision of Reality. This vision includes a view of what Reality is, an experiential and verifiable understanding of its various elements and the relationships between them, and a method of investigation that one can undertake to develop such understanding. The unfoldment of this understanding is a path of wisdom that can culminate in the embodiment of the vision. This embodiment is a particular actualization of the human potential, which manifests as the maturity of the human being.

This vision is particularly significant for our contemporary situation, and has the possibility of returning us to the fullness of our experience and world; because it emphasizes the direct, intuitive, and contemplative approach to truth, while embracing the discursive mental faculty, with its logic, reason, and science. We have seen that the vision recognizes a fundamental unity underlying these two ways of knowing, in a manner that enriches both of them, without compromising either.

It is clear that we do not need to dispense with reason and the scientific method in order to deal with modern emptiness and angst. Our approach has been more of finding a ground of mind and knowing that can support our modern scientific method but at the same time end its isolation, at least in terms of how it views Reality, from direct and contemplative experience. In other words, this vision embodies a way of knowing and an approach to perception and experience that is not in conflict with reason and scientific research. Thus we can acquire and live from both precise spiritual understanding and holistic scientific knowledge, and ultimately from the unified ground in which they are known never to have been actually separate.

Appropriate Vision

Our situation is not simply that we live in a Western culture whose primary mode of thought is the separation of God/Being, world/cosmos, and soul/self. West and East are not as separate from each other as they have been in the past; we can no longer think of them as two isolated traditions. Times have changed. Our era is witnessing the rapid development of a global culture, a world community. Advances in transportation and communication have rendered national and cultural boundaries nearly transparent. Cultures are coming into contact with each other to an unprecedented extent; and, in contrast to other times where there developed pockets of cultural diversity, very few places on Earth now remain untouched by this wave of universalization. Even these isolated or resistant pockets seem likely to be swept up in this inexorable homogenizing current.

Our time is marked by the collapse of major geopolitical divisions, by immense political, economical, cultural, social, and technological changes. The values of Western culture, including notions of democracy, human rights, a free market economy, an emphasis on material comfort and the technology that supports it, and the primacy of individual freedom and autonomy, are spreading over the globe. Steadily these seem to be becoming global human values, interacting in various ways with local and regional values. Furthermore, Eastern influences are beginning to spread in the West, as evident in the availability of Eastern religious practices and literature in many Western locales, as well as the spread of various Asian and African communities in most Western countries. All this is facilitated by accessible and rapid transportation and electronic communication, which are the products of the scientific advances whose history began with the fragmentation of the basic triad.

We are in the midst of this transformation, right at the cusp of the rising wave, and as a result our lives are changing at a dizzying pace. Styles of life, ways of being and doing, and standards of value, are naturally going through an intense process of destructuring and restructuring. The traditional or established ways are rapidly disappearing, mixing with each other, in various degrees of harmony or conflict. It is important to note that one of the main areas of difficulty that many of the traditional cultures experience in coming to terms with modernity is its attendant secularism, and the emptiness and meaninglessness that result from the loss of traditional cultural modes and values.

This advancing globalization, happening at the same time that we are becoming increasingly aware of the subtle emptiness of modern secular Western life, is resulting in many people feeling confused and questioning, consciously or unconsciously, what it means to be human in our times.[9] The destructuring effect of cultural diversity is making many feel the stripping away of the substance of their value systems, reflecting the denuding of the three elements of the triad. They feel it as the loss of the sense of living in a meaningful world. Many now have no sense of having a world that can psychologically hold them and their aspirations in a clearly meaningful way. The pervasive questions become: What is life on Earth? What should life be? How will we live? What are our values? What is important? What is real? What will work? What is appropriate for our times?

If we do not want to simply regress to past solutions, as many fundamentalist movements are trying to do, we will have to ask: What is the vision of being human that is appropriate for our times? To refer to the past for solutions would involve our interpretations of what that was like; this is what fundamentalism does. However, going to the past will not enable us to reach the true underlying fabric that can bring unifying meaning into our life; this fabric is the presence of true nature, which is always in the now, and beyond ordinary mind.

The vision we have been elaborating is also a vision of human existence appropriate in a society that is multicultural, multiracial, and democratic; a society teeming with many philosophies, a multiplicity of points of view, and a plethora of spiritual teachings; and a society enlivened by a free-market economy, where both personal excellence and freedom are important. Our vision of Reality includes a vision of human beings appropriate for our times, for it includes the following considerations.

1. The decline of the sense of cosmos is understood in a way that provides a new and more appropriate sense of a hospitable and meaningful world. Because the perspective of essential aspects and the uniqueness of individuation implicit in the realization of the personal essence are grounded in the boundlessness of true nature, in which manifest reality is seen to arise from a ground deeper than any particular cultural norms and traditions, this vision can serve a world of cultural diversity. Because the sense of world originates from a dimen-

sion of experience deeper than the particular cultural structures, this vision is able to contain them without eliminating differences.

2. Both technical developments and cultural diversity are rendering our society increasingly complex, and our lives barely livable, because of the sheer number of influences, impacts, and demands with which we need to contend. However the ground of our vision is a simplicity beyond content, the simplicity of the absolute. In its realization we are grounded beyond the details, and stable within life's varying and complex stimuli. This simplicity is necessary for us to deal with such amazing complexity without losing our center and balance.

3. We also saw in chapter 21 that this simplicity is solid and fundamental, and hence gives us the capacity to be grounded enough to retain our authenticity and personal uniqueness in the homogenizing global tide.

4. At the same time, this solid simplicity is able to express itself not only as a multileveled consciousness that can unify logical mind and contemplative spirit, but also in a multifaceted personal embodiment that can respond to the variety and multiplicity of impacts and intersections. In other words, in the realization of the microcosm pearl we are able to embody a multifaceted realization of our human potential, which makes it possible for us to respond adequately to the increasing variables in our society. An adequate response here means we can respect and value the truth and uniqueness of each variable, without having to resort to a schizoid isolation, devaluating aggression and vilification, or a reduction of the richness of complexity to a dead and superficial homogenizing unity. In other words, the vision allows for the individual, and for the group, a rich actualization of various and varying elements of the human potential.

5. The speed of change and transformation in our times requires a flexible and open mind that can grow and develop with the acceleration, rather than becoming scattered and lost, or impeded and stuck. This openness is available to us through the realization of the spacious quality of true nature and the flexibility of the soul's dynamism.

6. The vision fulfills the way the Western mind values life, by providing an understanding and a path that can lead to an integration of the various dimensions of being a human being living a normal life

on Earth: physical, psychological, spiritual, social, political, ethical, and so on. In other words, the vision provides answers and solutions to such questions as: How can a stockbroker be spiritual? Is it possible? Can one be an expert in a scientific field and not lose one's spiritual connection? Can one be spiritual and not forget that there are many people hungry, or that there are constant wars in many places on the Earth? How can one pursue personal excellence in a human community and still fully engage in the inner quest for liberation and spiritual realization? How can one have a job, family, friends, interests, creative activities, and so on, and experience them as mutually supportive with one's inner quest for meaning and liberation? How can one pursue personal excellence and the inner quest but find this not only nonconflictual with but supportive of others' well-being?

This vision of Reality can satisfy the burning need of the individual who wants to live an authentic life, one who wants to find out what real humanity is, one who is hearing the inner call and feels moved to engage the soul's quest for ultimate truth, liberation, and realization. Traditional religions and spiritual teachings arose within much more isolated communities, where life was simpler and the choices more limited, where the demands on one's intelligence were considerably less complex. All these religions and spiritual traditions, as well as many more recent developments, including various forms of philosophy and psychology, are presenting their visions of what a human being is or should be. Our time is unique for such individuals in that all of these visions, ancient and new, are available. Each ancient tradition presents its vision as it originated, or in one or another of its developments throughout the years, or modified to one degree or another to address our times. Many new approaches are being developed, some original and some eclectic.

Each teaching is an embodiment that presents to the world a certain vision of Reality, including an understanding of what it is to be a human being. A spiritual school is successful if it actually embodies its vision. That is the contribution of the school to the community at large, and not just to the individuals involved in it.

However, most of us, when we feel the inner urge for meaning and liberation, may simply want to hook into a psychological, philosophical, or spiritual teaching that will respond to this most primordial call. It is only after a very long time, maybe years, until some realization and fulfillment, that we have the capacity to ask how this is appropriate to life on the planet in this century, at this time. For most people at the beginning of the spiritual journey, it is in some sense an idle question, because we are so hungry, consumed with a passionate desire to just find the connection to Being for ourselves.

Each teaching presents us with a vision of what it is to be human, but few actually offer one that attempts to resolve the Western predilection for separation and specialization or to address the cultural and intellectual complexity of our times.

Epilogue

THE INNER JOURNEY IS MANY THINGS. It is a journey of adventure and discovery; a journey of maturation and completeness; a journey of truth and authenticity; a journey of love, devotion, passion, and union; a journey of compassion, giving, and service. It is a journey of realization of the nature of soul and reality; a journey of insight and learning; a journey of fulfillment of life and human potential; a journey of liberation from suffering and limitation; and a journey of inner freedom.

Yet, all these reflect one thing, and only one thing. For the journey is essentially a journey home, to our original primordial ground and source. To be at home is to be whole, contented, and at peace, for no reason but that we are abiding in our true nature. There is no need then, no restlessness, no stirring of dissatisfaction, no ambition for anything at all.

Abiding at home, we can live any life that fits our circumstances, and it will be a life redeemed, where one's fulfillment is identical with serving others. Such connection can take us through the vicissitudes of life and its unavoidable adversities, with grace, dignity, and maturity.

Appendix A

Western Concepts of Soul

All of the wisdom traditions work with the concept of the soul, for the soul is the vessel of all experience and awareness. However, how the soul is conceptualized and what properties and faculties she is seen to have, and how these are described, changes from one teaching to the other. We find significant variations even within the same tradition, although a set of fundamentals is shared by the various schools of each tradition. And since it is the same referent that is conceptualized, we will find a great deal of overlap among the various traditions. However, since the soul is infinite in her potential and manifestations, there are bound to be differences. In this and the next two appendixes, we will give a short description of how several wisdom traditions view the soul, and how this informs their understandings of inner development and enlightenment. This will clarify how our view relates to these more well-known perspectives, and how we use some of their conceptualizations.

In this appendix we will briefly describe the view of the soul in the Western tradition, specifically as it has been conceptualized in the Platonic and Neoplatonic traditions and Christianity. The Sufi tradition belongs here, for it developed partly though the interaction of Neoplatonism and a revealed monotheistic religion from the Middle East, similar to ones we will discuss here. However, we will address that tradition in a separate chapter, because Sufism has a highly developed and organized knowledge of the soul, which we will discuss in some detail.

The reader should keep in mind that the descriptions we give of particular teachings are interpretations—both our own, and those of the authors we quote—and not definitive accounts.

1. Platonic and Neoplatonic Traditions

Ancient Greek conceptions of soul are the primary sources of all Western views of soul, including those of Islam and Judaism. In fact, it is Socrates who is credited to be the father of the Western conception of soul, for he was the first to recognize that a human being is his soul. Homer, the Orphics, the Physicists, and the poets all used the term *psyche* before Socrates, but they used it in ways that now seem alien to us. In his extensive scholarly study of the history of ancient philosophy, Reale writes that "no one prior to Socrates had understood by soul what Socrates understood by it, and after Socrates, the whole of the West. . . . the soul for Socrates was identified with our consciousness when it thinks and acts with our reason and with the source of our thinking activity and our ethical activity. In short, for Socrates the soul is the conscious self, it is intellectual and moral personhood." (Giovanni Reale, *A History of Ancient Philosoph: From the Origins to Socrates*, p. 202.)

"The soul was now objectively recognized as the centre of man's life. From the soul came all men's actions. . . . in the writing of Sophocles, [*soul*] meant not only the 'shade' of a dead person in the Homeric sense, but also an element in human nature, the seat of feeling, thought, and will, and by natural extension, the person as a whole." (W. David Stacey, *The Pauline View of Man*, p. 69.)

This made possible the Orphic insistence that knowing and caring for one's self means caring for the normal personal consciousness. Work on moral and spiritual development became clearly grounded in one's subjective experience; for it became possible now to understand that "to know 'your self' does not mean to know your own name, nor your own body, but rather to examine interiorly and to know your own soul, just as to care for your self does not mean to care for your body but for your soul." (Giovanni Reale, *A History of Ancient Philosophy: From the Origins to Socrates*, p. 203.)

Socrates also regarded this soul as possessing deeper dimensions; for she is not only what rules our minds and lives, but she is the part of us that connects us with divinity and spirituality. Both Plato and Xenophon, the two who wrote of Socrates, understood this, as Reale writes: "But even Xenophon, in agreement in the final analysis with what Plato has said, affirms in fact that for Socrates the soul is that which in us participates in the Divine and that which in us rules." (Ibid., p. 206.)

Socrates saw human moral and spiritual development as interior liberty and autonomy from external temptations, through *enkrateia*, a moral self-control in the face of pleasure and pain and in the presence of urges and passions. "To lay the foundation of *enkrateia* in the soul means to make the soul the ruler over the body, and reason the ruler over the instincts. . . . In fact, before him liberty had an almost exclusively juridical and political meaning; with him it took on the moral meaning of the control over animality." (Ibid., pp. 214–215.)

This developed in his notion of *autarcheia*, the autonomy of virtue and the virtuous human being, where the development of the soul became synonymous with the development and rule of virtue in life; in his view, this happens through control of and independence from the soul's animal nature that binds it and limits its experience to the body. "In the concept of *autarcheia* there are two characteristic features: a) autonomy with respect to physical needs and impulses through the control of reason (the psyche), and b) reason (the psyche), which alone is sufficient to achieve happiness." (Ibid., p. 216.) His dialectic, what is referred to as the Socratic method, became his way of achieving this inner liberty from the everyday compulsions of the animal nature of the soul, "for the correct interpretation of the Socratic 'method' of philosophizing it is necessary to refer to the new concept of the psyche . . . The dialectic of Socrates with all the complex means which support it, in fact, consciously points without deviation toward the soul and toward concern for the soul." (Ibid., p. 239.)

This method is that of examining the inner experience of the soul to arrive at her moral and spiritual perfections, those of the virtues like courage, humility, and truth, and then to the spiritual ground of the soul, the Good. He did not enunciate truths; rather, he questioned his listeners and motivated them to recognize their lack of true knowledge. This allowed them to begin true inquiry into the nature of their soul, for he saw that the "psyche is cared for by simply destroying its pretensions to wisdom and bringing it to the acknowledgment of its unknowing." (Ibid., p. 254.)

Plato basically systematized the Socratic way of philosophy in his metaphysical system, where he established a clear and distinct supersensible dimension, that of the eternal ideas, the counterpart to the physical and sensory. The ideal or intelligible dimension is composed of eternal realities, perfect and heavenly, and the soul is "the intelligible and immaterial aspect of man, and it is eternal as the intelligible and immaterial is eternal." (Giovanni Reale, *A History of Ancient Philosophy: Plato and Aristotle*, p. 140.)

He believed that the soul is eternal, and saw this as necessary for her to be able to know the immutable and eternal ideas. This means that he believed the soul to originate from this spiritual dimension, an idea we find echoed later in the Koranic revelation, but not only containing the spiritual. "We have now learned, not only that Plato considers the soul to be immortal but that he considers it to be in some essential way akin to the eternal Forms, changeless, simple, without parts, ever the same . . . we shall find the soul gradually absorbing all of man that is not sheer physical matter." (G. M. A. Grube, *Plato's Thought*, p. 129.)

He systematized Socrates' notion of the virtues by connecting them to the world of the ideas, and saw the development of the soul as a purification that enables her to perceive such supersensible realm. Reale sums up Plato's view this way:

"Plato states the Socratic commandment, but adding a mystic coloration, by explaining that the 'care of the soul' means 'the purification of the soul.' This purification is realized when the soul, going beyond the senses, is possessed by the pure world of the intelligible and spiritual, and communing with it, as with that which is connatural and similar in kinship . . . It is not an ecstatic and alogical contemplation, but a cathartic effort of inquiry and progressive ascent of knowledge . . . Hence the soul is cured, purified, converted and elevated by knowing. And this is virtue." (Reale, *A History of Ancient Philosophy: Plato and Aristotle*, p. 166.)

Aristotle adds something different and unique to the concept of soul, even though he departs from the Platonic tradition. Aristotle's view of the soul can be seen as a synthesis of the pre-Socratic view that the soul is something intrinsically united to the body, with the Platonic one that is ideal in nature. He defines soul, in his *De Anima*, using his philosophic categories of form and substance or matter, where all entities are material substances structured by their intelligible forms. "The form is the intimate inward structure, the 'thingness' of the thing; the matter is just the possibility of being that or another thing which is made actual for the time being by the reception of a particular form. . . . Matter then is simply the element of possibility, of changeableness in things. Form is the stable, permanent, knowable, scientifically definable element in things." (A. H. Armstrong, *An Introduction to Ancient Philosophy*, p. 79.)

Aristotle thought that for a human being the body is matter, and the soul is the form, the intelligible principle of life and being, that structures this matter. "His definition of soul is 'the first actuality of a natural body potentially having life; that is, organic.' (*De Anima* 412a, 27.) The soul is the actuality which realizes the potentiality of a body capable of life; it is the formative principle which makes a living body a living body." (Ibid., pp. 91–92.)

Aristotle also introduced distinctions in the soul that were later adopted by the various monotheistic traditions. First, there is the vegetative soul, accounting for birth, nutrition, and growth; second there is the sentient or animal soul, possessing movement, appetites, and sensation; and third is the rational soul, possessing knowledge, deliberation, and choice. He thought that there is only one soul for a human being, which possesses a tripartite nature. "Consequently the plants possess only the vegetative soul, the animals the vegetative and the sentient, human beings the vegetative, the sentient, and the intellectual soul." (Giovanni Reale, *A History of Ancient Philosophy: Plato and Aristotle*, p. 35.)

Plotinus continued the Platonic tradition, but extended it in such original ways that he became the father of Neoplatonism. Neoplatonism in time became the primary ancient wisdom tradition whose integration with the three monotheistic religions functioned as an important structural component in the development of their mystical currents. Plotinus formulated his system in terms of the triad of the One, Mind (*nous*), and Soul (*logos*). The One is the absolute source of all manifestation, and *nous* is the first manifest. *Nous* is the universal mind, the intelligible dimension which is both being and knowing, and is populated by the Platonic Forms. *Nous* manifests Soul, which is the universal creative principle underlying the structure of the physical world. Soul is here universal, and constitutes one of the three hypostases; however, individual souls are individualizations of this all-soul, originally inseparable from it but in their descent into bodies they lose sight of their heavenly origin:

"So it is with the individual souls; the appetite for the divine Intellect urges them to return to their source . . . In the Intellectual, then, they remain with the All-Soul, and are immune from care and trouble; in the heavenly sphere, inseparable from the All-Soul . . . the souls indeed are thus far in the one place; but there comes a stage at which they descend from the universal to become partial and self-centered; in a weary desire of standing apart they find their way, each to a place of its very own. This state long maintained, the Soul is a deserter from the totality; its differentiation has severed it; its vision is no longer set in the Intellectual; it is a partial thing, isolated, weakened, full of care, intent upon the fragment; severed from the whole, it nestles in one form of being." (Plotinus, *Enneads*, p. 338.)

Plotinus thinks of this descent into the physical as nonvoluntary, made possible by the necessity of the universe to actualize all of its possibilities. This view has two important implications. First is that the soul originally knows her source, and its intelligible spiritual perfections, giving Socrates' idea of recollection its metaphysical grounding. Second is that the soul is originally one with the all-soul, being inseparable from it in the spiritual dimension. In other words, the individual soul is never completely cut off from her spiritual source, being permanently inseparable from it in some place in herself, a place that is not necessarily known consciously to us. Because of this, Plotinus thinks of the inner journey as a return to the origin, through a process of recollection that becomes possible through detachment from the body and the physical world:

"Recollection (*anamnesis*) is formally different from memory, . . . it consists in a permanent preserving in the Soul of what is co-natural to the Soul itself insofar as it derives it from its original and formal contact with the supernal realities. Our higher Soul, in fact, is eternally bound to Mind (Nous). . . . The highest cognitive activity of the Soul consists, hence, in the thought which grasps the Ideas and Mind (Nous). Beyond this the Soul also possesses the meta-rational power of accepting the One itself and 'uniting itself' with Him." (Giovanni Reale, *A History of Ancient Philosophy: The Schools of the Imperial Age*, p. 380.)

Plotinus, however, introduces something new in the inner journey of the soul to the One, which is that even though the process is of knowing through detachment, the detachment will need at some point to be from knowing itself. In other words, the soul must cut away words, discourse, and discursive reason, all and any differentiation from the One: "In sum, we must withdraw from all the external, pointed wholly inwards; no leaning to the outer; the total of things ignored, first in their relation to us and later in the very idea; the self put out of mind in the contemplation of the Supreme; all the commerce so closely There that, if report were possible, one might become to others reporter of that communion." (Ibid., p. 544.) We see here that Plotinus finds the salvation of the soul in complete mystical union.

2. *The Christian Tradition*

Christian thought shared much of the Greek's conception of soul, but it developed its own unique way of seeing her nature and development. The soul is still the nonphysical part of the person, the person's psychic self, endowed with mind, heart, and will. Yet, because Christianity is a revealed religion, believing in a creator God, and especially because of the centrality of Christ, the nature of the soul, her relation to the spiritual, and her development, all have a unique flavor. Questions of love, faith, and grace attain an importance not found in Greek thought.

However, there is no unified Christian view of the soul, divinity, and their relationship; there are various doctrinal positions held by the various churches, and the accounts of individual mystics and saints. Since there are major commonalities that make all of them Christian, we can speak of a Christian tradition of wisdom. Because of this we give a selective account of some of the major views.

The soul was created by God, and not eternal as it was for Plato, and because of the doctrine of creation *ex nihilo*, her relation to her creator becomes an important point of controversy, that is finally solved in a way that gives Christianity much of its uniqueness. For the Greeks, as we have seen especially with Plotinus, the soul is originally inseparable from the Divine, and her inner journey is then a return to origins, which is the same as a deepening of self-knowledge. "Christianity, on the other hand, speaks of the Incarnation of God, of his descent into the world that he might give to man the possibility of a communion with God that is not open to him by nature. And yet, man is made in the image of God, and so the movements of ascent and descent cross one another and remain—as a fact of experience—in unresolved tension." (Andrew Louth, *The Origins of the Christian Mystical Traditions*, p. xiv.)

Initially, many Christian fathers thought the soul was eternal and had divine origins, as we see in the work of Origen, one of the first fathers. He thought of soul as originally spiritual, wholly *nous*, before the fall; but Origen believed that, after the fall, the soul loses her spiritual nature and becomes simply *psyche*: "Originally, all spiritual beings, *logikoi*, were minds, equal to one another, all contemplating the Father through the Word. Most of these minds (all except the future mind of Christ) grew tired of this state of bliss and fell. In falling their ardour cooled and they became souls (*psyche*, supposedly derived from *psychesthai*, to cool). As souls, they dwell in bodies which, as it were, arrest their fall and provide them with the opportunity to ascend again to contemplation of God by working themselves free from their bodies and becoming minds, *noes*, again. As *nous*, the spiritual being can contemplate the Ideas and realize its kinship with this realm." (Ibid., p. 61.)

Origen posited five spiritual senses as belonging to the soul, each of which need to be developed for the soul to arrive at her goal. They help her discriminate good from evil, sensitize her to the will of God, and enrich her experience of contemplation and union. These are contrasted to the physical senses, but understood as expressions of the *nous* capacity. Vices hinder their operation; hence grace and spiritual practice are necessary for their development.

Origen also developed the idea of three stages of the mystical life, which were later called the purificatory, the illuminative, and the unitive ways of life. The purificatory is the stage of struggle against the passions and development of the virtues. The illuminative is that of contemplation, of seeing the transience of life, and the desire to pass beyond it to the realm of the ideas. The unitive life is not in the soul's hands and does not depend on her efforts, but upon her reliance on God's grace and mercy. This is the union with God, and knowledge of him, but again within the unique Christian flavor: "Knowing God is being known by God, and that means that God is united to those who know him, and gives them a share in his divinity." (Ibid., p. 73.)

The relation of the soul is to a personal God, and not just to a divine or intelligible realm; the journey of return can happen only through the grace of the Father through the Son: "The ascent begins, or is made possible, by what God has done for us in Christ and made effective in us by baptism. The mystical life is the working-out, the realizing, of Christ's union with the soul effected in baptism, and is a communion, a dialogue between Christ and the soul." (Ibid., p. 53.) In other words, the soul purifies herself to be fit for union with Christ, and through this union she shares Christ's contemplation of the Father. Christ, the Word, is seen as the necessary intermediary, the only possible access to the Father.

Origen believed in the notion of original sin, which makes it necessary for the soul to rely on God's mercy. The idea of original sin became one of the differentiating features of Christianity, and connected with that of the need for grace, for "according to St. Ambrose grace is primarily understood as the forgiveness of sins and not as a deification." (Paul Tillich, *A History of Christian Thought*, p. 102.)

A related element in Origen's work is that union with God is not self-knowledge, but God's knowledge of himself, a doctrine to which the gnostic Christians did not subscribe. For them union happens as gnosis, where gnosis is not only direct spiritual knowing, but a self-knowledge: "It is the fact of self-recognition which introduces the 'deliverance' from the situation encountered and guarantees man salvation. For this reason the famous Delphic slogan 'know thyself' is popular also in Gnosis and was employed in numerous ways, especially in the Hermetic gnostic texts." (Kurt Rudolph, *Gnosis*, p. 113.) Because of this and other beliefs the gnostics were declared heretics. One interesting gnostic belief is that the soul comes to earth partly to retrieve something precious, a precious pearl, implying that the fall has developmental implications.

The council of Nicaea, held in 325, not only refuted the gnostics, but rejected some elements of Origen's thought. The main controversy around the meaning of creation *ex nihilo* was resolved in the doctrine that the soul was not only created, but had no divine origin. The gulf that separated God from the physical world also separated the soul from Him. This led to the development of the unique character of Catholic spirituality and psychology, which is that the soul has no spiritual essence, and her inner journey is not toward divinization. In other words, spirit belongs only to God, and only through his grace can the soul be spiritualized.

Athanasius, the theologian whose name is most closely associated with the Nicene orthodoxy, offered the image of the mirror to describe the soul. "So Athanasius' metaphor for the soul as mirror in which God is reflected suggests that there is a real similarity between the soul and God, and preserves the notion that self-knowledge is itself a way of knowing God. But it does this without suggesting that there is a natural kinship between the soul and God. There is no ontological continuity between the image in the mirror and that of which it is the image; so, in the case of the soul reflecting the image of God, this similarity discloses a much deeper dissimilarity at the level of substance." (Andrew Louth, *The Origins of the Christian Mystical Traditions*, p. 80.)

The ideas of original sin, the wretchedness of the soul, the need for God's love and grace, the reliance on faith, and the unknowability of God now develop and take center stage in Christian thought, second only to the doctrines of trinity and Christ's divinity. Contemplation becomes less of a *nous* knowledge and more of a heart feeling the touch of God's presence; this development leads Gregory of Nyssa to develop the idea of spiritual senses as those related to feeling: "In the dark night, the soul cannot see, but she can feel the presence of the Word: the Word 'gives the soul some sense of his presence'. . . . And the senses that Gregory shows most interest in are precisely those that are concerned with presence: smell, taste, and touch or feeling." (Ibid., p. 94.) We see here how the soul is now able to experience spiritual textures and tastes, fragrances and delicacies. Furthermore, the idea of divine darkness begins to take root.

In the Christian tradition, it is important to recognize that when the soul experiences purity and spiritual presence inside her she knows it is not her nature or essence, but the presence of God. Augustine developed this idea within a Neoplatonic metaphysics. First, he believed in the value of truth, and love of truth, which opened introspection and psychological self-scrutiny, for he found truth in the interior of the soul. In fact, for him the "soul is the inner realm . . . The discovery of the soul in this sense is one of the most important cornerstones of Christianity. It includes the world as the sum of all appearances. In contrast to the Greeks, where the soul is a part of all things, the world now becomes an object. The world is an appearance for the soul, which is the only real thing." (Tillich, *A History of Christian Thought*, p. 113.)

For Augustine the inner journey first brings self-knowledge, but this is seen as a first step and not as the final result. "The first step to God is discovery of self, discovery of the self as a spiritual being that contains and transcends the material order." (Louth, p. 143.) In other words, the first step is the discovery of the soul. But when the soul finally discovers ultimate truth it is God's presence within her, not her truth. "So Augustine says: After going into your soul, transcend yourself. This means that in your soul there is something which transcends your soul, something immutable, namely, the divine ground." (Ibid.)

Augustine saw the soul as possessing will, which formed her center, instead of the intellect being the center. "If man is seen in his essential relationship to God, . . . then he is seen by Augustine as a will whose substance is love . . . this essential nature of man is distorted by what Augustine calls sin, especially original sin." (Ibid., p. 122.) For Augustine, all sin is pride, which begins with the soul turning away from God, desiring to be autonomous and to stand on her own. This leads to lust and concupiscence.

In the Middle Ages, the spiritual organ of the soul was increasingly seen to be not intellective but affective. This led to the notion that the intellect needs to be transcended, as in Denys the Areopagite's *Mystical Theology*, and the well-known *Cloud of Unknowing*. This finally develops into Saint John of the Cross's work, typified by *Dark Night of the Soul*. Here the inner journey of the soul is that of purification, the struggle with the passions. This is made possible through God's dark light in the soul, which appears in the soul as faith: "The dark night is an inflowing of God into the soul, which purges it from its ignorances and imperfections, habitual natural and spiritual, and which is called by contemplatives infused contemplation, or mystical theology." (Saint John of the Cross, *Dark Night of the Soul*, p. 100.)

Saint John divides the process of purification into two stages. The first is the purification of the sensual soul, from her animal passions or capital sins, those of pride, avarice, luxury, wrath, gluttony, envy and sloth. The second is the purification of the spiritual part of the soul, from her attachments. This leads to mystical poverty, where the divine "assails the soul in order to renew it and thus to make it Divine ... destroys and consumes its spiritual substance, and absorbs it in deep and profound darkness." (Ibid., p. 104.) Here the soul arrives at the point of recognizing that she has and owns nothing, not even her substance, that it all comes from God. Such emptiness and poverty become the necessary conditions for union with God. Then the soul will be adorned with the virtues, those of serenity, humility, equanimity, courage, sobriety, innocence, faith, and love.

The process of the inner journey is no longer simply the detachment from the body and its appetites, but purification of all passions, attachments, ignorance and complete divestment of possessions, including knowing, perception, and existence.

Christian thought is vast and varied; here we have presented just a few representative examples to give some flavor of the Christian concept and sense of the soul. For example, some later Christian mystics did not participate in the Nicene doctrine, and believed that the soul is continuous with divinity. "The soul is thus in its essence uncreated, as Julian of Norwich implies. It is, as E. I. Watkin says with reference to Julian's teaching, 'outside the time series in the eternal Now of God.' ... Eckhart, indeed, was condemned for saying (as was alleged): 'There is something in the soul that is uncreated and uncreatable.'" (Sidney Spencer, *Mysticism in World Religion*, p. 244.) This is similar to some Protestant mystics, for example Sebastian Franck, who taught that "there is a divine element in us, which is the inmost essence of the soul." (Ibid., p. 279.)

Appendix B

Eastern Concepts of Soul

The various conceptions of soul in the Eastern traditions—schools of Buddhism, the various kinds of Hindu and Kashmiri teachings, and Taoism—have many things in common, just as with the Western traditions. All these traditions think of soul as a nonmaterial consciousness that transmigrates through many lifetimes. They all subscribe to the idea of karma, that past actions determine future lives and actions. They all believe that enlightenment is final liberation from the need to return to physical life, and that it occurs partly through the exhaustion of old karma and the lack of accumulation of new karma. There are similarities but also differences in the conceptions of soul among these traditions, and hence in their views of the path of liberation. They all employ yogic techniques, using breath and subtle centers and energies. Many of them use meditation methods; these may either deepen concentration practices or expand awareness.

1. *Raja Yoga*

This is the yoga of knowledge, one of the main yogas in Indian spirituality; we will discuss it according to Saraswati's model. This yoga is based on Kabila's Samkhya philosophy and Patanjali's yoga sutras. The individual self or "I" is considered to be made up of two principles (*tattvas*): *prakriti* or *jada* (matter), and *purusha* or *chetan* (consciousness). Consciousness abides and is hidden in matter, its abode. Consciousness is associated with the soul or self, referred to as the *atman*. The meaning of *atman* is self or self-nature. Its abode consists of three coextensive bodies, comprising five sheaths. The first body is the physical or gross body, composed of two sheaths, *annamaya kosha* (food sheath) and *pranamaya kosha* (vital air sheath). In other words, it is composed of the properly physical body and the energy or pranic body, the subtle body of energetic centers and channels. The second body is the astral body, composed of two sheaths, the mind and intellect. The third body is the causal, composed of the bliss sheath, which has several layers. The main layers of this body are the *ahamkara*, the ego principle that gives the self the sense of being a separate individual; *chitta*, which is the consciousness medium, where all inner impressions happen; and the innermost *atman*. The astral is subtler than the physical, and the causal subtler than the other two.

The psychic part of the self consists of the last two bodies, composed of the last three sheaths. Another way of describing this psychic organism is that it consists of the *atman*, the conscious self that abides in and uses the *antahkarana* (psychic apparatus). "Antahkarana has fourfold characteristics: Manas (mental faculty of concept and imagination), Buddhi (intellectual or reasoning faculty, the leader of the mind), Ahamkara (the sense of individuality or egoism), and Chitta (the 'mind-stuff' of memory and emotion)." (Swami Yogeshwaranand Saraswati, *Science of Soul*, p. 89.)

One interesting belief of Saraswati's is that consciousness resides only in the *atman*, which then vivifies and enlivens the psychic apparatus and the body, giving them life and consciousness. In other words, even though *chitta* is the "consciousness stuff" he believes that its consciousness comes from the *atman*. Hence, he thinks of the *atman* as the soul, while our conception of the soul, which is similar to the various Western views, is that the *atman* or the spiritual principle inseparable from the *antahkarana* is the soul. This is significant for the path of liberation in this yoga; however, Saraswati does see the *chitta* as a dynamic field that functions as the locus of all experience: "If we say that the Chitta has infinite and endless forms it is no exaggeration. Through its identity with its functions (Vritti Sarupaya), Chitta has the natural capacity of receiving the impressions of all objects of the world in the present and which are to come in the future, because Chitta can be coloured by all the objects of the three periods of time. . . . Chitta undergoes different types of modifications, e.g., Dharma (pertaining to its own nature), Lakshana (pertaining to characteristics) and Avastha (pertaining to state)." (Ibid., pp. 217–218.) In other words, all experiences and realization are the function of the *antahkarana*, while *chitta* is the stuff or medium of these experiences.

Being impressionable in its subtlest parts, the *chitta* also retains the impressions of all past experiences: "All the subtle functions and subtle feelings of pleasure and pain and all the gross actions, gross objects and gross knowledge, as well as gross functions, cast their impressions on the subtlest and most sensitive part of the Chitta and are termed Samskaras.... Chitta keeps in its womb the Samskaras of all the thoughts, of knowledge, realization and ignorance, and of action and inaction." (Ibid., pp. 122–123.) These *samskaras* or impressions become the seeds of karma, which then determine the character of further experiences.

The *chitta* can flow outward toward the world and its concerns or inward toward the *atman*. Its outward flow happens under the impact of *rajas* (energy or activity) or *tamas* (inertia and dullness), and hence it is never calm, while *sattva* (related to clarity and tranquillity) characterizes its inward flow. The *samskaras* affect the flow of *chitta* depending on whether their quality is rajasic, tamasic, or sattvic. Another thing that affects the flow of *chitta* is the *vrittis* (concepts), whose abode is the buddhi (the intellect), and the *vasanas* (tendencies) related to both.

The *atman* is a nondimensional point of light and consciousness that resides in the deepest and subtlest level of the *chitta*, situated in the region of the physical heart that falls right at the center of the chest. The *atman* is the witness, the essential presence and awareness that surveys all the modifications of the *chitta*, under the influence of the *samskaras*, *vasanas*, and *vrittis*. "From the point of view of size in this creation, the orb of Atman, the soul, is smaller than an atom, and from the point of view of subtlety, it is similar to Brahman.... Through its association with Chitta, it assumes the same colour and form that Chitta assumes. This Jivatman or individual soul exists in the form of an extremely subtle point or dot." (Ibid., p. 208.)

The individual is normally not aware of the *atman* or the *antahkarana*, its psychic abode. The yogic practice is then a path of awareness and knowledge where one first becomes aware of the *antahkarana* with its various components, discriminates and understands them, and then discriminates and realizes the *atman* itself. This means that there is first identification with the three bodies, and the process is of discriminating them clearly and recognizing that they are not the real self, until one recognizes the *atman* as the unchanging true self. This happens by entering and clarifying the various sheaths, starting from the most gross and moving to the subtlest. The initial entry is through the physical body, and the practice is a form of renunciation oriented toward the withdrawal of the senses from the external world and reversing the outward flow of *chitta*. This is done partly through physical postures and breath control, which then leads to the capacity to check thoughts and imagination, necessary for concentration. Concentration is developed by keeping the mind one-pointedly focused on an external object or on one of the *chakra* centers. This leads to the penetration of the first sheath, and the awakening of the *kundalini*, which in turn pierces and awakens the various seven *chakras* of the *prana* sheath. One becomes able to discriminate the various sheaths and to understand their functions.

By now one has been able to develop various degrees of *samadhi*, or superstates of concentration: *savikalpa samadhi* (concentration in the presence of subject and object), *savitarka samadhi* (concentration with reasoning, or identifying the object and absorption into it with the presence of the reasoning mind), *savichara samadhi* (concentration with desire to know the truth of object, as in a subtle element or *chakra*), *nirvichara samadhi* (concentration with total absorption, where the object shines alone without distractions or duality; *chitta* flows in a continuous stream of bliss), *asmitanugta samadhi* (the realization of "I am," where *chitta* realizes the *atman*), and lastly, *asamprajnita samadhi* (concentration without support, where the *atman* stands alone, not needing any support, not even that of the *chitta*). The last is also called *nirbija samadhi*, concentration without seed, meaning all *samskaras* and *vrittis* are inactive.

As one develops subtler *samadhis*, one penetrates deeper and subtler sheaths, which correspond to progressively higher *chakras*. "Through Savichara and Nirvichara Samadhi one attains realization of the causal body, Anandamaya Kosha (Bliss Sheath in the heart) together with its six constituent elements: subtle Prana, Ego, Chitta, Jiva (individual soul), Prakriti (matter), Brahman (the Absolute)."

(Ibid., p. 4.) Then there ensues the perception and understanding of the relationship of these six factors. By penetrating and going beyond the *ahamkara*, or ego principle, one attains to concentration without individual consciousness. Then the *samskaras* are dissolved: "By the practice of Asamprajnata Samadhi (illumination without individual consciousness) the Samskaras (mind impressions) are dissolved or made inactive." (Ibid., p. 5.) This clarifies the *chitta*, the consciousness substance, and makes it transparent to the *atman*.

The next step is the development of dispassion and discriminating wisdom. The first is needed for detachment from the effect of the *gunas* (inertia, passion, and purity); for until these are transcended the soul is bound to worldly experiences and tends toward external flow. The second has to do with developing the subtlest function of the *buddhi* (intellect), what is called *ritambhara prajna*, meaning truth-bearing intellect: "The power of that intellect which grasps the truth completely and does not accept even a trace of untruth is known as truth-bearing intellect.... Through its truth-bearing nature it aids a man to realise the subtlest knowledge of the difference between Purusa and Prakriti, known as discriminative understanding or Viveka Khyati." (Ibid., p. 171–172.)

This discriminating understanding that the essential intellect is capable of is recognized by this yoga as the particular capacity needed for liberation: "The direct means of attaining Moksha is Viveka-Jnana or discriminative knowledge." (Ibid., p. 139.) It makes it possible for the individual to discriminate truth from falsehood, and to discriminate the true form and meaning of subtle realities. Its function becomes specifically necessary at the final subtle stages of practice, for discerning and realizing the *atman*. This is seen as having utmost significance because the body and the *antahkarana* not only function as the abode of the *atman*, but also function to hide it from awareness. The final step of distinguishing one's true self from the various levels of its vehicle is to differentiate it from *chitta* itself. *Atman* is the *purusha*, which is the witness of the changes of *prakriti*, the most subtle part of which is the *chitta*. It is the unchanging that is constantly witnessing the changing field of experience, but is normally not isolated from it. "This small Chitta becomes so luminous, so bright due to the luminosity of Atman, and becomes so coloured by the idea of ego, that although it is not impossible, it is certainly difficult to separate—to pick out the minute subtle Atman—in this ego-coloured luminous Chitta." (Ibid., p. 126.)

When the intellect reaches its level of *ritambhara*, meaning it is full of the presence of truth, it attains the discriminating capacity. This happens when the rajasic and tamasic tendencies are transcended through supreme dispassion, allowing the intellect to be totally sattivic, full of purity and clarity. "Then, in the gentle light of Sattwa, there shines Viveka-Jnana or discriminating knowledge which shows the difference between Chitta and Atman." (Ibid., p. 239.) The luminous white *chitta* becomes transparent and clear, revealing the crystal light of the *atman* like a crystal star. In our language, this means the true essential self is realized when it is discriminated from the changing field of the soul. However, the *chitta* does not cease after its clarification from the *samskaras*, *vrittis*, and *vasanas*; it becomes established in *atman*: "Because of the cessation of all distractions merely caused by Vrittis or thought-waves and the pairs of opposites of the world, the Chitta remains established in its essential nature." (Ibid., p. 250.)

The last step is that of recognizing the oneness of *atman* with *brahman*, the transcendent absolute. The *atman* is the reflection of the infinite absolute in the individual *chitta*, and by recognizing it and discriminating its subtlest form it becomes the entry to the absolute, with its vastness and transcendence. There are more substages and realizations, but this is only a short exposition. (See *The Point of Existence*, chapter 4, for further discussion of the self-realization of *atman* in *raja yoga*, and its relation to our view.)

Here we will simply mention one other important Indian concept of soul, that of Aurobindo. His term for the soul is "psychic being." (Aurobindo, *The Life Divine*.)

2. Nondual Kashmir Shaivism

Since this tradition is nondual it does not regard the individual soul as separate from true nature. For this teaching, the nondual true nature is the Self, Shiva. Shiva is the ultimate spiritual nature, but inseparable from all manifestation. So the Self is all of the universe, in all of its levels and dimensions. Shiva is eternally inseparable from Shakti,

Shiva's creative energy, while Shakti manifests the universe as an extension of herself. It is central in this teaching that the ultimate truth is not only presence and awareness, but also dynamism and creativity, expressing Shakti, and is usually referred to as *spanda*, meaning pulsation or vibration. In the *Spanda Karika*, one of the central texts in Shaivism, it is said: "Therefore, it is perfectly valid to say that the Lord whose nature is consciousness brings about the emergence of the world in the form of congealment of His essence (i.e., He materializes His essence in the form of the world)." (Jaideva Singh, *The Yoga of Vibration and Divine Pulsation*, p. 289.) This is a nondual view through and through, where unity reigns supreme as the Self, Shiva.

Shiva manifests the universe through degrees of delimitation, manifesting himself as successive *tattvas* (elements or principles). Each succeeding *tattva* is more limited than the one before it; at the summit is Shiva in his absolute purity and transcendence, and at the bottom is physical matter. The individual soul does not appear in this scheme of manifestation until the twelfth *tattva*, that of *purusha*. This, however, occurs after the preceding *tattvas*, which are related to *maya* (illusion and its related coverings). The individual soul is, therefore, considered a limitation of Shiva, where Shiva conceals his infinity and freedom in the form of a limited individual. In other words, the individual soul is inherently Shiva, but Shiva that has limited his nature through different levels and kinds of coverings.

The individual soul is composed first of the two *tattvas*, *purusha* and *prakriti*, composing the subjective and objective poles of the experiencing limited individual: "Siva through Mayasakti which limits His universal knowledge and power becomes Purusa or the individual subject. . . . Purusa is also known as *anu* in this system. The word *anu* is used in the sense of limitation of the divine perfection. . . . While Purusa is the subjective manifestation of Siva, Prakriti is the objective manifestation." (Jaideva Singh, *Siva Sutras*, p. xxvi.) The Samkhya system in India conceives of one universal *prakriti*, or original substance, while Shaivism believes that each *purusha* has a different *prakriti*. *Prakriti* is the matrix of all objectivity. "Purusa is the experient . . . and Prakriti is the experienced." (Ibid., p. xxvii.)

In other words, *purusha* is the subjective witnessing awareness, while *prakriti* is the medium and content of all experience of self. This *prakriti*, or the manifest field of experience, further differentiates into *antahkarana* (the psychic apparatus), *indriyas* (senses), and *bhutas* (matter). The psychic apparatus is the inner instrument of the individual, which is further differentiated into three *tattvas*:

1. *Buddhi*, which is the ascertaining intelligence, or intellect, that reflects both internal and external objects. It is the agent of discrimination and decision.
2. *Ahamkara*, the ego or "I" principle, the power of self-appropriation. It creates the sense of a limited and separate "I."
3. *Manas*, or mind. With the senses it constructs perception, and by itself it creates images, concepts, and thoughts.

This does not mean that *ahamkara* is limited but not *purusha*, as believed in other Hindu teachings. *Purusha* is limited through the five *kanchukas*, coverings, that veil the infinity of Shiva: "In Saivism, *purusa* is not a realized soul. *Purusa tattva* is bound and limited just as *ahamkara tattva* is. The only difference that exists between *purusa* and *ahamkara* is that *purusa* is connected with subjectivity and *ahamkara* is connected with objectivity. And this *purusa* is entangled and bound in five ways which are the five *kancukas*. . . .

"First there is *niyati tattva*. The function of *niyati tattva* is to put the impression in *purusa* that he is residing in such and such a particular place and not in all places. . . .

"Next comes *kala* [*kāla*] *tattva*. The word *kala* means time. The action of *kala tattva* is to keep *purusa* in a particular period. . . .

"The third *tattva* by which *purusa* is limited is known as *raga tattva*. *Raga* means attachment. This is that attachment which results from not being full. The action of *raga tattva* is to leave the impression in *purusa* that he is not full, that he is not complete, and that he must have this and that to become full. . . .

"The *fourth tattva* which limits purusa is *vidya tattva*. *Vidya* means knowledge. The action of *vidya tattva* is to put the impression in *purusa* that he has this or that particular and limited knowledge, that he is not all knowing for he knows only some limited things. . . .

"The fifth and final bondage and limitation for *purusa* is *kala* [*kalā*] *tattva. Kala tattva* creates the impression in *purusa* that he has some particular creativity." (Swami Lakshman Jee, *Kashmir Shaivism*, pp. 7–8.)

Through covering and limiting his omnipresence, eternity, boundless bliss and abundance, omniscience, and omnipotence, Shiva assumes the limitations of the *purusha*, and becomes a limited individual, *anu*. However, the five coverings are expressions of *maya*, or illusion, another universal *tattva* that points to ignorance of nature:

"These five bondages of *purusa* are caused by *purusa's* ignorance of his own nature. And this ignorance is another *tattva* which is known as *maya tattva*. These five *tattvas* are created by *maya* for *purusa*. That *purusa*, therefore, who is the victim of *maya*, does not know his own real nature and becomes bound and entangled by these five (*kancukas*) and thus becomes a victim of *prakriti*. He takes on individuality and becomes a limited individual." (Ibid., p. 8.)

This is the process through which the infinite and nondual Self becomes a limited soul, which now operates through intellect, mind, and individuality, by using the senses. Kashmir Shaivism, in effect, believes that bondage is due to innate ignorance. Shiva is originally pure awareness and consciousness, but also freedom of action and knowledge, as we see in the first sutra of the *Siva Sutras*: "Awareness which has absolute freedom of all knowledge and activity is the Self or nature of Reality." (Jaideva Singh, *Siva Sutras*, p. 6.) But this pure presence of awareness becomes the limited individual due to an innate ignorance, the result of Shiva limiting his nature:

"The bondage of the individual is due to innate ignorance or *anava mala*. It is this primary limiting condition which reduces the universal consciousness to an *anu* or a limited creature. . . . It is owing to this that the *jiva* considers himself to be a separate entity cut off from the universal stream of consciousness. It is consciousness of self-limitation and imperfection." (Ibid. p. xxix.) In other words, the soul does not recognize her original nature because of *anava mala*, which has two sides. The first side is the ignorance of her awareness nature, with all of its limitlessness, and the other is the identification with being a limited and separate individual, with the *antahkarana*, or the psychic apparatus. Along with *anava mala*, *maya mala* and *karma mala* contribute to the limitations. We have discussed the effects of *maya* through its coverings, and karma points to the learned identifications and limitations due to previous actions. *Anava mala* is the innate ignorance of true nature, which makes the soul identify with the three *tattvas* constituting the *antahkarana*.

Inner work is then a matter of recognizing one's original nature, and not that of improving or developing oneself. The soul is inherently the dynamic and creative cosmic field of awareness, and she needs to wake up to this fact experientially. Kashmir Shaivism employs several ways, or *upayas*, toward this end, depending on the degree of awakeness and capacity of the student. They range from nonmethod, which depends on the grace of the gurus or Shiva, through a yoga of discriminating understanding that establishes the true nature of the soul, to that of yogic techniques that employ mantra for the activation of *kundalini*. The *Siva Sutras*, the primary text of Shaivism, is basically a description of these three kinds of yoga, and their results. In his introduction to the *Siva Sutras*, Jaideva Singh describes in his introduction to this text the most advanced *upaya*, called *sambhava yoga*: "This comes about, not by seeking, not by choice, not by discipline, but spontaneously when the mind has ceased cogitating and surrenders itself completely to the effulgence of the Divine Presence within." (Ibid., p. xxxiv.)

The process of awakening is not necessarily sudden, but goes through successive stages of refinement of consciousness as the soul progressively realizes deeper or more universal *tattvas*. Basically, the central idea is that the coiled kundalini at the root of the spine represents Shakti herself, the dynamic *spanda*. Upon being awakened, she brings about, through her dynamism and energy, an unfoldment of the soul toward subtler and less limited *tattvas*, until the realization of the Shiva *tattva*. Paul Muller-Ortega writes: "Thus, from the relatively superficial activities of sense perception to the progressively subtler forms of inner awareness, there spans a unified spectrum of levels of the *spanda* which lead inwards until the most delicate and powerful tendrils of individuality merge with the infinitely fast vibration of the ultimate consciousness." (Muller-Ortega, foreword to Singh, *The Yoga of Vibration and Divine Pulsation*, p. xix.)

The ideal of Shaivism is not only universal liberation, the usual Indian ideal of going beyond the cycle of life and death. It is rather *jivanmukta*, liberation of the individual soul in life. The liberated human being lives as a liberated soul, a soul that is the direct expression of the transcendent Shiva, but also identified with Shiva's freedom and limitlessness. It is interesting that this type of liberation is seen as requiring both the experiential realization of Shiva and the intellectual comprehension of the philosophy: "When, however, at the same time you also attach Buddha *jnana* to *purusa jnana*, which means that on the one hand you practice on your own Being and on the other hand you go into the depth of the philosophical thought of the monistic Saiva texts and elevate your intellectual being, then you become a *jivanmukta*, one who is liberated while living." (Swami Lakshman Jee, *Kashmir Shaivism*, p. 100.)

3. Buddhist Schools

Buddhism does not employ the concept of soul as do other Indian traditions, hence the notion of *jiva* or *atman* as the real self is alien to it. In fact, Buddhism teaches the opposite notion, that of *anatman*, or no-self, which expresses the Buddha's primary insight that the individual has no unchanging abiding self or essence. This developed in the Mahayana teaching into the notion of *shunyata*, emptiness, which the Madhyamika school took to deny the inherent existence not only of the self but of all perceivable phenomena. Buddhism does, however, share many of the Indian notions regarding soul, like the ones above in yoga and Shaivism. It seems that the Buddha formulated his understanding partly in response to an extreme Hindu focus on self. It is not that his teaching does not include the various categories known in his time, but he formulated them in a way that avoids or minimizes the pitfall of reification. The notion of emptiness is not so much the negation of soul as it is a destructuring of reification of self, objects, and essences in general. We also should mention that Buddhism has developed many schools and subschools, with various and differing conceptualizations, where the differences are frequently quite subtle. We can only refer here to some general notions of a few of these schools.

The Buddha's teaching regarding the self is that it is not an abiding and unchanging entity but a bundle of five psychophysical constituents, five *skandhas*: form, feeling/sensation, perception, mental process, and consciousness. An older version renders them as color-form, feeling (judgments), concepts and conceptual process, motivation, and consciousness in the specific sense of perception. These relate to the phases of any conscious experience. The idea is that because the skandhas appear in experience as a unity we believe they are an autonomous entity, as Nagarjuna states:

> *As long as there is the belief in the skandhas,*
> *There will come from them . . . a belief in a self.*
> *When there is a belief in an ego, then there is karma.*
> *From this, there will come (re)birth.*
>
> GUENTHER AND KAWAMURA,
> *Mind in Buddhist Psychology*, p. 3

The fifth skandha, consciousness, is further divided into six types of consciousness, depending on its object: consciousness of sight, hearing, smell, taste, the tactile sense, and mental consciousness, *manovijnana*. The last of these is necessary to account for the construction of sensory input into coherent perception and experience. With this came the dynamic nature of consciousness, likened to a river that is in constant flow and change but still preserving its direction and relative identity. The earliest Buddhists, the Theravadins, called it the stream of consciousness. "In spite of the incessant flow and the continual change of its elements, the existence of the stream cannot be questioned. Its factual reality consists in its continuity (*santana*) and in the steadiness and regularity of the relations prevailing within its changing components." (Lama Anagarika Govinda, *Foundations of Tibetan Mysticism*, p. 73.)

This perspective of consciousness as consisting of various kinds and levels flowing in a dynamic stream was extended by the Yogachara (sometimes referred to as the Vijnanavada) school, one of the two main schools of Mahayana Buddhism. Combining this continuity of consciousness with Buddha's original insight of no-self they taught that "although there exists no permanent unchanging entity or substance called 'the self,' still there exists a *vijnana-santana* or 'stream of consciousness,' an unceasing flow of states of consciousness. This stream of consciousness flows through many different lifetimes like a river flowing through different landscapes; it is the same river throughout its course, and yet it changes from moment to moment." (John M. Reynolds, *Self-Liberation through Seeing with Naked Awareness*, p. 90.)

This psychologically more sophisticated Buddhist school developed the famous doctrine of "eight consciousnesses," the six above, and two more fundamental levels that underlie the continuous stream of consciousness. "The observation of this continuity is what gives rise to self-consciousness, which is described by the Vijnanavadins as a function of *manas*, the seventh class of consciousness, which is thus distinguished from the mere co-ordinating and integrating of sense-impressions in the 'thought-consciousness' (*mano-vijnana*)." (Govinda, *Foundations of Tibetan Mysticism*, p. 73.) The object of this seventh consciousness is not the external world of sense but the continuous stream of experience throughout various lifetimes, the ever-flowing river of inner forms; for "the continuous stream of consciousness flowing through them does not only contain on its surface the causally conditioned states of existence, but the totality of all possible states of consciousness, the sum total of all experiences of a beginningless 'past,' which is identical with a limitless 'future.' It is the emanation and manifestation of the basic universal consciousness, which the Vijnanavadins called the eighth or 'Store-Consciousness' (*alayavijnana*)." (Ibid., p.73.)

The idea is that the stream of consciousness is only what we are conscious of from the infinite potentiality of the storehouse consciousness. This *alayavijnana* is like an ocean, a universal consciousness that contains all potentialities of experience. It is beyond all individual distinctions and limitations. Kennard Lippman writes, "In this Yogachara system, it should be remembered that the term potentiality of experience or experiencing process (*sems, citta*) is equivalent to the 'fundamental structure of all experiencing,' the so-called eighth stratum of experiencing, the other seven being specifications or 'transformations' of this." (Manjusrimitra, *Primordial Experience*, p. 15.)

Yogachara included the mind-only school, Chittamatra. The main understanding of this school is that all is mind, consciousness, or experiencing—*chitta*. This primacy of experience was described by Vasubandhu, one of the main originators of this school, in the verse: "Nothing exists for ordinary people and Noble Ones apart from the continuum of their own experiencing." (Ibid., p. 15.) In other words, we cannot say self or objects exist. There is only experiencing, only mind or knowledge; for that is all that we can be aware of. The *alayavijnana* is then an underlying ground, universal and limitless, with structure that we term experience of self and universe. Its self-structuring appears as the operation of the other seven levels of consciousness.

This theory of consciousness basically describes any ordinary experience, for all of the eight are present in all experience. There is always one or more of the sense kind of consciousness. There is always the mind that recognizes and labels. There is always the intellect that conceptualizes, discriminates, and develops ideas and belief systems. And there is always the ground consciousness, the source of all content.

The process of delusion, the belief that there is a separate and abiding self, is due to the intellect consciousness, "which takes the eighth, a momentary flow in which habituating tendencies are 'built up' and 'discharged,' as an enduring entity called one's 'self.'" (Ibid., p. 15.) Ego-centered perceptions develop out of this structuring through the other six types of consciousness. Now there is experience of a separate self—perceiving objects, while in fact there is only experiencing, which is a continuously flowing self—structuring consciousness. There is no objective or subjective experience, no outside or inside, no world or self. Yogachara understood this to be what the Buddha meant by emptiness. The other Mahayana school, the Madhyamika, did not agree with this, and believed emptiness meant that no object in perception possesses any independent essence or abiding entity. This included the *alayavijnana*. Buddhist Mahayana schools, as well as those of Vajrayana, adhere to one brand of Yogachara or Madhyamika, or some combination or development of them.

The teaching of eight levels or strata of consciousness, which are a different structuring of the stream of consciousness, is the closest thing in our understanding to a concept of soul in Buddhism. In fact, it is quite similar to yoga and Shaivism, as we described above, with the flavor of carefully avoiding reifying this stream as a self or entity. The main difference is that this stream is not taken to mean a flowing medium, but a perceptual and sometimes mental consciousness. Yet, this is not true of all Buddhist schools, for the stream, and more exactly the *alayavijnana*, is referred to sometimes as the source and potential of all experience, both *samsara* and *nirvana*.

The *manas* consciousness is considered the fulcrum of delusion or liberation, for its conception of the universal consciousness is what determines whether it goes to one or the other. This is because it is the consciousness that mediates between the universal *alayavijnana* and individual experience. "Intuitive-mind (*manas*) is one with Universal Mind (*alayavijnana*) by reason of its participation in Transcendental Intelligence (*arya-jnana*) and is one with the mind-system (the five senses and the intellect) by its comprehension of differentiated knowledge (according to the six classes of *vijnana*) . . . *Manas* is that element of our consciousness which holds the balance between the empirical-individual qualities on the one side and the universal-spiritual qualities on the other. . . . Manas is the principle through which the universal consciousness experiences itself and through which it descends into the multiplicity of things." (Govinda, *Foundations of Tibetan Mysticism*, pp. 74–75.)

It seems there are differences in Buddhist schools in terms of which of the eight levels of consciousness is the seventh, some saying it is the *mano-vijnana*, as in the case of Vasubandhu, and others saying it is the *manas*, as does Govinda. There is agreement that the *manas* is the way we experience the *alayavijnana*, but that the discriminating intellect conceives of this current of experience in terms of a reified self, so "error is not committed by *manas* but by the intellect which therefore is also called *klista-mano-vijnana*, 'afflicted' (namely, by error) 'intellectual consciousness.'" (Ibid., p. 79.)

When mind or *manas*, then, is freed from the ego-creating function of the intellect, it can turn from the objects of the physical world inward, toward its primordial ground, which then leads it to enlightenment: "But in the moment in which *manas* turns away from sense-consciousness and from the intellect and directs its attention upon the primordial cause of its being, upon the universal source of consciousness, the illusion of the ego-concept becomes apparent and the experience of *sunyata* reveals itself in its depth and magnitude." (Ibid., p. 77.)

The process of liberation in many schools of Buddhism is basically the recognition that there is no abiding and eternal self, and then the more basic recognition of the emptiness of all existence, that nothing exists on its own. Meditation is the central tool, but various yogic techniques are employed by the tantric schools of Buddhism. Some schools of Buddhism, including the Tathagatagarbha (Buddha nature) schools, such as Zen, and some of the Tibetan teachings, such as Dzogchen and Mahamudra, consider enlightenment to be not only the realization of emptiness but of the primordial ground of awareness.

These schools integrate much of the Yogachara teachings, especially the theory of consciousness, but disagree with its conception of the *alayavijnana* as the primordial ground, and hence with its view that everything is mind. Referring to the ground as *kunzhi*, a Bon teacher of Dzogchen writes: "In Dzogchen the *kunzhi* is the base of everything and corresponds to self-originated wisdom and to the enlightenment principle. This explanation is not the same as that of the *kunzhi* or '*alayavijnana*' in the Sutric Cittamatra system, where the *kunzhi* is described as a kind of mental consciousness that contains all the categories of thought and karmic traces that give rise to virtuous and nonvirtuous tendencies and actions." (Tenzin Wangyal, *Wonders of the Natural Mind*, p. 111.)

This view of *alayavijnana*, common among these schools, seems different from Govinda's understanding, but Govinda's understanding reflects some currents in Buddhist teaching. Actually, the fact that the Yogachara's view of mind, at least in some of its interpretations, seems to imply this mind to be a mental consciousness differentiates its stream of consciousness from the consciousness or *chitta* as used by some of the Indian schools, as in Shaivism and *raja yoga* above. For these latter teachings *chit* or consciousness is not a mental consciousness, but a medium or presence, a mass of awareness. Because of this, it is important to recognize the difference in the usage of the word consciousness (*chit*, *chitta*) by Buddhists and its usage by other Indian traditions. What Shaivism, for instance, calls consciousness will be referred to as awareness by Buddhists. Throughout this book, we have adhered to the Shaivite view of consciousness, which is the equivalent of pure awareness in Buddhism.

Vajrayana can be seen as a development of Yogachara but also an original development that integrates elements of both Yogachara and Madhyamika. It uses the notion of eight consciousnesses in a different way than Chittamatra, as does Dzogchen. Govinda states that the essence of Buddhist tantra developed from Yogachara: "This is the essence of Tantrism, as developed with logical necessity from the teachings and religious practice of the Vijnanavadins and Yogacarins . . ." (*Foundations of Tibetan Mysticism*, p. 93.) Regarding the development of Dzogchen, Guenther states: "On the other hand, the Yogachara thinkers' process-oriented view, which emphasizes the human system's process of unfolding, fitted well into the rDzog-chen view, which emphasizes the system's self-renewal and freedom." (Herbert Guenther, *From Reductionism to Creativity*, p. 4.)

On the other hand, the schools that equate liberation with the realization of the primordial ground of awareness, even though integrating much of the Yogachara, criticize its mind-only or experience-only view on the ground that this view negates phenomena; they then proceed to replace the alayavijnana with the primordial ground of awareness, viewed as Buddha nature or nonconceptual presence, this way allowing the existence of phenomena independent from our experiencing, but still holding them to be the manifestation of this presence. So we see, for instance, the principal writer of Dzogchen, Longchenpa, stating that all phenomena are the expressions of *rigpa*, presence-awareness: "The way things appear has always been a radiance not existing internally nor externally apart from being a mere play of the creativity (of pure and total presence). It is not found as something mental or other than mental, but is held to be merely how things present themselves interdependently when secondary conditions are present." (Manjusrimitra, *Primordial Experience*, p. 27.)

We see here very subtle differences between the various schools, but they are reflected in the path and in the conceptualizations of realization. The Vajrayana teachings conceptualize the process of liberation as the transformation of the eight strata of consciousness, into what are called the awarenesses or wisdoms of the Buddha, meaning that the eight appear the way we have described them in our normal experience before enlightenment, but appear differently after that. They become manifestations of enlightened awareness, and categorized according to the Buddha families. These are the tantric categorization of five groups that include the *skandhas*, qualities of consciousness, poisons or passions, colors, stones, and so on. According to one version, the fifth *skandha*, that of "individual consciousness (*vijnana-skandha*) turns into the knowledge of the universal law and ultimate reality (*dharma-dhatu-jnana*) represented by the Dhyani-Buddha Vairocana, 'The Radiating One.' ... The *alaya*-consciousness is transformed into the consciousness connected with the Knowledge of the Great Mirror ..., which in Tibetan is called the Mirror-like wisdom ... and is represented in the Dhyani-Buddha Aksobhya, who is the embodiment of the immutability of this wisdom. ... Feeling (*vedana*), which is self-centered, as long as *manas* plays the role of self-consciousness and produces the illusion of the separateness and difference of being, now turns into the feeling for others, into the inner participation and identification with all that lives: into the consciousness connected with the Knowledge of Equality ..., embodied in the figure of the Dhyani-Buddha Ratnasamhava. ... The empirical thought-consciousness (*mano-vijnana*), the discriminating, judging intellect, turns into the intuitive consciousness of inner vision, in which 'the special characteristics of all things' (*dharmas*) becomes clearly visible. ... It is called 'the consciousness connected with ... Discriminating Wisdom.' ... The embodiment of this ... is the Dhyani-Buddha Amitabha. ... The functions which are characterized by the group of mental formations (*samskara-skandha*) are thus transformed into 'the consciousness connected with the Knowledge of the Accomplishment' ... symbolized by the Dhyani-Buddha Amoghasiddhi." (Govinda, *Foundations of Tibetan Mysticism*, pp. 83–86.)

The Nyingma school of Tibetan Buddhism conceptualizes a ninth consciousness, related to the whole field of experience, and not only to one's experience. This way it divides the nine into five categories, where the first five, related to sense consciousness, are seen as one, and then mind, ego-conceptualizing intellect, *alayavijnana* and the ninth make up the rest of the five. These five consciousnesses are seen to correspond to the five Buddha families. And since each of these families is connected with one of five passions, the transformation of the five passions is related to the five types of enlightened awareness. This teaching takes the view that the ground awareness and presence, primordial presence, displays five differentiations, as clear light of different colors, associated to the five Dhyani Buddhas, where each is a union of clear light and emptiness or openness. In his commentary on the *Kungejapa*, Longchenpa addresses this: "Thus, desire becomes discriminating awareness, the unity of bliss and openness. Aversion becomes the mirror-like awareness, the unity of clarity and openness.

Stupidity becomes the reality-field's awareness, the unity of appearance and openness. Pride becomes the awareness of utter sameness, the unity of pure presence and openness. Envy becomes the all-accomplishing awareness, also the unity of pure presence and openness." (Longchenpa, *You Are the Eyes of the World*, p. 42.)

Wisdom of the reality field is usually given the color blue, but sometimes white; it apprehends the inseparability of awareness from the appearance of all forms. In the realized state the mere awareness is inseparable from awareness of emptiness. The essence of awareness is absolute emptiness. It is the simple empty awareness of expanse, the field where all phenomena appear. This precedes all other perception. There is awareness and there is emptiness at the same time, occurring together. So that is the mere minimum; the bare minimum of any experience is awareness.

The mirror-like wisdom, given the color white or crystal, sometimes blue, means now there is not only awareness, but there is also the awareness of the forms that are present. This awareness is completely transparent; it sees everything as it is. Sometimes it is called clarity, or nonconceptual awareness. When we recognize the experience of the soul there is the presence of awareness and the awareness has form but the awareness of the form is not separate from the form. When this awareness of the form is completely nonconceptual it is called mirror-like wisdom.

Next is the wisdom of equality, assigned the color of yellow or gold, which is that although there is awareness of forms, the forms make up one reality; everything is of one taste. This is the perception of unity; for although there is perception of form, forms are differentiated, oneness still remains. The forms are all forms of the same field; they are modifications in the field, shapes in the same field. The wisdom of discrimination, given the color red, means that not only is there an awareness of forms and an awareness that these forms do not make separations or partitions in experience, but there is also a cognition of these forms, a knowledge of what they are. The all-accomplishing wisdom, given the color green, sees that the differentiated yet singular awareness composed of knowledge, which is the totality and unity of all the above four, is always unfolding in a dynamic creativity.

Just as the nine consciousnesses describe the structure of normal egoic experience, the five awakened awarenesses describe the structure of enlightened experience. They are not exactly states, but facets of enlightened consciousness, all present as one gestalt.

The stream of consciousness, which is structured through the eight strata of consciousness, does not disappear in enlightenment. It is not only that the various strata of consciousness transform to the various Buddha wisdoms, but the current of consciousness remains and becomes the subtle body of the awakened one. For example, in the Mahamudra teaching of the highest yoga tantra of Vajrayana it is seen to be clarified, through meditation on emptiness, and to transform into what is called the illusory body. This illusory body is a subtratum of individual consciousness formed by the union of clear light and emptiness. In a Mahamudra text, Nagarjuna writes that "the very subtle wind upon which is mounted the all empty mind of clear light is the basis for attaining the illusory body . . . while the gross body and mind are temporary bases upon which the 'I' is imputed, the primary and continuously residing bases of imputation are the very subtle mind and its mounted wind . . . there are two types of body: the gross and the subtle. . . . The subtle body of the continuously residing continuum on the other hand, never dies. . . . The temporary gross body is like the house in which this continuously residing body is temporarily dwelling. At the time of death this subtle body leaves its temporary dwelling and moves on to another life." (Geshe Kelsang Gyatso, *Clear Light of Bliss*, p. 195.) This view is not shared by all schools of Buddhism.

This subtle body is exactly what other traditions, even the Western ones, including our view, refer to as the soul, which is a stream of awareness. It is not only a mental stream of consciousness, as Yogachara had emphasized. The illusory body is then the clarified soul, for it is an awareness that is at the same time a dynamic presence and awareness inseparable from emptiness. The illusory body itself goes through a process, for it has two stages: the impure and pure illusory body, the latter connected with the *vajra* or diamond body. Gyatso connects the illusory body to the primary deities of Vajrayana practice: "Three additional terms for the illusory body are the 'complete enjoyment body,' 'Vajrasattva' (the *vajra*-being) and 'Vajradara' (the *vajra*-holder)." (Ibid., p. 201.) This is because this Mahamudra teaching considers the illusory body necessary for final enlightenment; for it is the basis of a Buddha's form body: "To become a buddha you must attain a buddha's form body and the illusory body is its primary or substantial cause." (Ibid., p. 188.)

Appendix C

Soul in Sufism

The Sufi tradition is grounded in Islamic spirituality, but employs many Neoplatonic notions. The four terms the Sufis use to refer to the nonphysical dimension of man are *ruh*, *nafs*, *qalb*, and *aql*, which are roughly translated as spirit, soul or self, heart, and intellect, respectively. These terms are often used interchangeably, for they all represent the substance or meaning of the individual while the body is merely the form. However, most of the time the emphasis is on *ruh* as the pure spirit or essence, connected to the divine; *nafs* as the self that goes through transformation and purification but that exists initially at the animal and sensuous level; *qalb* as the integration of the two that stands for what is truly human and that functions as the inner locus of divine manifestation, and *aql* as the intellect in the Greek sense, as *nous* or the discerning quality of spirit. The ambiguity in Sufi writings in relation to these terms reflects the fact that they are the same reality but on different levels and dimensions, which is the same as saying that the human subjectivity is one that has many potentials on various dimensions. We see this ambiguity especially in Sufi poetic writings, as in the following from Rumi, where he uses intellect to mean our meaning of essence, and spirit as our meaning of soul:

> *The body is outward, the spirit hidden; the body is like the sleeve, the spirit the hand.*
> *Then intellect is more hidden than spirit: The senses perceive the spirit more quickly.*
> *You see a movement, you know there is life. But you do not know it is filled with the intellect. . . .*

> *The spirit of prophetic revelation is beyond the intellect; coming from the Unseen, it belongs to that side.*
>
> WILLIAM CHITTICK,
> *The Sufi Path of Love*, p. 41

There have been many Sufi orders and teachers, and hence many varieties of concept of soul; we will present what is most common, and hence most general, about this concept in Sufism. This is possible because Sufism is not a disparate collection of saints and movements, but a coherent tradition that includes various schools or orders that have been in constant communication and contact.

Sufism divides spirit into several levels, with the lower functioning as the form and body of the higher. The lowest is the animal spirit, then the human, then the angelic, then the universal or Muhammadan spirit, then the divine spirit, or God. Spirit is recognized as awareness or consciousness capable of discernment. Rumi says:

> *Experience shows that the spirit is nothing but awareness.*
> *Whoever has greater awareness has greater spirit.*
> *Our spirit is greater than the animal spirit. Why? Because it has more awareness.*
> *Then the angel's spirit is greater than ours, for he transcends the rational senses.*
> *Then the spirit of the saints, the Possessors of Hearts, is even greater. Leave aside your astonishment.*
>
> (Ibid., p. 31)

Some of the ambiguity can be clarified when we recognize that the Sufis think of the spirit (*ruh*) as created by God from His own spirit, and from spirit comes soul (*nafs*), as we see in the following passage from a famous Sufi text, where the translator renders *ruh* as soul: "*Nafs* is the result of *ruh*; *ruh*, of order. Because by His own self, without any cause (whereto the order is the hint) God creates the soul; and by means of *ruh* (whereof creation is the hint), the crown of created things." (Suhrawardi, *The Awarif U'l-Ma'arif*, pp. 136–137.)

The *ruh* is connected with Adam, and hence seen as active and male, while *nafs* is associated with Eve, and hence conceived of as female and passive to *ruh*:

"The existence in the material world:

(a) of Adam became the stage of *ruh* in the hidden world.

(b) of Hawa (Eve) the stage of the form of *nafs* in the hidden world.

Hawa's birth from Adam is like unto the birth of *nafs* from *ruh* (the soul); and the effects of the marriage of *nafs* and *ruh*, and the attraction of male and of female, became assigned to Adam and Hawah." (Ibid., pp. 137–138.)

The connection between *ruh* and *nafs* is sometimes seen in the sense that the *nafs* is the animal spirit, as in the case of Rumi, who "often refers to the animal spirit by the term *nafs*, which is most commonly rendered into English as 'soul' or 'self.'" (Chittick, *The Sufi Path of Love*, p. 33.) The implication is that as spirit becomes more limited it becomes *nafs*, or soul. However, *nafs* or soul is the body, the outer garment, of spirit or *ruh*. The most important implication for the path is that since *nafs* comes originally from spirit, and spirit from God, the inner journey is that of return, where *nafs* or soul first becomes one with spirit, and then one with the divine spirit, from whence it has come. "All souls are made of that essence, which is the essence of the whole manifestation. In every soul there exists some part of that essence, however little. The quality of that essence is that it absorbs all that is around it and in time develops, so that it will merge into its own element which is divine." (Hazrat Inayat Khan, *The Soul: Whence and Whither*, p. 26.)

Sufis see God as the macrocosm, the totality of all of existence, as one dynamic unified Being. This is most clearly and fully developed by Ibn 'Arabi, the Andalusian Sufi, who also saw individual human beings as the microcosm, reflecting the divine in their completeness when they undergo the full spiritual transformation. "The microcosm reflects the macrocosm in two ways which are of particular significance for Ibn al-'Arabi's teachings: as a hierarchy of existence and as a divine form, a theomorphic entity. The three basic worlds of the macrocosm—the spiritual, imaginal, and corporeal—are represented in man by the spirit (*ruh*), soul (*nafs*), and body (*jism*)." (William Chittick, *The Sufi Path of Knowledge*, p. 17.)

Ibn 'Arabi, like Rumi, understood the soul to be our individual awareness, and also recognized that she is the bridge that connects the spiritual and the physical dimensions, the *barzakh*. Ibn 'Arabi saw her as possessing unlimited potential for experience and development because God has placed in her all of His attributes. Thus she is potentially the true microcosm: "No connection can be established between the one and the many, the luminous and the dark, without an intermediary, which in man's case is the soul, the locus of our individual awareness . . . The soul—that is to say, our own self-awareness—represents an unlimited possibility for development, . . . 'God created Adam upon His own form' means that He placed within man every one of His attributes, just as He placed all of His attributes within the cosmos." (Ibid., p. 17.)

Rumi believed the soul exists on the mineral level, the vegetal, the animal, the human, and the angelic, meaning that she has the various attributes of all these dimensions of reality. We see a similar statement in the following passage from Ibn 'Arabi: "There is nothing but a rational soul, but it is intelligent, reflecting, imagining, remembering, form-giving, nutritive, growth-producing, attractive, expulsive, digestive, retentive, hearing, seeing, tasting, smelling, and feeling." (Ibid., p. 84.) This passage reflects the Sufi understanding of the various properties and faculties of the soul, which span the physical, the vegetal, the animal, the mental, and the spiritual. But Ibn 'Arabi does not see these as parts used by the soul, but as forms of her own functioning, as he writes: "Moreover, the soul perceives all these affairs, and the diversity of these names. Yet it is nothing to any of them; on the contrary, it is identical with the form of each." (Ibid., p. 84.)

The Sufis see *nafs* as the inner consciousness of the human being, the real self that needs to be awakened and transformed. She is both animal and angel, or as Rumi says: "The creatures are of three kind. First there are the angels, who are sheer intellect . . . Second are the beasts, who are pure sensuality and have no intellect to hold them back . . . There remains poor man, who is compounded of intellect and sensuality. He is half angel and half beast." (Chittick, *The Sufi Path of Love*, p. 86.) The development is a matter of a harmonization of the two where the angelic or spiritual side becomes dominant.

The *nafs* exists in the beginning, in our adult life, as *nafs ammara*, the commanding self, the soul predominated by the animal and sensuous tendencies. The Persian Sufi Alaoddawleh Semnani sees this soul as connected to the second of the seven organs of subtle physiology, the subtle body that contains the *lataif* or subtle centers or organs: "The second organ is on the level corresponding to the soul (*latifa nafsiya*), not the one which is the seat of spiritual processes, but of the vital, organic processes, the *anima sensibilis, vitalis*, and which consequently is the center of uncontrolled desires and evil passions; as such it is called *nafs ammara* in the Quran . . . This means that the level to which it corresponds on the subtle plane is the testing ground for the spiritual seeker." (Henry Corbin, *The Man of Light in Iranian Sufism*, p. 124.)

This initial stage of the soul or self is regarded as the barrier to spiritual illumination because it lacks the necessary refinement and is ruled by the animal passions. She is frequently given the location in the belly, for that is the place of her operation in her initial condition: "The secondary, or 'Commanding' self—which rules the personality most of the time and which provides the barrier against extra-dimensional perception—is not one of these Subtle organs, but it has a 'location,' in the area of the navel. Concentration on this spot may be said to be connected with the attempt to transform this Self." (Idries Shah, *A Perfumed Scorpion*, p. 89.)

Sufi work deals with the *nafs* by transforming her from her initial condition, through stages of development, this way becoming more receptive to her spiritual sources until she becomes one with spirit. It is a process of purification from animal tendencies and drives, from human passions and from confusion and ignorance. So the movement is from animal to human to angelic soul.

"The Self, called Nafs, goes through certain stages in Sufi development, first existing as a mixture of physical reactions, conditioned behaviour and various subjective aspirations . . . The seven stages of the Self constitute the transformation process, ending with the stage of perfection and clarification. Some have called this process the 'refinement of the Ego.'" (Ibid., p. 82.) There are various ways of describing this process, but the general scheme consists of seven stages: the commanding self, the accusing or blaming self, the inspired self, the tranquil or pacified self, the satisfied and fulfilled self, the satisfying and fulfilling or fulfilled-by-God self, and finally, the purified and completed, or perfected self. Another version presents five stages, where the first three are the same as above, and the last two are those of safety, then knowledge: "The fourth is Salimah, who has arrived at a point where, though he be in the midst of the life of the world, he can yet rise above it . . . He is one of whom it may be said that he is in the world, but is not of the world . . . And there is the fifth, 'Alimah, or God-consciousness . . . It is this soul which proves the fulfilling of that purpose for which it came to earth." (Hazrat Inayat Khan, *The Soul: Whence and Whither*, pp. 94–95.)

We can think of the first stage, the commanding self, as corresponding to the animal soul, the last one, the pure and complete self, as corresponding to the angelic soul, and the other five are the various stages of development of the human soul. However, the commanding self is not only the animal soul; it is a development of consciousness dominated by the animal element, which means it is the normal condition of most people: the average self which is the normal sense of ego that is based on conditioning but mostly run by the animal soul. So the animal soul is in command here, which is why it is called the commanding self. It commands you because it drives you; the instincts and drives are what command the soul and her life. The need to satisfy and gratify the appetites and drives is in command here. That is why the Sufis often refer to it as the unregenerate soul.

The commanding self is recognized by the Sufis as the source of "blamable" qualities, the passions, those that are not only reprehensible in the eyes of society but function as barriers to spiritual illumination. Suhrawardi lists ten primary blamable qualities: "(1) *Hawa'* (desire). *Nafs* desireth to advance as to its desires; . . . (2) *Nifaq* (hypocrisy). In many outward states, *nafs* is not concordant with its interior; . . . (3) *Riya'* (hypocrisy) . . . abundance of property or boasting thereof. Pride. Violence. Independence. . . . (4) The claim to Godship, and obstinacy against God. *Nafs* ever desireth that people should praise it; should obey its orders; should love it above all; . . . (5) pride and self-beholding. *Nafs* looketh at its own beauteous qualities; regardeth with contentment the form of its own *hal*. . . . (6) Avarice and parsimony . . . (7) Greediness and asking for more . . . (8) Levity and light-headedness . . . (9) Haste to fatigue . . . (10) Negligence." (Suhrawardi, *The Awarif U'l-Ma'arif*, pp. 130–133.)

The first movement is from the commanding self to the blaming self, the accusing self. This has to do with the beginning of the development of the human, which is the beginning of conscience. It is more accurate to say that the commanding self and the blaming self together is where most people are. The blaming self develops through the function of religion; by following the precepts of exoteric religion the soul can develop a conscience, where there is caring for others, and a self-reproach for being a self-centered animal driven by instincts. The superego is mostly a fake conscience based on the internalization of external prohibitions and rules, while the blaming self is based on real concern, conscience, and remorse. The blaming self is based not on external influence, but on the influence of reality and experience. Just by having experience over and over again you know what is good and what is not good, what works, what doesn't work. This generates concern, remorse, sorrow, shame, guilt for using others, misusing them and misusing oneself, for betraying oneself, for wasting one's energy and self, by seeing the blamable or harmful qualities, passions, and actions of the soul. It is a matter of the soul beginning to discriminate. At the beginning the animal soul has no consideration of consequences; here consequences are taken into consideration, and that is why it is the beginning of the human soul. There is the discrimination, responsibility, and practicality necessary for human life.

Next is the movement to the inspired self, the soul inspired by insights, glimpses, flashes, intimations, intuitions from the essential realm, or as the Sufis say, from the world of spirits and from the divine realm. The soul is inspired about the possibilities of the human soul because she is now open and receptive to certain experiences, certain tastes, that intimate her own greater possibilities and those of reality in general. This is usually the stage at which people want to start the inner work. It is more of a spiritual inspiration, indicating more refinement, more understanding, more refined experience, becoming aware of the possibilities of aliveness, that there is another universe that is much more beautiful, or a way of experiencing the universe that is more sublime. The soul is already moving out of the usual level of civilized society. "When the depraved or commanding self and the reproaching or accusing selves have done their work, the organ of perception and action becomes susceptible to the entry of perceptions formerly blocked. For this reason it is termed the Inspired Self. In this stage come the first indications, albeit imperfect ones, of the existence and operation of a reliable higher element, force, power or communication system." (Idries Shah, *A Perfumed Scorpion*, pp. 83–84.)

The next level is *nafs mutma'inna*, the secure and safe self, the soul that has finally recognized and accepted that she has a spiritual nature, and is aware of it. Here essence is recognized and realized as one's inner nature; here there is basic trust based on love, faith, and hope. She is secure and safe because of this trust and faith, because of direct recognition of spirit, not merely insight and inspiration. The transformation has gone much deeper. The Arabic word, *mutma'inna*, is difficult to translate. The literal translation is something like security, safety, and peace. There is the security of being held by the divine, guided by Him. There is "serene balance, equilibrium of the individuality." (Idries Shah, *The Sufis*, p. 395.)

The next movement is to *nafs radhya*, the satisfied and the contented self. Here it is not just peace and serenity, but there is also a definite fulfillment and a realization of spiritual fullness and richness. This is a movement toward the angelic soul, where spiritual qualities begin to dominate the soul. The heart is more present, the essential heart of love, joy, and contentment. One experiences "power of fulfillment, new ranges of experience not susceptible to description beyond approximate analogy." (Ibid., p. 395.)

The sixth, and penultimate, level is *nafs mardhyah*, the contenting and satisfying self, in which the sense of fulfillment has been integrated and understood to the extent that the person now can guide other people to it. There are apparent differences among Sufis in the meaning of this stage. The term *mardhyah* literally means satisfied by another, in this case the soul is not only satisfied but satisfied by God, in her relationship to Him. This is the sense that comes from the Qur'anic passages. However, the other interpretation relates to the word *murdhyah*, which means satisfying the other. The two meanings are connected. Also, this latter meaning implies that there develops a "new activity and function, including extra dimensions of the individuality." (Ibid. p. 395.)

The seventh and final stage is the pure and complete self. *Pure* implies purification of the drives and the passions, and from confusion, conditioning, and ignorance. The soul is purified, clarified, and at the same time refined to her original state of total receptivity. *Pure* means purified all the way so she is totally receptive to spirit. Hence she is completely spiritual, an angelic soul. Totally nondual with spirit, the soul is completely spiritualized and her potential is available to her in its totality. Here we have "completion of the task of reconstitution, possibility of teaching others, capacity for objective understanding." (Ibid., p. 395.)

The soul in the angelic level is not like the human level. The human soul is transparent to essence. For instance, she is transparent to love; the love comes through her. But on the angelic level the completed soul is not only transparent to the love, the soul is loving, completely loving, where love is her innate expression. It is the difference between the soul possessing an essential heart and the soul being totally essential. However, this final stage is more than simply the angelic soul; it is the human soul that has attained complete spiritualization. The soul becomes totally transparent to the spiritual world, and hence is one with it. The soul here has integrated her full potential, which according to Ibn 'Arabi, includes all of the divine names and qualities. Hence, this stage is that of the complete human being, the true microcosm. This is not a matter only of God-realization, but of this realization functioning as the ground and center of being a human individual, a fully mature human being. According to Ibn 'Arabi, "the Perfect Man is endowed with a perfect 'comprehensiveness.' And because of this 'comprehensiveness' by which he synthesizes in himself all the existents of the universe not individually but in their universality, the Perfect Man shows two characteristic properties that are not shared by anything else. One is that he is the only being who is really and fully entitled to be a perfect 'servant' ('abd) of God. All other beings do not fully reflect God, because each actualizes only a single Divine Name; they cannot, therefore, be perfect 'servants.' The second characteristic feature of the Perfect Man consists in his being in a certain sense the Absolute itself." (Toshihiko Izutsu, *A Comparative Study of Key Philosophical Concepts in Sufism and Taoism*, p. 227.)

In other words, the complete transparency of the soul makes her transparent, above all else, to the very essence of divinity, the absolute truth: "The Perfect Man is the one whom the Absolute penetrates and whose faculties and bodily members are all permeated by the Absolute in such a way that he thereby manifests all the Perfections of the Divine Attributes and Names." (Ibid., p. 232.)

The Sufi work on the soul is based on Sufi ontology and metaphysics, primarily the notion that the absolute essence manifested creation to behold His perfections and all of His possibilities, and specifically created the human soul out of His spirit to be the complete mirror for all such perfections. The impulse for creation is love, and hence this love appears in the soul as love of God, and a passionate desire to know and serve Him. To serve Him is to become a complete vehicle for all His perfections. The love between the soul and her creator is the magnetic force behind the inner journey.

The Sufi methodology is primarily that of *dhikr*, the remembrance of God through His divine names. This is done through invocation and repetition, singly and in groups.

Various orders employ many other methods and attitudes including renunciation, seclusion, self-observation, contemplation and meditation, and so on. The primary thrust is to purify the soul and refine her in order to be receptive to divine effulgence, *tajalli*. The work is understood as being done by the individual soul, but the grace of a teacher or shaykh and, most important, that of God, are indispensable. Some of the Sufi orders employ a specific Sufi subtle physiology, oriented toward the activation and development of the five subtleties, the *lataif*. Both *dhikr* and color visualization are employed here, but an initial development and refinement of the soul is necessary for this activation. "The organ of stimulation of the Five Centers is the transformed consciousness, the personality originally found in the form of the Commanding Self, when it has been through its refining process." (Idries Shah, *A Perfumed Scorpion*, p. 90.)

As these centers are activated, and the divine names and qualities experienced and integrated, they impel the soul toward her refinement and development through the seven stages. It is this individual consciousness that goes through the development, functioning as the specific organ of evolution that through its refinement leads to balance and integration: "The frequent references to refining, purifying and discriminating are connected with this. The dervish refines his consciousness so that he can become aware of states of mind and conditions of reality which are only crudely grasped by the ordinary mind . . . When what we have called the Organ of Evolution is developed and working, the functions of instinct, emotion and intellect are transmuted and work in a new key." (Idries Shah, *The Sufis*, pp. 303–304.)

The process of refinement that opens up the soul to her spiritual sources is frequently described as a marriage between the soul and spirit, *nafs* and *ruh*, leading to a new organ, called technically *qalb*, heart, meaning that the soul now possesses spirit as her inner core and center. This marks the establishment of the human level of soul or spirit. The heart, however, is not only a matter of integrating the spiritual riches; it means that the soul has developed into an organ that is receptive to divine effulgence, and hence can function as the locus of divine manifestation. Furthermore, the marriage ends the contrary tendencies of *nafs* and *ruh*, for the heart's "form (is) pictured with the essence of love; and its vision, illuminated with the light of beholding. . . . From the marriage of the two loves (*ruh* and *nafs*) was born the heart's form; like to Barzakh, it intervened between the sea of *ruh* and the sea of *nafs*; to both inclined; and between them became the hinderer of contentions." (Suhrawardi, *The Awarif U'l-Ma'arif*, p. 208.)

The soul increasingly receives God's gifts as *hals*, spiritual states, which advances her development to new *maqams*, stations or established stages of development. The process of refinement goes through repeated deaths and rebirths, until the soul reaches the station of poverty, where she recognizes that all of her riches, even her spiritual substance and existence, come from her creator. This allows a complete surrender and openness where she experiences extinction into the divine presence, termed *fana'*. This then develops into *baqa'*, remaining in the divine presence, as His expression and servant, as the completed and perfected human.

Appendix D

Essence in Childhood Experience

To appreciate our understanding of how human infants and young children experience essence requires taking into consideration two important distinctions we make in regard to the experience of true nature. The first distinction we make, as discussed in chapter 9, is between true nature as the ground of all manifestation, and its arising as the inner nature of the soul. When it arises as the nature of the soul we call it essence; otherwise we term it Being. It is the same ground, but we can experience it in its fullness or in a more or less limited way. The difference between the two is the position of the soul in relation to true nature. When the experience is transcendence of the individual soul, and all other particular manifestations and forms, we experience it as the true nature of everything and recognize it as the ultimate ground transcendent to all manifestation. Here we can experience true nature in its objective and full purity, as presence-awareness-emptiness. However, we can experience this same true nature from within the individual form of the soul, and recognize it as the inner and true nature of the soul. This is not an experience of transcendence, but it is a direct experience of true nature. In this kind of experience we can be aware of true nature with varying degrees of subtlety and objectivity, or more or less fully and completely. (See *Luminous Night's Journey*, chapters 10–12.)

It seems to us that thinkers who believe that infants do not ordinarily experience their essential nature do not take into consideration this distinction, and other distinctions we make. An important example is Ken Wilber, who takes the position that the neonatal experience is basically physical: "The infant at birth is basically a sensorimotor organism, a holon containing within it cells, molecules, atoms. . . . Of course, the self isn't actually or merely physical, but it is still predominantly oriented to the lowest and most basic dimension of all, the material and sensorimotor. . . . There is nothing particularly spiritual about this state. It cannot take the role of the other; it is locked into its own egocentric orbit; it lacks intersubjective love and compassion. . . . This is the shallowest and most cramped consciousness you can imagine." (Ken Wilber, *A Brief History of Everything*, pp. 158–159.)

In *The Eye of Spirit*, Wilber discusses the Diamond Approach briefly, with an encouraging and appreciative attitude toward it as an example of an integrated approach relevant for our times. Then he adds in a lengthy note a more detailed critique of the Diamond Approach. He does this by a selective review of two books by the author, *Essence* and *The Pearl Beyond Price*. Within his larger attitude of agreement and appreciation he criticizes some of the points brought out in these books. Wilber raises good questions, and addresses crucial elements of childhood experience, an area of research still in its infancy. By addressing some of his main points we will have the opportunity to clarify some of the subtlety and complexity of infant experience, as well as some of the relevant discoveries of the Diamond Approach. We will also be able to redress some of the unclarity and incompleteness in our previous publications in regard to infant experience.

Wilber's main disagreement with the Diamond Approach is with the notion that infants and babies can experience essence, a disagreement that does not primarily depend on actual observation and direct experience, but takes its stance according to mostly theoretical considerations. It seems, first, that Wilber always refers to the first kind of experience of true nature, in the distinction we make above, when he discusses spirit or true nature. For him experience of Spirit seems to always mean experience of transcendent and total purity and objectivity. So it is always experience of infinite Spirit and boundless clarity, emptiness, or nonduality, which is what he tries to refute as the experience of the neonate, as we see in the following passage describing infant experience: "But in no sense is the infant fully in touch with Dharmakaya or Spirit (except insofar as Spirit is the Ground of all things, including infants). . . . the infant is primarily a bodyself, instinctual, vital, impulsive, narcissistic, egocentric; living for food, its God is all mouth." (Ken Wilber, *The Eye of Spirit*, pp. 362–363.)

This stance, we believe, comes partly from the fact that he mostly is addressing authors who hold views like this, for example, Washburn, who thinks of the psyche as having two poles, the ego and the Dynamic Ground. By *ego*, Washburn means something different from our usage of the term; his term seems to be close to our notion of soul or self, as he himself writes: "The ego is a self; it is a self-conscious subject with a unique personal identity." (Michael Washburn, *The Ego and the Dynamic Ground*, p. 244) His view of the psyche is similar to ours, but we do not see the soul and the ground as a polarity, but as organism and ontological ground of the organism. For Washburn the original condition is that of being embedded in the ground, which he sees as the ground of both spirit and libidinal energy: "In the state of original embeddedment, the ego is only minimally differentiated from the Dynamic Ground. It therefore exists primarily as an ego germ immersed in the Dynamic Ground, the original source of life." (Ibid., box on p. 23.)

Therefore, Washburn thinks of the infant's consciousness as abiding in spirit and living in plenitude: "Although alert, engaged in complex interactions with caregivers, and otherwise responsive to its environment, the newborn is prone to give way to states of undivided, boundless fullness. It is prone to 'dissolve' into states of blissful absorption in the Dynamic Ground." (Ibid., p. 49.) This is somewhat similar to our view of infant experience. But rather than seeing the neonate as immersed in the ground of Being, we believe this ground forms the neonate's ontological ground, its existence. However, our view of the quality of early experience lies intermediate to those of Wilber and Washburn.

Also intermediary between the approaches of Wilber and Washburn, but on a more specific cognitive-affective level of developmental analysis, is Harry Hunt's view that essential states, when recognized as such experientially, involve complex or abstract synesthesias, which place them beyond the capacity of ordinary childhood experience. [Hunt, Some developmental issues in transpersonal experience, *Journal of Mind and Behavior* 16 (1995): 115–134, and Experiences of radical personal transformation in mysticism, religious conversion and psychosis: A review of the varieties, processes, and consequences of the numinous, *Journal of Mind and Behavior* 212 (2000): 353–398.] Accordingly, the many examples of adult recall of very early essential states are understood as developmental precocities within a line of spiritual intelligence, much as one would view musical and mathematical prodigies, but here seen as direct exteriorizations of abstract imaginal processes that are also part of the deep structure of the ordinary felt meanings underlying all symbolic cognition. Some indirect support for such an imaginal-metaphoric precocity model of childhood transpersonal states is found in Hunt's research showing superior spatial abilities in adults who recall early essential experiences from childhood, and some indication of poorer adult spatial performance in those with predominant childhood nightmares and night terrors.

For Hunt, as in the Diamond Approach, very young children and infants would manifest more normative stage-specific essential experience in terms of their spontaneity, love, energy, etc. But without the gradually developing capacity for self-referential awareness, these would lack the more abstract synesthetic mediation that would render them as specific states, precocious or otherwise. Infant cross-modal synthesizing experience would instead be limited to the more concrete forms of facial and gestural mirroring. In contrast to Wilber, Hunt rejects the notion that later essential realization, as in classical mystical experience, requires a postformal operational cognitive development in the sense of Piaget. Rather, it can be more parsimoniously understood as the rarely achieved level of formal cognitive operations within what Piaget called the affective schemata, and which he thought were inherently cut off from the abstract formal development he traced within the intellectual schemata. The physiognomies of the lataif as described within the Diamond Approach would, for Hunt, show the beginnings of this abstract development within feeling, also the basis of the arts, but rendered more fully independent of a concrete medium within the developmental line of spirituality. It would be abstract spatial metaphors, synesthetically animated, as in the direct sense of light, flow, color, darkness, depth, etc., per se that make the early essential beingness of the infant recognizable and experienceable as specific transpersonal states, rarely and precociously in early childhood and as a more uniform potential in later development, where our more typical egocentricities of affect and self have been surmounted, whether briefly or more permanently. Accordingly, for Hunt, adult essential development does return to a line of unfoldment generally interrupted in childhood, as with Washburn, but adds to it, at least in part with Wilber, the abstract imaginal processes of mediation that would transform early beingness into the self-referential being experiences of transpersonal states.

It seems to us that Wilber's position is due to his system of categorizing spiritual experiences into four stages, of which the third and fourth are those of pure spirit: "These four stages I call the psychic, the subtle, the causal, and the nondual . . . These are basic structures, and so of course each of them has a different worldview, which I call, respectively, nature mysticism, deity mysticism, formless mysticism, and nondual mysticism." (Wilber, *A Brief History of Everything*, p. 200.) Therefore, when he disagrees with our view he seems to be understanding us to be asserting that the infant lives in the causal stage, of pure boundless Spirit. There is the implication here that causal spirit can only be experienced in this transcendent mode.

To believe that this is the only way we can experience true nature, or pure Spirit, is not only untrue, but will invalidate the experience of most practitioners in the wisdom traditions. This view stems from the naive belief, promulgated in the 1960s, that one either experiences enlightenment or does not, and there is no middle ground. In reality, the experience of true nature—Spirit in its causal or nondual dimensions, to use Wilber's terminology—ranges over a whole continuum. We can experience true nature in its ultimate or absolute ground to various degrees of fullness and completeness. This depends partly on how clarified our soul or individual consciousness is, and partly on the frame of reference from which we experience it.

Wilber apparently criticizes our position on infant and childhood experience because he interprets it as meaning we believe the infant is always in the full experience of true nature. We agree with him that this kind of experience is not the place where an infant, especially the young child, lives. We have never suggested that babies are realized in this way. In fact, we see that our usage of the term *self-realization* for young children's experience can be misleading, because the term is more normally used to refer to the transcendent and complete experience of true nature. Although we always qualify this usage, it has obviously led Wilber to a reading we did not intend.

The actual situation is, however, not so clear cut. Our observation is that infants do experience true nature, but normally from the second perspective, from within the individual form of the soul. The infant's soul is present fundamentally as true nature, but usually in a limited way. This is in part because the infant's soul is not transcendent; in addition, true nature for the infant is usually mixed with various forms that the infant is not able to discriminate from it, and some of these forms are opaque and/or animalistic. First, the soul's plasmatic medium is mixed with true nature, and this medium can be in various conditions of clarity. Furthermore, the baby can be identified with a particular form emerging within the ground of true nature, which tends to limit its luminosity.

An infant's soul can be, and normally is, present in one degree or another of embodiment of true nature. It is not easy to exactly know how completely, but most likely the infant is dimly aware of the presence of true nature, but without recognition, discrimination, or ability to distinguish it from the various forms that enchant it much more powerfully with their color and variety. Infants are present as presence but most likely experience it differently from a self-realized adult.

The infant does not experience true nature unconsciously, but rather without self-recognition or cognitive discrimination. This is an important distinction that Wilber does not seem to consider, even though he is familiar with the teachings of Dzogchen and Kashmir Shaivism, both of which teach that true nature is always present and accessible, but we simply do not recognize it. They both emphasize *recognition* as the central necessity for enlightenment, termed *rigpa* in Dzogchen and *pratyabhinja* in Kashmir Shaivism. Dzogchen teaches that the barriers to the realization of true nature are basically of two kinds, innate and acquired, the latter through mental obscurations. An example of this distinction in ignorance of true nature (*ma-rigpa*) is the following verses from "The Wish-Granting Prayer of Kuntu Zang-po," a revealed text of Riddzin Godemchan:

> *Since the cause of sentient beings' delusion*
> *Is unmindfulness and absence of Knowledge,*

> *Through this, my wish-granting prayer, the Buddha's aspiration,*
> *May everyone recognize Knowledge spontaneously.*
> *"Innate ignorance"*
> *(Accompanying each moment of perception)*
> *Implies unmindful, distracted cognition,*
> *And "conceptual ignorance"*
> *(Selecting, structuring and labeling)*
> *Implies dualistic cognition.*
> *This twofold ignorance, innate and conceptual,*
> *Forms the basis of all beings' delusion.*
>
> KEITH DOWMAN,
> *The Flight of the Garuda,* p. 150

The innate ignorance indicates that recognition is not something lost, but that it is originally absent, which requires an awakening to our true nature. If we want to adhere to Wilber's notion of involution, we can see that it is this recognition that is lost in involution.

Kashmir Shaivism, which is sometimes referred to as the system of *pratyabhijna*, views this absence of recognition as a forgetting by Shiva, the ultimate ground, as it manifests itself in the form of individual soul. It is an integral part of this teaching that Shiva is the actual true self, the inner and true nature of the individual soul, and that the soul achieves liberation upon recognizing this truth. Jaideva Singh writes in the introduction to his translation of one of the main texts of Kashmir Shaivism: "Liberation, according to this system, means the re-cognition (*pratyabhijna*) of one's true nature." (Jaideva Singh, *The Doctrine of Recognition,* p. 25.) Paul Muller-Ortega, in his preface to the same book, writes, explaining the meaning of recognition in this teaching: "In the spiritual process of recognition, because what we recognize is our Self, we re-cognize, re-member, what we already have always known. We remember that we remember. . . . This shift, which radically restructures our self-experience, is more than memory, however. It is a synthetic activity of consciousness which creates a new and liberating gestalt of wholeness, in which reality is seen as it really is." (Ibid., p. xi.)

These sources are clearly open to interpretation; we rely on our own understanding, which is based on direct observation. We use such references to support our understanding for the reader, and to demonstrate its continuity with traditional teachings. But the real proof of a perspective is whether it leads to actual results in practice, whether by applying the understanding individuals open up to their true nature in a way that develops their soul. The proof, in other words, is in the pudding.

Our own observations indicate that there are two modes of experiencing true nature, in terms of recognition. Some individuals actually and consciously have the experience, but do not recognize it for what it is; they do not recognize it to be what they are. In other words, one can experience true nature without recognizing it as one's true nature. But the experience can also arise in such a way that one not only recognizes the phenomenological characteristics of true nature, but recognizes it to be what one truly is. This is not only experience, but recognition, awakening. Furthermore, when one awakens to one's true nature the experience is not that of finding something that was not present before, but of recognizing what has always been present for what it is. When we recognize our normal awareness for what it is we immediately recognize the pervasive field of presence, as Muller-Ortega writes: "Thus, in the process of recognition, ordinary awareness comes to encompass its own unbounded source." (Ibid., p. xii.) It is as if the recognition brings to focus the full truth of true nature. (See *The Pearl Beyond Price*, chapter 37, for further discussion of the awakening to the field of presence.)

The implication of this for early experience is that the soul is in touch with her ground true nature, but does not recognize it as such. She swims in the water, feels the fluidity, and sees the transparency, without discerning it as the water necessary for her existence. The recognition requires the full development of the soul's cognitive faculty. However, our observation is that the infant's soul, though immersed in true nature at times of psychophysical equilibrium and feeling its characteristics, not only does not recognize it for what it is, but also her direct awareness of it is dim and tends to be obscured by the dominance of the forms that arise in her experiential fields. Some of these forms are aspects of essence, of various colors and textures; but even though perceived and felt, they are not recognized for what they are. Some of the arising forms, mostly not aspects of essence, become gradually integrated into her sense of self, an identity that begins to function as a lens through which consciousness looks, further obscuring her ground true nature. The final result is that she is prevented from recognizing her true nature, and also from directly experiencing it, due to the duality arising from the development of ego structures. This is the acquired ignorance described by Buddhism. What remains of it is our ordinary awareness as we normally experience it. In the reverse process, that of self-realization, she needs to penetrate this acquired obscuration, but also to wake up to the arising presence as her deepest nature.

There exists another, more subtle, consideration, that might be a factor in the infant's inability to recognize its ground. It is known that the infant is initially not self-reflective, and that self-reflection develops at some point in early experience. Since the infant is not self-reflective, but at the same time experiences itself immediately, its state of being might be what is known in spiritual traditions as witnessing. This is actually the claim of some spiritual traditions, as later quotes will attest. In pure witnessing the soul is so completely her ground that her posture of awareness is complete witnessing of arising phenomena without any self-reflection. The witness does not reflect on itself. In this case there is awareness of the various arising forms, but no perception of the ground that is the source of awareness, even though one is totally being the ground. This means one is totally being one's true nature, but there is no discrimination of it in consciousness. This is not unconsciousness; this is total awareness. It is being oneself so completely, so intimately, that one has no perceptual or cognitive awareness of it. One is so much one's ground that there is no distance that allows self-reflection. This is the characteristic mode of awareness in the self-realization of the absolute. (See chapter 22.) We see this as a possibility at the earliest times of infancy, but have no observational evidence for it or against it. And if it is present in infancy, it is bound to be only at the very earliest stages, and remains after that only as an intermittent state.

Wilber believes that the researchers who hold that infants are naturally in touch with their spiritual nature are participating in what he calls the pre/trans fallacy; that is, they are confusing prepersonal states, the natural states of the infant before ego development, with transpersonal states, which according to him require the personal development of ego. He singles out Washburn as the main researcher engaged in this fallacy. But according to Washburn, this is not exactly his view. Cortright clearly describes Washburn's view: "Washburn believes the issue is more complex than a simple either/or dichotomy, that these two are intimately related . . . Washburn proposes that the nonegoic potentials (the dynamic ground) when expressed through an ego that is immature or weak look prepersonal. Whereas, these very same nonegoic potentials when expressed through a mature, strong ego appear transpersonal." (Brant Cortright, *Psychotherapy and Spirit*, p. 86.)

This is similar to our understanding. The essential potential of the soul is the same for all stages of development, for it is eternal. It is available to the soul at any of these stages when her consciousness experiences itself directly and immediately. However, the fullness, completeness, and purity of experience depend on the maturity and development of the soul. In infancy, the soul experiences herself directly, so she is in touch with her spiritual ground; but she is immature and undeveloped in many ways, which makes this experience incomplete, vague, and limited. In other words, the essential ground is always experienced through the consciousness of the soul, and hence the quality of this experience will naturally depend on the condition of this consciousness.

Our main reason for believing that the infant's soul is in touch with her true nature, but without recognition, is that we know from experience that when the soul is not perceiving through a construct, a construct that normally develops by the third year of life, her experience of herself is immediate. We also know that when the soul is experiencing herself immediately, without the intermediacy of such constructs, she experiences presence. Actually, this is true almost by definition: the experience of presence is nothing but the soul experiencing herself with immediacy. What else will the soul experience herself as but as presence, when she is experiencing herself immediately? To recall our comparison of experience of the soul to the views of light as wave and particle: From the perspective of true nature, the wave side of Reality, there is only presence. The experience of physicality, the way we experience it as adults, is not possible before we develop the cognitive and ego structures that make it possible for us to experience it this way, as the particle side of Reality. In other words, the infant's experience cannot initally be predominantly of the physical body because, in some sense, there is no physical body yet. The experience of the physical body as we know it in adulthood is due to ego development, as asserted by developmental psychology, and we would be guilty of being adultomorphic to think of the infant experiencing itself this way. (See *The Point of Existence*, chapter 6, for more discussion of the experience of body in the immediacy of presence.)

To take the position that the infant or baby does not experience itself as presence is to believe either that the infant's experience is not immediate or that the physical body is more fundamental than the presence of true nature. In the first case we need to account for what is responsible for the intermediacy. It will be impossible to account for it when we know that structures in the mind that the infant is born without and that develop in the first few years of life are what create intermediacy. It has been known from ancient times, by the various wisdom traditions, that what obscures perception of true nature is nothing but the representational-discursive-thematic mind, a mind that the infant has not developed. This mind is actually what accounts for our experience of ourselves as physical bodies and the world as composed of discrete objects. Without the presence of the cognitively developed mind, how can we say the infant is experiencing things not immediately, or that it acts as a physical body?

In the second case, to believe that when the infant's consciousness is immediate it experiences its body will imply we do not yet understand what immediacy or presence means. Or it will mean that we believe the body is more fundamental than true nature, which is to take the atomistic positivist view that physicality is ultimate; this contradicts all the spiritual teachings of humanity, particularly the nondual ones. In self-realization one knows that when true nature is not perceived it is due to the obscurations of our mental constructs. This is not only our observation; it is the fundamental principle upon which most nondual teachings base their methods, as we see in the following passage from Kashmir Shaivism: "In the *jiva* or empirical individual, Reality or Siva or the Divine transcendental Self is Light-

Bliss that is ever shining within its glory but is hidden from our gaze on account of our thought-constructs. Reality is an Eternal Presence within ourselves. It is *Siddha*, an everpresent Fact, not *sadhya*, not something to be brought into being by our efforts." (Jaideva Singh, *Siva Sutras*, pp. xxxiii–xxxiv.) These thought-constructs obviously do not exist in infancy.

Furthermore, essential presence is a fundamental dimension of the soul, one that she cannot be without. It is her ontological dimension, what gives her existence. In fact it is her true mode of existence. Therefore, the combined factors that essence is the ontological ground of the soul and that she experiences it when she experiences herself without mediation, removes this experience from the considerations of stages and phases of development, for it is eternally present, and experienced whenever we experience ourselves immediately.

Our view, which is based primarily on direct perception of infants and on extensive familiarity with the nature of presence of true nature, is that the essential experience of infants is obvious and self-evident. Nevertheless, we have actually rarely discussed the infant's experience of true nature the way we are discussing it here, as the experience of the ground true nature. To understand this we need to discuss another important distinction we make regarding the experience of true nature. As we see in chapter 9, we make a clear distinction between true nature or essence as the ground of the soul, and the aspects of essence. This is a distinction that Wilber does not seem to appreciate or take into consideration when discussing childhood experience. He misunderstands us when we discuss the infant's experience of the essential aspects, such as love, identity, or personalness, and treats such discussion as if it were about the basic ground of true nature, in its transcendent infinity. We see this perspective in the following passage, where Wilber comments on our description of the baby's experience, where we clearly state that it is an experience of a particular aspect of essence, that of love: "But if sweet, cute, adorable, and fluffy are characteristics of pure Love and essential Being, then kittens are totally Self-realized." (Wilber, *The Eye of Spirit*, p. 368.) We also see it in the following quote, when he addresses our view that with the subtle perceptual capacities we can see that the young child's experience includes Essence. "In fact, with enlightened awareness you can see Essence radiating from dirt; that's not the point. The point is, what is the actual form of Essence that manifests at any given stage?" (Ibid., p. 367.)

We fully agree, but we mean something different when we discuss forms of Essence. We do not mean Wilber's psychic or subtle forms of experience; we mean aspects of essence.

An essential aspect, such as love, is not always manifest, and not explicitly present in the true nature, which is the ground of all manifestation. Hence it may arise in an individual soul's experience, or it may not; it is a transitory though universal manifestation. Only the fundamental dimensions of the ground true nature are eternally present, like awareness and emptiness; essential aspects arise depending on situations. So the presence of an essential aspect is not always everywhere, as in the dirt, as Wilber seems to imply. Only the ground true nature is everywhere, eternally.

Our perception is that the infant's experience is mainly of the individual soul that is only dimly aware of the ground, but much more fully aware of a mix of essential aspects and animal forms and impulses. The infant's soul is bound to be grounded in true nature, as everything is. But since it is a soul with consciousness that is experiencing without the intermediacy of mental constructs, it is bound to have some in-touchness with its true nature, regardless of how dimly or incompletely. We believe it is possible for the infant to fully go into states of ultimate ground, but these will be occasional excursions. The infant does not consciously live in such transcendence, and here we are in agreement with Wilber. We are also somewhat in agreement with Washburn here, and differ only in degree. The infant is in touch with the ground of Being, but only dimly, and goes into boundless bliss and fullness only during peak experiences of fulfillment and satisfaction. The infant's normal experience is mostly a mixture of essential aspects and animal desires, and hence of various degrees of mixture and alternation of well-being and frustration.

It seems, from what we know of Wilber's system, that he does not have a place for the aspects of essence as we understand them, and this might be the central reason for his disagreement with our view of childhood experience. The way he formulated his system excludes the reality of this important dimension of our Being. So when he is considering our discussion of essence in one of its aspects, he takes the view that we are discussing Spirit, or ground true nature, or that we are discussing elements from what he calls the psychic or subtle dimensions. This reflects his system much more than it reflects our understanding.

From our perspective, the causal level is a ground, but this ground differentiates itself into qualities. The ground is pure presence, or the absolute that is presence inseparable from emptiness, but this presence differentiates into qualities, which are qualities of the same presence. The only difference in experience is that the first is nondifferentiated and without qualities, while the second is differentiated into a particular quality. The fact of presence is common to both, the same for both, and it is this fact of presence that is most important about true nature, or Spirit. In other words, we cannot situate the essential aspects in any of the dimensions that Wilber's system posits. It would be inaccurate to put them in the psychic or the subtle levels, for this would put them in the category of energies and visions, which they are not. (See *Essence*, chapter 2.)

It is this lack of appreciation of the essential aspects, and the implications of this lack of understanding, that accounts for why Wilber believes that we vacillate in our view between a retro-romantic Wilber-I and a developmental Wilber-II model. In fact, this difference reflects the truth of two essential aspects; the personal essence, the pearl beyond price; and the essential identity, the point of existence. The personal essence is an aspect that functions as the prototype of individuation of true nature, and hence its integration is a development. The essential identity functions as the prototype of self-realization of true nature, and hence its integration is a discovery and not a development. This is why we published separate books to explore these aspects, *The Pearl Beyond Price* and *The Point of Existence*.

That infants experience essential aspects is something of which we are certain. It is not a theoretical position. The important point, however, is not only that Wilber misunderstands our view because of his apparent lack of appreciation of essential aspects, but that his view neglects this dimension of Being that we have found, in the Diamond Approach, to be of great usefulness for individuals who want to connect to their true nature. The perspective and understanding of essence in its aspects is one of the greatest strengths of the Diamond Approach, and one of its main contributions to the knowledge of Spirit and its realization. This understanding, and the perspective of how to work with these aspects in relation to particular sectors of our ego-self, is not only central to the Diamond Approach, it is its most distinguishing characteristic. To not understand or appreciate it is tantamount to not understanding a central and foundational tenet of the Diamond Approach.

The importance of the essential aspects is that they are more accessible than the ground true nature to the normal adult soul. They are more accessible because they embody qualities that the soul can recognize and to which she can readily relate. They are qualities, like love, compassion, and will, that the soul knows she needs and is happy to learn about. On the other hand, true nature in its ground, what Wilber calls Spirit or causal spirit, is not only not so easy to access, but also more difficult to understand or to relate to, and vastly more difficult to integrate into our lives.

At the same time, the essential aspects embody the same presence as that of the ground true nature. They are its differentiations, just as the colors of the rainbow are the prismatic differentiations of white light. Therefore, when we become familiar with the essential aspects, it is an easy step to recognize and appreciate this ontological presence. By focusing then on the presence common to all essential aspects we can connect more readily to nondifferentiated presence, the ground true nature, transcendent spirit. These are actually some of the major stages of traversing the path in the Diamond Approach. We have found this approach very effective in helping individuals connect with their true nature, and because of this most of the author's books are devoted to the understanding of one essential aspect or another. *The Pearl Beyond Price* is devoted to the understanding of the aspect of personal essence, *The Point of Existence* to the aspect of essential identity, and so on.

An important element of our understanding of essential aspects is what we have termed the theory of holes. (See *Essence*, chapters 3 and 4.) Part of this perspective is that as the soul loses touch with her essential aspects in childhood she experiences these losses as holes. The soul ends up experiencing a deficient emptiness instead of the presence of essence with a particular quality. These holes become repressed as part of the process of the development of ego structures, leaving these structures standing on a ground of deficient emptiness.

Wilber does not dispute the existence of such holes, but explains them as the absence of upcoming development, a longing emptiness anticipating the arrival of essence, and hence not reflecting a previous loss: "This experiential aspect of the hole is not the emptiness of something once present but repressed, but of something new struggling to emerge. The experiential emptiness is a profound yearning for the greater tomorrow, not a lament at the loss of a lesser yesterday." (Wilber, *The Eye of Spirit*, p. 367.) We do observe that such longing emptiness anticipates the arrival of a development, especially when new dimensions of essence are about to emerge. However, this kind of emptiness is not the same thing as the holes we discuss in the theory of holes. The holes we discuss are not only forms of emptiness, but the emptiness feels specifically like a lack, accompanied with pain about something missing. When we investigate such deficient emptiness, what arises is normally not a longing toward something new, but a pain, a wound of loss. Sometimes the emptiness will appear with a longing for what is missing, but when we investigate this longing emptiness it will also lead to the same wound. This wound, instead of reflecting a lack of new development, reveals, upon investigation, a childhood history of loss. Both the emptiness and the pain reveal one's personal history of how the particular aspect became disconnected from one's experience. It is usually when such childhood content is fully understood that the essential aspect emerges in consciousness.

Wilber believes that the childhood content definitely needs to be worked through to allow for new development, for example, the emergence of essence, because such content blocks its emergence. It is true, in our observation, that such content blocks the emergence of essence, but such content does not en masse block the emergence of essence in general, as Wilber believes. We find the content quite specific and precisely particular to the aspect arising, with different kinds of content arising for different essential aspects. Also, the content explicitly contains childhood memories of essential aspects, and childhood issues about these particular aspects. Many of the case vignettes we give in

The Void, The Pearl Beyond Price, and *The Point of Existence* clearly demonstrate this.

Wilber's theory does not explain this phenomenon; it explains a different kind of emptiness that also occurs in the spiritual path. However, Wilber's belief that childhood content blocks in a general way the emergence of new developmental states, as those of essence, is the common belief in transpersonal psychology, and is also held by some spiritual teachings. This view is what gives validity to transpersonal psychology, which correctly takes the position that spiritual work requires working on the conflictual history of childhood. But this generalization may lead, in our view, to the wrong view of how our psychological issues are related to our true nature. That is why we do not subscribe to the view of transpersonal theory that one first needs to work on one's psychological issues, and then on spiritual development. Both Wilber and Washburn subscribe to this view. However, Wilber has been softening his stance on this position, and Washburn's position is not absolutely linear in this way. Washburn writes: "Once regression in the service of transcendence has returned the ego to the Ground, a developmental reversal occurs: the dark night of the soul comes to an end and a period of psychic renewal begins. The period of regressive deconstruction is over and the ego enters a period of healing reconstruction, a period that, adopting traditional terminology, I shall call regeneration in spirit." (Washburn, *The Ego and the Dynamic Ground*, p. 203.)

We find this view too linear to reflect the reality of experience; nor does it take into consideration the existence of essential aspects. The Diamond Approach begins with the idea that we need to work on our psychological issues, which will include regressive processes, if we are serious about our spiritual development. But then the process becomes much more specific, and much less linear. We find that psychological issues and spiritual development do not arise one after the other, consecutively. Rather, we find that the psychological issues are completely intertwined with the phenomenology of Spirit, and with the specific characteristics of essence and its various aspects. Psychological issues, which have their genesis mostly in childhood, plus necessary regressions, continue, as a result, into the most advanced stages of spiritual development. Furthermore, childhood content does not block essence in a general way. Specific segments of our childhood issues and ego structures block particular spiritual states. And it is our finding that the correspondence between psychological issues originating in childhood and particular essential states appears to be universal to all souls, hence the possibility of a particular body of knowledge that maps such correspondence. The Diamond Approach contains such knowledge. All the books we have published are elucidation of elements of this knowledge.

The specificity of understanding essence and its aspects, and the precise relation of particular essential states to corresponding psychological issues and ego structures, is the hallmark of the Diamond Approach. To not understand this is to not understand the Diamond Approach, and hence to not understand the reason for our attempt to put this knowledge out in published form.

We are grateful to Wilber's critique partly because it has alerted us to the difficulty of understanding the essential aspects, as well as to the inadequacy of our writing to address this difficulty. It would seem that frequently the reader believes he or she understands what we mean about an essential aspect when in reality this is not so, and sometimes the perspective of aspects completely escapes the reader's attention. Then the reader misses the fact that this is a new paradigm different from the traditional ones, as we see clearly in the next passage from a transpersonal psychologist: "There is some lack of clarity about what essence is in relationship to other spiritual systems. Although Ali says that essence is how humans experience spiritual Being, he uses this to mean different things at different times. He positions himself in the nondual tradition with its accompanying biases and accepts the Buddhist notion of no-self, yet speaks of essence as something that mediates between the individual and the Absolute. Sometimes he seems to equate essence with *atman* or Buddha-nature while at other times he attributes qualities and feelings to essence that do not appear in any classical descriptions of *atman* or Buddha-nature." (Brant Cortright, *Psychotherapy and Spirit*, pp. 93–94.)

To understand what essential aspects are would clarify all these points, but it seems that this is not an easily accessible understanding. This difficulty is partly due to the fact that spiritual matters are not easily accessible to the discursive mind, partly to the personal limitations of the author in communicating his knowledge, and partly because the perspective of essential aspects is a new perspective, different from the conceptualizations in the various traditional teachings. Most readers seem to assume that the perspective of essential aspects is the same as, or parallel to, that of one traditional teaching or another, and in this way misapprehend our teachings.

The theory of holes—which includes the distinction between essence as the ground of the soul and essence as aspects, as well as how each aspect relates to a particular psychodynamic issue or ego structure—is a new discovery, a paradigmatic shift particular to the Diamond Approach. As usual, it is not easy to recognize or accept a paradigmatic shift in a particular field of research, and the tendency is to conflate it with other, older paradigms. But this misses the advantages of the new development.

We believe it is this kind of conflation and lack of recognition of this new paradigm, a lack of understanding that is crucial to appreciating our view of childhood experience of essence, that makes Wilber lump the Diamond Approach's view of childhood experience with the camp he calls "romantic," and makes him believe that this view is not new or original, but dates back to the classic romantic philosophers: "But at this point Ali is committed to a very strong Romantic model. 'Our understanding of how Essence arises in children and then is put aside in favor of ego identifications is a new and rather surprising set of observations.' Of course, it is neither new nor surprising, but the two-centuries-old Romantic developmental scheme." (Wilber, *The Eye of Spirit*, p. 361.)

Wilber seems to believe, perhaps due to not taking the two distinctions we have discussed above into consideration, that if abiding in presence the infant should not be capable of having animal reactions. This position disregards the knowledge that the condition of most realized individuals is that they abide in presence, but are definitely capable of animal reactions. This is what we mean when we say that something, in this case animal reactivity, is potential in the soul. For us, spirit is not only a potential for the soul; it is her ontological ground. And the animal is an inherent dimension of our potential; it will arise in the experience of the realized individual in its gross forms until this individual learns to harmonize it with the essential ground.

But the animal is not the ontological ground of the soul, at any stage of its development.

Wilber actually believes that the infant is capable of experiencing spiritual states, as when he writes: "This is also why I have never denied that transpersonal experiences of various sorts are available during the preegoic period; I have simply denied that they are due to any preegoic structures." (Ibid., 179–180.) This he attributes to what he calls "the trailing clouds of glory," a phrase of Wordsworth with which he refers to the end of the process of involution. He also attributes to Tibetans and others that the human child does not lose touch with his essential nature until around the age of three, which is exactly our understanding: "The traditions vary on how long it takes, in infancy, for these 'trailing clouds of glory' of the psychic/soul witnessing to fade. Teachers I have talked to (and various texts themselves) suggest that it seems to vary from a few weeks to a few years, depending primarily on the 'strength' of the transmigrating soul-drop." (Ibid., p. 181.)

This view is similar to ours, down to the timing, but differs in terms of the source of the experience. Wilber explains these early essential experiences with his notion of the binary soul. He seems to take the Tibetan view of two types of indestructible drops, and Aurobindo's notion of the dual soul—that the soul has both divine and animal dimensions—to mean that the human being possesses two separate souls, one spiritual and the other animal, the spiritual goes through transmigration and the animal dies with the body: "This, as we will see, is also similar to Aurobindo's distinction between the frontal consciousness, which develops in this lifetime, and the deeper/psychic being, which transmigrates." (Ibid., p. 180.) He believes that the infant is the animal soul only, and that essential perceptions are occasional penetrations from the divine soul, which the child is normally not experiencing. This position actually contradicts the Tibetan view that he cites, for this view is that the consciousness loses touch with its ground gradually in the first few years of life, instead of the ground appearing in occasional flashes as he asserts here.

Furthermore, there is no indication that Aurobindo regarded these two souls as separate, apart and different, or as two stratified hierarchical but dissociated systems; otherwise he would have believed in ultimate duality. He actually called the chapter that discusses this question "The Double Soul in Man," and not "the two souls in man," and his discussion is clearly of two different dimensions of the soul, even though his terminology sometimes seems to imply two entities: "So too we have a double psychic entity in us, the surface desire-soul which works in our vital cravings, our emotions, aesthetic faculty and mental seeking for power, knowledge and happiness, and a subliminal psychic entity, a pure power of light, love, joy and refined essence of being which is our true soul behind the outer form of psychic existence we so often dignify by the name." (Aurobindo, *The Life Divine*, vol. 1, p. 220.)

The argument also applies to the tantric Tibetan view. It is not clear whether Wilber actually adheres to such duality, but his explanation of early essential experiences seems to imply it. To take the notion that the soul has different dimensions and potential to mean having different and separate souls can lead to problematic conclusions. It will mean, for instance, that we interpret the Sufi notion of the evolution of the soul through mineral, plant, animal, human, and angelic souls to mean that human beings possess five separate souls: mineral, plant, animal, human, and angelic. Even though the Sufis refer to animal and vegetal soul and so on, it is clear that they mean different stages of evolution of the same soul, corresponding to the integration of the various dimensions of her potential.

Our view of the animal and divine souls is that there is one soul that has both divine/angelic and animal potentials of experience. Her ultimate ground is always the divine or true nature, but she is capable of manifesting various forms of experience on all levels of experience. In other words, the soul has many dimensions of potential, one of these is the animal, and another is the essential; but it also has others, as in the mental and emotional. The soul manifesting an animal form of experience, characterized by desire and aggression, does not indicate that there is another soul. All forms of experience, whether animal desires or essential aspects, are momentary and transitory manifestations; only her ground of true nature wedded to its dynamism is lasting. The soul in her natural condition is open to the totality of her potential: the divine, the animal, and others. (See chapters 5 and 10.)

Wilber's idea of two souls seems to be an attempt to support his theory of involution, which he seems to think is necessary for his theory of evolution. Wilber's theoretical position relies on his formulation that evolution occurs after involution. He believes that spirit first devolves gradually, moving from absolute void spirit to soul to mind until it becomes matter. He believes it is the perennial philosophy's view that "self becomes alienated from spirit during involution, not during anything that happens in evolution. Involution is the prior (but also timeless) movement whereby spirit goes out of itself to create soul, which goes out of itself to create mind, which goes out of itself to create body (*prana*), which goes out of itself to create matter. .... Evolution then proceeds to unfold and remember that which was enfolded and forgotten." (Wilber, *The Eye of Spirit*, p. 362.) Evolution then proceeds in the reverse order of involution.

He bases this position on the notion of the great chain of Being, which position he believes such thinkers as Plotinus and Aurobindo promulgated. Involution ends with Spirit becoming matter, and that is the point at which the human being is born. According to this theory the infant is all physical, or all animal, for it is at the point of greatest involution, and hence it cannot ordinarily experience essence. (See quotation on pages 527–528.) But he is not completely clear in his position. On the one hand he believes that the infant at birth is basically a sensorimotor organism, a holon containing within it cells, molecules, atoms; on the other hand he insists the self isn't actually or merely physical, that there is nothing particularly spiritual about this state, either. If the self in infancy is not actually physical, but there is nothing spiritual about it, then what is it?

One can deduce an involution theory by reading the accounts of the great chain of Being. For these accounts can sound as if Being or God hides himself in the process of creation, in descending worlds of manifestation, ending in the physical world where we can perceive no spirit. We see this clearly in Kabbalistic accounts, in the idea of God constricting His light in each successive world of creation, as in the following passage:

"These levels or stages of creation therefore fulfill two very important functions. First, by concealing God's light through successive constrictions, they allow for the existence of countless independent creatures, culminating in man. Second, they provide man with a ladder with which he can climb to the highest spiritual rungs and thereby infuse his earthly life with greater and greater awareness of God." (Aryeh Kaplan, *Inner Space*, pp. 97–98.)

This can be seen as involution only if the higher stages become inaccessible somehow to the lower ones, or by completely changing into them. The above quote contradicts the first possibility, for it would then be difficult to account for the presence of a ladder of ascent. In his view of childhood experience, Wilber seems to move close to this second interpretation, even though he clearly understands the great chain of Being as a nested hierarchy. Therefore, we can only assume he assumes the first possibility, which means that the higher stages become inaccessible in principle to the lower ones. But then we need to account for how this inaccessibility occurs, from our experience and observation of both lower and higher stages. Experience shows that the inaccessibility is due to the veils of representation, identification with partial manifestations, etc., that stand at the roots of ignorance. These kinds of veils are clearly developmental, and are not present in infancy. In other words, inaccessibility to these higher levels of Being is due to acquired ignorance. The only veil that is possible in such early times is the one in relation to recognition of true nature, and understanding it for what it is, which forms the innate ignorance of the soul.

It seems to us that Wilber's understanding of involution is a misreading of both Plotinus and Aurobindo. It is true that Plotinus taught that spirit moves from absolute spirit to mind to soul to matter. First, Plotinus's notion of mind is different from that of modern Western thought, the latter of which Wilber understands and uses in his theory of involution and evolution. By *mind*, Plotinus meant what he called *nous*, Intellectual Principle, knowing inseparable from being: "in the Intellectual-Principle itself, there is complete identity of Knower and Known . . . there, no distinction exists between Being and Knowing." (Plotinus, *Enneads*, p. 241.) It is related to what we refer to as basic knowledge in chapter 4, as discriminating awareness in chapter 18, the way of knowing that Western thought has collapsed into representational knowing. And by *soul*, Plotinus was referring to universal soul, and not to the individual soul. It is the dimension of creative dynamism in our perspective, the dimension of the logos. (See chapter 20.)

The important point, however, is that Plotinus did not speak of involution. He did not say that spirit actually transforms gradually until it becomes only matter, or that by moving to the next phase it loses, in principle, contact with its source, which seems to be Wilber's inference, and the idea that makes his position about infancy experience intelligible. It has been clear to thinkers and philosophers for a long time, and is actually the accepted understanding of Plotinus, that he meant that spirit has different dimensions of manifestation, with each level emanating the next one. But he never suggested that spirit ceases to be on its original level, or loses contact with it, through the emanation of successive levels. He explicitly taught the coexistence of the various dimensions where each emanated dimension can contemplate its source, an important and repeated teaching in his *Enneads*.

If we can discern a notion of involution in Plotinus's thought, it is only in the sense that the individual soul can lose touch with, or forget, her deeper dimensions. Hence his thought is primarily that of return to the original purity of the soul—not a development in the sense Wilber presents—by becoming detached from preoccupation with the body and its physical world, a theme he shared with Plato and most other Greek thinkers. In fact, Plotinus clearly thought of the soul as having a part of her always in the spiritual dimension; the soul never completely becomes physical or totally dissociated from the spiritual: "Even our human Soul has not sunk entire; something of it is continuously in the Intellectual realm." (Plotinus, *Enneads*, p. 342.) We see Plotinus's view of the chain of being clearly in the next passage: "In two ways, then, the Intellectual-Principle enhances the living quality of the Soul, as father and as immanent presence; nothing separates them but the fact that they are not one and the same, that there is succession, that over against a recipient there stands the Ideal-Form received." (Ibid., p. 350.)

The next quotation clearly shows Plotinus' view that the ideal world of *nous* is nothing but the true nature of the ordinary world. In other words, the ordinary world is not separate and fallen in principle, but it is the same as the spiritual world, except that we do not see it as it is. Hadot, one of the twentieth century's best interpreters of Plotinus, writes about the latter's view of the spiritual world, the world of forms: "By this method, there appears before our eyes the world of forms, which thus turns out to be the visible world freed from its materiality; that is to say, reduced to its beauty . . . What, then, is the relationship between the visible world and the world of Forms? If the latter can be seen through the former, and if the vision of the spirit can prolong the vision of the eye, it is because there is continuity between the two worlds: they are the same thing, at two different levels. Plotinus insists strongly on this continuity. 'Our world,' he writes, 'is not separated from the spiritual world' (II, 9, 16, 11). . . . The Spirit's vision, prolonging and developing the vision of the eye, allows us to glimpse, behind the material world, a world of Forms. The material world is nothing other than the 'visibility' of these Forms, and is therefore to be explained by them." (Pierre Hadot, *Plotinus or the Simplicity of Vision*, pp. 37–39.)

The accepted view of the great chain of Being among both Eastern and Western mystical thinkers is that of emanation, not involution. The other contending view is that of manifestation, or immanence, which means that a dimension of spirit does not emanate the next one, it merely manifests it within its own field. This is the view of the higher nondual teachings, such as Dzogchen and Mahamudra, Kashmir Shaivism and the most elevated teachings in Sufism, for example those of Ibn 'Arabi. Both views conceive all the dimensions of being as coexisting, the first hierarchic in grades and levels, and the second as coemergent and mixed, each one containing the next one, as we see in the following quote from Sufism: "The theory of Emanation supposes the Universe to descend in successive, widening circles of being from the supreme. . . . The theory of Immanence (Shuhudiyya School) declares that God is everywhere present. The Observer is one and the mirrors are multitudinous. The multiplicity of mirrors does not affect the oneness of reflection in the numerous mirrors . . . The theory of Emanation is compared to a pyramid which extends from a point on the top downwards to the base in expanding gradations. The symbol of Immanence is a point in the centre, which expands all round towards the sphere." (Sirdar Ikbal Ali Shah, *Islamic Sufism*, p. 122.)

This indicates that the soul always has the fundamental dimensions of being as potentially accessible at any stage of development. True nature as pure spirit is also always potentially accessible because it forms our ontological ground. Thus only obscurations, as in Buddhism, or attachment to the bodily world, as in ancient Greek thought, can limit this access. The difficulty of accessibility is not metaphysical but psychological. It is acquired ignorance.

We think that the notion of the soul's potential, a potential that includes both the animal and the spiritual, is consistent with Wilber's theory of evolution of spirit, and corresponds far more closely with direct experience and the spiritual literature of humanity. We are in general agreement with his theory of evolution of spirit, and appreciate the breadth and depth of his vision. We disagree with his theory of involution, which we see as a misreading of the great spiritual thinkers of the wisdom traditions, and with his ideas of the infant's range of experience.

If, however, we want to preserve the notion that Spirit goes through involution, then we need to explain what Wilber's Tibetan and Indian sources say, that involution does not come to completion until the third year of life. Then our understanding of how the soul loses touch with her essence will function as an adequate explanation of how this occurs. Furthermore, Wilber's evolutionary theory will be much closer to the notion of soul's development we have in the Diamond Approach, to which this book has been devoted.

We wish to express our appreciation for Wilber's bold attempt to create a transpersonal theory and to situate it within a larger cosmic evolutionary perspective. We also wish to appreciate the fact that he recognized in the Diamond Approach a true synthesis of the psychological and spiritual, the individual and universal. It is true that he seems not to take into consideration the new conceptualization in the Diamond Approach of aspects of causal spirit or ground essence, but he is open enough to recognize the new integration that our approach makes, and is courageous enough to acknowledge it publicly.

Our work is not in the same line as that of Wilber or Washburn, in the sense that we are not trying to create a transpersonal theory. Our writings constitute an introduction of the Diamond Approach, a path of inner transformation, to interested readers, and in the process make a contribution to the knowledge of Spirit. However, we find ourselves to be moving in the same current of thought, where there is a great deal of agreement in the ideas, with some differences, which are natural in such circumstances.

Appendix E

Soul as Autopoietic System

The paradigm of self-organization has become increasingly influential in the past few decades in various fields of science, especially evolutionary theory. The process of self-organization links inanimate systems of matter and living creatures; this paradigm is applied in the understanding of biological, social, ecological, and cultural structures. Although self-organization has long been understood as a basic property of living systems, animals, and plants, only since the 1960s has it been applied to inanimate matter as well.

This development involved considerations of thermodynamics, a branch of physics that began as the study of the statistical properties of large aggregates of particles. It concerned itself mainly with the study of isolated systems, systems of components not operating in exchange with an environment. The second law of thermodynamics states that an isolated system moves irreversibly toward entropy, an increasing state of disorder, culminating in equilibrium at maximum disorder. The isolated system, when left to itself, irreversibly moves toward dissolution of whatever structure it started with, toward increasing disorganization. For example, if we pour hot water in one side of a pan, and cold water at the other side, the system initially has a structure, with two different thermal sides. However, left to itself it gradually and inexorably moves toward loss of this structure, toward becoming one homogeneous system of lukewarm water, i.e., with no structure.

It was recently discovered that the second law of thermodynamics does not always apply, especially not to systems open to an environment. This was the discovery of a Nobel laureate in chemistry, Ilya

Prigogine, and his collaborators, which he developed into the theory of dissipative structures. (Prigogine, Nicolis, and Babloyantz, "Thermodynamics of Evolution," and Prigogine, "Irreversibility as a Symmetry Breaking Factor.") He discovered some chemical reactions that demonstrated that open chemical systems can spontaneously develop structures, when they exchange energy and matter with their environment. In other words, they eliminate the extra entropy in their exchange, becoming coherent evolving systems, now called dissipative structures. These open systems evolve structures through the capacity of importing energy from the environment and exporting entropy. They are nonequilibrium dynamic systems, continuously destructuring old structures and developing new ones. Prigogine showed how nonequilibrium can be a source of order and organization, resulting in the recognition of a new ordering principle, termed *order through fluctuation*, but most importantly pointing to the possibility of self-organization in open systems in general.

This principle of self-organization is now applied to the study of the evolution of living and nonliving systems such as cells, microorganisms, brain structures, the biosphere, planets, stars and galaxies, the whole universe; it is also used to understand the development and functioning of cities, groups, cultures, and so on. All these are open dynamic systems that have the property of self-organization. (Erich Jantsch, *The Self-Organizing Universe*.)

A self-organizing open living system has a central function, which is that of autopoiesis, a concept introduced by the Chilean biologist Humberto Maturana, who further developed it with cognitive scientist Francisco Varela. (Maturana, *Biology of Cognition*; Maturana and Varela, *Autopoietic Systems*.) Autopoiesis is the mechanism that makes living beings into autonomous systems; it is the function of continuous self-renewal through exchange with the environment and the regulation of this process in such a way that integrity of structure is maintained. Such a "dissipative structure continuously renews itself and maintains a particular dynamic regime, a globally stable space-time structure." (Jantsch, *The Self-Organizing Universe*, p. 31.) An autopoietic system is one primarily characterized by self-renewal, rather than being allopoietic, geared primarily toward the production of a product or function, as in the case of a machine. The human fetus is a clear example, for it continuously renews and develops itself into a coherent dynamic living system, in constant exchange with its uterine environment, a process that continues after birth with increasing autonomy.

Thus an autopoietic system is one that can renew itself by constantly dissolving old structures and developing new ones, through the exchange with the environment and the metabolism of this exchange in interaction with the system's own dynamic potentials.

We can now formulate in the language of systems theory our previous discussion of the soul as an organism of consciousness. Understanding the soul as an autopoietic system illuminates various properties that are central to the soul's development, functioning, and transformation. In short, the soul is an open dissipative dynamic system of consciousness capable of self-organization. The soul, like all living organisms, lives within a context, in this case a space-time environment with emotional, mental, spiritual, social, aesthetic, political, and cultural dimensions, among others. She is in constant exchange with her environment, and through the metabolism of this exchange she develops and matures. She constantly dissolves inner structures and builds new ones, through the interaction of her inner potentials with her contact with the environment.

As a self-organizing (autopoietic) system, the soul has the following intrinsic properties:

- She is a dynamic continuous system, a field.
- She is an open system in interaction with an environment, not a closed or isolated system.
- She renews herself through the interplay of what she receives from the environment with her inner potentials, which results in output into the environment.
- She is not a static structure, but a dynamic and evolving consciousness. In other words, it is inherent to the soul that she is both presence and process, inseparable as presence in dynamic self-renewal.
- She is an evolving system of consciousness.
- She evolves through the dissolving of older structures as new ones develop. In other words, her development involves constant restructuring.

- She is self-organizing, developing through the evolution of more complex higher-order organization. This means that new structures do not simply replace old ones, but include them in a higher order of organization. This inclusion involves temporary dissolution of structures preceding the emergence of higher structures that include in their constituents the developments of the early structures.
- She is a non-equilibrium open system, which allows her to maintain a coherent order with openness, through fluctuation or change.

The soul is actually the prototype of self-organizing systems, which can be experienced directly as a self-organizing Riemannian manifold. Appreciating the characteristics of self-organization and autopoiesis can help us understand some of the difficulties we encounter in our inner journey of development. It shows that the flexibility and malleability of the soul are necessary for her self-renewal, for her to continue to function as an autopoietic system, rather than a machine.

Consequently, the rigid and fixated structures created through ego development can be seen as barriers to the function of autopoiesis. For the soul to mature, she cannot retain the same structures that she develops at any particular stage of her evolution. To become attached to these structures, which is the hallmark of egoic life, means active resistance to self-renewal. The hallmark of egoic existence is the permanent identification with structures created in early life. Through this attachment to established structures the soul tries to remain in static equilibrium, antithetical to her nature of open non-equilibrium. She attempts to maintain order through fixation, which necessitates isolation, while her nature is to be open, which means she needs to find order through fluctuation, i.e., through change. Or as Jantsch puts it: "Autopoiesis and evolution, global stability and coherent change, appear as complementary manifestations of dissipative self-organization." (Ibid., p. 44.)

Hence, egoic life constitutes an attempt to turn the soul into a machine, a closed and relatively isolated system. The rigidity and fixity of the ego-self point to how the soul has become mechanical and isolated, and explains the primary reasons for its lack of vibrant living unfoldment. Furthermore, the second law of thermodynamics will impel the rigidly structured soul toward entropy, toward less order, more disorganization, and hence ultimately toward disintegration. This accounts for the continual suffering of ego life, and its hopeless and incessant attempts at balancing itself. Egoic life is bound to lead toward disorganization and breakdown, not renewal and evolution.

To move toward renewal, the soul must recognize and respect her dissipative nature, and allow the process of autopoiesis to resume, or to resume more fully. This becomes the process of inner work, in which older structures are made transparent, dissolve, and allow for new structures of experience to emerge in a way that integrates the learning of the old structures. This is a metabolic process where the conscious medium of the soul is liberated from its rigid structuring, and develops by becoming increasingly structured by her essential nature and qualities. This process leads to realization and liberation, which is the regaining of the full autopoietic function of the self-organizing principle of the soul. More precisely, this function is the way the soul's inherent creative morphing dynamism expresses itself in evolutionary self-renewal, culminating in self-liberation.

Liberation, then, is not the attainment of a static state or ground. It is rather the freedom of the soul to fully engage in autopoiesis, that is, to reach the flexibility and impressionability, combined with mature autonomy, that allow her to be transparent to the fullness of her potential, in a dynamic responsiveness to her environment. Her self-renewal becomes a continuous dynamic morphogenic process, where she constantly and spontaneously restructures herself, expressing the richness of her potential in attunement with the demands and needs of her environment.

We see that egoic life basically does not respect the autopoietic nature of the soul; it tends to make the open, living system that is the soul into a closed and isolated one, more like a machine. The difference between the egoic and the essential life is not absolute, for the soul cannot become completely a machine. She is inherently an open and dynamic system, and hence rigid ego structuring only limits this openness and constrains her dynamism; it cannot completely eliminate them. When the soul is extremely closed and isolated, she will generally move toward breakdown and disorganization. More accurately, the more rigid and fixed is the ego structuring of the soul, the more she will be subject to the second law of thermodynamics. In contrast, greater self-organization and autonomy are the natural outcome of dissipative autopoiesis, with its dynamic self-renewal. Therefore, inner work is a matter of liberating and expanding the autopoietic function of the soul, optimizing her capacity for self-renewal. This freedom is a central part of liberating the soul's creative dynamism.

Appendix F

Consciousness Research

In the past few decades the study of consciousness has become a very active interdisciplinary field with intense research and debate, spanning the disciplines of philosophy, psychology, neuroscience, and even physics. The attempt to study consciousness scientifically has run into many difficulties due to the nature of the subject matter, but has also resulted in some fertile lines of inquiry. By *consciousness*, the researchers mean either the capacity for perception or the awareness of sentience or subjectivity; the emphasis changes according to the particular study. The area of greatest disagreement is the question of explaining subjective experience. Researchers generally fall into two major camps on this issue, divided by the mode of access emphasized in the research. Guzeldere describes it this way: "But as far as the epistemology of the matter goes, there appears to be a genuine asymmetry between the *mode of access* to facts of one's own consciousness and the mode of access to facts about other's conscious states.

"This asymmetry is what grounds the important distinction between systematic approaches to consciousness from the *first-person perspective* and the *third-person perspective*. Further, this distinction is important because it is what, in turn, determines the central methodological axes of what are loosely referred to as the *phenomenological approach* and the *physicalist approach*." (Guzeldere, "Problems of Consciousness," *Journal of Consciousness Studies*, 115.)

Thus the two camps are the researchers who believe that consciousness should be studied by observing the phenomenological characteristics of our subjective experience, and those who believe we should study it by seeing its externally observable role in perception, cognition, and behavior. The field as a whole studies what are called the problems of consciousness, as in the questions of what it is, its media and mechanisms, its locus, who is characterized by it, why it exists, how it arises or emerges, and so on. The hardest problem turns out to be the question of how to account for the inner characteristics of conscious experience, the inner feel and sense of it, its *qualia*. This is where there is the greatest and most heated disagreement and debate, for the spectrum of "positions with respect to qualia extends from taking qualia to be non-physical properties that require a new ontology, to reductively identifying qualia with neurophysiological properties." (Ibid, p. 135.)

The subjective versus objective approaches to consciousness culminate in field theory emergence and localization reductionism, where consciousness is regarded as causal with respect to functioning or as an epiphenomenal by-product, respectively. The attempt to localize consciousness is not uniform, and tends to be seen in terms of localization of functions of consciousness in various parts of the brain or nervous system. These attempts utilize the latest findings in brain research, and their impetus is that consciousness is a by-product of the evolutionary complexity of brain organization. It is an epiphenomenon of brain activity, where "[e]piphenomenalism is the view that (phenomenal) consciousness, or the mind in general, has no causal powers, and hence exhibits no effects in the world, even though it may be the effect of some other cause itself." (Ibid., p. 136.) This means that the qualia of experience, the actual subjective content, is only a by-product, while mental functioning happens through brain activity that is out of conscious experience. This view, in turn, becomes connected to artificial intelligence, and the notion that consciousness is the result of algorithmic processes, as we discuss below.

Emergentism, or field theory, is the notion that consciousness is not caused and produced by brain activity, but that it is a causal emergent when evolution reaches a certain degree of self-organization. One of the first to posit the idea that subjective consciousness is an emergent function from higher-order organizational processes of the brain was the neurologist Roger Sperry. He regarded the consciousness of sentience as possessing its own holistic properties and functions that are not reducible to neural structures of the brain. (Roger Sperry,

"In Defense of Mentalism and Emergent Interaction"; "Structure and Significance of the Consciousness Revolution.") However, there are different forms of emergence theory, some requiring the development of complex neural networks and some not.

One uses artificial intelligence (AI) modeling, especially in parallel processing theories, where a sufficiently complex net of binary switches would develop the feedback that defines consciousness as a function, called weak AI, and the extreme form, called strong AI, which believes that such a system would actually be sentient, would have its own qualia. This computer modeling believes that if a computer is complex enough it will have consciousness, for consciousness is the function of a complex algorithm, a computational process. "According to strong AI, it is simply the algorithm that counts. It makes no difference whether that algorithm is being effected by a brain, an electronic computer, an entire country of Indians, a mechanical device of wheels and cogs, or a system of water pipes. The viewpoint is that it is simply the logical structure of the algorithm that is significant for the 'mental state' it is supposed to represent, the particular physical embodiment of that algorithm being entirely irrelevant ... The mind-stuff of strong AI is the logical structure of an algorithm." (Roger Penrose, *The Emperor's New Mind.*)

Penrose, a mathematical physicist, does not subscribe to this view; he tries to refute it in the above book, but believes mathematics and physics hold the hope for explaining consciousness: "In my own arguments I have tried to support this view that there must be indeed something essential that is missing from any purely computational picture. Yet I hold also to the hope that it is through science and mathematics that some profound advances in the understanding of mind must eventually come to light." (Ibid., p. 448.) Penrose explains such a field through quantum events in cell microtubules. (Roger Penrose, *Shadows of the Mind.*)

Although this is vibrant and exciting research, it is clear to us that all these views subscribe to the Cartesian dualism of mind stuff and physical phenomena, hence to the basic triadic split of Western thought in general. Furthermore, even though some suggest giving consciousness its own ontological status, there is no attention paid to what this ontological status is. In other words, all these views discuss consciousness in terms of its function, and the question of qualia has not reached the point of asking what the qualia qualify that is consciousness. The phenomenological camp considers subjective experience and its qualia to be central in the study of consciousness, but there is yet no appreciation of the relation between experience and consciousness. In other words, the concept of pure consciousness, consciousness in itself, does not seem to figure in the debate.

It is interesting that although it is obvious that understanding the ontological status and nature of consciousness will be helpful in understanding the qualia of consciousness, and in answering many important questions in the field, there is no attempt to go to the sources that claim precisely such ontological knowledge. Detailed and precise knowledge of consciousness resides in the various wisdom traditions of mankind; in fact most of these teachings are mainly methodological paths toward the exact experience and understanding of the ontological nature of consciousness. The field that emergentism tries to understand is clearly known, with a great degree of agreement by many of these teaching traditions, as a field of consciousness. Consciousness is recognized as a field on its own, understood as more fundamental than physical matter. In fact, matter can be seen as only one dimension of consciousness, but it is not generally recognized as consciousness due to limitations in our epistemological stance.

Only recently has there been some interest in this direction, but it has not penetrated mainstream consciousness research. There have also been some published studies of consciousness from the perspective of meditational disciplines, for instance by some practitioners of Transcendental Meditation. A recent example is the work of Harry Hunt, in his attempt to synthesize the various disparate fields that study consciousness, especially those of cognitive, phenomenological, and transpersonal approaches. He relies on the ecological perspective of Gibson, whose theory is that perception is a function of navigation with an inherent proprio-location or self-location emerging directly from the patterned flow of the world. (J. J. Gibson, *The Ecological Approach to Visual Perception.*) He derives from this a view of perceptual awareness as the core of a consciousness potentially shared across species, and uses Norman Geshwind's theory of symbolic cognition, based on a capacity for cross-modal translation and transformation among multiple perceptual modalities, to develop a view of self-referential symbolic consciousness. (Norman Geschwind, "Disconnection Syndromes in Animals and Man.") Hunt employs this understanding to include spiritual or transpersonal experiences, seeing them as maximal abstract synesthesias, thus shedding light on the nature of consciousness. He thinks that "transpersonal states show the structures of symbolic cognition unfolding presentationally, for their own sake. Accordingly, these states will show most directly the cross-modal, hierarchic syntheses normally hidden within the pragmatics of representational symbolism." (Harry Hunt, *On the Nature of Consciousness*, p. 199.) Even though he is a phenomenologist, he seems to go further in his phenomenology of consciousness than current debate by giving consciousness a clearer ontological status and connecting it to studies of Heidegger and of Buddhism. He writes: "In the much-debated relation of consciousness and mind I reduce the latter to the former. Consciousness is not a 'mechanism' to be 'explained' cognitively or neurophysiologically, but a categorical 'primitive' that defines the level of analysis that is psychology. Its existence may become a fundamental problem for a holistic, field-theoretical biology of the future, but for the human sciences it is the context of our being." (Ibid., p. xiii.)

Appendix G

Logoi of Teachings

If one has only a cursory familiarity with the wisdom traditions of humankind, it can be easy to assume that they are very different, possessing diverging meanings and concerns, and aspiring to different kinds of spiritual experience and purity. Some people believe that one or another of the wisdom traditions is actually not spiritual, or has mistaken views. If all these teachings profess to know the correct and objective view of reality, and they differ greatly from each other, then, logically speaking, some of them are bound to be mistaken, or at least limited. A deeper familiarity with these teachings might bring one to the opposite conclusion, that they are actually different ways of expressing the same truth. We may aspire, then, to a unification of all traditions, because it seems that the differences between them are not fundamental. This is the view of the perennial philosophy, which views many teachings as valid and correct views of reality, expressed as different formulations of the same truth.

A deeper experiential inquiry into these teachings will reveal to us that these two extreme views express a naïve and linear appreciation of reality. It is true that we find commonalities and differences, but to think of these as determining the validity of a spiritual path is a limited way of looking at spiritual truths and how they appear to individuals. Different spiritual teachings do not have to be similar for them to be valid, nor do they have to be speaking about the same truth, nor need they involve the same experiences. Also, the fact that different traditions and teachings differ in their conceptualizations, experiences, and even their ultimate aims does not mean that some have to be mistaken. Reality is more intelligent, magical, and loving than either of these extreme views suggests.

All genuine teachings are expressive of the universal logos, the creative matrix of all reality. Since the logos has an optimizing property that tends, if cooperated with, to unfold experience toward its own harmony and the peace of its absolute ground, all these teachings will express an optimizing intelligence and a movement toward a maximization of experience. Yet, how this optimization occurs, what it means, the phases it goes through, the various experiences involved in it, and the concepts best used to describe these experiences and their direction, can be different. In other words, the universal logos is too creative and intelligent for it to be constrained to unfold in one particular valid way, a way that we can term the true and objective view of reality. The logos is responsive to situations and actual needs of real people, and these are determined by historical epochs, culture, language, forms of logic and psychology, major events, and so on. Therefore, how it unfolds its wisdom as a teaching will have to take into consideration all these factors, and many others. This is an expression of its optimizing and loving intelligence, and its total freedom. This amounts to recognizing that the logos can unfold experience through different and varying logoi.

The universal logos is the ordered pattern of the flow of manifestation, as we discussed in chapter 20. It is the flow of embodied concepts as cosmic speech, which articulates its intelligent optimizing force. But the term *logos* also means a particular pattern of change, flow, and development, with its own logic and conceptualization. This latter meaning implies that there can be logoi, different forms of logos that apply to different situations or systems. All the logoi must reflect and express the universal logos as an ordered pattern of unfoldment, but they can differ in their conceptualizatons, their logic, and the particulars of the phases of development.

It is possible to see that each teaching is an expression of a particular logos. The logos of a particular teaching has its own unique view of ultimate reality or truth, self or soul, and spiritual path. Each possesses a different and unique technical language, logic of experience and understanding, ideals of development or realization, phases of unfoldment of experience and understanding, and kinds of experience, perception, and knowledge. Furthermore, each possesses an approach to spiritual work or practice, determined by its view of ultimate truth and realization. This necessitates different methods and approaches, and varying spiritual technologies, that are often different in principle.

Most important, this implies differing views of ultimate truth, final realization, and spiritual experience, which amounts also to different ways of conceptualizing spiritual dimensions and qualities. An obvious example is the difference of conceptualization in the view of ultimate reality between Buddhism, Vedanta, and Taoism on one hand, and the monotheistic traditions on the other. Buddhism and Taoism conceptualize the ultimate truth as an impersonal truth, a ground of existence, emptiness, or Tao, from which everything spontaneously arises. The monotheistic traditions think of the ultimate truth as not only a personal and personally responsive God, but as one who actively manages creation.

The idea that each teaching has its particular logos does not mean that there are many universal logoi. Rather, it means that all these logoi are expressions of the one universal and cosmic logos, the creative dynamism of transcendent truth. They are different ways that the universal logos manifests its wisdom and teaching about reality. Each is absolutely valid, and possibly complete as a teaching. They are all different, each leading to a different kind of spiritual experience, a different terrain in the inner journey, sometimes a different meaning for spiritual development and enlightenment, and frequently to different ways of experiencing spiritual reality and understanding. Yet, each is accurate and objective. Each expresses and describes reality faithfully. For each is accurate within its own logos, and leads to the kind of experience and realization that its own logos dictates. This is similar to traveling to a faraway country from different directions. One will encounter a different terrain, will have a different experience, will need different supports, and so on, depending on the route one takes. The experience and needs of a person traveling by air will be different from those of a person traveling by land or sea. Even if two individuals travel on land their experiences can still be quite different, depending on their means of transportation.

When they all finally arrive at the same destination they will have some similar perceptions, but they will not necessarily agree on how they see it, what they value about it, which part they value, which aspect they focus on, how to relate to it, and so on. They are all right in what they see and value, but their routes determine to some extent how they see the destination and how they relate to it.

Thus the different logoi will lead to different experiences and realizations but still are all accurate depictions of reality. The metaphor of travel is necessarily limited because the various logoi are all expressions of the universal logos, intelligently unfolding a path appropriate for the situation and needs of the people in it. Reality is so rich and amazing, so loving and compassionate, that it will reveal itself in the ways that will most effectively liberate the particular people. There will be common realizations like selflessness, generosity, compassion, and so on, but how the individuals experience the ultimate truth and how they view it and relate to it can be quite different. In fact, how they experience selflessness and compassion subjectively is frequently different.

In other words, each genuine teaching is absolute in the sense that it is an objective perception and understanding of reality. But each is absolute relative to its own particular logos, a logos that reveals reality objectively and truly, but differently than other logoi. The principle that explains the differences and similarities in the wisdom teachings is, then, relative absolutism. It is neither absolutism nor relativism.

Each teaching is the expression of a particular logos, an authentic way reality manifests itself to individuals. It is not the creation of an individual or a group of individuals, or even a historical or cultural context. These provide the channel, the clearing, or the invitation for a particular authentic way reality can manifest itself, but this way is the creation of the universal logos, the creative dynamism of the ultimate truth.

Because each teaching expresses and embodies a particular logos, it is not normally possible, or advisable, to consider that they are talking about the same thing, or that one will experience similar things by traversing their corresponding paths. It is also not possible to translate the experiences and conceptualization of two teachings in a one-to-one manner, for such correlation is frequently not present.

Furthermore, it is at best unrealistic to compare two teachings in terms of conceptualizations, experiences, and realizations.

In reality, just because we may understand the conceptualizations of one teaching does not qualify us to understand the conceptualizations of another teaching. The difference in logoi implies a difference in worldview and logic of experience; each teaching has its own secret code that will unlock its riches. To understand the language of a teaching, and to penetrate its experience, will necessitate breaking this code. To break the code of a particular teaching it is not enough to know the code of another teaching. It is not enough to familiarize oneself with the particular teaching's literature, or even practices. One has to immerse oneself in the particular teaching and its logos. One has to place oneself in its wisdom current, and traverse its path for some distance, before one is able to break its code. That is the reason adopting a teacher or teaching and doing the practices for some time frequently does not lead to much success. One has to first break the code, come to experientially know the logos of the teaching, before this logos begins to unfold within one's personal experience. When one finally breaks the teaching's code, things begin to make sense and the particular experiences and realizations of this teaching begin to flow in one's consciousness.

One corollary to this understanding is that it is folly and a waste of time to try to find a view that unifies all teachings. Such an endeavor is bound to be intellectual and partial, being largely the product of the imagination of the thinker. This thinker must literally immerse herself or himself in the currents of all these teachings, which cannot be done concurrently, and break their codes, before even beginning to understand these teachings. And the most one can do then is simply to learn from each teaching, and relate some things among the teachings. However, a complete integration is not possible, because each teaching is sufficient unto itself and absolute, though unique and different, in its view of reality.

One way to break the code of a teaching is to first achieve the realization of one's own teaching. Using our travel analogy, one has to first arrive at the country of destination. Then one can have some possibility of breaking the code of another teaching without full immersion and commitment. But it will still require some immersion and practice, appreciation of the difference of the other teaching, and respect for its validity, uniqueness, and originality.

One's Own Path

A genuine teaching is the expression of one out of many unique logoi, all different in many ways, but there is normally a great deal of overlap, because they are all expressions of the universal logos, the creative dynamism of the ultimate truth. The overlap differs in extent and kind depending on the particular logoi. Some logoi overlap a great deal, sometimes to the extent of seeing that they can be grouped together as constituting a larger logos. For example, it is easy to see that Taoism, Vedanta, and Buddhism are different and unique teachings, but have a great deal in common. So the three can be grouped together as constituting one overarching logos, the most pervasive in the East. In the West, Kabbalah, Sufism, and mystical Christianity each has its own unique logos, yet the three have so much in common that we can see that they are differentiations within a larger and overarching logos. There is also the shamanic logos, which contains many different logoi, all different and unique, from around the world, , but all share many common elements. There exist other overarching logoi, but all of the most well-known overarching logoi in turn intersect and overlap in complex ways.

On the other hand, each particular logos of a major wisdom tradition frequently contains sub-logoi, as different schools within the same tradition. They share the major tenets and principles of the particular parent logos, with its logic and language, but differ in some important ways. While these differences can be divisive, they frequently are quite enriching to the parent logos, revealing more of its possibilities. We see this in the various Sufi orders, in the plethora of Buddhist sects, in the many kinds of Christian mystics, and so on.

We can divide a particular logos all the way to personal logoi, where each person has his or her unique path, pattern of unfoldment, and unique experience. Any teaching will need to respect these personal differences if it is going to be effective with many individuals. However, this can get out of hand, when people believe that they have their own unique and different path and must follow their "own way," which frequently means not following any teaching or teacher. Such a view is obviously due to unresolved autonomy issues, because each personal logos is an expression of a particular teaching logos. To believe such an isolationist view is to regard all teachings as invalid. But teachings are valid not only because they are the expression of authentic logoi, but also because personal logoi overlap to such an extent that groups of them necessarily fall within a particular teaching logos. To believe that each human being has his own way and path, and hence cannot follow any teaching, is to disregard the truth of tremendous similarities between these personal logoi. It is also foolish and wasteful, for to take this view amounts to maintaining that each person will have to discover a logos of teaching, new and original. Not only is this impossible, there is no need for it in the overwhelming majority of instances. It is not a simple matter to discover a new logos, understanding and formulating it in a way that becomes an effective path. Anyway, this is never an individual choice; it is the universal logos that unfolds new paths, with its fathomless intelligence and love.

Nevertheless, the situation necessitates that each individual search for the teaching most appropriate for her or him. This is especially true in our postmodern times, where all the teachings of humankind are available. The presence of such plethora of teachings, both ancient and new, can present quite a dilemma to the seeker. The seeker will have to be intelligent and sensitive in his or her choices to be able to connect with an appropriate teaching, which means a teaching that possesses a logos that has a great overlap with the seeker's personal logos. Under normal circumstances, this means the seeker, in approaching various teachings, needs to be sensitive to which one he or she seems to resonate with. In other words, the choice is not only dictated by the quality of the teacher, which is also very important, and not by the reputation or the glorious stories of a particular teaching. One has to feel a real resonance with the teaching, and intuit that it makes sense somehow, even though one will not be able to tell precisely how, until one breaks the teaching's code.

Another way of stating this is that one must be sensitive to the direction and promptings that the universal logos is unfolding within one's experience. It is the universal logos that unfolds our experience, and if we listen to its guidance and intimations we may discern which way it is taking us. In other words, the universal logos is the force that directs our destiny, including which path to follow. We need to discover the direction its optimizing intelligence wants to take us, which is the same as finding and following our destiny. The path we follow is, in some very deep way, not a personal choice, but a destiny. That is why a genuine teacher does not recruit or try to enlist students, but simply follows the unfolding of the logos, accepting what it does in terms of which students to bring into the teaching and which it sends away.

Logoi of Spiritual Dimensions

We will discuss two major examples to illustrate the understanding of relative absolutism, concerning the view and conceptualization of spiritual dimensions and qualities. Though many of the wisdom teachings conceptualize reality in terms of dimensions, there are exceptions. Buddhism, for instance, does not conceptualize dimensions of reality, especially not hierarchical dimensions. One perceives reality or one does not. One can perceive it in various degrees of accuracy, but this does not imply different levels of reality.

However, the teachings that conceptualize hierarchical levels of reality differ in their conceptualizations. Most of them share the principle of hierarchical descent where the absolute is gradually veiled through the progressive manifestation of the world, but they employ different conceptualizations in terms of how they see this descent, and what they emphasize in viewing it. Kashmir Shaivism is one of the teachings that conceptualize different levels, termed *tattvas*, principles. They proceed in a descending order that reflects greater particularization of manifestation, which is the same as greater hiding of the ultimate truth, Shiva. In each succeeding *tattva*, Shiva is less in the foreground and manifest reality is more evident. Shaivism includes thirty-six *tattvas*, descending from the most nondifferentiated and subtle Shiva to the most particular and concrete physical reality.

Many logoi conceptualize five major levels of descent. Sufism uses the same principle of greater manifestation of the world and more obscuration of the ultimate truth. It calls its levels the five planes of Being, beginning from the unmanifest absolute to the physical world:

In the Sufi world-view, five 'worlds' (*'awalim*) or five basic planes of Being are distinguished, each one of them representing a Presence or an ontological mode of the absolute Reality in its self-manifestation.

1. The plane of the Essence (*dhat*), the world of the absolute non-manifestation (*al ghayb al-mutlaq*) or the Mystery of Mysteries.
2. The plane of the Attributed and the Names, the Presence of Divinity (*uluhiyah*).
3. The plane of the Actions, the Presence of the Lordship (*rububiyah*).
4. The plane of Images (*amthal*) and Imagination (*khayal*).
5. The plane of the senses and sensible experience (*mushahadah*).

TOSHIHIKO IZUTSU,
A Comparative Study of Key Philosophical Concepts in Sufism and Taoism, p. 11

The Kabbalah also conceptualizes five levels, called worlds, which are also in a descending order that reflects the same principle of hiding the ultimate truth as manifestation becomes more definite and concrete. Hence, Kabbalah shares an overarching logos with Sufism, yet both possess their own unique logoi. Because of this, it is erroneous to equate these five worlds with the five planes of Being of Sufism, even though there exist some correspondences.

In Kabbalah, the progression goes from Adam Kadmon, the concept of God's Will, which constitutes the underlying basis for all further existence; to the world of *atzilut*, which is the essence of existence that God desires to bestow to His creation; to the world of *beriyah*, which is the beginning of *perud*, independent existence and separation; to the world of *yetzirah*, which corresponds to the angelic world of spiritual forces that lies immediately beyond our physical domain; finally to the world of *asiyah*, where the spiritual actually interacts with the physical dimension. (See Rabbi Aryeh Kaplan, *Inner Space*, pp. 23–27.)

The Sufi conceptualization is similar in terms of the principle of descending order, that of greater veiling of the absolute as creation moves toward our normal world, but there are still differences. One of the main differences is that the first plane of Being of Sufism is *ahadi-*

yah, which is the absolute itself, and not God's will. Another is that the world of *asiyah* in Kabbalah has no exact counterpart in the Sufi five planes. One way of stating the difference between the two logoi is that Kabbalah looks at the descending order in terms of God's action of creation, while Sufism looks at it in terms of the results of God's action, or more specifically, as the planes of His existence.

We have discussed in the present book five boundless dimensions of Being, but they are not related to the same principle of descending order or obscuration of true nature. In other words, even though the Diamond Approach uses the conceptualization of five boundless dimensions, the principle of differentiation is different. We can say that the first two worlds of Kabbalah are boundless in the sense we mean in our discussion of boundlessness, for the world of *beriyah* is the beginning of separation. In the Diamond Approach, all the five dimensions are boundless, where no separation exists. In other words, the five worlds of Kabbalah are a way to understand how creation happens in five stages, where God's essence becomes hidden as our ordinary world of experience comes to view. The same is true of the Sufi schema. The five dimensions in the Diamond Approach are the five facets of Reality when we view it in its objective and unobscured truth. All of them together reveal reality, and express different potentials of the ultimate truth. They have a descending order, but a different principle of such. It is a matter of lessening subtlety, or increasing the number of real concepts, what we have called universal concepts. Yet, all the dimensions are coemergent, and appear consecutively only because of the soul's limitation. The schema of the Diamond Approach differs from the Sufi and Kabbalistic one in that it is not primarily a schema of creation or God's manifestation, for all the five dimensions are dimensions of the purity of true nature; thus they do not include the physical world or the imaginal world of spirits and angels.

The five dimensions of the Diamond Approach are actually more similar to the five awarenesses of the Buddha in some branches of Buddhism. (See chapter 16.) The five awarenesses or wisdoms are not hierarchical, they are the facets of enlightened awareness. Because of this we can find a homology between them and the five boundless dimensions of the Diamond Approach. However, it is a homology, a general one-to-one correspondence, but not an identity, for each is an expression of a different logos.

Spiritual Qualities

The situation is even more complex with spiritual qualities, the qualities of spiritual presence, true nature, or ultimate truth and qualities like love, eternity, perfection, mercy, and so on. Many people seem to think there exists a set of qualities that all spiritual teachings use, perhaps with different names or descriptions. Nothing is further from the truth. It is true that many of the wisdom teachings utilize spiritual qualities, but how they define them, how they relate to them, and how these qualities relate to the ultimate truth, changes according to the logos of the teaching. The differences are so profound that much misunderstanding occurs, to the detriment of both teachings and individuals. To recognize and understand the logos of the teaching is quite important for understanding and appreciating the qualities of a particular path. And the understanding of these qualities is frequently central to the teaching, and important for traversing its path.

To illustrate, we can begin with Buddhism. The logos of this wisdom tradition does not include spiritual qualities as a primary element in it. However, some of its schools do refer to and enumerate them. The most relevant part of Buddhism here is that of the Tathatagarbha schools, where Buddha nature is seen as to have inseparable qualities, such as perfection, permanence, bliss, and compassion.

These are the qualities of Buddha nature, true nature before differentiation into dimensions or aspects. They are its inseparable qualities. They are the timeless qualities of nondifferentiated and ultimate true nature. In other words, using the conceptualization of the Diamond Approach, they are not related to any of the five boundless dimensions or the many essential aspects; for the former are the differentiation of true nature into dimensions, and the latter into explicit and discernable qualities. In the Diamond Approach, the spiritual qualities are aspects of essence, the way true nature appears in the experience of the soul in a differentiated and discriminated way, a way that is relevant for both the inner path and everyday life. The Buddhist logos does not include this kind of differentiation of true nature, in contrast to its importance in the logos of the Diamond Approach. The logos of the Diamond Approach includes the understanding that true nature is originally nondifferentiated, which includes in an implicit and undifferentiated manner various perfections. These are qualities of its presence, its being, and its truth, that become instrumental in manifest reality when they arise in a differentiated and explicit manner. In other words, these are qualities of manifest true nature, one of the primary ways it appears in manifestation. They appear in an explicit, differentiated, and even discriminated way; they are capable of being experienced individually and known for what they are. True nature is like white light, and the essential aspects are like the rainbow colors that are its prismatic differentiations.

We can actually say that the Buddha qualities are quite general, for they apply to all dimensions and aspects of true nature, just as they apply to the ultimate truth before differentiation and conceptualization. It is like they are the qualities of white light, while the essential aspects are the prismatically differentiated colored lights. The Buddha qualities also do not appear individually. They are the general characteristics of true nature in general, similar to the qualities of white light. As a result the Buddhist logos does not utilize them much in its practices while the essential aspects are central to the methodology of the Diamond Approach.

Kabbalah has a system of spiritual qualities, the *sefirot*, that differ somewhat from both essential aspects and from qualities of true nature. They express a logos similar to that of the Diamond Approach, but not identical. They are similar to the essential aspects in the sense that they are differentiated attributes through which true nature appears in a limited way: "The Sefirot are generally referred to as Midot, which means literally 'measures' or 'dimensions,' and by extension, attributes or qualities. It is through the Sefirot that God limits His infinite essence and manifests specific qualities that His creatures can grasp and relate to. As such, the Sefirot act variously as filters, garments or vessels for the light of Ain Sof that fills them." (Aryeh Kaplan, *Inner Space*, p. 40.)

Upon closer examination we find that the *sefirot* are more complex qualities than the essential aspects, for they are the principles by which the world of manifestation is structured: "The ten sefiroth represent the spiritual archetypes not only of the Decalogue, but also of all the revelations of the Torah. They are the principal determinations or eternal causes of all things." (Leo Schaya, *The Universal Meaning of the Kabbalah*, p. 21.) They are usually arranged hierarchically, from *keter* to *malkhut*, structuring each of the five worlds of Kabbalah. They are not separate, however, for each *sefirah* is clothed in the one descending from it: "Thus the Sefiroth themselves appear to be wrapped within one another, in their hierarchic order, and so closely interrelated that nothing but a single principal whole can be perceived. In reality, their unity is indivisible: it is the totality of the divine powers, which are expressed in their specific aspects only when they are manifested in the midst of cosmic separativity. All distinct manifestations, all the variety of things, are only the effects and symbolic 'wrappings' of the Sefiroth; they are ordered and linked together by the Sefiroth and re-absorbed into them, into their unity which is the one, universal cause, the only God." (Ibid., pp. 25–26.)

In other words, the *sefirot* are an expression of the Kabbalistic logos, which is a schema of creation and its stages and levels, a schema that is not analogous to the logos of the Diamond Approach. The essential aspects do not possess any hierarchy or arrangement. They are like the colors of the rainbow, differentiations from the white light; we cannot say that one color of the rainbow is closer to white than the rest. Furthermore, it is important for the Kabbalah that there exist only ten *sefirot*, while the number of essential aspects has not, and perhaps cannot, be conclusively determined. However, we are aware of many more than ten.

If we content ourselves with the descriptions of essential aspects and *sefirot* we can easily make the mistake that they must be the same set of qualities, for both are considered lights or possessing luminousity, and they both appear on the five dimensions of each logos: "the Sefirot are Orot, Lights or Luminaries that serve to reveal and express God's greatness . . . , the basic concepts of the Sefirot come into existence in Atzilut, but become more manifest at the lower levels of the spiritual dimension. This means that the inner structure of each universe consists of the same Ten Sefirot." (Aryeh Kaplan, *Inner Space*, pp. 40–41.) We see some of the differences in the following passage: "It is the Sefirot that make it possible for an infinite and transcendental God to interact with His creation. For they allow us to speak about God's immanence in creation, what He does, without referring directly to what He is." (Ibid., p. 39.) In other words, the *sefirot* point to God's action, not his Being, which is different from the essential aspects. This is because the Kabbalistic logos is primarily about the structure of God's action of creating the world, and hence "each Sefirot is a specific power or mode through which God governs and sustains His universe." (Ibid., p. 40.)

One way to illustrate the difference in the logoi of spiritual qualities between the Diamond Approach and Kabbalah is to use the metaphor of the physical body and its constituents. The *sefirot* are like the major organs: the brain, heart, lungs, liver, and so on, which are the organizing and functioning centers of the body; while the essential qualities are more similar to the elementary elements of the body necessary for its life and functioning, such as amino acids, neurotransmitters, enzymes, hormones, and so on.

The more frequent confusion about the essential aspects is to equate them with the Sufi divine qualities and names. There exists an overlap between the two sets of qualities, but the logoi of their differentiation are different and unique. The essential aspects are the differentiations of the absolute as reflected in the dimension of pure presence, or universal *nous*. So they are differentiations of the presence of true nature, as noetic forms, which also appear on the dimension of pure awareness as prenoetic forms. On the other hand, the Sufi divine names are more generally the differentiations out of the macrocosm, the divine being (see chapter 23), but mostly out of the pattern of the logos that discerns the relations of the absolute to manifest reality. Such differentiation sometimes uses some of the noetic forms as constituting some of the divine names, like love and truth, which creates the overlap with the essential aspects of the Diamond Approach. But the great majority of the ninety-nine divine names are those of relational action or functioning, or simply relating to manifestation, for example "the compassionate," "the life giver," "the avenger," "the first," "the last," and so on.

Such differentiation does not apply to the essential aspects, for they are the explicit differentiations of the perfections of the presence of the ultimate truth, regardless of its relation to manifestation. Love, for instance, can be seen in relation to manifestation, but it is the inherent quality of true nature regardless of any manifestation. Existence is another essential quality, which is not necessarily relational.

In reality, all the essential aspects are important and significant for manifestation, especially for sentient beings, and they do relate the soul to her true nature, but not in the anthropomorphic way that the divine qualities use in their language and logic. Because of the centrality of the concept of God the creator in their common overarching logos, both Kabbalah and Sufism use anthropomorphic language in their differentiations of spiritual qualities.

Another possible area of confusion with the essential aspects is the Christian virtues, like charity, sobriety, humility, and so on. However, this is again a different logos. The virtues are not the essential qualities themselves; they are actually not qualities of spiritual presence or the divinity. They are the manifestations of a soul that has integrated her true nature, the qualities of her attitudes, expressions, and actions. It is not what the soul experiences within herself, which is more the qualities of spirit, but what other people perceive in her actions and expressions.

It is important to recognize that all of these sets of qualities appear in experience. However, what the individual focuses on, discerns, or finds valuable changes depending on the logos he or she follows. This focus and value system will naturally invite the logos of the particular wisdom teaching, which will then unfold the individual's experience more along the lines of the qualities of its logos. One of the laws of the universal logos is that whatever the soul focuses on and pays greater attention to tends to increase and expand. So the focus on and familiarity with a particular logos will unfold the individual's experience to reveal more of the qualities of the particular logos. This is natural and necessary, and there is no way to avoid it. That is how reality functions.

This does not mean the qualities of other logoi will not manifest in one's experience. They will manifest, but will most likely be seen from the perspective of one's particular logos. For an example, if one follows the Tibetan system of deity yoga, one visualizes a particular deity or bodhisattva. Because of the creative basic imagination of the soul given to it by the universal logos, the visualization will invoke a presence that appears as this deity or bodhisattva. The individual will experience a luminous presence with scintillating lights, jewels, precious metals and robes, skulls, and so on. This will be a particular state of presence, or spirit, which is meaningful within the logos of Tibetan Tantra. But, seen from the logos of the Diamond Approach, each color of light, each particular gem or robe, will represent an essential aspect. The student of the Diamond Approach will tend to focus on each of these, and in time one's experience will unfold not in the form of Tibetan deities, but more in the form of single essential aspects or diamond vehicles, the latter being the Diamond Approach's way of experiencing and making sense of constellations of aspects. The reverse will happen to Tibetan students when an essential aspect arises in their experience. They will not likely discern it as an essential aspect, but will try to relate it to their deity practice, which will, if the deity practice is continued, naturally invoke the experience of the visualization deity.

In this exploration, our intention has not been to elucidate the correspondences or differences between the wisdom traditions, for the correspondences and relationships we have discussed can be considered simplistic or at least incomplete; rather, our intention is to illustrate the fact of the existence of different logoi, and how they may overlap or not. We can learn from various logoi, for they are all the expression of the ultimate truth of existence. Each adds to the richness of humanity's knowledge, experience, and appreciation of reality. Yet, for one's personal fulfillment and liberation, one needs to delve into a particular logos as deeply as possible, and not desultorily skip around from one logos to another. Liberation is not an eclectic path, but always the fruit of a genuine logos.

Notes

CHAPTER 1. SOUL OR SELF

1. The Judaic tradition was similar to the Greek; we see this clearly in the Kabbalistic notion of the five souls. The five souls indicate five levels to the soul, each dominating depending on her stage of development. The first of these levels, that of *nefesh*, is the one that most closely corresponds to our contemporary usage of the term *self*. The third, that of *neshama*, corresponds more closely to our contemporary concept of soul, but is more like what the ancients meant by spirit. (See appendix A.)

The notion of soul in the Christian tradition is similar to that of Greek and Judaic thought, with a difference in relation to the soul's spiritual essence. The Greeks believed that the soul is inherently and essentially spiritual, and its spiritual journey is a matter of return to an original perfection and purity. The orthodox Christian position became one that held that the soul was without an inherent spiritual purity, but that it is given this spiritual dimension upon baptism, or by believing in and opening oneself to the Christ as the Word become flesh. It seems that the modern concept of self is more of a development of, or maybe just similar to, the Christic conception of the soul, more than any of the other ancient modes of thought. Yet the Christian position did not conceptualize a soul as distinct from a self. (See appendix A.)

Islam uses the term *self—nafs—*to refer to what classical Greek philosophy, Christianity, and Judaism meant by *soul*. In speech, the terms *self* (*nafs*) and *spirit* (*ruh*) are usually used interchangeably, depending on whether the emphasis is on the worldly or the spiritual, respectively. Another distinction is that *nafs* is used to differentiate one from others, while *ruh* is used to refer to the spiritual part of the same self. In terms of Islamic spirituality, as seen in Sufism, the soul or self (*nafs*) has seven degrees or levels of development, with increasing spiritual purity. The first two, the commanding self and the accusing self, correspond more closely to our contemporary concept of self. (See appendix C.)

Hindu thought uses the term *atman* to refer to the self, but for them this is more like our contemporary concept of soul. In fact, it is closest to the Western concept of spirit, but it is a unique concept to Hinduism, unlike self in Western languages. Hindu philosophy and religion use the term *jivatman* to refer to the ancient Western concept of soul, as the overall subjective self, distinct from the body.

But for them *atman* and *jivatman* are two sides of the same thing or two manifestations or levels of the same self. In fact, it is also central in Hindu thought that *atman* is fundamentally identical to *brahman*, the ultimate reality. That is the reason that they view the *brahman* as self, even though the highest self. In other words, for Hindu thought there is no such thing similar to our contemporary concept of self, especially as reflected in Western psychology. (See appendix B.)

Buddhism is more complex and subtle when it comes to the question of self or soul. An important reason for the way the Buddha formulated his teaching is that it was a response to what he perceived to be an excessive Hindu emphasis on the *atman*, at his time. Therefore the Buddhist primary thrust of teaching is called *anatman*, that there is no such self. However, this is quite a subtle subject and even Buddhist schools themselves have different understandings of what it means. The most general formulation of the Buddhist view is that the sense of being an autonomous and eternally unchanging entity is not real but illusory. But as we will discuss further on, Buddhism does have, in some of its branches, an understanding of soul similar to the classical Western usage, but with characteristic Buddhist flavor. The main difference from the Western concept is that it is not an independently abiding existent. One example of this Buddhist concept is the Yogacharin notion of the eight consciousnesses, where the eighth consciousness comes closest to the Western notion of soul. (See appendix B.)

2. Stephen Mitchell, a psychoanalyst and historian of psychoanalytic thought, writes: "The most striking thing about the concept of self within current psychoanalytic thought is precisely the startling contrast between the centrality of concern with self and the enormous variability and lack of consensus about what the term even means. The self is referred to variably as: an idea, or set of ideas in the mind; a structure in the mind; something experienced; something that does things; one's unique life history; even an idea in someone else's mind . . . and so on." (Mitchell, *Hope and Dread in Psychoanalysis*, p. 99.)

3. Many ancient wisdom traditions regarded the soul as the bridge between our world and the invisible spiritual world. She is the intermediary between spirit and body, making it possible for spirit to inhabit the body. The Sufis call her *barzakh*, meaning bridge or connecting link.

It thus makes a great deal of sense to know the soul first in attempting to know God or spirit. We find ourselves normally in physical reality, and to move our sensitivity to the invisible spiritual dimension, the connecting link between the two, the soul, becomes the natural entry, the jumpgate. Yet it is also the instrument for knowing the world.

4. Some branches of transpersonal psychology have attempted to bring soul back to psychology. The most notable of these is the work of James Hillman and his brand of archetypal psychology, a development from Carl Jung's work. Hillman clearly recognizes how modern psychology has lost its soul, and how it turned soul into self, in accord with modern science and philosophy: "Psychology, whose very name

and title derives from soul (*psyche*), has stopped soul from appearing in any place but where it is sanctioned by this modern world view. Just as modern science and metaphysics have banned the subjectivity of souls from the outer world of material events, psychology has denied the autonomy and diversity of souls to the inner world of psychological events . . . Psychology does not even use the word soul: a person is referred to as a self or an ego . . . We have all been de-souled." (James Hillman, *Re-visioning Psychology*, pp. 2–3.)

He shares with us the understanding that the modern view of Reality has led to the loss of soul not only in psychology but even in science, metaphysics, and theology. His view of soul is similar to our own in some respects but not in others. It is similar when he writes: "It is as if consciousness rests upon a self-sustaining and imagining substrate—an inner place or deeper person or ongoing presence—that is simply there even when all our subjectivity, ego, and consciousness go into eclipse. Soul appears as a factor independent of the events in which we are immersed. (Ibid., p. xvi.) His view differs from ours when he writes: "By soul I mean, first of all, a perspective rather than a substance, a viewpoint towards things rather then a thing in itself." (Ibid., p. xvi.) Our view is that soul is not only a perspective, but an actual ontological presence, a field of consciousness that functions as the ontological ground of all inner events. (See chapters 2 and 3.)

It seems to us that Hillman emphasizes particular dimensions of the soul, in keeping with his archetypal and mythological psychology, where image, poetry, and metaphor are seen as the way to grasp and appreciate soul: "Here I am working toward a psychology of soul that is based in a psychology of image. Here I am suggesting both a poetic basis of mind and a psychology that starts neither in the physiology of the brain, the structure of language, the organization of society, nor the analysis of behavior, but in the processes of imagination." (Ibid., p. xvii.) We share with him the view that soul cannot be understood only through analysis, and that ambiguity seems to be inherent to her experience. However, our view is grounded more in ontology, where we can directly experience and recognize the soul, as we will see in detail in the next few chapters, as a living organism of consciousness, a presence that holds the imaginative and poetic content as particular dimensions of its potential.

In other words, it seems to us that Hillman views the soul in a way that counterbalances the modern Cartesian view of self, but also in a way that sees it as connected to depth and meaning. His view partly corresponds to the common expressions we mentioned in the chapter relating to loss of soul as loss of depth, meaning, and integrity. He recognizes that soul is who and what we are, but emphasizes her traditional connotations of depth, significance, and spirituality, bringing him closer to the common understanding of soul in our times. Our view is more neutral and hence more inclusive, where we see soul as who and what we are, which we can experience and appreciate the way Hillman does, but which we can also experience as the normal self and its conventional or superficial experiences, or as the spiritual ground with all of its purity and perfection.

His view is useful in counterbalancing the modern Cartesian view of reality, but our intention is different. We are trying to present a view that integrates the modern conception of self and world in a larger matrix, as one particular expression of its possibilities.

Hillman's emphasis is clearly articulated by one of his students, Thomas Moore, who devoted a book to bringing the soul back to life, instead of to psychology as Hillman does: "'Soul' is not a thing, but a quality or a dimension of experiencing life and ourselves. It has to do with depth, value, relatedness, heart, and personal substance. I do not use the word here as an object of religious belief or as something to do with immortality. When we say that someone or something has soul, we know what we mean, but it is difficult to specify exactly what that meaning is." (Thomas Moore, *Care of the Soul*, p. 5.)

This emphasis, even though useful as a counterbalance to modern thought, will, if taken to be an inclusive definition of soul, limit our understanding and appreciation of the many dimensions and infinite potential of the human soul. We will see in the following chapters where this emphasis of archetypal psychology falls in our view of soul. This is not to deter from the value of this emphasis and the perspective it expresses, for our times do need to regain soul.

5. Psychology has tried to be part of the study of cosmos/world, namely science, but it has not been able to effectively do that. Freud thought of psychoanalysis as a branch of biology, but biology has not accepted that. And when psychology tries to align itself more closely in its methods with physical science it loses its connection with soul even more, as one sees in behaviorism and cognitive psychology.

6. Some branches of Eastern thought—for example, some Buddhist practices—utilize reasoning and logical analysis as part of their spiritual practice. We see this in the approach to the concept of emptiness, where the student studies and logically proves the emptiness or nonexistence of all things.

Most of the time this is reminiscent of the approach of Western theology, in its attempts to prove the existence of God. This is not the kind of integration we have in mind when we think of integrating reason with mystical knowledge. We do not mean using reason to convince ourselves of some truth, and then doing a spiritual practice to contact such truth, which seems to be part of the practice of some Buddhist schools.

We mean using reason to open up our minds, partly by removing its unreasonable stances and assumptions, and partly to sharpen and focus its awareness. This imbues our awareness with a precise objectivity and an intelligent penetrating power that can look at our experience and challenge it in such a way as to open it up. This opening up can then reveal whatever the truth of the soul is, whether its ground is God or emptiness, or something else. Some Buddhist schools do use such an approach, but this does not seem to be the prevalent way of using reason. In other words, we are thinking of integrating our reason in our spiritual inner work to help illuminate experience and arrive at spiritual truth.

7. Reason and logic were used extensively by theologians and some mystics in the major faiths, but in a way that contributed to convincing Western thought that it

is incompatible with spiritual experience. In the monotheistic religions it was used primarily to attempt to prove the tenets of the faiths, particularly to find proofs for the existence of God. This clearly has failed, and must have helped erode the notion that matters of the spirit have anything to do with reason. But logically proving the tenets of religion has been mostly the concern of theologians, not of mystics and spiritual adepts. Furthermore, the failure here is more appropriately seen not as the failure of the reasoning mind, but as revealing that the whole endeavor was and still is the result of a mentality that firmly believes in the split between God, world, and soul. The failure is due to applying reason separate from gnosis to an area where reason has not yet separated from gnosis. Reason is bound here to be misguided, and it is bound to fail because it is undertaking an ill-conceived project from the start.

Plato did not use reason to prove the existence of the divine; he used it as a facet needed for the development of a way of knowing that can experientially penetrate to the divine. Reason helped to open direct spiritual knowing to a precision and capacity for objectivity that is necessary for it to be accurate.

8. The conviction in this matter-centered universe is so powerful that many of our scientists and thinkers are busy trying to figure out how consciousness has developed out of the evolution of the brain. These researchers and thinkers believe that consciousness—the most basic property of the soul—is an epiphenomenon of matter, merely a result of the brain reaching a certain complexity. Matter here is more fundamental than consciousness, and hence soul. This view is behind the theories about artificial intelligence that believe that it can at some point be indistinguishable from the operation of consciousness. (See appendix F.)

9. Western thought has been awakening to this impoverishment of our world and world view, as we see in the various perspectives or paradigms characterizing modern alternative thought. Ken Wilber describes this insight this way: "the downside of the enlightenment paradigm was that, in its rush to be empirical, it inadvertently collapsed the . . . interior depths into observable surfaces, and it thought that a simple mapping of these empirical exteriors was all the knowledge that was worth knowing. This left out the mapmaker itself—the consciousness, the interiors, the Left Hand dimensions—and, a century or two later, it awoke in horror to find itself living in a universe with no value, no meaning, no intentions, no depth, no quality—it found itself in a disqualified universe, ruled by the monological gaze, the brutal world of the lab technician. (Wilber, *A Brief History of Everything*, p. 89.)

10. How is this soul-self related to the body? Is it apart from the body, as the ancients thought of it, or does it include the body, like the total self of some psychological theories? The answer to this question is not as simple as it seems, and requires understanding the wholeness of the soul in a more complete way than possible at this point in the book. This understanding, in its turn, will require the larger understanding of the relation between God/Being and cosmos/world, for it will depend on how we understand the relation between the spiritual and the material. To cast our question in the form of whether the soul includes the body or is a part of it will

indicate an adherence to a point of view conditioned by the triadic split. At the least, such split will dictate our understanding of the possible answer, while we wish to present a vision that does not participate in such separation. Therefore, we will have to deal with this question further on in our exploration.

11. Some spiritual traditions may dispute this. Theistic religion, specifically Christianity, states that true knowledge, or the knowledge of Reality, can only come from God, or from some divine origin, through revelation. But even though this point is fundamental to Catholic thought, it is a theological and/or epistemological subtlety, which becomes relevant mainly at the deeper stages of spiritual life.

For the present stage of our discussion it is enough to recognize that even the monotheistic traditions, including the most orthodox Christian theology, will accept that whatever the source of true knowledge—a divinity independent of our consciousness or an inner awareness—we are the medium that recognizes and knows. Our consciousness is indispensable for perception, knowledge, and recognition of truth. Even the experiences that are considered God's own fall within inner direct perception.

12. This is exactly what the ancient explorers of inner truth, both Eastern and Western, did. The Buddha observed and studied his own mind, and developed methods of meditation that enabled others to do the same. Almost all of Indian philosophy and spirituality begins, and ends, with the study of the self, the *atman*. The Delphic injunction, "Know thyself," became through Socrates and Plato the primary foundational principle of the Western wisdom tradition, which in turn became central for Neoplatonism: "To find ourselves is to know our source." (Plotinus, *Enneads*, p. 544.) Christian spirituality, as seen through the teachings of the desert fathers, begins with the knowing of the soul and the purification of the soul that is needed for it to mirror or be receptive to divine inspiration. The cornerstone of Islamic spirituality and philosophy is the saying attributed to God: "Whoso knoweth himself knoweth his lord."

CHAPTER 2. ORGAN OF EXPERIENCE

1. Some teachings include the understanding that the inner and outer mandalas or vessels appear as two only at the beginning of the path, and the path leads to the recognition of their unity in the fullness of realization.

2. The Diamond Approach is a path of wisdom, an approach to the investigation of Reality and work on oneself that leads to human maturity and liberation. Because of our particular vision of Reality, it is not completely accurate to think of this approach as spiritual work, for this work does not separate the spiritual from the psychological. Neither does it see these two as separate from the physical everyday life and scientific investigation of the content of perception. However, because we live in a society where the prevailing thought is that of the separated facets of Reality, the closest category recognized in this mentality, to our approach, is that

of a spiritual path or exploration. We prefer the expression *essential work* to refer to our approach, because it is based on the essential nature of Reality, meaning the essence of the three disciplines that developed from it.

3. The difficulty in knowing and understanding the soul has been recognized by many spiritual traditions, each teaching explaining it according to its own perspective. It is understood in the Sufi tradition, as we see in the following quote from a Sufi classic, where soul is usually referred to as *nafs*, and knowledge as *mar'ifat*: "The ma'rifat of *nafs* is in all qualities difficult, for *nafs* hath the nature of the chameleon . . . The recognizing of *nafs* in all its qualities, and the reaching to a knowledge of it, is not the power of any created thing. Even so difficult is the reaching to the substance of ma'rifat of God, and even so, to the ma'rifat of *nafs*, as 'Ali hath said." (Suhrawardi, *The 'Awarif U'l-Ma'rif*, p. 127.)

In the Christian tradition, we see this in many well-known writings, as in the following quote that describes how knowledge of the soul is viewed in the *Macarian Homilies*: "The soul, they say, is like a tree with many limbs and branches: it is very difficult for us to grasp all these parts of the soul. A man's soul is vast and unfathomable to himself . . . The self that he thinks he is is but a part." (Andrew Louth, *The Origins of the Christian Mystical Tradition*, p. 116.) The perspective of these homilies is that only with the help of spirit is full knowledge of the soul possible, but this is viewed from the orthodox Christian perspective, which is that spirit can only come from God, but not from the soul herself. We will see further on that our understanding is that the soul can be fully known only with the realization of spirit which we, however, view as the essence of the soul.

4. In the third Ennead, Plotinus discusses whether souls are parts of universal soul, and concludes that it is all one soul, because soul is indivisible: "But again: 'Everywhere unity' applies both to Soul itself and to its various functions . . . But since the soul is a rational soul, by the very same title by which it is an All-Soul, and is called the rational soul, in the sense of being a whole (and so not merely 'reasoning locally'), then what is thought of as a part must in reality be no part but the identity of an unparted thing." (Plotinus, *Enneads*, p. 255.)

5. For reports and discussion of near-death experiences see Raymond Moody, *Life after Life*; Kenneth Ring, *Life at Death: A Scientific Investigation of Near-Death Experiences*; Michael B. Sabom, *Recollections of Death: A Medical Investigation*. For out-of-body experiences see Robert Monroe, *Journeys Out of the Body*.

One of the most famous reports of out-of-body experience is that of the late Ramana Maharshi, the well-known Vedantist saint, who awakened to his spiritual dimension by finding himself apart from his body and observing it from above. (B. V. Narasimha Swami, *Self-Realization: The Life and Teachings of Sri Ramana Maharshi*, chapter 5.)

6. It might seem at the face of it that we are adhering to a dualistic view of the soul, namely, that to discuss individual location will mean we believe in separate and

autonomously existing individual souls. This impression will alert all good Buddhists. However, nothing is further from the truth; for we have only mentioned differentiated location, and differentiation does not mean separation. A wave in the ocean is an individual wave, differentiated from other waves, but this does not make it separate from other waves, or from the ocean itself. The question of individual soul, and the existence of autonomous entities, is a deep and subtle one. As we will see in chapters 17, 18, and 22, our view is that there are individual souls, but there are no such things as autonomously existing entities. We will also see that such view does not only not contain contradiction but that it is necessary to account for the various levels of experience.

7. The scientific atomistic view, that our experience is only a matter of neuronal firings and messages—and its reflection in our naive normal belief that inner events are discrete happenings in a vacuum—is actually not tenable in the view of our contemporary science. Quantum field theory, and quantum theory in general, understands all physical phenomena as basically wave phenomena, as perturbations of a field, a unified fabric of excitations. This scientific view indicates that it is more accurate to think of our body basically as a field of some sort, and hence all its inner events as perturbations or waves in such field.

If we take the materialist positivist view that matter is all there is, then we stop here, but if we want to continue pursuing our project of finding a ground that unifies the scientific and spiritual, then the physical cannot be this ground. We are interested in finding a nonreductionistic understanding of Reality.

8. This becomes clear when we are able to experience our soul directly, for at times of expansion of consciousness we can be aware of our sensitive interiority extending beyond the physical confines of the body. We can then experience inner events, like states of consciousness, within the body but extending further. The more expansion the larger the radius of our sense of interiority. This directly points out that our interiority is not exactly physical, but that it normally coincides with the physical. We will discuss in some detail how this happens in the process of development of our sense of self, and see that the limiting of our interiority to the confines of the body is due to identifying ourselves through the body image. (See chapter 12.)

9. This point might invite certain objections from the perspective of some spiritual teachings. Buddhism, and other teachings based on awareness, may object that both the site and agent of all experience and perception is pure awareness itself. This does not contradict our view, for as we have seen, the soul expresses this pure fundamental awareness in the world of space and time as the capacity for individual experience. We will discuss in some detail, in chapters 4 and 5, how the soul is related to awareness in terms of perception and experience, and the necessity for the individual soul to account for presence of locus of perception.

The reader can find a specific discussion about the relation of the soul to pure boundless awareness in *Luminous Night's Journey*, chapters 10–12.

10. It is part of our normal awareness that the self is the agent of action. This characteristic of self, that of agency, has also been recognized in depth psychology. Daniel Stern, for instance, believes agency to be an important and defining characteristic of the self, and assigns its development to a particular age. His view of the self is that it has four dimensions: emergent self, core self, subjective self, and verbal self. Agency is characteristic of the core self: "A tentative list of experiences available to the infant, and needed to form an organized sense of a core self includes (1) self-agency, in the sense of authorship of one's own actions and nonauthorship of the actions of others: having volition, having control over self-generated action (your arm moves when you want it to), and expecting consequences of one's actions (when you shut your eyes it gets dark) . . . ." (Daniel Stern, *The Interpersonal World of the Infant*, p. 70–71.)

This kind of understanding may bring some objection to our view of soul as agent. Teachings that understand the ultimate doer as God—mystical thought in the monotheistic traditions, or higher self in Hinduism, will object to our notion of soul as agent of action. Again, there is really no contradiction here, for the individual soul is like the wave of the ocean, and whatever the wave does can also—in fact, more fundamentally—be attributed to the ocean. We will discuss this view of the nonduality between the soul and cosmic being in chapters 17, 18, and 23, but the reader can also find some account of this in *Luminous Night's Journey*, chapters 13–14.

The question here is not a matter of only reconciling our notion of soul with these teachings. The question is a fundamental one, which is the necessity of the soul for any individual experience and awareness, and hence any experience or perception. Ibn 'Arabi, the main writer and systematizer of Sufi thought, conceptualized this as the reciprocal need between God and the soul.

Corbin states Ibn 'Arabi's view when discussing the completed human being, which "is to have achieved the state of the Perfect man, to whom the totality of the divine Names and Attributes are epiphanized and who is conscious of the essential unity of divinity-humanity or Creator-creature. But at the same time, the Perfect Man discriminates between the two modes of existentiation encompassed in the essential unity, *by virtue of which he is the vassal without whom his Lord would not be, but also by virtue of which he himself would be nothing without his Lord.*" (Henry Corbin, *Creative Imagination in the Sufism of Ibn 'Arabi*, p. 211; italics added.)

11. This observer is the result of ego development, meaning it is due to a mental construct. The development of this separate internal observer is related to the ego identity, the sense of recognition of a self that is a separate subject. See *The Point of Existence*, p. 110. Identifying with this ego structure gives the egoic experience its character of separation of subject and object. When we are able to experience directly, without mentally identifying with this structure, we begin to recognize the nondual character of our experience, and see that its phenomenology has always been this way, even when we where identified with the ego identity observer. To recognize the absence of duality in our inner experience is to experience the primordial condition of the soul, soul before ego structure.

CHAPTER 3. ORGANISM OF CONSCIOUSNESS

1. Consciousness has recently become a subject of study and research in various scientific fields, as in cognitive psychology, neuropsychology, brain research, artificial intelligence, and others. Yet these fields do not approach the ontology of consciousness, as we do in this chapter.

In this chapter and the next few, we unfold a view of consciousness, and its relation to perception, cognition, and the qualia of experience, that emerges from the direct discriminating experience of this consciousness in the process of inner transformation.

We use the term consciousness in this chapter, and in the rest of this book, to refer to the conscious or aware medium of the soul. This usage is similar to many Indian schools, especially that of Kashmir Shaivism. The reader needs to be aware that the Buddhist schools use the term *consciousness*, which is the same Sanskrit term *chit* or *chitta* used by Shaivism, to mean something else. Buddhism uses the term *consciousness* in the perceptual and mental sense, and not in the ontological sense. For the ontological sense, meaning the field of presence that is conscious, Buddhism uses the term *awareness*. At least, this is how it is rendered in English translations.

2. When we say direct experience we do not mean flashes or intuitions. We mean a sustained perception, of varying degrees of depth and range, for many years of study and exploration. We refer to a current of experience that becomes a coherent body of knowledge.

3. Physical fields are usually associated with certain forms or properties of matter. Quantum fields, for example, are usually associated with elementary particles. Quantum theory views the field and particles as two manifestations of the same reality. This is formulated in what is called the complementarity principle, which is that a particle is how our senses—or instruments—perceive some of the regions in this field. A particle is an interaction of waves in the field, and this node of wave interference is a particle. The two formulations, particles and waves, are equivalent and complementary, and we cannot say one of them is real and the other is not.

This can bring up the question of the relation of the soul to the body. From the perspective of our vision the soul and body form a complementarity, similar to wave and particle. This metaphor is not a complete description, but valid for our physically embodied experiences. We also find it to reflect direct perception of soul more accurately than the contemporary scientific theories about consciousness. Physical fields are inseparable from their particles, being two sides of the same reality, but this does not hold completely for the soul and body. It does not hold completely because it obviously does not explain a disembodied soul, which is what individual experience after death means. This is also seen in out of body experiences.

To recognize the full complementarity principle in relation to the soul we need to view it from the larger perspective of Reality, where the question is not about the relation of soul and body, but about spirit and matter in general. We discuss this universal complementarity principle of spirit and matter when we discuss the relation of physical reality to Being. (See chapter 23.)

4. Sufis think of the soul as being like a vapor that fills the body. They also use the metaphor of butter in the buttermilk to refer to the relation of soul to body. But it is always that the soul pervades and interpenetrates the body. A Sufi writer said it this way: "Though the individual soul is a limitation it is free from matter and extension and from colour and form. It is cognizant of self and not-self, but not liable to be sensed by any of the senses. The limitations of Ruhi-Azam [the Great Soul] are the souls of men, and when such limitation is manifest in body it becomes animal-spirit. It is subtle in nature, and each particle of it is connected with each particle of the body." (Sirdar Ikbal Ali Shah, *Islamic Sufism*, p. 140.) We see here the similarity between this view and that of Plotinus, as described in note 4 of chapter 2, and in the following note.

5. Plotinus took the view that the soul is not composed of parts, and hence the individual soul is not different from the all soul, universal soul. His discussion of this property of indivisibility of soul is similar to what we now term a holographic property, where each region includes the characteristics and functions of the whole. (See the chapter entitled "The Problems of the Soul," in Plotinus, *Enneads*, pp. 253–255.

Some brain researchers, like Karl Pribram, have thought of the brain functioning in a holonomic way, where the various functions and memories are spread through all brain cells and dendrites. This begins to make greater sense when we recognize the holographic property of the soul, and remember it is our individual consciousness. The principle of complementarity is bound to be even more complete between the consciousness of the soul and the brain. (See Pribram, *Brain and Perception*.)

6. Many spiritual traditions conceive of pure consciousness, the essence of the soul, as presence. (See *The Point of Existence*, appendix B.) Some traditions shy away from this as an expression of their particular theology. Orthodox Christianity, for example, traditionally attributes ontological presence only to God. This position sometimes manifests personally for some Christians pursuing an inner path of transformation. It is difficult for some of these individuals to recognize themselves as presence because of consciously or unconsciously adhering to this orthodox position about presence. To recognize oneself as presence can cause to the Christian student deep conflicts and guilt, for only God possesses such presence.

Christian orthodoxy has thought of spiritual or existential presence as characterizing God but not the soul because it had taken the position of an extreme duality of God and soul, where God is the creator and the soul is a creation out of nothing, not out of the being of God. This position became Christian orthodoxy only at the famous council of Nicaea. "The Council of Nicaea, held in 325, marks a watershed in the history of Christian theology." (Louth, *The Origins of the Christian Mystical Tradition*, p. 75.) The council came down on the side of one of two main Christian thoughts at the time, represented by Athanasius and Arius, who both believed in the doctrine of creation out of nothing, but creation "ex nihilo means for them that there is a complete contrast between God and the created order, between the uncreated and self-subsistent, and that which is created out of nothing, by the will of God." (Ibid., pp. 75–76.) Nicene orthodoxy placed the soul with the created order, hence devoid of self-subsistence, or ontological presence. For this orthodoxy "the doctrine of creation ex nihilo implies that the most fundamental ontological divide is between God and the created order, to which latter both soul and body belong. The soul has nothing in common with God; there is no kinship between it and the divine." (Ibid., p. 77.)

Islamic spirituality possesses a similar view to Nicene orthodoxy, in the position that all being belongs to God, but differs in that the soul possesses a real ontological presence, bestowed upon it by God. In other words, this spirituality recognizes a continuity between God and the soul, just as it sees the world as a theophany, God's expression of himself.

In our experience and observational research, one can experience the soul as devoid of everything and that she gets everything from God or the divine, including being, this way resembling the Nicene position. This occurs particularly in the experience of mystical poverty, as the soul approaches the absolute dimension of Being, the luminous darkness and mystery of Being. But we differ in that we understand this to be due to the soul still experiencing herself through a mental construct, that of the image of being a separate entity. When she is able to shed this mental concept of herself, and experiences her reality completely nonconceptually, she finds no distance between the absolute and her essence. (See *The Point of Existence*, chapter 41, for a more detailed account of this understanding. Also, see *Luminous Night's Journey*, chapter 8.)

We recognize the soul as basically an ontological presence because the experience of presence is nothing but the experience of ourselves when it is direct and unmediated, when it is free of mental self-images, reifications, and concepts.

7. This paradigm has come under attack from various realms of postmodern thought, for isolating the self from its world, and as a result impoverishing both self and world. This paradigm is known by many names: the Enlightenment paradigm, the representational paradigm, the mirroring paradigm, and so on. "This is the idea that you have the self or the subject, on the one hand, and the empirical or sensory world, on the other, and all valid knowledge consists in making maps of the empirical world, the single and simple 'pregiven' world. And if the map is accurate, if it correctly represents, or corresponds with, the empirical world, then that is 'truth.'" (Ken Wilber, *A Brief History of Everything*, p. 59.)

8. Postmodern deconstructionist thought has done something similar, which also tends to rob our knowing of its ontological ground. Such extreme deconstructionism, as seen in the followers of Derrida and Foucault, in cultural constructivism, in relativism, understands all reality and truth to be ultimately a construction, cultural and personal. For such philosophy there is no such thing as universal truth. Now,

this is fundamentally true for ego experience of self and world, for our sense of self and world develops, as has been amply understood by object relations theory, through the development of ego structures, which always occur within object relations, which imply a social and cultural context. (See *The Point of Existence*, chapters 5 and 6, and *The Pearl Beyond Price*, chapter 2.)

Deconstructionism reduces all truth and all reality to nothing. This is actually what occurs when we first deconstruct ego in paths of inner transformation. However, as these wisdom teachings know, this deconstruction is only the first step of the transformation, the next is the arising of true reality, free and independent of any construction. In fact, this reality is understood as primordial, unoriginated, and nonconceptual. And we experience this reality as presence, beingness independent of construction. Understood from the perspective of gnostic traditions, deconstruction is nothing but a new form of nihilism, for it leaves only construction and deconstruction, but no universal or ultimate truths.

What deconstructionism cannot deconstruct is the existence of the consciousness that does the deconstructing. This is not solved by resorting to the Buddhist concept of emptiness, which says that everything, including the self, is empty of any ultimate existence. Emptiness in Buddhism does not negate the presence of individual consciousness, or the world. It merely corrects our understanding about their ultimate mode of existence. In fact, the higher teachings of Buddhism see this emptiness as inseparable from clarity, and the coemergence of the two as presence. Buddhism, just as most wisdom traditions, believes it is possible to the see the world in its true and real condition, which is that of presence that unites emptiness and clarity, meaning the mode of being of Reality is beyond the concept of existence and its opposite nonexistence. Deconstructionism, however, believes that the true condition of Reality is nothing, nonexistence. What is called relative truth in Buddhism, contrasting it to absolute truth or emptiness, is not what the deconstructionists call relative. Buddhism calls it appearance, but it does not hold the view that this appearance is necessarily constructed by humans. It deconstructs the conventional experience of appearance through the experience of emptiness, but then appearance does not completely disappear, but rather reemerges redeemed, released from construction. Now appearance appears, spontaneously and independent of our constructions, coemergent with emptiness, and we experience this Reality as presence, as in the following quotation from Longchenpa, one of the main exponents of Maha Ati of Tibetan Buddhism:

"The way things appear has always been a radiance not existing internally or externally apart from being a mere play of the creativity (of pure and total presence). It is not found as something mental or other than mental, but is held to be merely how things present themselves interdependently when secondary conditions are present." (Manjusrimitra, *Primordial Experience*, p. 27.)

We see here that both positivistic and deconstructionist philosophies lose the ontological ground, which we experience as presence. Positivistic thought believes in the perspective of ego as ultimate reality, while deconstructivist thought deconstructs this perspective. It shows it to be ultimately relative and amounting to nothingness, but stops short of Reality.

9. As we will discuss later in much more detail, this type of knowing is known by various wisdom traditions. It is referred to in Sanskrit as *jnana*, in Tibetan Buddhism as *yeshe*, in Sufism as *dhoug* (taste), by the Gnostics as *gnosis*. It was the accepted meaning of mind in Greek thought, in the notion of *nous*: "This means that *nous* and its derivatives have a quite different feel from our words, mind, mental, intellect, intellection, etc. Our words suggest our reasoning, our thinking; *nous*, noesis, etc., suggest an almost intuitive grasp of reality . . . *Nous*, then is more like an organ of mystical union than anything suggested by our words 'mind' or 'intellect.' And yet *nous* does mean mind; noesis is a deeper, simpler, more contemplative form of thought, not something quite other than thinking." (Louth, *The Origins of the Christian Mystical Tradition*, p. xvi.) Plotinus was very clear and definite that in *nous* (Intellectual-Principle), being and knowing coincide: "Hence we may conclude that, in the Intellectual-Principle itself, there is complete identity of Knower and Known, and this not by way of domiciliation, as in the case of even the highest soul, but by Essence, by the fact that, there, no distinction exists between Being and Knowing." (Plotinus, *Enneads*, p. 241.)

10. If consciousness is only a function, then it must be a function of something. We are then bound to conclude that it is a function of the brain and the nervous system. However, if we see it as a function but a function of the soul, then we will ask what soul is. If we do not reduce soul to something physical, then we are bound to see it as presence. And Being is the simplest and most fundamental that presence can be.

11. A question may arise here about the relation of pure consciousness to awareness, and whether the ultimate truth of the self is emptiness, as Buddhism teaches. This is a matter of subtlety in the experience of the presence of consciousness. Emptiness is the ultimate truth of the soul not in the sense that a soul does not appear to awareness, but that her mode of existence is beyond our normal concept and feeling of existence. This mode is called emptiness, and feels like spacious absence of any substance. Yet this emptiness is also inseparable from a transparent clarity—as formulated by Buddhist schools—both constituting a unity that characterizes both soul and universe. When we experience the coemergence of emptiness and clarity we recognize it as pure awareness, and feel it phenomenologically as presence. Awareness is then consciousness, but consciousness experienced inseparable from emptiness.

Therefore, we are at this point discussing consciousness and not awareness, not because we do not think that the ground of the soul is awareness, but because to discuss awareness accurately we need to first understand emptiness. We will do this later in chapters 19 and 21, but continue our discussion here without explicitly differentiating consciousness from awareness. This subtle differentiation is not material at this point of the discussion.

CHAPTER 4. NOESIS

1. The most common scientific understanding of this perception is that the nerves in the chest detect the stimuli in the region, sending messages to the brain. Then

the brain recognizes the messages, an event that happens in the brain. The organization of the stimuli into meaningful knowledge arises as the brain interpretations pass through our sense of self. This is a cybernetic and atomistic view of perception, but has long been confirmed experimentally. This is obviously what happens on the physical level, but we now need to understand it further because we have seen that consciousness is not only a matter of the activity of the brain. Consciousness is a field of conscious presence. The question is how perception appears from the perspective of presence. It will not necessarily nor obviously correspond with our physical model, but neither do we take this to contradict the physical model. We need to remember the complementarity between the body and soul, brain-nervous-system and consciousness, where phenomena can be explained in two or more different ways, without them contradicting each other.

2. This statement contradicts the extreme currents of constructivist thought, for it shows that when our mind is not involved at all there remains perception. Further, this perception is not only of an amorphous nothing, but also of forms, shapes, colors, and movements. Actually, Buddhism refers to this level of consciousness as mirror-like awareness, indicating that it is a faithful reflection of reality, without distortion, addition, or subtraction. Reality possesses structure even when our constructing mind is not functioning. (See appendix B.) If this were not the case a true Zen master would be tripping over things all the time, for the realization involved in Zen is a matter of perceiving nonconceptually.

3. Except perhaps for some early introspectionist studies, consciousness research does not appear to address this fundamental level of consciousness.

4. Vajrayana Buddhism includes this as one of the fundamental dimensions of enlightened consciousness, one of the five awarenesses of the Buddha, mirror-like awareness. (See appendix B.) We discuss this dimension in relation to Being in chapter 19.

Zen bases its notion of satori on nonconceptual awareness, on pure perception free from the cognitive mind. Zen satori is basically the transcending of one's discriminating mind, as we see in the following quote from one of the most well-known Zen masters: "Mumon comments: 'In studying Zen, one must pass the barriers set up by ancient Zen Masters. For the attainment of incomparable satori, one has to cast away his discriminating mind. Those who have not passed the barrier and have not cast away the discriminating mind are all phantoms haunting trees and plants.'" (Zenkei Shibayama, *Zen Comments on the Mumonkan*, p. 24.) This reveals nonconceptual awareness, as we see in a quote from another master, Linji: "The pure light in a moment of awareness in your mind is the Buddha's essence within you. The nondiscriminating light in a moment of awareness in your mind is the Buddha's wisdom within you." (Thomas Cleary, *Zen Essence*, p. 4.)

5. We are discussing inner consciousness here, and inner experience, because we want first to understand the soul. When we come to investigating Being and world we will see that the dichotomy of inner and outer disappears.

6. Our normal geometry is Euclidean, where each dimension is a straight line that intersects the other dimensions in right angles. Riemannian geometry is a more general class of topographies, where dimensions do not intersect in right angles, as in the case of the surface of a sphere. Riemannian geometries can be quite complex and exotic, and there is no limit to the number of dimensions they address. Einstein used Riemannian geometry to give a mathematical expression to his general theory of relativity, but such geometries have many other applications in mathematical physics. We find the notion of such geometry to be quite useful in trying to understand and describe inner experience. Inner experience sometimes appears Euclidean, but most of the time it is Riemannian. The soul in particular can be most adequately visualized as a Riemannian space.

7. The view that the rope is also a construction assumes that all perception and experience is relative. It is relative to the individual, or at least to the culture that forms the mentality of the individual. But this leaves no room for universal truths, no true spiritual understanding, as we see in the following passage from Bataille, one of the most well-known structuralists: "With extreme dread imperatively becoming the demand for universality, carried away to vertigo by the movement that composes it, the ipse being that presents itself as a universal is only a challenge to the diffuse immensity that escapes its precarious violence, the tragic negation for all that is not its own bewildered phantom's change." (George Bataille, *Visions of Excess*, p. 174.) The relativist may believe that the understanding of absolute relativism is enlightenment, but the accounts of enlightenment and awakening which humanity has garnered in its history do not support this view. Things can become quite subtle in terms of what remains in perception in awakened consciousness, but none of the wisdom traditions postulate an amorphous nothing. And even then, we have the knowingness of this nothing.

The experience of enlightenment is knowingness free of relativism, personal or cultural. It is liberation because it is free from the confining constructions of both the individual and culture, and this liberates our Being to freely display its richness. This is a positive experience, rich with significance, vibrant with color and full of truth. In Buddhism, for instance, what is called relative truth is not what the relativists call such. Because when all construction is undone in enlightenment, awakened consciousness is aware of absolute truth, or emptiness, inseparable from relative truth. This relative truth does not go away with deconstruction; it merely reveals its true face.

8. It is interesting that our age is sometimes referred to as the age of information because of the phenomenal development of computers and communication technology. However, we are discussing a different form of information here, where it is not composed of binary bits, but of living impressions. Some proponents of artificial intelligence would like to believe that all consciousness can be encoded into binary bits, but the view of basic knowledge we give here shows the impossibility of this happening, for even the presence and functioning of computers and communication devices will also be nothing but basic knowledge.

9. This process, as we will see in chapter 12, is how ego and its structures develop. When our knowledge from the past structures our experience in the present in such a way as to obscure what actually is, then we are in the darkness of basic ignorance, the ignorance that inner work attempts to dissipate.

10. Here it might be useful to recall the categorization in the Sufi tradition of the faculty of cognition in the soul whose operation depends on the level of the soul. They say that each level of soul has a different form of cognitive faculty—the animal soul, the human soul, the spiritual soul, and then the universal essence, which is supposed to be God.

"The Sufis, however, characterize Nafs with desire, Qulb [*qalb*] with knowing, soul with sight, Ser with contemplating and Dhat with appearing." (Sirdar Ikbal Ali Shah, *Islamic Sufism*, p. 141.)

The animal soul form of knowledge is called desire, desiring. All the animal soul knows is desire, the object of desire, and the desiring of that. The cognitive faculty of the human soul is called knowing. The human soul means the level of the soul when she experiences essence as her heart. And her mode of knowledge is the normal knowing. The cognitive faculty of the spiritual soul is called seeing. This is what we have been discussing as basic knowing. For God, appearing and seeing are the same. Appearing means manifestation of everything, which is God's knowledge.

Desiring is knowledge based on duality. Knowing has a hint of unity to it, like when you think in your inner experience, "I know I am feeling a certain feeling." The feeling is part of you but you are somewhat separate from it; we call that *dual unity*. The soul is in dual unity with her experience. Seeing is nondual experience where the seer and the seen are completely the same thing. That is when the soul, the medium, is the same thing as the cognizer. Appearing is boundless and nondual.

11. The fact that thoughts arise in basic knowledge, and hence can embody it and express it, is utilized by some wisdom traditions in their methodologies. It is known that the soul can become developed and embodied enough for one to think consciously and intentionally, instead of thoughts arising on their own. Mentation becomes an activity of the soul that is basic knowledge; in other words, it is embodied thinking, presence appearing as thought. This could be what Gurdjieff meant by "objective mentation."

The Tibetan tradition utilizes this property of the soul in a different way, in some of its tantric teachings. This happens especially in the nondual teachings, where some of the meditation practices are oriented toward thinking. It is the recognition and the abiding in the nonduality of thoughts and nonconceptual awareness, where thoughts phenomenologically manifest as forms of presence.

12. The Greeks appreciated this fact, for some of their thinkers used reason and logic inseparably from gnostic knowledge. The words *reason* and *logic* did not mean to them what they mean to us now. They reflected their notions of *nous* and *logos*, which meant, respectively, mind in the sense of the knowingness of basic knowledge,

and reason as the harmonious unfoldment of this knowledge, seen as the "order of reality."

13. For a full understanding of this integration we need to be familiar with basic knowledge in relation to Reality as a whole, and not only in relation to the soul, as we are doing here. We need to understand basic knowledge as the ground of all manifestation, which we cannot discuss until we arrive at our exploration of the boundless dimensions of Being, specifically in chapter 18.

CHAPTER 5. POTENTIAL

1. The extreme schools of relativism and constructivism view our experience as determined only by the shutters. When the shutters are removed, nothing remains for knowledge to behold.

We also imply here that the knowledge of the wisdom teachings can be objective in the way scientific knowledge is. Even though it is a different kind of knowledge, it has similar criteria of objectivity. Like scientific knowledge of the physical world, this knowledge is verifiable.

2. It was Parmenides who believed that the soul is characterized by endlessness.

3. The following is the beginning of a Sufi story, "The Increasing of Necessity," that illustrates the Sufis' understanding of how necessity unfolds potential:

"The tyrannical ruler of Turkestan was listening to the tales of a dervish one evening, when he bethought of himself of asking about Khidr. 'Khidr,' said the dervish, 'comes in response to need. Seize his coat when he appears, and all-knowledge is yours.'

'Can this happen to anyone?' asked the king.

'Anyone capable,' said the dervish. . . ." (Idries Shah, *Tales of the Dervishes*, p. 195.)

Khidr is the secret guide of the Sufis, who reveals the mysteries of Reality, the land of truth.

4. Some Buddhist approaches have a notion of the seed of enlightenment, *tathagatagarbha*, usually translated as "Buddha nature." The idea here is that our true nature exists in us like a seed. We all have the Buddha nature, but in potential. It can develop into Buddhahood. This is similar to the conventional notion of potential, as something specific and special in us, but seen as universally true for all human beings.

Yet other Buddhist schools think of *tathagatagarbha* not only as a seed hidden in our soul, but as the actual nature of our soul. Dzogchen (Maha Ati), for instance, understands *tathagatagarbha* as our real nature, the presence that we can recognize and realize through inner practices. *Tathagatagarbha* does not develop, for it is already and primordially complete. In her study of the differences between the two philosophical currents in Tibetan Buddhism, those of Rangtong and Shentong, where the latter is seen as underlying the teachings of Dzogchen and Mahamudra, Hookham writes about the view that Shentong holds regarding the *tathagatagarbha*:

"The essential feature of a Shentong interpretation of Tathagatagarbhha doctrine is that the Buddha is literally within all beings as their unchanging, permanent, non-conditioned nature. Shentongpas explain scriptural statements that the Buddha is present as a seed to be figurative only, because Buddha is by all accounts considered to be non-conditioned, eternal, unchanging, bliss, compassion, wisdom, power, and so on. For Shentongpas the fact that Buddha is non-conditioned means the essence of Buddha is complete with all Buddha Qualities in a timeless sense. There is no question of them arising from a seed." (S. K. Hookam, *The Buddha Within* [Albany: SUNY Press, 1991], pp. 2–3.)

This is closer to the view of essence as potential that we are discussing in this chapter. Yet it is important to recognize that even though our true nature is primordially complete, this does not mean there is no unfoldment or development, for it is always in a state of revelation. In Dzogchen this is reflected by the view that *tathagatagarbha* is always manifesting its riches in fresh displays of forms.

5. The monotheistic traditions say that only God knows everything about the soul; it is not possible for the human being to know everything about it. We see this in the following passage from a famous Sufi text: "The recognizing of *nafs* in all its qualities, and the reaching to a knowledge of it, is not the power of any created thing." (Suhrawardi, *The Awarif U'l-Ma'arif*, p. 127.)

6. This understanding is similar to the Sufi belief that the spiritual soul (*ruh*) originates from the same place as angels, what is termed the angelic realm. At the spiritual dimension of the soul, its ontological ground, it is of the same nature as the angels, meaning completely spiritual. We will discuss angels in chapter 6, but we want first to add that this Sufi understanding is based on the Qur'anic passage that responds to a question put to the prophet Muhammad about the soul, as we see in the following passage: "To this the Quran says: 'They ask thee about the Soul, say 'Soul is the command (*amr*) of the Lord thy God (*Ar Ruhu min amr-I-rabbi*)." (Shah, *Islamic Sufism*, p. 140.) The world of command is the dimension of angels in Islamic thought.

The Platonic tradition also views the soul as originally divine, and thus views the inner journey as a matter of return. This is the reason that Platonism, Neoplatonism, Kabbalah, and other Western traditions conceptualize the journey of spiritual realization as a return to a lost perfection. In Christianity, the Nicene orthodoxy changed this, and declared the soul to be inherently lacking in spiritual purity, for it is not related to the divine directly. This is not true for all Christian contemplatives, but many of those who believed in the soul's original spiritual purity were condemned as heretics by the Church. Origen is a well-known example of this kind of contemplative; another is Evagrius of Pontus. "Evagrius explains that the objects which the mind contemplates are outside of it and yet contemplation of them is constituted within the mind itself, but that in contemplation of the Holy Trinity this is not so, for here this distinction is overcome, here there is essential knowledge, knowledge, that is, which is not knowledge of something else, but knowledge in which knower and known are one." (Louth, *The Origins of the Christian Mystical Tradition*, pp. 108–109.) Evagrius believed that prayer had the function of the soul recognizing her inherent spiritual nature, which he connected with the Greek term *nous*: "In prayer the soul regains its primordial state as *nous*." (Ibid., p. 110.)

The Eastern traditions are unanimous that the primordial nature of the human being is spiritual purity, what we call essence. These traditions are completely explicit about the inherent primordial purity, perfection, and completeness of ultimate reality, which is the true nature of human beings. We see this in Vedanta, Kashmir Shaivism, Buddhism, Taoism, and other Eastern traditions.

CHAPTER 6. MORPHING DYNAMISM

1. This intrinsic property of changeability was viewed in different ways by the various wisdom traditions. The Sufis saw it as an expression of God's mercy. Ibn 'Arabi, the most systematic Sufi writer, used an interesting image to illustrate the Sufi view in regards to this property of the soul. Sufis frequently use *soul* and *heart* interchangeably, especially in that the human soul is almost synonymous with heart. The word for heart in Arabic is *qalb*. It comes from the root word that means to turn, as in turning from one thing to another or from one side to the other. This root word, *qalab*, means both turn and change.

Ibn 'Arabi uses the image of God, here named the all-merciful (*al-rahman*), holding the heart between two of his fingers, turning it one way then another, continually. Our soul, the heart between God's fingers, is as a result always changing its state; it never stays the same. This he sees as the action of mercy, so the all-merciful is changing the condition of the soul continually, even though it might not feel good sometimes. That's the usual experience of being a human being; there's always change, one thing to another. It is the action of the all-merciful because it gives the soul the possibility of learning and growing.

Buddhism, on the other hand, sees this property in terms of transitoriness, as the truth that everything is transitory, which lies at the heart of Buddha's first noble truth, that of the fact of suffering. Transitoriness can be seen as the main source of human suffering because it indicates that we always lose whatever we have, whatever we love, whatever we need. To recognize, acknowledge, and accept the inherent transitoriness of all forms of experience we become nonattached, while attachment is a denial of this truth. This attachment is the main source of human inner suffering.

Viewing changeability as connected with God's mercy brings up for the Sufi love for God, which is the motive power energizing all Sufi inner work. By seeing it as the transitoriness at the heart of human suffering, the Buddhist develops compassion, which is the primary motive power for doing inner work in Buddhism.

2. This is similar to the Reichian concept of streaming, where energy is experienced as streaming through the body as its armor tension is released in therapy. "In armored human organisms, the orgone energy is bound in the chronic contraction of the muscles. . . . Genuine sensations of plasmatic excitation waves are experienced only when a whole series of armor segments, e.g., muscular blocks in the region of the eyes, mouth, throat, breast, and diaphragm, have been dissolved. When this has been accomplished, marked *wave-like* pulsations are experienced in liberated parts of the body which move up toward the head and down toward the genitalia." (Wilhelm Reich, *Selected Writings*, p. 155.)

Reich thought of this flow as energy, and at some point called this energy *orgone*. Experience of inner flow is usually of the movement and circulation of body fluids and energies, and this is probably what most often happens in Reichian and other body-centered therapies. However, flow can possibly be of the soul herself, of the conscious presence of the soul. However, if the practitioner does not have the concept of soul or presence, then she or he is bound to think of it in terms of flow of energy, and if it feels fluid, as circulation of body fluids. It seems that Reich was actually aware of the fluid presence, but thought of it as orgone, or life energy, or plasmatic flow, as we see in some of his writings: "Our theory tells us: what we subjectively perceive and what we call 'organ sensations' are objective movements of protoplasm. Organ sensations and plasmatic currents are functionally identical." (Wilhelm Reich, *Selected Writings*, p. 309.) See *Essence*, chapter 2, for more detailed discussion of the difference between presence and energy.

The notion of stream of consciousness is also familiar in many other traditions. We see it as central in the work of the American psychologist William James, and in the Yogachara teaching of Buddhism. (See appendix B.)

3. Csikszentmihalyi used the term *flow* to describe these kinds of peak experiences, while William James used the term *stream*. (Mihalyi Csikszentmihalyi, *Flow*; William James, *The Principles of Psychology*.)

4. The Sufis, in particular, use the experience of this stage of the inner journey to formulate their language for expressing the movement in this journey. They use the term *unveiling* (*kashf*) to point to new revelations, arising spiritual perceptions, and discoveries of inner realms and meanings. Unveiling indicates something is covered over, obscured by something. The previous form covers the next one, and so by the process of flow the previous form disappears, unveiling the next form, the deeper one.

This emphasizes the Sufi view that it is God who possesses all knowledge. We uncover this knowledge, unveil it, which the Sufis differentiate from revelation, which is God's revealing (*wahi*) his secrets, which he does only to the chosen, his prophets and messengers. So Sufism expresses the Islamic hermeneutics that revelation is special knowledge, given by God to his chosen messengers, as he did to

Muhammad by sending him Gabriel, al-Wahi. Unveiling (*kashf*), on the other hand, is a human activity, the result of inner practice and exploration. The Qur'an, similarly to the Torah, is then God's revelation, and all mystical knowledge and experience the Sufis come upon is unveiling.

5. Some of the Buddhist schools use this language of appearing, referring to the division of Reality into absolute, which is emptiness, and relative, which is manifestation. The relative, the manifest, is frequently referred to as appearance. We see this in the following passage from Padmasambhava, one of the foremost saints of Tibetan Buddhism:

> *Moreover, as for this diversity of appearances, which represents relative truth,*
> *Not even one of these appearances is actually created in reality, and so accordingly they disappear again.*
> *All things, all phenomenal existence, everything within Samsara and Nirvana,*
> *Are merely appearances (or phenomena) which are perceived by the individual's single nature of the mind.*
>
> JOHN M. REYNOLDS,
> *Self-Liberation through Seeing with Naked Awareness*, p. 24

The same schools, especially the nondual ones, also use terms like *display*, *radiance*, *glimmerings*, and sometimes simply *manifestation*.

6. This seems to be the origin of Heidegger's view of the relation of time to Being. He looks at the role of time differently from how we see it here, by looking at its dynamic instead of its linear passage. He believed time is intrinsic to Being because Being is always a result of becoming, and becoming is the future moving into the present, and through it to the past. Therefore, whatever appears to our perception comes from the future, as the "presencing" that time gives. He writes that we can escape indeterminacy "if only we look ahead toward Being as presence and towards time as the realm where, by virtue of offering, a manifold presencing takes place and opens up. . . . Insofar as there is manifest in Being as presence such a thing as time, the supposition mentioned earlier grows stronger that true time, the fourfold extending of the open, could be discovered as the 'It' that gives Being, i.e., gives presence." (Martin Heidegger, *On Time and Being*, p. 17.)

Tarthang Tulku also uses this image of appearance arriving from the future, and hence connects future with the openness of Being, where he also emphasizes time's dynamic instead of its passage. "Such times of vitality reveal the momentum of time as a thrusting, driving presence. When we awaken to this momentum, experience becomes something different from what it usually is. The interaction of identified entities gives way to shifting shapes unfolding in unbroken presentation." (Tarthang Tulku, *Dynamics of Time and Space*, p. 91.) Then he writes in the same chapter: "Instead of somehow passing on substance to the present, the future sustains the present through its coming. Though this 'coming' never arrives, its dynamic contributes the charged 'field' within which the aliveness of present experience can unfold." (Ibid., p. 96.)

Both Heidegger's and Tarthang Tulku's views on manifestation are counter to the conventional one, where it is a movement of forms from the past into the future. They obviously both have their stance in consciousness, instead of the material world or the rational mind.

7. This reminds us of the Hopi relation to time. This particular tribe of native Americans did not have our concept of linear time. They measured speed with intensity and fullness. "The Hopi language is seen to contain no words, grammatical forms, constructions or expressions that refer directly to what we call 'time,' or to past, present, or future, or to enduring or lasting, or to motion as kinematics rather than dynamic . . . Hence the Hopi language contains no reference to 'time,' either explicit or implicit." (Benjamin Lee Wharf, *Language, Thought and Reality*, pp. 57–58.)

8. The nondual wisdom traditions that recognize forms as inseparable from emptiness will describe manifestation here as nonarising, because there is no separation between the absolute source, which is emptiness, and the forms that constitute appearance. Appearance and emptiness are completely coemergent, totally mixed. One formulation of the path then, as in Dzogchen and Mahamudra, is that at the beginning there is experience of the flow of thoughts. In the middle of the path there is experience of alternation of the flow of thoughts and calm stillness, empty of thoughts. Real and natural realization is the end of the path, where the flow of thoughts and the calm emptiness are inseparable. As the *Heart Sutra* says: "Form is emptiness, emptiness is form." So at the deepest level there is always a flow, it never stops.

9. This inseparability of spiritual nature from dynamism has been formulated in various ways by the different wisdom traditions. Shaivism used the image of the eternal embrace of Shiva and Shakti, where Shiva is the ultimate ground and self, while Shakti is his energy and dynamism responsible for manifestation. The image of embracing male and female deities is common in Tibetan Buddhism, but the one that most specifically refers to our discussion is that of Samantabadra and Samantabadri, the absolute and his consort, in the Maha Ati teaching.

10. That is why we believe Wilhelm Reich had a deep insight into the soul when he thought the armor of the orgasm reflex is a constriction of an organismic deep movement, similar to that of a jellyfish-like flow. It seems he was perceiving that the soul can be free and dynamic, the way a jellyfish is. "The expressive movements in the orgasm reflex are, viewed in terms of identity of function, the same as those of a living and swimming jellyfish." (Wilhelm Reich, *Character Analysis*, p. 396.)

It is possible that recognizing how the constriction of the jellyfish-like movement of the organism interferes with genital orgasm contributed to the orientation of his therapy toward freeing sexuality. He saw freedom of genital sexuality, in other words, as the way toward the total freedom of the organism. He thought of the organism primarily as physical, but we believe he had some perception of the soul, in terms of her flow, dynamism, and pulsating movement.

CHAPTER 7. IMPRESSIONABILITY OF SOUL

1. The fictional idea here is of a being who does not have a specific form or shape, but assumes whatever form or shape that suits it at a particular time. This being is some kind of a living organic substance, a formless puddle of sort, malleable and endowed with the capacity to mold itself as needed. So this being can assume a humanoid form, a man or woman, but can just as easily change itself into a tree, a chair, a bird, part of the wall, and so on. It changes itself according to what it believes it needs to survive, learn and communicate. Movies and television shows have been using some recent advances in graphic computer technology, specifically morphing, to create characters like these on the screen. Some notable ones are the T1000 robot in the movie *Terminator 2*, and the changeling Odo in the *Star Trek* spinoff *Deep Space Nine*. This computer technology has been able to produce graphic art that resembles how the soul actually transforms.

2. Some wisdom traditions, especially the Eastern ones, think of this conditioning lasting numerous lifetimes. The idea of transmigration is wedded with that of karma, which is how one's actions in one particular lifetime determine the characteristics of the following lifetimes. This means that one's experience can impress one's soul so deeply that this impression can last many lifetimes. Usually, these lasting impressions are considered, as in Hindu thought, to survive as seeds (*samskaras*) that can be activated at some point, leading to experiences and life situations related to the ones that generated them, and general tendencies (*vasanas*) and characteristics for the particular soul. "By the very fact that their mode of being is that of 'potentiality,' their own dynamism forces the *vasanas* to manifest, to 'actualize,' themselves under the form of acts of consciousness . . . The *vasanas* condition the specific character of each individual; and this conditioning is in accordance with both his heredity and his karmic situation." (Mircea Eliade, *Yoga*, p. 42.)

3. Buddhism has recognized the unique situation of the human being in positing human life as the most auspicious of possibilities. In its teaching of transmigration it conceives that one can be born in various forms of life. It divides sentient beings into six categories: gods, jealous gods, human beings, animals, hungry ghosts, and denizens of hell. Yet it believes that human life is far more precious than the others, even than that of the gods, because it is the only form of life where learning can fully happen, which is necessary for enlightenment. For the monotheistic way of recognizing the unique position of the human soul, as in the Islamic story of Adam and Lucifer, see note 1, chapter 9.

4. Making the soul feminine, and essence (spirit or God) masculine, is standard in many traditional teachings; it is actually an important element of these teachings, and their theology and metaphysics. This is clear, for instance, in the Song of Songs

in the Old Testament, in the writings of many Christian mystics and theologians, as well as in Islamic and Sufi literature. The soul has been described as a bride to God or the Christ, and the completion of her journey is union with him.

Sufi literature makes this more specific, where the union of essence—as spirit (*ruh*) and soul (*nafs*)—is seen not only as important for spiritual development but as marking a particular marriage that results in an offspring, named heart (*qalb*). (See appendix C.)

Even some Hindu teachings use the masculine and feminine genders to distinguish essence and soul, but mostly in terms of cosmic manifestations. An example is that of Kashmir Shaivism, where Shiva is seen as masculine, and his counterpart, Shakti, is the feminine creative matrix of all manifestation. The sense of the feminine is seen as that of creativity, instead of merely receptivity, similar to the Sufi marriage between *ruh* and *nafs*. We have already discussed the creativity of soul in terms of her morphogenic and unfolding property, but receptivity points to this creativity in her relation to her ground of essence. In other words, the idea of a marriage or union between soul and essence, resulting in the complete human being, points to a particular process of morphogenic transformation, that of spiritual development, realization, and liberation. It points to it, and explains how it actually happens.

5. This process was seen by Heinz Hartmann, as described by Blanck and Blanck, as part of the process of inner ego organization: "As this proceeds, certain forms of behavior change in function. A process which had originated as a defense—for example, the essential mechanism of reaction formation in toilet training—acquires adaptive autonomy when the purpose changes to maintenance of hygienic habits and orderliness." (Blanck and Blanck, *Ego Psychology*, p. 32.)

6. This paranoia toward, and intolerance of, receptivity and impressionability depends on the strength of our ego structure. Strength of ego structure reflects its secure establishment, its cohesive integrity, and its reality or nearness to the actual experience of ourselves and the world. This strength expresses itself as a tolerance for change, as flexibility in openness for impressions, because of the resiliency of this ego. But when the ego structure develops weaknesses or lacks stable cohesion and integrity it will tend to be brittle and vulnerable, and hence will generally be more rigid, inflexible, and defensive.

In other words, the weaker the ego structure and the less secure our sense of identity, the more resistant we will tend to be toward greater malleability, impressionability, and receptivity. This vulnerable receptive state is experienced as quite intolerable. There is terror about it, and all kinds of splittings and distortions happen to avoid that impressionability. On the other hand, even though a strong ego structure can be rigid and defensive, it will be able to regain its structure after dissolving; it will regroup and be able to function. The soul of this individual has a flexibility that is lacking in weak structures.

The unusually weak structure will find it difficult to regroup and function after reaching this place of being completely impressionable because complete impressionability means there is no fixed structure here, no structure at all. To get to impressionability means dissolving whatever structure happens to be there in that particular part of the soul. For instance, if the soul has an identity of being a deficient person, she generally would be attached to feeling like a deficient person even though it is painful. This is because if she loses the deficient identity she will lose her familiar structure, and become for a time an undefinable structureless medium. But she has to dissolve the feeling of being a deficient person to be impressionable to other things. As long as she believes she is a deficient person, she is not truly impressionable. She can't be impressed by being a happy person, she can't be impressed by joy, she can't be impressed by strength, she can only be impressed by deficiency. She is set, she is fixed. There is a fixation on that deficiency because that fixation gives her structure and is a protection against feeling completely unprotected and open to whatever influence.

7. Traditionally this has been formulated as the soul changing from fearing people and creation to fearing God, as she progresses on the inner path. She listens more to the dictates of essence until essence becomes the center and ground of all of her experience. This is total faithfulness in and to spirit.

8. The classic study of this process of purification of the soul, a process by which the soul learns to be detached from her animal nature and its various attachments, is *Dark Night of the Soul* by Saint John of the Cross.

CHAPTER 8. LIVING PRESENCE

1. Using the language developed by Arthur Koestler, each of the forms that the soul generates is a *holon*, an entity or structure that is itself a whole and a part of another whole. In this language, the soul unfolds through a holarchic evolution, where the unfoldment appears in a *holarchy*, a natural hierarchy of increasing wholeness. Each holon emerges in a way that both transcends and includes the previous ones.

Ken Wilber, in *Sex, Ecology and Sexuality* and *A Brief History of Everything*, used the work of Arthur Koestler and many others, as well as systems theory, holism, and many of the postmodern new paradigm theories, to construct an overarching synthesis of a theory of evolution, on both the cosmic and individual scales. His synthesis argues for evolution through creative emergence: "Evolution is in part a self-transcending process—it always goes beyond what went before. And in that novelty, in that emergence, in that creativity, new entities come into being, new patterns unfold, new holons issue forth. This extraordinary process builds unions out of fragments and wholes out of heaps. The Kosmos, it seems, unfolds in quantum leaps of creative emergence." (Ken Wilber, *A Brief History of Everything*, p. 24.)

This view describes how the soul unfolds, as the creative emergence of forms of increasing levels of organization, each superseding but integrating the previously arisen ones. In fact, the soul seems to us to be the ontological archetype of such self-organizing and developing living systems. Relating this observation with Wilber's synthesis of it in terms of cosmic evolution raises the question of how the cosmos is like the soul, and the question then of a cosmic soul. We address this question in chapter 20.

2. This has been studied systematically by Piaget and other developmental psychologists. He recognized mental development as progressing through stages, where at each stage a new capacity and function emerges and develops. The overall development of mind is not that one stage displaces the one preceding it, but by developing a new form it subsumes and integrates the preceding one.

3. Examples are Dzogchen, Zen, and the higher teachings of Kashmir Shaivism.

4. Buddhism, among other Eastern wisdom traditions, believes in the possibility of complete enlightenment, where one can perfectly abide in the primordial completeness. This is the station called Buddhahood. But Buddhism clearly believes this is the result of a protracted process of learning and maturation. Not only did Buddha need about six years of dedicated search, but the tradition tells the stories of his thousands of previous incarnations, where he assiduously worked on developing and maturing his experience and understanding, collecting spiritual merit and capacity. The point is not whether one needs many incarnations, but the mythology clearly indicates the need for a period of learning and maturation.

5. Our life is all in our consciousness in a more fundamental way than we discuss here. We discuss our experience here as reflecting both the inner and the outer, but at certain stages of the inner journey, as we understand the relation between soul, Being, and world, the dichotomy between inner and outer collapses. Our life becomes the flow of consciousness, but not in the limited sense of the individual soul, as we discuss here. Our present discussion is an entry into this larger perspective, and for a fuller discussion of this perspective see chapters 17–22.

6. Buddhism, actually, refers to our experience as the "stream of consciousness." (See appendix B.) This is the usual Buddhist reference to the soul, as a current of consciousness, but most emphasized by the concept of the *alayavijnana* in the Yogachara school of Mahayana Buddhism. "The *alayavijnana* is sometimes understood as a flux of mental phenomena that constitutes a continuum existing beyond the individual's life." (E. K. Neumaier-Dargyay, *The Sovereign All-Creating Mind*, p. 11.) We will see shortly that this is a perspective of consciousness or mind that Buddhism shares with many of the other Eastern traditions, as in the case of Vedanta, and that this perspective tends not to emphasize life and what it means.

7. One of the first scientists to put out the idea that subjective consciousness is an emergent function from higher-order organizational processes of the brain was the neurologist Roger Sperry. He saw such consciousness of sentience as possessing its own holistic properties and functions that are not reducible to neural structures of the brain. (See Roger Sperry, "In defense of mentalism and emergent interaction,"

Journal of Mind and Behavior 12:221–46 [1987]; "Structure and significance of the consciousness revolution;" *Journal of Mind and Behavior* 8:37—66 [1987].)

8. How true this is remains a question for spiritual experience. Many of the wisdom traditions believe that consciousness is capable of self-consciousness and introspection independently of the brain, or of the body as a whole. These traditions believe that there is not only consciousness after death, but mental process and introspection. This is clear in the teachings of the *Tibetan Book of the Dead*, the major monotheistic accounts of the soul's experience after death, and others.

This might mean that the soul is capable of being conscious of herself independently of the body, but that this capacity becomes more complete, or sharper and more discriminating, with the assistance of the brain. Another possibility is that the soul can attain the capacity for self-consciousness and introspection only first with the assistance of the brain, but that it can develop to the extent that it does not need it at some point. This will mean that not all souls will retain this capacity after death. This is a speculation on our part, for we do not have direct experience of life after death.

The other and more plausible idea is that the body and its brain are necessary for the soul to operate in the physical dimension, this way extending her capacities to the physical realm. This means that she already has the capacity for mental functioning and introspection but not in the way or to the extent we have them when our soul is embodied in a physical organism.

9. What arises from understanding the relation of world to Being can be summed up by saying that matter is not what we think it is. Matter is one way we experience the appearance of the universe, namely through the use of our senses. It is the particle side of reality, which appears to our perception this way because of our route of approaching it. Approaching it differently, from the inner subjective side, we can experience its wave aspect. This application of the metaphor of the complementarity principle reveals that the wave aspect of matter is pure consciousness. From this perspective all the theories about the arising of consciousness need to be revised in a radically different light, for consciousness is not a product of matter because matter itself is a certain level of organization of consciousness. Pure consciousness is more fundamental than and ontologically prior to matter. Therefore, inner or subjective consciousness is a further organization of consciousness, and not something that suddenly arises when brain neural networks reach a certain high degree of organization. The evolution of the brain seems to be necessary for this property of consciousness to emerge, but it does not depend only on brain complexity. The inherent pure consciousness is its necessary ground.

Hence, the AI theory, and possibly the emergence theory, proves to be inadequate. This is to be expected, for both are expressions of our modern thought that has dissociated the basic triad. And since consciousness and its relation to matter lie at the very heart of this dissociation, we will be fooling ourselves if we believe that theories grounded in this dissociation can give us an adequate understanding of the relation of matter and consciousness.

10. Therefore, physical phenomena that used to be described mechanically can now be understood using terms borrowed from the properties of life, as we see in the following passage from Jantsch's application of this new theory of systems to evolution in various dimensions of reality: "This new type of science which orients itself primarily at models of life, and not mechanical models, spurs change not only in science . . . The basic themes are always the same. They may be summarized by notions such as self-determination, self-organization and self-renewal; by the recognition of a systemic interconnectedness over space and time of all natural dynamics; by the logical supremacy of processes over spatial structures . . ." (Erich Jantsch, *The Self-Organizing Universe*, p. 8.)

11. We are not implying that consciousness is the actual wave side of particles. We are not adopting the complementarity principle of quantum theory, and asserting that the wave side is consciousness. We are using the complementarity principle as a metaphor, which we apply to understand the gross perception of matter, as our physical bodies and other physical objects are observable with our physical senses. We use this metaphor to illustrate our understanding that our perception of such physical objects is due to a certain type of observation, and that if we adopt a different mode of observation, that of witnessing from the perspective of the spiritual ground of the soul, we will see this matter as a medium of consciousness, as particular forms within a field of sensitivity.

In quantum mechanics, the wave side of particles is still seen as something physical, measurable with physical instruments. In our understanding, we are not challenging or changing this view, but applying the complementarity principle as a metaphor to a different polarity, that of matter and spirit.

12. Plotinus postulated the world soul, logos, or reason-principle that underlies our physical universe: "The Reason-Principle presiding over visible Shape is the very ultimate of its order, a dead thing unable to produce further: that which produces in the created realm is the living Reason-Principle—brother, no doubt, to that which gives mere shape, but having life-giving power. . . . the total Logos with its two distinguishable phases, first, that identified not as Nature but as All-Soul and, next, that operating in Nature and being itself the Nature-Principle." (Plotinus, *Enneads*, p. 235.)

Christian mysticism and Sufism postulated something similar, the universal logos. Scheller and Hegel thought of world history as the evolution of Spirit, as we see in the following passage from Weiss's introduction to Hegel: "What it means is that the changing world and all its history is none other than this principle's own manifestation, the revelation of itself in various modes of consciousness or stages of unity culminating in philosophic thought, which alone adequately exhibits the full development of Spirit as nothing other than the raising of itself to truth. 'Truth,' Hegel says, 'aware of what it is, is Spirit.'" (Frederick Weiss, *Hegel: The Essential Writings*, p. 5.)

We deal with this question more completely in chapter 20.

13. David Bohm is one of the few scientists who developed a similar idea by using the physical theory of quantum mechanics. He postulated what he called an implicate order, as a sea of energy that underlies all phenomena, the complement to the explicate order, the physical universe: "This sea is to be understood in terms of a multidimensional implicate order . . . while the entire universe of matter as we generally observe it is to be treated as a comparatively small pattern of excitation. This excitation pattern is relatively autonomous and gives rise to approximately recurrent, stable and separable projections into a three-dimensional explicate order of manifestation . . ." (David Bohm, *Wholeness and the Implicate Order*, p. 192.)

He thought this implicate order to be related to consciousness, or the underlying ground of our normal consciousness and matter: "That is to say, we are suggesting that the implicate order applies both to matter (living and non-living) and to consciousness, and that it can therefore make possible an understanding of the general relationship of these two, from which we may be able to come to some notion of a common ground both . . ." (Ibid. p. 196.)

He even thought that life, as a result, is inherent to the universe because it is implicit in the implicate order: "Indeed, the holomovement which is 'life implicit' is the ground both of 'life explicit' and of 'inanimate matter,' and this ground is what is primary, self-existent and universal." (Ibid., p. 195.)

14. Some new paradigm systems theorists reach a similar conclusion, considering the self-organizing property of the universe, and its sub-systems, as signifying life. We see this view in the following passage: "Thus, self-organization dynamics becomes the link between the realms of the animate and the inanimate. Life no longer appears as a thin superstructure over a lifeless physical reality, but as an inherent principle of the dynamics of the universe." (Erich Jantsch, *The Self-Organizing Universe*, p. 19.)

Systems theory, however, stops short of recognizing the actual living conscious presence that forms the ground of all forms, whose life appears in the physical universe as self-organizing dynamics.

15. This clearly implies that most adult human beings become less in touch with their souls as they physically mature, but most importantly that most of humanity is out of touch with the living presence of its soul, the source of true life. This is actually the contention of all wisdom traditions, and can be seen clearly when one begins to actually experience one's soul directly and fully.

16. A question remains: What does physical life add to the life of the soul? This is an interesting question, one that has many answers, depending on what ancient teaching we consult. For us, it remains a mystery, requiring further research and investigation. It is possible that by assuming a body, life expresses itself in more dimensions, allowing different possibilities, invoking more potential. This is similar to the view of some ancient Greek philosophers, such as Plotinus. It is also possible that biological life is one of the stages of the growth of the soul: necessary, but a stage nevertheless.

CHAPTER 9. SOUL AND ESSENCE

1. The recognition that potential is a property of the soul and not essence has led some of the wisdom traditions, such as Islamic gnosis, to think of human beings as more precious than angels. Angels are the primordial spiritual perfections, the inherent perfections of ultimate truth, whether we see this ultimate truth as God or pure Being. Hence, angels can be seen as standing for the aspects of essence, since these aspects are the explicit differentiations of the perfections of essence, pure consciousness. The following quote from a Sufi text points to this fact:

"If the World of the Real Supernal contains Light-substances, high and lofty, called 'Angels,' from which substances the various lights are effused upon the various mortal spirits, and by reason of which these angels are called 'lords,' then Allah 'Lord of lords,' and these lords have different grades of luminousness." (Sirdar Ikbal Ali Shah, *Islamic Sufism*, p. 198.)

Other teachings will see them within their particular categorization of divine perfections. For Islamic gnosis, the human soul is more precious because she has infinite potential, where an angel has no potential. An angel is perfect, primordially pure and free. Nevertheless, an angel can only be this particular quality of perfection. It cannot develop to embody other qualities. The soul, on the other hand, can be miserable and wretched in its everyday experience, but she does not only have infinite potential, she has all of essence, with all of its aspects and dimensions, as part of this potential. She has the potential to develop in such a way as to embody all the aspects of essence, all the perfections of ultimate truth. Rumi, calling spirit or essence *intellect*, puts it this way: "He whose intellect dominates his sensuality is higher than the angels, and he whose sensuality dominates his intellect is lower than the beasts." (William Chittick, *The Sufi Path of Love*, p. 86.)

The Qur'an tells the story of how Lucifer, called Iblis, the most glorious and beautiful of all the angels, fell and became Satan, the devil. The story tells that when God created Adam he created him from earth but breathed into him from his spirit. He asked all the angels to kneel to Adam, this way acknowledging his superiority to them. But Lucifer rebelled, protesting that he, Lucifer, is perfect, a being of light, while Adam was a being of mud. Chittick quotes this Qur'anic verse in his study of Rumi:

"In the Koran God addresses humanity as follows: "We created you, then We shaped you, then We said to the angels: 'Bow yourselves to Adam.' So they bowed themselves, save Iblis. He was not of those that bowed themselves. Said He, 'What prevented thee to bow thyself when I commanded thee?' Said he, 'I am better than he; Thou createdst me of fire, and him Thou createdst of clay' (VII 11–12)." (Ibid., p. 83.)

This indicated that Lucifer did not understand and appreciate Adam, standing for human potential. He did not see that Adam has the potential to be greater than all the angels, for they are each a perfection of the divine, while Adam can be the actualization of all of these perfections. In other words, Lucifer did not understand that man was created in the image of God. This, the story goes, angered God, who then threw Lucifer out of the divine court.

2. We do not mean the customary meaning of *concept*, that is, a notion that refers to a category of percepts. By concept we mean something more basic, which in some sense can be called a primitive concept, or a preconcept, a recognition of a percept before it is connected to a whole category of percepts.

3. Plato said that Socrates called it recollection, but by this Plato did not mean remembering something one experienced in previous occasions. He meant the soul opening to a dimension of herself already present in her. He meant she knows such spiritual qualities because they are her nature, a nature from which she had become alienated. When she finally accesses this dimension, she recognizes the qualities because it is inherent to her to know them. He called such knowing the knowing of intelligible forms, the ideas, as we see in the following passage from Reale's study of Plato: "The things that we grasp with the bodily eye are physical forms; the things that we grasp with the 'eye of the soul' are, instead, non-physical forms: the vision of the intellect grasps intelligible forms, that are precisely pure essences. The 'Ideas' are thus these eternal essences of the Good, the True, the Just, and similar things, that the intellect, when it is stretched to its maximum capacity, and moved in the pure realm of the intelligible, succeeds in 'determining' and 'grasping.'" (Giovanni Reale, *A History of Ancient Philosophy: Plato and Aristotle*, p. 48.)

This type of knowing was appreciated not only in Greek philosophy, but also by some Eastern teachings. We see it in the Zen mode of realization, where being and knowing are identical, as expressed by Suzuki: "Self-nature, otherwise expressed, is self-knowledge; it is not mere being but knowing. We can say that because of knowing itself, it is; knowing is being, and being is knowing. This is the meaning of the statement made by Hui-neng that: 'In original Nature there is Prajna-knowledge, and because of this, self-knowledge. Nature reflects itself in itself, which is self-illumination not to be expressed in words.'" (D. T. Suzuki, *Zen Buddhism*, p. 173.)

This kind of basic knowing is usually referred to by the Sanskrit term *jnana*, similar to Tibetan concept of *yeshe*, indicating an inherent and fundamental knowing, in contradistinction to normal thematic knowing, as we see in the following quote from Guenther's study of Dzogchen: "It seems that at the one extreme of the experiential spectrum there is a high-energy optimal awareness (*rig-pa*) operating in and as a pristine cognition (*ye-shes*) coincident with a formal gestalt as the external expression of an inner meaning (*sku*), carrying with it the feeling of certainty and undivided wholeness. At the other extreme there is a stepped-down awareness (*ma-rig-pa*), which manifests as the thingness of thought and its reductionist programs . . ." (Herbert Guenther, *Matrix of Mystery*, p. 22.)

This is important for Dzogchen, the nondual teaching of Vajrayana, where this basic knowing is reflected in the notion of *rigpa*, which is true nature as basic knowingness, as fundamental illumination, as presence inseparable from knowingness: "In Nying-ma it is called the '*mind-vajra*'; this is not the mind that is contrasted with basic knowledge in the division into basic knowledge (*rig pa*) and mind (*sems*) but the factor of mere luminosity and knowing, basic knowledge itself." (Dalai Lama XIV, *Kindness, Clarity and Insight*, p. 210.)

It is not an accident that most people find it difficult to understand Plato when he writes about the recollection involved in knowing the *eidos*, the universal ideas. Most think of it as simple remembering, perhaps from past lifetimes. This is because such knowing is missing in our ego experience, for this experience develops with and is based on discursive representational knowledge, ordinary knowledge. As a result, our modern and most postmodern thought conceives of concepts as merely constructs we form in our discursive mind. There is no recognition of a different level of concepts, of inherent discrimination in reality that our soul can spontaneously discern. (See *The Point of Existence* appendix C, and chapter 4 of the present book.)

4. What are called the virtues—courage, sobriety, innocence, serenity, humility, truthfulness, equanimity, detachment, and so on—are the soul's being transparent to essence in her actions and expressions. They are not aspects of essence, and are not ordinarily experienced as states of presence, but they are the adornments of the soul that has realized her essence. As a result they are observable from the outside, by others, and not by oneself.

The virtues that Plato mentioned in his dialogues are sometimes one or another of the cardinal virtues, such as courage, but sometimes the effect of essence on the perception of the soul, as in beauty, and sometimes the effect of essence on the action of the soul, as in justice. Sometimes they are the actual presence of an essential aspect, as in truth or intelligence. Sometimes they are true nature in its nondifferentiated mode, as in his notion of the Good.

5. See *Elixir of Enlightenment* for the role of essential aspects in traversing the path of inner transformation and liberation, *The Void* for detailed investigation of the effect of the presence of spaciousness on the soul, *Spacecruiser Inquiry* for the function of the aspects in the practice of inquiry, understanding, and inner guidance, *The Pearl Beyond Price* for detailed investigation of the aspect of personal essence and its role in ego development and its integration, and *The Point of Existence* for exploration of the aspect of identity and its role in narcissism and self-realization. Most of the books by the author are detailed explorations of various of these essential aspects.

CHAPTER 10. ANIMAL SOUL

1. Aurobindo, the Indian philosopher sage, termed this dimension of soul the desire soul, and referred to the essential dimension as the divine soul: "So too we have a double psychic entity in us, the surface desire-soul which works in our vital cravings, our emotions, aesthetic faculty and mental seeking for power, knowledge and happiness, and a subliminal psychic entity, a pure power of light, love, joy and refined essence of being which is our true soul behind the outer form of psychic existence we so often dignify by the name." (Sri Aurobindo, *The Life Divine*, vol. 1, p. 220.) However, Sufism, Kabbalah, and many other wisdom traditions have consistently used the term *animal soul*, while Christianity has tended to call it the sense or sensual soul.

2. The Greeks believed that the primitiveness and animality of the soul, and hence all of her passions, attachments, and wretchedness, owe to her association with the physical body. This assumption guided most of their philosophers, including Plato, to believe that leaving the body is the sure way for the purification and liberation of the soul. In other words, they blamed the body for all the inner ills of the soul. Others have shared aspects of this view, including many ascetics of various religions.

3. The Sufis regard the heart as the result of the marriage between essence and soul, what they call *ruh* and *nafs*. (See appendix C.)

4. A classic account of work with the animal soul and harmonizing it with the spiritual nature is *Dark Night of the Soul* by Saint John of the Cross. This is only one way of bringing maturity. Another is the Eastern path of tantra, wherein the passions are not purified and transcended but embraced and transformed into positive qualities.

5. Freud saw this when he believed that repression and sublimation are the best things that our society has found to deal with our instinctual drives. He recognized by this the benefit to society in the development of a superego that embodies the ethical and moral rules of society.

He saw no alternative other than this sublimation, because our civilization in general has found no other solution. However, it has been the function of inner work schools the world over to find and apply ways of dealing with the animal soul in a way that integrates it harmoniously with the rest of our potential. In fact, to truly deal with the animal soul is to seriously move toward enlightenment.

6. Other researchers have recognized the potential for such experiences, as in some of the wisdom traditions. Some modern researchers have made similar discoveries, the best known being Grof's research in LSD experiences, and later work with therapeutic hyperventilation. Grof, exploring LSD experiences, describes three major types of animal experiences: "Genuine animal identification is a clearly transpersonal experience and has a primary quality; it is a phenomena sui generis that cannot be derived from other unconscious material and interpreted symbolically. The three LSD experiences related to animals—animal autosymbolic transformations, animal identifications, and phylogenetic memories—each have their specific characteristics." (Stanislav Grof, *Realms of the Human Unconscious*, p. 181.)

He thinks of phylogenetic memories as including the sense of time regression, while animal identification is devoid of this sense: "The major difference between them is that simple animal identification is not accompanied by the sense of time regression and by the feeling that the individual is exploring the evolutionary lines of phylogenetic development." (Ibid., p. 181.)

The animal experiences we are discussing do not have this sense of time regression, but they do seem to include all forms in our phylogenetic history. In describing phylogenetic animal experiences, Grof lists forms that are familiar to us from exploration of the animal potential of soul: "The objects of identification are most frequently other mammals, birds, reptiles, amphibians, and various species of fish. Occasionally, they can be much less differentiated forms of life, such as insects, gastropods (various snails), brachipods (shellfish), cephalopods (octopus and squid), and coelenterates (sea anemones and jellyfish)." (Ibid., p. 172.)

7. This will obviously be the explanation given by those who believe in the theory of transmigration of the soul. This theory will easily explain our observation by the idea that the soul has actually experienced all these organic forms in its many reincarnations. We do not find this to be a compelling explanation, partly because it assumes a subtle physical reductionism, as we will see in our subsequent discussion.

8. Some of the wisdom traditions have understood this from ancient times. The most well-known example is the Sufi belief that the soul develops within an even wider range of experience. They believe that the soul has a potential that includes plant life and even inanimate matter. So the evolutionary history for the soul is cast as development from mineral, to vegetal, to animal, to human, to angelic and further as we see in the following discussion of Rumi's work by Chittick: "According to Rumi's teachings, the spirit must manifest itself as each of the four elements and only then enter into the three kingdoms. When it appears within the world in the form of a mineral, it begins its return to its own world. Through successive stages it is transformed from mineral to plant, to animal and finally to man. When it assumes the form of human being, the spirit is ready to begin disengaging itself from the material world." (William C. Chittick, *The Sufi Path of Love*, p. 74.)

The understanding that such forms of experience are potential to the soul has also been part of Sufi knowledge: "The human spirit embraces within itself innumerable possibilities of outward manifestation. It can throw down uncountable shadows or forms. Since 'Adam was taught the names,' the meanings of all things are contained within man's spirit. And each of these meanings can become manifested as a corresponding form." (Ibid., p. 74.)

Our observation corresponds with this Sufi knowledge, that the soul potential includes all possible forms of manifestation, whether organic or not, regardless of size and shape. So the soul can experience herself, as happens frequently on the spiritual journey, as a star, a planet, a galaxy, a universe, a rock or mountain, rain or clouds, an ocean or a river, a jewel or a crystal, a metallic or an organic form, and so on. The experience is not physical, but feels similar to the physical. It is an inner experience, and the forms are forms of consciousness, but they are the closest a human being can experientially know these manifestations.

Encountering these experiences in his LSD research, Grof considered them to be a particular variety of transpersonal experience. In his system of classification, these experiences fall within the category of Spatial Expansion of Consciousness. (Stanislav Grof, *Realms of the Human Unconscious*, pp. 178–190.)

Furthermore, each of these inner forms of experience has a psychological meaning. Star is identity, planet is organization, galaxy is expansion, and so on. This is a concrete and precise way of recognizing the ancient idea that the human being is a microcosm of the universe. We will discuss this in detail further when we discuss the nature of the universe and its relation to the soul.

9. Wilhelm Reich, the psychoanalyst who founded breathwork therapy, thought he was observing the actual flow of physical protoplasm when he noticed protoplasmic flow in the body. (See chapter 6, note 2.) We believe it is more likely that he was observing the flow of the basic substance of the soul, but that he thought of it within his own conceptual framework. He thought of it as a physical substance that had a physical movement because he was looking at things from the perspective of his research into the body and its energies.

CHAPTER 11. NORMAL DEVELOPMENT OF THE SOUL

1. It is difficult to know the infant's state because we usually do not remember such times, and it is not so easy to get into the consciousness of an infant. So most infant research merely observes infants' external behavior and draws conclusions accordingly. We find this quite unacceptable. How can we draw conclusions from such external referents about inner states when we know that the infant does not experience things like us, adults? We know that infants' cognitive, emotional, and ego capacities are not developed and integrated as with the adult. So how can we apply the perspective of a consciousness that can only see things with its developed mind and cognition to one that does not have such development? The possibility of adultomorphism is omnipresent, and actually unavoidable. Anyone who has done enough inner work to free their consciousness from the dictates of ego and cognitive structures, which an adult normally possesses, knows how almost impossible it is to do, and how pervasively such structures influence our perception, understanding, and attitudes. It is our observation that most infant researchers are trapped in this dilemma, and their conclusions can only be taken provisionally. We recommend that before a researcher tries to study infants' inner states that she or he first learns to experience inner states without the structures that developed from childhood on; otherwise the danger of adultomorphism is unavoidable.

Because of this situation we resort to two other sources of information to supplement such behavioral research. The first is from adults' memories of early childhood experiences. There is mounting evidence that we can have memories from early infancy and prenatal life. Also in this category is the reconstruction work done in psychoanalysis. The second source is the subtle capacities of perception that develop through the inner journey. These capacities include the ability to see directly into somebody else's consciousness, and the ability to feel directly the details of another person's inner state. These subtle capacities can develop to a great degree of discrimination and refinement, but they are also subject to distortions and projections more than our physical senses. We do not need to take these observations at their face value and accept them as facts, but we can use them as pointers to what the infant might be experiencing.

We also work on freeing our consciousness from the adult's ego consciousness by learning about inner states of consciousness that are free from ego structures.

Knowing about these states, especially those that can go beyond conceptualization and formal cognition, gives us perspectives similar to what the infant experiences, because the infant's early states are still largely preconceptual. This brings our perspective closer to the nonperspective of the infant, at least closer than the capacity of the normal adult ego.

We integrate the findings of some infant experimental research with observations from the above two sources of information, but viewed from the enlarged perspective of knowing both the ego states that the infant develops into and the states of consciousness that transcend conceptualization and formal cognition, to arrive at an appreciation of infant's inner states. We take such understanding as more likely to be accurate than merely using infant experimental research or subtle perceptions. Nevertheless, we do not present our understanding as fact, but as the most likely possibility. In other words, when we discuss the infant's inner experience we want the reader to understand that we still take our knowledge as provisional, but as the best we know at present.

2. This kind of observation has led some thinkers to take the position that the human infant is not capable of experiencing essential states, and that it is completely animal. The most well-known and vocal advocate of this position in our times is the transpersonal theorist Ken Wilber. For fuller discussion of childhood essential experience, and of Wilber's view, see appendix D.

3. According to cognitive research, images begin to emerge in childhood experience at the age of seven months, and symbols during the second year, and both are necessary before concepts dominate awareness, which happens between the ages of four and seven. (See Gruber and Voneche, *The Essential Piaget*.)

4. Recent infant research has discovered that infants possess capacities for knowing that are not representational in a mental fashion, that do not require the cognitive and conceptual development necessary for normal representational knowing. This has been used by some psychoanalysts to study experience occurring before the development of object relations, which requires cognitive development. Kumin uses it, among other findings and considerations, to study what he calls pre-object relatedness, which he associates with this early prerepresentational phase, with its mode of apprehension: "The prerepresentational phase refers to an innate presentational capacity in human infants that precedes and makes possible the development of the semiotic and symbolic function necessary for re-presentation as conscious and unconscious thought. The prerepresentational state is characterized by sensori-motor processes, intermodal matching . . . , and nonsymbolic, concrete, psychosomatic apprehension." (Ivri Kumin, *Pre-Object Relatedness*, p. 25.)

The assertion seems to be that infants are able to discriminate, not through concepts and representations, but through "nonsymbolic, concrete, psychosomatic apprehension." What is this "innate presentational capacity" that infants possess? This seems to us to be a clear reference to what we have been referring to as basic knowledge, most likely at a primitive stage of its presentation.

5. Individuals interested in the various lines of development may consult the literature of the various research fields. For instance, in cognitive development there is Piaget's valuable work. In ego development there is the totality of psychoanalytic developmental psychology, in child development there is a great deal of recent research in the cognitive and psychoanalytic schools, etc.

Some thinkers, like Washburn, Wilber, and Grof, have been developing various theoretical models of human development, as part of the attempt at developing a transpersonal psychology. We find in these attempts at synthesizing many lines of development. The most comprehensive is the developmental model of Ken Wilber, which we find quite satisfactory for a general theoretical ground. At the same time, we believe that Washburn's model is more accessible for practical use than that of Wilber, even though it is not as comprehensive and thorough. Grof's model includes important elements not present in the other two.

Because of our general thrust we will address issues and questions in the various research fields only when they are relevant to our task.

6. There are many theories about the fall of man; each tradition has its own story of explaining how the human soul got to be in her normal and unregenerate condition. One of the earliest comes from Empedocles, in his famous fragment:

"There is an oracle of necessity, a decree of the Gods from of old, everlasting, with broad oaths fast sealed, that, whensoever one of the daemons, whose portion is length of days, has sinfully stained his hands with blood, or followed Strife and sworn a false oath, he must wander thrice ten thousand seasons away from the Blessed, being born throughout the time in all manner of mortal forms, passing from one to another of the painful paths of life.

"For the power of the Air drives him seaward; and the Sea spews him out on the dry land; Earth hurls him into the rays of the blazing Sun, and Sun into the eddies of Air. One from another receives him, and he is loathed of all.

"Of these now I am also one, as exile from God and a wanderer, having put my trust in raging Strife." (F. M. Cornford, *From Religion to Philosophy*, p. 224.)

Christianity believes in the actual fall of Adam and Eve from Paradise, as told in the Old Testament, but there exist also mystical and gnostic interpretations of the story. The Sufis believe the same thing and also adopt the Islamic view that souls are born with various faculties, qualities and endowments due to God's choice and will. This is the theistic way of accounting for how everybody finds themselves in different places and with different capacities.

This is contrasted with the Indian theory of reincarnation and karma, where each soul is born with karma from previous lifetimes, which accounts for human variations. The theory of karma does not really completely answer the question of how it all starts. Buddhism believes in an endless beginning, so there is always karma.

The view we give in this book does not rely on either of these classical positions, but neither does it contradict them. It can be taken as the way the soul develops to her present condition, or as an additional factor in this development. We do not take the view that this development is an error or wrongness, but rather as a natural developmental stage, necessary for further stages of the soul's development.

7. This is similar to Wilber's notion of involution that precedes evolution, but happening in the lifetime of the soul. (See Wilber, *Sex, Ecology, Spirituality*.) Evolution in this case includes involution as one of its stages, leading ultimately to a greater development.

8. This original and primal condition has been relegated by some religions to some ancient unspecified date, as in the biblical story of Adam and Eve living in Paradise. Some modern researchers attempted to capture it in one kind of psychological concept or another. Freud, for instance, tried to capture it in his definition of primary narcissism, an inadequate concept that, nevertheless, contains his insight that the infant's homeostatic equilibrium state is a kind of psychosomatic wholeness. There is, and has been, much debate about whether the infant's original state of homeostasis is actually positive in this way or more conflictual and painful. The views of Washburn and Wilber seem to be diametrically opposed in this respect.

Washburn believes that the neonate is absorbed in a dynamic ground, which functions as the source of both numinous spirit and libidinal psychic energy: "Libido or psychic energy on the one hand and numinous spirit on the other, I propose, are different manifestations of the power of the Dynamic Ground." (Michael Washburn, *The Ego and the Dynamic Ground*, p. 5.)

This is similar to our view that the soul is originally coemergent with her essential ground, the presence of Being, but not identical. Washburn thinks of this primal absorption as a state of plenitude, overflowing with energy: "This state of absorption which I shall call *original embedment*, is a condition of dynamic plenitude. It is a state that is overflowing with upwelling energy. The newborn is bathed in the 'water of life,' which arises from the Ground and flows freely through the newborn's body." (Ibid., p. 48.) Thus he considers the original condition of the neonate to be one of unalloyed positivity: "It follows from the fact that the original embedment is a condition of dynamic plenitude that it is a state that is contented and fulfilled, without felt lack or need, and therefore that it is a condition that is psychically (although not physically) self-sufficing." (Ibid., p. 49.)

Wilber, on the other hand, argues that spirit goes through involution then evolution: "Spirit manifests as the entire world in a series of increasingly holistic and holarchic spheres, stretching from matter to body to mind to soul to spirit itself. But all of these different dimensions are actually just forms of spirit, in various degrees of self-realization and self-actualization . . . Involution (or efflux), this general view continues, is the process whereby these dimensions are manifested as forms of spirit, and evolution (or reflux) is the process of recollection and remembrance . . ." (Ken Wilber, *The Eye of Spirit*, p. 157.)

He views the neonate as in the condition resulting from the involution of spirit into matter: "In this scheme, the infantile self might indeed be trailing clouds of glory . . . but it is primarily adapting to the dimensions of spirit-as-matter and spirit-as-prana (sensuality, emotional-sexual energies, elan vital, diffuse polymorphous life and vital force) as well as the very early forms of spirit-as-mind (images, symbols, protoconcepts)." (Ibid. p. 158.) Thus Wilber holds a view opposite to that of Washburn in terms of the quality of experience of the neonate and considers the latter's view to be retro-romantic: "But the retro-Romantic theorists simply eulogize the prior frostbitten state, and see that as prefiguration of the Divine awakening, as being itself a type of unconscious Heaven. But the fusion state is not unconscious Heaven, it's unconscious Hell." (Ken Wilber, *A Brief History of Everything*, p. 167.)

9. The primal nondual condition includes the inseparability of the body from the soul. The infant does not experience itself as a soul with a body, or the reverse. Soul and body are coemergent and coextensive, not differentiated in the baby's experience. See *The Point of Existence*, chapter 6, for a fuller account of how the body appears in nondual presence.

10. This is the dimension of divine love, one of the five basic dimensions of the ground true nature. True nature appears with this dimension dominant in its presence depending on the situation of the soul; one of these major situations is that of adequate holding. (See *Facets of Unity*, chapters 4, 5, and 6, for greater detail.)

11. These are the autoplastic and alloplastic ways of adaptation that Hartmann thought of as primary ego functions of the human organism. (Heinz Hartmann, *Ego Psychology and the Problem of Adaptation.*)

12. Winnicott, the British object relations analyst and pediatrician, wrote extensively about the child's need for adequate mothering, and specifically understood the consequences for the child's experience of environmental inadequacy. He is one of the few psychoanalysts who used the term *being*, as in his notion of "continuity of being," to describe the child's original and natural state. He described how inadequacy leads to inner reactivity of the child, a reaction that annihilates the child's sense of being. He writes: "As a result of success in maternal care there is built up in the infant a continuity of being which is the basis of ego-strength; whereas the result of each failure in maternal care is that the continuity of being is interrupted by reactions to the consequences of that failure, with resultant ego-weakening." (D. W. Winnicott, *The Maturational Processes and the Facilitating Environment*, p. 52.)

He recognized that psychological development of a healthy self depends on adequate holding, which allows the soul's potential to become an individual, while inadequate holding leads to a personality based on reactions, and hence a false self: "With 'the care that it receives from its mother' each infant is able to have a personal existence, and so begins to build up what might be called a continuity of being. On the basis of this continuity of being the inherited potential gradually develops into an individual infant. If maternal care is not good enough then the infant does not really come into existence, since there is no continuity of being; instead the personality becomes built on the basis of reactions to environmental impingement." (Ibid., p. 54.)

We use his work more than others' in understanding the needs of adequate environmental holding, and the consequences of its inadequacy or absence. We find Winnicott's view to be similar to ours, but as we will see, our view includes other elements that Winnicott did not study.

13. We treat this subject matter in much more detail in *Facets of Unity*. The first part of this book is a detailed discussion of the question of basic trust, holding environment, inadequacy of holding, the result of this inadequacy, the reactivity to the inner disruption or difficulty, and so on. There is also a more detailed discussion of the role of the dimension of divine love in the feeling of holding and our work to regain it. In *Facets of Unity*, we refer to divine love as *living daylight*, for it is experienced as both love and light. This part includes discussion of resulting issues in relation to God, or goodness in the universe.

The second part of the book is a more detailed account of the inner difficulty resulting from inadequate holding. We use the map of the enneagram to study nine different ways of experiencing this inner difficulty and nine ways of reacting to it. The nine ways depend on the nine types of the enneagram, but explored from the perspective of the holy ideas. The holy ideas are nine facets of Reality as seen from a realized perspective.

When holding is lost or inadequate the soul loses the sense of one of the holy ideas, which results in a particular delusion about reality. There result then nine particular delusions, corresponding to the nine holy ideas. These delusions color the soul's experience of the inner difficulty and her reactions to it. Hence there results nine ways of experiencing the inner difficulty and nine ways of reacting to it. The three: the delusion, the particular difficulty, and the specific reaction constitute a psychological complex that becomes the seed for a particular personality type.

This development is a process that takes several years but ends up in the ego-self differentiating into nine types. Our discussion of the question of the holding environment in the present book deals mostly with the early issues of its inadequacy.

14. This understanding of narcissistic disturbances is similar to that of the major theories in psychoanalysis. The main differences are: first, we see this disturbance as related primarily to the identity of the self, and not to the total self and, second, we include the dimension of essential presence as one of the major potentials of the soul or self, a dimension alien to psychoanalytic theories.

We mostly use Kohut's formulations to understand the various structures and issues related to narcissism. We regard his psychology of self, as discussed in *Analysis of the Self* and *Restoration of the Self*, as the most developed understanding of the narcissistic sector of the self. (See *The Point of Existence*, chapters 5–8 and 16, for a detailed discussion of depth psychological theories of self and narcissism.)

CHAPTER 12. EGO DEVELOPMENT OF THE SOUL

1. This is actually one of the main insights of psychoanalytic developmental psychology, as in ego psychology, self psychology, and the various forms of object relations

theory. The accepted wisdom now is that the self develops the sense of individuality and identity, which means these are ego structures built through ego development in the first few years of life. We see this explicitly in the following passage from Mahler: "The task to be achieved by the development in the course of normal separation-individuation process is the establishment of both a measure of object constancy and a measure of self constancy, an enduring individuality as it were. The latter achievement consists of the attainment of the two levels of the sense of identity: (1) the awareness of being a separate and individual entity, and (2) a beginning awareness of a gender-defined self-identity." (Margaret Mahler et al., *The Psychological Birth of the Human Infant*, pp. 223–224.)

2. This is a summary of the main tenets of object relations theory. See Otto Kernberg's *Object Relations Theory and Clinical Psychoanalysis*, and Greenberg and Mitchell's *Object Relations in Psychoanalytic Theory*.

Our major divergence from this psychoanalytic theory is that we recognize the self as a field and organism of consciousness, the soul, instead of the vague psychoanalytic concept of self. This difference clarifies that what becomes structured is the soul's field, something that is left poorly addressed in object relations theory.

3. Representation in psychoanalytic theory is not only mental representation. It embodies affective and drive components, as we see in Kumin's definition: "I use the term 'representation' in the psychoanalytic sense, to convey enduring charged affective mental images of the self and significant others that are experienced as acting in a private internal space, or internal representational world." (Ivri Kumin, *Pre-Object Relatedness*, p. 25.) Yet such affective representations include and depend on, as ground, ordinary mental representations, such as images and concepts.

4. Washburn, in his transpersonal theory of psychology, recognizes the dissociation from the ground, but uses different terminology, which with other factors gives his work a different emphasis from our discussion here. He uses the term *ego* somewhat similarly to our usage of the term *soul* or *self*. He sees the ego's (soul's) loss of its ground occurring through ego development, but his treatment of the subject is different from ours. He sees the dissociation as resulting from psychodynamic factors, mostly repression and splitting because of early conflicts: "The shift from nonegoic ascendancy to egoic one-sidedness that occurs during the transition to the egoic stage is predicated on a repressive separation of the ego from the nonegoic potentials of life. Following Freud, I shall call the repression that occurs at this point primal repression." (Michael Washburn, *The Ego and the Dynamic Ground*, p. 18.)

He gives a clear account of how such early conflicts lead to the soul repressing her ground. However, it seems because his concept of the ground in early childhood is primarily energetic he does not address the factors we are discussing here that reflect the nature of presence and ego development.

Psychodynamic factors that reflect early conflicts do not seem to us sufficient to explain the inclusive universality of dissociation of the ground. Recognizing that the primary dimension of the ground is the ontological presence of the soul, and contrasting that with the mental nature of ego development, clearly demonstrates how the soul has no choice in the matter and that the dissociation does not depend on only accidental or even common conflicts in early childhood. To view the dissociation from the perspective of the structures that ego development constructs is to recognize the fundamental and inherent determinant of such dissociation.

Furthermore, to understand the dissociation as only psychodynamic will tend to limit our discussion to the psychological dimension of the soul, and not to her spiritual nature and development. Washburn attempts to build a transpersonal theory applicable to therapy, and because of that he constructs his model with spiritual development in mind, as it reappears later in life in the reintegration of the ground. This may work, but it seems to us then that the characteristics of the spiritual ground of the soul, as in the fact that it is a presence which is immediacy of nondual experience, are not considered in the understanding of how its alienation occurs. The result will be that the process of reintegration will also not fully consider, and hence not benefit from, these characteristics. This view, we believe, will limit our capacity to regain the spiritual ground. It will tend to orient Washburn's theory toward psychotherapy grounded in a spiritual view of the self, but not the inner work of spiritual transformation. This actually might be Washburn's intention or interest, for he explicitly presents his model as a psychology, albeit a transpersonal one.

In the Diamond Approach, the characteristics and phenomenology of spirit or presence, and the physiognomy of essential aspects are central to understanding the dissociation, and hence they can be readily utilized in our methods of inner work. This, combined with the view of essential presence, seems to help the soul orient herself more readily toward inner transformation than repair of past conflicts. (See *Spacecruiser Inquiry* for a discussion of how characteristics of essence are reflected in the practice of inquiry.)

Washburn's model of dissociation, also reflected in his approach to reintegration, subscribes to the general transpersonal notion that psychological or psychotherapeutic work and spiritual development are separate, with the former preceding the latter. His approach is not as linear as that of Wilber, but it is still largely so, for ego work seems to precede spiritual work, at least in terms of the emphasis of his stages of reintegration. We believe this linearity, in Washburn, Wilber, and transpersonal theory in general, is due to their not truly incorporating actual knowledge of our true nature, with its aspects and dimensions, into their theories of the self and its development. Spiritual and inner work teachings, such as Kabbalah and Sufism, tend to include the details and specifics of the dimensions of Being in understanding the self and its development. It seems to us that transpersonal theorists have been unable to liberate themselves from this quite general and linear, and hence limiting, paradigm of inner work, as first ego, then spirit.

Washburn's model is, however, a valuable contribution to the understanding of the psychodynamics of the original dissociation. His approach clarifies areas we do not focus on, for he utilizes both Freudian and Jungian concepts to explore the original repression and its consequences, and connects this to object relations. In chapter 11 of the present volume, we have discussed the question of holding environment and the narcissistic limitations of the caregivers. The reader can also find a different area of discussion in *Essence*, chapter 3, about the psychodynamics of the loss of essential aspects. Our approach actually combines the psychodynamic and the phenomenological-epistemological together, for we view them as inseparable.

5. This is actually the claim of psychoanalytic developmental psychology, but its implications are usually not contemplated. This theory believes that the self-representation and the totality of ego structures pattern and structure the ongoing experience of the self. The implications of this are normally not contemplated because of the belief that by the self developing these structures she becomes able to recognize and live in the real world. In other words, the implicit position of these theories is that reality structures the mind, and hence the more realistically this structure reflects experience the more balanced and normal is the individual.

Developmental depth psychology, it would seem, takes the position that by the self developing its ego structures it becomes able to perceive, relate to, and function in reality. This is of course due to the pervasive triadic split in Western thought, a split that automatically reduces the soul to a mental self in a physical organism. Because of this there is no recognition or appreciation of how these ego structures alienate us from our essential ground, and how they limit the creative dynamism of our soul.

6. We explore in detail the experience of being a separate individual, a person capable of relating to other persons, in *The Pearl Beyond Price*. We develop the understanding of how ego development occurs through the building of identification systems of images and object relations, and contrast these with the experience of essence, which is simply Being. For this more exhaustive discussion see chapters 2 and 4 in that book, which focuses on the development of the ego structure related to separateness and individuality, and the essential aspects associated to it. *The Point of Existence* focuses instead on the ego structure related to identity, and the aspects associated to it.

7. Ken Wilber, in his critique of the view that childhood experience contains identity with essence, ridicules it by believing it is a position that says the baby is unconsciously conscious. Hence he believes it is a self-contradictory view. Wilber's understanding of this view is obviously incorrect, for there is no implication of unconsciousness. He does not seem to appreciate the importance of recognition, that one may be aware of true nature without recognizing it, or not recognizing it as such; this is the view in the Diamond Approach. (See appendix D.)

8. This is the reason why when the ground true nature, pure nondifferentiated presence, is recognized by the soul, the experience is not a remembering in the usual sense of the word. It is more of a recognition of something that has always been present. It is a discrimination of something in experience that we tend not to discriminate because we are too focused on the forms of experience, while this is the

ground of all the forms. By recognizing it, true nature intensifies and becomes more dominant in experience.

When students remember essence from very early childhood it is usually the remembering of essential aspects. The aspects have very particular characteristics that can be retained in memory. When the individual remembers these vividly, the aspects may arise with the presence that is qualified by them, by their invoking the presence, not by remembering it.

9. One important thing we see here is that there is no ego separate from the soul. The proverbial ego of spiritual terminology is nothing but the ego-self, the soul structured through ego development. There is no ego as an entity; there is only the soul that can become ego by becoming structured with mental forms. Therefore, the idea of ego death is a misnomer. There is no entity that dies, for the soul does not die. All that happens in such experiences is that an ego structure dissolves, and the soul field is liberated from its influence. More accurately, the soul ceases to structure her experience through these mental forms. This can bring about the dissolution or transcendence of one's identity, but this identity is a feeling that arises from the soul being structured by a particular self-representation. A representation dies, but no entity.

Depth psychology itself, as in psychoanalytic theory, does not recognize an ego that is an entity. Ego in psychoanalytic thought is nothing but a mental structure, or a system of mental structures, and the processes and capacities that go into its development and functioning. In fact, some theoreticians consider the ego to be nothing but the organizing process itself: "The basic proposition we wish to develop is that the concept of ego, as it has evolved through its several definitions in the course of psychoanalytic theory construction, has become synonymous with organizing process." (Blanck and Blanck, *Ego Psychology* II, p. 15.)

10. Object relations theory normally considers only the mental kind of structuring, and so the tendency is to view structure not existing quite early in life. This is part of the reason why many depth psychologists do not believe that prenatal experience can contribute directly to ego development. But this has been changing because of the presence of experimental evidence that neonates can develop structure before specifically mental cognition and memory are developed enough to construct mental images. These research findings, however, do not cast their exploration and understanding in the context we develop here, that the soul is a medium that can be structured. The findings are instead used to extend psychoanalytic theory to earlier forms of experience.

Daniel Stern used this fact to support his notion that the neonate develops senses of self before its memory and other cognitive capacities are developed enough for mental ego structuring. He first establishes that the baby develops the capacity for preverbal representation of direct impressions of episodes: "What we are concerned with, then, are episodes that involve interpersonal interactions of different types. Further, we are concerned with the interactive experience, not just the interactive events. I am suggesting that these episodes are also averaged and represented preverbally. They are Representations of Interactions that have been Generalized (RIGs)." (Daniel Stern, *The Interpersonal World of the Infant*, p. 97.)

Stern believes that one of the earliest senses of self, the core self, develops through these representations, which are integrations of direct experiential impressions: "RIGs can thus constitute a basic unit for the representations of the core self. RIGs result from the direct impress of multiple realities as experienced, and they integrate into a whole the various actional, perceptual, and affective attributes of the core self." (Ibid., p. 98.)

11. Bass and Davis write about the effects of sexual abuse: "The long-term effects of child sexual abuse can be so pervasive that it's sometimes hard to pinpoint exactly how the abuse affected you. It permeates everything: your sense of self, your intimate relationships, your sexuality, your parenting, your work life, even your sanity." (Bass and Davis, *The Courage to Heal*, p. 37.) There are by now many books and articles written on the question of abuse, and its lasting impressions are increasingly becoming public knowledge.

12. There are at present many schools of thought regarding the treatment of trauma. Particularly effective ones known to the author are Bodynamics, EMDR (Eye Movement Desensitization and Reprocessing), and the work of Peter Levine.

13. This clearly demonstrates that work on trauma and abuse is necessary if the individual is serious about inner transformation. We have observed that some individuals do not become aware of their trauma or abuse history until they go deep in their inner journey. But we have also observed the limitations such history places on the individuals who do not deal with it effectively. Our recommendation is that individuals who know that they have such history try to confront it and deal with it therapeutically before fully engaging the inner journey. Otherwise, this unmetabolized history not only limits one's capacity to traverse the path, but also distorts it and its experiences.

14. See *The Tangled Wing*, by Melvin Konner, for an excellent discussion of the biological roots of human behavior and emotions. Regarding the role of chemical imbalance, see, for example, *The Successful Treatment of Brain Chemical Imbalance* by Martin T. Jensen, and *Panic Attacks and Phobias*, by Shahidul Islam.

15. Buddhism holds that in order to become a Buddha—that is, to become fully realized and enlightened—one must be born in a perfect body. The mythology lists some of the observable physical characteristics of a Buddha, but we suspect that this implies the insight that the body must be perfect in its inner functioning and balance, including its chemical balance and genetic makeup.

"The yogi who attains enlightenment does so in the form of the complete enjoyment body.... First, the complete enjoyment body is adorned by the thirty-two noble symbols and eighty noble examples. These symbols and examples are the distinctive characteristics of a buddha's form indicating the many ways in which an enlightened being is superior to ordinary sentient beings. Such characteristics include the crown protuberance (*ushnisha*), wisdom hair curl, elongated ears, and other marks that symbolize and exemplify the unsurpassable qualities of a fully awakened buddha." (Geshe Kelsang Gyatso, *Clear Light of Bliss*, pp. 222–223.)

16. Developmental theory has determined that the self-representation has the body image as its core, for "the kernels of the early infantile self-images are the memory traces of pleasurable and unpleasurable sensations, which under the influence of autoerotic and of beginning functional activities and of playful general body investigation become associated with the body image." (Edith Jacobson, *The Self and the Object World*, p. 20.)

Yet there is, as far as we can tell, no clear discussion or study about how the early ego structures are animalistic, and how, as a result, the ego-self is mostly the animal soul with a veneer of civilization. Instead, the question appears in psychoanalytic research in the debate over whether drive theory (pioneered by Freud and his immediate students) or object relations theory (pioneered by Fairbairn, Guntrip, Kernberg, and Kohut) provides a more accurate account of the development of the self.

Our perspective recognizes no such division. We share the view of those researchers who hold that the drives and object relations are inseparable at the early stages of development, and at later stages they both continue to be important, but sometimes in different stages of development.

17. This transition has not been explored much. We believe that the possible mechanism by which the soul learns to discriminate forms includes cross-modal translations. (See Harry Hunt, *On the Nature of Consciousness*.)

18. We have referred to it as the essential *nous*, using the Greek word for intellect, because the Greeks understood intellect in this way. For them intellect is not only understanding, but understanding inseparable from being.

In fact, this Greek notion was used and extended by both Islamic and Jewish philosophy and mysticism in the concepts of active intellect, derived from Aristotle, as we see in the following quote describing one of the early Islamic philosopher's view of the intellect: "Alkindi invoked Aristotle's distinction between the active intellect—an intelligence which contained eternally intelligibles outside the soul—and the possible intellect, in the soul. The possible intellect, under the impact of the active intellect, is able to pass into act and receive from it knowledge of the intelligibles." (Gordon Leff, *Medieval Thought*, p. 146.)

Both Islamic and Jewish schools of inner transformation—and to some extent Christian thought—have recognized the unique role this higher intellect plays in the inner journey. Similarly to the Greek philosophy, especially the teachings of Plato and Plotinus, Sufism has emphasized that it is the higher intellect that is needed for the inner transformation. In his study of Rumi, Chittick writes: "By its very nature the spirit possesses the faculty of discernment, which is known as the 'intellect.' The differences in spiritual levels among human beings derive to a large extent from the different degrees to which the light of the intellect penetrates the veil of the ego." (William Chittick, *The Sufi Path of Love*, p. 34.) Chittick then quotes Rumi: "The intellect is of two kinds: The first is acquired. You learn it like a boy at school. From books, teachers, reflection and rote, from concepts and from excellent and new sciences. . . . The other intellect is a gift of God. Its fountainhead lies in the midst of the spirit." (Ibid., p. 34.)

19. Psychoanalytic developmental psychology, as in object relations theory, has as its main achievement the understanding of how ego development basically serves to develop a sense of an autonomous individual capable of relating to others. This is referred to as self and object constancy, which are the primary outcomes of the separation-individuation process. McDevitt and Mahler write: "The attainment of a certain degree of object constancy, the achievement of a definite individuality, and a more enduring development of psychic structure—these are the three major tasks of the fourth and final subphase (from 24 to 36 months) from the point of view of the separation-individuation process." (Lax, Bach, and Burland [eds.], *Self and Object Constancy*, p. 11.)

20. Wilber posits a stage called *vision-logic* as preceding actualization of the essential potential: "Vision-logic or network-logic is a type of synthesizing and integrating awareness. Formal operational awareness is synthesizing and integrating in many important ways, but it still tends to possess a kind of dichotomizing logic, a logic of either/or rather like Aristotelian logic. But vision-logic adds up the parts and sees networks of interactions. . . . When the self's center of gravity is identified with vision-logic, when the person lives from that level, then we tend to get a very highly integrated personality, a self that can actually inhabit a global perspective, and not merely mouth it." (Wilber, *A Brief History of Everything*, p. 191.)

21. It is important to recognize that the personal essence is a particular aspect of essence. Some readers of our books seem to think we mean individual essence, as opposed to cosmic or boundless essence, when we use the expression *personal essence*. We do not use *personal* in this sense, and hence when we use the term *personal essence*, we mean there are many aspects that boundless ground essence manifests in the individual soul, and personal essence is a particular one of these. We have found that our concept of the personal is not easy to understand, and that most people can only think of personal in contradistinction to universal or cosmic on one hand, or the ego sense of personal, which means related to personal history and individual characteristics, on the other. We mean neither; we mean the essential prototype of the second. (For a clear discussion of this sense of the "personal," see *The Pearl Beyond Price*, especially chapter 5.)

The individuation development of the soul is known by some of the Sufis, who know the personal essence as the pearl beyond price, or Muhammadan Pearl, indicating it is the station of the mature and complete human being, as we see in the following passage describing Alauddin Semnani's understanding of the *lataif* or subtleties of the soul: "The third subtle organ is that of the heart (*latifa qalbiya*) in which the embryo of mystical progeny is formed, as a pearl is formed in a shell. This pearl or offspring is none other than the subtle organ which will be the True Ego, the real, personal individuality (*latifa ana'iya*)." (Henry Corbin, *The Man of Light in Iranian Sufism*, p. 124.)

Sufism, as a result, is one of the rare wisdom traditions that view spiritual development as not only the realization of true nature but of also individuating it in life in the world. This becomes one of their leading mottoes: "to be in the world but not of it."

22. Winnicott seems to have understood this important function of ego development, a function not appreciated by most other object relations theorists. The soul does not merely develop into an individual, but learns to inhabit the body, a process that Winnicott called personalization: "Personalization was the word used by Winnicott to describe psychosomatic collusion, or the 'psyche indwelling in the soma.' . . . Psychosomatic collusion is largely taken for granted by most people, but Winnicott saw it as an achievement. It is a development from 'the initial stages in which the immature psyche (although based on body functioning) is not closely bound to the body and the life of the body.' . . . Personalization means not only that the psyche is placed in the body, but also that eventually, as cortical control extends the whole of the body becomes the dwelling place of the self." (Davis and Wallridge, *Boundary and Space*, pp. 40–42.)

CHAPTER 13. LIBERATING THE SOUL

1. As we will see in the second half of this book, true nature's primordial dimensions include also those of nonconditional love-bliss and ontological emptiness.

2. The soul has a natural pattern through which she develops, with its own stages and forms of experience. It is a universal pattern of development, where individual variations occur, but more in the nature of variations on the same theme. We discuss this notion in more detail in *Facets of Unity*, chapter 15, within the context of the holy ideas, the nine facets that Reality manifests. We refer to it as the holy plan, meaning the inherent plan for the evolution of the soul given to her by her true nature, the holy essence.

3. It is obvious that this constraint is bound to generate a great deal of frustration, suffering, incompleteness, and unfulfilled longing. This suffering becomes added to the suffering of alienation, with its meaninglessness and emptiness. Suffering tends to motivate many individuals to undergo the inner journey, and many of the wisdom teachings couch their conceptualizations in terms of freedom from this suffering. However, it is clear that since it is natural for the soul to grow and develop, reflecting her immense potential, the movement of this maturation will have its own pressure, which the soul can experience as frustration, but also as love of truth, reality, discovery, learning, expansion, and growth.

4. Kashmir Shaivism takes this position in a very explicit manner. This nondual teaching considers enlightenment to be not only abiding in pure presence of awareness, but also to have freedom of will and action, reflecting the view that true nature, Shiva or highest Self, is awareness inseparable from freedom of activity, as clearly enunciated in the first sutra of the Shiva Sutras: "Awareness which has absolute freedom of all knowledge and activity is the Self or nature of Reality." (Jaideva Singh, *Siva Sutras*, p. 6.)

5. One important implication of this freedom is that the journey cannot be oriented toward any static end, even if this end is absolute truth. To orient her toward any end is to try to constrain her dynamism to flow according to our own beliefs and preferences. Besides the certain possibility of a prejudice dictated by some structure, we can never second-guess our creative dynamism. The intelligence of this dynamism is completely beyond our personal knowledge, and there is no way for us to know what is best to unfold next, or what will actually manifest next. Any attempt to orient or push the dynamism toward a particular state will most certainly block or constrain her freedom of flow. The best approach we can take is to be completely open and receptive to her creative display. (See *Spacecruiser Inquiry*, chapter 2, for more complete discussion of this important point.)

6. This is one reason a teacher is needed in the inner journey, for the availability of essence in the presence of the teacher is a great help in allowing this inquiry to go to deeper dimensions. When essence is not available in oneself or the helper, the inquiry will tend to stay on the psychological level, and will at best be therapeutic.

7. See *Spacecruiser Inquiry*, for detailed discussion of this process of inquiry. It is important here to point out that psychodynamic work is not sufficient on its own to liberate the soul from her limitations; neither is it sufficient to lead on its own to the point of effectively working with ego structures. The presence of essence is required in challenging, confronting, and clarifying these structures.

8. This discussion is a short summary of the process of working through ego structures. A more complete exploration of this process can be found in *The Void*, which is devoted entirely to this process, but particularly to the study of essential space or inner spaciousness. *The Pearl Beyond Price* also deals with this process, but the emphasis is on the arising qualities of essence and how they structure the experience of the soul.

9. This is an important point, for many psychologists take the position that ego structure can change, as in therapy. This is usually referred to as ego structuring or restructuring therapy. What we observe is that the change is not in the specific ego structures one works on, but in the overall experience of the self. Therapy may bring into consciousness hidden, repressed, or split-off structures. These begin to structure experience more than they have in the past, resulting in overall changes in personal experience.

Another source of change is that by working on some problematic structures the therapy patient will learn to disidentify from them, and they will have less power over his experience. They will not change their particular patterning, but their influence will be ameliorated. This amelioration of the influence of problematic structures, combined with the strengthening of already existing wholesome ones, will appear as an overall change in the experience of the individual. This does not mean that one can actually change the patterning of a particular structure. We cannot change the form of the impression in the soul, but we can change its depth and power, and hence its importance in the overall economy of experience.

10. Many classical techniques, awareness meditation, for example, work on structures; others, such as concentration techniques, do not. However, all the classical techniques are part of a complete teaching, where the techniques are only part of the path. The teachings normally include various kinds of disciplines, moral and ethical guidelines for behavior, extensive preparatory exercises, and interaction with the teacher. All of these work on ego structures indirectly, by impacting their manifestation in behavior and attitudes.

11. This does not mean that one cannot have access to spirit and experiences of enlightenment without clarifying all of one's structures or resolving one's neurotic manifestations, a fact that has been recognized for ages and has recently been formulated in the language of transpersonal psychology, as demonstrated in the following quote: "To believe spiritual attainment is the right only of the psychologically 'well adjusted' does not square with the facts. There are a number of very disturbed or crazy, borderline, and highly neurotic saints and spiritually advanced or enlightened beings . . . The suggestion that all shamans, psychics, clairvoyants, saints, and sages have worked through their childhood wounds and neurotic distortions is not supported by historical or clinical evidence." (Brant Cortright, *Psychotherapy and Spirit*, pp. 77–78.)

This fact does not mean, however, that spiritual attainment is independent of one's mental health. The perspective we have been unfolding is that of how the rigidity and opaqueness of ego structuring obscure our true nature from our awareness. The more transparent are the structures of the self, the more access we can have to the dimension of true nature. There can be breakthroughs when for one reason or another one's obscuring structures are not in force. This may result from making some of the structures transparent, so they allow access to essence, but other structures may remain unclarified and manifest in neurosis or distortion. Furthermore, a borderline might have a weak ego structure, making his or her structure not only not cohesive, but also, and as a result, not so able to block such deep potential. So such an individual might develop an access to true nature, while still being a borderline. However, this access is bound to be limited one way or another. Furthermore, this access is not going to affect one's life in the balanced and integrated way necessary for Spirit to integrate life into its dimension, which is an important part of spiritual attainment.

Cortright, like many other transpersonal psychologists and new age pundits, has developed the mistaken idea of the sick guru or the neurotic enlightened individual. The idea is that one can be enlightened and neurotic at the same time. But this view does not appreciate the nature of the process of spiritual unfoldment, where there can be degrees and levels of spiritual realization. The view we take, which happens to be the view of the major traditional spiritual teachings, is that spiritual attainment has many levels, and that psychological health improves with the deepening of this attainment. The latter will be the integration of one's spiritual attainment in one's life, an important dimension of spiritual maturity. Therefore, spiritual attainment might coexist with neurosis; however, spiritual attainment that does not heal one's psyche is incomplete, or imbalanced.

Furthermore, enlightenment is not only spiritual attainment. Enlightenment is the completion of the attainment, its perfection. One is then a buddha, in Buddhism; a perfect master, in Hinduism; a complete human being, in Sufism, and so on. When one is truly enlightened one cannot be neurotic or suffer emotional pain. To not see this is to dilute the concept of enlightenment, the possibility of complete integration of psyche and spirit, and all other dimensions of existence. This dilution might seem compassionate and gentle, but it is ultimately uncompassionate for it robs us of the view of true spiritual maturity, which has been seen traditionally as completeness, balance, integration, wholeness, inner health, and liberation.

Cortright takes the view that while "sometimes there may be a correlation between the psychological and spiritual lines of development, they do not seem to be identical." (Ibid., p. 80.) Whether there are two lines of development or not, there is no appreciation in this view of the fact that what obscures our true nature is the belief in a self that is structured through history and mind. This structuring contains all the psychological makeup of the individual, as developmental theory has amply demonstrated. So one can have access to the spiritual dimension and still have psychological problems, but this points to the incompleteness of one's spiritual attainment. As the self-structures are made transparent in the inner journey they are clarified or purified, which means they are divested of their historical imprints, among other things. Neurotic and emotional difficulty is part of the imprint, and if it survives it is bound to have an obscuring effect on one's contact with true nature. Cortright cites some spiritual teachers as examples to illustrate his view, but his examples only underscore the fact that these teachers have not attained full enlightenment, but are, or were, at best partially realized. This does not negate their attainments and usefulness, but situate them in the larger picture of spiritual realization. To be enlightened is to be liberated from all limiting impressions; neurosis and childhood conditioning of any kind are obviously instances of such limitations.

We believe it is this understanding of the liberation from all limiting impressions, as in the case of ego structures, that makes Buddhism define enlightenment or Buddhahood as complete absence of all obscurations, and complete absence of the possibility of all obscurations. One has not only made transparent all limiting influences, but one cannot now be influenced by any. The definition is not only the "abiding in true nature," but also the "absence of obscurations," as we see in the following:

> *Beings are the very Buddha (in their true nature),*
> *But their (nature) is obscured by adventitious obscurations.*
> *When the obscurations are cleansed, they themselves are the very Buddha.*
>
> TULKU THONDUP,
> *Buddha Mind*, pp. 8–9

Buddhism actually divides obscurations into two kinds, mental and emotional, and the latter clearly includes neurotic and structural issues. When we begin to appreciate the true meaning of full realization we understand why Buddhism believes that a Buddha, or a fully enlightened individual, appears only every five thousand years. If we really take this to be true we will then need to conclude, since the last Buddha lived only twenty-five hundred years ago, that there has not been a completely enlightened individual since then and there will not be for at least the same amount of time. The important point is to recognize that there is such a thing as enlightenment, and that this is a condition of complete liberation, not just a partial liberation, limited to one dimension of human existence. This view actually protects us from the individuals who profess enlightenment and still manifest disharmony, discord, or mental imbalance. We can then develop an objective level of trust, and accurately see what we can learn from them.

12. Michael Washburn formulates his theory of reconnecting with the spiritual ground as a regression: "Because the physicodynamic pole of the psyche is originally lost via repression, it can be restored only via regression." (Michael Washburn, *The Ego and the Dynamic Ground*, p. 171.) This exposed him to criticism, mostly by Wilber, who believes that this is a retro-romantic view that does not accord with fact, for the regression returns consciousness to primitive content and not to the spiritual ground: "In my view, 'regression in the service of ego' is thus a return to, and a recontacting of, the alienated feelings, emotions, affects, or emotional-sexual energies that were dissociated in the early fulcrums. Once these are integrated into the self-system, then growth can more easily move forward into the higher and transegoic realms. Thus, regression in service of ego is sometimes a prerequisite for transcendence of ego, but it is not the actual mechanism of transpersonal growth itself." (Ken Wilber, *The Eye of Spirit*, p. 148.)

Washburn, however, responds to this by saying that his regression is not the usual one in the service of ego, but rather in the service of spirit: "The dark night is not a regression in the strict sense, for it is not a merely retrograde movement to earlier or more primitive modes of functioning. Nor is the dark night a regression in the service of the ego, for it does not serve in the long run to consolidate the ego in a position of supremacy within the field of consciousness. . . . The dark night is, then, more a regression in the service of spirit than it is a regression in the service of the ego." (Washburn, *The Ego and the Dynamic Ground*, pp. 171–172.)

See the next note for further discussion of this debate. We discuss our understanding of how regression works for the service of spirit in the present chapter.

13. We saw in the above note that Wilber disagrees with Washburn that regression is the way to essence, or Spirit, but he bases his disagreement on his view that the

soul does not experience essence in early childhood. Our view recognizes that one cannot go back to childhood for essence, but that is because essence is outside of time, and not because we did not experience it in childhood.

Wilber believes that the soul is basically animal and physical in childhood, so regression will merely take her to the animal soul, not to essence. (See appendix D.) We agree that regression tends to take the soul to her animal structure, so if we just do regression work this will be all that happens. However, this is not because she was only animal at the time. We have discussed how ego structuring leads to preserving the animal dimension by structuring it into the normal sense of self, at the same time that it dissociates the soul from her essential presence. In our work, some essential qualities arise in the regression, especially when working with primitive structures, but this is not the primary way Essence arises.

14. We follow R. D. Fairbairn, the British object relations theorist, in this terminology. He saw the self as developing with a central ego that one consciously identifies with, and that has a relatively harmonious and integrated sense of self resulting from the good-enough relation to mother in early childhood. This is the relationship that the child has been able to develop with its mother in which it was able to integrate both painful and pleasurable impressions. In other words, it is the outcome of the central object relation to the mother, the crucible for the development of the conscious sense of self. In this object relation the central ego relates to the good mother, so it is a generally good object relation.

The central ego is the normal self that normally interacts with people in the light of consciousness. The part of the relationship to mother that is bad or difficult to tolerate, the bad object relation, is not included in the central ego and its central object relation, but split off and defended against, by primitive splitting and/or repression. This bad object relation is, differently from most other object relations theories where there is only a bad and a good object, in turn split off, by splitting the bad mother or object. In other words, Fairbairn does not only posit a bad mother but two types of bad mother, split off from each other, and each engaged in a separate relation. One is the frustrating or libidinal object relation where a desirous self (libidinal ego) wants a good and wonderful mother but is frustrated because it cannot have her; the other is the antilibidinal object relation where a bad and hostile mother is internalized and directed against the libidinal ego. (See W. Ronald Fairbairn, *Psychological Studies of the Personality*.)

We follow his terminology but modify his theory somewhat in the formulation of the third object relation, which we call the rejection object relation and describe as a scared and small self, interacting with a big and hostile object. We find Fairbairn's formulations to correspond very closely with our observations, and his understanding of the original and primitive condition of the self to correspond closely with our notion of the animal soul.

CHAPTER 14. PRIMITIVE STRUCTURES OF THE SOUL

1. In the Diamond Approach, we organize the knowledge of the soul child in a typology according to the enneagram. We discriminate nine types, depending on the

ego types known as the enneagram of fixations. We find that each ego type is typified with a particular type of soul child, which is how this type experienced itself as a young child. What differentiates the type of soul child is the presence of an essential aspect that functions as the predominant positive quality of the soul in childhood. Uncovering the soul child, experiencing and developing its particular essential aspect, becomes a powerful way of liberating the soul from her particular enneatype fixation. We see this as the core of the psychodynamic work on the enneagram of fixations.

The ego fixation characterizes the central ego, but not the soul child, where the latter is characterized by the fixation's psychodynamic source or antecedent.

2. The soul child is the repository of both animal and essential forms from which the soul has become alienated, but that still possesses some structuring of a primitive type that makes it into an entity patterned by the body. However, we are not implying here that by its repression essence is lost primarily through classical repression. We mean that when this primitive structure of the soul emerges it is not rigidly structured, making it possible for it to be transparent to essence. Therefore, it is easier to experience essence when this structure is present, giving this structure an aliveness and dynamism normally missing from the more advanced ego structures.

3. This is the animal soul in Sufism, the sensual soul in Christianity, the irrational soul (*nefesh*) in Kabbalah and Hasidism, and the desire soul in Hinduism. These traditions see this primitive soul manifestation as the primary barrier to spiritual development, because its drives and instinctual appetites form the most formidable impediment to the inner journey, always orienting the soul away from her inner aim and promising her sensual satisfactions. This is the reason why many of these traditions have developed inner disciplines and ascetic practices to do their work, with the understanding that subtle spiritual discrimination happens much easier when the soul is purified of her animal tendencies.

The task of purifying the soul of her animal drives and appetites is the theme of the first half of Saint John of Cross's *Dark Night of the Soul*. He calls this work of purification the "night of sense," differentiating it from the "night of spirit," which is work on attachment to the fruits of the inner journey.

4. This is known in depth psychology as the defense of primitive splitting, common in early childhood. The consciousness dissociates part of her experience from the rest by setting it aside, disowning it, and relegating it to a part of the soul that has no experiential or conscious contact with the rest. The classical example is that of splitting the self or object into good and bad self or object, where the two parts are experienced separately and hence help the young child protect from its own badness either its own goodness or that of its mother.

It seems that society's revulsion toward the pure animal potential of the soul and the incapacity to deal with it, which manifests in the parent's attitudes toward the child, impel him to regard it with the same rejection and hence to split it off by psychologically disowning it.

5. This is similar to Freud's finding that the id contains two primary drives: the erotic and sexual, and the aggressive and destructive. However, the libidinal or animal soul corresponds more closely with Fairbairn's notion that early in its development, the self is not an unstructured id, a pool of instinctual energy and drives, but a structured organism driven by the two instincts. In other words, Freud thought of the id as the original container of the drives, but Fairbairn thought the drives make sense only to an integrated functioning organism, which he termed the libidinal ego: "The 'libidinal ego' also differs from the 'id' in that it is conceived, not as a mere reservoir of instinctive impulses, but as a dynamic structure comparable to the 'central ego,' in its more infantile character, in a lesser degree of organization, in a smaller measure of adaptation to reality and in a greater devotion to internalized objects." (Fairbairn, *Psychoanalytic Studies of the Personality*, p. 106.)

6. The libidinal soul desires to possess and swallow the object. But it also desires pleasure, nourishment, and erotic contact with it. The libidinal desire does not differentiate between the desire for the object and the erotic aim of satisfying the desire. Psychoanalytic theory split at some point between drive theory and object relations theory, but we see here that the two are inseparable at the beginning.

7. See chapter 39 in *The Pearl Beyond Price* for a discussion of the soul's development that resolves the central object relation. We call this development the diamond pearl, meaning it is an essential individuation that integrates essence in its aspects and dimensions.

8. Individuals who are familiar with deep states of meditation or are developed enough in the inner journey know that it is possible to be in the nonconceptual dimension of Being and still have insights. Zen stories and koans are a good example of this situation.

9. Developmental theory explores the building of structure that requires the cognitive capacities to be mature enough to construct representations from memory traces. Thus object relations theory sees ego development beginning with the symbiotic phase, at around a few months of age. A. N. Meltzoff and his coworkers have recently found that neonates have significantly more sophisticated representational (but prelinguistic) competence than was previously thought. Meltzoff writes that neonates "can represent adult behavior in non-modality specific terms that not only encode the event but also serve as the basis of self-action. On this view, visual perception and motor productions are closely linked and mediated by a common representational system right from birth." (Meltzoff, "Perception, Action, and Cognition in Early Infancy," pp. 75–76.)

We have already quoted some psychoanalytic researchers in their usage of this intermodal matching of neonates in their theories. For example, Daniel Stern, in *The Interpersonal World of the Infant*, posits the establishment of senses of self as occurring earlier than psychoanalytic theories have previously held. Ivri Kumin used these findings to support his research into early relatedness and affect development before conceptual representational capacities develop, in *Pre-Object Relatedness*.

Most psychoanalytic developmental theory does not explore structure building before birth, and considers it to begin after birth. However, there has arisen in recent years a mounting body of evidence of prenatal memories, regression, and experiences related to this period of the life of the organism. Some writers have explored the kind of prenatal experiences that may happen that will have later ramifications for experience and development. Laing argued that prenatal life has its own affective and psychological dimension, and that it affects later development: "It is still not a commonplace to recognize a formal similarity between a known embryological sequence of patterns, for example the transformation of the relation of embryology and trophoblast to psychological and mythological sequences. We shall try to bring into focus some of the morphemes or formal factors in each domain." (R. D. Laing, *The Voice of Experience*, p. 109.) See also Laing's *The Facts of Life*. Citing both recent and older sources, he discusses the effects of the birth experience, embryological processes and their disruption, the prenatal bond, and so on, on later psychological experience.

Other contributions to understanding the impact of embryological experience on later psychological development include Francis Mott's Configurational Psychology, in Mott, *Nature of the Self* and *Biosynthesis*; Frank Lake's Clinical Theology in Lake, *Studies in Constricted Confusion*; and Otto Hartmann's Dynamic Morphology in Hartmann, *Dynamische Morphologie*.

David Boadella's work synthesizes the findings of these studies with Reich's work, and that of other body-centered approaches into what he calls Biosynthesis, which depends on the notion of embryological kind of memory: "There is mounting evidence that the excitation patterns of the foetus, both pleasurable and unpleasurable, and the reflexive movement patterns associated with these, are retained in some form that may be recoverable. If this is so, then it is legitimate to assume that the laying-down process of the memories of these experiences will also shape and direct the organism.... Some system of primitive recall of past organismic states seems the property of even single cells." (David Boadella, *Lifestreams*, p. 28.)

These explorers investigated early experiences to study their impact on later experience, but did not focus on the psychic structuring necessary for this influence to survive to later times. Experience is a momentary structuring of the field of the soul by the arising of inner forms, while structure is the permanent or semi-permanent structuring through the impressions or traces left by these forms. Only such lasting impressions can leave a mark on later experience. We have already discussed how this structuring happens through the impressionability and malleability of the soul's field of consciousness.

Boadella views this in terms of a "primitive recall," but he has developed an understanding of how prenatal experience contributes to the sense of self, which is a way of discussing structure building: "Before the birth of language, before any word is uttered, the basic sense of identity, or lack of it, is already formed. It flows from the matrix of umbilical pulsations which stop when the cord is severed and are replaced by the rhythms of breathing and suckling. It is stroked into being by the contact of skin to skin, which replaces the movement of the womb fluid over the lanugo hairs, and the rhythmic sounds of the voice caressing the ear, familiar from the inter-uterine period. It is born out of the spontaneous movements of the body, which, contained for nine months in the cushioning fluids of the womb, now stretch out and experience the immeasurable finality and solidity of the earth." (Ibid., p. 63.)

10. Boadella writes about the effect of umbilical structure on later affects: "Umbilical affect is the flow of feeling associated with the sense of life and energy being pumped into the centre of one's body through the umbilical cord (endodermal). Positive umbilical affect carries a sense of well-being and vitality, a golden glow in the pit of the stomach. Negative umbilical affect carries a sense of malaise, anxiety, despair and loss of well-being; it is a dark sense of being poisoned or blackened at the source of life." (Ibid., p. 18.)

11. The effects of the mother's state on prenatal experiences have been reported by Grof in *Realms of the Human Unconscious*, Liley in *Fetus as a Personality*, and others: "If the mother is stressed, tense or full of bad body-feelings, these can be communicated to the foetus, as can feelings of rejection, guilt or hostility about the growing baby. Based on memories of patients in therapy of this early life-period we can conclude that the foetus is sensitive not only to gross disturbances of its existence, such as mechanical pressures, loud sounds and intense vibrations, but distress if the mother is ill, exhausted or intoxicated." (Boadella, *Lifestreams*, p. 32.)

12. Some of the researchers cited above recognize the birth experience to be specifically significant. Grof has taken this significance much further, making it the emblem for universal and spiritual processes, affecting all future life transitions, in his notion of perinatal experiences: "The connection between biological birth and perinatal experiences is quite deep and specific. . . . This makes it possible to use the clinical stages of delivery in constructing a conceptual model that helps us to understand the dynamics of the perinatal level of the unconscious. . . . In spite of its close connection to childbirth, the perinatal process transcends biology and has important psychological, philosophical, and spiritual dimensions." (Grof, *The Adventure of Self-Discovery*, p. 9.)

We do not find the birth experience to be universally important for all individuals, even though it seems to structure some individual's souls. This might reflect our limited experience with it, or that it is important only for some individuals, depending on their particular experiences at birth.

13. Boadella uses Otto Hartmann's work to study how early embryological anatomy determines later psychological experience, which he organizes according to "three fundamental energetic currents or lifestreams flowing in the body, associated with the cellular germ-layers (ectoderm, endoderm, and mesoderm) in the fertilized egg

out of which the distinctive organ systems are formed." (Boadella, *Lifestreams*, p. xiv.)

Using Hartmann's work he describes how this embryological process includes bulges and tubes: "The embryo is built from the outside inwards. Otto Hartmann has described how the three embryological layers or discs are formed. . . .

"Two hollow elliptical cell-bubbles form—the amniotic sac and the yolk sac. . . . from the cells lining the lower surface of the amniotic sac, the ectoderm develops, which later becomes the outer layer of the body. From the cells lining the upper surface of the yolk sac develops the endoderm, the inner lining of the body. . . .

"The three layers of the original disc—outer (ecto), middle (meso) and inner (endo)—each have an associated tube system. Along the back of the outer ectodermic layer a groove forms and the edges fold in to enclose the neural canal, a sealed tube full of fluid that will soon swell out at the head end into three bulges. We are watching the emergence of what will become the three parts of the brain—forebrain, midbrain and hindbrain." (Ibid., pp. 24–25.)

It seems, for example, that the ectoderm structures the soul in such a way that leaves a trace that becomes later telescoped with the skin boundary of the body to form the separating boundaries of the sense of individual entity. This means that a deeper layer of this boundary structure is formed through the impression of the ectoderm, and earlier yet by the amniotic sac.

14. Laing explains some dream images as the effects of fetal implantation, rather than the customary interpretation involving the fantasy of the return to the womb: "I can see no warrant to regard all those entry themes of rapturously sinking into a bed of bliss, or of being sucked in, of being swallowed in quicksand, of subsiding into a swamp, of being buried alive, as reversed birth symbols. Their biological analogue of implantation is staring us in the face." (R. D. Laing, *The Voice of Experience*, p. 143.) (Also see David Boadella, *Embryology in Therapy*.)

CHAPTER 15. THE INNER JOURNEY

1. We use the Sufi term *lataif* because it is the same system of centers of subtle physiology, which is different from the Indian *chakra* system. The *chakra* system operates with subtle energy, *prana* or *shakti*, while the *lataif* centers operate with essential presence. (See *Essence*, chapter 2.) The way we activate and use the *lataif* is not exactly the same as the methods of the Sufis, who themselves use different methods depending on the particular Sufi order or teacher. Some Sufis do not use the *lataif* system. We use the same color code as the Sufis, because these colors happen to be the colors of the aspects operating through each center. However, the Sufis use the centers as organs of functioning of consciousness, while we activate them primarily to access the essential aspects that operate through them.

2. This is equivalent to the development of the soul that the Sufis refer to as the "human" soul, related to the stages of the inspired and pacified soul.

3. The ancient stories have the Pearl always in the world, guarded by a fearsome monster, symbolizing the ego. This is because the realization of the Pearl is a matter of integrating one's essential development in the world as a human person. So everyday life is the arena where it arises and develops. The following is an excerpt from a story that appears in The Acts of Thomas, titled "The Hymn of the Soul": "If thou go down into Egypt and bring back thence the one pearl which is there in the midst of the sea girt about by the devouring serpent, thou shalt again put on the garment set with gems and the robe whereupon it resteth and become with thy brother that is next unto us an heir in our kingdom." (Cecil, Rieu, and Wade, *The King's Son*, p. 5.)

4. Essentialization of the soul is not the self-realization we have just discussed in the chapter. In self-realization the soul becomes essence, while in essentialization the two become one. In the first instance the soul is essence and not soul, while in the second the soul continues to be soul while she is essence. The difference experientially is that between the essence being identity, and the totality of the soul, with her dynamism, being essence. Self-realization is a first step, necessary for essentialization, which is a more complete and hence more difficult integration.

5. This stage of development is equivalent to the *pure and complete soul* in Sufism.

6. All the wisdom traditions recognize this level of experience as central to enlightenment and realization. Each presents and describes this level in its own peculiar language and within its own metaphysics. We give an example from Zen, in the words of one of Zen's most illustrious masters, Dogen, from his masterpiece, *Shobogenzo*:

"Studying the Buddha Way is studying oneself. Studying oneself is forgetting oneself. Forgetting oneself is being enlightened by all things. Being enlightened by all things is causing the body-mind of oneself and the body-mind of others to be shed. There is ceasing the traces of enlightenment, which causes one to forever leave the traces of enlightenment which is cessation." (Dogen, *Shobogenzo*, p. 32.) The next quote, from a Christian classic, gives the monotheistic flavor: "He is his own being and the being of everything else. Of him alone may this be said: and thus he is wholly separate and distinct from every created thing. And thus, also, he is one in all things and all things are one in him. For I repeat: all things exist in him; he is the being of all." (William Johnston, *The Cloud of Unknowing*, p. 150.) There is a difference here from the above Zen perspective, which is the Christian position that this is God experiencing Himself, and not the soul experiencing her ultimate divine nature. This is a subtle point, for how can we be aware of God's experience of Himself if not through the soul?

7. In *Facets of Unity*, we give a detailed account of this ego delusion, by analyzing it into nine different delusions, each characterizing one of the enneatypes. We see in this book that each delusion reflects an ignorance of a particular facet of reality. Collectively, these facets are referred to as the *holy ideas* in the enneagram teaching.

In appendix B, we discuss some of the views of Eastern wisdom teachings regarding the soul, and we find that the delusion of being a separate self is recognized by all of them as the primary ego delusion.

8. One of the best terms for this barrier is the Zen phrase from Mumon: "the gateless gate." The following poem is from the preface to the Mumonkan, by Mumon himself: "Gateless is the Great Tao, There are thousands of ways to it. If you pass through this barrier, You may walk freely in the universe." (Zenkei Shibayama, *Zen Comments on the Mumonkan*, p. 10.)

9. This is reminiscent of the view of the Western monotheistic traditions of angels functioning as messengers from God to humans. In fact, we believe the idea of messenger angels is an alternative way of describing the diamond vehicles. Some Hindu gods also function in this manner, and descriptions of some Buddhist deities and *bodhisattvas*, like Vajrasattva and Vajradhara, seem to also be descriptions related to what we call the diamond vehicles.

10. We have not, however, found in any of the wisdom teachings a description of these vehicles that resembles ours in its presentational characteristics. The various traditions always present these messengers or teachers from true nature in anthropomorphic forms, possessing arms, legs, heads with eyes and noses, and so on. Tibetan deities may have many arms or heads, but the form is still the human body. In the Diamond Approach, there is no anthropomorphizing or metaphorizing, these vehicles appear in the field of the soul in shapes and forms that have their own logic, but the logic seems to be more geometric and architectural than anthropomorphic.

11. We do not have sufficient experiential knowledge of the other wisdom traditions that use the expression *diamond body* to know whether it is the same meaning as we are discussing here. Buddhism, Taoism, and other traditions teach of the inner work producing at some point an inner body of light or consciousness, and some call it the "diamond body" or the "vajra body," as we see in the following quote about its development from the "illusory body," the subtle body developed in *anutarayoga*: "Finally, when the illusory body is called 'vajra body' this means that the impure illusory body is like the vajra body while the pure illusory body is the actual vajra body itself." (Geshe Kelsaang Gyatso, *Clear Light of Bliss*, p. 201.)

Possibly, the vajra body referred to here as part of the *anutarayoga*, is the ninth diamond vehicle in the Diamond Approach, for the latter has properties similar to the descriptions in this tantra.

12. Most of the knowledge specific to the Diamond Approach originates directly from the diamond vehicles, and their dimension of essential diamonds, with their associated universal wisdom. This is the most direct and concrete reason we call our work the Diamond Approach. And it is the main reason why we recognize this approach as a path of wisdom, for it is the teaching of these essential vehicles of wisdom.

It must be clear to the reader by now that the Diamond Approach is not the intentional synthesis of a person, the author or somebody else. The scope and depth of knowledge is simply beyond the personal mind of the author, not to mention that it is not knowledge in the ordinary sense. It is gnostic knowledge, noesis, direct unveiling of Reality. It cannot be arrived at through an intellectual process or synthesis, for the mind simply cannot go to such realms of wisdom.

It must also be by now clear, by the same token, that the Diamond Approach does not come from a previous wisdom tradition and was not learned from another teacher. It is true that the author received it from a source, but the source is true nature itself, that has communicated this teaching by manifesting its diamond vehicles of wisdom.

13. We use a variant spelling of the Hebrew word for chariot (*merkavah*), as in the chariot of Ezekiel—Markabah in Arabic—which happens to also be the word for "vehicle."

14. Strictly speaking, the first love object and object of gratification for the soul is the breast, but we are assuming that the breast functions in ego development as a forerunner for the mother-object.

15. This truth about pleasure and happiness is universal to all the wisdom teachings. Hinduism, in its various branches, makes this truth primary in its formulation of true nature, as *satchitananda*. *Ananda* (bliss) is seen here as inseparable from *sat* (truth or being) and *chit* (consciousness).

16. The *dorje* is a ritualistic and symbolic object used by Tibetan Buddhism in the shape of two diamonds connected together to form an elongated shape. It is sometimes composed of four sides, or diamonds, making a cross. The object symbolizes the skillful means of enlightened consciousness.

CHAPTER 16. TRUE NATURE

1. In his *Critique of Pure Reason*, Kant held that time and space are *a priori* concepts, beyond the capacity of our mind to transcend. He saw them as the natural and given context where all knowing has to take place. We see here that this is true for ordinary knowledge, but not for basic knowledge. Basic knowledge, specifically the discriminating knowingness of true nature, can know outside of time and space. The timelessness and spacelessness we are discussing in the present chapter is only one example, the most extreme and radical. But spiritual cognition can perceive in other ways that are beyond time and space.

Isaac Newton thought of time and space as ultimate, but in the sense that they exist in God's mind. They are beyond the human mind, for this mind exists within this time-space context. This is similar to the view we are discussing in the present chapter, if we think of God's mind as something like true nature.

Albert Einstein challenged elements of this Newtonian universe, by seeing that time and space are relative to each other, and to the speed and location of the observer. As we continue in our discussion, we will see that Einstein's view simply points to further properties of true nature, and its relation to time and space.

2. Buddhism refers to this manifest world as appearance, for from the perspective of true nature it simply appears. It is, also, not what is; it is the appearance of what is. It refers to true nature in this context as the absolute. Or it formulates them as the relative and absolute truth.

Plotinus refers to the nonmanifest true nature as the One, while the Sufis refer to it as the Divine Essence, and the Kabbalah calls it Ain Sof. Some consider it comparable to the "Father" of the Christian Trinity. Manifestation would be the creation. In Hinduism, Vedanta calls the unmanifest *parabrahman*, and manifestation *maya*.

3. Compare this with the following passage from the celebrated essay "Being Time," by Zen master Dogen: "When one reaches the state of suchness, it is one blade of grass, one form, it is understanding forms, not understanding forms, it is understanding grasses, not understanding grasses. Because it is only right at such a time, therefore being time is all the whole time. Being grass and being form are both time. In the time of time's time there is the whole of being, the whole world. For a while try to visualize whether or not there is the whole being, the whole world apart from the present time." (Dogen, *Shobogenzo*, pp. 104–105.)

4. Christianity calls it the divine darkness, where the deeper the soul penetrates and the closer she is to this transcendent truth the less she discerns and knows. She is increasingly enveloped in divine darkness, which robs her of mind, even consciousness. Gregory of Nyssa writes, in *The Life of Moses*, describing the final stages of the soul's journey: "It thus leaves all surface appearances, not only those that can be grasped by the senses but also those which the mind itself seems to see, and it keeps on going deeper until by the operation of the spirit it penetrates the invisible and the incomprehensible, and it is there that it sees God. The true vision and the true knowledge of what we seek consists precisely in not seeing, in an awareness that our goal transcends all knowledge and is everywhere cut off from us by the darkness of incomprehensibility. Thus that profound evangelist, John, who penetrated into this luminous darkness, tells us that 'no man hath seen God at any time' (John 1:18), teaching us by this negation that no man—indeed, no created intellect—can attain a knowledge of God." (Quoted in Andrew Louth, *The Origins of the Christian Mystical Tradition*, p. 87.)

Sufism thinks of it as the divine essence, unknowable in its absolute transcendence. The Sufis think of God as both divine essence and divine being, where the first is the transcendent and unmanifest source and self of the divine being, while the latter is the true existence of all things. The divine being is knowable but not the transcendent source. The following is from Ibn 'Arabi, quoted by Chittick: "He who has no knowledge imagines that he knows God, but that is not correct, since a thing cannot be known except through positive attributes of its own self, but our knowledge of this is impossible. So Glory be to Him who is known only by the fact He is not known! The knower of God does not transgress his own level. He knows that he knows that he is one of those of who do not know." (William Chittick, *The Sufi Path of Knowledge*, p. 154.)

Kabbalah also thinks of the Ain Sof as essentially unknowable, as we see in the following passage where it is equated with *keter*, the first *sefirah*: "The absolute infinity of the supreme essence, the pure selfness of *kether [keter]*, excludes all otherness and consequently all knowledge of it: *'en sof* [Ain Sof] cannot be known, nor how it makes beginning or end . . . .'" (Leo Schaya, *The Universal Meaning of the Kabbalah*, pp. 36–37.)

Yet many Kabbalists and Sufis describe their experiences of the divine essence, as do many Christian mystics of the divine darkness, and how its realization is necessary for completing the journey.

The Eastern traditions do not think of it as unknowable, for it is for them consciousness itself, pure illumination and knowing.

There seems to be a paradox between assertions of unknowability and accounts of its experience, a paradox we hope to illuminate in the present chapter.

5. This is one reason that Dzogchen, for instance, takes the view that true nature is fundamentally characterized by constant manifestation of forms. It is inherent in it to be displaying forms, and transcendent true nature devoid of forms is an impossibility. Dzogchen goes so far as to assert that an experience of true nature devoid of forms is only a form that true nature takes and is not the true ultimate ground. It is only a *nyam*, a transient experience.

6. Kashmir Shaivism has incorporated this fact into its system. It takes the view that ultimate reality, Shiva, manifests the world in ontological stages, where these stages are increasingly dominated by manifestation, until it arrives at normal perception, where only manifestation appears to awareness. The inner journey is then a path of ascent, where self-realization is increasingly dominated by the pure consciousness of Shiva, where manifestation increasingly takes a second place until the truth of Shiva completely outshines it. Each step of ascent is a matter of experiencing a deeper *tattva*, or element, and there are thirty-six of these *tattvas*. The path of ascent retraces the stages of the descent of Shiva into manifestation: "The glorious great Lord by His power of absolute Freedom . . . in the process of gradual descent, displays by way of the play of concealing His inner nature, the succeeding aspects by suppressing the preceding ones, though they serve as the substratum for the succeeding aspects." (Jaideva Singh, *The Yoga of Vibration and Divine Pulsation*, p. 11.)

We see the flavor of this approach in the following quote from a Shaivite teacher: "I will give the explanation of the tattvas in the way of rising not coming down. We must rise up to Parama Siva. . . . I will, therefore, explain the grossest element 'earth' first and then proceed to explain subtler and subtler elements until we reach the subtlest element, the finest, which is Parama Siva." (Swami Lakshman Jee, *Kashmir Shaivism*, p. 1.)

Sufism has a similar system, but not as detailed in its explication of the varying dominance of the two sides of reality. It starts with transcendent unity, then with manifest unity, then oneness or unicity, then the world of difference, and so on. The following passage is how one major Sufi sage puts it: "The distinction between the Unity (*al-ahadiyah*), the Unicity (*al-wahaidiyah*) and the 'Quality of Divinity' (*al-uluhiyah*) consists in the fact that, in the Unity, none of the Names and the Qualities manifest themselves; it corresponds then to the pure Essence in its immediate actuality, whereas in the Unicity the Names and the Qualities and their activities are manifested, but with regard only to the Essence, not in a separate mode, so that each one therein is the essential determination for the other. As for the 'Quality of Divinity,' there the Names and the Qualities are manifested according to that which is appropriate to each one of them." (Abd Al-Karim Al-Jili, *Universal Man*, p. 24.)

Sufism takes the position that the transcendent source is unknowable, while Kashmir Shaivism believes that the ultimate state of Shiva is its inseparability from manifestation, in the form of Shakti, which is knowable in experience as Shiva being the world while still transcending it.

7. This is the experience of cessation in Buddhism, considered the ultimate attainment in its Theravada branch. In Sufism, it is total extinction in the divine essence. In some forms of Vedanta it is the experience of the absolute truth.

8. Writing of the view of Gregory of Nyssa, Louth underscores this path of going into increasing darkness: "The progress is a progress from light to deeper and deeper darkness. The initial stage is the removal of the darkness (*skotos*) of error by the light of the truth. But, from then on, the further the soul progresses the deeper is the darkness into which it enters, until eventually the soul is cut off from all that can be grasped by sense and reason." (Andrew Louth, *The Origins of the Christian Mystical Tradition*, p. 83.) This view is not unique to Christianity; it is shared by some schools of Sufism, and Jewish mysticism, as we see in the following passage by Philo of Alexandria, quoted by Louth: "'So see him enter into the thick darkness where God was, that is, into the innermost sanctuary—formless conceptions concerning being.'" (Ibid., p. 32.)

9. Some Sufis have recognized, along with certain Christian and Jewish mystics, that the divine darkness is a luminous light, a black light, that is actually the light of the divine essence. Some Sufis called it "midnight sun" and thought of it as the source of all other lights. The following passage is from Lahiji, a Persian Sufi: "I saw myself [writes the Shaykh] present in a world of light. Mountains and deserts were iridescent with lights of all colors: red, yellow, white, blue. I was experiencing a consuming nostalgia for them; I was as though stricken with madness and snatched out of myself by the violence of the intimate emotion and feeling of the presence. Suddenly I saw that the black light was invading the entire universe. Heaven and earth and everything that was there had wholly become black and, behold, I was totally absorbed in this light, losing consciousness. Then I came back to myself." (Henry Corbin, *The Man of Light in Iranian Sufism*, p. 112.)

This passage is also relevant for the previous note, demonstrating how the cessation or extinction occurs. Corbin writes of the Sufi view of black light: "We shall learn further . . . that the 'black light' is that of the divine Ipseity as the light of revelation, which makes one see. Precisely what makes one see, that is to say, light as absolute subject, can in nowise become a visible object. It is in this sense that the light of lights (*nur al-anwar*), that by which all visible lights are made visible, is both light and darkness, that is, visible because it brings about vision, but in itself invisible." (Ibid., p. 102.)

10. Compare this with the Sufi belief that God has said: "I was a hidden treasure, and I created the world in order to know myself." In other words, the divine essence before manifestation does not know itself the way we think of knowledge, as perception and discrimination. Hence He required the mirror of creation to see and know himself.

11. This is the view that the late Nisargadatta Maharaj took. He believed that even though the absolute truth is pure awareness, it is not aware of itself when there is no manifestation. In such condition there is no consciousness or awareness of anything. There is neither experience nor perception. Consciousness arises as manifestation arises, forming its ground. He writes: "As Absolute, I am timeless, infinite, and I am awareness, without being aware of awareness. As infinity I express myself as space, as timeless I express myself as time. Unless there is space and duration I cannot be conscious of myself. When space and time are present there is consciousness, in that the total manifestation takes place and various phenomena come into being." (Jean Dunn, *Prior to Consciousness*, p. 72.)

Meher Baba took a slightly different perspective. He believed that God has three basic conditions: limitation or helplessness, which is that of normal human experience; awakeness or all-powerfulness, which is the conscious experience of God-realization; and sleep, which is that of cessation and no awareness. In other words, when in total transcendence God is as if in deep slumber: "God experiences three conditions of consciousness: (1) His Original State; (2) Helplessness; (3) All-powerfulness. The Original State. In this state God, unconscious of His Infinite Power, Bliss and Existence, is perfectly at peace. This state can well be compared with the sound sleep state of a person." (Meher Baba, *The Everything and the Nothing*, p. 95.) This is actually similar to the Sufi perspective, but Meher Baba did see himself as connected to Sufism.

12. The understanding that the unknowing of the divine darkness is actually the true knowing of the transcendent truth has been known by many of the Western mystics. Plotinus saw it as knowing through presence, not through intellection, a knowing specific to the knowing of the One, for "the main source of the difficulty is that awareness of this Principle comes neither by knowing nor by the Intellection that discovers the Intellectual beings, but by a presence overpassing all knowledge." (Plotinus, *Enneads*, p. 539.)

The most well-known Western mystic of divine darkness is Denys the Areopagite, who speaks of the ascent of the soul using the analogy of Moses' ascent of the holy mount, demonstrating that he saw the divine darkness as the ultimate knowing: "And then Moses is cut off from both things seen and those who see and enters into the darkness of unknowing, a truly hidden darkness, according to which he shuts his eyes to all apprehensions that convey knowledge, for he has passed into a realm quite beyond any feeling or seeing. Now, belonging wholly to that which is beyond all, and yet to nothing at all, and being neither himself, nor another, and united in his highest part in passivity (*anenergesia*) with Him who is completely unknowable, he knows by not knowing in a manner that transcends understanding." (Quoted in Andrew Louth, *The Origins of the Christian Mystical Tradition*, p. 173.)

13. Buddhism is the most well-known wisdom tradition that makes emptiness the center of its understanding of ultimate reality. But Buddhism has many schools, with various views of what emptiness means. The view we are presenting here will be more consonant with the Prasangica school of Madhyamika. In his excellent introduction to Tsong Khapa's masterpiece, *Essence of True Eloquence*, Thurman sums up this view of emptiness: "The proof of realitylessness is the logical iron rail that directs the cognition to full confrontation with the total dissolution of all subjectivity and objectivity into an experience of absolute nothingness. But it is also the catapult beyond this great cognitive 'black hole' of absolute compression, since its critical wisdom energy dissolves the apparent objective existence of objective nonexistence. Thus, emptiness dawns immediately as the magnificent panorama of relativity, through its absolute negation of the intrinsic reality of nothingness." (Robert Thurman, *The Central Philosophy of Tibet*, p. 169.) Tsong Khapa, the founder of the Gelug school of Tibetan Buddhism, puts it this way: "The perfect, the objective selflessness of things, is the pure object, and hence also the ultimate. It is manifest in the unreality of the selves of things, and, because it is established by that fact alone, it is called 'the intrinsic unreality of things,' and hence the 'ultimate-unreality.'" (Ibid., p. 197.)

14. The nondual wisdom traditions, including those known as the Tathagatagarbha school of Buddhism, and Mahamudra and Dzogchen in particular, consider this ground to be the ultimate true nature, Buddha nature or the nature of mind: "And when the mind is in tranquil equipoise, there emerges a union of awareness and void that is vivid, transparent, and unblemished. This is nonconceptual awareness of intrinsic reality." (Takpo Tashi Namgyal, *Mahamudra*, p. 78.) Furthermore:

> *The great awareness exists*
> *In the bodies of all sentient beings,*
> *Neither as duality nor nonduality,*
> *Neither as substance nor nonsubstance,*
> *But as the supreme state*
> *Pervading all things, dynamic and static.*
>
> *Ibid., p. 221*

This conflicts with other schools of Buddhism that consider emptiness to be the ultimate nature of mind. These schools consider clear light to be not permanent, as in the experience of cessation. Even some schools of Dzogchen consider clear light or the factor of luminosity to be impermanent, as evident in the following passage from a Bon Dzogchen book about *dharmakaya*, the ultimate truth body: "All manifest bodies are impermanent; even the Dharmakaya has two forms—the wisdom Dharmakaya (the awareness side), which is impermanent, and the nature Dharmakaya (the empty side), which is permanent . . . Generally we say that Dharmakaya is permanent but the kayas are impermanent; but here the Dharmakaya has two divisions. We say that the Buddha's knowledge is purified but that it is impermanent; what is permanent is the nature of emptiness. The Buddha's mind is not permanent." (Shardza Tashi Gyaltsen, *Heart Drops of the Dharmakaya*, pp. 79–80.)

15. The nondual wisdom teachings, including Kashmir Shaivism and Dzogchen, tend to take this view. Shaivism refers to this inherent dynamism as *spanda*, which is inseparable from Shiva, as we see in the Spanda Karikas: "Thus the essential nature of the Lord is perpetual spanda (creative pulsation). He is never without *spanda*. . . . our nature is identical with that of Sankara who is full of *spanda sakti*, the essence of which consists in quivering light." (Jaideva Singh, *The Yoga of Vibration and Divine Pulsation*, p. 10.)

16. Dogen expresses this in his unique Zen prose: "At the time the mountains were climbed and the rivers crossed, you were present. Time is not separate from you, and as you are present, time does not go away.

"As time is not marked by coming and going, the moment you climbed the mountains is the time-being right now. If time keeps coming and going you are the time-being right now. This is the meaning of the time-being.

"Does this time-being not swallow up the moment when you climbed the mountains and the moment when you resided in the jeweled palace and vermilion tower? Does it not spit them out?" (Dogen, *Moon in a Dewdrop*, pp. 77–78.)

CHAPTER 17. DIVINE LOVE AND LIGHT

1. Hindu thought has a precise term for this barrier: *ahamkara*. This term refers to the "I am" concept, the concept of separate individual existence. The various Indian spiritual traditions consider this illusion basic to the ongoing experience of the soul, and see it as the primary barrier to enlightenment.

2. This is reminiscent of Plato's name for the highest truth, "The Good." (See Plato's *Republic*.)

3. Psychoanalytic developmental psychology understands affects to develop in early childhood through various processes, among them increasing differentiation. "As the infant's ego begins to develop signaling and receiving functions, these new capabilities assist in affect development. According to Krystal, affect development includes

the differentiation, tolerance, symbolization, and desomatization of affects." (Ivri Kumin, *Pre-Object Relatedness*, p. 32.) We are not, however, aware of any studies linking these differentiated affects to love.

4. Hence, it is this dimension of true nature that inspires love, melting, poetry, and surrender. The experience of this dimension makes sense of the attitudes of love, adoration, devotion, humility, prayer, and supplication in relation to true nature. The soul tends to spontaneously exhibit such attitudes when touched by this heavenly love, and it is easy then for her to relate to true nature as a loving divinity, a good divine mother. Spiritual practices built around devotion and love of God tend to invoke this dimension as God's love, mercy, and grace. The path becomes that of surrender to and adoration of the divinity.

Such orientation dominates some of the wisdom traditions, as those of Christian mysticism, Sufi orders, Hindu *bhakti yoga*, and others. The Diamond Approach utilizes and depends on this orientation, but not as the central element of the teaching. It forms one of the major elements in the orientation of the approach, in the love of truth and trust in true nature to guide and hold the soul's unfoldment.

5. The reader may wonder how universal is this experience, and how much it is the influence of background, culture, and popular beliefs and tales. Our observations point to its universality, for it seems that childhood religion is not determinative. The individuals who spontaneously came up with these images, without prior introduction, were Christians, Jews, and Muslims mostly, which might predispose them toward religious indoctrination. However, the images and patterns that unfold in this issue reflect exactly the Christian story of the Beast, its symbology and stages, which neither Jews nor Muslims share.

Knowing that the soul possesses a potential of many forms and images, many of which are known in some cultures and tales, predisposes us to believe that these forms are primal and primitive ones, and are actually the true and original source of the cultural and popular stories and images. Therefore, we think of the Biblical story of the devil as a particular process through which the soul manifests some of her potential and deals with its associated issues and conflicts. This is similar to Jung's idea of archetypal images and processes.

6. This painful situation, so prevalent in the human experience, has plunged the theologians of the main monotheistic faiths into a great dilemma about God, of how to reconcile the experience of suffering and deprivation in the world with the notion of God's omnipotence and boundless benevolence. The resolution we find in the Diamond Approach, as we will see, depends on the objective understanding of true nature, and its relation to world and soul; that is, there is no dilemma or paradox when we objectively understand Reality.

7. Such separateness has been seen by many mystics as the original fall, the true meaning of the biblical story of the fall. In other words, separateness is one way of understanding the Christian concept of original sin, for it leads naturally and

automatically to all the ugly passions, and ultimately to hatred, even hatred of goodness and love. In Islamic thought, the devil was an angelic soul that was cast out of heaven. In other words, we may see that the casting out of heaven as the loss of the paradisal state of divine love, which results in separateness, isolation, opposition, and loss of love. (See *Facets of Unity*, chapter 11.) Absence of love, combined with the privations of separateness, breeds hatred, becoming personified in the figure of the Beast.

8. Some ancient Greeks viewed beauty similarly. We see this in the work of Plato and Plotinus, and many others, as in the following passage: "Let us, then, go back to the source, and indicate at once the Principle that bestows beauty on material things . . . We hold that all the loveliness of this world comes by communion in the Ideal-Form." (Plotinus, *Enneads*, p. 47.)

9. Such relation is midway between the religious and mystical paths to spiritual life. Religion, especially in its theistic forms, views the soul as an individual entity that needs God for salvation and well-being. From this perspective, God is viewed as some kind of force or presence separate from the soul, to which divinity the soul relates in some kind of object relation. In other words, most theistic religions do not view Being as the true nature of the soul, but as a God that transcends her. She then relates to God within a personalized relationship, where she prays to, devotes herself to, adores, and loves the divinity. In this process she loses her rigidity and surrenders to God; God becomes her shepherd, and she His obedient servant. This process of growing nearness to God, which can take many forms of feelings and relationships, can end in a union with the divine presence, as in the Song of Songs in the Old Testament. Love, humility, and obedience lead ultimately to union. There are many varieties of this union and many theological positions regarding what forms of it are possible for a human being.

The mystical path is that of identity with the divinity of true nature, of finding the unity and oneness of Reality. The religious path can be seen as a stage toward the full mystical realization, which is how many mystics view it.

In the Diamond Approach, the religious attitude is useful, sometimes, to deal with the deep identity with the separate soul, taking her from where she is, and employing its perspective of personal relationship to the divine, but then to transcend this perspective in the mystical self-realization.

The true relationship of the individual soul to the ultimate reality of Being seems to be a midway station between the religious and mystical types of experience. But it is, more accurately, seen not as a relationship, but a mode of manifestation of true nature, as it unfolds some of its deepest potentials. See chapter 12 for further discussion of these questions.

10. Each wisdom tradition conceptualizes different forms, by focusing on the essential manifestations of true nature from different angles. The forms we mention here are specific to the Diamond Approach.

CHAPTER 18. BEING AND KNOWLEDGE

1. Many wisdom teachings contain similar formulations. Buddhism, for instance, has a similar classification in its three bodies of the Buddha, the fully enlightened soul. True nature before differentiation is referred to normally as *dharmakaya*, the body of truth. The essential differentiations are referred to as *sambhogakaya*, the body of enjoyment. The normally perceived level of manifestation is usually referred to as *nirmanakaya*, the body of manifestation. These three "bodies" are considered to be coemergent and inseparable. The last two are sometimes put together as *rupakaya*, the form body. "Dharmakaya is a term for Being-as-such, experienced as an absolute value; Rupakaya is its representation in a perceptible way, that is, through being a Nirmanakaya man represents the ultimate value of Being, and through simultaneously being a Sambhogakaya, he is empathetically one with the ultimate value of Being." (Herbert Guenther, *The Tantric View of Life*, p. 45.)

The monotheistic traditions resolve Reality into three realms: the divine, the subtle or angelic, and the material. There are differences between the various traditions, but this general plan obtains in each.

2. An aspect is then one of the veils of light, according to Sufi thought. Such idea comes from the Sufi notion, taken from the Qur'an, that God is hidden by thousands of thousands of veils, of darkness and light. The Kabbalah holds a similar view.

3. This understanding demonstrates that as true nature manifests in forms, it does not change into them completely. It only manifests these forms within itself, while it continues to be their ground and nature. This is different from our understanding of the theory of involution of Being as, for instance, promulgated by Ken Wilber. His view seems to be that when true nature manifests various levels of forms, it ceases to be its purity and fully involutes into the forms themselves. (See appendix D.)

4. Sufi thought has made Being into the fundamental truth, prepared first by Islamic philosophy's understanding of the true station of Being. Al-Kindi, Al-Farabi, and Ibn Sina discussed existence as the original truth of reality, existence that is independent from existents. They associated such existence, or Being, with God, and hence considered it more fundamental than the forms of manifestation. Forms are accidents, dependent on true existence, which is the truth of the Supreme Being. Sufi thinkers such as Ibn 'Arabi, Al-Jili, and Shabistari, extended this philosophic view into mystical experience, and viewed the divine being in terms of this fundamental existence, pure Being.

Izutsu, in his study of the Sufi's principal notion of *wahdat al-wujud*, the unity of existence, makes this very clear: "All so-called things are adjectives or adjectival in nature, modifying and qualifying the sole reality called 'existence.'" (Toshihiko Izutsu, *Creation and the Timeless Order of Things*, p. 73.) And again: "The moment existence is grasped as an object, it ceases to be itself. Existence in its original indetermination can never be taken hold of as an object. It can only be realized as the subject of all knowledge in the form of man's self-realization, for it is the ultimate Subject." (Ibid., pp. 77–78.)

This view that the ultimate truth is the being and existence of everything is common to most teachings, including Christianity, regardless of the Nicene doctrine that separates God from creation. We see this in the following passage from a famous Christian text: "For I repeat: all things exist in him; he is the being of all." (William Johnston, *The Cloud of Unknowing*, p. 150.)

5. Kashmir Shaivism includes this distinction in its system of manifestation, as two of the highest *tattvas*, or principles, *sadashiva* and *sadvidya*, where the following passage describes the differences between these stages of realization: "The experience of this stage is 'I am this,' but the 'this' is only a hazy . . . experience. The predominant side is still 'I.' The Ideal Universe is experienced as an indistinct something in the depth of consciousness. *Sadasiva tattva* is the first manifestation. . . . In the *Sadvidya tattva*, the 'I' and the 'This' side of experience are equally balanced like the two pans of an evenly held balance." (Jaideva Singh, *Siva Sutras*, pp. xxii–xxiii.)

Sufi thought also uses this distinction, making unity and oneness the first two levels of manifestation, where unity (*ahadiyah*) is first, and oneness (*wahidiyah*) the next rung of manifestation: "Thus, the *wahidiyah* is not existential unity pure and simple as is the case with *ahadiyah*, but rather a comprehensive unity of an infinity of different things. The *wahidiyah* in this sense is unity with inner articulations. . . . The *ahadiyah*, considered in itself is pure and absolute Oneness, there being not even a shadow of multiplicity." (Toshihiko Izutso, *Creation and the Timeless Order of Things*, p. 90.)

The same distinction exists in Taoism, evident in these words of Chuang-tzu: "What is the ultimate limit of Knowledge? It is the stage represented by the view that nothing has ever existed from the very beginning. This is the furthest limit (of knowledge), to which nothing more can be added . . .

"Next is the stage at which there is the consciousness of 'things' being existent. But (in this consciousness) 'boundaries' between them have never existed from the very beginning . . ." (Toshihiko Izutso, *A Comparative Study of Key Philosophical Concepts in Sufism and Taoism*, pp. 354–355.)

6. In the notes to chapter 16, we have given passages from Zen about the relation of time to true nature, but other traditions address this in their own distinctive way. Calling the nowness of Being pre-eternity (*azaliyya*), the Sufi Al-Hamadani writes: "For not only is pre-eternity 'with' every unit of time and 'in' every unit of time, but it comprehends in itself every unit of time and precedes every unit of time in existence, whereas time cannot comprehend pre-eternity just as no place can comprehend knowledge." (Toshihiko Izutso, *Creation and the Timeless Order of Things*, p. 138.)

7. One may argue that the original concept is not being, but emptiness. But emptiness is nonbeing, which is the other side of being, and is nonsensical without the concept of being. In actuality, being and nonbeing, being and emptiness, is the first

dichotomy. They arise together, for every basic concept appears as a pair, as a dichotomy. (See *Diamond Heart*, Book 4, chapter 14, for a discussion of concepts and conceptualization in relation to knowing.)

We will see in the next chapter how the transcendence of the conceptual dichotomy of being and nonbeing takes us to true nonconceptuality. This will be a simpler dimension of true nature than pure presence, and more fundamental, but we are discussing here pure presence, and its characteristics, among which an important one is that it is the beginning of concepts.

8. A protoconcept is a primitive concept that precedes the development of conceptualization in the cognitive development of the mind, according to Piaget. The mind can recognize an object, like a chair, but has not developed to the extent of knowing that there is a whole category—chair—that includes many other chairs. The mind knows chair as the particular chair in awareness. A normal or formal concept is an idea that stands for a whole category, but this takes us to representation and away from Being and the direct experience of presence.

9. This understanding of essential aspects is close to Plato's understanding of the qualities of pure spirit. He thought of the original archetypes of virtue and purity of spirit as ideas, *eidos*. He obviously recognized that they are conceptual or cognitive forms, but of a different kind of cognition than the one ordinarily known. He thought of them as qualities of spirit, even though he called them ideas:

"The things that we grasp with the bodily eye are physical forms; the things we grasp with the 'eye of the soul' are, instead, non-physical forms: the vision of the intellect grasps intelligible forms, that are precisely pure essences. The 'ideas' are thus these eternal essences of the Good, the True, the Beautiful, the Just, and similar things. . . . Actually for Plato there is a metaphysical connection between the vision of the eyes of the soul and to what we owe this vision. Intellectual vision implies as its reason for being what the Intellect sees: that is the Ideas. For this reason the Idea implies a radical concise nexus, that is, precisely a unified structure between vision–the object of vision–form–being." (Giovanni Reale, *A History of Ancient Philosophy: Plato and Aristotle*, pp. 48–49.)

It is possible that by "ideas" he meant what we call here "universal concepts." This is actually clear in Reale's passage above, and in later Platonic and Neoplatonic thought, as in Plotinus's case. See below for a discussion by Plotinus of the divine mind. The notion of essential aspects is the closest thing we know to Plato's concept of the Ideas.

10. This view is reminiscent of that of Chittamatra, the mind-only school of Mahayana Buddhism. It is called *mind-only*, because its understanding of emptiness is that all manifest forms are manifestation of mind. Only mind exists; all phenomenal appearances are empty, possessing no independent self or essence, because they are manifestations of mind, totally dependent on the universal mind.

11. We recognize here the source of the cognitive function, that it is grounded in one of the fundamental dimensions of true nature. The knowability of forms in this

dimension points to the source of all scientific knowledge, and the source of its possibility. We will discuss shortly how the noetic capacity becomes the normal knowing capacity used by our Western science, but recognizing the noetic function on this dimension of true nature reveals to us that Western science, and all other human modes of knowledge in all times and cultures, is a natural potential of Reality. Western thought has simply tapped into a possibility provided to us by our true nature. It has tapped into the possibility of discriminating knowing of the forms of manifestation, of nature and mind. Western thought recognized that these forms can be known and understood in a precise, detailed, and objective manner. It saw that we can know them correctly, that each has its own pattern that can be penetrated and seen for what it is. It did not look at them as unknowable or inherently mysterious, or impervious to precise and objective understanding. It took this potential of the human consciousness and developed it greatly. It has in the process forgotten that the precise pattern of forms is not the only thing that can be known about them. It forgot that discriminating knowing can also know the ground and source of these forms. It did not recognize this possibility partly because it participated in, and even developed as part of, the view of the dissociation of the original triad. This dissociation did not allow Western thought to recognize that the ground of its discriminating knowing capacity derives from a place more fundamental than the discrimination itself, more basic than the differentiations. It did not see that knowing is made possible by the ground of Being, the ground that it believes to be separate and irrelevant to its precise knowing.

This understanding can also be seen as providing the possibility of bridging the two: the precise discriminating knowing and the ground of Being. The bridge is clearly the dimension of pure presence, for it is the dimension where the ground of Being and discriminating knowing are inseparable.

12. In chapter 4 we discussed how the soul's field, at one of its dimensions, is pure knowledge, pure knowing. We see here the cosmic and universal source of this property of the soul, as the cognitive dimension of true nature.

13. This view is almost identical to Plotinus' conception of *nous*, his second hypostasis. He wrote in his *Enneads* that the first manifestation out of the One, which is the first hypostasis, is *nous*, Intellectual-Principle, or divine mind or intellect, and that it is both being and knowing: "Hence we may conclude that, in the Intellectual-Principle itself, there is complete identity of knower and Known, and this not by way of domiciliation, as in the case of even the highest soul, but by Essence, by the fact that, there, no distinction exists between Being and Knowing." (Plotinus, *Enneads*, p. 241.)

Plotinus also wrote that it is infinite and boundless, beautiful and magnificent, containing all space and time: "For here is contained all that is immortal: nothing here but is Divine Mind; all is God; this is the place of every soul. Here is rest unbroken.... All its content, thus, is perfect, that itself may be perfect throughout, as holding nothing that is less than the divine, nothing that is less than intellective. . . . this is pure being in eternal actuality; nowhere is there any future, for every then is a now; nor is there any past, for nothing there has ever ceased to be . . . and the total of all is Intellectual-Principle entire and Being entire." (Ibid., p. 351.)

He also saw it as the container of all the Platonic forms. He saw that all forms, in whatever dimension, appear in the *nous* as ideas, as forms of knowing: "The Intellectual-Principle entire is the total of the Ideas, and each of them is the (entire) Intellectual-Principle in a special form." (Ibid., p. 432.)

This demonstrates that Western thought knew of the dimension of being-knowing, where everything is both presence and knowledge. Many others in the Western world—Platonists, Neoplatonists, Christian mystical theologians, Kabbalists, Sufis, and various philosophers—knew of this dimension, wrote about it, and included it in their wisdom teachings. This means that Western thought, at least in some of its important quarters, knew of the indivisibility of knowing and Being. Yet, we find Western thought in our times viewing these two as inherently separate and dissociated. This indicates that some historical development must have occurred that severed these roots of Western thought, and established the view that being and knowing are separate things, alienated from each other.

Eastern thought is also familiar with this Being dimension of knowing. The Sanskrit term *jnana* and the Tibetan terms *yeshe* and *rigpa* refer to such basic knowingness. Kashmir Shaivism considers the ultimate Self or ground to possess not only pure awareness but freedom of knowing. The Buddhist teaching regarding the five wisdoms or awarenesses of the Buddha includes the wisdom of discrimination, which also refers to an inherent discriminating dimension to true nature. (See appendix B.)

Nevertheless, Eastern thought has not given this dimension the kind of attention and importance that Western thought did. None of the Eastern teachings, as far as we can see, made it as central as Plotinus, who described it in as much detail as we are doing here. Western thought has obviously seen discriminating knowing to be of central importance, and has developed it into the form we know it in modern and postmodern times. It has become the bedrock of Western civilization.

14. It was Piaget who first systematically studied the development of the perception of an object in early cognitive development. He realized that the baby does not see discrete objects the way adults do, that the baby does not have the concept of an object existing independently and on its own. He termed the development of a concept of an object the *attainment of object permanence*, which is now believed not to occur until five months of age: "Emde . . . described the first weeks of life as essentially 'prerepresentational,' and Brazelton and Cramer . . . claimed that object permanence does not occur until four to five months of age." (Ivri Kumin, *Pre-Object Relatedeness*, p. 15.)

Object relations theory has used this research of early cognitive development in its formulation of how the child develops the sense of being a separate self relating to a separate other. This is not only a cognitive development, but an emotional one that utilizes the achievement of object permanence to establish the concept of a love object in a relationship, the human other. According to Margaret Mahler, this is the attainment of object constancy: "From the point of view of the separation-individuation process, the main task of the fourth subphase is twofold: (1) the achievement of a definite, in certain aspects lifelong, individuality, and (2) the attainment of a certain degree of object constancy. . . .

"The establishment of affective (emotional) object constancy . . . depends upon the gradual internalization of a constant, positively cathected, inner image of the mother. This, to begin with, permits the child to function separately . . . despite moderate degrees of tension (longing) and discomfort. Emotional object constancy will, of course, be based in the first place on the cognitive achievement of the permanent object, but all other aspects of the child's personality development participate in this evolution as well. . . ." (Margaret Mahler, *The Psychological Birth of the Human Infant*, p. 109.)

Neither cognitive research nor object relations theory include the view we take here of the original experience being of a true oneness of all forms. They both believe that the two achievements are the development of the capacity to experience reality correctly, taking the adult ego's view of reality as true reality, as what truly exists, not seeing how this development has lost the unifying ground of Being, regardless of the fact that it is necessary for cognitive and normal emotional development. In other words, there does not seem to be present in these disciplines an awareness of the influence of adultomorphic thought, which is normally egomorphic.

15. *Oxford English Dictionary*, 2nd ed., defines *reification* as "the mental conversion of a person or abstract concept into a thing." To *reify* means "to convert mentally into a thing, to materialize." For example, "when people make or find a new abstract noun, they instantly try to put it on a shelf or into a box, as though it were a thing, thus they reify it."

16. Positivist philosophy, the basis of our Western mode of science, believes that the reified world is the real world. Hence, it has no place for God or Being, spirit or soul. It recognizes only the reifying mind, its ordinary knowledge composed of reifications, and the reified world of discrete objects and processes. It calls this "reality," the exploration of which is science. Science is very good at dissecting the world and studying its components, resulting in our technological advances. It has accumulated much true knowledge about the noetic forms it studies, but as long as it bases itself on positivist philosophy, which is actually an expression of naïve realism, it is bound to miss the ground of all manifestation, the omnipresent field of true nature. It will not be able to penetrate to the ultimate nature and truth of its objects of study.

Science need not take the positivist position. Its objective research can proceed within a view that recognizes the ultimate unity of all things; this unity allows for the presence and reality of knowable forms. This deeper and more accurate view may actually aid scientific research, adding another dimension of reality to its study, making this study more complete and objective, and making available to researchers more subtle capacities for perception and research.

On the other hand, extreme constructionist philosophy, popular in postmodern times, takes the opposite view. It sees the world as composed not of reified noetic forms, but only of mental constructs. In deconstructing the view of naïve realism, it veers toward extreme nihilism, lacking the recognition that the constructs of the mind are not completely without basis. It does not see that the basis of the reified world is the oneness of existence of basic knowledge. It does not see that the mind cannot be so original, that it is bound to borrow its concepts from direct basic experience of truly arising forms. It wants to liberate us from the belief in independent objects, but it ends up robbing us of the luminous richness of basic knowledge, with its myriad noetic forms. It is true that these noetic forms do not exist independently on their own, but they are not completely the creation of our individual minds. They are the inseparable forms of the universal mind. Reality lies midway between the visions of positivism and of extreme constructionism.

17. Western science has itself debunked this wrong view. Quantum field theory shows that reality is actually a field, where objects are nothing but manifestations of this field, and are perceived as objects because of our mode of observation.

18. This becomes the crystallized belief in a separate and ultimately self-existing entity we call the self. Seeing that such self is a belief in a reified concept was the Buddha's central discovery. He said there is no self or no soul, meaning that there is no discrete and ultimately self-existing entity we can call self. Buddhism clearly sees this situation, and how reification is a spiritual and fundamental problem. Reification manifests in the normal mind as the belief that each object exists independently from others and has its own inherent essence or ultimate existence. Buddhism calls this the belief that phenomenal objects possess a self, meaning a truly abiding independent existence. Seeing the fallacy of this view became the central element of the wisdom teaching of Buddhism. The teaching becomes then a path toward understanding the process of reification, which leads to the realization of true nature.

The view that absence of an abiding self means recognizing that separateness is due to a mental reifying process, and then seeing that all forms are inseparable forms of universal mind, became the view of emptiness according to the Yogachara school of Mahayana Buddhism. The view of emptiness according to the Madhyamika school will become clear as we discuss true nature in another of its other boundless dimensions, in chapter 21.

19. The process of de-reification can be seen as a destructuring process for it is a matter of destructuring the reified concepts of the mind. However, this is an incomplete understanding of this process. De-reification can also be misinterpreted and abused when understood exclusively as destructuring. Because the penetration of reified concepts leads not simply to chaos or annihilation of experience, but to the ground of basic knowledge, the process is more accurately understood as that of restructuring. The structuring of experience by ordinary knowledge dissolves and is replaced by the authentic and spontaneous structure of basic knowledge.

20. Inquiry reveals the barriers to liberation and realization in various degrees of subtlety. It reveals them as the effect of the past on the present, as the process of identification with the content of experience, as the limiting structures of the soul, or as the reactivity that dissociates the soul from presence, and so on. The way we understand the nature of the barriers changes and evolves depending on the deepening of our understanding of Reality. At some point this understanding matures to the understanding of reification, and then becomes even subtler.

We find that even though it might be tempting to guide the student from the beginning of the inner journey to view the situation from the perspective of reification, this endeavor will most likely become intellectual. A student may understand the meaning of reification and its process intellectually, but this is a far cry from actually and experientially understanding it. Furthermore, the process of de-reification is impossible without the support and guidance of essence. We are aware of many who talk of destructuring and de-reification, but our observation is that the largest majority of these individuals are engaged in a clever intellectual exercise. The soul, or the mind, cannot truly de-reify without standing on the real ground of true nature. When this supportive ground is not available the soul is bound, mostly unconsciously, to rely on a subtle reified ground. If this were not the case, then many of the very intelligent individuals who intellectually understand reification would be liberated.

To truly understand reification and work with reified concepts from this subtle level of understanding requires the sharp subtlety of the guidance of Being. In the Diamond Approach, this occurs with the assistance of the no-diamond guidance, whose diamonds are the concept diamonds. At this dimension of realization we understand more fully the function of diamond understanding. We see that it reveals the basic knowledge of Being because it is an essential vehicle structured by the concept diamonds, which are the original discriminated differentiations of pure presence. It is constituted by the essential concepts, the universal concepts. It thus has the capacity to reveal the most basic concepts in basic knowledge. Because it is constituted by the sharp, precise, and objective basic knowledge of the qualities of true nature, it can challenge all reifications, all the way to the reification of essential qualities.

CHAPTER 19. AWARENESS AND THE NONCONCEPTUAL

1. The possibility of this state of awareness can be derived from our knowledge of the condition of early infancy. The infant may recognize a few things, but generally does not recognize most of the forms in its environment. The forms are present around it, and some forms of experience arise within its own organism, but it does not know what it is perceiving.

We cannot say it perceives only what it recognizes; otherwise it would be perceiving mostly darkness. If we accept that its perceptual capacities are developed, then it does not merely perceive darkness, or a blur, and we have to accept that it perceives the forms we perceive in the environment, without necessarily differentiating them out as separate forms or recognizing them.

2. The following Zen passage refers to this perception: "You are thoroughly lucid and transparent like a crystal. Subject and object, in and out, being and nonbeing are just one, and this one ceases to be any longer . . . Hakuin said, 'It was like sitting in an ice cave a million miles thick.'" (Zenkei Shibayama, *Zen Comments on the Mumonkan*, p. 28.)

3. Zen is the most well-known tradition that uses the transcendence of the discriminating mind. We see this in the following passage, in which "Mind" refers to awareness: "Mind is the Buddha, while the cessation of conceptual thought is the Way. Once you stop arousing concepts and thinking in terms of existence and nonexistence, long and short, other and self, active and passive, and suchlike, you will find that your mind is intrinsically the Buddha, that the Buddha is intrinsically Mind, and that Mind resembles a void." (John Blofeld, *The Zen Teaching of Huang Po*, p. 67.)

We see this clearly also in the following passage from a text of the Rinzai sect of Zen: "Mumon comments: 'In studying Zen, one must pass the barriers set up by ancient Zen Masters. For the attainment of incomparable satori, one has to cast away his discriminating mind. Those who have not passed the barrier and have not cast away their discriminating mind are all phantoms haunting trees and plants." (Zenkei Shibayama, *Zen Comments on the Mumonkan*, p. 24.)

Because of this, Zen has utilized *koans*, enigmatic statements and stories that cannot be penetrated by the intellect, but only by going beyond it. So to penetrate a *koan* is to experience the nonconceptual truth, Reality before discriminating knowing. The *koans* simply point to this truth beyond mind, as we see in the following famous *koan* about the Buddha, referred to as the "World Honored One," from a famous text of the other major sect of Zen, Soto: "One day the World Honored One ascended the seat. Manjusri struck the gavel and said, 'Clearly observe the Dharma of the King of Dharma; the Dharma of the King of Dharma is thus.' The World Honored One then got down from the seat." (Thomas Cleary, *Book of Serenity*, p. 3.)

The other major method of Zen is *zazen*, sitting meditation without an object or a doing of any kind. It is simply sitting, being the truth without attempting to accomplish anything. Zen seems to be the wisdom tradition that focuses on the realization of true nature through nonconceptual awareness, and hence, it has the most developed understanding of nonconceptual truth.

4. To see that the differentiation of forms precedes knowing, we recognize that the dimension of nonconceptual awareness is appreciated mostly in Eastern wisdom traditions, as in Zen. The Western traditions have almost all but neglected it, as we see in Plotinus' system. An exception is Kabbalah, which sometimes characterizes the *sefirah hochmah* as nonconceptual mind. For Plotinus, the dimension of being is that of the *nous*, where being and knowing are inseparable, similar to our dimension of pure presence. But he has no dimension deeper than this that includes differentiation of forms. The dimension beyond the *nous* in his system is that of the One, but the One has no differentiation of forms, besides not having knowingness.

We find this situation in almost all the major Western traditions of wisdom, where the final reality is considered as mystery or unknowing, but not a nonconceptual awareness. We will see in the next chapter that the One of Plotinus, or the divine darkness in the monotheistic traditions, corresponds more exactly with what we refer to as the absolute dimension. In other words, the Western traditions have emphasized the *nous* dimension, while the Eastern ones the nonconceptual dimension. We think this is possibly the reason why the concept of enlightenment and liberation has become the interest of the Eastern traditions, while that of union and annihilation in God has become the Western idea, which is going from knowing to the darkness of unknowing. Unknowing is merging with the divine darkness, while enlightenment is the clarity and light beyond mind.

5. Even though Zen has developed the nonconceptual perspective more than any other wisdom tradition, it is also important in some other Eastern traditions. Generally speaking, Buddhism has found this dimension to be of central importance, Zen has developed it most, but other Buddhist schools have also understood the importance of nonconceptual or pure awareness. It is particularly important in the nondual teachings, as in Mahamudra and Dzogchen. In the following passage from a famous and ancient Dzogchen text, we see the reference to the nonconceptuality of awareness, and the unity and inseparability of ground and manifestation:

> *Listen: the pristine awareness of the creativity of the universe*
> *Is nonjudgmental and free from all discursiveness.*
> *Serene and insubstantial, like the sky,*
> *We call it unborn.*
> *Without stirring from the unity of self-refreshing pristine awareness,*
> *The details of experience are clearly differentiated without being contrived.*
> *Whoever fully comprehends and actually experiences this*
> *Is called a child of the majestic creativity.*
>
> LONGCHENPA,
> *You Are the Eyes of the World*, p. 49

6. It is customary in Zen to refer to the nonconceptual reality, the unity of true nature and manifestation, with the terms *suchness* or *thusness*. Dogen writes: "Whereby do we know suchness exists? It is as if to say body and mind together appear in the whole world, and because they are not self, we know they are thus." (Dogen, *Shobogenzo*, p. 49.) The translator, Thomas Cleary, explains the terminology: "The word used for 'such,' *Imo* in Sino-Japanese, is a colloquial word which is equivalent to a classical word used in Buddhism for the term thusness, being-as-such, the all-inclusive reality." (Ibid., p. 47.)

But such, thus, suchness, or thusness is not a conceptual category; rather, the expressions are an attempt to go beyond concepts. Dogen explains how these signifiers point beyond conceptual dichotomies: "Truly, because it cannot be grasped at all, as such or not such, therefore it cannot be grasped as such, it cannot be grasped as not such. Such means thus. It is not limited needs for the way, it is not unlimited needs for the way. Suchness should be studied in nongrasping, and nongrasping should be sought in suchness." (Ibid., p. 55.)

7. In arriving at this insight, Zen resorts to cognition even less. This is evident in a story related to the famous koan about "Mu," which stands for the Zen truth: "In the biography of Master Hakuin we read the following moving story of his first encounter with his teacher, Master Shoju. Shoju asked Hakuin, 'Tell me, what is Jushu's 'Mu'?' Hakuin elatedly replied, 'Pervading the universe! Not a spot whatsoever to take hold of!' As soon as he had given that answer, Shoju took hold of Hakuin's nose and gave it a twist. 'I am quite at ease to take hold of it,' said Shoju, laughing aloud. The next moment he released it and abused Hakuin, 'You! Dead monk in a cave! Are you self-satisfied with such 'Mu'?' This completely put Hakuin out of countenance." (Zenkei Shibayama, *Zen Comments on the Mumonkan*, p. 22.)

8. If this were not the case Zen masters would not talk at all. However, their *koans* are constructed of words, not only of actions.

9. Immanuel Kant included these dichotomies in his "categories of understanding," necessary as conditions for the possibility of knowledge. Even though he thought of knowledge as due to the synthetic activity of the knowing subject, and not pure presence, he recognized that such dichotomies are necessary for our cognitive universe: "In his analysis of theoretical reason, Kant attempts to establish the conditions of the possibility of knowledge. In the *Critique of Pure Reason*, he maintains that knowledge is the product of the synthetic activity of the knowing subject. Through *a priori* forms of intuition (space and time) and categories of understanding (unity, plurality, totality, reality, negation, limitation, substance/accident, cause/effect, action/patience, possibility/impossibility, existence/nonexistence, and necessity/contingency), the subject bestows unity and coherence upon the confusing manifold of sense data." (Mark Taylor, *Deconstruction in Context*, p. 5.)

10. This seems to be the reason some nondual wisdom teachings tend to not value philosophical approaches to reality. We see this in the case of Buddhist schools, where the nondual teachings of Dzogchen and Zen disagree with the philosophical schools, as those of Madhyamika, in terms of approach to truth.

11. There is a famous story about one of the founders of a major Zen school that illustrates the difficulty of this realization. In old age, decades after his enlightenment, he was asked about his realization. He answered: "Fine, thank you. However, after all these years the body is still having a hard time going along with it."

Zen expresses this realization in *koans*, as we see in the following famous example: "Once a monk made a request of Joshu. 'I have just entered the monastery,' he said. 'Please give me instructions, Master.' Joshu said, 'Have you had your breakfast?' 'Yes, I have,' replied the monk. 'Then,' said Joshu, 'wash your bowls.' The monk had an insight." (Zenkei Shibayama, *Zen Comments on the Mumonkan*, p. 67.)

In the *Shobogenzo*, Dogen refers to this realization as being enlightened by the myriad dharmas, as we see in Yasutani's commentary, referring to this realization as the actualization of enlightenment: "To completely discard one's own views and oneself, and then, moved by one's intrinsic nature itself, to carry out the activities of daily life as one's intrinsic nature—going and returning home, getting dressed, eating and drinking, defecating and urinating—that is 'to be enlightened by the myriad dharmas.' That is the actualization of enlightenment, the full manifestation of original enlightenment, the full manifestation of the absolute nature." (Hakuun Yasutani, *Flowers Fall*, p. 36.)

12. Taoist literature abounds with the paradoxes of nonconceptuality, which frequently appear as absurdity or indifference. We present a few verses from the *Tao Te Ching*:

> *In truth, is there any definite difference*
>   *between "yes" and "no"?*
> *Between "good" and "evil," is there any*
> *Absolute distinction?*
> . . . .
> *The people of the world excitedly pursue*
>   *merry making*
> . . . .
> *I alone remain quiet and indifferent.*
> *I anchor my being to that which existed*
>   *before Heaven-and-Earth were formed.*
> *I alone am innocent and unknowing as a*
>   *newborn babe.*
> *Unoccupied by worldly cares, I move*
>   *forward to nowhere.*
>
>   HUA-CHING NI,
>   *The Complete Works of Lao Tsu*, pp. 15-16

13. Zen master Dogen, in his *Genjokoan*, puts this noncognitive realization this way: "When buddhas are truly buddhas they do not need to be aware of being buddhas. However, they are actualized buddhas and further actualize buddhahood." (Hakuun Yasutani, *Flowers Fall*, p. 30.)

14. Zen expresses this by saying, "When you meet the Buddha on the road, kill him." Zenkei Shibayama comments: 'This expression is often misunderstood. Zen postulates absolute freedom in which all attachments and restraints are wiped away. The Buddha therefore is to be cast away and so are the Patriarchs. Any restraints whatsoever in the mind are to be cast away. For the one who has passed through the abyss of Great Doubt, transcending subject and object, you and I, and has been revived as the True Self, can there be anything to disturb him? The term 'to kill'

should not be interpreted in our ordinary ethical sense. 'To kill' is to transcend names and ideas.'" (Shibayama, *Zen Comments on the Mumonkan*, p. 29.)

15. This is similar to the understanding of the great Sufi shaykh Ibn 'Arabi:

"If a gnostic ('*arif*) is really a gnostic he cannot stay tied to one form of belief. That is to say, if a possessor of knowledge is cognisant of the being in his own ipseity, in all its meanings, he will not remain trapped in his own belief. He will not decrease his circle of belief. He is like materia prima (*hayula*) and will accept whatever form he is presented with. These forms being external, there is no change to the kernel in his interior universe." (Muhiyddin Ibn 'Arabi, *Kernel of the Kernel*, p. 1.)

CHAPTER 20. LOGOS AND CREATIVE DYNAMISM

1. This seems to contradict the biblical account in the first chapter of Genesis, in which all the universe was created at some point in the past, with this creation requiring seven days, and time then passing on this creation. In other words, according to the usual understanding of the story of creation in the bible, the universe is old. Yet, this is one interpretation, and it is possible to conceive that the continual creation itself, not the old creation, began at some point and continued to the present. This will be an attempt to harmonize with the biblical account, but most of the time the mystics and seers who understand continual creation do not find it necessary to engage in such speculation. Many of the wisdom traditions understand continual creation, and such understanding in fact forms a significant part of the mystical side of all the monotheistic traditions that adhere to the biblical account of creation.

We see this most clearly in the Sufi tradition, as in the following quote where the author writes of Jami, the famous Persian Sufi poet: "This universe, he continues, consists of accidents all pertaining to a single substance, which is the Reality underlying all existences. This universe is changed and renewed unceasingly at every moment and at every breath. Every instant one universe is annihilated and another resembling it takes its place, though the majority of men do not perceive this, as God most glorious has said: 'But they are in doubt regarding the new creation.'" (Sirdar Ikbal Ali Shah, *Islamic Sufism*, p. 148.)

In another passage he elaborates on the newness of existence: "Thus it never happens that the Very Being is revealed for two successive moments under the same guise of the same phenomena. At every moment one universe is annihilated and another similar to it takes its place. But he who is blinded by these veils, to wit, the constant succession of similar phenomena and like conditions, believes that the universe constantly endures in one and the same state, and never varies from time to time. (Ibid., p. 151.)

2. That all objects constituting the universe, at all levels of experience and perception, are nothing but the forms that Being assumes, means that creation is not out of nothing in the sense that this nothing is not Being. Creation is out of the very

substance of Being, from the very presence of divinity. Sufis have stressed this insight, connecting it with the understanding of continual creation. We find this most clearly in the work of Ibn ʿArabi, the greatest shaykh, as in the following passage from Corbin's study of this Sufi's work:

"And His creation springs, not from nothingness, from something other than Himself, from a not-Him, but from His fundamental being, from the potencies and virtualities latent in His own unrevealed being. . . . The Creation is essentially the revelation of the Divine Being, first to himself, a luminescence occurring within Him; it is a theophany (*tajalli ilahi*). . . . The Divine Breathing exhales what our Shaikh designates as *Nafas al-Rahman* or *Nafas Rahmani*, the Sigh of existentiating Compassion; this Sigh gives rise to the entire subtle mass of a primordial existentiation termed Cloud (*'ama*). Which explains the following *hadith*: 'Someone asked the Prophet: Where was your Lord before creating His (visible) Creation?—He was in a Cloud; there was no space either above or below.'" (Henry Corbin, *Creative Imagination in the Sufism of Ibn 'Arabi*, p. 185.)

Writing about creation as new creation he says:

"Creation as the 'rule of being' is the pre-eternal and continuous movement by which being is manifested at every instant in a new cloak. The Creative Being is the pre-eternal and post-eternal essence or substance which is manifested at every instant in the innumerable forms of beings; when He hides in one, He manifests Himself in another. Created Being is the manifested, diversified, successive, and evanescent forms, which have their substance not in their fictitious autonomy but in the Being that is manifested in them and by them. Thus creation signifies nothing less than the Manifestation (*zuhur*) of the hidden (*batin*) Divine Being in the forms of beings: first in their eternal hexeity, then—by virtue of renewal, a recurrence that has been going on from moment to moment since pre-eternity—in their sensuous forms." (Ibid., pp. 100–101.)

Such view, that all the forms of the manifest world are forms that true nature takes and not separate from it, is prevalent in most nondual teachings of the East. We see it in the following passage from a study on Kashmir Shaivism:

"'This world even when it comes out from Him rests in Him, by whose light, it being manifest rests in Him as that light itself, with whose light it is identical, whose light alone considered in its entirety is sufficient for its (the world's) proof.' . . . . The sense of this verse is that nothing appears as different from the Light of manifestation, since the manifest world is one with the Light of manifestation." (Jaideva Singh, *The Yoga of Vibration and Divine Pulsation*, p. 30.)

3. Plotinus had a similar view of individual souls and their relation to the universal soul, what he called Soul, implying universal and boundless soul, which he saw as the creative and ordering force behind the universe. He considered Soul as the third of his hypostases, after the One and the *nous*. Reale writes of Plotinus's view of Soul, what we have been calling dynamic presence:

"Now consider that Soul's 'looking to' the things which come after it, this 'ordering,' 'ruling,' and 'commanding' is identical with its producing, generating, and vivifying of these very things. The Soul . . . is the first born productive cause, the creative and vivifying principle of all things. Here are some of the numerous affirmations of Plotinus in this regard:

"Soul, then, in the same way, is intent upon a task of its own; in everything it does it counts as an independent source of motion. . . .

"Let every Soul recall, then, at the outset the truth that Soul is the author of all living things, that it has breathed the life into them all, . . . it is the maker of the sun; . . . and it is a principle distinct from all these to which it gives law and movement and life, and it must of necessity be more honorable than they, for they gather or dissolve as Soul brings them life or abandons them, but Soul, since it never can abandon itself, is of eternal being.

"The Soul is consequently not only a principle of movement, but it itself is movement:

". . . Soul arises out of motionless Mind (Nous)—which itself sprang from its own motionless prior—but the Soul's operation is not similarly motionless; its image is generated from its movement. It takes fullness by looking to its source; but it generates its image by adopting another, a downward, movement." (Giovanni Reale, *A History of Ancient Philosophy: The Schools of the Imperial Age*, pp. 353–354.)

4. Plotinus had a similar understanding of the relation between individual souls and Soul, or boundless dynamic being. Reale writes of Plotinus's understanding:

"The Soul, by producing the sensible and entering into relations with the sensible . . ., even if it is not originally and primarily divisible, 'it becomes divided into bodies.' When bodies are divided, it happens that the Soul which is in them is also divided, not in the manner in which bodies are divided, but by remaining 'in its entirety in each of the parts.' The division of Soul, in sum, does not mean its breaking up into separate parts as occurs in bodies, but its being in its wholeness in all the parts of the divided bodies, since Soul does not have magnitude. Therefore, divisibility remains a characteristic specific to bodies, while the Soul has the capacity to enter totally into all its parts." (Ibid., p. 355.)

5. Kashmir Shaivism conceptualizes the ultimate nature as Shiva, but also that Shiva has a creative side, Shakti, which is inseparable from Shiva. This teaching refers to this creative dynamism as *spanda*, pulsation or throbbing: "This *sakti* of the lord who is non-moving, being of the nature of consciousness . . . is known as *spanda* in accordance with the root meaning of the word signifying slight movement . . . Thus the essential nature of the Lord is perpetual *spanda* (creative pulsation). He is never without *spanda* . . .

"This *spanda-sakti* consists of the compact bliss of I-consciousness which holds in its bosom endless cycles of creation and dissolution." (Jaideva Singh, *The Yoga of Vibration and Divine Pulsation*, p. 10.)

6. That is why even Buddhism, in some of its nondual teachings, uses the language of creation and creator to refer to this characteristic of true nature. We see this in

the words of Longchenpa, one of the primary teachers of the Tibetan tradition of Dzogchen:

[Because my creativity is beyond all affirmation and negation]
I determine all events and meanings.

. . . .

[Because all buddhas, sentient beings, appearances, Existences, environments,
    and inhabitants]
Arise from the quintessential state of pure and total presence,
One is beyond duality.

. . . .

Because all phenomena do not exist apart from me,
One is beyond duality. I fashion everything.

LONGCHENPA,
You Are the Eyes of the World, pp. 34–35

7. The monotheistic traditions express this in the language of divine will and destiny. This language is also used by some of the Eastern teachings, as we see in the following quote from Kashmir Shaivism:

"Sutra 2: By the power of her own will [alone], she (*citi*) unfolds the universe upon her own screen [in herself, as the basis of the universe]." (Jaideva Singh, *The Doctrine of Recognition*, p. 45.)

This then confronts us with the thorny theological problem of free will and divine will, and the possibility of conflicts between them. It is easy to see from the perspective of dynamic presence that there is only one will, and only one doer, always and eternally. The question of free personal will arises only when our realization of true nature is limited and we do not see the unity of being and its holy will. (See *Facets of Unity* for a fuller discussion of holy will and its relation to personal will and choice.) More precisely, the problem of personal will versus predestination arises only when we are aware of a universal will but still experience a personal will due to our limited understanding. We do not know yet that it is our understanding and realization that is limited, and hence experience a conflict between two wills. We cannot resolve this dilemma from this limited perspective, for it is the result of this limitation, but we can make a practical resolution that may lead to a fuller realization and understanding of true nature. The usual resolution taught by these traditions is that we need to recognize the free will that God gave us, and use it to follow His will, instead of going against it. In this way we harmonize our personal will with the divine will, and union with God's presence.

This is a valid practical solution, for by denying our free will we deny the truth of the situation, which is that we have a limited understanding, the necessary result of which is the experience of having a free will and personal choice. In other words, we need to start from the state we find ourselves in and move from there, otherwise we will be merely parroting mental ideas. Irrespective of the fact that our state is due to not recognizing the limitations of our understanding, we must start from a place we understand if we are going to move deeper into the truth. As discussed in chapter 22, this insight is part of the wisdom of one of the diamond vehicles of the journey of descent. (For a detailed discussion of how beginning from where one is one may go deeper into true nature, see *Spacecruiser Inquiry*, chapter 9, about the personal thread in spiritual inquiry.)

In other words, the mere knowledge that we are all Buddha does not mean that we can ignore that we are not enlightened. We cannot say there is no such thing as individual will and choice and give up our responsibility for our action and behavior. To do this amounts to surrendering to the forces of ignorance that motivate the actions and choices of the ego-self.

It is also possible to see that it makes sense to think that God gave us free will. Since all manifestation is the action of Being's dynamism, or divine will, then our condition of being a limited individual is due to this same will. In other words, since there is only one will, this will manifests the world in such a way that we find ourselves with a limited understanding that constrains us to the experience of free will. To pursue this point will take us to the action of grace and the need for the dynamism of Being for personal liberation, subjects we will discuss in the present chapter.

8. It is believed by scholars that it was Heraclitus who first used the word *logos* to mean the ordering principle of the universe. Subsequently, the Greeks used this term *logos* to mean reason, rationality, but more fundamentally order, which Western thought later termed *natural order*.

To quote Heraclitus (trans. J. Owens): "Out of all things can be made a unity, and out of unity, all things. Having listened not to me, but to the logos, it is wise to agree that all things are one.

"In conclusion, if things have a reality only as far as they change, and its changing is from opposites which are related to each other and their opposition is reconciled in a higher harmony, then it is clear that in the synthesis of opposites lies the principle which explains the whole of reality, and it is evident, consequently, that in this synthesis of opposites precisely consists God and the Divine." (Giovanni Reale, *A History of Ancient Philosophy: From the Origins to Socrates*, p. 51.)

It is clear from this passage that Heraclitus understood the logos to be the divine power or principle that both creates and orders the universe. Some believed he meant reason, but by reason he actually thought of the order that the universe possesses in the ways it changes and transforms, as we see in the following passage from Reale:

"The very famous Fragment forty-one, given different translations and interpretations, can be rendered as follows:

"There is only one wisdom: to recognize the intelligence who steers all things through all things.

"It seems almost certain that Heraclitus called this principle logos, which, as many maintain, does not really mean reason and intelligence, but rather a rule according to which all things are accomplished and a law which is found in all things and steers all things and generally includes rationality and intelligence." (Ibid., p. 53.)

From this we recognize that Heraclitus, and ancient Greek thought after him, thought of reason as reflecting the natural order of things, an order that is fashioned by the logos. Such an understanding may help us recognize the source of what we have come to understand by reason, that by following the rules of reason we are actually recognizing and following the order and harmony that naturally exists in the universe, which order expresses the creative force of Being. Heraclitus thought of reason as the way to live the spiritual life, but Western thought has developed by dissociating the original triad to the extent that reason became divorced from its true source, the creative reality that Heraclitus called logos. Through this dissociation reason became the governing principle of mental thought, divorced from the living qualities of dynamic presence and creativity of the logos. This development aided Western thought in evolving the scientific method whose aim is to find the laws of the universe, which means to discern and understand the natural order of things. It is obvious that the ancient Greek's concept of logos as order and reason is one of the main sources of Western science's interest in finding the laws of the universe. In other words, the idea that the universe follows natural laws is of Greek origin, and it is the concept of logos.

At the same time, by becoming dissociated from its roots in the living divine logos, reason has lost its spiritual power. In fact, through this development reason has become, for many of the religious traditions of the West, the enemy of the spirit. The spiritual gradually became the domain not available to reason, but accessible only by transcending reason, through faith or love.

Our study in this book is partly an attempt to redeem Western thought by redeeming knowing and reason. We discussed in chapter 19 how knowing can be redeemed by understanding the dimension of pure presence, where being and knowing are not separate, understood by the ancient Greeks in the concept of *nous*. We see in this chapter how the Greek concept of logos corresponds to the dimension of dynamic presence, and how by understanding the characteristics of this dimension of true nature we can see one way reason can be redeemed: we can recognize it as a reflection of the order through which the logos unfolds the universe. We see in Heraclitus' concept of logos a direction for this redemption. By recognizing reason to be a reflection of the order created by the logos, we can use it to reconnect with the ordering dynamism of the logos, and this way realize the dynamic presence of true nature. We can do this without having to cast out reason in its entirety. In fact, we can do this while embracing the advantages that reason has given to our scientific and logical thought.

Science is a way to study the logos, but it is a partial way. It studies the order of the natural universe, but not the source of order. At the same time, spiritual understanding also studies the logos, but it also tends to be partial in this study. It studies the dynamic force behind the existence of the universe, but tends not to value the order, or laws, that govern all manifestations, not just the physical.

There is no necessity for such dissociation. Scientific and spiritual understanding can be complementary and, in fact, mutually helpful. There is no reason why we cannot understand reason in such a way that supports both scientific research and spiritual realization, for reason is ultimately the order of the logos. The logos is the fashioner of all manifestation, both physical and spiritual, and its order patterns both. We discuss more aspects of this point later in the present chapter.

9. The Diamond Approach includes two perspectives about the relation of the boundless dimensions to each other. That of the journey of ascent views them as hierarchically ordered in increasing subtlety and fundamentality, while that of the journey of descent views them as inseparable and always coemergent. The Western traditions have in general seen them as hierarchically ordered. We have seen this in Plotinus, who saw the hierarchy as beginning with the unknowable One, which manifests the *nous* or divine mind, which then manifests the Soul, or what we are calling at this point logos. He viewed the logos as responsible for manifesting experienced and corporeal reality. Many of the Neoplatonists followed his lead, but this hierarchic view is also shared by other Western thinkers and traditions. It is shared by the mystical traditions of the three major monotheistic traditions. One of the first who used such hierarchy in terms of the logos was Philo of Alexandria, a Greek-educated Jew. His view of the logos became the foundation upon which not only Jewish but most Christian spiritual thought was built. We see this in the following passage from Reale:

"God, Philo explains, wanted to create the sensible world in an appropriate way, so he produced the intelligible world first, which has the function of being an incorporeal model according to which the corporeal world is to be realized the way an architect 'creates' who wants to construct a city. First of all he creates the project mentally and only afterward is it translated into reality. So the divine Logos is the activity or power of God which creates the intelligible reality which functions as a model or idea paradigm." (Giovanni Reale, *A History of Ancient Philosophy*, The Schools of the Imperial Age, p. 191.)

Sufis sometimes consider the logos an archangel. The archangel logos, who is called the holy angel (*malak muqaddas*), is considered the first manifestation from the unknowable God. From the logos everything proceeds, or is created.

10. It seems that the East has emphasized the nonconceptual perception of the pattern, while the West has emphasized the noetic side that is frequently connected with the love dimension. The West, in fact, seems to be generally unaware that the logos can be perceived nonconceptually, and hence that it can be experienced beyond the word. At the same time, this emphasis has allowed the West to understand the logos as the Word, as a pattern that can be read. It makes sense then that it was the West that developed the power of the word and of reason to its current heights.

11. It must be remarked that Christian thought conceived of Christ in terms of the logos, and sometimes referred to the Christ-logos as the pattern. Christianity included the notion that the logos is the creative matrix of existence, from the perspective that it was the first born of God, that is, the first dimension to emerge from the

absolute Father. Sufi thought developed a similar idea, linking the logos with the Muhammadan spirit, which was supposed to have existed before the creation of the world. Sufi thought also conceived of creation as some kind of a pattern impressed on an original material, or universal soul, by an original intellect, called "the Pen":

"*Aql-I-kul* is the form of Existence of God's knowledge. It is called *Qalam-i-Aala* (The Exalted Pen) in the language of the Sharia. All individual souls are contained in this; and are as embodiment of one soul, called Ruhi Azam (The Great Soul): and out of this individual souls manifest themselves. . . . Nafs-i-Kul is the breath of the Dhat and the embodiment of God's knowledge of Creation. All forms of Existence are impressed on it. It is also called Lawhi-Mahfuz (the Preserved Tablet). Whatever was or is to happen is, as it were, written down by the Exalted Pen on this Tablet." (Sirban Ikbal Ali Shah, *Islamic Sufism*, pp. 138–139.)

In other words, the pattern of all that exists and how it is going to change and develop is written on a tablet, pointing to another quality of this pattern. The pattern of the logos is composed of words, and can be read. In other words, this pattern can be discerned, that is, the universe can be understood. In fact, the first word in the Muhammadan revelation, that of the Qur'an, is God's word to Muhammad: "Read." This points to an uncanny similarity between the Greek interest in understanding the manifest world, as in the concepts of *nous* and logos, and that of the monotheistic revelations, as we have just described for Islamic thought, and as it is well known in Christianity in the view of Christ as the Word. We will pursue the notion of logos as word that can be read in the present chapter.

12. It is interesting to observe that while *reason* originally referred to the natural order of the flowing pattern of manifestation as basic knowledge or noesis we have come to know it through the dissociation of the basic triad only as the orderly flow of ordinary knowledge, or representational knowledge. Yet, this points to the correspondence between ordinary knowledge and basic knowledge. As we have seen in chapter 18, ordinary knowledge is a reflection of basic knowledge in the discursive mind. We see now the same correspondence in relation to reason; ordinary reason is a reflection of original or basic reason, which is the order of the flow of the pattern of the logos, in the discursive mind. By recognizing this correspondence we may be able to redeem reason by reconnecting it with its ground of dynamic presence.

13. Understanding the original and basic meaning of rationality, as the reasonable flow of reality, we can appreciate the ancient definition of man as the rational being, or the idea of the development of the human soul into a rational soul. The human being is a rational creature because human beings can discern the pattern of the logos. The developed and mature human soul is a rational soul who lives according to the harmonious pattern of the logos.

14. We may term this *basic thinking*, contrasting it with ordinary thinking. This may help us realize that ordinary thinking is a reflection of the flow of the logos. In other words, our thinking mind is a reflection of the logos, creating new thoughts and concepts similar to the creative logos. Such understanding may lead us to the recog-

nition that our thinking can arrive at objective thinking, where it is not only the rational flow of mental thoughts, but the orderly flow of insight. This is a possible realization in the inner journey, where our thinking mind becomes connected with its essential ground, and hence thinks not only rationally, but with the universal concepts of noetic forms. This is similar to Gurdjieff's concept of *objective mentation*, but also to Kuhlewind's *pure thinking*, which he sees as an approach to investigating spiritual realities and to realizing presence:

"Such pure thinking, if applied to other fields, could create the possibility of thinking with mathematical precision about spiritual realities. Thereby the activity of the Spirit in man would truly begin. Awareness of the Logos could be kindled by pure thinking about the light of consciousness. Perceiving the Logos, the spirit could assume its true function: to investigate the obstacles that stand in the way of realizing consciousness-in-the-present, and to develop methods for removing these." (George Kuhlewind, *Becoming Aware of the Logos*, p. 90.)

15. Ibn 'Arabi was one of the most well-known Sufis to popularize the idea that God possesses a universal imagination through which He creates the universe, as we see in the following passage from Corbin:

"We encounter the idea that the Godhead possesses the power of Imagination, and that by imagining the universe God created it; that he drew this universe from within Himself, from the eternal virtualities and potencies of His own being; that there exists between the universe of pure spirit and the sensible world an intermediate world which is the idea of 'Idea Images' as the Sufis put it, the world of 'supersensory sensibility,' of the subtle magical body, 'the world in which spirits are materialized and bodies spiritualized.'" (Henry Corbin, *Creative Imagination in the Sufism of Ibn 'Arabi*, p. 182.)

Such cosmic imagination has its counterpart in the individual soul, as the creative imagination of the soul. We must caution the reader that by imagination we do not mean the ordinary imagination, which is under the sway of the desires and ignorance of the ego-self. We mean a more basic imagination that is the embodiment of the logos's imagination in the soul. However, we can also observe that our ordinary imagination is a reflection of the basic imagination of the soul, a personalization of the power of the logos to create through imagining.

In the basic and creative imagination of the soul, given to it by the logos, each name or word possesses a quality, color, feeling, and image. Words, feelings, and images are interchangeable in this realm, which we experience more as a faculty of the heart than the mind.

We recognize in this capacity of creative and basic imagination one of the higher faculties of the soul. The soul possesses many higher faculties, with their corresponding lower or ordinary ones. We have discussed that of knowing, thinking, reason, imagination, and will discuss further in this chapter the faculties of speaking and expressing in general. All these higher faculties are important for spiritual practice, and eventually for the realized life. In practicing, however, we always have to begin with the normal and lower faculty, and by integrating it with presence, or immediacy of experience, it connects us to the higher faculty.

16. Philo was the first to unify the Greek concept of logos as reason and ordering principle with the biblical word of God, even though it is Christianity that made this central to its theology. He understood logos to be divine thinking and reason, and connected these with God's creative power. Reale writes about Philo's notion of logos:

"In these passages the divine Logos would seem to be the same as the activity of divine thinking, that is, with divine reasoning, or better, with the divine Nous, with that which is not distinct from God himself.

"But Philo immediately distinguishes the Logos from God and makes it almost a hypostasis, even calling it 'first born of the uncreated father,' 'second God,' 'image of God.' . . . The Logos of Philo expresses, in addition (and this is very important), the fundamental connotations of the biblical notion of "wisdom" as well as of the biblical 'word of God,' which is creative and productive word . . .

"In all these meanings the Logos signifies an incorporeal reality which is beyond the sensible, a transcendent. But because the sensible world is construed according to an intelligible model, that is, according to the Logos, and, in fact, by means of the instrumentality of the Logos, there is in this way, a Logos immanent to the sensible world, or better, an immanent aspect of the Logos, which is simply the actions, and hence, the various effects of the incorporeal Logos in the corporeal world. In this immanent sense, the Logos is the bond which holds the world together, the principle which conserves it, the rule which governs it, and so on." (Giovanni Reale, *A History of Ancient Philosophy: The Schools of the Imperial Age*, p. 192.)

17. Various traditions refer differently to this divine self-expression. Some Hindu thought conceived this self-expression as *lila*, the playful expression of joy. The Sufis think of it as a consequence of God's love to be known. The Kabbalah conceives of it as the expression of God's goodness and generous love: "God had absolutely no need to create the world. God Himself is absolute perfection, and He has no need for anything, even creation. Thus, to the best of our understanding, we can say that God created the universe for the purpose of bestowing good upon man." (Rabbi Aryeh Kaplan, *Inner Space*, p. 9.)

18. Philo might have been the first to connect the logos to speaking. He connected it to God that speaks and gives the biblical revelations, but also to the divine creative activity:

"It is well known that Philo's doctrine is a development of the Stoic idea of the divine logos or reason that underlies and fashions all things. For Philo, with his pronounced doctrine of a transcendent God . . ., the Logos becomes a mediator between the transcendent God and the world, and has both transcendent and immanent aspects. There is however another strand in Philo's doctrine of the Word that is much less remarked on. This develops not out of the idea of the divine reason, logos, but from the idea of God as one who speaks—*ho legon*—an idea of God without parallel in Greek thought. There is no difficulty in relating this to the idea just mentioned of the divine reason fashioning the universe, since, in the account of the creation in Genesis 1, creation is a result of God's speaking." (Andrew Louth, *The Origins of the Christian Mystical Tradition*, p. 27.)

It was, however, Christian thought that developed this idea of God as the speaker who creates everything through the Word: "Whoever can speak is not of this world. This world exists for and through the speaker, through the logos. Nothing is un-sayable; it is a logos-world." (George Kühlewind, *Becoming Aware of the Logos*, p. 19.)

In the same book, Kühlewind discusses the Christian concept of the logos in a way that reveals its mystical and experiential aspects, making it available to personal experience. He understands the primary cosmic function of the universal Christ or logos as that of creation, and how it is the dimension of divinity behind all creation. He also views creation as divine expression and self-revelation. He writes:

"The Logos is the first-born of creation (Col. 1.15; Rev. 3.14): nothing can have come into being before it. As soon as the Creator moves out of His immobility, steps out of His silence, with the first movement, the Logos is there; . . .

"The Creator gives up his immobility, his stillness, and points—through the Word—to creation. In pointing with the word, he shows himself, and is revealed. This is the primal revelation, creation itself. . . . The Father has no secrets from the Son, for the Creator himself becomes through the first creation the Logos." (Ibid., p. 26.)

Close to our view, Kuhlewind is also very clear that the logos is not simply an expression; that even though it creates by speaking, it is presence and being, not simply an expressive act: "The speaker is pure presence, in every sense. . . . In order to cognize the speaker, consciousness must be raised into the present . . . The revealer, the being who reveals itself in man through speaking, is the I-am-here: 'here' in the sense of presence. This is also his name: I-am-here." (Ibid., pp. 62–64.)

19. Kashmir Shaivism, for instance, considers Shakti to be the creative dimension of true nature, as the inseparable companion of Shiva, the absolute truth: "Sakti, however, is not separate from Siva, but is Siva Himself in His creative aspect. . . . Hahesvarananda puts it beautifully in his Maharthamanjar . . .: 'When He becomes intent to roll out the entire splendor of the Universe that is contained in His heart (in a germinal form), He is designated as Sakti." (Jaideva Singh, *The Doctrine of Recognition*, p. 10.)

Hence *shakti* is a concept similar to our concept of the logos. This teaching also considers *shakti* as the activating and transforming force in the inner journey. It is the inherent inner dynamism, responsible for change and transformation, including inner and spiritual development and evolution. This teaching believes that it is *shakti* that appears as *kundalini*, coiled at the base of the spine as a cobra of energy and vitality: "*Kundalini*: The creative power of Siva; A distinct *sakti* that lies folded up in three and half folds in *Muladhara*." (Jaideva Singh, *Siva Sutras*, p. 241.) When this *kundalini* awakens it brings about the inner transformation and development that takes the soul back to intimate union with Shiva, through the revelation of the mysteries of Being. This has become one of the central methods of Kashmir Shaivism and its many developments and offshoots, as in the case of the Siddha path, that was represented in the West by Baba Muktananda and now by Gurumai.

The monotheistic religions consider themselves to be revealed religions, revealed through the word of God. Judaism is based on the Torah, the words of God to Moses, who literally spoke to him and gave him the tablets with written inscriptions on them. Islam's central power is the Qur'an, God's word to Muhammad, carried to him by the archangel Gabriel. Christianity considers Jesus to be the logos become flesh and born within humanity. It does not only consider Christ to be the only born of God, but that he is the only way to the Father. In other words, it recognizes that it is the logos that can bring about the revelation of spiritual mysteries leading to redemption and liberation. This is a clear recognition that the logos is the dimension of revelation, which is solely responsible for any spiritual transformation. Such view is similar to that of Kashmir Shaivism above, and to most of the world wisdom traditions. The Christian view differs from the other traditions in its connection of the dimension of the logos to the person Jesus, and its belief that only through this person can one go to the Father.

20. Tibetan Buddhism has developed this way of communication to a fine art. It refers to it as *abhisheka*, meaning transmission, empowerment, or direct introduction. It delineates three types of communication: through words, mainly through the lama's speaking or the reading of scriptures; through symbols, mainly through rituals that include body postures, hand movements and the use of ritual objects and procedures; and mind-to-mind transmission, which is from the consciousness and presence of the lama to the consciousness of the disciple.

21. This is the reason traditional teachings consider certain languages to be sacred; that is, they closely correspond to the patterns of Reality, and their vocabulary and structure can connect us with its presence and truth. It would seem that a language fulfills such a function if it is based primarily on the universal concepts of the *nous*, and its grammar and syntax approximate the orderly flow of the logos. The most well-known example is Sanskrit, whose syllables are chanted as sacred names to invoke the timeless truths of true nature. Kashmir Shaivism includes a teaching based on language, where the process of manifestation of the world is seen in terms of letters and words. (Swami Lakshman Jee, *Kashmir Shaivism*, chapter 3.)

Another example is Hebrew; much of the teaching of Judaism, including the Kabbalah, is intertwined with the Hebrew alphabet. The Hebrew texts constantly expound the teachings of the Torah through a complex exegesis, where the words and letters carry implicit and symbolic as well as explicit meanings.

Arabic is another example, for it is the language of the Qur'an, Muhammad's primary miracle. Muhammad was very successful in transmitting his message within the span of his own life; this is rare in religious movements. A primary reason for his success was the language of the Qur'an, which was so aesthetically beautiful, so precise and faithful to the experience of his hearers, that many of them could not but have their minds open and their hearts melt, or their beliefs shaken, by merely hearing a recitation of a passage from the Qur'an. In fact, the Qur'an is considered to be Muhammad's primary miracle because its language is the most perfect usage of the Arabic language, a logos language used so skillfully that the minds and hearts of many of the contemporaries of Muhammad had to believe it must have come from God. Muhammad was illiterate; how other than miraculously could he have produced the most perfect manifestation of the Arabic language?

22. Kuhlewind based his understanding of the language structure of the world on Rudolf Steiner's anthroposophy. He writes about the alienation of language from the logos:

"The more we consider concepts as abstractions, the more they will seem to lack in being, compared to the concrete particular we perceive. This tendency is reinforced by the existential, 'being' character of perception, which contrasts sharply with the unreality of finished thoughts and concepts." (George Kuhlewind, *The Logos-Structure of the World*, p. 37.)

In other words, the more abstract our concepts become the more they become alienated from Being, which is the presence of the logos, the ground of language: "For the attentive observer the world will appear, in every phase of cognitive life, to be structured by the word, or Logos. Only an I-being has a 'world.' And I-beings have a world only because the world has the nature and structure of the word, the Logos, which in turn is accessible only to I-beings." (Ibid., p. 17.)

Language reflects the logos pattern of the world, because its original vocabulary is simply a demarcation of the word-concepts that appear as noetic forms, given to our perception and not invented by us. So it is true that language structures our world, as many linguists and philosophers have seen, but its structure has its origin in the structure of the world given to our perception. More precisely, the pattern of the logos is pre-given, and it possesses a richness of word-concepts, but these concepts are not demarcated in the logos. They appear as a continuity, forming some particular details of the pattern. A language demarcates some of these concepts, but another language may demarcate differently, at different junctures of the pattern, this way producing different concepts. Yet all of these concepts are actually pre-given, for they have always existed as part of the universal pattern. Kuhlewind puts it this way: "The system of concepts provided by language structures the unified, given perceptual world. The only concepts we know are those our language gives us. The systems of speaking and thinking are one and the same; in Humbold's words, we are in the 'energetic' phase of language development. In this phase languages do not simply label something that already exists; rather they demarcate and define the 'somethings.' Concepts indicate where 'something' ends, where its boundary is, for 'in the given there actually are no discrete entities, but everything is in continuous connection.'" (Ibid., pp. 56–57.)

He is very clear in the next passage, where he critiques the nominalists, that concepts originate from a pre-given reality: "The nominalists did not realize that even their own theory presupposed a primal language. The collective concepts, which they regarded as 'mere' names, presupposed wordless, 'nameless' concepts." (George Kuhlewind, *Becoming Aware of the Logos*, p. 67.) These wordless and nameless concepts are the noetic forms, or their ontological precursors, the prenoetic forms. Such critique also applies to the relativists and constructionists, for it demonstrates that Reality has its own structure, pre-given to our consciousness and mind.

23. We see at this point that the self-organizing properties of open systems simply express the optimizing dynamism and unfolding order of the logos. When such self-organization reaches a particular threshold it becomes biological life; when it reaches a further threshold it becomes conscious life; and when it reaches the threshold of consciously and knowingly integrating the timeless truths of true nature it becomes realized life. Therefore, life, consciousness, and realization are the inherent properties of the logos.

Such appreciation of the optimizing force and intelligence of the logos may help us understand its role in the inner journey, and why the wisdom traditions have seen it as the savior. The inner journey is basically the action of the optimizing intelligence that unfolds the experience of the soul toward maximization of her openness to and realization of her true nature. Such optimization can appear through the agency of *shakti* and its *kundalini*, grace and its love, guidance and its compassion, or any other force that the particular wisdom teaching employs, but they are all dynamic methods that utilize the wisdom of the logos.

24. Tarthang Tulku uses the term *Great Time* to refer to real time: "By opening ourselves up to 'time,' it can act and speak more freely through us. Our speech and gestures become totally irrepressible and spontaneous, welling up from 'time,' the dynamic center of our being. Everything we are and do becomes a direct and overtly faithful expression of the inner structure of 'time' itself." (Tarthang Tulku, *Time, Space and Knowledge*, p. 191.)

CHAPTER 21. THE ABSOLUTE AND EMPTINESS

1. Such a discovery is not easy, and normally requires a deep and sustained inquiry or practice of some kind. Made well known by Ramana Maharshi, the Vedantic practice of asking "Who am I?" is one such method. In the Diamond Approach, we use a more general inquiry into experience, and this inquiry will, at some point, reveal the witnessing background awareness. We explore the movement to the silent witnessing background in *Luminous Night's Journey*, chapters 2 and 3, and discuss some of the personal issues and situations that need to be understood. Such movement is made immeasurably easier if we are already familiar with the experience of the unfolding pattern of the logos. However, our discussion in chapter 3 of the above book is of the silent universal witness, which is not the full experience of the absolute, but the beginning of such experience. We do not discuss the full experience of the absolute until chapter 7 of the same book.

The movement from the flow of manifest experience to the unmanifest background is not the only route to the absolute. There are no set ways, and various teachings approach the absolute via different routes. We discuss alternative routes that use inquiry in *The Pearl Beyond Price*, chapter 38; *The Point of Existence*, chapter 41; and *Diamond Heart Book 5* (forthcoming).

2. This is a common teaching of many of the wisdom traditions. A clear example is the teaching of the great Sufi shaykh Ibn 'Arabi. In his study of Ibn 'Arabi's work, Izutsu writes: "From the particular viewpoint of the Divine self-manifestation (*tajalli*), . . . the Absolute in the state of unconditional transcendence is said to be at the level of 'unity' (*ahadiyah*). There is as yet no *tajalli*. *Tajalli* is only expected of it in the sense that it is to be the very source of *tajalli* which has not yet begun. And since there is actually no occurrence of *tajalli*, there is absolutely nothing recognizable here. . . . The stage of Unity is an eternal stillness. Not the slightest movement is there observable." (Toshihiko Izutsu, *A Comparative Study of Key Philosophical Concepts in Sufism and Taoism*, pp. 23–24.)

3. We find references to this luminous darkness in many of the wisdom traditions. Even though it is usually the Western teachings that refer to divine darkness, it is possible to find references to it in Eastern teachings, as in this Zen passage: "You are thoroughly lucid and transparent like a crystal. Subject and object, in and out, being and nonbeing are just one, and this very one ceases to be one any longer. Rinzai said, describing this state, 'The whole universe is sheer darkness.'" (Zenkei Shibayama, *Zen Comments on the Mumonkan*, p. 28.)

4. It is interesting that Kabbalah discusses the creation as involving a constriction (*tzimtzum*) of the light of the absolute, Ain Sof, as a process where the absolute vacates a spherical space for manifestation, as the next quote from the *Etz Chaim* indicates: "When it arose in His simple Will to create all universes, He constricted His infinite light, distancing it to the sides around a center point, leaving a vacated space in the middle of the light of Ein Sof . . . This space was perfectly spherical. . . . After this constriction took place . . . there was a place in which all things could be brought into existence (Atzilut)." (Aryeh Kaplan, *Inner Space*, p. 120.)

We do not necessarily share this notion of constriction, for in our understanding creation does not require it. The absolute simply manifests within itself all of creation, by manifesting a dimension out of itself that is coemergent with its vastness. Coemergence allows the absolute to be in its pristine perfection while everything appears within it. It would seem that the idea of *tzimtzum* is the Kabbalah's understanding of the biblical creation *ex nihilo*, just as the Nicene orthodoxy of Christianity understood it to mean that creation is separate from God. The Kabbalah's understanding has creation coming out of God, but through the intermediary of a spherical nothingness that is not exactly the absolute. Our view is that there is no intermediary necessary, and that the *nihilo* is simply a facet of the absolute, and not a normal nothingness.

5. Such experience is well known in Vedanta, as the experience of realization of this wisdom teaching. We find this clearly exemplified by the late Nisargadatta Maharaj,

who takes this experience to mean that the absolute is not aware of itself, but only of manifestation, as it unfolds. He understands the absolute to be pure awareness, or the source of awareness, but not aware of itself. See note 11 of chapter 16, for quotes from Nisargadatta Maharaj.

Yet, we think it is more accurate to view this experience of cessation as the focus on, or the absorption into, the absolute, which is not any particular content. Since there is no content to be aware of, and since the absolute is the darkness prior to light, we experience the exclusive focus on it as the absence of awareness and perception, as the experience of cessation. This is similar to the Buddhist view that cessation is a transitional experience of total absorption into emptiness.

6. Such experience demonstrates that in deep sleep the soul dives into the depths of her true nature, all the way to merging with the absolute darkness. Such absorption and annihilation into the source accounts for the rejuvenation that good sleep gives us, for the absolute is the primal source of energy. After sleep we tend not to experience the clarity and awakeness that we experience after the experience of cessation, because we wake up by going through the dream state, which brings back the mind and its content.

7. Here we see the truth of the biblical account of creation, that it is creation *ex nihilo*. Yet, our perception and understanding gives us a different interpretation than that of the Nicene council. The *nihilo* is not simply the nothing of ordinary knowledge, but the absence of presence that forms the absolute essence of all reality. It is the absolute nature of reality and, as we will see, the essence of God. This *nihilo* is absolute majesty and the greatest peace, the mysterious darkness that is the source of all creation. It is the father of the logos and the beginning and end of all creation.

8. Many of the wisdom traditions subscribe to this view of the absolute, and see this nonbeing as the last dimension that the soul needs to realize in her inner journey. One such tradition is Taoism, as shown in the following passage:

"At this last stage, the man is completely unified not with the ever changing 'ten thousand things'—as was the case when he was in the previous stage—but with the 'Mystery of Mysteries,' the ultimate metaphysical state of the Absolute, at which the latter has not yet come down to the sphere of universal Transmutation. The man is here so completely one with the Way that he has not even the consciousness of being one with the Way. The Way at this stage is not present as the Way in the consciousness of the man. And this is the case because there is no 'consciousness' at all anywhere, not even a trace of it. The 'oblivion' is complete. And the actualization of such perfect 'oblivion' is to be accounted for in reference to the metaphysical fact that the ultimate Absolute, the Way, is in its absolute absoluteness Something which one cannot call even 'something'. Hence the usual custom in oriental philosophies of referring to the Absolute as Nothing." (Toshihiko Izutsu, *A Comparative Study of Key Philosophical Concepts in Sufism and Taoism*, p. 346.)

9. From this discussion, we see that sensation is not necessarily of the body. Physical sensation is simply the reflection of the sense of presence that is the ground of our consciousness.

10. This is exactly the Buddha's teaching: what the individual takes himself to be is really nothing but a bundle of tendencies and qualities, at all levels of existence, held together for a span of time. And when we see through that, we realize emptiness as selflessness, *anatta*. So it seems that Buddha nature can be seen as the absence of nature, because there is no self or entity that is a buddha.

11. Such freedom and spontaneity will normally arouse one's fears of being inappropriate or making mistakes. But this simply demonstrates the remnants of inner conflicts, possibly some self-images or suppressed aggression. We then have the opportunity to see these limitations and understand them, which is necessary if we are going to integrate the realization of the absolute in daily life. Only when we have no more unconscious reasons to be afraid of spontaneity can we integrate such realization. But such realization will also require the integration of the understanding that true nature is pure intelligence and love, and that being it will only mean we will act with these undefiled qualities of Being.

We are not discussing the various issues and structures that we encounter in the inner journey as we discover and realize the absolute, but this does not mean they do not exist. We are simply focusing on exploring the absolute itself and how it affects our experience, but we need to remember that the issues and obscurations in the way of such realization are the deepest and the subtlest. The absolute challenges our deepest held beliefs and positions about ourselves and reality.

12. Emptiness is the traditional designation used generally by Buddhism. Emptiness is also referred to, in Buddhism, as selflessness. The emptiness of things is their ultimate selflessness, that they do not possess an essence that is ultimately self-existing. Buddhism, however, has many schools, with different interpretation of emptiness. The understanding we have been exploring is similar to that of the school called Prasangica Madhyamika, developed by Chandrakirti and others.

13. This is the teaching of the Hare Krishna school, which believes the ultimate is a personal Krishna who lives on some kind of a heavenly planet. The leader of this teaching writes as part of his commentary on the *Bhagavad Gita*: "Therefore, Krsna is the original Supreme Personality of Godhead, the Absolute Truth, the source of both Supersoul and the impersonal Brahman." (A. C. Bhaktivedenta Swami Prabhupada, *Bhagavad-Gita As It Is*, p. 18.) Because of this the realization of the impersonal *brahman* is simply the first step toward realization of the ultimate: "Brahman is the beginning of transcendental realization; Paramatma, the Supersoul, is the middle, the second stage of transcendental realization; and the Supreme Personality of Godhead is the ultimate realization of the Absolute Truth. Therefore, both Paramatma and the impersonal Brahman are within the Supreme Person." (Ibid., p. 225.)

This is because the *brahman*, which is similar to our notion of absolute, is considered to be an effulgence of Krishna, who is the absolute source: "Such mental speculators do not know that the Absolute Personality of Godhead is Krsna, that the impersonal Brahman is the glaring effulgence of His transcendental body, or that the Paramatma, the Supersoul, is His all-pervading plenary representation. Nor do they know that Krsna has His eternal form with its transcendental qualities of eternal bliss and knowledge. The dependent demigods and great sages imperfectly consider Him to be a powerful demigod, and they consider the Brahman effulgence to be the Absolute Truth." (A. C. Bhaktivedanta Swami Prabhupada, *Sri Isopanisad*, pp. 40–41.)

14. Dzogchen is one of the nondual teachings that recognize an absolute that is not nonbeing. However, it gives this absolute three facets, properties, or dimensions: essence, nature, and energy or manifestation. Energy or manifestation seems to refer to the logos creative dynamism; nature to the nonconceptual pure awareness, and essence to the nonbeingness of the absolute. Padmasambhava said:

> *It is certain that the nature of the mind is empty and without any foundation whatsoever.*
> *Your own mind is insubstantial like the empty sky.*
> *You should look at your own mind to see whether it is like that or not.*
> *Being without any view that decisively decides that it is empty,*
> *It is certain that self-originated primal awareness has been clear*
> *(and luminous) from the very beginning,*
> *Like the heart of the sun, which is itself self-originated.*
> *You should look at your own mind to see whether it is like that or not.*
> *It is certain that this primal awareness or gnosis, which is one's intrinsic awareness, is unceasing,*
> *Like the main channel of a river that flows unceasingly.*
> *You should look at your own mind to see whether it is like that or not.*
>
> JOHN M, REYNOLDS,
> Self-Liberation through Seeing with Naked Awareness, pp. 14–15

15. We saw in chapter 18, note 9, that some Sufis consider the absolute, the source of light, to be black light. Yet, this does not make it similar to the clear light of pure awareness, for it is a light prior to the light of awareness and vision. It is actually so mysterious that to call it light is simply an attempt to understand it through familiar categories, but it actually fails as an ultimate and final description if we think of it in terms of our familiar experience of light. However this does not contradict the Sufi perspective, which holds that we never actually see light, but always see its sources or its reflection. Even when we experience clear light we are actually experiencing the effect of light; namely, we experience in this case the clear, colorless, and transparent qualities of the medium, made visible by the light. And when we finally

experience light we see blackness, for there is no form or medium that is illuminated by it; we simply see it, the light that makes vision possible.

16. This is reminiscent of a similar situation in Buddhism, where the concepts of true nature and the expanse that manifests it are sometimes used interchangeably and sometimes not. The original expanse is referred to as *dharmadhatu*, and true nature as Buddha nature (sometimes *rigpa* or *shunyata*), two terms that are obviously intimately related but not identical.

17. Discussing the absolute, Nisargadatta described it thus: "By itself the light can only be compared to a solid, dense, rocklike, homogeneous and changeless mass of pure awareness, free from the mental patterns of name and shape." (Sri Nisargadatta Maharaj, *I Am That*, p. 34.)

18. In the experience of cessation the apprehending consciousness dissolves in the absolute. Subsequent experiences of consciousness apprehending the absolute nonbeing do not lead necessarily to annihilation, but to the mixing of the two. The apprehending consciousness becomes one with emptiness, resulting in the coemergence of being with nonbeing. The deepest coemergence is of the absolute dimension itself, the luminous black fullness of emptiness.

Some Tibetan Buddhist schools view the realization of Buddhahood similarly, as a consciousness that apprehends the absolute, which is complete emptiness. By apprehending the emptiness, it mixes with it and becomes an empty presence or empty awareness, the coemergence of presence and absence. In one of his teachings, the Dalai Lama makes a distinction between two absolutes, the nonaffirming emptiness and the affirming emptiness. The first is pure emptiness, the second is emptiness mixed with consciousness. He describes how a consciousness approaches emptiness and mixes with it, this way apprehending the nonaffirming negative: "According to the Ge-luk and other interpretations, during meditation only the absence of inherent existence is taken as the object of one's mode of apprehension, not anything else—just the mere negative of the inherent existence which is the object of negation. The practitioner seeks to remain in meditation without losing this object. A consciousness ascertaining this meaning must have the aspect of realizing a non-affirming negative, a negation which does not imply anything positive in its place."[Dalai Lama XIV, *Kindness, Clarity, and Insight*, pp. 214–215.)

Coemergence of mind and emptiness as the ultimate nature is common in Buddhism and not only in Tibetan Buddhism, as we see in the following passage from Zen: "When all the Buddhas manifest themselves in the world, they proclaim nothing but the One Mind. Thus, Gautama Buddha silently transmitted to Mahakasyapa the doctrine that the One Mind, which is the substance of all things, is co-extensive with the Void and fills the entire world of phenomena. . . . So full understanding can come to you only through an inexpressible mystery. The approach to it is called the Gateway of the Stillness beyond all activity." (John Blofeld, *The Zen Teaching of Huang Po*, p. 79.)

19. This understanding of the ultimate truth as extensionless, which makes all manifest forms actually one, an absolute identity, might be the reason behind the name some of the ancient Greek philosophers gave to the absolute: *the One*. Both Plato and Plotinus referred to the absolute as *the One*, and it is obvious that at least Plotinus was aware of the extensionless character of the One. Plotinus extolled the One's unity as "great beyond anything, great not in extension but in power, sizeless by its very greatness as even its immediate sequents are impartible not in mass but in might. We must therefore take the Unity as infinite not in measureless extension or numerable quantity but in fathomless depths of power." (Plotinus, *Enneads*, p. 542.)

20. The most famous mystic philosopher who arrived at this insight was Nagarjuna, the founder of one of the main schools of Mahayana Buddhism: Madhyamika, the Middle Way. His main point is that by *shunyata*, emptiness, the Buddha meant reality is ultimately indeterminate, that nothing positive can be said about it without our being able to prove it false. He basically disproved any position about emptiness that asserts or posits anything positive about it. The following is stanza 9 from his famous "Seventy Stanzas": "Because contaminated things arise in dependence on one another they do not exist inherently as permanent phenomena nor do they exist inherently as impermanent phenomena; neither as phenomena with self-nature nor without self-nature; neither as pure nor impure; neither as blissful nor as suffering. It is thus that the four distortions do not exist as qualities which inhere in phenomena, but rather are imputed to phenomena." (David Ross Komito, *Nagarjuna's "Seventy Stanzas,"* p. 112.)

The Taoist sage Chuang-tzu attempted to describe such mystery beyond being and nonbeing by the use of successive negations. Izutsu quotes him:

"In the same manner, (we begin by taking notice of the fact that) there is Being. (But the moment we recognize Being, our Reason goes further back and admits that) there is Non-Being (or Nothing). (But the moment we posit Non-Being we cannot but go further back and admit that) there has not been from the very beginning Non-Being. (The concept of No-[Non-Being] once established in this way, the Reason goes further back and admits that) there has been no 'there-having-been-no-Non-Being' (i.e., the negation of the negation of Non-Being, or No-[No Non-Being])." (Toshihiko Izutsu, *A Comparative Study of Key Philosophical Concepts in Sufism and Taoism*, p. 379.)

Some Sufis took a similar view, that the divine essence is unknowable because it is beyond any determination. The idea is that any positive determination becomes a delimitation, and the absolute is the unlimited and undelimited truth: "Those who think this way—'Abd al-Karim Jili is one of them—take the position that the absolutely ultimate stage of existence must be beyond even the condition of unconditionality and transcendence. And since existence at this stage is unconditional to such an extent that it is not delimited even by being unconditional, it cannot but be absolute Nothingness from the point of view of human cognition. It is in this sense called the *ghayb al-ghuyub*, the 'Mystery of Mysteries.'" (Toshihiko Izutsu, *Creation and the Timeless Order of Things*, pp. 87–88.)

21. We use theistic language here to illustrate a point, but we must remember that we do not make an absolute distinction between true nature and God. See chapter 23 for discussion of the relation between the two concepts.

22. Christian mystics called it the divine darkness, and Sufis the divine essence. (See chapter 18, notes 4, 8, 9, 12. See the same chapter also for a more detailed discussion of divine darkness.)

23. Plotinus put it this way: "Yet this absence of self-knowing, of self-intellection, does not comport ignorance; ignorance is of something outside—a knower ignorant of a knowable—but in the Solitary there is neither knowing nor anything unknown. Unity, self-present, it has no need of self-intellection: indeed this 'self-presence' were better left out, the more surely to preserve the unity; we must eliminate all knowing and all association, all intellection whether internal or external. It is not to be thought of as having but as being Intellection." (Plotinus, *Enneads*, p. 543.)

24. Ken Wilber, in his view of four quadrants, thought of consciousness as the dimension of depth, just as the physical world is the horizontal dimension. (Ken Wilber, *A Brief History of Everything*, chapter 5.)

25. This is the perspective of most schools of Hinduism, as in the case of Vedanta and yoga. The term for the absolute is the *parabrahman*, the transcendent self.

26. Zen symbolizes this final stage in its ox-herding pictures as that of the man in the market place, simple, ordinary, like everyone else, but totally settled and nonattached. We see the invisibility of this man's inner realization in the following Zen comment on this stage: "Inside my gate, a thousand sages do not know me. The beauty of my garden is invisible. Why should one search for the footprints of the patriarchs? I go to the market place with my wine bottle and return home with my staff. I visit the wineshop and the market, and everyone I look upon becomes enlightened." (Paul Reps, *Zen Flesh, Zen Bones*, p. 154.)

CHAPTER 22. THE JOURNEY OF DESCENT

1. Some traditional teachings believe that it is the destiny of some individuals to be stabilized at this station, where the realization of the absolute becomes the final realization, but that the destiny of others is to move on to other stations, as we will discuss further in the chapter. Some traditions, as that of Vedanta, believe the self-realization of the absolute is the final realization, and further stages are not contemplated. Other traditions, like the Sufi one, envisage further phases, conceptualized as further stations on the path but not as further or deeper dimensions of true nature.

2. Many of the wisdom traditions, especially the mystical teachings of the monotheistic religions, conceptualize this station as the surrender to God's will. They recog-

nize that the realization of union with God is easier than that of surrender to His will, and that the latter is a more profound and total surrender and realization. In the words of the Sufi master Qunawi: "If God now wants him to return to the World of the Visible in order to bring about the perfection of others, or himself (i.e., so that he may attain even higher stations of Perfection related to the Outward), or both together, man will return (to the Visible World) by undergoing a supra-formal composition after Opening (i.e., after having attained Union). This composition corresponds to his decomposition (which he underwent during his spiritual-ascent)." (Fakhruddin Iraqi, *Divine Flashes*, p. 164.)

3. This is one place in the understanding and wisdom in the Diamond Approach that is equivalent to the station of surrendering to God's will.

4. This is reminiscent of the Sufi holy saying: "I was a hidden treasure; I wanted to be known so I created the universe." This indicates not only that the whole of manifestation is a hidden treasure within the mysterious depths of the absolute, but that it is the manifestation of the divine being itself. The world, in other words, is a theophany.

5. This dimension gives credence to emanationism, the mystical metaphysical school of thought that views the process of manifestation or creation as emanation. This school considers the absolute to be absolutely transcendent to creation, for all creation is its emanation, and not its ontological truth. This contrasts with manifestationism, the school that views the process of creation as a manifestation within the absolute.

Our discussion in this chapter sheds light on the truth that emanationism tries to express, which is that the absolute is always transcendent to manifestation, an important truth that is sometimes overlooked in the nondual schools of manifestationism.

6. Many of the wisdom traditions use the metaphor of the sun and its light to refer to the relation of the absolute and manifest forms. The sun has been used to symbolize the absolute from ancient times, and this dimension clearly reveals how the absolute is actually the spiritual sun. The Sufis also refer to the absolute as the midnight sun, alluding to the darkness of its mystery.

We should not confuse this metaphor of the sun with the essential form of the sun. For one of the essential forms is that of the sun, as a radiant disc of light, of one color or another. Such essential form embodies the realization that we are the source of one thing or another: an insight, an idea, or creation.

7. This seems to be the realization of the well-known Indian Vedanta teacher Ramana Maharshi: "The Self is present in all perceptions as the perceiver. There are no objects to be seen when the 'I' is absent. For all these reasons it may undoubtedly be said that everything comes out of the Self and goes back to the Self." (Ramana Maharshi, *The Spiritual Teaching of Ramana Maharshi*, p. 32.)

8. It is possible to consider the virtual dimension to be the cusp demarcating the transition from ascent to descent. Hence, the absolute dimension will be the first dimension of descent. But the virtual dimension is not a manifest dimension at all, for it is simply the absolute in its absoluteness, before it becomes a dimension. Hence, we prefer to think of the absolute dimension as the cusp separating ascent and descent. It is the end of ascent and the beginning of descent.

9. This perception forms the core wisdom in the notion of chain of Being, common to many of the ancient wisdom traditions, including Neoplatonism, Kabbalah, Sufism, Kashmir Shaivism, and others. All of these wisdom teachings describe existence as composed of a hierarchy of planes of Being, originating in the absolute and ending in the physical universe. The teachings differ in their conceptualization of the chain of dimensions, their number, and so on, but all share the view that each succeeding dimension clothes the one more fundamental than it, but also contained by it.

The integrated dimension reveals the truth that the hierarchy in the chain of Being is not temporal or spatial, but ontological. It also reveals the truth that even though the planes of Being constitute a hierarchy they are all simultaneous and cooperative, all necessary for existence and experience. They are not stacked like bricks, but clothed one within the other. This dimension further reveals the usefulness of the view of the chain of Being.

10. It is interesting that some of the schools of Tibetan Buddhism think of the primordial condition as represented by the Adi Buddha, Samantabadhra in Tibetan. The Adi Buddha usually appears in iconography as a blue naked Buddha, while the primordial condition is frequently referred to as deep blue or blue black.

11. This is similar to the understanding of the *Heart Sutra* from the *Prajnaparamita*, one of the major texts of Mahayana Buddhism, that "form is emptiness, emptiness is form." However, the wisdom here is more specific, for it refers to the ground of reality as the coemergence of presence and absence, which is the same thing as a self-luminous emptiness. This is actually similar to what the Maha Ati of the Nyingma Tibetan school of Buddhism refers to as *dharmakaya rigpa*, the highest condition of *rigpa* or nondual presence.

12. This is reminiscent of the dawn clear light that some schools of Buddhism believe to herald the arising of Buddhahood. Clear light is seen to unite with emptiness through several stages until it arrives at the final stage, Buddha's enlightenment, characterized by the dawn clear light. This also corresponds with the fact that the Shakyamuni Buddha attained his enlightenment at dawn: "Eventually the yogi will attain enlightenment. As was the case with the meaning clear light, this enlightenment will be achieved at dawn, the symbol of the all empty clear light. . . . .

"With the total annihilation at dawn of the obscurations preventing omniscience, your mind of meaning clear light will become the resultant body of a buddha and your pure illusory body will become the resultant form body." (Geshe Kelsang Gyatso, *Clear Light of Bliss*, pp. 220–221.)

13. This is the major insight of the metaphysical school of manifestationism, which includes the major nondual teachings of mankind. The teachings of Ibn 'Arabi, the grand shaykh of the Sufis, as well as those of Dzogchen and Mahamudra, for example, fall within this view.

Yet, we see in our exploration of the quintessential dimension that the view of manifestation does not negate that of emanation, which has historically been seen as the opposite view. Manifestation basically shows that the emanating light never leaves the absolute, that emanation is simply self-lumination.

CHAPTER 23. REALITY

1. This understanding corresponds to some traditional nondual teachings. We see a similar view in Kashmir Shaivism, Dzogchen, Mahamudra, and some of the forms of Sufism and Kabbalah.

2. Quantum theory has shown us that physical objects appear so only due to our way of observing them, and that matter is fundamentally a field phenomenon, composed of quantum waves in vacuum. So the quantum field is the closest thing we know to a field of matter, but only some of the wave phenomena and not the whole field become observed as matter. In other words, there is no such thing as a continuous field of matter.

3. See *The History of God* by Karen Armstrong.

4. Sufism and Kabbalah do exactly that. Sufism, for example, thinks of God as two formless dimensions. There is the divine essence, and there is the divine being. The divine essence is the unmanifest essence of the divine being: the absolute and transcendent truth, which is inseparable from it. The divine being is the totality of Being with all of its dimensions, which Ibn 'Arabi believes the word *Allah* signifies. Chittick writes about Ibn 'Arabi's view: "God may be considered in respect of Himself, in which case He is referred to as the Essence, or in respect of His level, in which case He is referred to as the Divinity . . .

"Allah is called the 'all-comprehensive name,' which means that it designates every name and attribute of God. Hence, as we have seen, the 'Divine Presence'—that level of reality which pertains to the name Allah—includes the Essence, the attributes, and the acts." (William Chittick, *The Sufi Path of Knowledge*, p. 66.)

The Sufi term *divine essence* seems to refer to what we have been discussing as the *absolute*, and the *divine being* or *Allah* to what we have been referring to as *Being*. However, the Sufis think of God as personal, and not only impersonal. More accurately, the divine being can be personal or impersonal.

5. The notion of a personal God is most developed in the Western traditions, while the Eastern traditions have emphasized impersonal Being and true nature. Besides our discussion until this point in the present chapter, we see another element that may be crucial in this difference. Recognizing the soul's, and the logos's, quality of

life can help us understand this important difference between Western and Eastern thought. Eastern thought tends to emphasize pure consciousness in its spiritual view of Reality, much more so than Western thought. We see this in Buddhism, Taoism, and most parts of Hinduism, as in Vedanta and Kashmir Shaivism. As a result, spiritual completion becomes mostly the realization of true nature, the ultimate or absolute truth. True nature or absolute truth tends to be an impersonal ground, whose realization is independent of, and transcendent to, evolution and development: emptiness or Buddha nature in Buddhism, Tao in Taoism, Brahman in Vedanta, Shiva in Kashmir Shaivism. There is no emphasis on the property of life, for Being or for true nature. The ultimate is pure consciousness or awareness, beyond life, primordially perfect and complete. And even in the Eastern traditions that tend to be theistic, such as Shaivism, life is not usually referred to as an important characteristic of this ultimate truth.

This is quite in contrast to the Western spiritual traditions, especially the three prophetic religions. Life is an important quality of the ultimate, and hence this ultimate becomes God. God is characterized not only by consciousness and presence, but also by life. Islam gives God ninety-nine names, an important one being the living (*al-hay*), where *hayat* means life. The Sufis use this name, *al-hay*, as one of their main *dhikrs*, invocations, and it is important for the Sufi not only to not be of the world, but to also be in it. Jesus said not only that he was the truth, he said he was also the life. The closest that the Eastern teachings come to the quality of life is in the dynamism and creative manifestation. We see this in Dzogchen's view of energy, display, resonance or manifestation, as one of the three fundamental facets of the ultimate nondual truth, besides the facets of emptiness and clarity. Kashmir Shaivism emphasizes dynamism and creativity in the notion of Shakti, who is in eternal embrace with Shiva. However, Shakti is seen mostly as creative energy, and even though life is sometimes related to her, it is not emphasized.

It is possibly this quality of life that, at least in part, makes the monotheistic religions think of God as living and acting. The notion of God in the monotheistic religions is that there is a God who is alive, and part of God's aliveness is that God does things, is active. This is one reason why there is a tendency to anthropomorphize God: it is difficult to think of the living quality separate from the body. There is a tendency to believe God has a body because we associate life with the body.

When we see that life is an intrinsic property of the soul, which is the individualization of the logos, then we do not need to think of God in the form of the human body. When we recognize and understand the soul, we realize she doesn't need to have a form of the body, that she is fundamentally formless, yet still alive. To understand formless living presence, we realize God doesn't need to have a specific form, let alone an anthropomorphic one.

The appreciation of the property of life orients us not only toward dynamism, as a creative energy, but also toward unfoldment, evolution, and development. Because of this, we find it unsurprising that Western thought became interested in questions of development and evolution, how one thing leads to another in an organic process of growth. Eastern thought in general has not shown that much interest in looking at reality in terms of evolution, obviously not as much as Western thought has.

We might think that the East appreciates and understands self-organization and evolution, because it has appreciated dynamism and creativity, but these are not the same. Herbert Guenther, for example, uses the language of self-organizing autopoietic systems to describe elements of Dzogchen teaching and to point out the presence and usage of process thinking in this teaching. (See Herbert Guenther, *Matrix of Mystery* and *From Reductionism to Creativity*.) However, as far as we know there is no indication that Dzogchen emphasizes development and evolution. Evolution is not only process; it is more than process. In fact, the most important tenet of the Dzogchen view is that the true nondual state is primordially total and complete, and one only needs to recognize it. It eschews developmental and evolutionary paths, because it believes there is nothing to develop or evolve. Enlightenment is recognition and realization of nondual awareness, which is primordially and eternally perfect, the great perfection.

This difference of emphasis between Western and Eastern thought has actually had remarkable consequences, including the development of thought itself. Western mind tends to think of the notion of understanding, for instance, as evolving and maturing, where even the process of understanding itself is seen as an unfoldment, a gradual revelation. Understanding delves into experience, revealing increasing depths of its truth, until it finally arrives at the goal. Eastern thought generally thinks of understanding as recognition of truth, a one-step, or even multi-stepped process. It is not an increasing understanding, rather it is a penetration to the truth. It is process thinking, but not evolutionary thinking. Hence it tends not to be evolutionary and revelatory, but more of a recognition and discovery.

This general difference in emphasis is one of the main reasons that we consider our work, the Diamond Approach, to be an expression of the Western current of thought. (See *Spacecruiser Inquiry* for discussion of how understanding happens in the Diamond Approach.)

Another consequence and implication of the difference of emphasis on the property of life is that the East in general looks at human life differently than the West. For the East, enlightenment is basically a liberation from the cycle of life and death. It is usually seen as the end of reincarnation; the fully enlightened Buddha or *sadguru* does not come back after physical death, while all others have to come back until final enlightenment. This is different from the Western traditions, where spiritual realization is the fulfillment of life, the completion of life on Earth. Even Christianity, which has leaned more toward the rewards of the afterlife, sees spirituality as the fulfillment of life: Jesus promised to bring the kingdom of heaven down to earth.

This general difference in emphasis leads to a tremendous distinction that orients inner work differently, in terms of its ideals, methodology, and disciplines. All these develop differently. If our orientation is that we want to leave this life because it is basically a place of suffering, then out of compassion we practice and help ourselves and others to get the hell out of here. Actually Buddhism values life greatly, and frequently points to the preciousness of human life, but it is usually seen as precious because it is the best form of life for inner work and enlightenment, an enlightenment that finally transcends life and even leaves it happily. Life is valuable, but not for its own sake.

If our orientation is that we can fulfill life on earth, then out of love of life, truth, and humanity we practice to complete life on earth for ourselves and others. The East celebrates enlightenment as the release from life, while the West celebrates enlightenment as the fulfillment of life. That is why the ideal in the Kabbalah or Sufism is not the *arhat* or the *bodhisattva* of Buddhism, but the Perfect Man, who is the complete human being, the vice-regent of God on earth.

As we have said, it is only a matter of general emphasis, with many important exceptions, as clearly seen in Taoism, where life is appreciated in such a way that its prolongation becomes part of the tradition. This is contrasted with a lack of appreciation of life in Platonism and Stoicism, where life is generally seen as a preparation for death. As we saw in the first half of the book and in chapter 20, these are complementary orientations, depending on whether we take the side of conscious presence or the side of living presence, the side of essence or of soul. As we have already discussed, the two are actually coemergent and nondual, but can be differentiated. Yet it is important to remember that the differentiation of the ground of pure consciousness from the organism of living presence has resulted not only in differences, but in greater development of knowledge in both East and West. Where the East's knowledge of the ground is generally much more differentiated and developed than in the West, the West's knowledge of development, evolution, and individuation is generally more differentiated and developed.

6. We see no contradiction between the belief in a personal God and belief in impersonal Being, for both are valid expressions of true nature. We also see no reason to rate the two or put them in a hierarchy, as some of the ancient traditions do. We are referring to the comparative judgment in which the followers of many of the ancient traditions engage. For example, adherents of the monotheistic traditions commonly believe that their views are deeper and higher than those of the Eastern traditions, because the personal God is a higher reality than true nature or impersonal Being. Nontheistic practitioners often take the position that the belief in a personal God is naïve and limited, because impersonal Being obviously transcends any notions of God.

7. A good approximation to this unbounded and infinite pearl is Einstein's view of the universe as a boundless but finite universe. This is one of the solutions that his general theory of relativity gives for the size and shape of the universe. According to this particular solution the universe is an expanding four-dimensional sphere that possesses a finite diameter but has no end. This means that if we travel as far as possible in the universe to reach its end, we cannot reach it, but simply come back to where we started. Also this sphere does not exist in space, because it contains all space and time.

The macrocosm pearl is different because it does not have a size. However, it is reminiscent of one of the terms that Dzogchen gives to Reality: the "Great Thigle." *Thig-le* is the Tibetan term for drop. In his commentary on a Dzogchen text, Reynolds enumerates some of the names given to true nature: "Others call it *Tathagatagargha* or embryo of Buddhahood. Among the followers of the Tantras, some call it by the name of Mahamudra or Great Symbol . . . others call it the Unique Sphere (*thig-le nyag-gcig*) which is a Dzogchen term, or call it the *Dharmadatu* . . ." (John M. Reynolds, *Self-Liberation through Seeing with Naked Awareness*, p. 48.)

8. The microcosm pearl is the realization that corresponds to the Kabbalist and Sufi station of the complete, universal, or perfect man. The macrocosm is what the Sufis call the name of divinity: that is, Allah as comprising all dimensions of existence, which are planes of manifestation of absolute. And the microcosm pearl, termed the Perfect Man, is His vice-regent, created in His image. Ibn 'Arabi states it thus: "Here the Perfect Man is going to be explained. The presences that have been explained and the totality of the universes is encompassed and englobed in totality in Man. The Perfect Man is the possessor of the degree of unification; he is at the station of the Greatest Name (*al-ism-l'azam*). Just as the *ism-l'azam* collects and contains all the Names, in the same way the Perfect Man collects and contains within himself the universes of *mulk, malakut, jabarut,* and *lahut.*" (Ibn 'Arabi, *Kernel of the Kernel*, p. 13.)

9. The ancient traditions conceptualized this basic truth of existence differently. Buddhism sees it in the idea of the *bodhisattva* who diligently works toward the liberation of all sentient beings. The Kabbalah and Sufism see it in helping God in his work of bringing creation to completion and fruition, which means the realization of all its beings. The two points of view practically amount to the same thing, one with a theistic and the other with a nontheistic flavor. In both cases the human being becomes connected to something larger than himself, and becomes an expression of his true nature or divine source.

CHAPTER 24. SEPARATION OF SOUL, GOD, AND WORLD

1. Eastern thought tends to focus on the dichotomy of relative and absolute, contingent and ultimate, where the absolute or ultimate is isomorphic to the Western concept of God or Being, and the relative and contingent to cosmos or world. Soul or self is usually viewed as a distortion or contraction relating to the two primary concepts. Hinduism, in its various branches and varieties, considers the soul a mistaken or limited individualization of God/Being, and Buddhism tends to think of soul as illusory. (See appendixes A and B.) In other words, even though the triadic division is more Western than Eastern, it is not totally lacking in the East.

2. This has been the topic of studies for many years, but we mention one recent book, by Karen Armstrong, that explores how modernity and secularism developed in the West and the Middle East, within the context of the three monotheistic religions. It focuses on the rise of fundamentalism in these three religions in modern

times, as a consequence of an epistemological vacuum accompanying secularism. Armstrong attributes this to the rise of practical reason and logic, which she terms *logos*, as the dominant mode of thinking. This, she argues, has happened at the expense of *mythos*, related to religion and the fundamentals of existence, which she believes was always used side by side in the past with logos. She writes: "By the eighteenth century, however, the people of Europe and America had achieved such astonishing success in science and technology that they began to think that logos was the only means to truth and began to discount mythos as false and superstitious." (See Karen Armstrong, *The Battle for God*.)

3. Existential philosophy arose and developed mostly through this discovery and through the appreciation of modern angst and emptiness. Yet, this philosophy has not provided a way out, or a way of addressing the alienation that can truly heal it. It contends that existential "nausea" is the unavoidable lot of being human in modern times, and that the best we can do is to consciously acknowledge and embrace it. This is clear in Sartre's work, as well as that of Camus. Contemporary developments in Continental philosophy tend to go off on tangents arising from the basic existentialist insight, but no true and real attempt to find a living solution has arisen.

4. Ancient Western philosophy and religion can easily be seen as attempts to understand and appreciate the three elements of the triad and their interrelationships. This was often done explicitly, but any close study of the development of Western thought can easily discern the central importance of this triadic division of reality, as the interrelated study of *Deus*, *homo*, and *natura*.

It is not the subject matter of this book to study how the separation of the triad occurred, but many studies directly or indirectly address this development: for example Seyyed Hossein Nasr's *Knowledge and the Sacred*, and Arthur Koestler's *The SleepWalkers*. Nasr's is a clear discussion of the development of Western thought along these lines. His understanding and analysis is both deep and extensive. We generally agree with his discussion, but do not share his attitude of glorifying ancient times and finding our times lacking.

In Nasr's first chapter, he traces how knowledge dissociated into two diametrical types: Knowledge and its Desacralization. He agrees with many other scholars that Descartes acted as a central fulcrum for this development: "Descartes has been quite rightly called the father of modern philosophy for it is he more than his contemporaries, Spinoza and Leibniz, who epitomizes what lies at the heart of modern philosophy and even modern science, namely, the reduction of knowledge to the functioning of the individual reason cut off from the Intellect, in both its microcosmic and macrocosmic aspects." (Seyyed Hossein Nasr, *Knowledge and the Sacred*, p. 41.)

Descartes was pivotal in the dissociation of the original triad. Our era is in some sense the child of Descartes, who believed we can know our being only inferentially, through thinking. His famous "*cogito ergo sum*" is perhaps the ideal slogan for the split of the original triad. He separated consciousness from the world, where consciousness became subjectivity, and the world became dead matter that follows the laws of cause and effect, which are mapped mathematically. The soul became a self or subject separate from the world, studying it from a detached distance. The self as subjectivity became our modern notion of consciousness, so prevalent to this time that consciousness research is still seen as research of subjectivity. We have seen how far this is from the understanding of consciousness held by the wisdom traditions, and how it is a view that is bound to lead to collapsing the soul into a self. This way the world became also dissociated from God/Being.

Another pivotal figure in this dissociation is the work of Saint Thomas Aquinas, who emphasized the separation of faith from reason: "Accordingly, St Thomas, like Albert, made a sharp distinction between the two: faith came from revelation, and dealt with divine truths which were not accessible to reason; reason, on the other hand, had to start with what could be known through experience and demonstration." (Gordon Leff, *Medieval Thought: St Augustine to Ockham*, p. 215.) This illustrates how much of this dissociation occurred through the development of Christian thought.

We are not implying that ancient Western thought did not have what we now know as conceptual thinking, but rather that it recognized its roots in a deeper and more inclusive knowing, a knowing inseparable from Being. This is what Nasr called sapiential knowledge, and what the Greeks meant by *nous*, or intellect: "This means that *nous* and its derivatives have a quite different feel from our words, mind, intellect, intellection, etc. Our words suggest our reasoning, our thinking; *nous*, noesis, etc., suggest an almost intuitive grasp of reality.... *Nous*, then, is more like an organ of mystical union than anything suggested by our words 'mind' or 'intellect.' And yet *nous* does mean mind; noesis is a deeper, simpler, more contemplative form of thought, not something quite other than thinking." (Andrew Louth, *The Origins of the Christian Mystical Tradition*, p. xvi.) This view is similar to the understanding we have developed in chapters 4 and 18.

The dissociation developed most clearly in the Renaissance and the Age of Enlightenment, but became a well-established view through the positivist philosophy that became the ideological ground of modern physical science, as in the work of Auguste Comte and others.

5. There have appeared alternative attempts at explaining the dissociating development of Western thought. A recent example is *The Spell of the Sensuous: Perception and Language in a More-Than Human World*, by David Abram, in which he discusses this dissociation in the development of language and the alienation from ecological perception.

6. The Western mind regards truth as meaning, and hence meaningful within personal contexts. Truth is not only ultimate reality, but also how this reality is meaningful to persons and to personal life in the world. Hence, discriminating understanding, where the relationship of things are revealed, is necessary for West-

ern mind. This mind does not want to know such discriminating understanding only to move toward liberation, as in Eastern thought, but also because it appreciates and loves recognizing and seeing the particular details of truth. In Western thought, liberated life is the creative unfoldment of such meaning, not simply the transcendence of it. This particular logos has resulted in Western science and its technological advances. Science, as we know it, seeks to recognize the true properties and relationships of things we perceive because these are seen as inherently valuable and interesting, not because of any ulterior motives. The Western mind loves to discover, which is a passion independent from the need for gain. Without this openness there is no Western science.

7. Though many previous attempts to integrate science and religion differ from our own, some do overlap with our view. Ken Wilber, for example, attempts to preserve the integrity of both disciplines in *The Marriage of Sense and Soul: Integrating Science and Religion*.

8. The idea that humanity, and the universe as a whole, is evolving, is not a new one. A major thread running through much of the Kabbalah and Sufism, for example, is the view that humanity is evolving in a very slow process. Much of the work of these traditions is oriented toward global, not merely individual, evolution. Kabbalah actually takes the view that humanity's mission is to help God in evolving His creation.

9. Many currents of thought have recognized and described the emptiness and loss that results from such rapid destructuring and restructuring. However, these are usually pervaded by a view that does not take the fullness of human potential into consideration. Many take the position that there will be nothing left after destructuring, and conceptualize a featureless emptiness devoid of richness and personal uniqueness. Some use Buddhist philosophy to justify this position, envisioning the Buddhist concept of emptiness as identical to the emptiness they perceive arising upon destructuring.

This expresses an ignorance of the true condition of Reality, and fails to recognize that this featureless emptiness is a step on the way to true emptiness, but not it yet. Rather, it is a deficient emptiness that owes to the loss of culturally constructed mental structure. Buddhist emptiness does not nullify structure completely. It merely points to the mysterious ground underlying all perception and experience. It leaves the richness and color of our perceived world intact; in fact, it redeems it into a much more vivid but structured reality. This is usually expressed in the concept of the union of the ultimate truth and appearance, or that of the inseparability of emptiness and clarity, or the reality characterized by the five awarenesses of the Buddha. (See appendix B.)

References

Abram, David. *The Spell of the Sensuous: Perception and Language in a More-Than-Human World*. New York: Pantheon, 1996.
Al-Jili, Abd al-Karim. *Universal Man*. Trans. by Titus Burckhardt. English version by Angela Culme-Seymour. Lockerbie, UK: Beshara Publications, 1995.
Almaas, A. H. *Diamond Heart Book Five*. Berkeley, CA: Diamond Books, 1998.
———. *Diamond Heart Book Four: Indestructible Innocence*. Berkeley, CA: Diamond Books, 1997.
———. *Elixir of Enlightenment*. York Beach, ME: Samuel Weiser, 1984.
———. *Essence*. York Beach, ME: Samuel Weiser, 1986.
———. *Facets of Unity: The Enneagram of Holy Ideas*. Berkeley, CA: Diamond Books, 1998.
———. *Luminous Night's Journey*. Berkeley, CA: Diamond Books, 1995.
———. *The Pearl Beyond Price: Integration of Personality into Being: An Object Relations Approach*. Berkeley, CA: Diamond Books, 1988.
———. *The Point of Existence: Transformations of Narcissism into Self-Realization*. Berkeley, CA: Diamond Books, 1996.
———. *Spacecruiser Inquiry*. Boston: Shambhala Publications, 2002.
———. *The Void: A Psychodynamic Investigation of the Relationship between Mind and Space*. Berkeley, CA: Diamond Books, 1986.
Armstrong, A. H. *An Introduction to Ancient Philosophy*. Lanham, MD: Rowman and Littlefield, 1981.
Armstrong, Karen. *The Battle for God*. New York: Ballantine Books, 2000.
———. *A History of God: The 4,000-Year Quest for Judaism, Christianity, and Islam*. New York: Ballantine Books, 1994.
Aurobindo, Sri. *The Life Divine*, vols. 1 and 2. Pondicherry: All India Press, 1973.
Barasch, Marc Ian. *Healing Dreams: Exploring the Dreams That Can Transform Your Life*. New York: Riverhead, 2000.
Bass, Ellen, and Laura Davis. *The Courage to Heal: A Guide for Women Survivors of Child Sexual Abuse*. New York: HarperTrade, 1988.
Bataille, George. *Visions of Excess*. Minneapolis, MN: University of Minnesota Press, 1985.
Blanck, Gertrude, and Rubin Blanck. *Ego Psychology II: Psychoanalytic Developmental Psychology*. New York: Columbia University Press, 1979.

———. *Ego Psychology, Theory, and Practice*. New York: Columbia University Press, 1974.

Blofeld, John. *The Zen Teaching of Huang Po: On the Transmission of Mind*. New York: Grove Press, 1959.

Boadella, David. *Embryology in Therapy: Collected Papers from Energy and Character*. Rodden, UK: Abbotsbury Publications, 1984.

———. *Lifestreams: An Introduction to Biosynthesis*. London: Routledge & Kegan Paul, 1987.

———. *William Reich: The Evolution of His Work*. London: Vision Press, 1973.

Bohm, David. *Wholeness and the Implicate Order*. New York: Routledge & Kegan Paul, 1994.

Campbell, Don. *The Mozart Effect: Tapping the Power of Music to Heal the Body, Strengthen the Mind and Unlock the Creative Spirit*. New York: Avon, 1997.

Cecil, Robert, Richard Rieu, and David Wade (eds.). *The King's Son: Reading in the Traditional Psychologies and Contemporary Thought on Man*. London, United Kingdom: Octagon Press, 1980.

———. *The Sufi Path of Knowledge: Ibn Al-Arabi's Metaphysics of Imagination*. Albany: State University of New York Press, 1989.

Chittick, William C. *The Sufi Path of Love: The Spiritual Teachings of Rumi*. Albany: State University of New York Press, 1984.

Chödrön, Pema. *Noble Heart: A Self-Guided Retreat on Befriending Your Obstacles*. Audio Cassette. Boulder, CO: Sounds True, 1998.

Chopra, Deepak. *Quantum Healing: Exploring the Frontiers of Mind/Body Medicine*. New York: Bantam, 1990.

Cleary, Thomas (trans.). *Shobogenzo: Zen Essays by Dogen*. Honolulu: University of Hawaii Press, 1986.

———. *Zen Essence: The Science of Freedom*. Boston: Shambhala Publications, 1990.

Corbin, Henry. *Creative Imagination in the Sufism of Ibn 'Arabi*. Princeton, NJ: Princeton University Press, 1969.

———. *The Man of Light in Iranian Sufism*. New York: Omega Publications, 1971.

Cornford, F. M. *From Religion to Philosophy: A Study in the Origins of Western Speculation*. New York: Harper, 1965.

Cortright, Brant. *Psychotherapy and Spirit: Theory and Practice in Transpersonal Psychotheraphy*. Albany: State University of New York Press, 1997.

Csikszentmihalyi, Mihalyi. *Flow: The Psychology of Optimal Experience*. New York: Harper & Row, 1990.

Dalai Lama XIV. *Kindness, Clarity, and Insight*. Trans. and ed. by Jeffrey Hopkins. Ithaca, NY: Snow Lion Publications, 1984.

———. *An Open Heart: Practicing Compassion in Everyday Life*. New York: Little Brown & Company, 2001.

Davis, Madeleine, and David Wallridge. *Boundary and Space: An Introduction to the Work of D. W. Winnicott*. Harmondsworth: Penguin, 1983.

Dowman, Keith. *The Flight of the Garuda Dzogchen Teachings*. Somerville, MA: Wisdom Publications.

Dunn, Jean (ed.). *Prior to Consciousness: Talks with Sri Nisargadatta Maharaj.* Durham, NC: Acorn Press, 1997.

Eliade, Mircea. *Yoga: Immortality and Freedom.* Princeton, NJ: Princeton University Press, 1970.

Fairbairn, W. Ronald. *Psychoanalytic Studies of the Personality.* London: Tavistock Publications/Routledge & Kegan Paul, 1966.

Geschwind, N. "Disconnection Syndromes in Animals and Man." *Brain* 88 (1965): 237–294, 585–644.

Gibson, J. J., *The Ecological Approach to Visual Perception.* Boston: Houghton Mifflin. 1979.

Govinda, Lama Anagarika. *Foundations of Tibetan Mysticism.* London, UK: Rider and Company, 1973.

Greenberg, Jay R., and Stephen A. Mitchell. *Object Relations in Psychoanalytic Theory.* Cambridge: Harvard University Press, 1983.

Gregory of Nyssa. *The Life of Moses.* New York: Paulist Press, 1978.

Grof, Stanislov. *The Adventure of Self-Discovery.* Albany: State University of New York Press, 1988.

———. *Realms of the Human Unconscious: Observations from LSD Research.* New York: E. P. Dutton, 1976.

Grube, G. M. A. *Plato's Thought.* Boston: Beacon Press, 1958.

Gruber, Howard E., and J. Jacques Voneche (eds). *The Essential Piaget: An Interpretive Reference and Guide.* New York: Basic Books, 1977.

Guenther, Herbert V. *From Reductionism to Creativity: Dzogschen and the New Sciences of Mind.* Boston: Shambhala Publications, 1989.

———. *Matrix of Mystery: Scientific and Humanistic Aspects of Dzogschen Thought.* Boulder, CO: Shambhala Publications, 1984.

———. *The Tantric View of Life.* Boulder, CO: Shambhala Publications, 1976.

Guenther, Herbert V., and Leslie S. Kawamura. *Mind in Buddhist Psychology: A Translation of YeShes rGyal-Mtshan's "The Necklace of Clear Understanding."* Berkeley, CA: Dharma Publishing, 1975.

Guzeldere, Guven. "Problems of Consciousness: A Perspective on Contemporary Issues, Current Debates." *Journal of Consciousness Studies* 2, no. 2 (1995): 112–143.

Gyaltsen, Shardza Tashi. *Heart Drops of the Dharmakaya: Dzogchen Practice of the Bon Tradition.* Trans. by Lopojn Tenzin Namdak. Ithaca, NY: Snow Lion Publications, 1993.

Gyatso, Geshe Kelsan. *Clear Light of Bliss: The Practice of Mahamudra in Vajrayana Buddhism.* London: Tharpa, 1995.

Hadot, Pierre. *Plotinus or the Simplicity of Vision.* Chicago: University of Chicago Press, 1998.

Hartmann, Heinz. *Ego Psychology and the Problem of Adaptation.* New York: International Universities Press, 1958.

Hartmann, Otto. *Dynamische Morphologie.* Franfurt: Klostermann, 1950.

Heidegger, Martin. *On Time and Being.* New York: Harper & Row, 1972.

Hillman, James. *Re-visioning Psychology*. New York: Harper & Row, 1975.
Hsing-hsiu. *Book of Serenity: One Hundred Zen Dialogues*. Trans. by Thomas Cleary. Boston: Shambhala Publications, 1998.
Hunt, Harry. *On the Nature of Consciousness: Cognitive, Phenomenological, and Transpersonal Perspectives*. New Haven, CT: Yale University Press, 1995.
Ibn 'Arabi, Muhyiddin. *Kernel of the Kernel*. Translated by Bulent Rauf. Lockerbie, UK: Beshara Publications, 1981.
———. *The Wisdom of the Prophets*. Translated from Arabic to French by Titus Burkhardt. Translated from French to English by Angela Culme-Seymour. Lockerbie, UK: Beshara Publications, 1975.
Iraqi, Fakhruddin. *Divine Flashes*. New York: Paulist Press, 1982.
Islam, Shahidul. *Panic Attacks and Phobias: How the Chemical Imbalance in the Brain Is Affecting Our Mind and Body*. New York: Vantage Press, 1993.
Izutsu, Toshihiko. *A Comparative Study of Key Philosophical Concepts in Sufism and Taoism*. Berkeley: University of California Press, 1984.
———. *Creation and the Timeless Order of Things*. Ashland, OR: White Cloud Press, 1994.
Jacobson, Edith. *The Self and the Object World*. New York: International Universities Press, 1964.
James, W. *The Principles of Psychology*. New York: Dover, 1890.
Jantsch, Erich. *The Self-Organizing Universe: Scientific and Human Implications of the Emerging Paradigm of Evolution*. Saint Louis, MO: Elsevier Science & Technology Books, 1980.
Jee, Swami Lakshman. *Kashmir Shaivism: The Secret Supreme*. Albany: State University of New York Press, 1988.
Jensen, Martin T. *The Successful Treatment of Brain Chemical Imbalance*. Dubuque, IA: Kendall/Hunt Publishing, 1995.
John of the Cross, Saint. *Dark Night of the Soul*. Trans. and ed. by E. Allison Peers. New York: Doubleday, 1990.
Johnston, William (trans.). *The Cloud of Unknowning*. New York: Doubleday Publishing, 1973.
Kant, Immanuel. *Critique of Pure Reason*. Translated by F. Max Müller. New York: Doubleday & Company, 1966.
Kaplan, Rabbi Aryeh. *Inner Space: Introduction to Kabbalah, Meditation, and Prophecy*. Jerusalem: Moznaim, 1991.
Kernberg, Otto F. *Object Relations Theory and Clinical Psychoanalysis*. Northvale, NJ: Jason Aronson Publishers, 1990.
Khan, Hazrat Inayat. *The Soul: Whence and Whither*. New York: Sufi Order Publications, 1977.
Koestler, Arthur. *The SleepWalkers: A History of Man's Changing Vision of the Universe*. New York: Macmillan, 1959.
Kohut, Heinz. *Analysis of the Self*. New York: International University Press, 1971.
———. *Restoration of the Self*. New York: International University Press, 1977.
Komito, David Ross. *Nagarjuna's "Seventy Stanzas": A Buddhist Psychology of Emptiness*. Ithaca, NY: Snow Lion Publications, 1999.

Konner, Melvin. *The Tangled Wing: Biological Constraints on the Human Spirit*. New York, NY: Henry Holt, 1982.

Kühlewind, Georg. *Becoming Aware of the Logos: The Way of St. John the Evangelist*. Great Barrington, MA: Lindisfarne Books, 1985.

———. *The Logos-Structure of the World: Language as a Model of Reality*. Great Barrington, MA: Lindisfarne Books, 1986.

Kumin, Ivri. *Pre-Object Relatedness*. New York: Guilford Press, 1995.

Laing, R. D. *The Facets of Life*. New York: Allen Lane, 1976.

———. *The Voice of Experience*. New York: Pantheon Books, 1982.

Lake, Frank. *Studies in Constricted Confusion*. Nottingham: Clinical Theology Association, 1981.

Lax, Ruth F., Sheldon Bach, and Alexis Burland (eds.). *Self and Object Constancy: Clinical and Theoretical Perspectives*. New York: Guilford Press, 1986.

Leff, Gordon. *Medieval Thought: St. Augustine to Ockham*. Baltimore: Penguin Books, 1962.

Liley, A. W. "The Fetus as a Personality." *Australia & New Zealand Journal of Psychiatry* 6 (1972): 99–105.

Longchenpa. *You Are the Eyes of the World*. Ithaca, NY: Snow Lion Publications, 2000.

Louth, Andrew. *The Origins of the Christian Mystical Tradition: From Plato to Denys*. Oxford: Clarendon Press, 1983.

Maharaj, Sri Nisargadatta. *I Am That*. Durham, NC: Acorn Press, 1985.

Mahler, Margaret S.; Pine, Fred; Bergman, Anni. *The Psychological Birth of the Human Infant*. New York: Basic Books, 1975.

Manjusrimitra. *Primordial Experience*. Shambhala.

Maturana, Humberto R. *Biology of Cognition*. Report BCL 9.0. Urbana, IL: Biological Computer Laboratory, University of Illinois, 1970.

Maturana, Humberto R., and Francisco Varela. *Autopoietic Systems*. Report BCL 9.4. Urbana, IL.: Biological Computer Laboratory, University of Illinois, 1975.

Meher Baba. *The Everything and the Nothing*. Myrtle Beach, SC: Sheriar Press, 1989.

Meltzoff, A. N. "Perception, Action and Cognition in Early Infancy." *Annals of Pedatrics* 32: 63–77.

Mitchell, Stephen A. *Hope and Dread in Psychoanalysis*. New York: BasicBooks, 1993.

Moody, Raymond. *Life after Life*. Atlanta: Mockingbird Books, 1975.

Moore, Thomas. *Care of the Soul*. New York: Harper Perennial, 1992.

Monroe, Robert A. *Journeys Out of the Body*. New York: Doubleday, 1971.

Mott, Francis, *Biosynthesis*. Philadelphia: David McKay, 1948.

———. *Nature of the Self*. London: Wingate, 1959.

Namgyal, Takpo Tashi. *Mahamudra: The Quintessence of Mind and Meditation*. Boston: Shambhala Publications, 2001.

Narasimha Swami, B. V. *Self-Realization: The Life and Teachings of Sri Ramana Maharshi*. Tiruvannamalai: Sri Ramanasramam, 1985.

Nasr, Seyyed Hossein. *Knowledge and the Sacred*. Albany: State University of New York Press, 1989.

Neumaier-Dargyay, E. K. *The Sovereign All-Creating Mind: The Motherly Buddha*. A

Translation of the Kun Byed Rgyal Po'I Mdo. Albany: State University of New York Press, 1992.

Ni, Hua-Ching (trans.). *The Complete Works of Lao Tsu*. Santa Monica, CA: Sevenstar Communications, 1979.

Penrose, Roger. *The Emperor's New Mind*. New York: Oxford University Press, 1990.

———. *Shadows of the Mind: A Search for the Missing Science of Consciousness*. New York: Oxford University Press, 1990.

Prabhupada, Swami A. C. Bhaktivedanta. *Bhagavad-Gita As It Is*. Los Angeles: Bhaktivedanta Book Trust, 1990.

———. *Sri Isopanisad*. Los Angeles: Bhaktivedanta Book Trust, 1993.

Plato. *Republic*. Trans. by Desmond Lee. New York: Penguin Classics, 1955.

Plotinus. *Enneads*. Trans. by Stephen MacKenna. New York: Penguin Classics, 1991.

Pribram, Karl. *Brain and Perception: Holonomy and Structure in Figural Processing*. Hillsdale, NJ: Lawrence Erlbaum Associates, 1991.

Prigogine, Ilya. "Irreversibility as a Symmetry Breaking Factor." *Nature* 248 (1973): 67–71.

Prigogine, Ilya, Gregoire Nicolis, and Agnes Babloyantz. "Thermodynamics of Evolution." *Physics Today* 25 (1970): 23–28 and 38–44.

Ramana Maharshi. *The Spiritual Teaching of Ramana Maharshi*. Boston: Shambhala Publications, 1988.

Reale, Giovanni. *A History of Ancient Philosophy*. Vol. 1: *From the Origins to Socrates*. Albany: State University of New York Press, 1990.

———. *A History of Ancient Philosophy*. Vol. 2: *Plato and Aristotle*. Albany: State University of New York Press, 1991.

———. *A History of Ancient Philosophy*. Vol. 3: *The Systems of the Hellenistic Age*. Albany: State University of New York Press, 1990.

———. *A History of Ancient Philosophy*. Vol. 4: *The Schools of the Imperial Age*. Albany: State University of New York Press, 1990.

Reich, Wilhelm, M.D. *Character Analysis*. New York: Noonday Press, 1961.

———. *Selected Writings*. New York: Noonday Press, 1969.

Reps, Paul (ed.). *Zen Flesh, Zen Bones*. New York: Anchor Books, 1989.

Reynolds, John Myerdhin. *Self-Liberation through Seeing with Naked Awareness: An Introduction to the Nature of One's Own Mind in the Tibetan Dzogchen Tradition*. Barrytown, NY: Station Hill Press, 1989.

Ring, Kenneth. *Life at Death: A Scientific Investigation of Near-Death Experiences*. New York: Coward, McCann, and Geoghegan, 1980.

Rudolph, Kurt. *Gnosis: The Nature and History of Gnosticism*. San Francisco: HarperSanFrancisco, 1987.

Sabom, Michael B. *Recollections of Death: A Medical Investigation*. New York: Harper & Row, 1982.

Saraswati, Swami Yogeshwaranand. *Science of Soul: A Treatise on Higher Yoga*. New Delhi: Yoga Niketan Trust, 1987.

Schaya, Leo. *The Universal Meaning of the Kabbalah*. Baltimore: Penguin, 1973.

Shah, Idries. *A Perfumed Scorpion*. New York: Harper & Row, 1981.

———. *The Sufis*. New York: Anchor Books/Doubleday, 1971.
———. *Tales of the Dervishes*. New York: Dutton/Plume, 1970.
Shah, Sirdar Ikbal Ali. *Islamic Sufism*. New York: Samuel Weiser, 1971.
Shibayama, Zenkei. *Zen Comments on the Mumonkan*. San Francisco: HarperSanFrancisco, 1984.
Singh, Jaideva. *The Doctrine of Recognition*. Delhi: Motilal Banarsidass, 1998.
———. *Siva Sutras: The Yoga of Supreme Identity*. Delhi: Motilal Banarsidass, 2000.
———. *The Yoga of Vibration and Divine Pulsation*. Delhi: Motilal Banarsidass, 2000.
Spencer, Sidney. *Mysticism in World Religion*. New York: Peter Smith Publishing, 1969.
Sperry, Roger. "In Defense of Mentalism and Emergent Interaction." *Journal of Mind and Behavior* 12 (1987): pp. 221–246.
———. "Structure and Significance of the Consciousness Revolution." *Journal of Mind and Behavior* 8 (1987): pp. 37–66.
Stacey, W. David. *The Pauline View of Man in Relation to Its Judaic and Hellenistic Background*. New York: St. Martin's Press, 1956.
Stern, Daniel N. *The Interpersonal World of the Infant: A View from Psychoanalysis and Developmental Psychology*. New York: Basic Books, 1985.
Suhrawardi, Shahab-Ud-Din. *The Awarif U'l-Ma'arif*. Translated by H. Wilberforce Clarke. Delhi: Taj Company, 1984.
Suzuki, D. T. *Zen Buddhism: Selected Writings*. New York: Anchor Books, 1956.
Tanahashi, Kazuaki (ed.). *Moon in a Dewdrop: Writings of Zen Master Dogen*. New York: North Point Press, 1995.
Taylor, Mark (ed.). *Deconstruction in Context*. Chicago, IL: University of Chicago Press, 1986.
Thondup, Tulku. *Buddha Mind*. Ithaca, NY: Snow Lion Publications, 1989.
Thurman, Robert. *The Central Philosophy of Tibet: A Study and Translation of Jey Tsong Khapa's Essence of True Eloquence*. Princeton, NJ: Princeton University Press, 1991.
Tillich, Paul. *A History of Christian Thought*. New York: Simon & Schuster. 1968.
Tulku, Tarthang. *Dynamics of Time and Space: Transcending Limits of Knowledge*. Berkeley, CA: Dharma Publishing, 1994.
———. *Time, Space and Knowledge: A New Vision of Reality*. Berkeley, CA: Dharma Publishing, 1977.
Wangyal, Tenzin. *Wonders of the Natural Mind*. Ithaca, NY: Snow Lion Publications, 2000.
Washburn, Michael. *The Ego and the Dynamic Ground. A Transpersonal Theory of Human Development*. Albany: State University of New York Press, 1995.
Weiss, Frederick (ed.). *Hegel: The Essential Writings*. New York: Harper & Row, 1974.
Wharf, Benjamin. *Language, Thought, and Reality*. Cambridge, MA: MIT Press, 1956.
Wilber, Ken. *A Brief History of Everything*. Boston: Shambhala Publications, 1996.
———. *The Eye of Spirit*. Boston: Shambhala Publications, 1997.
———. *The Marriage of Sense and Soul: Integrating Science and Religion*. New York: Broadway Books, 1999.

———. *Sex, Ecology, Spirituality*. Boston: Shambhala Publications, 1995.

Winnicott, D.W. *The Maturational Processes and the Facilitating Environment*. London: Karnac Books, 1990.

Yasutani, Hakuun. *Flowers Fall: A Commentary on Dogen's Genjokoan*. Trans. by Paul Jaffe. Boston: Shambhala Publications, 1996.

Index

abandonment, 159, 170, 285, 295
absence, 396–397, 435–436
absolute, 376–409. *See also* brahman (absolute)
   freedom vehicle and, 455–458
   in journey of descent, 413–440
   relative absolutism, 570–571, 574
   in Sufism, 525–526, 575–576, 682–683n15, 686n4, 686n6
abstract imaginal processes (Hunt), 532–534
abstraction, 59, 61, 177, 317, 677n22
abuse, 96, 157, 159, 170–172, 227
accusing self, 523–524
action
   agent of, 452, 591n10
   of ego-self, 272
   of essential nature, 98–99, 296
   no personal action, 335–336, 340–341, 360–362, 380–381
   soul's malleability and, 95
actualization, 75–93, 101, 115, 162–163
Adam (biblical), 518–519, 613n1, 621n8
addiction, 173
Adi Buddha, 687n10
adolescence, 153
adults and adulthood
   abstract imaginal processes, 532–534
   aliveness in, 121–123
   early structures and, 95, 202, 212, 618n1
   ego development and, 153, 156, 197, 539, 658n14
   essential aspects and, 543

afterlife, 9, 690n5. *See also* death
aggression, 142–143, 147, 203–206, 227, 288
ahamkara (sense of egoism), 495, 496, 498–500, 502
alayavijnana (eighth consciousness), 507–510, 609n6
alienation, 5–8, 18, 100–101, 165–166
aliveness, 121–128, 359
aloneness, 231, 422
anatman (absence of self), 505, 584n1
angelic soul, 151–152, 225, 520–525, 549
angels, 601n6, 613n1, 643n9, 652n7
anger, 209–210, 227–228
animal forms, 92, 94, 146–148, 206–207
animal soul, 141–150
   Aristotle's view, 487
   domination by, 288
   soul development and, 152, 155, 174–176, 185–186, 203–204, 547–549
   in Sufism, 520–522
annihilation, 354–355, 384, 401
antahkarana (psychic apparatus), 496–499, 502, 503–504
anthropomorphism, 356, 581, 643n10, 689n5
anthroposophy, 677n22
anutarayoga, 643n11
anxiety, 172–173, 281
aql (intellect), 517
Aquinas, Saint Thomas, 694n4
Aristotle, 486–487, 629n18
Arius, 593n6
Armstrong, Karen, 692–693n2

706 Index

artificial intelligence, 117–118, 563, 587n8, 592n1, 598n8
artistic creativity, 19, 81, 532, 606n1
asceticism, 616n2
aspects, 139, 279, 286, 434–435. *See also* essential aspects
Assagioli, Robert, 6
Athanasius of Alexandria, 492, 593n6
atman (self), 495–500, 583–584n1, 588n12
attachment, 186–187, 237, 287–289, 294, 337–338, 502
Augustine of Hippo, 493
Aurobindo, Sri, 500, 548, 615n1
autonomy, 104–107, 282, 344, 452, 485
autopoiesis, 556–560
awareness. *See also* nonconceptual (pure) awareness; self-realization
  consciousness and, 596n11
  in dimensions of true nature, 296, 299, 306–307, 380
  in Eastern traditions, 501–503, 513–514
  of ego structures, 188–190
  environmental, 473
  in infants, 537
  reason and, 586n6
  repression and, 171, 227
  self-awareness, 20, 257, 387
  soul's, 15–23, 28, 33, 45–62
  in soul's inner journey, 242–243, 261–262

Baba Muktananda, 676n19
balance, 172–173, 244
Bataille, George, 598n7
Battle for God, The (Armstrong), 692–693n2
the Beast, 286, 651n5, 652n7
Being, 292–307. *See also* divine love; God; logos; nonconceptual (pure) awareness; pure (nondifferentiated) presence
  absolute and, 389, 401, 406
  actualization and, 447–456
  concept of, 308–309, 318–319, 327
  dimensions of, 225–226, 264–266, 348–362
  and doing, 335–336
  in early development, 159–161, 638n8
  great chain of, 551–554
  guidance of, 373
  Heidegger's view, 604n6
  and knowledge, 307–322, 365
  nonbeing, 258–261, 334, 384, 392, 430
  oneness of, 301–302, 338–340, 350–351, 381, 429–430
  pure, 261, 296–298
  soul and, 7–14, 20–21, 30–35, 58
  transcendence and, 256–257
belief
  in discrete objects, 320, 390–391
  in individual soul, 274, 634n11, 659n18
  inner journey and, 227, 258–259, 282
  nonconceptual awareness and, 331, 337–338, 342–343
  in personal God, 449, 691n6
belly center, 395–396, 521
biological life, 115–125, 127, 146–150
black aspect, 279, 286
bliss, 241, 293–294, 307, 338, 372, 409
blue aspect, 434
Boadella, David, 639–640nn9–11, 640–641n13
bodhichitta (seed of enlightenment), 600–601n4
bodhisattvas, 643n9, 692n9
body. *See also* diamond vehicles
  analogy to soul, 31, 37–40, 109–110
  bodies of *atman*, 495–497
  in coemergent nonduality, 442–443
  consciousness and, 27–28, 80–81, 514–515
  ego development and, 172–174
  of God, 453
  in Greek philosophy, 4–5, 616n2
  kayas in Buddhism, 628n15, 643n11, 653n1
  life and, 115–126
  of light, 275–277

Index   707

out-of-body experiences, 20–21, 128, 592n3
physical, 113–125, 182–183, 210–217, 498, 539
relation to soul, 149, 584n3, 587–588n10, 622n9
relaxation of, 273, 281
soul development and, 143–144, 152–153, 201–202, 210–217
soul's embodiment, 182–183
Bohm, David, 612n13
brahman (absolute), 497, 498, 500, 584n1, 681–682n13
brain, 76, 117–118, 173, 593n5, 596–597n1
buddhi (intellect), 496, 497, 499–500, 502
Buddhism. *See also* Tibetan Buddhism; specific schools of Buddhism
bodhisattvas, 643n9, 692n9
bodies in, 514–515, 628n15, 643n11, 653n1
Buddha nature, 577–578, 681n10, 689n5
cessation, 647n7, 680n5
discrimination, 657n13
emptiness, 505–510, 595n8, 649n13, 659n18, 681n12, 695n9
enlightenment, 600n4, 609n4, 634–635n11, 687n12
Hunt's theory and, 565
karma, 606nn2–3, 620n6
manifest world, 604n5, 645n2
nonconceptual awareness, 574, 597n2, 662n5
soul and, 505–515, 584n1, 586n6, 588n12, 602–603n1, 609n6, 659n18
true nature, 649–650n14, 683n16

Camus, Albert, 693n3
central ego, 200–202, 636n14
cessation, 382–386, 647n7, 648n9, 650n14, 680n5
chain of Being, 551–554, 687n9
chakra system, 445–446, 498
Chandrakirti, 681n12
change and changeability, 77–83, 88–95, 302, 348–362, 377, 475–476. *See also* dynamism; transformation
chariot vehicle, 236–241
childhood. *See* infancy and childhood
chitta (consciousness), 496–500, 507, 592n1
Chittamatra school, 507–508, 655n10
Christianity
beliefs, 645n2, 651–652n7, 689–690n5
demonic form, 651n5
divine darkness, 645n4, 647nn8–9
fall of Adam, 620n6
logos, 671–672n11, 674n16, 675–676nn18–19
nous (higher intellect), 629n18
revelation and, 588n11
soul, 489–494, 583n1
soul (council of Nicea and), 593–594n6, 601–602n6
soul (gender of), 99
soul (knowledge of), 589n3
soul (sensual), 615n1, 637n3
surrender to divinity, 651n4
ultimate truth, 642n6, 654n4
virtues, 581
citadel vehicle, 241–243, 343–344
clarity, 260–261, 275, 293, 325–326, 435–437
The Cloud of Unknowing (Denys the Areopagite), 493
coemergent nonduality, 437–447, 453
cognition. *See also* recognition
development of, 152–154, 211, 655n8
in dimensions of true nature, 138, 309–311, 324–325, 333
in early souls, 168–169, 174, 177–179, 536–540
essence and, 133, 138
research in, 620n5, 657–658n14
in Sufism, 599n10
color visualization, 222
commanding self, 521–524
compassion, 340–341, 603n1
computer technology, 21–22, 598n8, 606n1
concentration techniques, 222, 498–499

concept diamonds, 310–313, 322, 660n20
concepts. *See also* reification
   of Being, 308–309, 318–319, 327
   of God, 343
   "I am" concept, 498, 650n1
   soul development and, 152–153, 177–178
   transcending, 233, 257–261, 333–342
   universal, 134–135, 138, 310–313
   vrittis as, 497–498
conditioning, 97, 99–105, 153, 189, 227
conflict
   absence of, 387
   presence of, 156, 227, 230, 233, 238–239, 343
   soul development and, 101, 162, 166, 170–172, 186–187, 625n4
consciousness. *See also* awareness; cognition; pure consciousness; recognition
   autopoiesis and, 557
   blue aspect and, 434
   development of, 117–121, 149, 183–184, 208, 617n8
   in dimensions of true nature, 273–274, 289, 331–332, 383–384
   in Eastern traditions, 495–500, 506–514, 584n1, 592n1
   and essence, 128, 185
   five senses and, 51–52
   knowing and, 588n11
   knowledge and, 57–58, 65–67
   logos and, 678n23
   organ of, 26–41, 585n4
   receptivity and, 98
   research in, 561–565, 587n8
   self-consciousness, 168, 184
   soul's experience, 83–87, 109–110, 113–114
   in soul's inner journey, 234–236, 240, 249–251, 257, 265–266
   stream of, 79–80, 88, 506–509, 514, 603n2, 609n6
   in Sufism, 520–523, 526–527
   in Western thought, 3
constructivism, 597n2, 600n1, 659n16

contenting self, 524
control, 81, 104, 387
core dimension, 427–429
Cortright, Brant, 546, 634n11
creation. *See also* universe; world (cosmos)
   Christian views, 489–490, 492, 593–594n6, 654n4
   in dimensions of true nature, 352–354, 356, 361, 375
   in flow of experience, 82–83, 86
   Genesis account, 613n1, 665n1, 680n7
   in Kabbalah, 550, 679n4
   in Kashmir Shaivism, 666n2
   in Sufism, 648n10, 665–666nn1–2
creativity
   artistic, 19, 81, 532, 606n1
   dynamism and, 358–363
   limiting of, 100–101, 159–161
   Wilber's view, 608n1
Critique of Pure Reason (Kant), 644n1, 663n9
crystal vehicles, 331–333, 337–338, 343–344, 346
Csikszentmihalyi, Mihalyi, 603n3
culture, 72–73, 134–135. *See also* Eastern traditions; Western thought

daily life, 139–140, 198, 217, 642n3
Dalai Lama, 683n18
Dark Night of the Soul (Saint John of the Cross), 494, 616n4, 637n3
darkness
   of absolute, 378–382, 400–401
   of cessation, 385–386
   divine, 256–257, 401, 493, 645n4, 647nn8–9, 648–649n12, 662n4
De Anima (Aristotle), 487
death, 116, 123–125
   consciousness after, 610n8
   of ego identity, 244–245, 290, 302, 382, 627n9
   essence and, 127, 128
   fear of, 231, 243
   of God, 8, 461
   near-death experiences, 20–21
   psychic, 89

deconstructionism, 594–595n8, 598n7
defenses
    citadel vehicle and, 242
    divine love and, 281–283
    ego defenses, 101–104, 186–187
delusion, 230, 341, 508–509
demonic form, 284–285, 651n5
Denys the Areopagite, 493, 648–649n12
dependency, 106–107, 152, 161–162, 175
depression, 172–173
depth psychology, 35, 591n10, 626n5, 627n9–10, 637n4
Descartes, René, 34, 693–694n4
desire
    absence of, 295
    of animal soul, 142–144, 204, 287–289, 599n10
    for release, 272–273
desire soul, 207–210, 615n1
destiny, 574
destructiveness, 142–145, 147, 206, 284
development. *See also* infancy and childhood
    divine love and, 281, 283
    essential, 222, 226–234, 529–554
    logos and, 373–374
    mental, 78, 109, 633–635n11
    soul development, 131–184
    Sufic stages of, 521–527
developmental psychology
    ego, 101, 272
    insights from, 620n5, 623–624n1, 626n5, 630n19, 638–639n9, 650–651n3
dhoug (taste), 596n9
Dhyani Buddhas, 512
Diamond Approach, 62, 588–589n2, 643–644n12. *See also other* diamond *entries*
    actualization, 426, 445–446, 450, 463–464, 474–479, 624–626n4
    boundless dimensions, 282–283, 343–344, 358, 392–393, 576–577, 678–679n1
    essence, 594n6
    essential aspects, 135–136, 210

Hillman's views and, 584–586n4
Hunt's views and, 531–533
inquiry, 321–323, 328
soul, 3–4, 15–17, 636–637n1
Wilber's views and, 529–554, 626n7
wisdom traditions and, 581–582, 651n4, 652n9, 671n9, 679n4, 680n7
diamond body, 514–515
diamond guidance, 236, 275, 313, 331, 367–369, 660n20
diamond pearl, 455–456, 471–473, 638n7
diamond vehicles
    in dimensions of true nature, 272, 283, 322, 330
    in soul's inner journey, 226, 234–246, 265–267, 419–421, 424–429
diamonds
    absolute, 418–419, 431
    concept, 310–313
differentiation
    absence of, 255, 257–258, 407
    of absolute, 419–420
    in dimensions of true nature, 279, 295–303, 309–315, 328–330
    in Western thought, 466–467, 470
disabilities, 172–174
divine darkness, 256–257, 401, 493, 645n4, 647n8–9, 648–649n12, 662n4
divine essence, 645n2, 645n4, 688n4
divine love, 271–296, 431, 622n10
divine names, 525–527, 580–581
divine (universal) mind, 313–317
divine will, 668–669n7, 685–686n2
Dogen (Zen master), 642n6, 645n3, 650n16, 664n13
doing, 335–336, 361–362, 378–379, 451–452
dorje (Tibetan diamond symbol), 243
doubt, 664–665n14
dreams, 227, 248–251, 641n14
drive theory, 629n16
duality. *See also* nonduality
    desire and, 599n10
    of egoic realm, 176, 198–199
    overcoming, 185–187
    of soul and essence, 154–156, 176

dynamism, 348–362
  aliveness, 359
  ego structures and, 197
  essence and, 18–20, 139
  liberation and, 101, 186, 187, 188
  of logos, 372–374
  presence of, 358–363
  as property of soul, 51–52, 76–93, 557
  of Shakti, 501, 504, 650n15, 667n5, 675–676n19
  in soul development, 153, 159–161
  in soul's inner journey, 224–225, 262–263, 632n5
Dzogchen (Maha Ati)
  absolute, 682n14
  dynamism, 605n9, 650n15, 689n5
  emanation, 553, 688n13
  emptiness, 605n8
  enlightenment, 510–511, 534–536
  Longchenpa, 511–513, 595n8, 662n5, 668n6
  nondual presence, 687n11
  rigpa (fundamental knowing), 614n3
  true nature, 646n5, 649–650n14, 692n7

Eastern traditions. *See also specific spiritual traditions*
  interest in, 466–467
  in logoi of teachings, 569, 572
  primordial nature, 602n6
  soul, 15, 495–515
  transmigration, 606nn2–3, 617n7
  and Western compared, 9, 466–467, 470–471, 671n10, 688–691n5, 692n1, 694–695n6
Eckhart, Meister, 494
ego and ego structures, 164–184. *See also other ego entries*
  age and, 123
  ahamkara in Eastern traditions, 496, 498–500, 502
  Diamond Approach and, 210, 546
  Fairbairn's view, 638n5
  liberation from, 89–90, 185–199
  monster symbol for, 642n3
  reification and, 319–321
  soul development and, 10, 17–18, 148, 156, 202–203, 285–286
  soul's inner journey and, 222–224, 228, 230–231, 242–244
  types of, 200–202, 607–608n6, 636n14, 636–637n1
  Washburn's view, 624n4
ego boundaries, 275–276
ego defenses, 101–104
ego identity, 163, 244, 345
ego psychology, 623–624n1
ego regression, 195–197, 544
egoic experience, 22, 25, 58, 198–199
  autopoiesis and, 558–560
  in dark room analogy, 64
  and dynamism compared, 349–351
  liberation from, 29, 238–239, 322
  and self-realization compared, 254
ego-self, 271–273, 288–289, 300
  duality with essence, 144–145, 176
  Markabah vehicle and, 236–237
  transcending, 334, 390–391
"eight consciousnesses," 507–511
Einstein, Albert, 27, 376, 598n6, 644–645n1, 691n7
emanation, 420–421, 440, 553–554
emanationism, 686n5
embodiment of soul, 182–183
embryonic development, 89, 213–216
emerald aspect, 139, 279
emergence theory, 118, 564, 610n9
emotional child, 201
emotional forms, 298, 330–331
emotions. *See* feelings and emotions
Empedocles, 620n6
emptiness, 387–399, 596n11
  absolute as, 381, 604n5
  in Buddhism, 505–510, 595n8, 649n13, 659n18, 681n12, 684n20, 695n9
  as ground of forms, 86, 198–199, 213, 430–431, 605n8
  holes theory and, 544
  and inner spaciousness compared, 191
  logical analysis and, 586n6

of modern worldview, 461–464, 476
nonbeing and, 258–261, 654–655n7
presence and, 293, 304–307, 334
in quintessential dimension, 435–440
energy, 444–446
  in absolute ipseity, 408
  aliveness, 121–128, 359
  soul's, 81–83, 92–93, 110
  subtle (*prana*), 445–446, 498, 695n1
enlightenment. *See also* liberation
  absolute's mystery and, 400–401
  barriers to, 232–234
  in Buddhism, 600–601n4, 609n4, 634–635n11, 687n12
  ego structures and, 156, 193–196
  in other Eastern traditions, 504–505, 509–515, 534–536, 598n7, 632n4
  presence and, 33
  as primary religious concern, 9, 662n4
  rigpa (fundamental illumination), 614n3, 657n13, 687n11
  sudden *vs.* gradual, 74–75, 112
environment
  autopoiesis and, 555–559
  early dependence on, 106–107, 153, 175–176
  holding environment, 157–161, 173, 214–215, 278, 282–284
  intrusive, 103
  soul's growth and, 94–95, 101
  soul's potential and, 72–73, 162
epistemological issues, 232–234
essence, 38–41, 131–140. *See also other* essential *entries*; personal essence
  in Diamond Approach, 594n6
  in dimensions of true nature, 271–272, 275, 286–287, 334–335, 399–401
  distinct from soul, 98–99, 111–112, 127–128
  in infancy and childhood, 152–153, 202, 529–554
  liberation and, 185–186, 632n7
  plane of (*dhat*), 575
  potential and, 66, 73–75
  in soul's inner journey, 222–234, 240–241, 243, 258

essential aspects, 133–140
  actualization of, 441–446
  chemical imbalance and, 173
  in dimensions of true nature, 293, 297, 304–306, 310–313, 322, 330–331
  divine love and, 279
  infant's experience, 540–547
  lataif (subtleties of soul) and, 222
  logoi of teachings and, 578–581
  memory of, 627n8
  personal essence and, 182
  regression and, 196–197
  in soul's journeys, 227–230, 235, 244, 247–248, 261, 417–422, 427–435
  transparency to, 150
essential ground, 154–176
essential identity, 138, 224, 427, 542
essential nature, 102, 105–107, 144–146
essential *nous*, 179–180, 184
essential presence, 322
  actualization of, 424, 434–440
  ego development and, 171, 174, 181–182, 193–195
essential space, 190
eternity, 302–304
  eternal now, 263–264
  of soul (Plato), 486
Euclidean space, 306, 598n6
Evagrius of Pontus, 602n6
Eve (biblical), 519, 621n8
evil, 145, 283–284, 336–337
evolution
  holy plan, 631n2
  logos and, 363, 373–374
  of soul, 149–150, 155
  theories of, 117–121, 556–557, 608n1
  of Western thought, 471–473, 689–691n5
  Wilber's view critiqued, 549–550, 554
exercise, 126
existence, 300, 352, 363, 366
existential issues, 230–234
existential philosophy, 461–462
experience. *See also* egoic experience
  absence of, 257
  of absolute, 378–385, 393–397, 403–409

712 Index

actualization and, 76–93, 429–436, 454–456
of animal potential, 146–150, 174–175
in dimensions of true nature, 251, 273, 278–283, 295–307, 316–317, 321, 348–372
ego development and, 164–176, 191–193, 200–206, 211–215, 618n1
of essence, 134–135, 222–224
fear of losing, 274–275
flow of, 78–87, 113–114, 425–426
of growth, 109
knowledge and, 53, 55–58
nonconceptual, 49–51, 177, 327–333
of past and future, 59, 63–64, 72–73, 263, 604–605nn6–7
prenatal, 214–215, 627n10, 639–640n9
soul's, 15–25, 31–36, 45, 65–71, 96–98
in soul's inner journey, 231–233, 239–243, 251–255, 263–264, 329
transpersonal, 617n8
Ezekiel's chariot, 644n12

Fairbairn, W. Ronald, 636n14, 638n5
faith, crisis of, 343
fall of man, 620n6, 651–652n7
fear
absence of, 295
causes of, 101, 103, 172
of death, 231, 243
of loss, 148–149, 242, 274–275, 294, 331–332
of rejecting object, 205–206
of spontaneity, 681n11
feelings and emotions
agent of experience, 24–25
aloneness, 231, 422
bitterness, 284–285
in coemergent nonduality, 442–443
in dimensions of true nature, 279, 357, 403–409
inability to rest, 217
presence and, 33–34
shakti and, 446

soul development and, 153, 171–174
in soul's inner journey, 227, 233, 634n11
soul's properties and, 55–56, 78, 89–90, 95
fetal implantation, 216
field theory emergence, 562–563
flow
of experience, 78–87, 113–115, 367–368, 425–426
fluid quality of soul, 30–31, 80–83, 90
of forms, 260, 302, 371
of logos, 364, 372–375
protoplasmic, 618n9
soul's unfolding and, 94–95, 187–188, 357–359
stream of consciousness, 79–80, 88, 506–509, 514, 603n2, 609n6
food, desire soul and, 207–208
formlessness, 28–29, 39–40, 148–150, 190
forms. *See also* body; structures
absolute and, 392, 421
Aristotle's view, 487
Being and, 447–449
comprehension of, 51–59
of consciousness, 48
creation of, 86
diamond vehicles, 234–235
in dimensions of true nature, 258, 262–263, 286–287, 297–302, 326, 349–360
egoic, 166–167, 627n9
emptiness and, 260, 388–390, 430–431
flow of, 94–95, 114, 260, 302, 371
form body (*rupakaya*), 653n1
growth and, 108–112
noetic, 65, 313–315, 319–320, 365–368
in nonconceptual Reality, 50, 53–54, 327–330, 333
physical and essential, 291
Platonic, 125–126, 138, 657n13
prenoetic, 330, 348, 678n22

soul's properties and, 68–69, 90–91, 94–96
spiritual, 134–140, 299, 330–332
Franck, Sebastian, 494
freedom. *See* liberation
freedom vehicle, 267, 456–458
Freud, Sigmund, 203, 227, 586n5, 616n5, 621n8, 625n4, 638n5
frustration, 151–152, 204–208, 284
fulfillment, 209, 240–241, 280, 457–458
fullness, 70, 87, 304–307, 435–436
fundamentalism, 476
future, 59, 263, 604–605nn6–7

Gelug school, 649n13
gender, 99, 606–607n4
generosity, 280
Genjokoan (Dogen), 664n13
Geshwind, Norman, 564–565
Gibson, J. J., 564
globalization, 472, 475–476
gnosis (knowledge), 60, 243, 309, 491–492, 596, 613n1, 644n12
God
  in dimensions of true nature, 343, 353, 365
  divine *vs.* free will, 668–669n7
  hatred of, 285
  heart of, 282, 372
  isolation of, 7–9, 459–479
  knowledge of, 599n10, 603–604n4
  love of, 279–280, 602n1, 651n4
  presence and, 593–594n6
  proofs of existence, 586–587nn6–7
  in theistic religions, 489–494, 575, 606–607n4, 608n7, 652n9
Godemchan, Riddzin, 534
goodness, 277–278, 284–285, 336–337
Govinda, Lama Anagarika, 509–512
gratification, 237–238, 280, 287
greed, 142–145, 287–289
Greek philosophy, 58, 61, 599n12, 616n2, 629n18, 669–670nn8–9, 674n16. *See also individual philosophers*
Gregory of Nyssa, 492, 645n4, 647n8
Grof, Stanislav, 616–617n6, 617n8, 620n5, 640nn11–12

ground, essential, 154–176
ground dimension, 429–431
growth. *See* maturity and growth
Guenther, Herbert, 690n5
guidance
  of Being, 373, 660n20
  of caretakers, 162
  diamond, 236, 275, 313, 331, 367–369, 660n20
  inner, 185, 346–347
  personal logoi and, 573–574
  in Sufism, 526
  teachers, 368–369, 632n6
  toward true nature, 101, 233–324
Gurdjieff, G. I., 599n11, 673n14
Gurumai, 676n19

handicaps, 172–174
happiness, 173, 239–241, 457–458
Hare Krishna school, 681n13
harmony of logos, 370–372
Hartmann, Heinz, 607n5, 622n11
Hartmann, Otto, 640–641n13
Hasidism, 637n3
hatred, 205–206, 209–210, 284–285
heart
  absence of, 203
  crystal, 338
  in dimensions of true nature, 278–280, 294, 396, 404
  of God, 282, 372
  object relations and, 206, 209
  soul and, 40, 145, 222, 673n15
  in Sufism, 517, 527, 599n10, 602–603n1, 607n4, 616n3, 631n21
Heart Sutra, 605n8, 687n11
Hegel, Georg Wilhelm Friedrich, 120, 611n12
Heidegger, Martin, 33, 461, 565, 604–605n6
Heraclitus, 669–670n8
Hillman, James, 584–586n4
Hinduism. *See also* Kashmir Shaivism; Vedanta
  ahamkara ("I am" concept), 650n1
  conditioning, 606n2

714 Index

desire soul, 637n3
divinity, 651n4, 674n17
enlightenment, 634n11
gods, 643n9
soul, 583–584n1
true nature, 644n15
holding environment, 157–161, 173, 214–215, 278, 282–284
holes theory, 543–544, 547
holy ideas, 623n13, 642n7
holy plan, 631nn1–2
home, being at, 403–408, 483
Hopi tribe, 605n7
hormones, 172, 173
human being and humanity. *See also* soul
 animal soul in, 141–144
 essence of, 73–75
 serving, 457–458
 soul's potential and, 72–73, 221
 transmigration and, 606nn2–3
 vision of, 472–479
human soul (Sufism), 641n2
humility, 402
Hunt, Harry, 531–533, 564–565

"I am" concept, 498, 650n1
Ibn 'Arabi, Muhyiddin
 absolute stillness, 679n2
 creation, 666n2
 emanation, 553, 688n13
 God, 688n4
 knowledge, 665n15
 Perfect Man, 525, 692n8
 soul, 519–520, 591n10, 602n1
 universal imagination, 673n15
ideas
 holy, 623n13, 642n7
 Platonic, 54, 135–136, 486, 614n3, 655n9
identity. *See also* self
 with absolute, 406–407, 421–422, 457–458
 with divine love, 290
 ego development, 102–104, 163, 192–199, 244, 345
 essential, 138, 224, 427, 542

flux of, 77–78
soul development and, 148–150, 161–163, 169, 172, 214–215
transcending, 242–245, 251, 278
ignorance
 ego delusion, 642n7
 innate and acquired, 535–537, 551, 554
 in Kashmir Shaivism, 503–504
 as knowledge, 57
 transcending, 187, 256, 278, 295
illusory body (Mahamudra), 514–515
imagination, 59, 365–366, 532–533, 575
immanence, 439–440
impressionability, 94–107
 animal soul and, 142, 144, 174–175
 ego development and, 102, 181, 185, 211–214
 in young souls, 153, 169–170
Indian traditions, 495–500, 588n12, 615n1, 620n6, 641n1, 650n1. *See also* Kashmir Shaivism; Ramana Maharshi
individuality, 164
 absence of, 225, 275–276
 autonomy, 210
 dynamic presence and, 360–361
 essential pearl, 223
 freedom vehicle and, 456–458
 in Kashmir Shaivism, 503
individuation, 150, 180–183, 222–224. *See also* personal essence
infancy and childhood
 abuse in, 96, 157, 159, 170–172, 227
 aliveness in, 121–123
 awareness in, 660n1
 ego and soul development, 149–163, 166–169, 182–183, 200–210, 319–320
 essence in, 197, 529–554
 first love object, 238
 holding environment, 157–161, 173, 214–215, 278, 282–284
 intrusive environment, 103
 soul's properties, 95–96, 105–106
infiniteness
 of human potential, 72–73, 75

Index

of knowledge, 67–68
of true nature, 253
influence
   of ego structures, 197
   of logos, 373
   of ordinary knowledge, 321
   point diamond and, 428
   soul's impressionability, 94–107, 153, 169–170, 185
   inner balance, 160–163
   inner forms, 52–59, 94–96, 298, 387
   inner guidance, 346–347
   inner nature, 429
   inner order. *See* logos; self-organization
   inner (soul) child, 201–203, 209–210
   inner space, 190–191, 304–306, 598n6
   inner work and journey, 221–246. *See also* inquiry; realization
   autopoiesis and, 559–560
   basic spiritual insight, 131
   difficulty of, 101–103
   in East and West, 690–691n5
   end of search, 407–409
   issues encountered in, 195, 197–198, 204, 208
inquiry
   described, 189–191, 320–323, 345–347, 425
   diamond vehicles and, 235–236, 283
   ego structures and, 195
   existential issues, 231
inspired self, 523–524
instincts
   animal, 142–146, 237–238, 522
   in childhood, 175–176, 207
   liberation from, 186–187
integration, 145–146, 222–223
   of dimensions of true nature, 266–267, 282–283, 306–307, 336
   ego development and, 204, 212
   in journey of descent, 427–436
   of Markabah vehicle, 240
intellect, 179–180, 496, 497, 499–500, 517. *See also* logic and rational thought; nous (higher intellect)

intelligence of logos, 372–374
introspection. *See* self-reflection
intrusion, 103, 105, 159, 170
involution theory (Wilber), 535, 548, 549–554, 621–622nn7–8
ipseity, 406–409, 414, 457
irrational soul (*nefesh*), 637n3
Islam, 99, 583n1, 594n6, 629n18, 651n5, 652n7, 676n19, 689n5. *See also* Sufism
isolation of soul, 104, 271–272

James, William, 603nn2–3
Jesus Christ, 491, 676n19, 689–690n5
jivatman (soul), 497, 498, 583–584n1
jnana (fundamental knowing), 499–500, 505, 509, 596n9, 614n3, 657n13
journey of ascent, 266–267, 413–416, 432–434
journey of descent, 266–267, 413–440
joy, 168, 201, 239–240, 380, 404–405
Judaism, 99, 583n1, 629n18, 647nn8–9, 651n5, 676n19. *See also* Kabbalah
Julian of Norwich, 494
Jung, Carl, 6, 584n4, 625n4, 651n6

Kabbalah
   Ain Sof, 645n2, 646n4, 679n4
   aspects in, 653n2
   chain of Being, 687n9
   creation, 550, 695n8
   divine self-expression, 674n17
   five worlds in, 575–576
   language, 676n21
   perfection, 601n6, 691n5, 692n8
   sefirot, 578–580, 661n4
   serving God, 692n9
   soul, 583n1, 615n1, 637n3
   and transpersonal psychology compared, 625n4
Kant, Immanuel, 376, 644n1, 663n9
karma, 495, 503–504, 620n6
Kashmir Shaivism. *See also* Shiva and Shakti
   and Buddhism compared, 510, 592n1
   chain of Being, 687n9

creation, 666n2
divine will, 668–669n7
emanation and immanence, 553
enlightenment, 534–536, 632n4
ignorance and knowing, 503–504, 657n13
language, 676n21
path of ascent, 646–647n6
self-realization, 539–540
soul, 500–505, 607n4
tattvas (principles), 495, 501–504, 574, 646–647n6, 654n5
Khapa, Tsong, 649n13
knowing. *See also* awareness; knowledge
blue aspect and, 434
in dimensions of true nature, 324–325, 328, 333, 342–343, 348
of essential aspects, 133–138
of Ideas (Plato), 614n3
infancy and, 152–153, 619n4
jnana (fundamental knowing), 499–500, 505, 509, 596n9, 614n3, 657n13
mind and, 14
noetic forms, 313–315
origin of, 307–309
soul as medium, 34–37, 584n3, 588nn11–12
true nature and, 253–257
knowledge, 45–46, 307–322
basic and ordinary contrasted, 52–68, 232, 244, 317–319
conceptualizing and, 177–178
diamond vehicles and, 235–236, 243
in dimensions of true nature, 326, 344–347, 364, 372, 401–403
God's, 603–604n4
Kant's view, 663n9
pure, 65–70, 315
and rational thought, 34–35, 58–62, 672n12
representational, 165, 167
self-reflection and, 183–184
of soul, 22–25, 485–486
soul's unfolding and, 84
and spiritual maturity, 179–180

transmission of, 368
vidya tattva, 502
koans (stories), 638n8, 661n3, 663nn7–8, 663n11
Koestler, Arthur, 608n1
Kohut, Heinz, 623n14
Koran. *See* Qur'an
Krishna, 681–682n13
Krishnamurti, 122
Kühlewind, George, 673n14, 675n18, 677n22
Kumin, Ivri, 619n4, 624n3, 638n9
kundalini (creative power), 445–446, 498, 504, 675–676n19

Laing, R. D., 639n9, 641n14
language, 369–370, 676n21
lataif (subtleties of soul), 222, 521, 532, 630–631n21, 641n1
learning, 97–105
diamond vehicles and, 241, 245
embodiment and, 182–183
soul development and, 159–161, 166–167, 178
liberation, 185–199, 341–347
autopoiesis and, 559–560
in Eastern traditions, 499–500, 504–505, 509–515
from egoic experience, 29, 89–90, 238–239, 322
freedom diamond vehicle, 267
in journey of descent, 423–424
logos and, 582
from ordinary knowledge, 57, 232, 244
of potential, 71–72, 75, 81–84, 97, 101
from primitive structures, 210, 216–217
libidinal soul, 203–210
life, 110–125. *See also* adults and adulthood; infancy and childhood
Eastern *vs.* Western views, 689–691n5
logos and, 678n23
prenatal, 155, 170, 213–217, 639–640n9
protoplasmic forms and, 149–150

pure, 125–128
purpose and, 340
right living, 241–243
light
  of diamond vehicles, 235, 239–240, 243
  divine, 271–291
  of divine darkness, 256–257, 401, 647n9
localization reductionism, 562
logic and rational thought
  in cognitive development, 178
  of diamond vehicles, 643n10
  essential *nous* and, 180
  knowledge and, 34–35, 58–62, 672n12
  original meaning, 672n13
  in religious thought, 8–9, 586–587nn6–7
  in study of soul, 13–14
  universal thinking and, 365
  vision-logic (Wilber), 630n20
logos, 364–375
  absolute and, 379–382
  in Greek philosophy, 362–363, 487, 599n12, 611n12
  in journey of descent, 424–426, 431
  logoi of teachings, 567–582
  personal Being and, 451–453, 572–574
  and *shakti* compared, 675–676n19
Longchenpa, 511, 512–513, 595n8, 662n5, 668n6
loss, 124–125, 414, 544
love
  in dimensions of true nature, 340–341, 399, 403–405
  distrust and, 103
  divine, 271–296, 431, 622n10
  ego development and, 208, 209
  as essential aspect, 136–138
  fear of losing, 294
  as field, 158–160, 278–279
  of God, 526, 602n1
  in infants and children, 96, 151, 157–158
  in soul's inner journey, 224–225, 237–239, 256

lovemaking, 92
loving-kindness, 139
Lucas, George, 288
luminosity, 149–150, 260–262

macrocosm pearl, 454–455
Madhyamika school, 505, 508, 649n13, 659n18, 681n12, 684n20
Maha Ati. *See* Dzogchen (Maha Ati)
Mahamudra
  emanation and immanence, 553, 688n13
  emptiness, 605n8, 649n14
  enlightenment, 510–511
  Nagarjuna, 506, 514–515, 684n20
  nonconceptual perspective in, 662n5
Maharaj, Sri Nisargadatta, 648n11, 679–680n5, 683n17
Mahayana Buddhism, 655n10, 687n11
  Madhyamika school, 505, 508, 659n18, 681n12, 684n20
  Yogachara school, 506–507, 510–511, 603n2, 609n6, 659n18
malleability of soul, 94–97, 169–170
  animal soul and, 142, 144
  constraining of, 100, 102
  in infants, 153
manas (mind), 496, 502, 507, 509
manifestation. *See also* forms
  body of (*nirmanakaya*), 653n1
  in dimensions of true nature, 254–255, 297–298, 334–335, 352–363, 371–372, 397
  goodness in, 277
  ground of, 263–265, 329, 437–439
  in journey of descent, 415, 423–424, 431–434, 438–447
  prakriti as, 495, 498, 499, 501–503
  soul's unfolding and, 86
  unmanifest and, 251–252, 355, 376–382, 416–418
manifestationism, 686n5, 688n13
Markabah (chariot) vehicle, 236–241
master of knowledge, 344–347
materialism, 12, 21–22, 27, 238, 287–289, 587n8

matter
  Aristotle's view, 487
  consciousness and, 118–120, 610n9
  involution of soul into, 621–622n8
  physical life and, 116–117
  in *tattvas* (principles), 487
  world perceived as, 34
Maturana, Humberto, 556
maturity and growth, 108–112
  in dimensions of true nature, 302, 373–374
  ego development, 159–161, 168–169
  integration and, 222–224
  of personal essence, 452
  soul's liberation and, 185, 187, 210
  soul's unfolding and, 84, 97, 105–106
  spiritual, 179–180, 545, 633–635n11
  of universe, 120–121
maya (illusion), 501, 503–504
meditation
  methods, 79, 222, 498–499, 514, 633n10, 661n3
  use of, 324, 599n11, 638n8
Meher Baba, 648n11
Meltzoff, A. N., 638n9
memory
  in dimensions of true nature, 317, 319, 326
  ego development and, 164–165, 169–170, 181, 211–213
  embryological, 639n9
  in infancy research, 618n1
  psychodynamic issues and, 227
  soul's properties and, 53–54, 57–58, 97
mental development, 78, 109, 633–635n11
mental forms, 298
merging essence crystal, 332
microcosm diamond pearl, 471–473
Middle Way. *See* Madhyamika school
mind
  absolute and, 396–397
  Being and, 34–35, 309, 313
  God's, 316–317, 644n1
  manas as, 496, 502, 507, 509
  noetic forms and, 135, 319–320
  ordinary, 317–319
  perception and, 539
  rest for, 273, 280
  soul and, 16, 22, 39–40
  in soul's inner journey, 230, 249–251, 252
  transcending, 64, 326–328, 597n4
  universal, 313–317, 509
mind-*vajra*, 614n3
mirror analogy with soul, 49–51, 68–69, 96, 492
mirroring, 162–163, 169
modern worldview, 3–6, 12, 34, 61, 460–464, 584–585n4
monotheistic traditions. *See* Christianity; Islam; Judaism
Moore, Thomas, 586n4
mothers and motherhood
  ego development and, 164, 636n14
  gratification and, 237–238
  libidinal soul and, 204–205
  Markabah vehicle and, 237
  separation from, 229–230, 233, 295, 332
  true nature as, 651n4
motivation, 340–341
movement
  absence of, 255
  in coemergent nonduality, 442–443
  in dimensions of true nature, 302, 335–336, 348–362, 377, 399–403
  in infants, 175–176
  journey of descent, 413–440
  soul's, 19, 77
  of thoughts, 51
  toward inner truth, 238–239
movies and television, 51, 85, 350, 356–357, 440, 606n1
Muhammad, Prophet, 604n4, 672n11, 676–677n21
Muhammadan Pearl, 630–631n21
Muhammadan spirit, 518
music, 19, 59, 222, 239
mystery
  of absolute, 379–380, 399–409, 420

of soul's unfolding, 84–87
true nature as, 257
mystical experience and knowledge, 60–61, 256, 264, 338–340, 652n9. *See also* oneness of Being; unity
Mystical Theology (Denys the Areopagite), 493

nafs (soul or self), 517–522, 527, 583n1, 589n3, 607n4
Nagarjuna, 506, 514, 684n20
narcissism, 107, 144, 153
   in caretakers, 161–163
   Freud's view, 621n8
   transcending, 223–224, 289–290
Nasr, Seyyed Hossein, 693–694n4
natural growth, 109–110
natural order, 362, 669n8
nature. *See also* true nature
   desire nature, 144
   essential, 102, 105–107, 144–146
   growth in, 110
   self-nature, 407
   spiritual, 135–136, 605n9
nefesh (soul or self), 583n1, 637n3
Neoplatonism, 487–488, 588n12, 601n6, 671n9, 687n9
neurosis, 10, 634–635n11
New Age movement, 461
Newton, Isaac, 376, 644n1
Nietzsche, Friedrich, 8, 461
nihilism, 260
nirmanakaya (body of manifestation), 653n1
no-diamonds, 313
noesis (mode of soul's experience), 45–62, 243, 644n12
noetic forms, 65, 134–140, 313–315, 319–320, 365–368
nonattachment, 337–338, 343, 426, 664–665n14
nonbeing, 258–261, 334, 384, 392, 430
nonconceptual (pure) awareness, 49–51
   actualization of, 429–433
   as dimension of true nature, 301–302, 324–347, 364–366, 372, 393–394, 401

essence and, 111, 324–330, 591n9
forms arising from, 53–54
in infants, 177
knowledge and, 133–134, 401
preconceptual structures and, 211–212
realization of, 29, 186
nonconceptual Reality, 257–261, 328–347
nonconceptual trust, 157–161
nondifferentiated presence. *See* pure (nondifferentiated) presence
nonduality
   coemergent, 437–447, 453
   duality and, 339
   of essence, 138
   of knowledge, 56
   of primal condition, 155–156
   of seeing, 599n10
   of soul and essence, 127, 155, 607n4
   in soul child, 202
   in soul's inner journey, 224–225, 239, 252, 297–298
   of subject and object, 24–25
   of unity and oneness, 301
nothingness, 305–307
nous (higher intellect)
   diamond guidance as, 236
   essential, 179–180, 184
   in Greek philosophy, 466, 471, 596n9, 599n12, 694n4
   Origen's view, 490, 602n6
   Plotinus's view, 487–489, 656–657n13
now, 302–304, 379–380
Nyingma school, 512, 614n3, 687n11

object image, 164
object relations and object relations theory, 153
   central object relation, 638n7
   concept of self, 78, 623–624nn1–2, 629n16, 630n19, 657–658n14
   labeling of, 177–178
   libidinal soul and, 204–210
   parenting objects, 290

prenatal structures and, 638–639n9
Stern's view, 627–628n10
superego and, 198
objectivity. *See also* subjectivity
awareness and, 586n6
coemergent nonduality and, 442–443
of knowledge, 55, 61–62, 403, 600n1
noetic forms and, 314–315
objective thinking, 673n14
about pleasure, 241
about primitive structures, 206–207
of service, 456–458
use of reason, 13–14, 587n7
oceanic love, 273–278, 282, 286
oedipal child, 210
omnipresence, 262–264, 290, 345–346
oneness of Being, 301–302, 338–340, 350–351, 381, 429–430
openness
of absolute, 380
to all knowledge, 341–347
divine love and, 281
to dynamism, 632n5
ego development and, 102–104
to essential space, 190–191
nonbeing and, 306–307, 397–399
selflessness and, 387
order. *See* logos; self-organization
Origen of Alexandria, 490–491, 602n6
original sin, 491, 492, 493, 651–652n7
out-of-body experiences, 20–21, 128, 592n3

Padmasambhava, 604n5, 682n14
pain, 166, 170–172, 189, 544, 608n6
parents, 157–165, 210, 227–228, 290
Parmenides, 600n2
passions, 186–187, 512–513, 521, 522
past. *See also* memory
chitta (consciousness) and, 497
dimensions of true nature and, 263, 345, 352
experience of, 59, 63–64, 72–73, 263
time and, 604–605nn6–7
pearl
cosmos as, 454–455

diamond, 455–456, 471–473, 638n7
Muhammadan, 630–631n21
soul as, 222–224, 451, 454–456
Penrose, Roger, 563
perception
abstraction of, 177
cessation of, 385
of coemergent nonduality, 444
in dimensions of true nature, 324–325, 336, 348–354, 360–362, 371, 379–380
essence and, 138
in infancy research, 618n1
and mind, 539
pure, 49–51
soul's capacity for, 23–24, 47–48, 84
in soul's inner journey, 232–233, 255, 259–261
perfection
of essence, 111–112, 134–135
soul's potential for, 98
in Sufism, 521–522, 525–527
of true nature, 298, 310
person. *See* individuality; individuation
personal essence, 182, 630n21
as pearl beyond price, 222–224, 275, 408, 450–456, 542
stupa diamond vehicle and, 290–291
personal God, 449–453
personal logos, 572–574
phenomenological consciousness, 561–565
phenomenological issues, 232–234
Philo of Alexandria, 647n8, 671n9, 672n16, 674–675n18
philosophy. *See specific philosophies and philosophers*
phylogenetic forms, 146–150, 195–196
physical life and body, 113–125, 182–183, 210–217, 498, 539
physical world. *See also* matter
animal soul and, 142–144
diamond pearl and, 472–473
Plotinus's view, 488
true nature and, 248, 298–332, 446–447

Piaget, Jean, 532, 609n2, 620n5, 655n8, 657n14
Plato and Platonism. *See also* Neoplatonism
　beauty, 652n8
　body, 616n2
　concept of soul, 3, 485–486, 601n6
　"The Good," 650n2
　Ideas, 54, 84, 135–136, 614n13, 655n9
　life, 691n5
　the One, 684n19
　Platonic forms, 125–126, 138, 657n13
　recollection, 614–615n3
　spiritual training, 9
　study of self, 588n12
　use of reason, 587n7
　virtues, 615n4
pleasure
　diamond vehicle of, 236–241
　of energy, 446
　soul development and, 142–143, 151, 156, 207–209
Plotinus, 589n4, 611n12, 612n16
　beauty, 652n8
　concept of soul, 487–489, 593n5
　knowing of absolute, 685n23
　logos, 671n9
　nous, 551–553, 596n9, 656–657n13, 661–662n4
　the One, 645n2, 648n12, 684n19
　universal soul, 666–667nn3–4
　Wilber's theory and, 551–552
poetry, 19, 651n4
point diamond vehicle, 424–429
positivist philosophy, 469, 658–659n16, 694n4
posttraumatic stress disorder, 95, 171
potential
　in absolute, 417–418
　actualization of, 76–93, 187–188, 455–456
　of animal soul, 141–150, 174–176
　autopoiesis and, 557
　awareness of, 221
　in dimensions of true nature, 304, 358–359, 367, 374, 384

Index　721

　environment and, 162
　essential aspects and, 136
　individuation and, 180–182
　for life, 126–127
　limitations to, 100–101, 172–174
　as property of soul, 63–75, 97, 108–112, 538, 613n1
poverty state, 383, 527
power, 142–143. *See also* dynamism
　of Being, 355
　force of logos, 372–374
　kundalini (creative power), 445–446, 498, 504, 675–676n19
　in libidinal soul, 205–210
Prajnaparamita, 687n11
prakriti (manifest field of experience), 495, 498, 499, 501–503
prana (subtle energy), 445–446, 496, 498, 641n1
Prasangica Madhyamika school, 649n13, 681n12
pratyabhinja (recognition), 534
prayer, 602n6, 651n4
preconceptual structures, 198, 210–217, 346
prenatal life, 170, 639–640n9
prenoetic forms, 330, 348, 678n22
presence. *See also* essential presence; pure (nondifferentiated) presence
　absence of, 258
　in dimensions of true nature, 308–309, 334, 358–362, 384–386
　infant's experience, 539–541
　journeys in, 221–226, 239–243, 261–267
　knowledge as, 66
　of life, 108–128
　of logos, 371
　of potential, 70
　of pure consciousness, 131–133
　soul development and, 149–150, 165–166, 209
　soul's experience, 32–36, 47–48, 58, 80–83
　in spiritual traditions, 593–594n6
present, 302–303, 352

Pribram, Karl, 593n5
Prigogine, Ilya, 118
primitive structures, 146–150, 175, 198–217, 346
profane, concept of, 335
psyche. *See* soul
psychoanalysis, 618n1, 623n14
psychodynamic issues, 89–90, 193–197, 227–230, 545
psychology, 5–9, 459–470, 586n5. *See also* developmental psychology; transpersonal psychology
   depth psychology, 35, 591n10, 626n5, 627nn9–10, 637n4
   ego psychology, 623–624n1
   new metapsychology, 7, 11–14
   self in, 582n2, 584–586n4, 623n14, 623–624n1
psychosis, 228
pure awareness. *See* nonconceptual (pure) awareness
pure Being, 261, 296–298
pure consciousness, 30–31, 111, 593–594n6
   awareness and, 596n11
   essence and, 38–39, 131–138
   matter and, 610n9
   mental knowing and, 59–60
   as presence, 35
   and subjective compared, 32–36
pure depth, 405–406
pure knowledge, 65–70, 315
pure life, 125–128
pure (nondifferentiated) presence, 292–315
   in diamond presence, 431
   in dimensions of true nature, 322–323, 331, 344–345, 366–370
   ego structures and, 194–195
   essence as, 74, 132–135
   learning and, 100–101
   love and, 158–160, 622n10
   recognizing, 111, 168–169, 185–186, 543, 626–627n8
   self-reflection and, 184
   in soul's inner journey, 225–226, 235, 244

pure perception, 49–51
pure potential, 70–71
pure (spiritual) forms, 134–140, 299, 330–332
purity and purification
   of absolute, 440
   of essence, 74, 98, 132, 602n6
   of nonconceptual, 335
   Plato's view, 486
   Saint John of the Cross's view, 494
purpose, 340–341
purusha (subjective awareness), 495, 499, 501–503
Pythagoras, 9

qalb (heart), 517, 527, 599n10, 602–603n1, 607n4, 616n3, 631n21
qualia of consciousness, 561–564
quantum theory, 119, 590n7, 592n3, 611n11, 659n17, 688n2
quintessential dimension, 434–440
Qur'an, 601n6, 604n4, 613n1, 653n2, 672n11, 674n19, 676–677n21

raja yoga, 495–500
Ramana Maharshi, 589n5, 678n1, 686n7
rational soul (Aristotle), 487
rational thought. *See* logic and rational thought
Reality
   constructionist view, 658–659n16
   deconstructionist view, 594–595n8
   in Diamond Approach, 474–479, 588–589n2
   ground of, 391, 430–431
   knowledge and, 56–57, 60
   in logoi of teachings, 567–570
   nonconceptual, 257–261, 328–347
   nondual, 127, 297–298
   ontological hierarchy in, 433–434
   as a Riemannian manifold, 301–302, 433
   soul/essence duality and, 154–155
   soul's experience as, 20, 225
   unity of, 12, 266
   waking to, 18, 54–55

realization. *See also* enlightenment; liberation; self-realization; transformation
  of absolute, 406
  of boundlessness, 274–275
  de-reification, 321–323
  of diamond vehicles, 241–243, 457–458
  of essence, 74–75
  in integrated dimension, 434
  logos and, 569–570, 678n23
  of nonconceptual awareness, 333–338
  soul's unfolding and, 84
  traditional view, 54–55
  in Zen, 614n3, 663–664n11
reason. *See also* logic and rational thought
  awareness and, 586n6
  in diamond guidance, 313
  in Greek philosophy, 485, 611n12
  knowledge and, 672n12
  and logos compared, 364, 669–670n8
  in religious thought, 586–587n7
receptivity, 98–101, 105, 159–161, 222, 632n5
recognition
  of absolute source, 422
  enlightenment and, 534–536
  essence and, 133, 138
  of inner forms, 52–59
  of mental dichotomies, 333–334
  of nothingness, 312
  of soul's qualities, 221–222, 276–277
  in young souls, 168–169, 534–536
recollection, 488, 532–533, 614–615n3
red essence, 233
redemption of Western thought, 154–155, 467, 471–474, 670n8
reflection. *See* self-reflection
regression, 195–197, 545
Reich, Wilhelm, 603n2, 605n10, 618n9, 639n9
reification, 319–323, 344–345, 351, 356, 444
reincarnation, 617n7, 620n6
rejecting object relation, 204–207, 216, 636n14

relative absolutism, 570–571, 574
relativism, 598n7, 600n1
relativity of time and space, 376, 644–645n1
relaxation
  brain and, 173
  distrust of, 103
  experience of, 273, 403
  loving presence and, 158–160, 281
release, 81–83, 272–273, 283
religion, isolation of, 7–10, 31
representation, 165–167, 169–170, 627n9
repression
  age and, 123
  child abuse and, 170–171
  ego development and, 201–204
  Freud's view, 616n5
  psychodynamic issues and, 227–228
  Washburn's view, 624n4
restructuring therapy, 632–633n9
revelation
  bodhichitta and, 601n4
  of essence, 258
  mystical knowledge and, 61, 588n11
  of pure presence, 225–226
  in Sufi thought, 603–604n4
Riemannian manifold
  of cognitive forms, 314
  dimensions of Being, 264–266
  ego structures and, 169
  essential aspects and, 134
  Reality as, 301–302, 433
  soul as, 51–52, 88–89, 94
rigidity
  autopoiesis and, 558–560
  diamond dome vehicle and, 244
  liberation from, 103–104, 185–190, 283
  oceanic love and, 276
rigpa (fundamental illumination), 511, 534, 614n3, 657n13, 687n11
ruby aspect, 139, 279
ruh (spirit), 517–519, 527, 583n1, 601n6, 607n4

724   Index

Rumi, Jalaluddin, 517–520, 613n1, 617n8, 629–630n18
rupakaya (form body), 653n1

sacred, concept of, 335
sage, invisible, 409
Saint John of the Cross, 494, 616n4, 637n3
Saint Thomas Aquinas, 694n4
samadhis (concentration states), 498–499
Samantabadra and Samantabadri, 605n9, 687n10
sambhava yoga, 504
sambhogakaya (body of enjoyment), 653n1
Samkhya system (Indian), 501
samskaras (seeds of karma), 497, 498–499, 606n2
Saraswati, Swami Yogeshwaranand, 495–497
satchitananda (true nature), 644n15
satisfied self, 524
satori (transcending of discriminating mind), 64, 336, 597n4
Scheller, Max, 611n12
schizoid defenses, 104, 186–187
schizophrenia, 172
science and scientific method
    cognitive development and, 179
    consciousness and, 26–27
    experience and, 21–22
    isolation of, 7–9, 459–470, 585n4
    logos and, 362, 670–671n8
    in new metapsychology, 11–14
    noetic forms and, 315
    ordinary knowledge and, 318
    origins of life, 116–118
    physical feelings, 596–597n1
    positivist philosophy, 498, 658–659n16, 694n4
    second law of thermodynamics, 555–556, 559
    systems theory, 109, 118–120
science fiction, 88, 94, 288–289
secularism, 6, 460, 462, 475–476
secure self, 524

seeds
    of enlightenment, 600–601n4
    natural growth, 110–111
    potential as, 71, 72–73, 91
    samskaras as, 497, 498–499, 606n2
sefirot (spiritual qualities), 578–580, 661n4
self. *See also other* self *entries;* ego-self; soul
    absence of, 385–387, 422–423, 505, 584n1
    atman, 495–500, 583–584n1, 588n12
    duality with spirit, 9–11, 154–155, 176
    isolation of, 58
    liberation of, 29
    in object relations theory, 78, 623–624nn1-2, 629n16, 630n19, 657–658n14
    in psychology, 582n2, 584–586n4, 623n14, 623-624n1
    reification and, 320
    in religious traditions, 583–584n1
    Shiva as, 500–505, 605n9, 667n5
    Stern's view, 591n10, 628n10
    ultimate, 406–407
self-awareness, 20, 257, 387
self-consciousness, 168, 184
self-identity, 64, 198–199
self-images, 77–78, 102
    ego structures and, 189–193, 198, 205
    liberation from, 90, 186–187
    and memory, 164–165
    weak, 229
selfishness, 142–145, 206, 288
selflessness, 145–146, 280, 385–387
self-object dichotomy, 36–37
self-organization, 88–89, 108–109, 302–303
    in evolution theory, 116–119, 555–560
    logos and, 373–374
    personal essence and, 452–453
    of planet Earth, 472–473
self-realization
    autonomy and, 107
    in dimensions of Being, 266, 289–291, 323, 407–409

and essentialization compared, 642n4
infancy and, 534–536, 539–540
lacking in parents, 163
in soul's inner journey, 223–224, 254, 262–264, 423–424
self-reflection, 183–184
absence of, 138, 387
in infants and newborns, 168, 537
self-representation, 166–167, 169–170
self-respect, 96
Semnani, Alaoddawleh, 521
sensations, 53, 171, 255, 385–386
senses
consciousness and, 51
in dimensions of true nature, 298, 381
direct experience and, 13–14, 23
external stimuli and, 94–95
in Kashmir Shaivism, 502–503
in Markabah vehicle, 239–241
memory and, 58
Origen's view, 490
in Sufism, 575
sensual soul, 615n1, 637n3
separation
as existential issue, 233
from mother, 229–230, 233, 295, 332
servant of God (Sufism), 525–527
service, 456–458
sexuality
ego development and, 204, 207–208
orgasm, 92, 126
in Reichian therapy, 605n10
sex instinct, 142–144
sexual abuse, 170
Shaivism. *See* Kashmir Shaivism
shakti (subtle energy), 445–446, 641n1
shapes
absence of, 148–150, 203
of diamond vehicles, 234–235
of preconceptual structures, 211–213
of soul, 90, 134–135
Shibayama, Zenkei, 597n4
Shiva and Shakti, 500–505
creative dynamism of Shakti, 667n5, 675–676n19, 689n5
true nature and, 646–647n6, 650n15
union of, 605n9, 607n4, 675n19

Shiva Sutras, 503, 504, 632n4
Shobogenzo (Dogen), 642n6, 645n3
shunyata (emptiness), 505–510, 595n8, 649n13, 659n18, 681n12, 684n20, 695n9
Siddha path, 676n19
silence of absolute, 377–381
silver white aspect, 279
simplicity, 409, 477
skandhas (psychophysical constituents), 505–507, 511–512
sleep, 382
social instinct, 142–144
society, 145–146, 202–204, 477
Socrates, 3–5, 9, 11, 484–486, 588n12
Song of Songs, 606n4, 652n9
soul, 3–41. *See also* animal soul
absolute depth of, 405–407
as autopoietic system, 556–560
Buddhist views, 505–515, 584n1, 586n6, 588n12, 602–603n1, 609n6, 659n18
Christian views, 99, 489–494, 583n1, 589n3, 593–594n6, 601–602n6, 615n1, 637n3
development of, 131–163, 529–554
diamond pearl, 455–456
ego development, 164–184, 200–217
essence and, 38–41, 98–99, 111–112, 127–128, 131–140
in Greek and Western thought, 3–5, 9, 11, 483–494, 588n12, 601n6
inner journey of, 221–246
isolation of, 459–479
in Kabbalah, 583n1, 615n1, 637n3
in Kashmir Shaivism, 500–505, 607n4
knowing the, 584n4, 589n3
liberation of, 185–199
physical forms and, 291, 592n3
properties and functions, 45–128
in psychology, 584–585n4
in Sufism, 517–527, 583n1, 589n3, 593n4, 599n10, 601n6, 607n4
universal, 359, 666–667nn3–4
space
in dimensions of true nature, 315, 354, 375–378, 394, 397–399

inner space, 190–191, 304–306, 598n6
physical forms in, 447
presence and, 33
relativity of, 644–645n1
soul's experience of, 81, 84–87, 98, 105–106
in soul's inner journey, 242, 249–252, 262–264
space aspect, 139
spanda (creative dynamism), 501, 504, 650n15, 667n5
Spanda Karika, 501
speech, 178, 327, 333, 366–370
Sperry, Roger, 562–563, 609n7
spirit and spirituality. *See also other* spiritual *entries; specific spiritual traditions*
duality with self, 9–11, 154–155, 176
Hegel's view, 120, 611n12
incompleteness of spiritual traditions, 73
inner order and, 362
isolation of, 7–8, 176, 459–470
lataif and, 532
logoi of teachings, 569–570, 577–582, 661n4
matter and, 335, 611n11, 621–622n8
Muhammadan spirit, 630–631n21
in new metapsychology, 11–13
reason and, 669–670n8
ruh (spirit), 517–519, 527, 583n1, 601n6, 607n4
soul and, 3, 5–6, 18–19, 583–584n1, 584n3
spiritual potential, 144
Wilber's view, 530–533
spiritual awakening. *See* enlightenment; liberation; realization
spiritual forms, 134–140, 299, 330–332
spiritual maturity, 179–180, 545, 633–635n11
spiritual nature, 135–136, 605n9
splitting, 176, 202–206, 208, 624n4, 636n14
spontaneity, 387, 453, 454
Star Wars, 288
Steiner, Rudolf, 677n22

Stern, Daniel, 591n10, 627–628n10, 638n9
stillness, 91, 377–381
Stoicism, 691n5
stream
of actualization, 79–80
of consciousness, 79–80, 88, 506–509, 514, 603n2, 609n6
strength aspect, 139, 227–230
strong AI theory, 117–118, 563, 610n9
structures. *See also* ego and ego structures
autopoiesis and, 555–558
freedom from, 89–90, 187–197
globalization and, 475–476
of language, 369–370
primitive, 146–150, 175, 198–217, 346
in soul's inner journey, 228–230, 240–241
stupa diamond vehicle, 283
subjectivity, 3, 5, 22, 114
emptiness and, 259
freedom from, 89–90
object perception and, 390–391
subjective consciousness, 32–36, 562–563
sublimation (Freud), 616n5
suffering, 97, 144–145, 631n3
absence of, 387
in Buddhism, 602n1
over existential issues, 230
yearning for essence, 271–272
Sufism. *See also* Ibn 'Arabi, Muhyiddin
absolute, 525–526, 575, 682–683n15, 686n4, 686n6
angels, 671n9
Being (planes of), 574–576, 687n9
Being (as fundamental truth), 653n4
complete human being, 630–631n21, 634n11, 691n5, 692nn8–9
creation, 648n10, 665–666nn1–2
divine darkness and, 647nn8–9
divine essence, 643n2, 645–646n4, 647n7, 684n20
divine names, 525–527, 580–581
divine self-expression, 674n17

end of inner journey, 685n1
evolution of humanity, 695n8
fall of man, 620n6
heart (*qalb*), 517, 527, 602n1, 607n4, 616n3
logos and, 672n11
soul (explained), 517–527, 583n1
soul (knowledge of), 584n3, 589n3
soul (primal condition), 617n8
soul (relation to body), 593n4
soul (subtleties of, *lataif*), 222, 521, 532, 630–631n21, 641n1
soul (types of), 599n10, 601n6, 615n1, 637n3, 642n5
surrender to divinity, 651n4
time, 654n6
and transpersonal psychology compared, 625n4
unity, 647n6, 654n5
veils of light, 603–604n4, 653n2
Suhrawardi, Shahab-Ud-Din, 522
superego, 198, 203–204, 208, 228, 616n5
surrender, 280–283, 425–426, 527, 651n4
survival instinct, 142–144
sutras, 495, 503, 504, 632n4
systems theory, 109, 118–120

tantra, 511, 514, 599n11, 616n4
Taoism, 643n11, 654n5, 664n12, 680n8, 684n20, 689n5, 691n5
Tathagatagarbha Buddhist schools, 577, 649n14
tattvas (principles), 495, 501–504, 574, 646n6, 654n5
television and movies, 51, 85, 350, 356–357, 440, 606n1
therapy, 603n2, 605n10, 628n13, 632–633n9
Theravada Buddhism, 506, 647n7
thinking and thoughts, 109. *See also* logic and rational thought
  abandoning, 232
  capacity for, 58–60, 178
  in coemergent nonduality, 442–443
  concentration techniques and, 222, 498–499
  in dimensions of true nature, 313, 333, 365
  Eastern and Western views contrasted, 690n5
  external stimuli and, 95
  movement of, 51
  obsessive, 90
thusness, 328–330
Tibetan Book of the Dead, 610n8
Tibetan Buddhism
  abhisheka (transmission), 676n20
  Adi Buddha, 687n10
  dorje (diamond symbol), 644n16
  Gelug school, 649n13
  meditation practices, 599n11
  Nyingma school, 512, 614n3, 687n11
  Padmasambhava, 604n5, 682n14
  selflessness, 683n18
time, 604–605nn6–7
  awareness of, 51
  in dimensions of true nature, 33, 302–304, 349, 352, 354, 375–378
  essence and, 98, 197
  forms and, 86–87, 447
  life outside of, 126
  relativity of, 376, 644–645n1
  soul's impressionability and, 97
  in soul's inner journey, 225, 245–246, 249–252, 262–264
Torah, 604n4, 676n19
transcending and transcendence
  of absolute, 248–251, 421
  concepts, 233, 257–261, 333–342
  identity, 242–245, 251, 278
  ignorance, 187, 256, 278, 295
  and immanence, 439–440
  knowing and unknowing, 255–257
  mind, 64, 326–328, 597n4
  motive, 340–341
  narcissism, 223–224, 289–290
transformation. *See also* personal essence
  deconstructionism and, 595n8
  in dimensions of true nature, 302, 349, 352–360
  globalization, 475–476
  graphic art resembling, 606n1

of knowledge, 60
obstacles to, 100–101, 628n13
soul development and, 180–182, 185–186, 193, 209
soul's capacity for, 15–18, 22, 76–93, 99
in Sufism, 521–522
transitoriness, 602n1
transmigration, 548, 606nn2–3, 617n7
transmission of logos, 368–369
transparency
blocking of, 100
in dimensions of true nature, 286–287, 293, 325–326
essence and, 145, 195, 222–225
of protoplasmic soul, 150
of pure soul, 525–526
soul's capacity for, 90, 103
and spiritual attainment, 633–634n11
transpersonal experience, 532–533, 617n8
transpersonal psychology, 6–7, 545–547, 584–585n4, 620n5, 625n4, 633–634n11. *See also* Washburn, Michael; Wilber, Ken
transubstantiation, 88, 90, 93, 182
trauma, 95, 157, 170–172, 227
true nature, 247–267. *See also* Being; essence
awakening to, 536
dimensions of, 271–409
ontological hierarchy in, 431–434
quintessence and, 436–437
Reality and, 441–458
satchitananda as, 644n15
trust, 103, 157–161, 281–286
truth
awareness of, 221
of Being, 131
body of (*dharmakaya*), 653n1
buddhi in *raja yoga*, 653n1
of coemergent nonduality, 443
in dimensions of true nature, 321–322, 341–342, 372, 397–403, 594–595n8
Eastern and Western views contrasted, 694–695n6
about ego structures, 188–190
in logoi of teachings, 569–570
reason and, 586n6
relative *vs.* absolute, 570–571, 574, 598n7
serving, 457–458
soul's turning toward, 237–243
truth crystal, 332
Tulku, Tarthang, 604–605n6, 678n24
turning wheel, 245–246

unconscious (Freud), 227
unfolding. *See also* unfolding of soul
absolute and, 377–378
of cosmos, 120, 358, 362
of forms, 108–112
of logos, 571, 572–574
unfolding of soul, 83–87, 91–93, 114, 358–359
diamond dome vehicle and, 245–246
logos and, 367, 373
structures and, 187–188, 214–215
union
with God, 374, 491, 652n9, 686n2
mystical (Plotinus), 489
of Shiva and Shakti, 605n9, 607n4, 675n19
unity. *See also* nonduality
of action, 361
appearance of, 276
in dimensions of true nature, 293, 299–302, 338–339
of humanity, 472–473
of knower and known, 55
of knowing and being, 34
of manifestation, 266
of mind and body, 81–82
of rational and spiritual, 62
of Reality, 12, 266
of soul, God, and world, 463–465, 467
of soul and essence, 155, 607n4
in Sufism, 647n6, 654n5
wisdom traditions and, 567, 571
universal concepts, 134–135, 138, 310–313
universal consciousness, 507–510

universal mind, 313–317, 509
universal soul, 359, 666–667nn3–4
universe. *See also* physical world
  absolute and, 381
  in dimensions of true nature, 277–280, 298, 358–363, 402–403
  dream universe, 248–251
  human being as microcosm, 618n8
  in quintessential dimension, 436
  in systems theory, 119
  unfolding of, 120–121
unmanifest, 251–252, 355, 376–382, 416–418
unveiling (*kashf*), 603–604n4

Vajrasattva and Vajradhara, 643n9
Vajrayana Buddhism, 508, 510–511, 514, 597n4. *See also* Dzogchen (Maha Ati)
Varela, Francisco, 556
vasanas (tendencies), 497, 606n2
Vasubandhu, 507, 508
Vedanta, 645n2, 647n7, 678n1, 679n5, 685n1, 685n25, 689n5. *See also* Ramana Maharshi
vehicles. *See* diamond vehicles
Vijnanavada school. *See* Yogachara school
virtual dimension, 418, 687n8
virtues, 485, 491, 581, 615n4
vision-logic (Wilber), 630n20
visualization, color, 222
vrittis (concepts), 497–498
vulnerability, 97, 103–107, 153

Washburn, Michael, 620n5, 621n8, 624–626n4, 635–636nn12–13
  and Diamond Approach compared, 531–533, 541, 545
  Wilber's criticism, 538
water aspect, 139
Western thought. *See also* science and scientific method
  concepts of soul, 3–6, 58, 154–155, 459–470, 484–494
  and Diamond Approach compared, 671n9
  and Eastern compared, 466–467, 470–471, 584n1, 688–691n5, 692n1, 694–695n6
  globalization and, 475–476
  knowing and Being, 656n11, 657n13
  in logoi of teachings, 569, 572
  logos, 366–368, 671n10
  nonconceptual awareness, 661–662n4
  perfection, 601n6
  reason, 586–587nn6–7
  redemption of, 154–155, 467, 471–474, 670n8
wheel of time, 245–246
Wilber, Ken
  depth dimension, 685n24
  and Diamond Approach compared, 529–554, 695n7
  evolution theory, 608n1
  infancy and childhood, 619n2, 621n8, 626n7
  involution of being, 621–622nn7–8, 653n3
  vision-logic, 630n20
  and Washburn compared, 620n5, 625n4, 635–636nn12–13
  on Western thought, 587n9
will
  changeability and, 40
  diamond, 283
  divine, 668–669n7, 685–686n2
  of ego-self, 272
  free, 668n7
  freedom vehicle and, 456–457
  of inner truth, 273
  of true nature, 361
Winnicott, D. W., 622n12
wisdom
  of ancient philosophers, 465
  of crystal vehicles, 331
  of diamond vehicles, 266, 272
  in Eastern traditions, 499–500, 513
  of logos, 374, 678n23
  of nonarrival, 425–426
  nous and, 180
withdrawal, 104
womb, 214–215, 278

word, logos as, 366–368, 671–672nn11–12
word-concepts, 366–368, 677n22
world (cosmos). *See also* physical world; universe
   Being or God and, 448–449, 453
   in coemergent nonduality, 443–444, 447
   ego development and, 102
   isolation of, 58, 459–479
   leaving, 294–295
   in new metapsychology, 7, 11–14
   perceived as matter, 34
   in quintessential dimension, 440
   soul/essence duality and, 154–155
   soul's evolution and, 608–609n1
   soul's learning and, 100
unfolding inner forms, 95
world soul (Plotinus), 611n12

Xenophon, 485

yeshe (fundamental knowing), 596n9, 614n3, 657n13
yoga, 445, 495–500, 504, 643n11, 651n4, 685n25
Yogachara school, 506–507, 510–511, 603n2, 609n6, 659n18

zazen, 661n3
Zen. *See also* Dogen (Zen master)
   "gateless gate," 643n8
   invisible sage, 685n26
   luminous darkness, 679n3
   nonattachment, 664–665n14
   nonconceptual awareness, 597n4, 661n2
   nonconceptual reality, 638n8, 661–663nn3–7
   realization, 614n3, 663–664n11
   selflessness, 683n18
   soul's experience of herself, 642n6
zygotes, 216

The Diamond Approach is taught by Ridhwan teachers, certified by the Ridhwan Foundation. Ridhwan teachers are also ordained ministers of the Ridhwan Foundation. They are trained by DHAT Institute, the educational arm of the Ridhwan Foundation, through an extensive seven-year program, which is in addition to their work and participation as students of the Diamond Approach. The certification process ensures that each person has a good working understanding of the Diamond Approach and a sufficient capacity to teach it before being ordained and authorized to be a Ridhwan teacher.

The Diamond Approach described in this book is taught in group and private settings in California and Colorado by Ridhwan teachers.

For information, write:

Ridhwan
P.O. Box 2747
Berkeley, California 94702-0747
www.ridhwan.org

Ridhwan School
P.O. Box 18166
Boulder, Colorado 80308–8166

Satellite groups operate in other national and international locations. For information about these groups, or to explore starting a group in your area, taught by certified Ridhwan teachers, write:

Ridhwan
P.O. Box 2747
Berkeley, California 94702-0747
www.ridhwan.org

Diamond Approach is a registered service mark of the Ridhwan Foundation.